Real World Adobe GoLive 4

Real World

Adobe
GoLive 4

by

Jeff Carlson

Glenn Fleishman

with

Neil Robertson

Agen Schmitz

For Kimberly and Lynn D., ever patient

Real World Adobe GoLive 4

By Jeff Carlson and Glenn Fleishman
With Neil Robertson and Agen Schmitz

Copyright © 2000 by Jeff Carlson and Glenn Fleishman

Peachpit Press

1249 Eighth Street
Berkeley, CA 94710
510/524-2178 or 800/283-9444 (voice)
510/524-2221 (fax)

Find us on the World Wide Web at: http://www.peachpit.com
Peachpit Press is a division of Addison Wesley Longman

Real World Adobe GoLive is published in association with Adobe Press.

For resources mentioned in this book, see: http://www.realworldgolive.com

Editors: Corbin Collins, Marty Cortinas
Production Coordinator: Amy Changar
Copy Editor: Toby Malina
Proofreaders: Kimberly Carlson, Liane Thomas
Researcher: Lynn D. Warner
Interior design: Jeff Carlson
Cover design: Lynn Brofsky Design
Cover illustration: Jeff Brice

Colophon

This book was created with Microsoft Word 98, DeBabelizer 3 (Mac), Exposure Pro, HyperSnapX, and QuarkXPress 4.0.4 on an iMac, three PowerBooks, and two Pentium IIs. The fonts used were Adobe Minion and Formata.

ISBN 0-201-35474-8

9 8 7 6 5 4 3 2 1

Printed and bound in the United States of America

Preface

If you're like us, you're fond of coffee, of average height, and have unruly hair. But more importantly, you like to balance efficiency with a learning curve. You want to learn enough to make yourself not exactly lethal, but certainly dangerous. You want to reduce the amount of tedium in your production and design work without eliminating too much control. You also don't want to spend most of your time learning features and memorizing commands. You want to be able to learn a little and then sit down and produce.

GoLive is our favorite Web tool because it fills all of these needs from the newest user to some of the most experienced producers. Our colleagues, relatives, and friends have all related stories of using GoLive (as we sit around the monitor browning marshmallows over the vent) to create simple sites with a couple images, all the way up to 1,000-page juggernauts with JavaScript, DHTML, CSS, and other acronyms not suitable for public forums.

The reason GoLive fits the approach of so many users is its flexibility and straightforwardness. Most features in GoLive involve selecting or inserting an object—such as a table—and manipulating its contents or characteristics through dragging, clicking, or entering values in a structured palette. No hand coding is required except for a very few advanced tasks and tweaks.

We used to find ourselves turning to SimpleText or WordPad to write pages, especially simple ones, as it was much easier than wrestling a visual editor to the ground. However, since the release of CyberStudio GoLive 3, later updated to Adobe GoLive 4, our preference is to fire up GoLive, not a text editor—it's just easier to create content visually.

Who's GoLive For?

Many of you may never have touched actual HTML; others may disdain the notion of ever using a WYSIWYG approach to creating pages. But for both ends of the spectrum, GoLive can make sense.

GoLive rarely squeezes HTML's round pegs into a browser's square holes. With the exception of a kludge popularized by other visual editors and that is truly demanded by users—grids—GoLive structures itself around HTML instead of pushing HTML around to achieve dubious results.

The novice Web designer or production person can fire up GoLive and know, with some certainty, that the pages they produce won't cause most browsers to react with horror; part of the function of this book is to help you avoid the situations in which a browser might break out in a rash.

The advanced HTML coder has probably already realized that the profusion of acronyms—XML, CSS, XSL, DHTML—has overwhelmed his or her ability to create complex documents and manage all the content in them. GoLive provides advanced management tools that offer consistent control over the most disparate elements on a page or across a site without a commensurate amount of work.

On its face, GoLive seems like a vast, fractal Swiss Army knife, with every attachment you unhinge revealing subattachments on to infinity. If you glance through the manual and palettes, and click buttons that look like little footballs, stairs, and grids, you might think you've bitten off more than you can chew. But don't rely on first impressions.

The GoLive Way

When you scratch the surface, GoLive has a relatively consistent approach to handling a huge number of complex tasks without making you manage them individually. The program tries to hide the ugliest bits of plumbing and wiring from view. GoLive lets you work generally in a visual mode, previewing items as you create and modify them, even enabling you to do insanely complicated tasks by just dragging and dropping items onto a Web page.

Just like a new homeowner, however, the more comfortable you are in your surroundings, the more likely you are to want to tinker: you turn off a circuit breaker and unscrew a light switch faceplate to solve a faulty wiring problem. GoLive offers several tools for the handyperson, allowing you access to JavaScript editing, raw HTML, and Cascading Style Sheet (CSS) management.

But if you're just a renter, content to let the landlord bring in workers to make structural changes to your surroundings, you can still get a lot out of just living there. Similarly, if you're content to let a Webmaster, IS department, or techie handle the more intricate matters, GoLive has a lot to offer.

The best part of using GoLive, and the best part of writing this book, is that although it isn't all things to all people, it certainly is most things to many people. Most users find themselves deep into the program within a short time, whether they're using it to work on a single page or a large site.

Who's This Book For?

We wrote this book with three types of users in mind:

The novice user. If you've just started using GoLive, or have spent some time with it and are trying to sort out the many, many features in the program, *Real World Adobe GoLive 4* offers Part 1, *GoLive Basics*. This part of the book provides a comprehensive overview of all the features, palettes, preferences, and interface approaches used in the program. Consider it a ramp-up guide to begin using the software.

The next two parts, *Pages* and *Sites*, focus on the nitty-gritty of production and working within and outside of GoLive's constraints.

The *Advanced* part is the icing on the cake: a section devoted to the extra goodies that you'll want to get to in time.

The intermediate user. Before starting on this book, we categorized ourselves between intermediate and advanced GoLive users; we're in the latter category now, after months of hard work pushing and pulling the program. We want to transfer that acquisition of knowledge to the intermediate user who needs to get more out of the program, but has reached a plateau in the learning curve.

The *GoLive Basics* part of the book offers a good reference guide to features when you just can't find that one Inspector palette tab (out of at least 100) that you need to accomplish a task; or you're mystified about where a given preference might live (just ask us about how to set the line break preference!).

The real meat for intermediate users is *Pages* and *Sites*, as we've ferreted out all the day-to-day, real-world tricks and techniques you need to accomplish your specific tasks. We also cover all the options, basics, and extras of tools to visually edit and manage pages and sites.

Part 4, *Advanced*, is where you, as an intermediate user, can really leap ahead. You might be interested, for example, in using JavaScript. Although the JavaScript chapter doesn't teach you how to code that language—we have some recommendations on where to learn in that chapter—it does get you quickly up to speed on how to use GoLive to carry out your codes. The same is true for DHTML, CSS, and other advanced topics.

The advanced user. For a program as vast and deep as GoLive, we find ourselves often wishing for a reference that tells us *everything* about the program, even the fiddly little bits like editing the XML source file that contains all the special characters.

Well, friends, this book serves that purpose. The *GoLive Basics* part of the book can serve as a reference for you, just as for an intermediate user, in quickly getting the correct value, method, or location for a given task. It also can be a great visual reference for plotting a plan of attack for a given project: making sure GoLive has a particular feature can save some time.

The *Pages* and *Sites* sections might be more of a review than a primer for an advanced user, but we've tried to include as much detail and advice as possible for achieving best results, or for learning new tips to improve your workflow. A review of selected chapters might help you eke out even more efficiency.

The *Advanced* part of the book is aimed at helping those users who already know the basics of a protocol GoLive supports, like DHTML or XML, to quickly use those features with GoLive's tools; or to bypass GoLive's tools with knowledge of how GoLive interacts with hand coding.

How This Book Is Structured

Real World Adobe GoLive 4 is broken into four parts:

GoLive Basics. This section covers all the details that make up GoLive. We start with a quick overview of using all the features in the program to build a page and then a site. We proceed to cover all the myriad appearances of the attribute-examining, many-tabbed Inspector palette, and then on to the palettes and parts of the interface that allow you to modify or insert elements. Next, we cover where all the settings and preferences in GoLive live, what they control, and how to "detail" your program (like a racing car) to match your needs.

Pages. GoLive has a fully integrated visual page editor that allows you to drag and drop elements onto a page, format text, add colors, and control tables, frames, and other structured elements. This part of the book fully delves into each area in turn. The section is organized by thematic chapters. We start with an overview, and then proceed through text and fonts, images, color, tables, frames, layout grids and floating boxes, and forms. We finish with a round-up of other page-related features that don't fit neatly into any of those categories.

Sites. GoLive shines at site management, which includes tracking content across a site—such as images, links, and colors—and correctly uploading new files to a remote Web server. This part walks through the overall organization of the Site window, in which site management is focused in GoLive, and then into individual tabs and subjects. We cover handling sitewide fontsets and colors through the Fontsets and Colors tabs; uploading, downloading, and synchronizing content through built-in FTP (File Transfer Protocol) support; and observing and prototyping a site through the Site tab.

This part also sports a chapter on the popular subject of importing an existing site created by hand or in another application. We finish up with site-based features not centered on any tab, including managing components—reusable code snippets that are centrally managed and used to update content placed throughout a site.

Advanced. It's always a judgment call when talking about what's "advanced" and what's not. However, we decided to group all the newer and browser-dependent parts of GoLive—which were complex enough to require a real grounding in knowledge found outside the scope of this book—into the *Advanced* section.

This includes the JavaScript scripting language; DHTML (Dynamic HTML), which we opted to break into the two discrete parts that GoLive has defined: animation and pre-defined Actions; CSS for controlling text ranges and text blocks; and the Web Database, which is a kind of GoLive command headquarters for organizing all the assumptions about HTML and CSS for the program.

The last chapter, *Plug-ins and Media*, covers the extras that GoLive includes for dealing with external add-ons to browsers and pages, such as QuickTime editing, Flash and PDF URL management, and using browser plug-ins in GoLive to simulate browser behavior.

Appendixes. But wait, there's more! In the appendixes for the book, we present Macintosh-specific issues and extras: a few things that are found only in the Macintosh version of GoLive, including AppleScript support and FTP download file mapping.

We also include an appendix featuring the excellent CSS compatibility chart from WebReview.com. This chart shows all the properties associated with Cascading Style Sheets, and which properties work with which browser releases by platform and version.

How to Read This Book

No, this isn't a trick headline: we really do have a recommendation. There's too much structured content in this book for a straight-through reading; many features aren't relevant to all users. Our recommendations for getting the most of this book:

- **Scan it first.** Glance through the whole thing to find out where we've put everything and why. The structure above helps, and you can, of course, use the table of contents and index. But it's a big book, and we want you to know the lay of the land.

- **Answer your pressing questions.** Are there subjects you just don't understand? Features that drive you nuts? Parts of the program you adore and want to know more about? Check out the index, and look up those parts of the book.

- **Find the right chapter.** We've tried to structure this real-world book around themes and subjects that we focus on in our professional work on the Web, and that people have told us they use in their working methods.

- **Read the whole thing.** If you can't restrain yourself, stay up til 5 a.m. and read the book cover-to-cover. You can even add animation to the book by drawing pictures in the bottom right corner and flipping through at high speed. Hey, it's your book now!

More Knowledge than Fits in Print

We've created a Web site at http://realworldgolive.com that's more than marketing (though we admit to a little of that; it is the Web, after all). Use it as a real resource for getting answers to your pressing questions and sharing information with other users, as well as the authors and contributors to this book.

The site will contain updates to the book, fixes to errata (no book or product is ever bug-free), references to online resources, excerpts or the entire text of articles written by us on GoLive specifics, advanced advice on using the program, and news about GoLive developments.

You'll also be able to participate in an active, moderated, archived forum on GoLive that will provide a way for you to get some real answers to some real stumpers.

All the examples noted in the book can be found at the site, as well; this is especially useful with some of the tutorial material in the *Advanced* part of the book.

Of course, you can also buy the book from the site—but, wait... you've already bought the book, haven't you? (If not, support your authors and booksellers by spending your hard-earned money to share our hard-earned knowledge.)

Our Relationship with Adobe

Although this is an Adobe Press book, it's also a Peachpit Press book. This may be confusing to some readers not intimate with the book industry. We're proud and happy to have the Adobe banner over this title, and they provided technical resources and feedback on drafts of this book. However, they aren't responsible for errors, omissions, statements of opinion, or the current color of our unruly hair.

But, more importantly, Adobe didn't direct or change the content of this book. Because this is a Real World book, we state our opinions and results of our research quite clearly; this book is not the product of a marketing department, nor do we pull punches about things that don't work. At the same time, we're just as positive about what does work; we love this program. This Real World book doesn't give you a tour through the program's menus (though by the end you'll know what each one does). Rather, it shares the knowledge we've gained from our own use of GoLive and that of designers working with it every day in the field.

Conventions Used in This Book

We believe in making text contextually self-explanatory, and have tried to keep fonts, formatting, and special dingbats to a minimum. However, a few conventions are worth highlighting.

Because this book covers both Macintosh and Windows versions of Adobe GoLive, we've made a lot of effort to be as inclusive of both platforms as possible. The screen captures you see throughout the book were made fairly arbitrarily on either platform to emphasize how similar they are. However, whenever something is significantly different between the display in the two platforms, we've included platform-specific screen captures.

Similarly, whenever a key command or menu item is specific to a platform, in the text you see a note such as, "To invoke the Link Inspector, press Command-5 (Mac) or Alt-4 (Windows), or select it from the Windows menu (Mac) or View menu (Windows)."

Tip: Tips Offer More Information Tips appear called-out in the margins (as with this one), and generally contain real-world advice, ideas on tweaking settings, or slightly extraneous bits of knowledge that you might enjoy.

Code samples are marked in Courier to indicate something you can type in:

```
.foobar { text-size: 1000 px }
```

Hey, Whatever Happened to CyberStudio?!

If you had ever heard of "GoLive CyberStudio," and now wonder why it's "Adobe GoLive," we have one word for you: acquisition. GoLive, Inc., the original company that created CyberStudio, was bought by Adobe Systems, Inc., in January 1999. GoLive, Inc., created several releases of the product, which had, over time, become the best visual editor and site-management software for the Macintosh, supplanting other Mac-based packages, and really competing only with Macromedia DreamWeaver.

Adobe quickly decided they liked the name GoLive better—more in keeping with InDesign and other product names, perhaps—and released the 4.0 update for Macintosh under the Adobe GoLive banner in March 1999. The first Windows release followed in June 1999.

Why Not Use DreamWeaver?

Dif'rent strokes for dif'rent folks, folks.

DreamWeaver, to us, seems focused on the most advanced features necessary to create Web sites, like DHTML animation. Although it offers a full set of features for creating and editing pages and sites, the depth and flexibility of these features seems dwarfed by GoLive.

On the other hand, GoLive may not be the ideal tool for advanced Web-based multimedia producers who spend all their time creating only advanced functionality. However, we're pretty happy with GoLive's DHTML, CSS, and JavaScript editors.

But it really depends on temperament. We like GoLive because it works the way we conceptualize creating Web sites.

Our Team

We couldn't have written this book without the help of some very fine people who shaped the book with their work and advice.

Contributing Writers

Agen Schmitz (now his real name) was the primary writer of the *GoLive Basics* part of the book, as well as Chapter 28, *Plug-ins and Media*. He has worked with electronic media for some years, starting with conference editorial planning, and moving to a "large, unnamed Redmond, WA-based company" to write for their Web site on certain "2000" products. He now is a freelance writer and editor.

Neil "JavaScriptStud" Robertson did the primary work on the *JavaScript, Animation, Actions*, and *Web Database* chapters. Neil is a multimedia and Web designer and producer, having created Web sites back in the days when people asked, "What's a Web site?" He works as a senior multimedia designer and programmer at Phinney-Bischoff Design House.

This is the first book the two have contributed to, and we're happy to provide them this introduction to the publishing world.

Editing and Production

Toby Malina steered us through the rocks and hard places—Scylla and Charybdis—of deadlines and style, copy editing our drafts until they made sense to people other than us. Her contribution to the style of the book was immense. (However, if you don't like our breezy, laissez-faire style, it's our fault, really.)

Liane Thomas put in an enormous amount of effort on short notice to proof the entire book. Her input, consistent style, and suggestions were extremely helpful as the book reached its 11th hour.

Lynn D. Warner and Charles Fleishman (any relation to Glenn?) both acted as researchers and touchstones to ensure the book kept its readership in mind. Adam Pratt provided some valuable last minute sanity checking as well, as did Agen Schmitz and Toby Malina (they deserve to be thanked twice or three times).

Acknowledgements

We'd like to thank the gang at Peachpit Press who have always made our work possible. Their patience and encouragement is inestimable. Glenn was able to convey his early excitement about GoLive to Nancy Ruenzel-Davis, Peachpit's publisher, who agreed that Adobe's purchase of GoLive marked a great opportunity to come out with a book.

We also want to thank Corbin Collins and Marty Cortinas—our first and second editors—and Marjorie Baer (our extra editorial booster) for keeping us going and providing encouragement, and acting as important liaisons to the folks at Adobe. Peachpit's production team is second to none; Amy Changar is brilliant, and we love her, and she continues to tolerate us. ("Amy, it'll be 800 pages. No, wait 760. No, wait…") .

At Adobe, we'd like to thank Irv Kanode who managed to read and comment on hundreds of pages of material in a way that was constructive and modified many subtle points between our understanding of the program's external behavior and what's actually going on deep inside.

Blue World Communications deserves thanks for generously running the GoLive Talk mailing list, which generates a vast number of questions and answers in any given day, that helped us better understand what real-world users were wrestling with. (See our Web site for a link to the list.)

We liked the Stubbs Island Charter site (http://www.stubbs-island.com/) so much that we asked the owner of the company, who is also the wildlife photographer who took the pictures on the site, if we could excerpt it in examples in the book. We want to thank Jim Borrowman, the owner, and Tim Cole, the Webmaster and designer, for their gracious permission.

Our Greenlake officemates are the best: Ole Kvern, David Blatner, Brett Baker, Toby Malina, and Agen Schmitz; their cajolery is legendary. Our downstairs neighbors—Tony Williams, Lesley Mettler, and Karin Goncalves of Always Running—kept us always smiling, and prevented us from pulling calf muscles during those layout sprints.

And, not quite most importantly, but certainly utmost in our mind at this writing, we thank the La Pavoni espresso machine in our office (under the direction of Ole Kvern) for keeping us awake when we thought we lacked the consciousness for writing just…one…more……word.

From Glenn: "I'd like to thank my love, Lynn D. Warner, for enduring many discussions of GoLive software features and book deadlines. Karl Bischoff and Leslie Phinney kept me busy and excited during a difficult 1998, for which I am eternally grateful. And my thanks and love to my parents, Charles and Audi Fleishman, and my grandparents Sydney and Hilda Fleishman, for their limitless support. My coffee-swilling co-author has my gratitude for agreeing to this 'little' project in the first place and seeing it through until the last word."

From Jeff: "People told us that writing a 700-plus-page book about Adobe GoLive would drive us insane, and, of course, they were correct. Despite some nights of sleep-deprived hallucinations and numerous discussions about capitalizing HTML tags, the project concluded—and we still seem to have a little sanity left. This is entirely due to the patience and generosity of my wife Kimberly, my parents and extended parents Larry & Janet and Susan & Ron, and the folks who were kind enough to ask how the project was going and make coffee when it was most needed. Thank you all. Special thanks also go out to my coauthor and friend, Glenn, who got the ball rolling and pushed it uphill for significant amounts of time."

Overview

PART 1   **GoLive Basics**.................................1

CHAPTER 1   *Getting Started*...............................3

CHAPTER 2   *The Inspector* 39

CHAPTER 3   *Palettes and Parts*...........................123

CHAPTER 4   *Preferences and Customizing*...................153

CHAPTER 5   *Layout, Source, and Preview*..................187

PART 2   **Pages**.......................................**203**

CHAPTER 6   *Page Overview*................................205

CHAPTER 7   *Text and Fonts*...............................211

CHAPTER 8   *Images*.......................................233

CHAPTER 9   *Color* 253

CHAPTER 10   *Tables* 263

CHAPTER 11   *Frames* 291

CHAPTER 12   *Layout Grids and Floating Boxes* 309

CHAPTER 13   *Forms* 323

CHAPTER 14   *Page Specials*................................341

PART 3   **Sites**......................................**351**

CHAPTER 15   *Site Management*..............................353

CHAPTER 16   *Files, Folders, and Links*....................367

CHAPTER 17   *Sitewide Sets* 401

CHAPTER 18   *Staging and Synchronizing Sites* 411

CHAPTER 19   *Site Maps* 435

CHAPTER 20   *Importing a Site* 459

CHAPTER 21   *Site Specials* 473

PART 4   **Advanced** **489**

CHAPTER 22   *Advanced Features* 491

CHAPTER 23   *JavaScript* 501

CHAPTER 24   *Animation* 517

CHAPTER 25   *Actions* 537

CHAPTER 26   *Cascading Style Sheets* 561

CHAPTER 27   *Web Database* 585

CHAPTER 28   *Plug-ins and Media* 607

Appendixes and Index **641**

APPENDIX A   *Macintosh Issues & Extras* 643

APPENDIX B   *Master List of CSS Compatibility* 657

Index 685

Table of Contents

PART 1
GoLive Basics...1

CHAPTER 1
Getting Started...3
   Installing GoLive...3
      Tip: Allocate Memory Before Starting......................................**4**
      Sidebar: Manual Dexterity..*4*
   Opening GoLive..5
      Tip: ToolTips...**5**
      Sidebar: Managing Windows and Palettes.................................*8*
      Tip: Overlaying Palettes...**10**
   Getting Started: Step by Step..10
      Creating a New Page..10
      Tip: Both Background Color and Image....................................**13**
      Tip: Quick Background Color..**13**
      Tip: Absolute Links in a Site..**14**
      Tip: Font Preferences vs. Fontsets.......................................**16**
      Inserting Elements..17
      Tip: Cell blocks..**19**
      Tip: Dragging the Line...**20**
      Tip: Making a Table Color Active...**22**
      Tip: Dragging Images from the Desktop...................................**22**
      Tip: Editing Long URLs...**23**
      Tip: Dynamic Resizing...**23**
      Tip: Resetting Image Dimensions..**24**
      Tip: Generating Low-Res Images...**24**
      Creating a New Site..25
      Tip: Keeping It Together...**26**
      Tip: Doubling Your View...**30**
      Tip: Deleting Files...**32**
      Tip: Point & Shoot on Demand...**34**
      Tip: Shoot the Toolbar...**34**
      Tip: Adding Anchors...**34**
   Big Picture Workout...37

CHAPTER 2
The Inspector..39
   Inspector Basics...39

Document Layout Inspectors 43
   Layout View Controller 43
   Page Inspector. 45
      Tip: Don't Broadcast Your Tool's Name. **45**
      Tip: Adding Descriptions to Page Titles **45**
   Text Inspector 48
      Tip: Creating a Text Link **49**
      Sidebar: Our Favorite Keyboard Shortcuts *49*
      Tip: Photoshop Versus GoLive Actions **51**
   Image Inspector 52
      Tip: Speedier Browser Rendering **53**
      Tip: Proportional Resizing. **53**
      Tip: Careful What You Check **56**
   Table Inspector 57
   Line Inspector. 60
   Line Break Inspector 61
   Comment Inspector. 62
   Spacer Inspector 62
   Layout Grids 63
      Tip: Moving Text boxes a Pixel (or more) at a Time **64**
   Marquee Inspector. 65
   Anchor Inspector 67
      Tip: Anchor Keyboard Shortcut **67**
      Tip: Setting Amount and Delay to Nil **67**
   Tag and Endtag Inspectors 68
   Floating Box Inspector 68
   Body Script and JavaScript Inspectors. 70
      Tip: Opening JavaScript Editor **71**
Head Inspectors 72
      Tip: Editing JavaScript Functions **72**
   Meta Tags. 73
      Tip: Adding Keywords from Text **74**
      Tip: Updating Keywords **74**
   Link Inspector. 76
      Tip: Dept. of Redundancy Dept. **76**
      Tip: Link Inspector Not, uh, Link Inspector. **76**
   IsIndex Inspector 77
   Base Inspector. 77
      Tip: Absolutely Absolute, I Think **78**
      Tip: Still Alive and Kicking. **78**
   Tag and End Tag Inspectors 79
   Comment Inspector. 79
   Headscript Inspector 79
Frame Inspectors 79
   Frame Set Inspector 79
      Tip: Mixing Up Frame Sets **80**
      Tip: Frame Colors **80**
   Frame Inspector 81
      Tip: Framing Size **81**
Site Inspectors. 82
   File Inspector 82

Folder Inspector 85
Site View Controller 85
    Tip: Dragging QuickTime Images **85**
    Tip: Extras Folders Don't Inspect **85**
    Tip: Toolbar Hierarchy Control **86**
Link Inspector 90
    Tip: Graphical Inspection **90**
Reference Inspector 91
Color Inspector 92
Group Inspectors 92
Font Set Inspector 93
Error Inspector 94
FTP File and Folder Inspectors 95
    Tip: FTP Connections **95**
    Tip: FTP Tab **95**
    Tip: Check Your Rights **96**
CyberObjects 97
Date & Time Inspector 97
Button Inspector 98
    Tip: Dragging and Dropping Button Images **98**
    Tip: Resizing Button Images **98**
Component Inspector 99
URL Popup Inspector 100
Action Headitem and Inline Action Inspector 100
Browser Switch Inspector 101
Form Inspectors 102
Form Inspector 102
    Tip: Watch the Switch **102**
    Tip: Multiple Alternatives **102**
Form Button Inspector 103
    Tip: Form End Tag Auto Insert **103**
Form Check Box Inspector 105
Form Radio Button Inspector 105
    Tip: Changing Button Types **105**
Form Fieldset Inspector 106
Form File Inspector 106
Form Hidden Inspector 106
Form Image Inspector 107
Form Keygen Inspector 107
Form Label Inspector 108
Form List Box and Popup Inspectors 108
    Tip: Changing List Types **108**
Form Text Area Inspector 109
Form Text Field and Password Inspectors 110
Web Database Inspectors 111
Form Text Field and Password Inspectors 110
HTML and Character Inspectors 111
Cascading Style Sheets 116
Web Database's CSS Tab 116
Style Sheets Editor 117
CSS Selector Inspector 118
Zat is Not My Dog! 121

CHAPTER 3
Palettes and Parts 123

The Palette 123
    The Basic Tab 124
    The Forms Tab 125
    The Head Tab 126
    The Frames Tab 126
        Tip: It's a Drag **126**
    Site Tab 128
        Tip: It's a Drag, Part 2 . . . . **128**
    Site Extras Tab 129
        Tip: Customizing Icons **129**
        Tip: It's a Drag, Part 3 . . . . **129**
    CyberObjects Tab 130
        Tip: It's a Drag, Part 4 . . . . **130**
    QuickTime Tab 131
    Custom Tab 132
The Color Palette 132
    Color Palette Basics 133
        Tip: Tabbing Through Fields **133**
        Tip: Turning Colors Gray **134**
        Tip: Sampling Desktop Colors **134**
The Toolbar 136
    Toolbar Basics 136
        Tip: Multiple Default Browsers **138**
    Text Toolbar 138
        Tip: Indenting **139**
    Layout Grid Toolbar 139
    Outline Editor Toolbar 140
    Site Toolbar 141
        Tip: Contextual Site Menu **141**
    Web Database Toolbar 142
    Style Sheet Toolbar 143
        Tip: Style Sheet Minutiae **143**
Advanced Feature Editors and Windows 143
    JavaScript Editor 144
        Tip: Opening the JavaScript Editor, Part 1 . . . . **144**
        Tip: Opening the JavaScript Editor, Part 2 . . . . **145**
    Timeline Editor 145
    Track Editor 148
        Tip: Timeline Editor Isn't the Track Editor **148**
        Tip: Return to QuickTime File **148**
        Tip: Moving to Minute **148**
    Style Sheet Editor 149
        Tip: Only Classes, not IDs **149**
Putting Pieces Together 151

CHAPTER 4
Preferences and Customizing 153

Preferences Basics 153

Tip: Navigating Preferences **153**
General Preferences 154
Tip: Negating Preferences. **154**
Tip: Swapping Preferences **154**
Image. 155
Tip: Designating Stationeries **155**
Tip: Importing Images in Windows **155**
Tip: Adding Format. **156**
Display. 157
Cache (Mac) 158
URL Handling 159
File Mapping. 160
Tip: Deleting File Formats **160**
GoLive Modules 161
Languages and Fonts 165
Fonts 165
Encodings 165
ColorSync (Mac Only). 166
Tip: Missing Subsets **166**
LiveObjects 167
Site 168
Export 169
Tip: Deleting **169**
Folder Names 170
Page Status 171
Tip: Status vs. Labels **171**
Site View 172
Previewing in Web Browsers. 172
Tip: Setting Colors First **172**
Document Editing 173
Tip: Setting Multiple Browsers **173**
Find 174
Spell Checking 175
Plug-ins 176
Network. 176
Tip: Adding Plug-ins. **176**
FTP Servers. 177
Up-/Download (Mac Only) 178
Code Appearance 179
Source 179
Tip: Dragging File Types. **179**
JavaScript. 182
Tip: Where's JavaScript? **182**
Site Settings 183
Web Database 185
Global Tab. 185
CSS Tab 186
Preferential Treatment 186

CHAPTER 5

Layout, Source, and Preview...187

Document Window Basics 187
    Tip: Double-clicking Mode Tabs. 188
Layout Editor 189
    Tip: Opening the Head Section 189
    Tip: Maximum Width 189
    Layout Editor Advanced Features 191
Frame Editor 193
HTML Source Editor 194
    Tip: Layout Editor Reflects Frame Changes 194
HTML Outline Editor 197
Layout Preview and Frame Preview. 200
    Tip: I Can Preview Clearly Now 200
    Tip: Previewing Using CSS Root 201
Turn the Page 202

PART 2

Pages...203

CHAPTER 6

Page Overview...205

Page Structure. 205
    Head Section. 205
        Tip: Other Head Tab Tags 206
    Body Section. 206
Base. 207
Meta 207
    Plain Meta Tag 207
        Sidebar: It's All Relative. 208
    Refresh. 209
    Keywords. 209
        Tip: Search Secrets. 209
Link 209
Head and Shoulders 210

CHAPTER 7

Text and Fonts...211

    Tip: More on Text in GoLive 211
Entering Text. 212
    Paragraphs and Line Breaks 212
        Tip: Pasting Text Corrects HTML Entities 212
Navigating Text 213
    Navigating with the Mouse. 213
        Tip: Make Macintosh Text Clippings 213
    Navigating with the Keyboard 213
        Tip: Navigating Without Moving 214
Formatting Text 214
    A Brief History of Formatted HTML Text 215

Text Styles 215
Tip: Don't Blink. **216**
Tip: Mix and Match Styles. **216**
Text Structure 216
Paragraph Formatting 217
Text Alignment 218
Text Size. 220
Sidebar: GoLive is in Charge of Font Size Tags *220*
Sidebar: Why Windows Web Pages Have Tiny Text. *222*
Lists and Indents 224
Tip: No Need to Select All Text. **224**
Tip: CSS Bullets **225**
Tip: Removing Bullets or Numbers **225**
Tip: Spacers are Netscape Only **225**
Text Color 226
Tip: When Adding "Color" Is Helpful. **226**
Using Fonts 227
Specifying Fonts 227
Editing Fontsets 228
Tip: Local, Global, and Sitewide Fontsets. **228**
Sidebar: Seen Onscreen. *229*
Tip: Where There's a Will-Harris. **230**
Tip: Default and Page Sets Don't Mingle **230**
Tip: Make Your Fonts Available **230**
Tip: Careful Typing Produces Better Typography. **230**
Sidebar: Zapfing Early Internet Explorer Users *230*
You Look Simply… Fontastic 231

CHAPTER 8
Images. 233

Image Formats 233
Tip: Patent Medicine **236**
Inserting Images 236
Drag-and-Drop Importing. 237
Tip: Merge Layers in Photoshop for Import **237**
Tip: Import Images Files Aren't Uploaded **238**
Tip: Clean Up Leftover Image Placeholders **238**
Image Attributes. 238
Tip: Dimensions in Files **239**
Tip: Other Dimensions. **239**
Lowsource Images 240
Tip: Padding with Pixels **240**
Tip: Use Any Image as Lowsource **241**
Tip: Clever Color Previews **241**
Tip: Animated GIF Lowsource **241**
Resizing Images 241
Tip: Resize While Designing **242**
Aligning Images 243
Tip: Place Images at the Front of the Line **244**
Tip: Easy Margin Control Using Alignment. **244**
Linking Images 246

Tip: Auto-Set Border to Zero **246**
Imagemaps 247
Tip: Client-Side and Server-Side **247**
Tip: Grab Imagemaps by Their Edges **248**
Tip: Windows Highlights **248**
Tip: Adding Points in HTML **249**
Tip: The Hidden Polygon Point **249**
Tip: Complex Polygons Increase File Size **249**
Tip: Reordering Directives **250**
Tip: Storing Other Links **250**
ColorSync (Macintosh Only) 251
Tip: ColorSync Installation in Mac OS **251**
Tip: Roll Your Own Profiles **251**
Tip: Great Idea, Minimal Support **252**
Tip: Embedded ColorSync Profiles **252**
Tip: Copy Profiles to Your Site Folder **252**
Imagine Great Images 252

CHAPTER 9
Color **253**
Tip: The Slightly Misleading ColorSync Name **253**
Color on the Web 254
Sidebar: A Bit About Bits *254*
Color Between Platforms 255
Tip: Adjusting and Simulating Gamma **255**
Applying Colors 257
Tip: Drag to Select a Background Color **257**
Tip: Applying Text Color Without the Text **257**
Applying Colors in Other Editors 258
Selecting Colors 258
Tip: The Color Palette's Color Palette? **258**
Tip: Slider Slickness **260**
Tip: Select a Color from Anywhere on the Screen **261**
Sidebar: Why So Much Color? *261*
The Art of Color 262

CHAPTER 10
Tables **263**
Creating a Table 264
Building a New Table 264
Sidebar: Working Around the Table Default 264
Sidebar: Where's the Column Tab? 265
Tip: HTML 4.0 and Tables **266**
Sidebar: Provide the Numbers—the Correct Numbers 266
Tip: Specifying Column Widths **267**
Tip: Sometimes Math Is Hard **269**
Tip: Fill Cells to Show Their Colors **270**
Tip: Check Paragraph Alignment **271**
Tip: Aligning Captions **272**
The Fine Art of Table Selection 274

Tip: No Undo for Accidental Table Resizing 274
Selecting the Contents of a Cell 274
Tip: Can't Get a Cursor to Appear 274
Tip: Selecting All Contents Within a Cell. 274
Tip: Use Tab to Move Between Cells 275
Selecting an Entire Table 275
Sidebar: Setting Type Characteristics for All Cells in a Table. 275
Selecting a Cell 276
Tip: Increase Cell Spacing for Easier Cell Selection 276
Tip: Use the Hidden Tab in Complex Tables 276
Tip: Table Editing Through Cell Selection 276
Selecting Multiple Cells 276
Selecting a Row or Column 277
Nesting Tables 277
Tip: Quick Cell Selection Without Leaving the Keyboard 277
Editing Tables 278
Resizing Cells and Tables 278
Tip: "Live" Resizing Display 279
Adding and Deleting Cell Rows and Columns 280
Tip: Add and Delete Apply to Rows and Columns 280
Cell Spanning 281
Sidebar: A Hidden Problem? Count Those Columns! 282
Tip: Inserting Oversized Contents into Spanned Cells 283
Adding Color to Tables 283
Tip: Nest Tables to Create Colored Borders 284
Tip: Don't Drag Colors to the Cell Itself 285
Importing Table Content 285
Tip: Choosing the Right Delimiter 286
Tip: Importing with a Cell Selected 286
Tip: Don't Span Cells Before Importing 286
Tip: Importing into a Populated Table 286
Applying Formatting to Multiple Cells 286
Tables as Structure 287
Fixed versus Percentage Measurements 287
Tip: Create Structural Templates 288
Tip: Stitching Together Split Images 288
Building Forms Using Tables 288
Converting Tables to Layout Grids 289
Sidebar: Turning Layout Grids into Tables. 289
Ubiquitous Tables 290

CHAPTER 11

Frames 291

Frames versus Framesets 291
Sidebar: Keep Your Framesets and Frames Separate. 292
Creating Frames 294
Building and Populating a Frameset 294
Tip: Single Frame Icon versus Other Frameset Icons 294
Tip: Frameset or Empty GoLive Document? 294
Tip: Identifying the Frameset Icons 295
Tip: Controlling How New Frames Are Inserted 295

Tip: Previewing Noframe Pages on Windows 297
Tip: Provide a Link to Unframed Pages 297
Tip: Point & Shoot for Anchored Links 298
Editing Frames 300
Sidebar: The Mystery of the Macintosh GoLive Preview 300
Tip: Frames and Search Engines 301
Moving and Resizing Frames 301
Tip: Awkward Inspector Display When Resizing 303
Tip: Balancing the Scales 303
Frame Borders 304
Sidebar: Border Skirmishes 304
Tip: Using Frames as Layout Elements 305
Naming and Targeting Frames 306
Tip: Point & Shoot Can Kill Mac Targets 306
Tip: Multiple Open Frameset Files 307
Tip: Renaming Frames 307
Are You Game for Frames? 308

CHAPTER 12
Layout Grids and Floating Boxes 309
Tip: You Can Never Go Home (Page) Again 309
Tip: When to Use Positioning 310
Layout Grids 311
Handling the Grid 311
Sidebar: Browser Compatibility 311
Sidebar: Behind the Grid 312
Grid Objects 313
Tip: Indecent Nesting 313
Sidebar: Behind the Box 314
Floating Boxes 318
Tip: German Lesson 318
Floating Box Inspector 319
Tip: Auto Width, Height 320
Floating Box Controller 321
You Control the Horizontal 322

CHAPTER 13
Forms 323
Parts of a Form 324
Tip: Form Elements and JavaScript 324
Tip: Where to Find Form Pieces 324
Sidebar: Front-end, Not Back-end 324
Tip: Using Tables for Forms 325
Form Container 325
Tip: Close Form New to CyberStudio Users 325
Tip: Auto End Form 325
Tip: No End Form Inspector 325
Tip: Avoiding mailto: as an Action 326
Input Elements 327

Tip: Password Isn't Encryption **328**
Sidebar: Naming Elements. *328*
Sidebar: Bad Wrap. *329*
Tip: Wrap on Mac, Visible on Windows. **330**
Tip: Editing Lists in Source **331**
Tip: Label in GoLive Isn't Label in HTML **331**
Tip: Radio Button Group Fails to Display **332**
Tip: Mass Button Production **332**
Tip: Easily Change an Existing Image to a Submit Button **333**
HTML 4.0 Features. 334
Focus and Field Modifiers. 334
Tip: Tab Numbering Bug **336**
Sidebar: HTML 4.0 Resources *336*
New Buttons 337
Better Labeling and Grouping 338
Tip: Pointing Out the Wrong Place. **339**
CGI and Forms 339
Form a Line 340
Sidebar: A Script to Test Forms. *340*

CHAPTER 14

Page Specials **341**

Find 341
Replace 342
Tip: Find in Files **343**
Spellchecking. 343
Tip: Worldwide Spellchecking **343**
Checking 343
Skipping 344
Document Statistics 345
Web Download 346
Tip: Relocating Imported Images. **346**
Tip: Unethical Behavior. **346**
File Mapping 346
Tip: Using File Mapping in Files Tab **347**
Tip: Internet Config (Mac) **348**
Sidebar: Methods of Opening *348*
Open Files 349
Now That We're on the Same Page. 350

PART 3

Sites **351**

CHAPTER 15

Site Management **353**

Setting Up a Site 354
Making a New Site 354
Importing a Site 354
Tip: Help on Importing a Site **354**

Site Folders 355
    Tip: Saving the Site File Regularly **356**
Site Window 357
  References and Files 358
  Site Map. 359
  HTML Attributes 359
Site Preferences 360
  Site 360
  Other Site Preference Tabs 361
Site Menu, Palette, and Toolbar 361
    Tip: Site Tab, Site Tab **362**
Set Your Sights. 365

CHAPTER 16
Files, Folders, and Links **367**

Files Inside GoLive 368
Working with Files in a Site 368
  Root Location 368
  File Information 370
    Tip: Typing to Select. **371**
    Sidebar: Absolute versus Relative *371*
    Tip: Accessing Options **372**
    Sidebar: Status Icons. *374*
    Tip: Creator Overridden by GoLive (Mac) **375**
    Tip: Setting an Alternate HTML Editor. **375**
    Tip: Opening Problems (Mac). **375**
    Tip: Changing Names. **376**
    Sidebar: Aliases and Shortcuts. *376*
  Adding Files to the Site 378
    Tip: Analyzing Added Files **378**
  Moving Files 381
  Creating Links 381
    Tip: More on Point & Shoot **381**
    Tip: External Linking **381**
    Tip: Spring Loaded (Mac) **382**
    Sidebar: Hunt the Wumpus *382*
    Tip: Movin' On Up!. **384**
  Modifying and Examining Links 384
    Tip: Hand-Editing Links. **384**
    Tip: To and To **386**
  Tuning Up 386
    Tip: Update vs. Rescan. **386**
    Tip: PDF Problem (Mac only) **387**
    Tip: Reparse Changed **387**
    Tip: Reparse While Rescanning **387**
    Tip: Image Thumbnails **388**
External Links 388
  Link Objects 389
  Managing Links 390
    Sidebar: Importing Bookmarks from Browsers *390*
    Tip: Link Inspecting URLs **391**

Tip: Editing Long External URLs. **393**
Checking Links. 393
Tip: Memory Full! (Mac) **394**
Tip: No Action! (Windows) **394**
Tip: Bypass GoLive Validation **394**
Extras 394
Tip: Other Split-Pane Items. **394**
Errors. 394
Tip: Shortcut for Editing Long URLs **396**
Sidebar: Omitting Certain Files. *396*
Trash 398
Managing Media Links 399
Tip: Other Media Links **399**
Tip: More on Formats **399**
Single File Ahead. 400

CHAPTER 17
Sitewide Sets **401**

Creating and Editing 402
Tip: Font Space Sets. **402**
Creating. 402
Tip: Select the Right Tab **402**
Sidebar: Style Sheets for Pages and Sites. *402*
Extracting 404
Viewing 404
Editing. 405
Tip: Renaming Colors and Fontsets. **405**
Applying 406
Removing Unused 408
Making Sitewide Changes 408
Sitewide Find and Replace 409
Color Me Fontsettable 410

CHAPTER 18
Staging and Synchronizing Sites **411**

Tip: FTP Server at Your Service. **412**
How FTP Works 412
GoLive's FTP Clients 412
Setting Up a Connection. 414
Tip: You Need an Account. **415**
Tip: Tabbing over the Port Field **415**
Tip: Don't Save Your Password. **415**
Sidebar: ISPs and Directories *417*
Connecting to the Server. 418
File Handling. 419
Tip: Problem Adding Multiple Folders on Certain FTP Servers. **421**
Tip: Don't Rename or Move Files on the FTP Server. **421**
Tip: You Can't Revert after Deleting **421**
FTP Inspectors 422
Tip: Why Execute Is Checked on Folders **423**

Sidebar: Aliases, Symbolic Links, and Shortcuts 423
Synchronizing 424
   Sidebar: May I, Please 424
   Getting Set to Synchronize 425
      Tip: Setting Publish State **425**
      Sidebar: Do You Have the Time? 426
      Sidebar: GoLive's Clever Hack 427
      Tip: Upload Options Ignored **428**
      Tip: Upload Settings Don't Appear (Windows) **428**
   Uploading 429
      Tip: Upload Overload **430**
      Tip: Mirror Upload Site **430**
   Downloading 431
      Tip: Overwriting the Home Page **431**
Troubleshooting 431
   Connection 432
   File List 433
   Can't Access Directory or Upload 433
Locked and (Up)loaded 434

CHAPTER 19

Site Maps **435**
      Tip: Site Tab Not Site Window **435**
      Tip: Parents, Children, and Siblings **436**
Viewing versus Building 436
Viewing and Organizing 437
   Moving around 437
      Tip: Zoom for Layout Not Thumbnails **438**
      Tip: 300 Percent View **438**
   Examining Links 439
      Tip: Collapse to Print **441**
      Tip: False Alarms **442**
   Editing and Accessing Items 442
      Tip: Creating Thumbnails **442**
      Tip: Updating Thumbnails on Windows **443**
      Tip: Editing Long URLs Causes Error on Mac **444**
   Customizing the Site Map 444
      Tip: Switching Between Hierarchies **445**
      Tip: Can't Rearrange Order (Mac) **446**
   Printing 450
      Tip: Print at 100% **450**
      Tip: Print to PDF **451**
      Tip: Printing the Outline View **451**
Prototyping and Modifying 451
      Tip: New from Site Resets Any Changes **452**
   Adding Links 452
      Tip: Displaying Not Yet Linked Objects **452**
      Tip: Existing Links Show Solid Lines **453**
      Tip: Sibling Directions **453**
      Tip: The Home Page is Special **453**
   Adding Pages 454

Working with Pending Links and New Files....................................455
The Big Picture 457

CHAPTER 20

Importing a Site 459
Importing 459
Cleaning..461
    Tip: Mandatory Reparse All **461**
Attributes Without Quotations 462
    Tip: What's an HTML Attribute?..**462**
Fully Qualified HTTP References...463
Subsite Paths...464
PageMill Remnant 465
No Background Color or Image...466
Improving 467
Replacing Imagemaps 467
    Tip: Retaining Both Sides **468**
    Tip: Converting Server-Side Imagemap Files...........................**468**
Turning Repeated Elements into Components 470
Renaming Files and Reorganizing Structures.................................472
Brave New World 472

CHAPTER 21

Site Specials 473
    Tip: Find & Replace Not Reversible **473**
Sitewide Find and Replace...473
Setting Up Find & Replace 473
    Tip: Floor Show (Mac) **474**
Using Site-Wide Find & Replace 475
Find Files in Site 476
Export Site...476
    Tip: Changing Export Folder Names **477**
    Tip: The PRE Tag and White Space.....................................**478**
    Tip: Global White Space Settings.....................................**478**
Clear Site 479
    Tip: Let's Klar Up This Site...**479**
Templates...480
Stationery 481
    Tip: Don't Drag Stationery to Files Tab **482**
Components 482
    Tip: Components and Full HTML Page Structure.........................**483**
    Tip: Use Components for Copyright Statement..........................**483**
    Tip: JavaScript References from Components **483**
    Sidebar: Always Use Absolute References *484*
    Tip: Window Overlaps **485**
    Tip: Why Use CyberObjects Component..................................**486**
    Tip: CSOBJ **487**
    Tip: Getting Rid of CSOBJ Tags When Uploading **487**
URL Mappings 487
    Tip: Don't Read This Section. **487**

Setting Up URL Mapping 487
Tip: Automatic Addition **488**
Tip: Macintosh Crashes **488**
A Very Special Site 488

PART 4
Advanced **489**

CHAPTER 22
Advanced Features **491**

Other Advanced Features 492
Regular Expression Find and Replace 492
Tip: Ignore Case Still an Option **492**
Tip: Prefabricated Expressions. **493**
Find 493
Tip: Put a Backslash in When You're Not Sure **494**
Replace. 496
Practical Example. 497
Modules 497
Tip: More on Modules **498**
Tip: Third-Party Modules. **498**
Sidebar: Default Modules *498*
Tip: WebObjects, LiveObjects, CyberObjects **499**
Macros 499
Ever Advancing 500

CHAPTER 23
JavaScript **501**

Browser Support. 501
Sidebar: Learning JavaScript *502*
Using JavaScript in GoLive 503
Why Not Actions?. 503
Sidebar: Client-Side versus Server-Side Scripting. *503*
Sidebar: What About VBScript and ASPs?. *504*
Adding JavaScript 505
Inserting a Script 505
Tip: You Only Need One Script. **505**
Choosing a Browser and Language Version 506
JavaScript Events and the Events Tab. 508
Tip: Event Handlers Associate Objects with JavaScripts **508**
Sidebar: External JavaScripts *508*
JavaScript Objects and the Objects Tab. 509
Tip: Naming Form Elements **510**
Example: The Button Rollover 510
Example: Simple Form Validation 512
Sidebar: Syntax Check *512*
The Future of JavaScript 516

CHAPTER 24
Animation **517**
The DHTML Promise 517
Tip: Ignoring Netscape's LAYER Tag. **518**
Floating Boxes and Timetracks. 518
Tip: Only 4.0 Browsers Know DHTML. **519**
Tip: Action Track. **519**
Tip: Adding Frames Doesn't Affect File Size. **521**
Tip: Start with Invisible Floating Boxes **521**
Creating Animations 523
Tip: Floating Box Transparency **524**
Tip: Selecting the Floating Box. **525**
Tip: Keyframe Connectors in the Timeline Editor **526**
Tip: Starting Animations after a Page Loads **527**
Throwing Some Curves. 527
Tip: Avoid Random Motion. **528**
Animating Multiple Elements 528
Tip: Use Layering to Display Elements **530**
Sidebar: Avoiding Timeline Editor Interface Quirks *530*
Animation Scenes. 531
Tip: Invisibility Applies Only to GoLive. **531**
Triggering an Action within an Animation. 533
The Hard Truth. 535

CHAPTER 25
Actions **537**
Tip: Actions and Browser Compatibility. **538**
Tip: Editing Actions by Hand **538**
Tip: Installing Actions Plus 1.0 . . . . **538**
CyberObjects. 538
Tip: Testing CyberObjects **538**
Internal Objects 538
Tip: Weird Dates and Times (Mac). **540**
Page Actions 540
Standard Actions 540
Tip: Supporting Older Browsers. **540**
Triggering Actions 541
Page Event Handlers 542
Text and Image Link Event Handlers. 543
Tip: Empty Links for Actions. **544**
Action Track Event Handlers 545
Unsupported Actions. 545
Configuring Actions. 545
Tip: Special Actions **546**
Getters 546
Sidebar: Field Entry Indicator *546*
Image Actions 547
Link Actions 548
Message Actions 549

Multimedia Actions 550
Others 551
Specials 552
Variables 553
Combining Actions 554
Rotating Banner Ads 554
Open a Remote Control Subwindow. 556
Shifting Scripts to an External Library File 558
Sidebar: Pros and Cons of External JavaScript Libraries 558
Tip: Rebuild for Actions. **559**
Building Action-Packed Web Sites 559

CHAPTER 26
Cascading Style Sheets 561

Tip: CSS1 and CSS2. . . . . **561**
Style Sheets Backgrounder 562
Ancient Times. 562
HTML and Style Sheets. 562
Sidebar: Simple CSS Coding. 563
Previewing Style Sheets 564
Targeting Browsers. 564
Previewing in GoLive. 565
Tip: GoLive's Default Browser Assumptions **565**
Previewing in Real Browsers. 566
Designing Style Sheets 566
GoLive Tools 566
Tip: Internal and External Style Sheets Editors **567**
Sidebar: CSS Resources 568
Sidebar: Using Import to Link Style Sheets. 569
Style Sheet Selectors. 570
Tip: Contextual Selectors. **571**
Tip: IDs in External Style Sheets. **571**
Style Sheet Specifications 571
Tip: Preview in Browsers for Best Results **571**
Sidebar: Character Styles and Paragraph Styles 571
Tip: Previewing the CSS Definition **572**
Units. 572
Tip: GoLive Converts **573**
Tip: Ideal Pixels. **573**
Tip: Em Height Versus Em Width **573**
Sidebar: Embedding Fonts in GoLive
Tip: Making Type the Same on All Platforms. **575**
Tip: Float and Clear **575**
Cascading 576
Sidebar: The Specificity Formula. 577
Tip: In CSS2, Readers Come First **578**
Applying Style Sheets 578
Applying Classes. 578
Tip: Block that Property! **579**
Applying IDs. 580

Tip: Floating Boxes Took Over My Style!. **580**
Advanced CSS 581
   Complex Selectors 582
   Psuedo-Selectors 582
   Browser-Specific Features 583
Designing with Style. 584

CHAPTER 27
Web Database **585**
The Web Database Doesn't 586
Previewing Output 586
   Sidebar: A Word of Warning. *586*
      Tip: Previewing (Mac) **588**
      Tip: Scrolling Source Sample (Mac). **588**
Global Tab 588
   Sidebar: Applying Changes Globally *588*
   HTML Formatting 589
      Tip: Why Switch Line Breaks?. **590**
   Style Settings. 590
HTML Tab. 591
   Examining Tags 591
      Tip: Windows Organization **591**
      Tip: Editing and Adding Values **593**
      Tip: Previewing Attributes with Create This Attribute **595**
   Adding HTML Tags 596
   Changing GoLive HTML Defaults. 599
Characters Tab 600
   Adding Characters 601
CSS Tab 603
   Browser Preview Settings 603
      Tip: Windows GoLive Preview **603**
      Tip: Fooling Around with Built-in Browser Settings **605**
   CSS Settings 605
Other Tabs 605
Give It a Try 606

CHAPTER 28
Plug-ins and Media **607**
Netscape-Style Plug-ins 607
Adding Plug-in Objects 609
   Plug-in Inspector 609
      Tip: Recognizing Plug-in Files, Part 1 . . . . **609**
      Tip: A MIME You Look Forward To Seeing **609**
      Tip: Recognizing Plug-in Files, Part 2 . . . . **610**
   Userdef Inspector (Mac Only) 614
Java Applets and ActiveX 616
   Java Applet Specifics 617
   ActiveX Specifics 619
      Tip: Streamlining Alt Text **619**
XML 620

XML in GoLive 621
    Tip: More XML Information **621**
QuickTime Editing 624
   QuickTime Inspector 625
    Tip: Playing Tricks **625**
    Tip: Flat QuickTime Files **626**
   Track Editor and Inspectors 627
    Tip: Track Inspector Super Tips **631**
ASP Support 637
WebObjects 638
Plug In, Log Out, and GoLive! 639

Appendixes and Index 641

APPENDIX A

Macintosh Issues & Extras 643
File Features 644
   Finder Label 644
   Type and Creator 646
    Tip: Change Creator Freeware **646**
Mac OS 8.5 Specials 647
   Appearance Themes Aware 647
   Use Navigation Services 647
AIAT 649
ColorSync 650
Internet Config 651
    Tip: Getting Internet Config **651**
   File Mappings 651
    Tip: Programs You've Never Heard Of. **652**
   FTP Up- and Download Mapping 652
    Tip: Use Always Can't Be Added To **653**
   Proxy Servers 654
AppleScript 654
Text Clippings 656

APPENDIX B

Master List of CSS Compatibility 657
Compatibility Chart 658
Glossary 673

Index 685

GoLive
Basics
PART 1

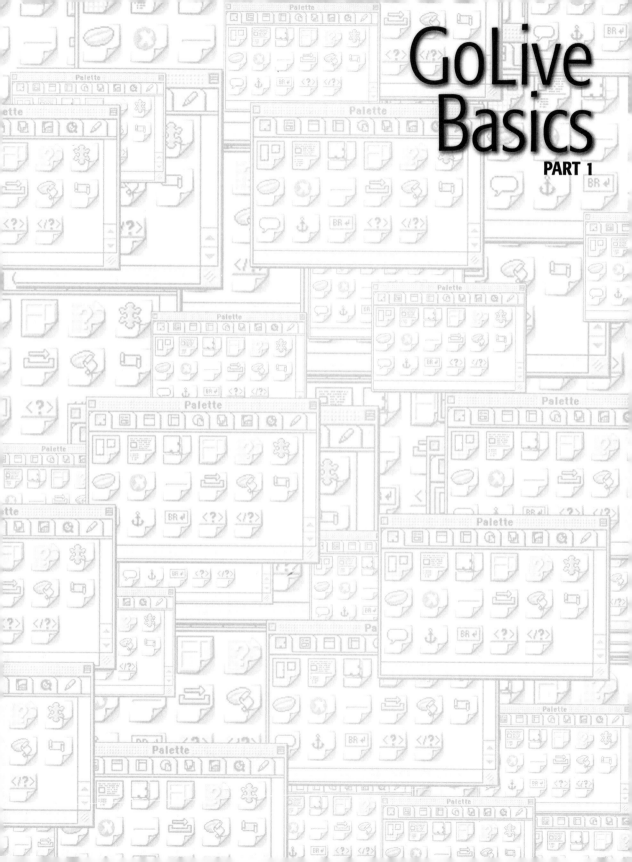

CHAPTER 1

Getting Started

Working with GoLive for the first time can seem like biting off an awfully big piece for one mouthful. This part of the book provides an overall guide to the program, walking you through each section of the program so you can become comfortable with its conventions and its interface. When reading other parts of the book, feel free to refer back to these first chapters to get a visual explanations of given interfaces or palettes. But our goal is to get you started quickly in using the program so you can learn how to accomplish your given tasks.

This chapter walks briskly through the whole process of using GoLive, so you can see every major feature of the program; the next four chapters in this section focus on individual areas and parts of the interface.

Installing GoLive

If you haven't installed GoLive yet, whip that CD out of its slipcase and stick it in your computer's CD-ROM drive. Under Windows, you can choose to install the program, its help files, and a set of tutorial files separately. On the Mac side, you can't configure the installation—all 34 megabytes get placed on your hard drive.

All installed parts are placed into the Adobe GoLive 4.0 folder (see Figure 1-1). This includes the GoLive application, folders for active and disabled modules (pieces of the program, such as WebObjects, PNG Support, and more, turned on or off in Preferences), imported images (which GoLive can render and display on the fly), and the GoLive cache (for pages and files that have been rendered before). In addition, there's also a Plug-ins folder where you can place various and sundry browser plug-ins from Shockwave to Flash to RealAudio.

Figure 1-1
GoLive's
installed files

Macintosh installation   *Windows installation*

Tip: Allocate
Memory
Before
Starting
Making large-scale changes to sites of more than a hundred pages or so can require extra memory. The Mac OS doesn't automatically allocate space to programs on demand, so before you start, find your installed copy of GoLive, select the application icon, and then either select Get Info from the File menu or press Command-I. (If you're using System 8.5 or later, select Memory from the Show popup menu.) Add 5,000K to 10,000K to both the Preferred and Minimum memory fields.

The Windows 98/NT/2000 operating systems don't allow you to set specific memory allocation for a program. The system can provide more memory to a program as it needs it. However, it's best to have as few other programs running as possible when performing these tasks to avoid odd problems that can arise.

You can turn virtual memory on in both the Macintosh and Windows systems, providing you with additional available memory for programs, although it slows down overall system performance because virtual memory involves reading and writing from the hard drive. (For details on turning virtual memory on or tweaking memory values, see http://realworldgolive.com/vm.html.)

Manual Dexterity

The first release of GoLive 4.0 for Macintosh—in March 1999—came with an 850-page horse-choking manual that covered Mac features (with lots of accidental inclusions of Alt keys and backslashes). This manual was a quick revision of the one that shipped with CyberStudio 3. Accompanying this hurking manual was a two-panel keystroke chart showing just the shortcut keys for tasks.

The first release of 4.0 for Windows showed up with a slimmed-down, redesigned, rewritten, approximately 450-page manual that covered both Mac and Windows. This smaller manual replaced the horsechoker that shipped with the Macintosh version starting in about June 1999. The new manual also came with a new keystroke chart with six panels, including the names and relationships of all the parts of the GoLive interface (customized for Mac and Windows).

Mac users who had gotten the bigger, less coherent manual complained fairly loudly on the GoLive Talk list (http://www.blueworld.com/blueworld/lists/golive.html) that they wanted the new manual. At the time of this writing, Adobe was planning on making the new one available for a shipping charge, but details weren't available as this book went to press.

Opening GoLive

Launch GoLive for the first time and you find the following four items populating your screen (see Figures 1-2 and 1-3):

- The Document window is where you build your page, as well as edit its underlying HTML, create frames, and simulate a preview in different browsers.

- The Palette features an arsenal of objects divided into categories and represented by icons that can be dragged to your page or site, from tables and images to QuickTime tracks and frame layouts (see Figure 1-4).

- The Toolbar contextually changes to fit a variety of tasks (see Figure 1-5). You see the Text Toolbar while carrying out most tasks in the Document window's Layout Editor, but other toolbars pop up from time to time, including the Layout Grid, CSS, and Site Toolbars.

- The Inspector palette contextually changes to allow modification of attributes to objects dropped into your page from the Palette (see Figure 1-6). For example, after dragging the Image icon from the Palette into a page, the Inspector becomes the Image Inspector; you can assign the image's source file, link it to another page, and configure an imagemap within its five tabs.

Tip: ToolTips   To make it easier to figure out the purpose of the sometimes-obscure icons that GoLive uses in its Toolbar and palettes, turn on ToolTips. Doing so causes the name of the item to pop up when you hover over it for more than a few seconds. On the Macintosh, select Show Hot Help from the Help menu; under Windows, the ToolTips appear automatically.

Figure 1-2
Macintosh
GoLive
first look

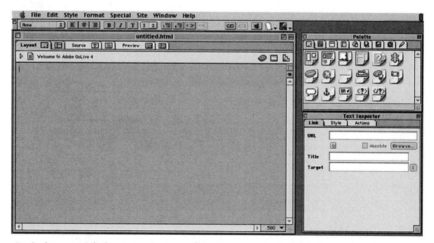

GoLive's essential elements, clockwise from the top: the Toolbar, the Palette, the Inspector palette, and the Document window.

Figure 1-3
Windows
GoLive
first look

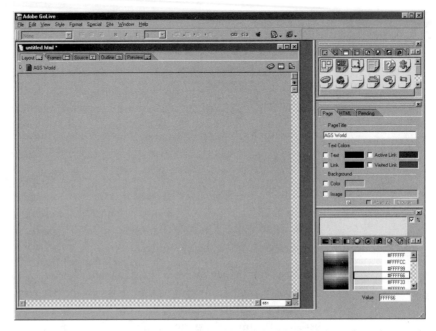

The same configuration under Windows, but with the addition of the Color Palette at the bottom right; the three palettes can group together into a docked palette bar.

ToolTips display when you hold your mouse over an icon in a tab or toolbar. In the Palette, the names of icons show up at the bottom of the palette whenever you move your cursor above any item.

You can control the visibility of these palettes along with the Color Palette, Link Inspector, and Floating Box Controller on the GoLive desktop by selecting the name from the Windows menu (Mac) or View menu (Windows), or by pressing the keyboard shortcut (see Table 1-1).

Table 1-1
Palette
keyboard
shortcuts

Palette	Mac (Windows menu)	Windows (View menu)
Toolbar	Command-0	Alt-0
Inspector	Command-1	Alt-1
Palette	Command-2	Alt-2
Color Palette	Command-3	Alt-3
Link Inspector	Command-5	Alt-4
Floating Box Controller	Command-6	Alt-5

Note: The missing number under the Mac shortcuts (Command-4) opens and closes the Web Database; on Windows, press Control-4.

Figure 1-4
Two Palette
tabs

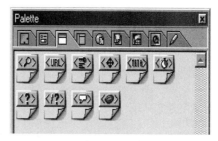

The Basic tab

The Head tab

Figure 1-5
Three toolbars

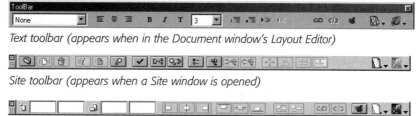

Text toolbar (appears when in the Document window's Layout Editor)

Site toolbar (appears when a Site window is opened)

Layout Grid toolbar (appears when a layout grid is selected in the Layout Editor)

Figure 1-6
Three
inspectors

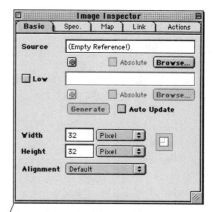

*Page Inspector (opens when the
Document window's Page icon is clicked)*

*Image Inspector (opens in Layout Editor
after placing an image placeholder, or
when editing a selected image)*

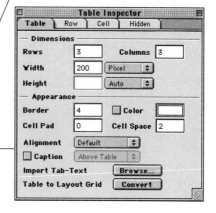

*Table Inspector (opens in Layout Editor
after placing a table placeholder, or
when editing a selected table)*

Managing Windows and Palettes

As you work with GoLive, your view of the program can become cluttered with a dizzying amount of windows, palettes, inspectors, and controllers (see Figure 1-7). However, GoLive provides a set of options to optimize and manage all the items on your display.

Managing on the Mac. On the Mac, you can minimize all GoLive's elements in two ways (see Figure 1-8):

- Control-click the title bar
- Drag the item to either the right side of the screen for floating palettes or the bottom of the screen for popup windows

The palette or window then becomes a tab, which you can maximize into its original form by clicking the tab or dragging it to an area on your screen. You can position the minimized tab by clicking the tab and holding, then dragging it along the edge of the screen where it rests.

You can also click the Windowshade box on the far right of any window or palette; or, double-click the title bar if you've checked the Double-Click Title Bar option in the Appearance control panel (System 8.5 and later), or the earlier Windowshade control panel. This "rolls up" the window, minimizing it to just a title. Unroll the window by clicking the Windowshade box again, or double-clicking the title bar.

As you drag palettes around the screen, notice that they tend to snap into place near each other to make them organize more neatly.

Minimizing problems with multiple resolutions. GoLive keeps track of where on the screen you minimized palettes the last time you did so, even if you're no longer viewing the screen at that same resolution. This becomes a problem when you switch resolutions on your monitor, such as when you're working at one resolution with a PowerBook on the road and then switch to a lower or higher resolution on a monitor back at the office.

Figure 1-7
That's a
lotta boxes

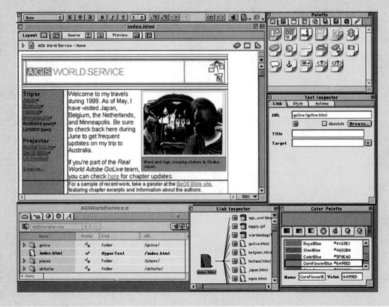

Figure 1-8
Grouping
palettes and
windows

Toolbar

Inspector palette

Palette

Color Palette

Link Inspector

Floating Box Controller

QuickTime Editor

Mac palettes minimize to square icons on the right of your screen, while Mac windows minimize to rectangular boxes (with window name) at the bottom of your screen.

Document window   *Palette*

untitled.html   Text Inspect

Document file tab

welcome.html

If you minimize palettes to the right side of the screen, quit the program, switch to a lower resolution, and run GoLive again, then those palettes are irretrievable. You have to change monitor resolution to be able to simply click them to expand them back to full size.

Worse, if you Control-click the titlebar to minimize a fully displayed palette—and the *last time* you minimized the palette was at a higher resolution—the palette's icon gets placed off your visible screen. Once again, you have to change resolutions to retrieve the palette's window.

(To change resolution, go to the Apple menu's Control Panels folder, and bring up the Monitors or Monitors & Sound control panel. You can select a higher resolution in most cases from the Resolution scrolling list.)

It's an unsolvable proposition if you're working on a PowerBook or at a screen resolution where you can't go any higher and yet your icons are still off the screen.

The only way to get the palette back is to close the application, go into the Preferences folder in the System folder, and trash the CyberStudio Preferences file. Reopen GoLive and all the many preference changes you've made to the program have been lost and you start from scratch.

Managing under Windows. The Windows version of GoLive lets you dock palettes on the right side of the screen (see Figure 1-9). Double-click the first palette to dock it and then Control-drag other palettes on top of it to add them to the docking area. You can resize palettes in this display, dragging the bar between them.

To break an individual palette out of this bar, drag it to a new location or double-click its top

Figure 1-9
Docking palettes
in Windows

Windows palettes group together in a bar on the right side of the screen

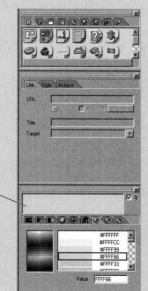

Double-click top palette border to break it out of the bar and into its own window.

Or, click, hold, and drag the palette to a desired screen location.

Managing Windows and Palettes, continued

bar; either action opens the palette in its own window. To return it to the palette bar, double-click its title bar or Control-drag it back into the palette bar area. Unlike the Mac version of GoLive, you cannot Control- or Alt-click a palette's titlebar to minimize it to a small icon. In addition, be careful where you drag a palette; dragging to the bottom of the screen can make it disappear.

For documents, Windows itself has a Minimize box on every window. Clicking this box reduces the item to just its title. You can drag this minimized item around on the page.

A GoLive resolution. We've noted that GoLive was designed with at least a 1,024-by-768-pixel window in mind. It's hard to display your HTML page and a couple palettes, along with the toolbar, without having a lot of overlaps at lower resolutions. If you're going to be dedicating more than 10 hours a week to using GoLive, we recommend getting at least a 17-inch monitor, if not a 19-inch one. Prices at this writing are as low as $650 for a high-quality 19-inch Sony Trinitron monitor with lots of bells and whistles.

Tip:
Overlaying
Palettes

If all your palettes and inspectors are fully visible (not covered partially or wholly by another palette or inspector), pressing their keyboard shortcuts make them disappear. However, if one of these items overlays another, pressing the keyboard shortcut for the hidden item brings it to the front.

More information. The wonderful world of the Inspector palette is covered in full in Chapter 2, *The Inspector*, while the Toolbar and Palette (and all their tabs and icons) are covered in Chapter 3, *Palettes and Parts*.

Getting Started: Step by Step

Now that you've opened up GoLive and looked under the hood, it's time to take it out for a spin and do some work. In this section, we introduce you to GoLive's basics by taking you step-by-step through creating a page, placing elements on it, and creating a site document.

Creating a New Page

GoLive defaults to opening up a new, untitled file when the program is opened. You can also create a new GoLive document by pressing Command-N (Mac) or Control-N (Windows), or by selecting New from the File menu.

Let's start by setting up some of the basic attributes of the page.

Page Title

In GoLive, the title of a page—the name that appears in a Web browser's top title bar—is set to "Welcome to Adobe GoLive 4" by default. To change the name, click anywhere within the Page Title field, located to the right of the Page icon at the top left of the main window. The entire title becomes highlighted and editable. When finished typing your title, press Return or Enter, and your cursor is placed at the beginning of the untitled document. For our example, we type AGS World Service.

This is simple enough. But for even more controls, click the Page icon to the left of the Page Title field to bring up the Page Inspector (see Figure 1-10). The inspector allows you to modify a page's title, text colors, background colors and images, and color profiles, as well as how GoLive handles other parts of the page.

Figure 1-10
Page Inspector

Clicking the Page icon brings up the Page Inspector, where you can set page title, colors, and other details.

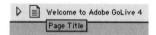

However, you can also click the Page Title text area to make it active and edit the page's title there.

To modify a page title within the Page Inspector, select the Page tab, then click within the Page Title field. Note that the entire field is not highlighted and that the cursor lands where you clicked. Enter your title, then accept the change by pressing either Return, Enter, or Tab, or by clicking the carriage return icon to the right of the field. (In our example, we added "- home" to the end of the title.)

GoLive in Action: Accepting Change

A large portion of a page's or a site's attributes are configured using the myriad of contextual inspectors. If you make a change to many, but not all, text fields—an area into which one types text—a carriage return icon appears to the right of where you enter the value into the field (see Figure 1-11).

That is your cue to either click the icon or press Return (Mac) or Enter (Windows) to have GoLive accept the edit to this field. You can also press Tab (both platforms) to jump to the next field in the inspector, which makes the change stick. If you click another tab or field within the Inspector or click back into your page without doing one of these actions, your change is not saved and the field reverts to what was there before.

Figure 1-11
Accepting new values

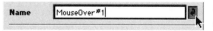

Click the carriage return icon, or press Return or Enter to stay in the field, or press Tab to move to the next field.

Text Colors

The Text Colors section of the Page Inspector allows you to change the color of a page's body text and links. The section is made up of four items—Text, Link, Active Link (the color that appears when a link is being clicked on), and Visited Link—each with a color field and a checkbox.

GoLive defaults to standard text colors, the names and values of which can be found under the Real Web Colors and Web Named Colors tabs on the Color Palette (see Table 1-2).

	Attribute	Name	Hexadecimal Value
Table 1-2 **Text Colors**	Text	Black	#000000
	Link	Blue	#0000FF
	Active	Red	#FF0000
	Visited	Magenta	#FF00FF

To modify the colors on our new page, bring the Page Inspector up by clicking the Page icon, and click one of the color swatches to display the Color Palette (or press Command-3 on the Mac or Alt-3 under Windows). Within the Color Palette, we choose Maroon from within the Web Named Colors tab (see Figure 1-12).

Figure 1-12
Dragging a
color swatch

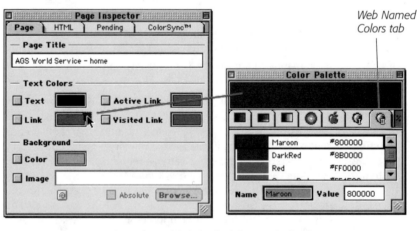

The Color Field is checked automatically after you drag a color swatch into it.

In the Color Palette, click the Web Named Colors tab (denoted by the circle icon with the Roman numeral 2) and find Maroon either by scrolling through the list, typing its name in the Name field and pressing Return or Enter, or by typing its hexadecimal value in the Value field and pressing Return or Enter. The Maroon color becomes highlighted in the list and the color is displayed in the preview pane.

Place your cursor over the preview pane (or over the color swatch in the list, to the left of the color's name), hold down your mouse, and drag a small color swatch to the Page Inspector. Drop the color sample over the Text Colors Link field. Maroon is added and the box to the left is checked automatically.

If you uncheck any of the Text Colors boxes, the color you chose for that field remains visible, but it is not active for that attribute.

More Information. For in-depth coverage of the Color Palette, see Chapter 3, *Palettes and Parts*, and Chapter 9, *Color*.

GoLive in Action: Undo

GoLive features only one level of undo (Command-Z on the Mac or Control-Z under Windows), and sometimes it even forgets that. For example, say you make a text change to a page while in the Layout Editor, then switch to another tab in the Document window; GoLive does not allow you to undo that last change when you return to the Layout Editor.

If you select a color from the Color Palette and drag it into the Color field on, say, the Page Inspector, then decide that's not the color for you, you cannot undo the dragged selection. To revert back, you must find that original color in the Color Palette and drag that back to the Color field. (Strangely, though, you can undo a selection made onto the Color field in the Table Inspector's Cell tab.)

Background

In the Background section of the Page tab, you can choose a color for your page as well as a tiled image (see Figure 1-13). To select a color, repeat the steps taken in the Text Colors section above. For this example, we use white. To place an image, check the box to the left of the Image field, making the field active and inserting an "(Empty Reference!)" reminder (see Figure 1-14).

Tip: Both Background Color and Image

Ancient browsers don't display a background image, although some of them display a background color. If you select both a color and an image, browsers that can show a background do; others display the color. Also, if your background image is large or takes time to load, the background color shows up while the image is loading.

Tip: Quick Background Color

If all you want to change is the background color and you don't want to mess around with the Page Inspector, simply drag a color swatch from the Color Palette to the Page icon and the color is added.

If you know the file destination of your desired image, type it in the Image field. Otherwise, click the Browse button, and navigate to an image in the Open dialog box. GoLive lets you import Web-friendly image formats like JPEG and GIF. The selected image is then tiled to fill the background of your page.

By default, the background image is referenced as a relative link: that is, its location is navigated as up or down folders from, or in the same folder as, the HTML

Figure 1-13
Tiled
background
image

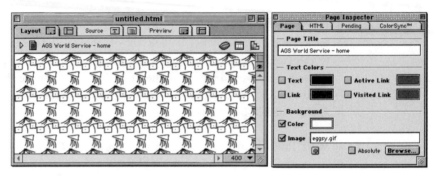

Figure 1-14
Empty
Reference
reminder

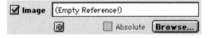

page that references it. If the image is in the same folder as the page, the file name is all that's needed to access it. However, if you move the HTML file later, the image becomes unreachable.

Checking Absolute provides a full URL to the image file, showing the entire file directory path (Figure 1-15). The HTML file which links to this image can be moved without losing the image.

Tip: Absolute
Links in
a Site

If you check the Absolute box when making a link inside the Site window, discussed later in this chapter, the link shows just the part from top of the site down, omitting the whole "file:///" messiness. GoLive knows where the site folder lives, so that part is implied, and you can drag files and images around at will inside the Site window; GoLive prompts you to rewrite the links to the new location.

Figure 1-15
Setting an
Absolute path

This is a rather annoying background image, so for this example we uncheck Image to get rid of it. Note that the name of the image file is immediately deleted from the Image field. Should you change your mind and check Image to return the background image, you are met with the "(Empty Reference!)" reminder again.

More Information. See Chapter 2, *The Inspector* for more on the Page Inspector's tabs. See also Chapter 8, *Images* and Chapter 9, *Color*.

Default Font

When you create an HTML page, the way the text on the page looks depends on how a viewer has configured his or her Web browser's font preferences (assuming they've even touched them). GoLive defaults to using the viewer's default font, unless you choose one of three default fontsets: Times New Roman, Arial, or Courier New.

Each fontset includes the named primary font choice, as well as additional font choices for viewers whose computers do not have the first choice or choices available (see Table 1-3).

Fontset	Font Attributes
Times New Roman	`<font face="Times New Roman,Georgia,Times">`
Arial	`<font face="Arial,Helvetica,Geneva,Swiss, SunSans-Regular">`
Courier	`<font face="Courier New,Courier,Monaco">`

Table 1-3
Fontsets

You can make changes to existing fontsets or create new global fontsets, or new sets for an individual page through the Font Set Editor (see Figure 1-16). For our example, we create a set for our individual page using Microsoft's favorite font, Verdana.

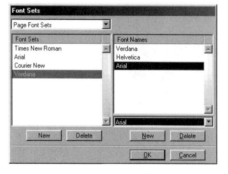

Figure 1-16
Font Set Editor
for page-based
fonts

Open the Font Set Editor by pressing Command-Option-F (Mac) or Control-Option-F (Windows), or selecting Edit Font Sets from the Font submenu of the Style menu. Select the Page icon in the left menu (Mac) or select Page Font Sets from the top menu (Windows) to work on sets for the open page.

Click the New button beneath the Font Sets menu and an Empty Font Set item is created, while a New Font item is created under the Font Names list. To name the fontset, either type a font name in the field where New Font appears below the Font Names list or select a font from the popup list to the right of the field. (If you type the name, be sure to press Return, Enter, or Tab to accept the change.) The selected font appears in the Font Names list, as well as the name of the Font Set.

To add additional fonts to this Font Set, click the New button below the Font Names list, then type the name (Mac only) or select a font from the popup list.

For our example, we select Verdana first, then add Arial and Helvetica as extra fonts to complete the set. When finished, click OK. You can check to see that the fontset now has been added to the page's Font Set list under the Font submenu.

To make the new fontset active on our page, we go to the Style menu's Font submenu, select Verdana, and start typing. Switch to the HTML Source Editor, and you see your text is surrounded by the proper Font tag and attribute.

```
<font face="Verdana,Arial,Helvetica">Witty text here</font>
```

If you have a piece of text typed on your page when you create this new set and then delete it, the fontset is also deleted.

More information. See Chapter 7, *Text and Fonts*, and Chapter 17, *Sitewide Sets*.

Tip: Font Preferences versus Fontsets

If you wanted to set the default font for your page, the first place you might look would be GoLive Preferences. Clicking the Fonts icon in the left menu window brings up the Fonts list box with attributes for Western font encodings, and includes attributes for Proportional and Monospaced, as well as the Cascading Style Sheet attributes Serif, Sans Serif, Cursive, and Fantasy Fonts (see Figure 1-17).

However, changing the default font in Preferences (by choosing an available font such as Verdana from the popup list at the bottom of the Fonts list box) only changes the viewable font within GoLive's Layout mode; even then it only changes text for the selected language encoding group—in this case Western.

Figure 1-17
Setting preferences for GoLive's viewable font

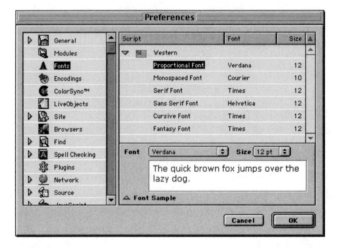

Text

When designing or editing a page, you see a lot of the Text toolbar, which allows you to control attributes of HTML text from paragraph style to setting bold and italic, to alignment in creating lists (see Figure 1-18). This piece of the contextual toolbar is visible and active in the Layout Editor and HTML Source Editor.

Figure 1-18
Text editing
part of Text
toolbar

This part of the Toolbar appears in the Layout Editor and HTML Source Editor

As is the case with much you discover about GoLive, the Toolbar is but one path of many you can choose to walk. If you love menus, many of these formatting controls can also be accessed through the Format and Style menus, while those who let their fingers do the walking can accomplish the same feats via keyboard shortcuts (see Chapter 5, *Layout, Source, and Preview*).

More information. Several other flavors of the contextual Toolbar are introduced in this chapter, but the complete assortment (from Text and Site to Outline and Layout Grid) is detailed in Chapter 3, *Palettes and Parts*.

Saving

At this point, we have a blank canvas to add more items to, so let's save this GoLive document and get on with adding some elements.

The Save command is really like any other Save command—press Command-S (Mac) or Control-S (Windows), or select Save from the File menu. Since you're saving the file for the first time, GoLive brings up the Save As dialog box so you can name the file and choose its location.

GoLive automatically adds the .html file suffix when using other methods of creating pages (such as in the Site window); for now, be sure to add .html or .htm to ensure that GoLive recognizes the file as a Web page.

Navigate through the file dialog box to where you want to place this saved file, and click Save or press Return. In this example, the file is saved as "ags-ws.html".

GoLive in
Action:
Opening
Files

Opening files in GoLive is like opening files in just about any other program—simply press Command-O (Macintosh) or Control-O (Windows) to display the Open dialog box and choose a file to open.

In addition, GoLive maintains a list of recently accessed files, and assigns three keyboard shortcuts to the most recently accessed files according to three file types: Command-1 for HTML documents, Command-2 for site documents, and Command-3 for other materials such as text files or QuickTime movies (see Figure 1-19).

Inserting Elements

Our page, so far, isn't very interesting. But, starting here, we begin to add elements from GoLive's huge palette of options. For our example, let's bring in a simple table and a couple images, two elements which often form the foundation of most Web pages.

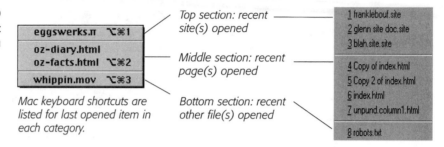

Figure 1-19
Open Recent
Files menu

Top section: recent site(s) opened

Middle section: recent page(s) opened

Bottom section: recent other file(s) opened

Mac keyboard shortcuts are listed for last opened item in each category.

Table

When in Layout mode, position the text-insertion point where you want the table to appear, then double-click the Table icon in the Basic tab of the Palette to place a table in your page at that point. You can also drag and drop the Table icon onto your page.

GoLive in Action: Drag and Drop

Here's your first encounter with GoLive's drag-and-drop, WYSIWYG interface. In the Palette, click the Basic tab and drag the Table icon into the body of the page (see Figure 1-20). Once plopped in there, notice that the Inspector palette now reads Table Inspector in its title bar.

You don't have to worry about dropping an icon in the wrong place. GoLive is smarter than you, and only lets you drag icons into what it deems an appropriate area (such as the Keywords icon into the Head section and a Table icon into the body area of the Document window).

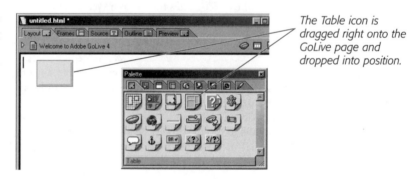

Figure 1-20
Dragging
a table icon
onto a page

The Table icon is dragged right onto the GoLive page and dropped into position.

GoLive places a three-row-by-three-column table that's 200 pixels wide; you modify the attributes within the Table Inspector, which appears when either the whole table or an individual cell is selected (see Figure 1-21).

To select an entire table, place your cursor over the top or left border of the table and click when the grabber hand cursor appears. A thin, black border surrounds your table and the Table Inspector displays the Table tab, where you make

Figure 1-21
Configuring
table attributes

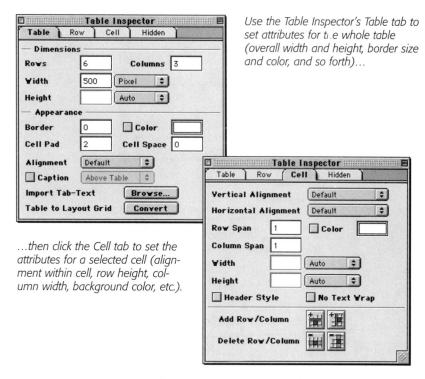

Use the Table Inspector's Table tab to set attributes for the whole table (overall width and height, border size and color, and so forth)…

…then click the Cell tab to set the attributes for a selected cell (alignment within cell, row height, column width, background color, etc.).

adjustments to the number of rows and columns, overall width, border appearance, and the table alignment. To select a single cell, click either the bottom or right border of the cell. This produces a thicker border that's set to black (if the Border field on the Table tab equals 1 or greater) or white (if the Border field is set to 0) to denote selection. The Table Inspector also opens to the Cell tab, where you can adjust width, height, vertical and horizontal alignment of elements, plus add and delete columns and rows. Placing your cursor within a cell brings up the Text Inspector or the Inspector palette of a specific element that is selected (such as the Image or Line Inspectors).

Tip: Cell blocks

Unlike some programs (like Microsoft Excel), you can't just click and drag to select multiple cells within a table. You must first select one cell, then Shift-click others (see Figure 1-22). You don't have to worry about hitting the exact border—go ahead, click right in the middle of additional cells. You can select cells that are directly adjacent or that are in some far off corner of the table (this is referred to as "noncontiguous selection").

To select all the cells in a table, first select a single cell, then press Command-A (Mac) or Control-A (Windows); or, Control-click (Mac) or right-click (Windows) and choose Select All from the contextual menu.

If you select the table as a whole (by clicking on the top or left outside border) and press Command-A or Control-A, you select the entire document.

Figure 1-22
Table
selections

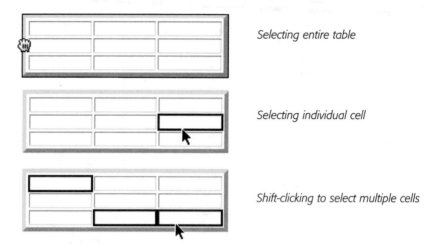

Selecting entire table

Selecting individual cell

Shift-clicking to select multiple cells

Starting with the Table Inspector's Table tab, let's configure a table that defines the layout of our page. In the Rows field, type 6 and press Tab to accept the change and move on to the next field. In the Columns field, type 3 and press Tab.

In the Width field, type 500 and press Return or Enter to keep your cursor within the field. In the menu to the right, Pixel is the default choice. If you select Percent, GoLive automatically calculates the percentage based on the width of the table in relation to the width of the GoLive document. Thus, a 500-pixel table in a 580-pixel GoLive document window is calculated as 86 percent. If you change the width of the document window (or, ultimately, the browser window), the table conforms to 86 percent of the total width. If you select Auto at this point with no cell contents, your table gets scrunched up into almost nothing. Remember, a table with no assigned width conforms only to the width of its contents.

Tip: Dragging the Line With Pixel selected as your Width measurement, place your cursor over the right outside border of the table (see Figure 1-23). It transmogrifies into a blue two-way arrow, signifying you can drag the table's outside border to a desired width. As you drag, notice that the measurement in the Width field changes dynamically. To change the width of a table's columns, press Option (Mac) or Alt (Windows) with the cursor over an interior border and drag: a light-blue two-way arrow appears.

Note that if Percent is selected, you can't drag the outside border of your table; you need to press Option (Mac) or Alt (Windows) to bring up the blue two-way arrow. However, Option/Alt-clicking and dragging the width of the table changes the measurement from Percent back to Pixel.

Finally, you can Control-Option-drag (Mac) or Control-Alt-drag (Windows) either the exterior or interior borders to make the table resize visually.

In the Table tab's Appearance area, click the Border field, type 0 (zero), and press Tab. In the Cell Pad field (which controls the amount of space by which ma-

Figure 1-23
Table
adjustments

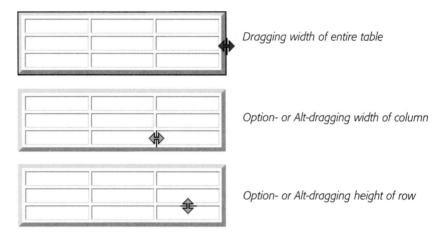

Dragging width of entire table

Option- or Alt-dragging width of column

Option- or Alt-dragging height of row

terial in a cell is offset from the separator or border on all four sides), type 2 and press Tab. In the Cell Space field (which controls the width between cells), type 0 (zero) and press Return.

The Alignment menu is automatically set to Default, which does not allow text or other elements to be placed on either side of the table. Choosing Left or Right allows you to flow text around the table. For this example, since we're creating a layout structure for the page, we choose Default.

If you check the Caption option, GoLive creates a new row at either the top or bottom of the table, selectable from the popup menu to the right of the Caption checkbox. The caption row has no border, spans the width of the table, and aligns the text in its center. (However, be wary of using this option, as it is not supported by all browsers.)

With the basic attributes of the table in place, we need to configure how the columns work. Select the top left cell by clicking its bottom border to display the Table Inspector's Cell tab. Here you can change how the text is aligned within the cell and how many rows and columns the cell spans. You can also define the width and height of an individual cell, or have those attributes define an entire column with one click.

The Width and Height fields default to Auto, which grays out the fields and prevents you from entering values. In the popup menu, select either Pixel to enter an exact measurement or Percent to assign a percentage. Setting the width for this cell sets the width for all the cells in the column (and, in turn, setting the height for a cell sets the height for all the cells in that row). For this example, we set the first column's width to 100 pixels and the width of the second to 10. If you select Percent from the Width popup menu, GoLive automatically calculates the nearest round percentage.

You can also set the background color for a cell or selection of cells. For our example, let's select the entire left column. First, select the top left cell by clicking its bottom border. Then, holding the Shift key, click anywhere within each subsequent cell below.

With the Color Palette open, select a color; for this example, choose Corn-FlowerBlue, #6495ED, from the Web Named Colors tab. Click the color in the Color Palette's preview pane, drag it over to the Table Inspector, and drop it on the Color field to the right of the Row Span field. The selected color now appears in the field, the box to its left is checked, and the selected rows are now filled with that color. To deselect this color for the selected cells, simply uncheck the box; the cells return to their original background color.

More information. See Chapter 10, *Tables*.

Tip: Making a Table Color Active	If you choose a background color for a table cell and do not place either text or an HTML element in it, the color does not show up in GoLive or in most browsers. To make the color viewable, place your cursor into the cell and press Option-spacebar to create a non-breaking space.

Image

Let's add a little life to our table by bringing in an image. From the Basic tab in the Palette, double-click the Image icon to place an image component within your document at the point where your text insertion point is. Alternatively, drag the Image icon from the Palette to a desired spot in your document.

At this point, the Inspector palette changes to the Image Inspector. Let's start with the Basic tab.

If you know the location of the desired image file, click within the Source field and type its filename and, if the file is located in another folder, its directory location. If you don't know the full path or filename offhand, click the Browse button, navigate to the file in the Open dialog box, select the file, then press Return or click the Open button.

Tip: Dragging Images	You can also drag an image file (in GIF or JPEG format) from the Desktop and place it anywhere within the GoLive document (see Figure 1-24).

Figure 1-24
Dragging images from Desktop

Tip: Editing
Long URLs Pressing Option (Mac) or Control (Windows) while the Image Inspector is open to the Basic tab changes the Browse button to Edit. Clicking Edit opens the Edit URL dialog box, where you can modify the image's URL (see Figure 1-25). This dialog duplicates the changes you can make in the Source field, but is extremely helpful in editing very long URLs.

Figure 1-25
Image
Inspector's Edit
URL dialog box

Once the image is placed, the Source field shows its file location relative to the GoLive document, and the Width and Height fields are automatically filled in with pixel dimensions. Select measurement units from the menus to the right of the Width and Height values; Percent calculates size based on the percentage of the area where the image resides, while Image omits the image measurements in the source code. (It's best to include pixel dimensions for your image to help browsers define the layout of a page while it's still loading an image.)

You can tell when a pixel dimension is selected by the blue resizing handles that appear at either the bottom or left of your image (see Figure 1-26). If both Width and Height are selected, a third resizing handle appears in the lower right corner.

Figure 1-26
Image resize
handles

To resize an image, click one of the blue resizing handles and drag—the bottom middle drags vertically, the corner drags diagonally, and the right middle drags horizontally.

Tip: Dynamic
Resizing On both Mac and Windows, if you Control-drag any of the resizing handles, the image displays dynamically as it's resized. Shift-dragging the corner box resizes the image proportionally, while Control-Shift-dragging the corner box proportionally resizes before your very eyes.

If you modify the size of an image from its actual dimensions, a resize warning icon appears on your image indicating that the icon might not display at its optimal resolution (see Figure 1-27).

Figure 1-27
Image resize
warning

Image resize warning icon

*Image resize warning button on
Image Inspector's Basic tab*

Remember, it's always best to modify an image's dimensions to the size you want before placing it on your page. A smaller image made larger looks jagged, while a larger image made smaller takes just as long to download and adds a burden on the browser to resize it down.

Tip:
Resetting
Image
Dimensions

If you modify an image's measurements too far for your tastes, click the image resize warning button to the right of the Width and Height fields to reset both measurements to the actual dimensions of the image. You can also individually select Image from the Width and Height popup menus.

Tip:
Generating
Low-Res
Images

If you have a fairly sizeable image that might take awhile to download in a browser, GoLive can automatically create a low-resolution placeholder image that loads first—it's black and white and somewhat pixilated, but much smaller than the original. Just click the Generate button on the Image Inspector's Basic tab to create a GIF file, the name of which is placed in the Low field.

To adjust how the image is aligned on the page—or, in this case, within the table cell—select one of the choices from the Alignment popup menu. In our example, we choose Top.

Click the Spec. tab of the Image Inspector. To add a border to your image, check the Border box and enter a value in the field to the right; it's unchecked by default. If you assign a link to an image, a border appears automatically around the image. To remove the border, check the Border box and enter 0 (zero).

While on the Spec. tab, you can also enter alternative (Alt) text, which appears on your page before your image has loaded, if a viewer has chosen not to load images, or is using a text-only browser—they still exist! If you want to use the image as a form button, check the Is Form box and type a name in the Name field.

More information. See Chapter 8, *Images.* For details on the Image Inspector, see "Document Layout Inspectors" in Chapter 2, *The Inspector.* For more on creating forms, see Chapter 13, *Forms.*

Horizontal Line

We add one more element to our page—a horizontal rule separating the top title image with the body text. From the Basic tab of the Palette, drag the Line icon to the desired point on your page, or place your cursor at that point and double-click the icon. Once again, the Inspector contextually shifts and becomes the Line Inspector, where you can adjust its style, width, and height (see Figure 1-28).

Figure 1-28
Line Inspector

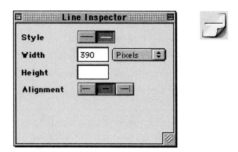

GoLive defaults to a Full width, but you can change to a percentage or pixel measurement by selecting the option from the popup menu to the right of the Width field. When Pixels are selected, GoLive automatically calculates the area's width and places that number in the measurement field. In addition, choosing one of these options allows you to select either left, center, or right alignment.

The Page

With the addition of our welcome text in the table cell below our horizontal rule cell, we have the beginning of a page (see Figure 1-29). True, it's not much to look at, but it's a blank slate that we can use to further build the page.

Now for the next horizon: building a site.

Figure 1-29
The completed
page

Creating a New Site

GoLive has excellent page-editing features, but its site management really shines. You could create pages eternally, but still have to manage all the links, objects, and references by hand without site management. By creating a GoLive site document that encapsulates all your files—pages and media—you get those management features and a whole lot more, including storage areas for site-specific colors and fontsets, frequently used external links, and the ability to transfer and synchronize your site onto an outside Web server using FTP.

Since we already have the beginnings of a site, let's choose to import the page we've been working on as the home page of our site. Under the File menu's New Site submenu, select Import from Folder or press Command-Option-O (Mac) or Control-Alt-O (Windows). For this site, we select the folder that encloses the ags-ws.html file and its placed image file, and save it as AGS-WS.site.

Tip: Keeping It Together

A good general practice to follow when setting up a site is to enclose all the files associated with the site's pages within a main directory folder. This is also important when importing files into a GoLive site from a folder. If, after importing, your site's pages continue to link to, say, image or media files outside of the site folder, those files are still referenced. However, when you upload your site to an outside server, those files do not automatically follow, although you can use other tools in GoLive to collect and copy them (see "Export Site" in Chapter 21, *Site Specials*).

To add these referenced files to your site, simply drag them from their current directory location into the Site window. GoLive then pops open the Copy Files dialog box, which asks whether you indeed want to update all files within the site that reference this file (see Figure 1-30). Make sure all desired files are checked, then click OK.

Figure 1-30
Copy Files
dialog

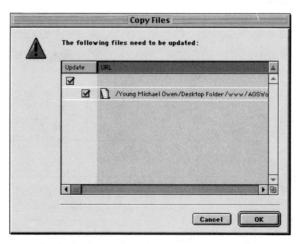

Copying referenced files into a site brings up the Copy Files dialog.

A quick examination of the site shows the HTML and image files collected in the site window's Files tab, as well as the color and font attributes, all listed as untitled under their respective tabs (see Figure 1-31). Notice that the colors include the HTML color name and are marked whether or not they're a Web-safe color. For this example, we label the colors according to their function ("left nav", "link",

Figure 1-31
Naming items
in the Colors
and Fontsets
tabs of the
Site window

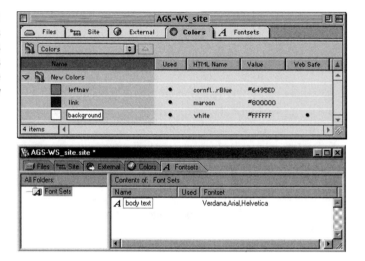

and "background") and we label the fontset as *body text*. This can be done by either clicking the color swatch and typing the name in the Inspector, or clicking the name and editing it within the name field.

More information. See Chapter 20, *Importing a Site*, and Chapter 17, *Sitewide Sets*.

File Inspector

Clicking the ags-ws.html icon in the Files tab of the Site window brings up the File Inspector, which, much like the Page Inspector, allows you to edit the file's basic attributes (see Figure 1-32).

On the File Inspector's File tab, you find information such as creation and modification dates, size of file, and file label. Note that when creating a blank site, GoLive defaults to naming the home page "index.html". You can change the

Figure 1-32
File Inspector

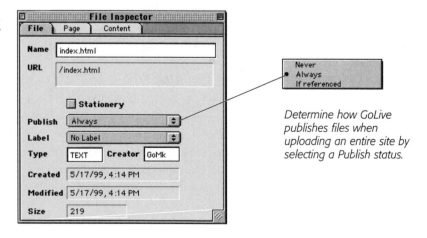

Determine how GoLive publishes files when uploading an entire site by selecting a Publish status.

default name in Preferences under the Site panel's Folder Names settings by typing a new name (such as "default" or "welcome", followed by your desired suffix) in the Home Page Name field.

If you want to use this file as a template for the rest of your site, check the Stationery box. (Alternatively, you can open up the split-pane of the Site window and drag a file to the Stationeries folder in the Extra tab.)

You can also determine under what circumstances a file gets uploaded to a Web server by selecting Always (the GoLive default), Never, or If Referenced from the Publish popup menu. Choosing the If Referenced option exports a file only if the file is linked to by at least one page in the site. Since ags-ws.html is our home page, we stick with Always.

Clicking the File Inspector's Page tab allows you to type a title that appears in the Web browser's title bar (see Figure 1-33). (This is just like the Page Title field in the Page tab of the Page Inspector...whew, what a mouthful!)

Figure 1-33
Changing a
page's title

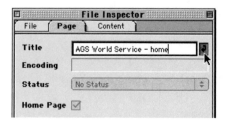

*Yet another way to modify a
page's title, via the Title field of
the File Inspector's Page tab*

The Home Page box is automatically checked (and grayed out) since this is the first file that's been added to the site. After more files have been added to the site document, you can choose another file as the site's home page by bringing up the File Inspector for that page and checking Home Page.

More Information. See Chapter 4, *Preferences and Customizing* to learn about setting up the Encodings and Status fields. For details on the File Inspector's tabs, see Chapter 2, *The Inspector*. See Chapter 18, *Staging and Synchronizing Sites*, to learn more about publishing, updating, and exporting your files.

Adding Pages to the Site

At this point, we have a very lonely home page. We could continue working on the design of that page, but let's start defining our site first. Using the Site tab of the Site window, GoLive allows you to create a hierarchy of empty placeholder files that can help you map out the site's structure. After laying down the site map, you can then go back into the individual pages and fill in content and add links.

After clicking the Site window's Site tab, find a file icon for the home page file that was just configured. Notice also that the Inspector palette becomes the Site View Controller (see Figure 1-34). For our purposes, make sure that Navigation

Figure 1-34
Site View
Controller

With the Site window open to the Site tab, click the eye icon in the upper right corner to open the Site View Controller.

Hierarchy is turned on, which allows us to create a flowchart-like map of our site. (Choosing the Link Hierarchy option only shows the real links between files in the existing site.)

Selecting the file icon brings up the File Inspector, but you can bring back the Site View Controller by clicking the eye button at the top right corner of the Site view window.

Place your cursor over the file icon and a small file icon inset within a gray box appears below. (Move your cursor away, and the box slowly disappears.) Click the gray box—the Create New Page button—and a new untitled page appears, connected to the first page by a green dashed line and arrow denoting a pending navigational relationship between the two files (see Figure 1-35).

The new file's icon includes a yellow construction marker, signifying that the page is currently devoid of content.

Figure 1-35
Creating a new
page with a
pending link

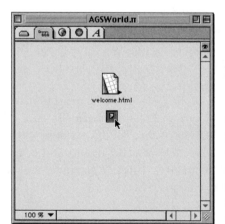

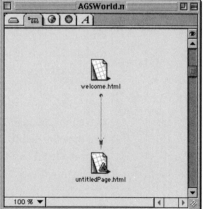

Add blank pages by clicking the Create New Page button (Mac on the left; very minimalist Windows version at right).

Files in the Site tab act like files in the Macintosh Finder or Windows Explorer: click the file's name, and the title becomes highlighted and editable. (Also, mousing over a file displays its name in the bottom bar of the Site window.) For our example, enter the name "australia.html" and press Return or Enter. You could also change the file name using the File Inspector, which appears when you select a file.

If you wish to create more placeholder files that live at this directory level, click one of the Create New Page buttons to the left or right of the file. A new untitled file appears with a pending connection to both the home page and the sibling page at this directory level. For our example, title this file "japan.html".

As you fill up the Site tab window with more placeholder files, things might get crowded. To collapse the hierarchy view, click the directional arrow to the left of the Create New Page button. This bunches all the files into one accordion-like file icon (with the active file being the one adjacent to the directional arrow clicked). Notice that the icon includes a directional arrow (denoting collapsed status) and a construction icon (denoting files that need content).

To change the view size of the Site tab, click the view popup menu at the bottom left of the Site Window. You can also hold down the Control (Mac) or Shift (Windows) key to turn the cursor into a magnifying glass. Additionally, holding down Command (Mac) or Control-Shift (Windows) brings up the grabber hand.

Tip: Doubling Your View If you're already at a view below 149 percent, the magnifying glass has a plus sign and clicking within the window doubles the size. Clicking again halves the size. If the view percentage is at 150 percent or above, a minus sign appears in the magnifying glass and you can only halve the percentage. You can also Control-drag (Mac) or Shift-drag (Windows) to select an area for magnification.

Now here's a question: Where do these files live? Click back on the Files tab of the Site Window to see a new folder entitled New Files has been created in the same directory folder as your home page (see Figure 1-36). This is GoLive's default folder name, which can be changed in Preferences under the Site pane's Folder Names settings.

To change the name of the folder, click the name to make it editable, type a new name, then press Return or Enter. (You can also click on the file icon and make the change in the File Inspector.) For this example, we enter "trips". You notice that the yellow construction icon also appears in the Status column for the australia.html and japan.html files. This icon continues to appear with these files until content is added to them.

More Information. See Chapter 19, *Site Maps*, and "Site Inspectors" in Chapter 2, *The Inspector*, for details on the Layout View Controller.

Figure 1-36
The NewFiles
folder in the
Site window

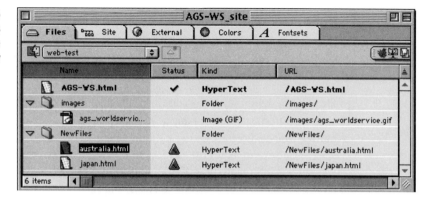

Adding Content to Pages

We could use the code we built for the Creating a New Page section by simply copying and pasting the source code. Within our example site we open the ags-ws.html home page file by clicking the Source tab, pressing Command-A (Mac) or Control-A (Windows) to select all, then pressing Command-C (Mac) or Control-C (Windows) to copy. We then open the japan.html file, go to the HTML Source Editor, select all, then press Command-V (Mac) or Control-V (Windows) to paste. But as you might suspect, this could become tedious if we have to repeat this process for each file in our site. The remedy to this problem is creating a template.

In our example, we open up ags-ws.html and then press Command-Shift-S (Mac) or Control-Shift-S (Windows) to bring up the Save As dialog box. On the Macintosh, click the site document button to the right of the encoding popup menu; under Windows, it's at the bottom right of the dialog box. This displays three directory choices: root folder of your site, or the Stationeries or Components folders within the site's .data folder (see Figure 1-37). Choose Stationeries and give the new file an appropriate name, then click OK. The saved file icon changes to look more like a notepad, denoting its status as a stationery file.

Figure 1-37
Save As
options

AGS-WS.html

*Save into a site's Root folder, or save as stationery or
component files into their respective GoLive folders.*

Mac Stationery icon

Now let's use this stationery to configure the three files of our site. In the Extra tab, double-click the stationery file (in our example, ags-station.html), and you're met with a dialog box asking whether you wish to modify the existing stationery file or create a new file (see Figure 1-38). Click the Create button, and an untitled

Figure 1-38
Opening a
stationery file

Mac and Windows dialogs vary slightly.

file with the attributes of the stationery file opens. (Be careful not to press Return or Enter and start banging away at your file; GoLive defaults to the Modify or Yes button, which edits the existing stationery file.)

For our example, we use Save As to overwrite the two files we created in the Site window's Site tab. Press Command-Shift-S (Mac) or Control-Shift-S (Windows), or choose Save As from the File menu. Click the site document button and choose Root folder or navigate to the root level of your site. Enter the name of one of the files (japan.html or australia.html), press Return or Enter, then click the Replace button to overwrite.

We've now set up a structure for our site using the visual capabilities of Go-Live's Site tab, and we've set the site's design by using GoLive's stationeries option. Now all that's needed is adding content and further formatting the pages.

More information. See Chapter 16, *Files, Folders, and Links.*

Tip: Deleting Files
If you want to delete files from your site, simply drag the files from the files list pane in the Files tab of the Site Window to the Site Trash folder in the split pane. You can also select a file and click the Delete button from the Site toolbar or press the Delete or Backspace button on the keyboard; these actions also move the files to the Site Trash folder. To move files from the Site Trash folder to the Trash (Mac) or the Recycle Bin (Windows), select the files within the Site Trash folder and click the Delete button on the Site toolbar.

Adding Links to a Site through Point & Shoot

A close cousin of Drag and Drop technology (a little older, a little wiser, and a bit more finicky), GoLive's Point & Shoot feature allows you to visually link items in a page on a site to other pages and files in the same or other Site windows (see Figure 1-39).

For example, say you want to link text from one page to another. After selecting the text and pressing Command-L (Mac) or Control-L (Windows), or clicking the New Link button from the Toolbar, the URL field on the Link tab of the Text Inspector becomes active with a subtle "(Empty Reference!)" reminder. You could type the URL to the page in the field, or click the Browse button to navigate the directory structure to your file. Or, if you have the other page open, you could use the Point & Shoot button (the one with the squiggly circle) below the URL field. (If you don't have the other page open, and you're not working with a Site window, Point & Shoot doesn't work, but more on that in a minute.)

Figure 1-39
Point & Shoot

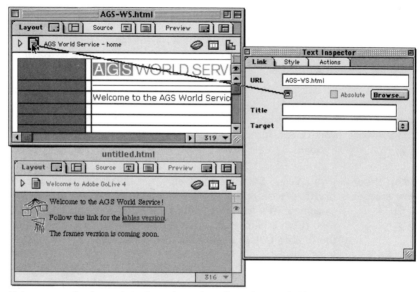

*Link to ags-ws.html page by using Point & Shoot from the untitled.html page's Text
Inspector to navigate to the destination page's Page icon.*

Clicking the Point & Shoot button and dragging your mouse around starts to
drag a rope-like connector emanating from the button. Drag the rope to the Page
icon of a Document window displaying the Layout Editor tab; a black border then
surrounds the Page icon. Notice that the name of the page has been placed in the
URL field of the Inspector. Release your mouse button to accept this link, and the
Point & Shoot rope disappears.

If you release your mouse button over anything that GoLive doesn't accept as
an end point for this link—such as the HTML Source Editor or a color reference
in the Site window—the rope snaps back and disappears.

This is pretty cool. However, insert an Image tag icon and try to drag from the
Point & Shoot button below the Source field on the Image Inspector's Basic tab to
a file icon, say on your desktop. You only get the snapped-back rope. GoLive only
allows you to link to files that are collected within a site document (and, therefore,
presented within the Site window). This is another reminder that GoLive's true
power is fully unleashed when working with its site-management features.

Just about any tag icon you add from the Palette that requires a reference to
either a source or destination file (such as images, Java applets, etc.) can be linked
to that file in the Site window using Point & Shoot. To access files in a lower directory location on the Mac, hold your mouse over the folder and, after a few seconds
delay, it opens to reveal its contents. If you want to go up a level, hold your mouse
over the up arrow to the right of the directory popup menu. In Windows, open up
your directory structure by holding your mouse over a folder's plus sign, then hold
the mouse over the desired folder to display its contents in the files pane.

Clicking the Toolbar's Site/Document icon also switches you from one window to the other (i.e., from document to site). However, to switch from document window to document window, click the down arrow to the right of the icon to display the Toggle Between Windows popup menu.

<table>
<tr><td>Tip:
Point & Shoot
on Demand</td><td>If you Command-drag (Mac) or Alt-drag (Windows) while hovering over an item (an image, an existing link, selected text), a squiggly Point & Shoot curl appears beneath your cursor. You can use it to bypass the Inspector's button and drag your Point & Shoot rope to the desired location.</td></tr>
<tr><td>Tip: Shoot
the Toolbar</td><td>If you have a Site window open while working on a GoLive document, you don't have to precisely position the windows to Point & Shoot between the two. From the Document window, select a range of text or an object and direct your Point & Shoot rope (from an inspector, or Command/Alt-dragging) to the Site document icon in the Toolbar. GoLive switches to the Site window while keeping your Point & Shoot lasso active.</td></tr>
<tr><td>Tip: Adding
Anchors</td><td>If you want to link to a specific point on the same or another page, drag the Point & Shoot button to that point. Releasing the mouse button creates an anchor tag placeholder, and enters a generic name in the Inspector's URL field. If you create this anchor on another page, the page's file name is placed before the anchor's pound sign (#).

To edit the anchor's name, go to the page where the anchor resides and select it; the cursor turns into a hand when mousing over an anchor icon. On the Anchor Inspector, type your anchor's new name in the Name field. GoLive asks if you wish to update all project files referencing this anchor; click the Update button to change the link reference on the original page (see Figure 1-40).

It's very important that you edit the anchor using the Anchor Inspector. If you were to edit the anchor's name from its reference point using the URL field of the Text Inspector's Link tab, the anchor in the URL reference would change its name, but the anchor that's referencing it would still have its generic, numeric name.</td></tr>
</table>

Figure 1-40
Update anchor
warning

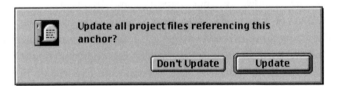

Uploading to a Site

After all this work, you want your site to be seen by the world. Working through the site file, you can post all or a selection of your pages. With the Site Window open, click the Site Settings button on the Toolbar, which opens the site Settings dialog box (see Figure 1-41).

GoLive opens to the General section, which shows an inactive field with the title of your home page. (If you need to designate a different home page, use the

Figure 1-41
Site settings

Site Settings button

Point & Shoot button and drag the rope to a file within the open Site window.) Clicking the FTP icon brings you to the settings for accessing your Web server.

In the Server field, type the server address. Clicking the popup button to the right and selecting Add Current Server adds this address to a global FTP list. If needed, you can specify a directory path in the Directory field (or, when connected to your server, you can click the Browse button to select a path). Type in your username and, if you want GoLive to remember your password, check the Remember Password box and type the password. Otherwise you are asked to type your password each time you connect—which can be good for security reasons (see Figure 1-42).

Figure 1-42
Connect
to Server
dialog box

If Remember Password is unchecked on the Site Settings dialog box, you encounter the Connect to Server dialog each time you connect, prompting you for the password.

In the Upload section, you can configure what is published to your site (see Figure 1-43). Checking the Honor Publish State of Groups and Pages boxes causes GoLive to use the individual file settings that you configured using the Publish popup menu on the File Inspector. If you uncheck either of these boxes, GoLive uses a complex set of criteria to decide which files to upload; see Chapter 18, *Staging and Synchronizing Sites.*

Click OK to accept your changes. Back on the Site toolbar, click the FTP Server Connect button to access your server. This automatically opens the FTP tab of the

Figure 1-43
Uploading
a site

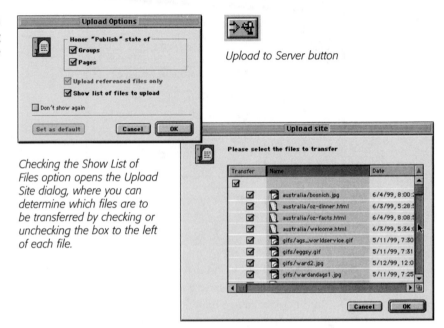

Upload to Server button

Checking the Show List of Files option opens the Upload Site dialog, where you can determine which files are to be transferred by checking or unchecking the box to the left of each file.

split pane if it's not already open, and turns the toolbar gray while connecting. Once connected, you see the directory structure of your Web server; for our example, since we're loading for the first time, it should be empty. You also notice that the directory level of your server address has been placed in the FTP pane.

Next, click the Upload to Server button on the Toolbar. You are then met with the Upload Options dialog box, where you can again configure what files are published to your site depending upon their publish state.

If you leave the Show List of Files to Upload checkbox marked, you get the Upload Site dialog box, where you can leave all files selected in your site to upload, or choose to uncheck individual files.

Click OK to begin transferring your files from your hard drive to your Web site (see Figure 1-44). If you've selected all the files from your site, the FTP pane should mirror the file structure in your files list when finished (see Figure 1-45).

Now that you're finished, click the FTP Server connect/disconnect button again—the status bar at the bottom of the FTP pan changes from connected to disconnected—and check your handiwork in a Web browser.

More information. See Chapter 18, *Staging and Synchronizing Sites.*

Figure 1-44
Uploading
files to a
remote site

Figure 1-45
Contents of
files list
parallel those
on the FTP site

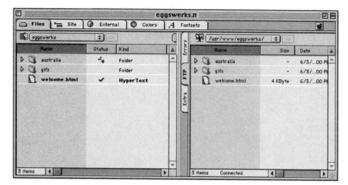

Big Picture Workout

Now that you've seen the big picture of GoLive from creating pages to uploading a site, and gotten a good brain and mouse workout, we can move on to more details of how the program works, from the many Inspector palettes, to other parts of the program, into setting preferences, and concluding with the basics of each editing view in the Document window.

CHAPTER 2

The Inspector

The shifting nature of GoLive's contextual Inspector palette is wonderful: it gives you the tools you need to complete most HTML tasks in one centralized location. The It ranges from controlling the attributes to a single tag of HTML code to creating a CSS style to helping you command and control the management of your site. That said, the fact that there are dozens of inspectors can come back to bite you if you don't have an idea of what to expect from an individual Inspector palette.

To give you an idea of what's ahead, see Table 2-1 for a complete list of the inspectors included in this chapter, divided into the GoLive sections where they play a part.

Inspector Basics

In the real world, inspectors are often investigators with an uncanny eye for detail; in GoLive, the Inspector is the tool used to narrow your focus on whatever item is currently selected (see Figure 2-1). With the item's inspector visible, you can control nearly all of its settings. Initially, the majority of inspectors—save for

Figure 2-1
A small sampling of palettes and inspectors

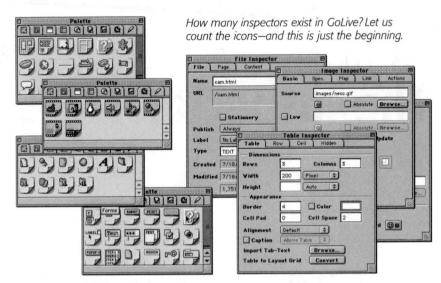

How many inspectors exist in GoLive? Let us count the icons—and this is just the beginning.

Table 2-1
Inspector list

Section	Total	Inspector
Document	22	Layout View Controller, Page, Text, Table, Line, Line Break, Comment, Spacer, Marquee, Layout Grid, Layout Text Box, Multiselection, Anchor, Plugin*, Userdef*, Tag, End Tag, Floating Box, BodyScript, JavaScript, Java Applet*, ActiveX*
Frames	2	Frame, Frameset
Head	10	Meta, Keywords, Link, Refresh, IsIndex, Base, Tag, End Tag, Headscript, Comment
Site	10	File, Folder, Site View Controller, Reference, Color, Group, Font Set, Error, FTP File, FTP Folder
QuickTime*	8	QuickTime, Video Track, Sound Track, Music Track, Video Effect Track, HREF Track, Chapter Track, Sprite Track
CyberObjects	7	Date & Time, Button, Component, URL Popup, Action Headitem, Inline Action, Browser Switch
Forms	14	Form, Button, Checkbox, Fieldset, File, Hidden, Image, Keygen, Label, Password, Popup, Radio Button, Text Area, Text Field
Web Database	8	CSS Selector, CSS Stylesheet, External Stylesheet, Attribute, Character, Enum, Section, Tag

* These features are advanced enough and used infrequently enough that a discussion of their use is found entirely in Chapter 28, *Plug-ins and Media*.

a few exceptions, such as the Layout View and Site View Controllers—are displayed when an icon is placed onto a page or into a Site window from the Palette. Just to make sure we have all of our bases covered before jumping in with both feet, here's a quick refresher on working with Palette icons.

- They can be dragged from a Palette tab to a specific spot in the appropriate work space, such as the Layout Editor's body section for any of the Basic tab's icons. You can also double-click most icons in the Palette to insert the object at the current text-insertion point.

- When you place an HTML tag icon into the Layout Editor, GoLive inserts a placeholder icon; this often remains a generic icon until you configure its attributes, such as specifying to an image's source file. Some placeholders, like anchors or comments, don't change appearance based on their contents. To edit the attributes for a placeholder, select it in the Document window, which displays the inspector that corresponds with its function.

Palette-centric information can be found in Chapter 3, *Palettes and Parts*, but you'll also find references to the Palette icons that partner with the individual inspectors in this chapter.

Common Attributes

While each inspector typically handles a single HTML tag or site-based object, many of the controls recur in each Inspector palette. This is because HTML tags share a limited set of values; the properties, or *attributes*, of HTML tags often include a URL or file location, a color name, or plain text. (This is discussed in more depth in Chapter 27, *Web Database*.) The following are some of the controls you run into most frequently.

Figure 2-2
Source
attribute

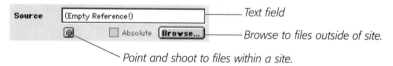

Source (also known as URL, File, and Base). When you need to define the path to a reference page or the source file for an image file, multimedia plug-in, or Java applet, you find a text-input field with "(Empty Reference!)" placed into it to remind you to grab the necessary file (see Figure 2-2). If you don't replace this text, "(Empty Reference!)" is literally inserted into your page.

You have three choices for entering the Source reference:

- Type the file name and directory location in the text field.

- Use the Point & Shoot button's lasso to rope that dogie...er, file. Remember, Point & Shoot works only in conjunction with files placed into site documents, or other open windows.

- Click the Browse button to navigate through your hard drive's file directory to the source file.

  In addition, check Absolute to use a full directory path from the root of the directory to the individual file instead of GoLive's relative default.

Target. If defining a link to another page, you are also given the choice of opening that link within another frame or in another window (see Figure 2-3). The standard four targets are:

- **_top:** loads the link into the full body of a window that replaces your current frameset.

- **_parent:** loads the link into the parent frame within a frame set.

- **_self:** loads the link into the same frame as the selected link.

- **_blank:** loads the link in a new blank window.

  If you're building a framed page and named the individual frames, those names also appear in the Target popup menu.

Figure 2-3
Target attribute

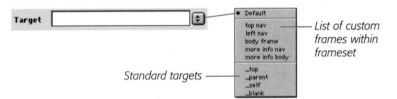

Color. As discussed in the previous chapter, you can set a background color (for a page or a table cell) by dragging a color swatch from the Color Palette into an inspector's Color field (see Figure 2-4). If the Color box is unchecked, the color within the field does not show up.

Figure 2-4
Color attribute

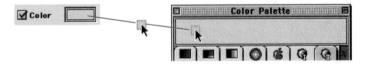

Alignment (also Align). To set the alignment of an object—such as an image file or media plug-in—choose one of the following (see Figure 2-5).

- **Top:** aligns the top of the object with the top of the largest item in a line.

- **Middle:** aligns the middle of the object with the text baseline.

- **Bottom:** aligns the bottom of the object with the text baseline; this does the same as Baseline, below.

- **Left:** places the object at the left margin; for most objects, like images or whole tables, this flows text around its right side.

- **Text Top:** aligns the top of the object with the top of text in the current line.
- **Abs Middle:** aligns the object's middle with the middle of the current line.
- **Baseline:** aligns the bottom of the object with the text baseline.
- **Abs Bottom:** aligns the object's bottom with the bottom of the current line.

Note that other elements (such as tables and marquees) have a different set of options in their Align or Alignment popup menus.

Figure 2-5
Align attribute

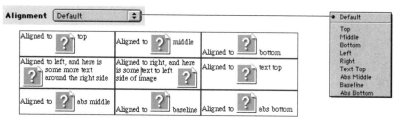

Document Layout Inspectors

The inspectors in this section appear when you add or edit page-based elements in the Layout Editor's body section. (Form elements, which are also placed into the body section, are a different breed unto themselves; we cover them in "Forms Inspectors," later in this chapter.)

Layout View Controller

Clicking the eye icon in the upper right corner of the Layout Editor reveals the Layout View Controller (see Figure 2-6). This inspector allows you to not only set basic viewing options within the Layout Editor, but also to disable the use of style sheets to help preview how a page appears in a browser that doesn't support Cascading Style Sheets (see Chapter 26, *Cascading Style Sheets*).

Figure 2-6
Layout View
Controller

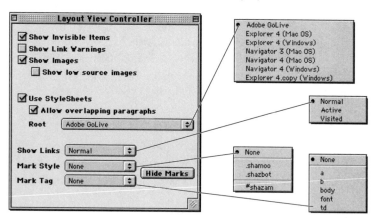

Showing Page Items

GoLive shows by default invisible items—carriage returns or icons indicating comments or forms—and images. Unchecking these items rids your page of the invisibles and turns images into generic image icons while continuing to show a box that corresponds to the image's original size.

Checking the Show Link Warnings box highlights any linked items that are broken; it also places a link icon within images that link to other pages (see Figure 2-7). Leaving Show Link Warnings checked highlights the URL field on the Link tab of the Text Inspector and places a green broken link bug icon below it to help identify that this is indeed a broken link.

Figure 2-7
Link Warnings

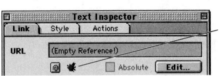

Selecting Link Warnings from the Layout View Controller highlights bad URL fields and adds the green bug warning below.

If you've created lowsource images for byte-intensive images, checking Show Low Source Images replaces the full-sized image with a much smaller black-and-white rendition of the original image. GoLive can create these automatically, so this is an easy way to preview its attempts.

Switching to Layout Preview also calls up the Layout View Controller, but the Invisible Items and Link Warnings options are grayed, as they have no effect.

Cascading Style Sheets (CSS)

While the options in the top half of the Layout View Controller are always available, unchecking Use StyleSheets [sic] effectively turns off the CSS options. The exception is the Show Links popup menu, which remains visible and allows you to preview the colors that have been chosen for active and visited links.

However, even if you're not using style sheets, leaving Use StyleSheets checked provides some helpful visual controls. Using the Root popup menu, you can view a simulated preview of your page as viewed in a number of different browser versions by operating system. The Mark Tag menu lists all of the tags used on a page, and selecting one highlights all instances of it.

If you are using style sheets, all individual classes and IDs are listed and, if selected, are highlighted on the page. (For more information about using style sheets, see Chapter 26, *Cascading Style Sheets.*)

Document Layout Controller

When you preview a page in GoLive using Layout Preview, the Inspector palette opens as the Document Layout Controller (see Figure 2-8). This is essentially the same as the Layout Controller save for the inactive Show Invisible Items and Show Link Warnings checkboxes.

Figure 2-8
Document
Layout
Controller

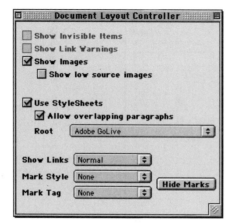

Displayed when viewing a page in Preview mode; invisible items and link warnings are inactive.

Page Inspector

The Page Inspector is used to set up the basic attributes of an individual page, from page title and link colors to whether a color profile is used (see Figure 2-9). While in the Layout Editor, click the Page icon in the upper left corner.

Page Tab

In the Page Title field, you can type a descriptive title that appears in a browser's top title bar. Remember to apply any changes to the Page Title field by pressing Return or Tab. GoLive defaults to "Welcome to GoLive 4", so be sure to remember to change the title to reflect your page.

Tip: We Know You Love GoLive, but… Because GoLive prefills the Page Title field, many people completely forget to change the title, or may not have realized they could or should. If you search on just the title of a page containing the word "golive" on AltaVista (by entering "title:golive" without quotes), you can see how many colleagues never made this change. A recent search brought up nearly 50,000 pages.

Tip: Adding Descriptions to Page Titles According to friends who specialize in promoting Web sites and understanding search engines, the text that appears in a page's title (in the Title tag set by GoLive's Page Title field) appears to be the most heavily weighted information that most search engines index. To get your site noticed, consider adding a longer description of your site in addition to the name of the individual page. GoLive doesn't seem to limit the number of characters within the Page Title field, so you can write as long a description as you want. However, a long page titles don't fit within a Web browser's title bar, and could look a little messy.

The Text Colors section allows you to set colors for body text, standard link text, active links, and visited links. To change one of these settings, open the Color Palette by pressing Command-3 (Mac) or Alt-3 (Windows), or clicking one of the color fields. Choose a color from the Color Palette and drag a swatch from the

Figure 2-9
Page
Inspector's
Page tab

Preview pane to the desired color field; this changes the field to the new color and the corresponding box becomes checked. If a color is added to one of the color fields which you then uncheck, that color does not show up in the page.

You can also set a background color or image to appear behind your page's text and images. For a refresher on using background images, consult Chapter 1, *Getting Started*.

HTML Tab

If you don't want your page to automatically include such basic tags as Html, Head, Title, or Body—for instance, if you were planning on bringing in customized HTML fragments later—you can uncheck these options on the Page Inspector's HTML tab (see Figure 2-10).

If one or more of the tags are unchecked, you can reset them all to be checked by clicking the Select All button.

Figure 2-10
Page
Inspector's
HTML tab

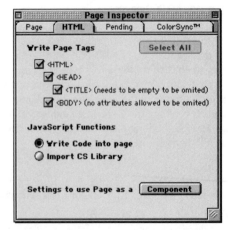

The JavaScript Functions options correspond to GoLive's Actions: prefabricated JavaScript code which allow you to accomplish sophisticated tasks without hand coding. GoLive defaults to Write Code into Page, which includes all necessary JavaScript code in the individual HTML page. If you're creating a site, however, select Import CS Library, which creates a separate file containing all of the necessary code for all Actions; your HTML page refers to this file, and a browser loads it separately. For the full details, see Chapter 25, *Actions*.

Pending Tab

GoLive lets you prototype and create sites in the Site tab of the Site window (yes, there are lots of bits named Site in this program). If you create pages or links through the Site tab, you wind up with a heap of HTML files but a paucity of actual links.

However, you can keep track of what pages still need to be linked via the Page Inspector's Pending tab, which lists all the files within a site (both HTML and assorted media) that are associated with or linked from an individual page (see Figure 2-11).

Figure 2-11
Page
Inspector's
Pending tab

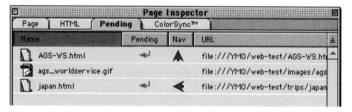

If a page is marked with a blue carriage-return icon in the Pending column, that page has been created within the site's navigation hierarchy in the Site tab, but the page you're examining doesn't have a link to it yet. The green arrows in the Nav column (pointing up, down, left, and right) indicate hierarchical direction in relation to the current page. (For more on these matters, see Chapter 19, *Site Maps*.)

The Pending tab also lists the files' directory location under the URL column (which is quite helpful when you have a plethora of "default.html" files). The Pending tab is blank unless a page is part of a site.

ColorSync Tab (Mac)

On the Macintosh, GoLive applies Apple's ColorSync 2.5 color-matching capabilities by default to all JPEG images collected on a page. The ColorSync tab lets you change GoLive's default settings (see Figure 2-12). You can select an external color profile by clicking the Profile radio button and either using the Point & Shoot button or clicking the Browse button to select the profile. You can also choose not to use any color profile; this is wise, as the integration of ColorSync color-management into browsers is currently limited to Explorer 4.0 and later on the Mac.

Figure 2-12
Page
Inspector's
ColorSync tab

If you choose an external color profile, be sure to check that it gets uploaded to your Web site, as GoLive's link parser does not monitor color profiles. See Chapter 8, *Images*, for more on ColorSync.

Text Inspector

The Text Inspector, the Inspector palette you see the most, is a grab bag of rather disparate items ranging from simple link fields to a tab for creating GoLive Actions to set complex browser behavior. To get to the Text Inspector, place your cursor in any piece of text or blank space in the body section of the Document window (see Figure 2-13).

Figure 2-13
Selecting
text in the
Document
window

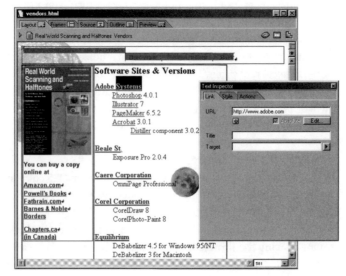

Link Tab

Using the Link tab, you build the interconnecting framework of your Web site, linking items on the current page to other pages within your site, or to external Web pages and other resources (see Figure 2-14). After selecting text and creating a new link, an "(Empty Reference!)" reminder appears in the URL field. At this point, you can either type the file name and path into the field, or use either the Browse or Point & Shoot buttons to navigate to the file.

Tip: Creating a Text Link   GoLive offers several ways to create a text link. After selecting text you can: press Command-L (Mac) or Control-L (Windows), click the New Link button the Toolbar, or click the New Link button in the Text Inspector's Link tab.

The Title field allows you to add a piece of text that appears in a balloon when you mouse over the link in recent versions of Internet Explorer and Netscape

Figure 2-14
Text Inspector's
Link tab

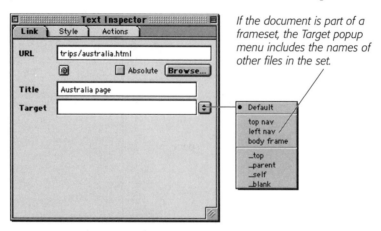

If the document is part of a frameset, the Target popup menu includes the names of other files in the set.

Our Favorite Keyboard Shortcuts

GoLive really, really wants you to use its Point & Shoot feature, which certainly isn't a bad desire. It might take a little practice to get used to, but it's handy. However, GoLive's relentless focus on driving you to use this feature comes at a sacrifice of better support for editing URLs by hand.

However, you can take advantage of a set of underreported keyboard shortcuts. Pressing Command-comma on the Mac jumps your text-insertion point from a linked text selection to the Text Inspector's URL field. Pressing Command-

semicolon returns the insertion point back to the text selection in the Document window.

This doesn't mean that we've moved our mice to the dustbin. We still access the URL field by clicking it with the mouse, but simply clicking is only half the job: the "(Empty Reference!)" text doesn't get replaced automatically, so be sure to drag across the field to select its entire contents.

If the URL exceeds the width of the Inspector palette, resize the window, or Option- or Alt-click the Browse button (which changes to Edit).

Communicator under Windows, but just Explorer on the Mac. Interestingly and somewhat inconsistently, you aren't required to press Return or Tab after entering text into this field to accept an edit.

If the page is within a frameset, you can set the destination frame in the Target menu by choosing the name of the frame or a standard location within a frame (_top, _parent, _self, or _blank).

Style Tab

If you've set CSS styles for a page, they'll be listed in the Style tab, and can be set for different units on a page by checking one or more of the boxes to the right of the style name (see Figure 2-15). The columns Inline, Par, Div, and Area correspond, respectively, to ranges of selected text, paragraphs in a selection (individually set), paragraphs in a selection (collectively grouped), and the entire body of the page or the contents of a table cell.

Figure 2-15
Text Inspector's
Style tab

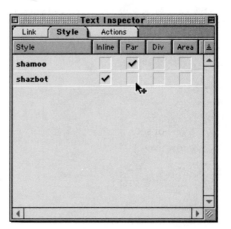

Click Par, for example, to add a style to all elements within any currently selected paragraphs or blocks of text, like lists.

For instance, suppose we set up a style called "shazbot" (nanoo, nanoo!) that turns text purple and increases its size to 16 pt. If we only want a few words to reflect this style, we select that range and then check the Inline column's box. (Notice that a green plus sign appears next to your cursor when it floats over an unchecked box, while a red minus sign appears when you mouse over a checked box.) Inline styles can only include items that affect type, not paragraph (also called "block") borders, backgrounds, or spacing.

If you want to set each paragraph in a selection to a style, check the box in the Par column. To apply a style around a selection, check the Div column, which creates a division (or Div) container around the selected paragraphs. (This works for borders, as one example, where you would want to differentiate between putting a border around each individual paragraph or around a whole set of paragraphs.)

Depending on where the text-insertion point is, checking the Area column's box applies a style to one of two places. If you're in a table cell, Area applies it just to that cell (via its TD tag). If you're elsewhere on a page, it affects the entire body section through the Body tag.

For more on Cascading Style Sheets, see Chapter 25, *Cascading Style Sheets*.

Actions Tab

GoLive Actions are prefabricated sets of code that you can combine to set up complex sets of actions attached to text, buttons, and animations. Actions can preload images, add sounds, dynamically change the content of images, open links in new browser windows, and other functionality.

Tip: Photo-shop versus GoLive Actions

GoLive Actions shouldn't be mistaken for the kin of Photoshop Actions, which are a series of recorded image-editing steps. GoLive does not currently allow you to record sequences like in Photoshop or CE Software's QuicKeys. (However, you could use QuicKeys to create sequences in GoLive as we frequently do.)

In addition to the Text Inspector, the Actions tab also appears in the Image Inspector (found later in this chapter in "Document Layout Inspectors") and the Button Inspector, found in "CyberObjects" (see Figure 2-16). The items in the Action tab are grayed out until you add a link to the current text selection.

To create an Action, create a link or click inside any range of text that has a link applied; the link can be empty—or set to the default "(Empty Reference!)"—without causing any problems running the Action. Next, click the Text Inspector's Actions tab. In the Events pane of the inspector, select a trigger, or a method by which the Action gets invoked by the user (see Table 2-2).

Figure 2-16
Text Inspector's
Actions tab

Selecting an Action...   *...allows you to configure its attributes.*

	Event Trigger	User Action
Table 2-2 Action triggers	Mouse Click	User clicks an item
	Mouse Enter	User moves cursor into item's area (mouseover)
	Mouse Exit	User moves cursor out of item's area
	Double Click	User clicks item twice in rapid succession
	Mouse Down	User holds down mouse button over item
	Mouse Up	User releases mouse button over item
	Key Down*	User presses any key
	Key Press*	User presses any key
	Key Up	User releases any key

* Key Down and Key Press are effectively the same; but, ideally, Key Down would capture an event only *while* the key is depressed.

After selecting an event, click the Plus button above the Actions pane, where a new Action titled "None" preceded by a question mark appears. A dot also appears to the right of the event name to indicate that an Action has been assigned to it.

Click the Action button below the Events pane to select from the list of Actions, and fill in the necessary information for that action in the lower half of the inspector; you may have to scroll or expand the Inspector palette to reach all of the options.

To add another action associated with this item, click the Plus button again. To delete an action, select it in the Actions pane and click the Minus button. (For more information on using actions, see Chapter 25, *Actions*.)

Image Inspector

Bringing an image into a GoLive document, either by dragging an image file from your hard drive or dragging the Image icon from the Palette's Basic tab, calls up the Image Inspector.

Basic Tab

If you use the Palette's blank Image tag icon, you can set the source of your image in the Basic tab by navigating to the image via browsing your hard drive or using Point & Shoot (see Figure 2-17).

Width and Height. The Width and Height fields are automatically filled in with the actual pixel dimensions of the image. You can choose a measurement unit through the field's menus if you want to change the image's actual dimensions. For instance, choosing Percent calculates an image's height and/or width based on the

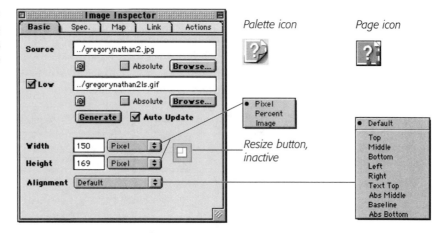

Figure 2-17
Image
Inspector's
Basic tab

current size of the browser window; this could dramatically resize an image depending on the user's browser window size.

If you want to change the dimensions of an image, click either the Width or Height fields, type a number, and press Enter or Tab. A resize warning icon appears within your image reminding you that the image may not look its best, and the resize warning button on the Image Inspector becomes active. If you want to return to the image's original width and height dimensions, click the resize button.

Tip: Speedier Browser Rendering   Specifying the width and height of images helps Web browsers render pages faster. If a browser knows how much space to reserve for the images it's receiving, it can flow text around that space first, giving your viewer something to read while waiting for everything else to appear. GoLive automatically imports an image's dimensions, so this really is a no-brainer.

Tip: Proportional Resizing   You can proportionally alter an image's size by Shift-dragging the lower-right corner handle. Adding Control (Mac and Windows) allows you to dynamically view the image resizing and the pixel dimensions in the Image Inspector. However, if you enter, say, a larger value in the Width field, then change the Height menu to Image, you achieve the same proportional resize.

Alignment. Below the Width and Height fields, you can choose the image's alignment on the page from the Alignment menu.

Lowsource. If you have a fairly large image that could take a while to load into a browser, specify a lowsource image, or an image that's identical in resolution to the larger image but has a lower bit depth or higher compression ratio, making it smaller in total bytes. To add a lowsource image, check the Low box and navigate to an existing lowsource image; or, click the Generate button to have GoLive create a black-and-white image for you. Checking the Auto Update option then updates the lowsource file each time the original image is modified.

Spec. Tab

The Spec. tab sports many miscellaneous items that don't fit into other categories (see Figure 2-18). In this tab you set a border for an image which appears when the image is also a link, control spacing around it, specify alternate text to show up if the image doesn't display, and handle form element details if your image is a form.

Figure 2-18
Image
Inspector's
Spec. tab

Checking the Form option...   ...calls up the Form Image Inspector

Alt Text. Alt Text appears in a browser if a user has chosen not to load images. It can also appear while images load in some browsers, or if a user has the not-entirely-rare Lynx text-only browser.

Border. GoLive defaults to an unchecked Border value of 0 (zero). A border appears when you apply a link to the image or turn it into an imagemap, although the Border value remains inactive. You must manually check the box and specify zero to get rid of the link border (see "Link Tab," below).

Hspace and Vspace. Adding a value to the Hspace (horizontal space) field adds that number of pixels to the left and right sides of an image, while a Vspace (vertical space) value adds pixel space to the top and bottom.

Is Form. If the Is Form option is checked to make the image a clickable form button, the Inspector changes to become the Form Image Inspector and the Alt Text and HSpace/Vspace fields become inactive. (In addition, the Map tab, where you set up imagemapping, becomes inactive.) The form options for the Spec. tab are covered later in this chapter in "Form Inspectors," and in Chapter 15, *Forms*.

Map Tab

Even though all graphics are rectangles by default, that doesn't mean you have to be stuck with rectagular links on your page. Imagemaps allow you to specify areas

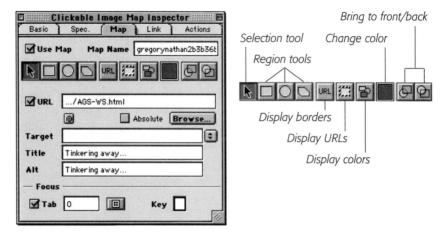

Figure 2-19
Clickable
Image Map
Inspector

of an image as unique "hot spots" with their own URLs. Check the Use Map box to configure a clickable imagemap. The Inspector becomes the Clickable Image Map Inspector; the link section of the Link tab becomes inactive and you must select a map region to apply an item from the Action tab (see Figure 2-19).

Map Name. GoLive assigns a semi-random Map Name, but you can call it whatever you want as long as it's not repeated for another map in the same Web page.

Region tools. To select an area of your image to map, click one of the Region tools (rectangle, circle, or polygon) and drag the shape to cover the desired area. Choosing the polygon tool allows you to click from point to point to create a shape within your image; if you want to later edit the points that you've created, double-click the shape with the selection (arrow) tool, then manipulate the points individually. To move completed shapes, use the selection tool. Shift-click to select multiple map elements within an image.

Display regions. The next four buttons control how an imagemap displays on a GoLive page. Clicking the Display URLs button toggles the display of the destination URL for each mapped area. Clicking the Frame Regions button turns on or off a border around each area. The Color Regions button toggles whether areas are filled with colors or not; you can drag a color swatch from the Color Palette to the Color Select button to change that fill. If you have overlapping map regions, you can use the Bring Region to Front/Back buttons to determine their stacking order.

Destination options. Add a destination URL to a region in the field below the buttons via normal link options. If you want to aim the link at a specific window within a frameset or open the link in a new window, choose one of the options from the Target popup menu or type the name in the Target field.

Alt and Title text. You can add names to the Alt (the same as Alt Text in the Basic tab) and Title fields for individual map regions.

Tab order. Checking the Tab option allows you to assign a Tabindex attribute to different field regions that controls the order in which tabbing on an imagemap takes a user through the regions; this only works under Windows browsers. Clicking the button to the right of the Tab field consecutively numbers additional map regions as you click them. Be sure to click the tab button again when finished setting the tab order, or the consecutive numbering continues even on map regions that have already been assigned a number.

Tip: Careful What You Check   If you set up a complicated imagemap, think twice before checking the Is Form option on the Spec. tab. Clicking this option erases all imagemap attributes that you meticulously set up; selecting Undo is futile, as it undoes nothing in this case.

Link Tab

Creating links for text or images reminds you that GoLive offers many ways to get there from here (see Figure 2-20). After selecting an existing image, you can:

- Press Command-L (Mac) or Control-L (Windows).
- Select New Link from the Special menu.
- Click the New Link button in the Toolbar.
- Click the New Link button on the Image Inspector's Link tab.

After creating a link, GoLive displays images with a default border. Checking the Border box and setting it to 0 (zero) turns off the border.

To set a link for the image, use the standard link options. You can set the image link's title and target, just as with a text link.

Figure 2-20
Image
Inspector's
Link tab

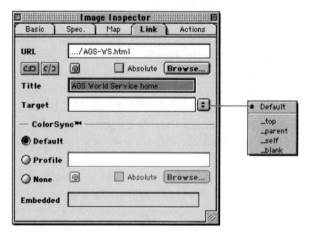

ColorSync (Mac). A true multi-tasker, the Link tab also includes the ColorSync options that were available in the Page Inspector. Choose the default ColorSync profile, or specify a profile for this image.

Actions Tab
See "Actions Tab" in the "Text Inspector" section earlier in this chapter.

Table Inspector

Tables have become a staple of any HTML page, from simple and logical presentations of data to elaborate layout schemes that are invisible to the viewer. But wrapping your brain around hard-coding TD and TR tags with precise pixel measurements seems a bit daunting. Generating tables with GoLive's Table Inspector can put you at ease immediately; it is one of the program's stellar performers.

To open the Table Inspector, drag the Table icon from the Palette's Basic tab; or, select an existing table by clicking its top or left border (you can tell you're on top of it when the cursor changes to a grabber hand). You can also click the right border, over which the cursor becomes a two-way arrow (which is used to increase the width of the table). Be careful not to click within the table and accidentally select an individual cell. (Selection is one of the hardest tasks associated with tables, and a big piece of Chapter 10, *Tables*, can help you with that task.)

Table Tab
If you've dragged a table placeholder from the Palette, GoLive drops in a default table that's 200 pixels wide, includes three columns and three rows, and features a 4-pixel border. The Table Inspector's Table tab is where you can edit these attributes, as well as row height, alignment of the table on the page, border size, background color, and cell space and cell padding (see Figure 2-21).

Figure 2-21
Table
Inspector's
Table tab

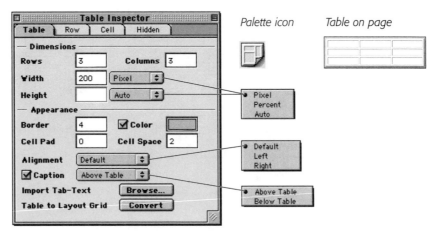

Palette icon   *Table on page*

Caption. To add a title to your table, check Caption and a row is placed above or below your table. GoLive defaults to centered text within the caption, but you can select the text and align it either left or right. However, this only shows up in Netscape's browsers; Internet Explorer continues to center the text.

Converting text to table. You can import pre-existing text into a table, but it must be a tab-delimited text file (.txt). Drag a table placeholder into your page, click the Browse button to the right of Import Table Text, navigate to the text file, and press Return or Enter. The default placeholder modifies itself to conform to the number of columns required by the tab separation and the number of rows equal to the number of lines of text.

Converting table to grid. Clicking the Table to Layout Grid Convert button transmogrifies your table into...another table, but one that doesn't seem like a table. For information on layout grids, see "Layout Grid Inspector," later in this chapter.

Cell Tab

Clicking on a cell within a table opens the Table Inspector to the Cell tab (see Figure 2-22). (Selecting the entire table opens the inspector to the Table tab.) In the Cell tab, you can:

- Choose alignment of text and objects within the cell using the Vertical and Horizontal Alignment menus.

- Span across a number of columns or down a number of rows.

- Set the background color for individual cells.

- Set width and height in pixels, as an automatic resize, or in percentages.

If you select a cell and change its Width measurement, that measurement is applied to all other cells within that column; a change to its Height measurement

Figure 2-22
Table
Inspector's
Cell tab

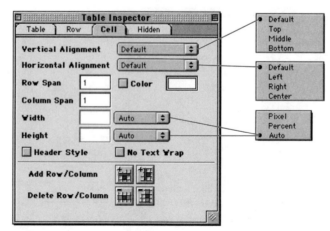

is applied to all cells within that row. For a refresher on sele ting table items, see Chapter 1, *Getting Started*, and Chapter 10, *Tables*.

Checking Header Style changes the source code of the cell to the HTML tag for table headers; this changes the preview for the text in that cell to bold, simulating how most browsers treat table headers. Checking No Text Wrap adds a Nowrap attribute to the table cell tag, which prevents text from wrapping in a table cell depending on the browser.

To add or delete columns or rows, select a cell by clicking either its bottom or right border, then click the appropriate button in the Cell tab. A new row appears above the selected cell's row, while a new column appears to the left of the selected cell's column. The new table items pick up the table attributes of the selected column or row (including cell alignment, and row height). However, a cell that spans multiple rows or columns produces a row or column formatted with all the original cells. In addition, any text formatting from the selected cell's row or column is not carried over.

Row Tab

The Table Inspector's Row tab allows you to change many of the same attributes found on the Cell tab, including background color, row height, and alignment of objects and text within table cells (see Figure 2-23). However, modifying attributes on the Row tab applies those changes across an entire row.

Figure 2-23
Table
Inspector's
Row tab

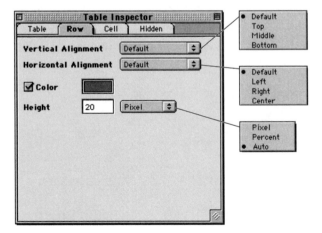

Hidden Tab

Normally, code other than HTML is signified by either an icon (such as the JavaScript icon) or colored foreign tags (for scripting languages like XML). However, foreign code doesn't show up in the Layout tab if it is embedded in your source code between table cells. To find this code, select an entire table or an individual cell and click the Table Inspector's Hidden tab to see a schematic of the table; instances of non-HTML code are indicated by a blue dot (see Figure 2-24).

To view the code, click a dot; an outer circle appears around the dot and the code appears within the table area in the Layout Editor. (The code is also editable at this point.) To return to the Layout Editor's table view, click anywhere within the table schematic or click one of the other Table Inspector tabs.

Figure 2-24
Table Inspector's Hidden tab

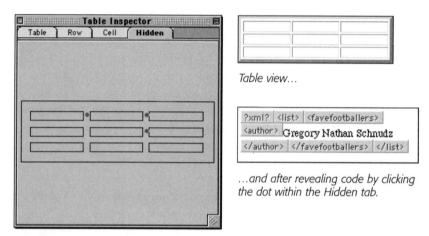

Table view...

...and after revealing code by clicking the dot within the Hidden tab.

Line Inspector

A horizontal rule is one of the few graphical elements that is generated by a browser without needing to load an image. To open the Line Inspector, double-click the horizontal rule icon in the Palette (or drag it into the page), or select an existing rule (see Figure 2-25).

Figure 2-25
Line Inspector

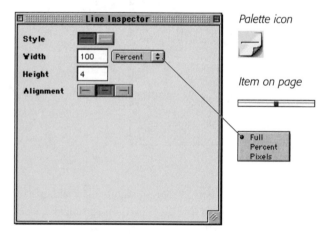

Palette icon

Item on page

Style. Choose between a solid bar (the left button) or the default shaded, three-dimensional line (the right button).

Width. GoLive defaults to Full, which spans the entire width of the area the rule occupies. Choosing either Percent or Pixels makes the Width field active, allowing you to enter a specific measurement.

Height. Here you can enter the Size attribute, which determines the rule's height in pixels. If this field is left blank, the line defaults to a height of 2 pixels.

Alignment. If you've specified a width measurement, you can choose an alignment (left, center, or right).

Line Break Inspector

In HTML, a line break (the BR tag) is a way to begin a new line without inserting any extra space between lines (which the P tag does). In GoLive, the easiest way to add a line break (a BR tag) is pressing Shift-Return (Mac) or Shift-Enter (Windows) with your cursor placed at the appropriate point in the body section of the HTML page. You can also drag the Line Break icon from the Palette into the page, although this is somewhat awkward. If you create a line break via the keyboard, the Line Break Inspector doesn't appear unless you select the icon on the page (see Figure 2-26).

If Clear is unchecked, you can choose All, Left, or Right from the Clear menu. Selecting either Left or Right stops the flow of text around an image until there are no more images aligned to either respective margin. Selecting All stops the flow of text around an image until there are no images aligned to either margin.

Figure 2-26
Line Break
Inspector

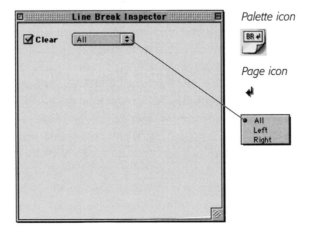

Comment Inspector

A helpful tool for any Web publisher is the comment tag, which in HTML starts with `<!--` and ends with `-->`. For example:

```
<!-- Ad insertion copy starts here -->
```

Any text or additional code that is placed within this tag container does not show up in a Web browser, though it is visible in the page's source code. This is perfect for adding reminders or placing page items or links that need to be added at a later date.

The Comment Inspector appears when the Comment icon is dragged from the Palette, or an existing Comment icon is selected on a page (see Figure 2-27). To add a comment, click within the blank notepad-like field and type away. Note that you don't have to press Return or Tab to accept any edits to this field; just click back to the Document window or any other GoLive element.

Figure 2-27
Comment
Inspector

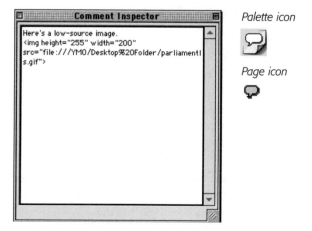

Palette icon

Page icon

Spacer Inspector

If you're producing Web pages for an audience that primarily uses Netscape (version 3 or later), you can add white space to a page using the Spacer tag, thus avoiding including invisible GIFs to space items out on a page. Otherwise, you may want to avoid using the tag, as it is ignored by all flavors of Internet Explorer.

After dragging the Horizontal Spacer icon from the Palette, you can configure the size of the blank space in one of three ways in the Spacer Inspector (see Figure 2-28): horizontally (which opens the Width field), vertically (which opens the Height field), or as a block (which allows you to edit its Width and Height, and its alignment).

You can also select the Spacer icon in the Document window and drag a blue handle to your desired size. Control-dragging dynamically resizes both the spacer icon as well as any surrounding text or images.

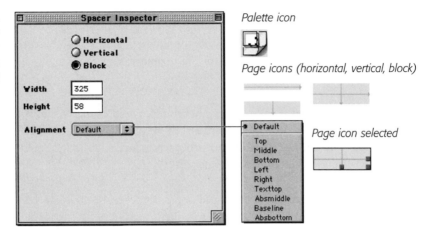

Figure 2-28
Spacer
Inspector
configuring a
spacer block

Palette icon

Page icons (horizontal, vertical, block)

Page icon selected

Layout Grids

At first glance, GoLive's layout grid looks a little wacky, letting you place objects and boxes of text any ol' place you want on a grid and have the placement appear accurately within a browser. HTML just doesn't do that, does it? A quick look at the source code, though, reveals that the layout grid is actually a complex HTML table, to which you can add the full range of HTML objects.

Layout Grid Inspector

On first placing a layout grid on a page (by dragging it over or double-clicking the Layout Grid icon in the Palette's Basic tab), the Inspector palette becomes the Layout Grid Inspector (see Figure 2-29). The Toolbar changes as well, but its fields are inactive. Once an object is selected, the fields and buttons come to life, allowing you to modify position and alignment within the grid, and size of the object. For more on this toolbar, see Chapter 3, *Palettes and Parts*.

Figure 2-29
Layout Grid
Inspector

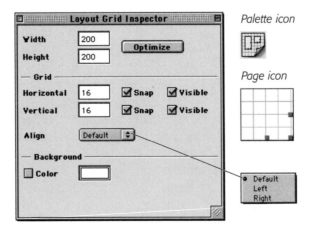

Palette icon

Page icon

GoLive defaults to placing a square grid measuring 200 by 200 pixels. You can use one of the three handles (on the right and bottom borders and bottom right corner) to drag the grid to your desired size, or you can use the Width and Height fields in the Layout Grid Inspector.

Optimize. The Optimize button to the right of these fields is grayed out and remains so until objects are placed onto the grid. Once active, clicking Optimize shrinks the right and bottom borders to be flush with the outermost borders of the objects contained within the grid.

Grid size. The default grid size is 16 pixels, but this can be changed for either Horizontal or Vertical measurements to produce smaller or larger grid patterns. If you want to view your layout without the background pattern or, say, only utilize vertical guides, uncheck the Visible option. In addition, if you're a free spirit and don't want your objects to automatically conform to being placed according to the grid pattern, you can uncheck the Snap option.

Background color. You can drag a color swatch to the Background color field to fill your grid with color.

Tip: Moving Text Boxes One Pixel (or More) at a Time	When Snap is checked for either or both Horizontal or Vertical Grids, you can press Option-arrow (Mac) or Control-Alt-arrow (Windows) to move a selected object one pixel at a time or press the arrow key by itself to move the object one full grid box at a time. However, unchecking either Horizontal or Vertical simply reverses the keyboarding: Option-arrow or Control-Alt-arrow moves by grid increments while just the arrow key moves items pixel by pixel.

Layout Textbox Inspector

To add text within this layout system, you must first drag in a Layout Text Box from the Palette's Basic tab, which brings up the Textbox Inspector (see Figure 2-30). (Yep, that's how GoLive spells it, even though it correctly spells the "Layout Text Box" tag icon in the Palette.) If you're selecting an existing text box, be sure to click on its outside border, indicated by the cursor changing to a grabber hand.

Unfortunately, there's not a whole heck of a lot going on with this inspector, with only a Background Color field that you can drag color swatches into and check or uncheck at your whim. It's up in the Toolbar where it's all happening, including the box's pixel location and the ability to change the its alignment within the grid.

Multiselection Inspector

Selecting multiple objects within a layout grid brings up the Multiselection Inspector (see Figure 2-31). The easiest way to select items is to drag and hit pieces of the desired objects (you don't have to surround an entire object to select it; just

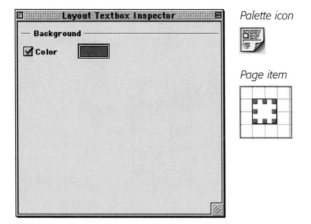

Figure 2-30
Layout Textbox
Inspector

Palette icon

Page item

Figure 2-31
Multiselection
Inspector's
Alignment and
Special tabs

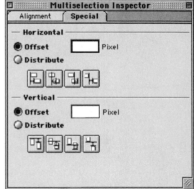

a corner). You can also first select one object , then gather others by Shift-clicking. No need to worry about being precise here either—if one object is selected, you can Shift-click anywhere within another object to select it, even finicky text boxes.

Marquee Inspector

To create a scrolling text message (which acts like a stock ticker), drag the Marquee icon in from the Palette's Basic tab. The Marquee tag that creates the scrolling information only works with Internet Explorer; you get just text—no scrolling and no background color—when viewed in Netscape Navigator.

Basic Tab

GoLive defaults to inserting a marquee that's 150 pixels wide, while the height adjusts to the selected text setting; for example, 14 pixels high for plain text set to a size of 3, or 28 pixels high for heading 1 text set to a size of 3.

You can adjust the width and height by dragging the handles of the marquee placeholder in the Document window, or by typing values in the Width and

Height fields in the Marquee Inspector's Basic tab (see Figure 2-32). To add horizontal and vertical space surrounding the marquee, enter values in the HSpace and VSpace fields.

Figure 2-32
Marquee
Inspector's
Basic tab

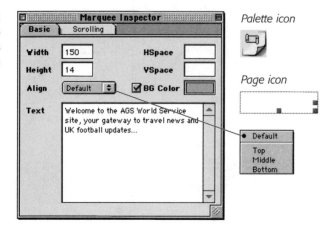

Palette icon

Page icon

If the marquee is placed within the flow of text, you can configure its placement (Default, Top, Middle, and Bottom) using the Align menu. If you want to choose a different background color, drag a color swatch into the BG Color field. Type in your desired message in the Text field; it's not necessary to press Return or Tab to accept edits.

Scrolling Tab

Click the Scrolling tab to configure the way your text moves across the screen (see Figure 2-33). The Behavior menu gives you three options:

- Scroll causes text to continually move across the marquee area.
- Slide scrolls text into the marquee area, then holds it onscreen; if this option is selected, make sure that text fits into the marquee box; otherwise ,your message could be cut off.
- Alternate scrolls text first left and then right across the marquee area.

Your marquee's message repeats endlessly unless you uncheck Forever and enter a set number of repeated scrolls in the Loops field. (These two options are inactive when Slide is chosen since the message is kept in the marquee box once it hits the screen.) Once the number of loops have completed, the marquee box remains blank. Entering a value of 0 (zero) automatically checks Forever.

To alter the scrolling speed, type a value in the Amount field. To set a delay between repetitions, enter a value in the Delay field. Choose to begin your text scrolling from either the left or right by clicking one of the Direction buttons.

Figure 2-33
Marquee
Inspector's
Scrolling tab

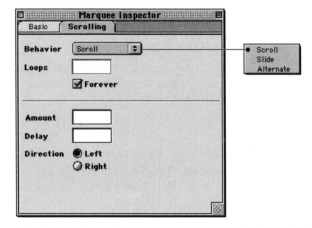

Tip: Setting GoLive defaults to entering no values in either the Amount or Delay fields. This can
Amount and look a little choppy, though, so it's advisable to enter a value. However, if after exper-
Delay to Nil imenting with Amount values you delete the value or type 0 (zero), no text shows up
in the marquee box.

Anchor Inspector

Anchors allow you to create a hyperlink to specific point on another page, or to a
designated position within the currently viewed document (see Figure 2-34). For a
refresher on creating anchors, see Chapter 1, *Getting Started*.

Tip: Anchor In addition to dragging the Anchor icon in from the Palette or using Point & Shoot ,
Keyboard you can also Command-Option-click (Mac) or Alt-click (Windows) within the text of
Shortcut an unselected text link (i.e., a text link that's not highlighted). This action adds an anchor icon to the left of the word; you can drag that to your desired location. In addition, the word within which you clicked appears in the Anchor Inspector's Name
field between "Anchor" and the number GoLive automatically assigns.

Figure 2-34
Anchor
Inspector

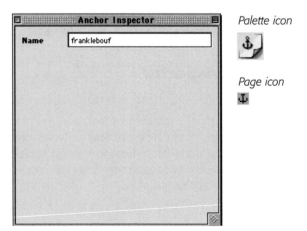

Palette icon

Page icon

Tag and Endtag Inspectors

HTML appears to be constantly shifting, but it's partly an illusion. There are many features that are part of the newest specifications for the language that haven't yet shown up in browsers, so it's unrealistic that GoLive should offer them all. The program makes some tradeoffs between previewing and inserting new tags that aren't compatible with many browsers, and limiting options to keep the HTML you generate pretty pure.

However, you can invent your Cake tag and use it, too, by inserting new tags with the Tag and End Tag icons: drag the icons from the Palette onto a page—you don't even have to hand code any HTML. The Tag Inspector allows you modify these objects' contents (see Figure 2-35).

Figure 2-35
Tag and End
Tag Inspectors'
Tag tab

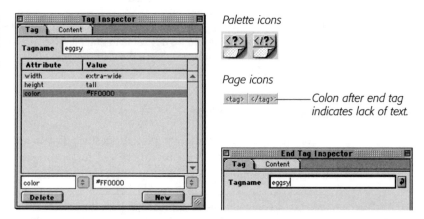

After adding the Tag placeholder, enter the tag's name in the Tagname field, then press Return. To add attributes, click the New button, type an attribute name in the Name field and its value in the Value field; repeat until you've had your fill of attributes. To get ride of an attribute, select it from the list and click the Delete button.

Many tags require a paired closing tag, so drag the Endtag icon from the Palette to the desired point in the Layout Editor to complete your HTML tag container.

Floating Box Inspector

Floating boxes could be the biggest thing in HTML since…tables!? That's right, tables. Remember when the Table tag and its ability to provide a rather complex layout scheme for your page seemed fresh, exciting, and downright cutting edge? A better question these days might be, "When *don't* you use tables?"

The floating box itself is a pretty handy way to create complex and dynamic layouts for 4.0 browsers and later by dividing up sections of a page into rectangular segments using the division (Div) tag and a Cascading Style Sheet definition. The ins and outs of floating boxes are discussed at length in Chapter 12, *Layout Grids and Floating Boxes*, as well as Chapter 24, *Animation*, but here's how to set up the basic elements.

Drag the Floating Box icon from the Palette into the Layout Editor and a floating box placeholder appears, featuring a tiny yellow box labeled "SB" offset from the top left corner of a 100 by 100-pixel box with a number in its bottom right corner indicating the order it was inserted into a page (see Figure 2-36). Placing your mouse over the box turns the cursor into a grabber hand.

Figure 2-36
Floating Box
Inspector

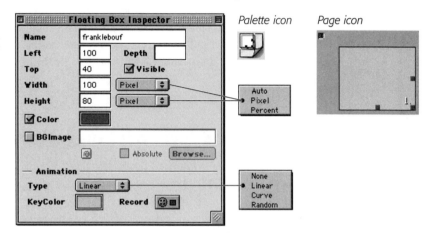

Dragging the box around the page changes its absolute x/y coordinates (as evidenced by the changing Left and Top values in the Floating Box Inspector), but the yellow floating box marker remains in the same position.

You can add HTML items to your floating box just as you would to the rest of your page, or within a layout grid or table cell. Drag in and configure images, Java applets, horizontal rules, and so on.

Name. In the Floating Box Inspector, enter a Name to identify a box.

Left and Top. To set how far the box sits from the left border of the browser window, type a pixel value in the Left field, then type a value in the Top field to place the box *x* number of pixels from the top of the window.

Depth. If you overlap floating boxes, you can choose their stacking order by entering a value in the Depth field. A floating box with a higher number is placed on the top of the heap, while the box with the lowest number is placed on the bottom.

Width and Height. Enter values in the Width and Height fields to modify the size of a box. (You can also click one of the blue handles within the floating box placeholder in the Document window and drag.) Choose Pixel for an absolute measurement, Percent for a measurement relative to the size of the browser window, or Auto to fit the content that's placed into the box.

Background. To add a background color to the box, drag a swatch from the Color Palette into the Color field. To add a background image, check BGImage and type the image file's URL or navigate to it using Point & Shoot or the Browse button.

Animation. Under the Floating Box Inspector's Animation controls, you can set the shape of an animation path (such as Linear, Curve, or Random), and the color for the Keyframe icon in the Timeline editor where you configure the bulk of your animation. Clicking the Record button allows you to set the path of an animation by dragging the floating box to desired points within the Document window. For more on creating floating box animations, see Chapter 24, *Animation.*

Body Script and JavaScript Inspectors

To start writing JavaScript, you need to choose whether to use a body script or a head script; consult Chapter 23, *JavaScript,* on making that choice. (Generally, you opt for scripts that appear in the Head section.)

If a body script is right for you, drag the JavaScript icon from the Palette's Basic tab onto your page. This calls up the Body Script Inspector (see Figure 2-37). (If you drag the Script icon from the Palette's Head tab into the Document window's head section, GoLive instead brings up an identical inspector named Head Script Inspector.)

The Body Script Inspector has blank fields for Name and Source when a Body Script is initially created. Choose browser compatibility from the Language popup menu, which then supplies the appropriate version of JavaScript (see Table 2-3).

	Browser Version	JavaScript Version
Table 2-3 JavaScript Languages	Navigator 2.*x*	JavaScript (the original version)
	Navigator 3.*x*	JavaScript 1.1
	Navigator 4.*x*	JavaScript 1.2
	Explorer 3.*x* and 4.*x*	JScript

If you have a text file with JavaScript code already prepared, check Source and type the name of the file and directory location or navigate to the file using Point & Shoot or the Browse button. However, if you still need to enter the script, click the Edit button to open the JavaScript Editor, where you notice the name you entered in the inspector is also displayed in the script name popup menu.

Figure 2-37
Body Script
Inspector

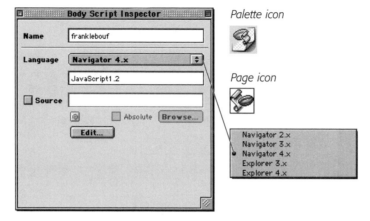

Palette icon

Page icon

**Tip: Opening
JavaScript
Editor**

In grand GoLive tradition, you have a number of options at the tip of your fingers to open the JavaScript Editor: click the coffee bean icon in the top-right corner of the Document window, click the Edit button in either the Head or Body Script Inspector, or double-click the placeholder icon in the Layout Editor.

Opening the JavaScript Editor also brings up the JavaScript Inspector. The Script tab mirrors the information found in the Body Script Inspector (name, language, source), but adds the Functions field, which lists all JavaScript functions found in an individual script (see Figure 2-38). Select an item from the Functions list and it becomes highlighted in the JavaScript Editor.

To add an event to your script, select from the list of available functions found under the Events tab and drag the item into the JavaScript Editor (see Figure 2-39). The function appears both in code in the Editor, as well as in the Event Code text box at the bottom of the JavaScript Inspector's Events tab. Notice that a description of the function appears to the right of the Event Code heading, and the selected function's icon now appears as active (that is, not grayed out).

Figure 2-38
JavaScript
Inspector's
Script tab

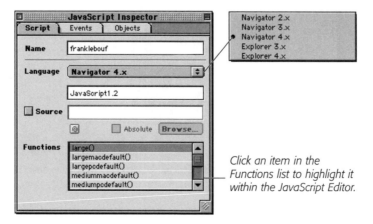

*Click an item in the
Functions list to highlight it
within the JavaScript Editor.*

Figure 2-39
JavaScript
Inspector's
Events tab

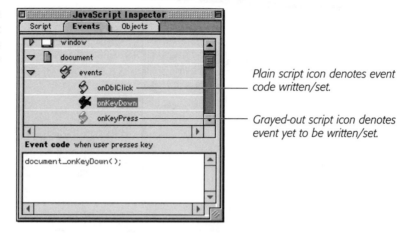

Plain script icon denotes event code written/set.

Grayed-out script icon denotes event yet to be written/set.

Tip: Editing JavaScript Functions   Adding a function to the JavaScript Editor allows you to edit its code in the Event Code field. Drag a function into the Editor, then make your edits or additions to the code. Select that function and drag it again into the Editor, and your edits appear in your script. Also, if you return to a function that has already been added (showing as active), selecting it adds a pen to the script icon, denoting that it is now editable.

To add objects and methods to the functions of your script, click the Objects tab, select from the list of available objects, then drag it to the desired point in the script (see Figure 2-40).

Figure 2-40
JavaScript
Inspector's
Events tab

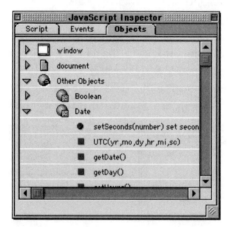

Head Inspectors

The Head section of an HTML page contains tags that describe the page to the viewer and to search engines, as well as identify foreign scripts, target frame or window destinations after a link is clicked, and even other miscellaneous items.

Head tags, the icons of which are found in the Head Section of the Palette, can only be placed within the head section pane of the Document window. GoLive defaults to placing three items of code in the Head section:

- `<META HTTP-EQUIV="content-type"content="text/html; charset=iso-8859-1">` identifies the character set used in the page, which can be changed in Preferences (see Chapter 4, *Preferences and Customizing*).

- `<META NAME="generator" content="Adobe GoLive4">` identifies GoLive as the creator of this page, which can be turned off in the General panel in Preferences under the Edit menu.

- The default title (`<TITLE>Welcome to Adobe GoLive 4</TITLE>`) appears in a browser's title bar; this can be changed by clicking and editing the field to the right of the Page icon, or editing the Title field in the Page Inspector

To add more tags, click the Head Section toggle triangle to open this area, or drag a Head tag icon from the Palette and hold it over the triangle. After a second or so, the Head section opens up, allowing you to place the icon.

Meta Tags

The workhorse of the head section, the Meta tag, lets you embed invisible information about your page, such as author's name, keywords, and description of the page's content. You can also control a page's refresh rate (for updating live information) or jump to a new destination after a set amount of time viewing the page.

GoLive offers a generic Meta Inspector for most of the settings you can apply to a page, but it also has the Keywords Inspector and the Refresh Inspector for managing those two specific tasks.

Meta Inspector

To add a Meta tag, drag its icon from the Palette's Head tab to the Document window's Head section; this brings up the Meta Inspector (see Figure 2-41). The Meta Inspector has a popup menu from which you can select either of the two most commonly used attributes for the Meta tag: Name and HTTP-Equivalent. Name is used for ordinary information, like the author's name, while HTTP-Equivalent can be used to insert values that are normally traded between a server and browser, such as a cookie setting or an expiration date for the page.

The popup button to the right of this field is inactive, so you don't have a list to choose from. See Chapter 6, *Page Overview*, for more details.

In the Content field, type the value that corresponds with the attribute. A page can have an unlimited number of Meta tags.

Figure 2-41
Meta Inspector

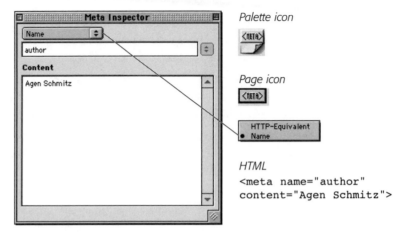

Palette icon

Page icon

HTML
```
<meta name="author"
content="Agen Schmitz">
```

Keywords Inspector

The Keywords Inspector lets you view, add, or edit a list of keywords describing your page's content (see Figure 2-42). For details on choosing keywords, see Chapter 6, *Page Overview*.

To add keywords to a page, drag the Keyword icon into the Document window's Head section, click within the text field, type a word or phrase and press Return or Enter, or click either the Add or carriage return buttons to add it to the list. Additional items are added into the list alphabetically. To delete an item, select it from the list and click the Delete button; to edit an existing item, select it from the list, make your edits, then click the Update button.

Shift-click on items to select consecutively; for example, shift-clicking the top and bottom items in a list selects all items. To select noncontiguous items, Command-click (Mac) or Control-click (Windows).

The Inspector lists the total number of keywords in the bar above the text input field. If you want to view the list in reverse alphabetical order, click the arrow to the left of the total.

Tip: Adding Keywords from Text
As you add or edit content in the Layout Editor, select a word or range of words and press Command-K (Mac) or Control-K (Windows) to add the selection to the keywords list, or choose Add to Keywords from the Special menu.

Tip: Updating Keywords
If you select an existing list item and edit it, you must click the Update button; pressing Return or even clicking the carriage return button at the end of the text input field adds a new keyword item to the list.

Now here's a wacky "feature": if you first select an item residing at the bottom of the alphabetical list (either in normal order or reversed), then select additional items above it using either Shift or Command/Control, the Update button becomes active. Clicking the Update button copies the item from the list's bottom to the top selected item (leaving all items in between unchanged). We're not sure how this might be helpful—but there it is.

Figure 2-42
Keywords
Inspector

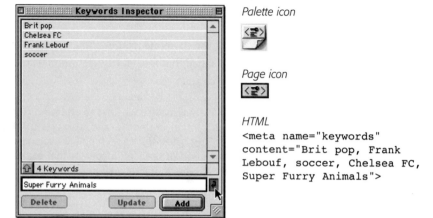

Palette icon

Page icon

HTML
```
<meta name="keywords"
content="Brit pop, Frank
Lebouf, soccer, Chelsea FC,
Super Furry Animals">
```

Refresh Inspector

Another member of the Meta tag family, the HTTP-Equivalent "Refresh" setting (as represented by the Refresh icon from the Palette's Head tab) allows you to control how often a page's content is refreshed. This might be useful for a page publishing minute-by-minute soccer scores or showing current traffic conditions. This same tag can be used to redirect a user's browser to another page after an automatic delay; this feature often gets used for introductory splash pages or for taking users to a new page after informing them that the page has moved.

In the Delay field of the Refresh Inspector, type a value in seconds for the refresh interval (see Figure 2-43). If you want to redirect the user to another page, click the URL radio button and type the file destination, or navigate to the file either using Point & Shoot or the Browse button.

Figure 2-43
Refresh
Inspector

Palette icon

Page icon

HTML
```
<meta http-equiv="refresh"
content="10;URL=../welcome
.html">
```

Link Inspector

The Link feature allows you to define relationships to other documents—such as style sheets or Web-formatted fonts—that require a special kind of external link in the Head section of a Web page.

Tip: Link Inspector Not, uh, Link Inspector.

GoLive offers the capability to visually track links to and from pages and objects in a site via the Link Inspector found under the Windows menu (Mac) or View menu (Windows); see Chapter 3, *Palettes and Parts*, for a full explanation of its use.

However, closer inspection of the Link Inspector that examines the Head section's Link object reveals it to be an entirely different inspector.

Tip: Dept. of Redundancy Dept.

GoLive has a few odd overlaps between similarly or identically named items like the two Link Inspectors or the Palette palette (it's a palette named Palette) or the Site window's Site tab. Try to make a visual identification of what GoLive displays to ensure you're viewing the correct item.

Drag the Link icon from the Palette's Head tab into the Layout Editor's Head section; this brings up the other Link Inspector (see Figure 2-44).

Figure 2-44
Link Inspector

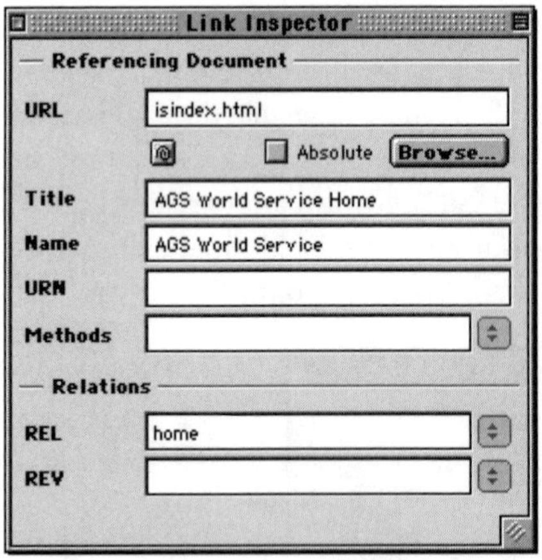

Palette icon

Page icon

HTML
```
<link href="welcome.html"
title="AGS World Service
Home" name="AGS World
Service" rel="home">
```

Select a linked document or page by entering its file information in the URL field or using the Browse button. (If the item is part of a GoLive site, you can also use the Point & Shoot feature.) Type the name of the file that is referenced in the Title field, then type the name of the link or anchor in the Name field. You can skip the URN (Uniform Resource Number) field, as that isn't supported, as well as the Methods field, which is rarely used.

You can enter values into the Rel attribute field to indicate the type of relationship this page has with the referenced file. Values entered into the Rev field indicate a reverse relationship to a file that is linking to the current page. Unfortunately, the popup menus for these fields are inactive in the 4.0.1 releases of GoLive; if you want to access these attributes you either have to type them from memory in the Link Inspector's fields or use the HTML Source Editor. None of these fields require you to press Return or Tab to accept edits. For more details, see Chapter 6, *Page Overview*.

IsIndex Inspector

The IsIndex feature dates back to Web antediluvian times when Web sites had only primitive tools. The Isindex tag designated a page searchable while simultaneously inserting a search field at the top of a page.

The IsIndex Inspector features one field—Prompt—which, when filled in, places the text to the left of the search field (see Figure 2-45). When a user types in text and presses Return, a new URL forms with the address of the current page, followed by a question mark and the keywords entered into the field (each separated by a plus sign).

GoLive—and the rest of the world—considers this tag obsolete, and the program doesn't preview it; you must preview the page in an external browser.

Figure 2-45
IsIndex
Inspector

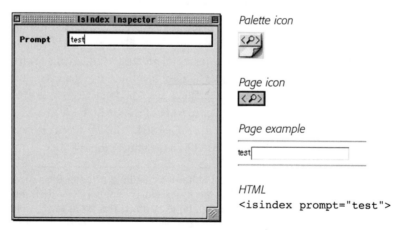

Palette icon

Page icon

Page example

test

HTML
`<isindex prompt="test">`

Base Inspector

Links and media file sources are typically written in code as relative to the current page. For example, if you're linking to an item at the same directory level, you only need to include the file name (i.e., "eggsy.gif"); if linking to a directory one level above, you'd type the HTML shorthand for moving up a level and include the directory name (i.e., "../gifs/eggsy.gif").

Using the Base tag, you can specify a URL that substitutes for the current page's location as the *base* on which to add or navigate any relative links on the page, including image and file references.

After dragging in the Base tag icon from the Palette's Head section, the Base Inspector appears (see Figure 2-46). Check the Base box and either enter the URL you want used as the page's base address or navigate to it. You can also designate a destination frame or window for all hyperlinks using the Target popup menu.

Figure 2-46
Base Inspector

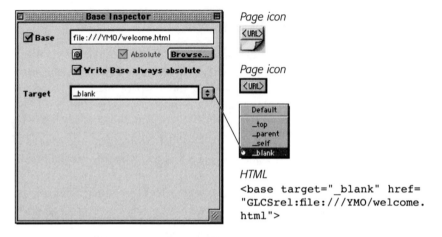

Checking Absolute below the Base field applies the absolute directory path to the item in the Base field if it's a local file (i.e., "file://YMO/welcome.html"); this applies to both the Base Inspector and to the underlying source code.

GoLive has two other kinds of identifiers that it appears to use for its own purposes, but which we can't figure out. Checking Write Base Always Absolute adds a GoLive-specific identifier to front of the URL: "GLCSabs:" if you've also checked the Absolute box above it, or "GLCSrel:". GoLive doesn't show this identifier in the Base field, but it does insert it in the underlying HTML.

Tip: Absolutely Absolute, I Think

Once you have checked either the Absolute or Write Base Always Absolute checkbox, click on any other tab in the Document window, then return to the Base tag icon in the Layout mode's head section. The Write Base... checkbox is now unchecked. (Additionally, on the Mac, if you've checked both Absolute and Write Base..., click on another tab, then return to the Layout Editor, the Absolute option is inactive while Write Base... is unchecked.)

However, a check of the Source tab shows that GoLive has absolutely carried out your wishes—it just doesn't keep track of it in Layout mode. This makes it a little confusing should you decide to turn off either of these options. To do so, simply check the option active again, then uncheck it to clear it.

Tip: Still Alive and Kicking

Adobe's manual says that the Base tag is obsolete. However, the latest HTML specification—version 4.0—that describes the language's features includes Base as a valid tag; it's useful, even, for page-wide behavior that doesn't require a lot of extra coding.

Tag and End Tag Inspectors

See the description for the Tag and End Tag Inspectors in "Document Layout Inspector," earlier in this chapter (see Figure 2-47).

Comment Inspector

See comments about the Comment Inspector in "Document Layout Inspector," earlier in this chapter (see Figure 2-47).

Headscript Inspector

If you want to add a script to a page's Head section, drag the Headscript tag icon in from the Palette (see Figure 2-47). This calls up the Headscript Inspector, which is virtually the same inspector as the JavaScript Inspector (see description in "Document Layout Inspector," earlier in this chapter), save for the name.

Figure 2-47
Miscellaneous
Head Inspector
icons

Head Tag and End Tag   Head Comment   Head Script

Palette icons   *Palette icon*   *Palette icon*

Page icons   *Page icon*   *Page icon*

Frame Inspectors

When viewing a page in the Frame Editor (after placing a frameset from the Palette's Frame tab), you run across two inspectors that control the behavior of framesets and individual frames.

Frame Set Inspector

The Frame Set Inspector appears immediately following the placement of a frameset icon from the Palette, or when you click on the border between two frames (see Figure 2-48). When a frameset is first inserted, the entire set is selected (indicated by a dark blue line surrounding all its frames), and any changes made on the Frame Set Inspector affect the entire set.

If you click on a frame border that divides several frames of the same orientation (either horizontal or vertical), GoLive places a blue boundary around those frames, and any modifications to the Frame Set Inspector affects just those frames.

Figure 2-48
Frame Set
Inspector

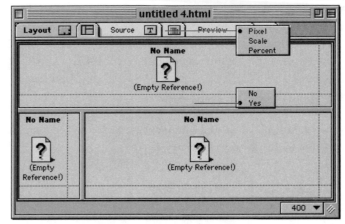

Orientation. A frameset's Orientation is set to either Horizontal or Vertical depending upon the way it sits within the frame layout. If you click the other radio button, your frameset flips to this orientation.

Tip: Mixing Up Framesets   If you have three or more frames on your page, you can rearrange how the frameset lays out by clicking one border and changing its Orientation, then clicking another border and changing its setting, and so on, and so on…

Sizing. You can set the size of two or more selected frames within a larger frameset. (If the entire frameset is selected, Size is inactive.) Choosing the default Scale automatically resizes the selected frames when a viewer alters a browser's size. Choosing Pixel sets an absolute measurement, while choosing Percent proportionally resizes based on the size of the browser window.

Border properties. Check BorderSize and enter a value in the field to the right to change its width; if checked, GoLive sets it by default to six pixels. To change the border's color, drag a swatch from the Color palette to the BorderColor field; GoLive sets it to gray by default. Checking BorderFrame outlines the frame with a thin, gray border; the default setting, when checked, is Yes.

Tip: Frame Colors   While you have to individually select each frame divider to modify border size and frame, you need only select one to set the color for all borders. The color chosen for that border bleeds into all other borders that do not have a color value assigned. Also, note that, unlike the color fields in the Table Inspector, you can't drag a color into the unchecked BorderColor field and have the color accepted; you must first check the option to make it active, then drag in your desired color.

Preview. To preview the frameset on the Mac without using the Frame Preview, click the Preview Set button. To return to file icon view, click the Stop Preview button. (This option is omitted in Windows GoLive 4.0.1.)

Frame Inspector

To begin setting the attributes of an individual frame, click anywhere within a frame except on the divider. You can set the measurement for a frame in the Frame Inspector by choosing either Pixel or Percent from the Size popup menu, then entering a value into its field (see Figure 2-49).

Figure 2-49
Frame
Inspector

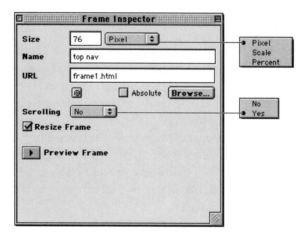

A frame's width is modified if its orientation—found in the Frame Set Inspector—is set to Horizontal, and its height is modified if a Vertical orientation is chosen. As with the Frame Set Inspector, if a frame's size is set to Scale, it sizes automatically when resized in a viewer's browser.

Choosing Pixel sets an absolute measurement that isn't resized, while choosing Percent proportionally resizes the frame relative to the overall width and height of the frameset. (You can also resize frames the old-fashioned way by dragging the frame divider.)

Tip: Framing Size   A frameset with multiple frames within an orientation (vertical or horizontal) specifies one frame's Size to Scale, while the other(s) are set to an absolute pixel size. This takes some of the burden off browsers when doing the math to accommodate different window sizes.

To link a page into a frame, enter the file name in the URL field, or navigate to the file. The question-mark file icon turns into a GoLive file icon, and the file name and directory information appears below. Next, give this frame a title in the Name field, which then appears above the file icon.

In the Scrolling menu, you can choose the default Auto option, which places a scroll bar (either vertical or horizontal) where text overflows the boundaries of the frame. If you choose Yes, a scroll bar is placed whether or not there is overflowing content, while choosing No does not produce a scroll bar even if content overflows.

GoLive defaults to leaving Resize Frame unchecked. If this is checked, a user can resize a frame in browsers that support this feature by dragging on a frame border and moving it left or right, or up or down.

On the Mac, you can preview a single frame by clicking the Preview Frame button. Click it again to turn off previewing and return to the file icon view.

Site Inspectors

The site-management features in GoLive are less focused on inspectors and more on the various tabs in the Site window, in which all management is centralized. The inspectors are still important, but many attributes and relationships in the Site window can only be, or also be, modified through dragging and dropping, or selecting an object and editing it directly.

The Site window is organized into five tabs: Files, Site, External, Colors, and Fontsets. These tabs handle, respectively, HTML and media files, site hierarchy and organization, external Web links and email addresses, sitewide color usage, and sitewide fontset usage. Each tab has its own set of inspectors that correspond to the kinds of objects stored in the tab.

File Inspector

The File Inspector helps you configure and view document basics, from static information such as creation date, to editable fields, including name, title, and "publish state." To invoke the Page Inspector, select a file—any file—in either the Files or Site tab.

File Tab

In the File Inspector's File tab, GoLive puts much of the same information you'd find in the Macintosh Finder or Windows Explorer, such as file type and creator (Mac only), creation and modification dates, and file size (see Figure 2-50). It also shows the file's location within the site in URL format.

Name. You can modify a file's name by editing within the Name field. If the file is referenced by others in the site, the Rename File dialog box appears and asks you whether you want GoLive to update all links with this new name. Check all boxes to the left of the file name that apply, then press Return.

Stationery. If you want to use a page as a template for designing other pages, check Stationery. The file then opens as an untitled GoLive document. (If you check Stationery for a media file, it opens in the application that created it, such as Acrobat or Photoshop, and add a "1" after the file's name.)

Figure 2-50
Site File
Inspector's
File tab

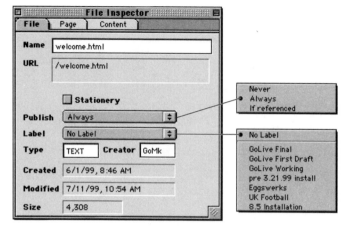

Publish state. In the Publish popup menu, choose a "state" for the document that controls how it interacts with GoLive's file synchronization feature. With Upload to Server in the Site menu set to observe the Publish state, setting a file to Never prevents its upload, Always forces its upload, and If Referenced checks first to see if the file is linked by a Web page before uploading it.

Label (Mac). The Label popup menu mirrors the Label color and title designations in the Macintosh Finder. (These settings can be modified via the Label control panel in System 7.5 and earlier, or in Preferences under the Edit menu in System 8.0 and higher.)

Page Tab

The Page tab only appears in the File Inspector when a GoLive document is selected (see Figure 2-51). Here you're able to modify a page's title just like you can in the Layout Editor via the Page Inspector, as well as view its encoding language.

Selecting the Status menu shows a list of options defined in the Site panel in the Preferences dialog box (for more information, see Chapter 4, *Preferences and Customizing*). Status works like Label on the Macintosh, described above, but allows a larger number to be defined, and it works on both Mac and Windows.

If you are viewing a page designated as the root page or home page for the entire site, Home Page is checked and inaccessible. To designate another page as the root, select that file, click the File Inspector's Page tab, and check Home Page. That causes the file's Home Page box to become checked and inaccessible, while simultaneously unchecking the previously marked home page.

Figure 2-51
File Inspector's
Page tab

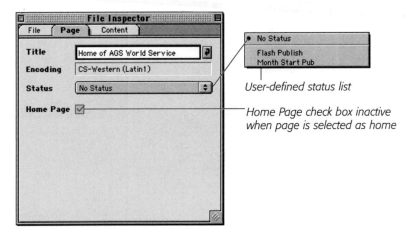

Figure 2-51
File Inspector's
Page tab

User-defined status list

Home Page check box inactive
when page is selected as home

Content Tab

Click the Content tab, and a thumbnail preview appears of the selected item if it's an HTML page or an image (see Figure 2-52). If the image is animated, it previews the animation in the Content tab.

If you select a QuickTime file, the QuickTime playback bar appears at the bottom, allowing you to preview the movie or sound file directly in the inspector. (A Pan button allows you to move the movie around.)

You can also preview other media files, like Shockwave and Flash, as long as you place their respective browser plug-ins into the GoLive plug-in folder. See Chapter 28, *Plug-Ins and Media*.

But wait—the Content tab isn't just for previewing! Click the thumbnail, drag it into an open document, and—voila—it's placed into the file with the correct file reference. You can also drag the thumbnail to another open Site window. If you drag the image into another folder within the site where the image already resides, a copy of the image is placed into that folder. This isn't usually advisable as there's more chance that Golive could get confused and break links in existing pages.

Figure 2-52
File Inspector's
Content tab

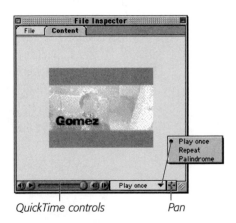

QuickTime controls   Pan

Tip: Dragging QuickTime Images

Select a QuickTime movie file from the Site window, scan through the frames to find a desired image, then drag it into an open document. A temporary GIF file is created with a generic numeric name and placed in the folder that's been designated as the Import Image folder within the GoLive application folder.

To make things go more smoothly, choose a location within your site as the Import Image folder (via Preferences's General panel under Image, where you can also choose an import file format). This saves you the trouble of dragging the image file into the site from an outside folder, as well as lets GoLive automatically update links to it.

Folder Inspector

Selecting a folder in the Files tab brings up the Folder Inspector, which is a truncated version of the File Inspector (see Figure 2-53). Here you find most of the same information found on that inspector's File tab, including name, location in the site, publish state, label (Mac only), and creation and modification dates.

Figure 2-53
Site Folder Inspector

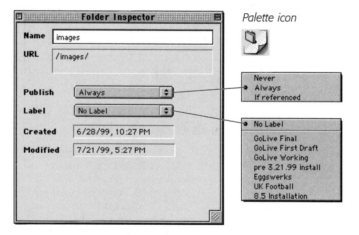

Tip: Extras Folders Don't Inspect

If you select a folder from the Extra tab in the right pane of the Site window, all editable fields and popup menus are rendered inactive.

Site View Controller

Click on the Site window's Site tab to see a map of the site you are building or managing. This brings up the Site View Controller, which allows you to customize what you see within this tab. If this controller doesn't automatically open in the inspector palette, like when an object has been selected, you can access the Site View Controller by clicking the Eye icon in the upper right corner of the Site window or just clicking into blank space within the window.

Arrange Tab

The Arrange tab allows you to control the basics of your site view, beginning with the two radio button choices at the top (see Figure 2-54).

- Clicking the Link Hierarchy button displays only the relationship between pages in a site that have actual links between them.

- Clicking the Navigation Hierarchy button displays the structural relationship between all pages in a site, including those that have pending links between them. This option also activates the Create New Page button, allowing you to add and link in new, blank pages to a site.

Figure 2-54
Site View
Controller's
Arrange tab

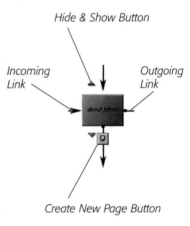

Hide & Show Button

Incoming
Link

Outgoing
Link

Create New Page Button

Link Hierarchy (left) shows only those files that are connected to other pages within a site.

Navigation Hierarchy (right) shows relationships between pages based on where files are placed within site; a thin, solid line denotes the pages are linked, while a dotted line denotes an existing file in the navigation scheme that's not yet linked.

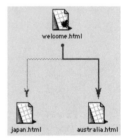

**Tip: Toolbar
Hierarchy
Control**
You can also choose between these two views by clicking the Navigation or Link Hierarchy toolbar buttons; for more information on using the Site Toolbar, see Chapter 3, *Palettes and Parts*.

Auto Arrange Items. Checking Auto Arrange Items allows you to also check the Stagger Items option. If Auto Arrange is unchecked, you can move files' icons anywhere you want within the Site tab. Checking it again resets the icons' positions; you can also click the Arrange Items button in the Toolbar.

New Page. Checking Use "Create New Page" Live Button allows you to click around an existing page to add blank pages to a navigation structure; it's only active when Navigation Hierarchy is selected. When you pass your mouse over a page or media file, a gray box with a small file icon appears above, below, left, or right of the file icon. If you click the box, a new, untitled GoLive document appears and is connected to the initial file by a dotted line, indicating it's not yet linked in.

Hide & Show. Checking Use "Hide & Show" Live Button allows you to collapse all or a portion of a site map by clicking the directional arrow that appears while a mouse hovers over a file icon that is connected to other file icons.

Side Knots. Checking Show Side Knots displays lateral and upward link relationships via two icons: the Incoming Link, a horizontal line with a dot on its left (indicating where a link begins); and the Outgoing Link, a horizontal line with an arrow on its right (showing which other files that file links to).

Hover your mouse over an Incoming Link and its color becomes muted; files at the same navigation level or above it that are linked to by this file have their ending side knot color muted. (Destination links to files below a file are denoted by a vertical line and arrow.)

T.o.C. To create a table of contents for a site in HTML text, click the button next to Create T.o.C. Page. This creates a static file that you can edit but which isn't dynamically linked up. (Under Windows, the button reads From Navigation, but on the Mac it displays as From Navigation or From Links based on the currently active hierarchy view.)

The table of contents is generated using links based on the hierarchy view you've chosen, nesting items in bulleted lists to show their depth in the site.

New From Site. To restore a modified Site tab after you've added links, pages, or dragged icons around, click the New From Site button. (If Navigation Hierarchy is selected under Windows, the button is labeled New From Navigation.)

Filter Tab

Checking or unchecking items on the Filter tab's Show Items list displays or hides icons representing different categories (see Table 2-4 and Figure 2-55).

Reachable and Unreachable. Under the Reachable by Home Page section, check If Reachable to view all pages connected to one another starting from the site's root page or home page. To see items that aren't part of that hierarchy, check If Unreachable. These items appear at the far right of the Site tab.

Table 2-4	Checking This...	...Displays This
File icons and filters	HTML Files	All GoLive Web pages
	Media Files	All images and multimedia files
	Folders	All folders, including those within GoLive data folder (Stationeries, Site Trash, and Components)
	URLs	All link objects found in the External tab
	Addresses	All email address objects found in the External tab
	Missing Files	All items listed as missing in the Errors tab of the Site Window (opened by clicking the green bug in the top right corner)

Figure 2-55
Site View
Controller's
Filter tab

Display Tab

Click the Display tab and choose how you want icons to be represented in the Site tab: file icons, thumbnails, frames, or precious little TV screens (see Figure 2-56). To identify files, choose to display either their file name (i.e., "default.html") or page title set in the Page Inspector and File Inspector (i.e., "Welcome to the AGS World Service").

Enter values in either the Horiz. or Vert. fields under grid spacing to modify the blank space surrounding site icons. GoLive defaults to 55 vertical pixels and 140 horizontal pixels. If you checked either thumbnails, frames, or TV screens, you can control their size by entering values in the Frame Size Width and Height fields.

To modify the way link lines are displayed, click one of the three Lines buttons (curved, diagonal, or straight). To display in a file directory view, click Display's Outline radio button.

Figure 2-56
Site View
Controller's
Display tab

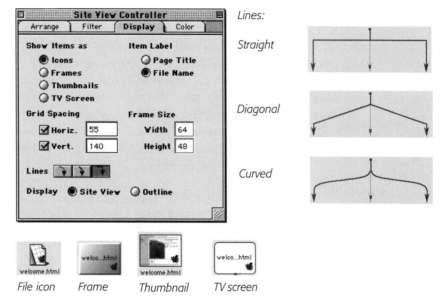

Color Tab

The Color tab is where you can modify the colors for the various items in the Site tab: navigation lines, link lines, file names, and background (see Figure 2-57). To change a color, simply drag a swatch from the Color Palette into a desired color field.

Under Item Color, you can override the default or custom colors used to display pages. Choosing Status Label colors each page according to its page status (assigned in the File Inspector and defined in Preferences the Site pane's Page Status settings), while choosing Monochrome allows you to select a custom color for all pages appearing in the Site tab. On the Mac, choosing Finder Label colors pages according the label colors assigned in the Finder.

Figure 2-57
Site View
Controller's
Color tab

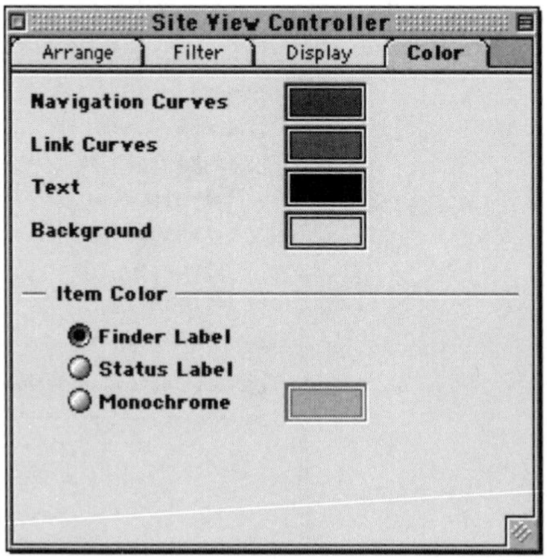

Link Inspector

The Link Inspector—found under the Windows menu on the Mac, but under the View menu under the Windows operating system—shows you the relationship between Web pages or certain kinds of media files (like Acrobat PDFs and Flash files that embed URLs) and the items that they link to or contain, like images, colors, fontsets, or other pages (see Figure 2-58).

You can bring up the Link Inspector from the menu mentioned above, by pressing Command-5 (Mac) or Control-5 (Windows), or by clicking on an Incoming or Outgoing Link in the Site tab.

Tip:
Graphical
Inspection

The Link Inspector graphically connects objects so that you can easily understand the relationships between them, relink items, connect missing references to the correct files. Technically, it's not an inspector like the other inspectors because it's got a graphical interface where all other Inspector palettes use a form interface with buttons, boxes, and fields.

Selecting any file or object in any of the Site windows tabs shows you all other objects on the site that point to the object (for media files and links) or contain the object (for colors and fontsets). If the item is a Web page—or an Acrobat PDF, QuickTime movie, or Flash animation with embedded URLs—the Link Inspector shows all outbound links as well.

You can use the Point & Shoot button to relink all the inbound links pointing to the selected item to any other item in its category. In the Figure 2-58, for exam-

Figure 2-58
Link Inspector
and Link View
Controller

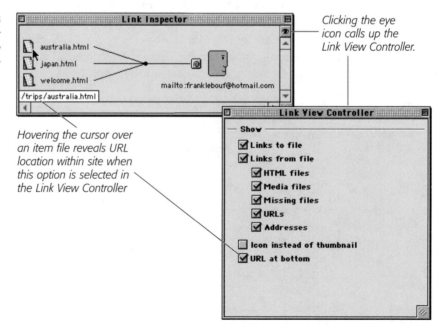

Clicking the eye icon calls up the Link View Controller.

Hovering the cursor over an item file reveals URL location within site when this option is selected in the Link View Controller

ple, you could relink "mailto:franklebouf@hotmail.com" by using Point & Shoot to select "mailto:pele@footie.com.br". You can also link to objects that are not in the same tab, like replacing a link to an email address with an HTML file.

Link View Controller. The items that GoLive displays in the Link Inspector can be controlled through the Link View Controller, accessed by clicking the eye icon in the upper-right corner of the inspector. (The controls are almost identical to the Site View Controller's Filter and Display tabs for setting up the Site tab.)

You can choose whether to show inbound and outbound links or both, and filter which outbound links to show. Pages with a large number of external links, for instance, can create a huge scrolling display in the Link Inspector.

Checking Icon Instead of Thumbnail displays the Finder icon (on the Mac) or a default icon (under Windows) instead of a Web page thumbnail. The URL at Bottom checkbox toggles the display of the item's location on the site.

Reference Inspector

GoLive automatically gathers all external Web addresses and email addresses used in a site and organizes them in the External tab. But you can also create these objects from scratch by dragging or double-clicking the URL or Address icon from the Site tab of the Palette into the External tab. (Note that double-clicking an icon places the item at the top level of the External tab's object manager.)

After creating a new address or URL, you must type a name in the highlighted field of the file icon and press Return to accept the edit before the Reference Inspector comes up (see Figure 2-59). Once it does appear, you can make further

Figure 2-59
Reference
Inspector and
Site Window's
External tab

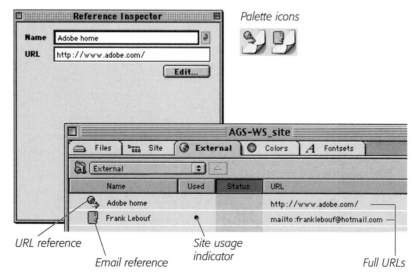

edits in the Name field and type in its URL for external Web links. If you have an especially long URL, you might want to modify it by using the Edit button, which opens the Edit URL dialog box.

Email addresses are automatically given a "mailto:" prefix if this option is selected in Preferences under the General pane's URL Handling settings.

Color Inspector

GoLive collects references to colors used anywhere in your site in the Colors tab. Selecting Get References Used from the Site menu scours the site for colors. Or you can create new color entries by dragging the Color icon from the Palette's Site tab. A new color requires a name before the Color Inspector appears (see Figure 2-60).

Figure 2-60
Site Color
Inspector

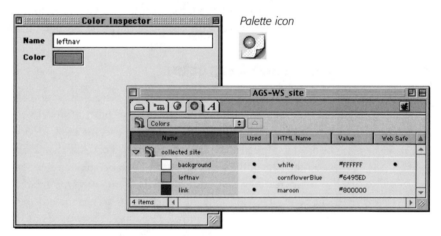

Change the color's title in the Name field, and modify the color by dragging a color swatch from the Color Palette into the Color Field. Double-clicking a color (either its swatch or any part of its name or attributes) opens the color in the Color Palette's preview pane.

Group Inspectors

Although sounding more like some cabal of oversight committees, GoLive's Group Inspectors centralize the attributes for working with external links, colors, and fontsets within a site.

External Group Inspector

Drag either the URL Group or Address Group icon from the Palette's Site tab into the External tab to create a folder where you can collect references to sites and email addresses. The Group Inspector allows you to modify the title of the folder, as well as assign one of four folder types: URLs, Addresses, New URLs, and New Addresses (see Figure 2-61). If you've just imported a site, GoLive carefully separates the two groups into New URLs and New Addresses folders.

Figure 2-61
Color and Font
Set Group
Inspectors

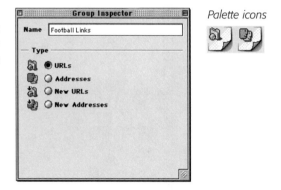

Palette icons

Color and Font Set Group Inspector

The Color and Font Set Group Inspectors win the award for most redundant items in the GoLive pantheon of palettes and inspectors (see Figure 2-62). Selecting a folder within either the Colors or Fontsets tabs of the Site window (or inserting that tab's group icon from the Palette into the tab) brings up the Color or Font Set Group inspector. Each of these two inspectors contain just one field—Name—which you could easily change by selecting the object in the Site window and typing your edits.

Figure 2-62
Color and Font
Set Group
Inspectors

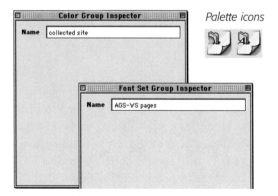

Palette icons

Font Set Inspector

To create a site-specific fontset, drag the Font Set icon from the Palette into the Site window's Fontsets tab; GoLive also gathers fontsets used in a site when you select Get Fontsets Used from the Site menu. Give your set a name by typing a title in the Name field in the Font Set Inspector (see Figure 2-63).

Figure 2-63
Site Font Set
Inspector

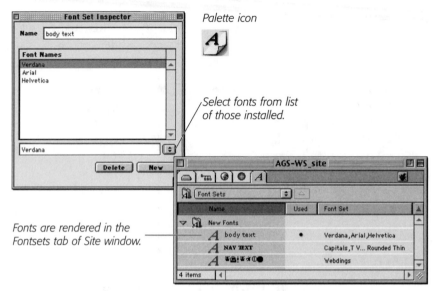

Palette icon

Select fonts from list
of those installed.

Fonts are rendered in the
Fontsets tab of Site window.

Click the menu to the right of the text field at the bottom of the inspector to see a list of your active system fonts. Selecting a font from the list places the font name in both the text field and in the Font Names list. You can also enter a name from scratch to add it to the fontset.

You can't reorder items in this list after adding them; you have to delete them and re-enter them in the preferred order. Click the New button to add additional fonts to this set; to do away with an individual font, select it and click the Delete button or select Clear from the Edit menu.

The fontset list displays each set using a preview of the first font's typeface.

Error Inspector

The dreaded green bug to the right of a file in the File tab's Status column indicates bad links on that page. To see a list of errors, click the Error tab in the second pane of the Site window. On the Mac, click the Aspect Control icon at the top of the window; under Windows, click the toggle arrow at the bottom of the window.

Unfortunately, the Error Inspector doesn't provide a lot of information; the only field included with the Inspector is a URL field with the usual Point & Shoot and Browse buttons to navigate to a solution (see Figure 2-64). And the inspector doesn't tell you what file this error appears in.

To get to the heart of the matter, select the error item, the press Command-5 (Mac) or Control-5 (Windows) to open the Link Inspector. The selected file is then connected to its source, allowing you to open up the infected file and stamp out any HTML bugs that have taken up residence.

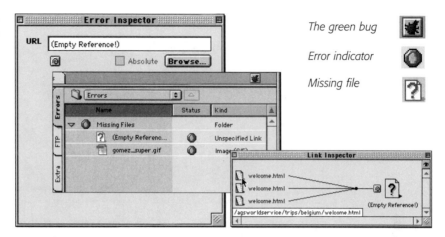

Figure 2-64
Error Inspector

FTP File and Folder Inspectors

Once you've uploaded your site to a Web server, you can view file information, change a file or folder's name, examine links (symbolic links, aliases, or shortcuts) to other files, and set up access permissions via inspectors.

Tip: FTP Connections Connect to your remote FTP server before following any of the directions below; if you don't yet have this set up, consult Chapter 18, *Staging and Synchronizing Sites*, to get everything in place.

Tip: FTP Tab The FTP tab on the Mac is found by clicking what Adobe calls the Aspect Control icon in the upper right of the Files tab; under Windows, that icon is found at the bottom left of the Files tab. Click the FTP tab in the revealed panel.

FTP Folder Inspector

When you select a folder from the FTP tab, the FTP Folder Inspector comes up (see Figure 2-65). If you want to change the title of a folder, type it in the Name field, making sure to press Return or Enter to accept the edit (there is no carriage return icon to remind you).

The fields below the name are informational only, displaying the URL for the FTP site and the date when the folder was last updated with a new file. The date-stamps of files or other folders that reside within the directory don't affect the datestamp on the FTP Folder Inspector when they are updated.

In the Rights section, you can view and change the access permission, or rights, to the folder in three categories: read, write, and execute. Permissions can be set for the owner of a folder, others in an associated work group, or everyone else in the world; the owner and group have to be set by the system administrator. When you change a checkbox's state, the Set Rights button becomes active and must be clicked to apply the change.

Figure 2-65
FTP File, Folder, and Link Inspectors

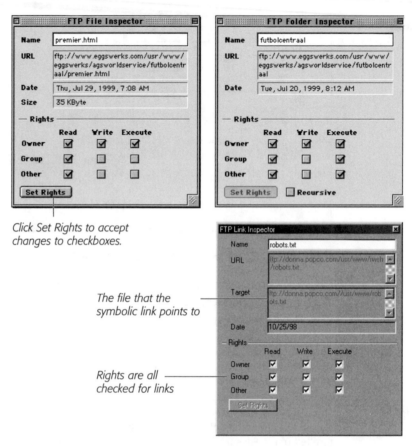

Click Set Rights to accept changes to checkboxes.

The file that the symbolic link points to

Rights are all checked for links

Tip: Check Your Rights   If Execute is unchecked for Owner, you can't even open a folder by clicking its toggle arrow; you'll only get an error message saying permission is denied. To change permissions to reflect Execute for Owner, select the folder and check the option. Execute must be set for Group or Other only if the group or world at large also has write permission to modify items in the folder or upload new items to it.

Checking Recursive applies all the permissions you've set for the folder to every item underneath the folder, including all nested folders and files.

FTP File Inspector

The FTP File Inspector mirrors the FTP Folder Inspector's items, save for the Recursive option and the addition of a Size informational field (see Figure 2-65).

To set a level of access for an individual file, select the item's icon in the FTP tab, then check or uncheck your desired options in the FTP File Inspector.

FTP Link Inspector

GoLive also has an almost identical inspector that works only with links to other files (see Figure 2-65). Under Windows, these links are called "shortcuts" and on the Mac, they're "aliases." In both cases, the file icons have italic type and an arrow symbol to indicate they point to another file; the FTP Link Inspector shows both the pointer's location and the destination's location.

Under Unix, the most common hosting platform for Web sites, these links are called "symbolic links," and they cannot be modified via GoLive. The subject gets dense pretty quickly; for an in-depth discussion, see Chapter 18, *Staging and Synchronizing Sites.*

CyberObjects

GoLive collects a number of cool tricks that can be inserted into pages from the Palette's CyberObjects tab, including automatic browser switching and effects such as timestamps and datestamps and URL popup menus. (These are discussed in the context of GoLive Actions in Chapter 25, *Actions.*)

Date & Time Inspector

To add a datestamp and/or timestamp to your page, which shows viewers the last time a page was updated, drag the Date & Time icon from the CyberObjects tab of the Palette into the body section of the Layout Editor. The time and date is read from your computer's built-in clock; the information is updated each time the file is saved.

From the Date & Time Inspector, choose the language format of how the date and time are written from the Format popup menu, then select the language and style displayed in the radio buttons below (see Figure 2-66).

Figure 2-66
Date & Time
Inspector

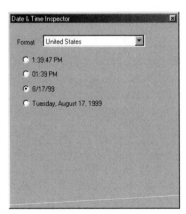

Button Inspector

You can set up a quick and simple effect with the Button Image CyberObject where moving the mouse over an image causes that image to change; this is called a "rollover," because the button's image changes when the cursor is rolled over it.

Drag the Button Image icon from the CyberObject's tab of the Palette into the body section of the Layout Editor to reveal the Button Inspector.

Basic. In the Basic tab, enter a unique name for the button in the Name field (see Figure 2-67). Select the Main icon and specify the image file you want to display without any mouse action when the page loads. A preview of the image replaces the Main icon, while the checkbox to the left of the field is inactive (and stays that way, since the main image has to be displayed).

Select the Over icon to swap in another image when a viewer's mouse passes over the image area; check the box to the left of the field below and navigate to the desired file. Do the same for the Click icon, which displays another image when a viewer clicks the object. (You can choose to apply just one or the other option.) In the Layout Editor, the main image is displayed in the button image placeholder.

Figure 2-67
Setting up a rollover in the Button Inspector

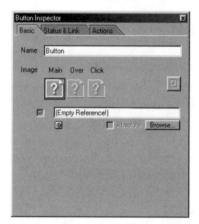

Tip: Dragging and Dropping Button Images   GoLive allows you to drag and drop images from either the Site window or your hard drive into the Button Image placeholder. For the Main image, drag a file as you would any other, where a thumbnail of the image is displayed in place of the Main icon. To add an Over image, Option-drag on the Mac or Control-drag under Windows. Shift-Option-dragging (Mac) and Control-Shift-dragging (Windows) assigns an image to the Click item.

Tip: Resizing Button Images   Dragging images into the Button Image placeholders, instead of using Point & Shoot, sizes the image according to the dimensions of the placeholder. To return the image to its actual dimensions, click the Image Resize button to the right of the three image previews in the inspector. (An inactive button means that the image is just fine.)

Also, if either the Over or Click option is unchecked but selected, the Image Resize button is active, and clicking it makes the placeholder return to its small default size. To fix this, select one of the images that's already placed and click Resize to bring back the true dimensions.

Status & Link and Actions tabs. Use the Status & Link tab to enter a message that displays at the bottom of a browser window in the Status field when you mouse over the Main image (see Figure 2-68). Check URL and assign the the link's destination, as well as a target window. The Actions tab works just as it does with the Text and Image Inspectors with the exception that if you create an action for a button, the link assigned in the Status & Link tab's URL field is deactivated.

Figure 2-68
Button
Inspector's
Status & Link
and Actions
tabs

Component Inspector

If you create a wide range of pages that need to have the same item updated frequently, consider using GoLive's centrally-managed component feature, a Cyber-Object placed onto a page that references a snippet of HTML saved as another page elsewhere. Components are discussed further in Chapter 21, *Site Specials*.

The simple Component Inspector has a single function: to allow you to specify the source of the Component CyberObject you've dragged onto a page or want to modify (see Figure 2-69).

Figure 2-69
Component
Inspector

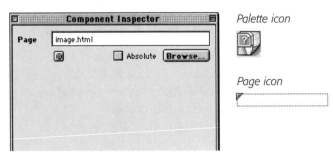

Palette icon

Page icon

URL Popup Inspector

To give your viewers easy access to other pages in your site without cluttering the page landscape with a lot of links, use the URL Popup CyberObject to create a popup menu that, when an item is selected, jumps to that designated page. To create this effect, drag the URL Popup icon into the main body section of the Layout Editor; this brings up the URL Popup Inspector (see Figure 2-70).

Figure 2-70
URL Popup
Inspector

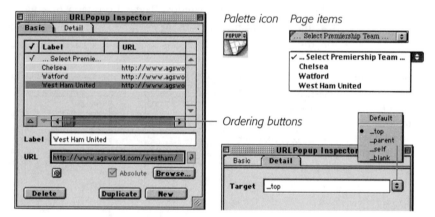

The top item in the Basic tab's list pane is the popup menu's label, the item that viewers see first before clicking to reveal the menu's items. GoLive defaults to placing Choose in the the Label field, but you can type another message in the list to entice your viewers.

Select the next item and enter a description of your first link in the Label field, then press Return, Enter, or Tab to accept the edit.

In the URL field, type a link destination or navigate to it using the usual methods. If you want to specify a target frame or browser window, select the Detail tab and choose or enter your destination window, method, or frame.

To add a new list item, return to the Basic tab and click the New button; or, click the Duplicate button. To reposition an item within the list, select it and click the up or down arrow to the left of the list scrollbar.

Action Headitem and Inline Action Inspector

Most Actions are triggered when the viewer does something, like clicking a link. To start an Action automatically, use the Action Headitem and Inline Action icons. Dragging an Action Headitem icon to the Document window's Head section, or dragging the Inline Action icon into the body section, inserts an Action placeholder that isn't attached to a text, image, or other hyperlink.

If you place an Action Headitem, you can choose to trigger the Action as the page loads or as the viewer leaves the page. To determine the trigger for a Headitem, select an item from the Exec. popup menu of the Action Inspector (see Figure 2-71). If you place an inline Action in the body of a page, the browser triggers that effect once the page load reaches the Action's position on the page as it parses.

For more information on setting up Actions, see the Action Inspector section earlier in this chapter. For more on Actions in general, see Chapter 25, *Actions*.

Figure 2-71
Action and
Inline Action
Inspectors

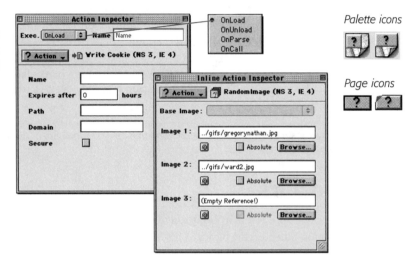

Browser Switch Inspector

To send viewers with an incompatible browser to another page with compatible content, drag the Browser Switch Headitem icon from the Palette into the Document window's Head section; this brings up the Browser Switch Inspector (see Figure 2-72).

Figure 2-72
Browser
Switch
Inspector

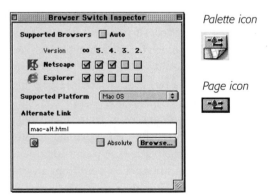

If you want GoLive to determine browser compatibility, leave Auto checked. GoLive then checks the appropriate items for the browsers listed below based on the content of your page: it checks only the 4.0 and 5.0 browsers if you've included Cascading Style Sheets, for instance; you would want to send viewers with browser version 3.0 and lower to an alternate page.

To determine your own options, uncheck Auto and check the browser versions that are compatible for your page. In the Supported Platform popup menu, select either All, or choose between Windows and Mac OS.

In the Alternate Link field, type a destination URL for the alternate page or navigate to it using the standard methods.

Tip: Multiple Alternatives   After configuring one Browser Switch Headitem for a particular platform, drag another Headitem icon into the head section from the Palette and set up an alternate switch for the other platform.

Tip: Watch the Switch   Browser switching does not work with version 2.0 browsers or Internet Explorer 3.01 for the Mac.

Form Inspectors

Working with forms in GoLive is the subject of Chapter 13, *Forms,* so here we just want to touch on the basics of inserting a form into your page and give you a feel for the different inspectors that you'll encounter.

Form Inspector

Every form starts with the Form tag, which is inserted by dragging the Form icon into the Layout Editor from the Forms tab of the Palette.

In the Form Inspector, type a unique name for this form in the Name field (see Figure 2-73). In the Action field, checked by default, set the destination file name and directory location of the CGI script that processes the information on the server when the form is submitted. (If you don't have a CGI set up, contact your system administrator who needs to configure it on the Web server.)

Set a target frame or window using the Target popup menu. If you're requesting the user to upload a file (a rare request), choose a setting from the Encrypt popup menu. Normal forms use "application/x-www-form-urlencoded", while file uploading uses "multipart/form-data". Don't let the name fool you: this field doesn't do any encrypting—a better title for the field should be Encoding. A system administrator would tell you if you needed to use any other value for that attribute.

Choose the way your information is sent from the Method menu: Get (GoLive's default) specifies that all of the data is sent as part of a URL; Post sends

Figure 2-73
Form Inspector

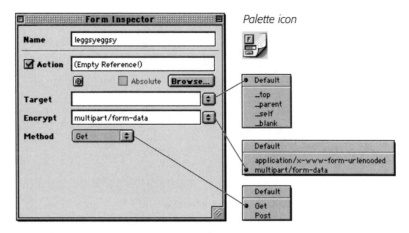

Palette icon

it behind the scenes, sending the data in a less public manner. Default omits a Method from the Form tag, but browsers default to Get.

After inserting a Form opener, you can start adding other form elements. When finished with a form, be sure to drag the End Form icon from the Palette after the last form element.

Tip: Form End Tag Auto Insert

If you click to another GoLive tab, then return to the Layout Editor, you find that GoLive has kindly placed an End Form icon after the last form element if you haven't done so already. Nice catch, GoLive!

Focus. You might notice that most Form inspectors include much of the same information in each inspector, but the Focus settings might be most mysterious. These features are all part of the HTML 4.0 specification, which no browser has fully implemented yet; Adobe has jumped ahead of the crowd by offering support for them. Some of the 4.0 and later browsers support a few of these features, but it's not safe to rely on any them.

The four items in the Focus area are Tab, Key, Readonly, and Disabled. The Tab checkbox, if selected, allows you to set an order by which pressing tab advances the text-insertion point from element to element in a form. You can click the button next to the Tab field and then click fields one at a time to set order. The Key field lets you select a keyboard shortcut for a user to type to jump to that field. Readonly and Disabled are modifiers which either render a field uneditable or dimmed back.

For more information on setting up the Focus section, see Chapter 13, *Forms*.

Form Button Inspector

The Form Button Inspector actually appears for three types of buttons found in the Forms tab of the Palette: the Submit Button, the Reset Button, and the customizable Button (see Figure 2-74). The difference between these three is subtler

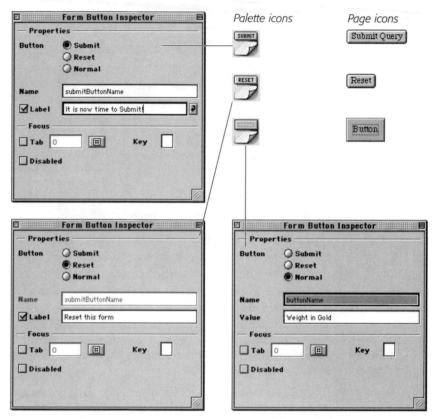

Figure 2-74
Form Button
Inspectors

Palette icons   *Page icons*

than appearances imply. There are really *three settings* and *two kinds of buttons* masquerading as three settings and three icons.

Dragging the Submit or Reset button from the Forms tab of the Palette creates one kind of button, a standard rounded-corner HTML button which dates back to 1993 or 1994, and which can be set to submit a page to a server for processing, reset its contents (erasing all entered values), or trigger a JavaScript (the Normal setting).

The other kind of button—really an HTML 4.0 Button tag behind the scenes—is created by dragging the Button icon from the Palette. This button defaults to the Normal setting, but it's substantively different from a rounded-corner button. It can contain any HTML whatsoever as its contents, including tables, form elements, images, and so on. Clicking in the button itself allows you to edit it and paste items into it.

Submit. A viewer presses the Submit button when he or she is ready to send the form's data to the server for processing. Enter a name for the form object, then enter the wording you want to appear in the button by checking the Label and typing in the field. If unchecked, GoLive leaves that value empty but previews it as Submit Value.

Reset. To enable a viewer to clear a form's data and start entering it again from scratch, insert a Reset button. The Name field is inactive, as HTML doesn't send a name for this button to the server. Use the Label field to customize the button's wording. If unchecked, GoLive leaves the value empty, but previews it as Reset.

Normal. The Normal setting creates a button—rounded-corner or advanced button variety—that has *no* action associated with it. You can create a JavaScript that has, as its trigger, a user clicking, mousing over, or otherwise manipulating this button. As with the other two inspectors, enter a name for the form object.

Tip:
Changing
Button Types

Any type of button can be changed to be a Submit, Reset, or Normal button. If you want a Normal button that has rounded corners, drag a Submit or Reset Button icon onto the page, then use the Button Inspector to change it to Normal. Likewise, if you want an advanced Submit button with rich HTML content in it, drag a Button icon to the document and then click Submit in the inspector.

Form Check Box Inspector

To add a checkbox within a form, drag the Check Box icon into your page from the Palette, type a unique identifier in the Name field, and enter a descriptor in the Value field (see Figure 2-75).

Figure 2-75
Form Check
Box Inspector

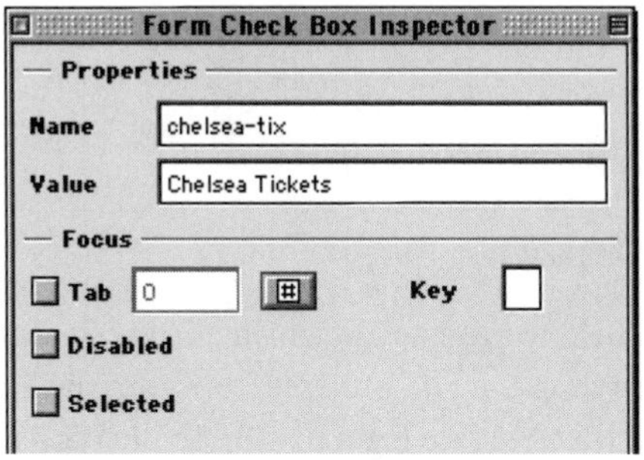

Palette icon

Form Radio Button Inspector

Drag the Radio Button icon from the Palette onto a page, and assign an individual value in the Value field (see Figure 2-76). The Group field acts as an umbrella for a set of radio buttons with different, exclusive values. Enter a unique name or select an existing Group from the menu displaying all groups in the form.

Figure 2-76
Form Radio
Button
Inspector

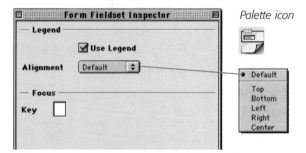

Form Fieldset Inspector

In HTML 4.0-compatible browsers, you can visually group a set of form elements using a fieldset, which is a box that surrounds a set of form elements. After dragging the Fieldset icon into the Layout Editor, you can add a title to the group by selecting the word "Legend" on the page and typing your desired descriptor.

To align the legend along the top of the boundary box, select an option from the Alignment popup menu, or uncheck Legend to turn it off (see Figure 2-77). Now you're ready to start adding content to this box by typing text and dragging form elements in from the Palette.

Figure 2-77
Form Fieldset
Inspector

Form File Inspector

To add a file-selection field to your form, which allows viewers to locate and upload files to your server, drag the File Browser icon from the Palette. In the Name field, enter the name of the field (see Figure 2-78). In the Visible field, type a number that determines the field's width on your page.

Form Hidden Inspector

Drag the Hidden icon from the Palette to create an input tag that is hidden from your viewer. Type a unique identifier in the Name field and a descriptor in the Value field (see Figure 2-79).

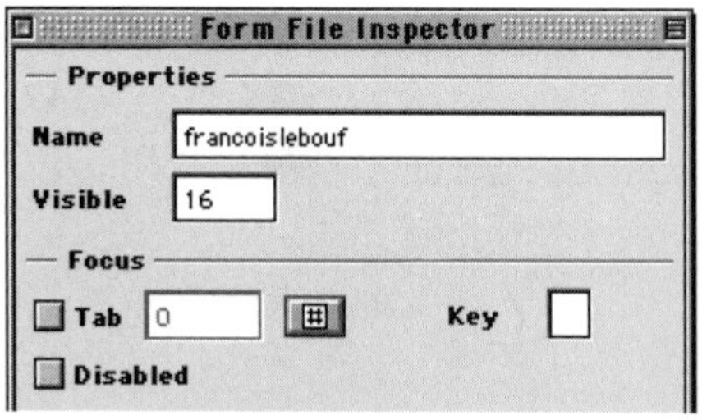

Figure 2-78
Form File
Inspector

Palette icon

Figure 2-79
Form Hidden
Inspector

Palette icon

Form Image Inspector

To add an image to your form as, say, a customized button, drag the Input Image icon into the Layout Editor. Alternatively, select an image already placed into your page, go to the Spec. tab, and check Is Form underneath the Form section; the Image Inspector then changes its title to Form Image Inspector, keeping all of its typical image controls while adding the Name field and Focus information to the Spec tab (see Figure 2-80).

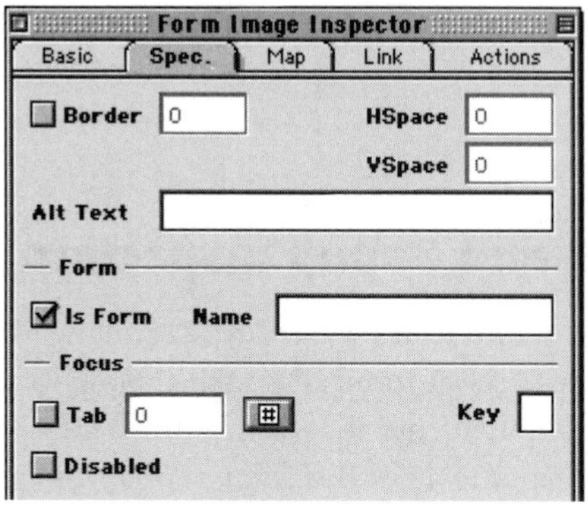

Figure 2-80
Form Image
Inspector

Palette icon

Form Keygen Inspector

Adding a Keygen icon to your page inserts a key generator tag that is used with certificate-management systems. (Chapter 13, *Forms*, talks more about generating keys). Type a unique identifier in the Name field, then type a security level in the Challenge field (see Figure 2-81).

Figure 2-81
Form Keygen
Inspector

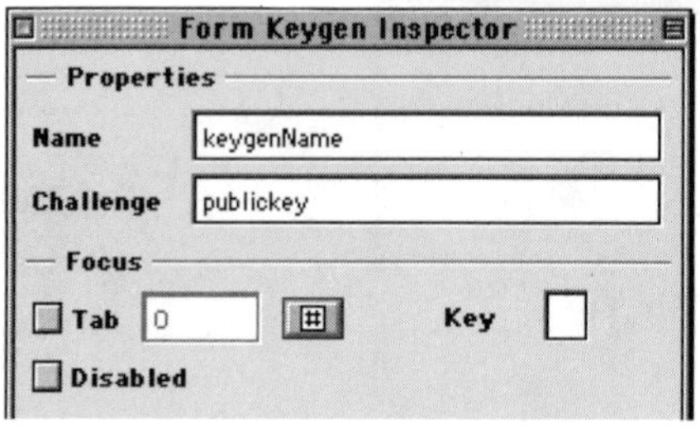

Palette icon

Form Label Inspector

For HTML 4.0-compatible browsers, you can add a descriptive label to a form control (such as a check box or radio button). Drag the Label icon into your page to add a "Label" placeholder. To change the name of the Label, click within the text and type your desired name. Click back on the outside border to select the Label element to bring the Form Label Inspector back up (see Figure 2-82).

Under the Reference field, use the Point & Shoot button to select a form element on the page, which adds an ID name/number to the field; you can also Command-drag (Mac) or Control-drag (Windows) to a form element from the Label's blue outside boundary. To show which form element is associated with this label, click the Show button to display a pointer to the element.

Figure 2-82
Form Label
Inspector

Palette icon

Form List Box and Popup Inspectors

Adding the List Box icon into your page creates a scrolling list offering multiple options for your viewer to select from; adding the Popup icon accomplishes the same effect but with a popup menu. To switch between the two inspectors, check Multiple Selection to change to a List Box from a Popup, or vice versa (see Figure 2-83). When Multiple Selection is unchecked, the value in Rows is 1, denoting that only 1 item shows in the page's form element (creating the popup menu).

Tip:
Changing
List Types
To create a one-row list box in some browsers, check Multiple Selection and type a value of 1 in the Row field. If you leave Multiple Selection unchecked, but type a Row value greater than 1, some browsers create a list box, others create a popup menu, and some list the contents of the box on a single line. Use at your own risk.

Figure 2-83
Form List Box
and Popup
Inspector

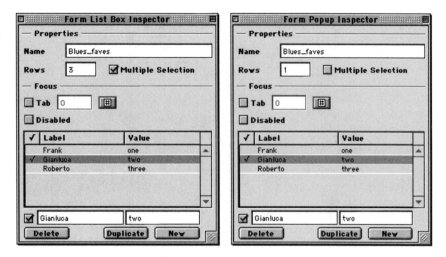

Palette icons   Page icons (popup, list box)

GoLive defaults to placing three numerical items in the list area. To add your own value, select one of the list items to activate the text input fields at the bottom of the inspector. In the first field (in the Label column), type the label you want to appear in the browser, then type a value in the second field (under Value) which gets sent to the server to identify that option. A checkmark to the left of the Label text field specifies that item as initially displayed as the selection, either shown in the popup menu or highlighted in the list box.

Form Text Area Inspector

To add an area on your page where viewers can type multiple lines of text, drag the Text Area icon from the Palette and type a unique identifier in the Name field (see Figure 2-84). In the Row field, type a value to determine the height in rows of text; in the Columns field, type a value to set its width in number of characters.

In the Wrap popup menu, select one of the following options to determine how text is displayed:

- **Off:** stops text from wrapping; lines are sent exactly as typed.
- **Virtual:** displays word-wrapping, but the breaks aren't sent to the server.
- **Physical:** displays word-wrapping, and the breaks are sent to the server.

If you want to add sample text that your viewer can overwrite, type that content in the Data text field at the bottom of the inspector.

Figure 2-84
Form Text Area
Inspector

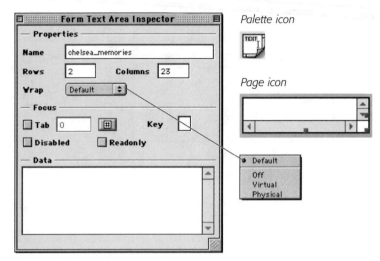

Palette icon

Page icon

Form Text Field and Password Inspectors

To add a one-line text field to your form, drag the Text Field icon from the Palette; to create a text field which hides characters as they're typed (i.e., "●●●●●●"), drag the Password icon into your form.

The Is Password Field option is checked when you drag a Password icon to the Document window. Check this field to turn a text field into a Password field and vice-versa (see Figure 2-85).

Type a name in the Name field. You can prefill a form by entering text in the Content field. You can control the width in characters for the field by entering a value in Visible, and the maximum number of characters entered through Max.

Figure 2-85
Text Field and
Password
Inspectors

Palette icons   *Page icons*

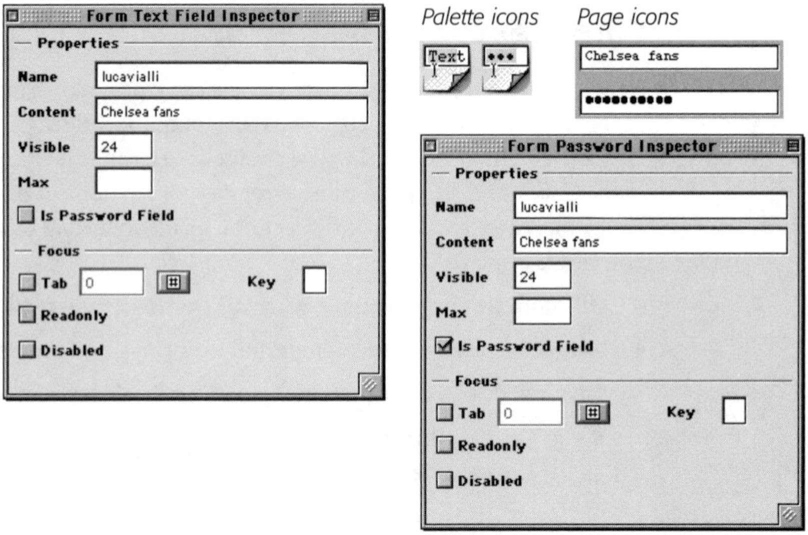

Web Database Inspectors

GoLive's Web Database is the control center for the code that GoLive generates, from HTML to XML to Cascading Style Sheets. This aspect of GoLive is covered in depth in Chapter 27, *Web Database*, but the individual inspectors associated with the Web Database are offered here for reference. The Web Database can be invoked through the Windows menu (Mac) or View menu (Windows), or by pressing Command-4 (Mac) or Control-4 (Windows).

HTML and Character Inspectors

The Web Database's HTML tab allows you to configure the entire library of HTML tags, while the Characters tab lets you control encoding for special characters.

Both tabs are viewed in a hierarchical file structure, with each level corresponding to a specific inspector (see Figure 2-86). In the HTML tab, click the top section level (if viewed in Structured mode) to view the WebDB Section Inspector. Clicking the next level down (the top level when viewing in Flat mode; see "WebDB Inspector," below) brings up the WebDB Tag Inspector. Expanding a tag and selecting an element below it calls up the WebDB Attribute Inspector; to define enumerations, one level below attributes is the WebDB Enum Inspector.

The Characters tab features two inspectors: the WebDB Section Inspector (when viewing the top file level in Structured mode) and the WebDB Character Inspector (which allows you to set characteristics for individual characters).

Figure 2-86
HTML and
Characters
tabs expanded
in Structured
view

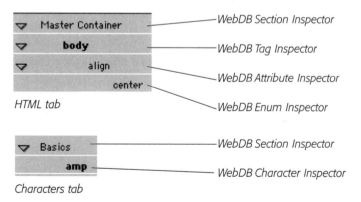

HTML tab

Characters tab

WebDB Inspector

This inspector is called up when you first access either the HTML or Characters tabs (see Figure 2-87). Choosing Structured arranges the respective list under defined headings (such as Forms and Frames under HTML), while choosing Flat lists the contents in alphabetical order.

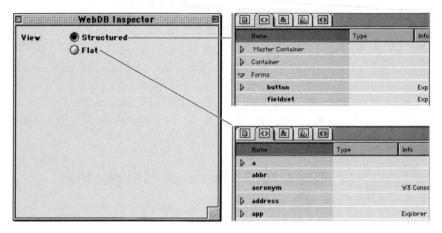

Figure 2-87
Web Database
Inspector

WebDB Section Inspector

When viewing either tab in Structured mode, click one of the section headings to bring up the WebDB Section Inspector (see Figure 2-88). You can modify its title in the Name field and add comments in the appropriately named Comment field.

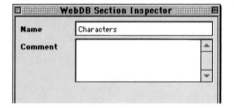

Figure 2-88
Web Database
Section
Inspector

WebDB Tag Inspector

On the Web Database's HTML tab, select one of the tags (displayed in bold face) to bring up the WebDB Tag Inspector.

Basic. The Basic tab displays the tag's name in the Tag Name field and a description of its function in the Comment field (see Figure 2-89). The Structure popup

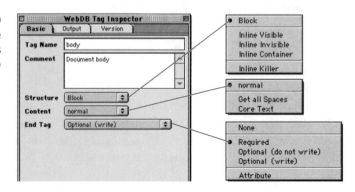

Figure 2-89
Web Database
Tag Inspector's
Basic tab

menu details the structural information about a tag; for instance, Inline Invisible denotes that content within a tag is visible in the browser, but the tag itself is not a visible element.

The Content popup menu displays how a tag's content is viewed in the HTML Source Editor; for instance, Normal indicates that content is displayed using line breaks, tabs, and spaces.

The End Tag popup menu controls whether an end tag is required.

Output. The WebDB Tag Inspector's Output tab allows you to control formatting of source code (see Figure 2-90) in the HTML Source Editor's layout. The Outside popup menu configures the vertical spacing between the tag and other elements above and below it, while the Inside popup menu configures vertical spacing of interior content between the start and end tags. Check Indent Content to add space horizontally before the beginning of a tag.

Figure 2-90
WebDB Tag
Inspector's
Output tab

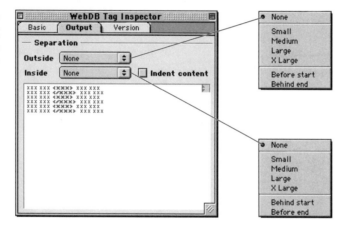

Version. The Version tab indicates which browser or HTML versions display this tag in order to flag errors by version with the HTML Source Editor's Check Syntax feature (see Figure 2-91). Checking Can Have Any Attribute prevents the syntax checker from flagging as an error attributes assigned to a tag that aren't listed in the Web Database's list of attributes for that tag.

WebDB Attribute Inspector

Click the toggle arrow to the left of a tag to reveal a list of its available attributes, then select one to bring up the WebDB Attribute Inspector (see Figure 2-92). Again, the name of the attribute and a brief description of its function is displayed. The Attribute Is popup menu displays whether the tag requires its inclusion or is optional.

Figure 2-91
WebDB Tag
Inspector's
Version tab

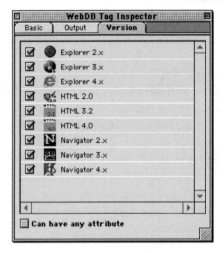

The Value Type popup menu indicates what kind of content the attribute's value can have (such as Number for numerical values only, or Enumeration for multiple options).

Check Create This Attribute to force GoLive to write the attribute even if it's empty; if you enter a value or choose it from the popup menu, GoLive inserts the value as the default for the attribute.

The Version tab is identical to the WebDB Tag Inspector; in this case, it controls whether the Check Syntax feature flags attributes as available for a given browser version or HTML specification.

Figure 2-92
WebDB
Attribute
Inspector

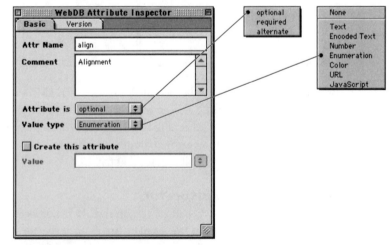

WebDB Enum Inspector

If an HTML attribute includes a toggle arrow to its left, click it to reveal a list of predefined values, or enumerations, associated with it; selecting one brings up the

WebDB Enum Inspector (see Figure 2-93). The value's name is listed in the Enum Name field, while a brief description may be displayed in the Comment field. Click the Version tab to see which browser versions support this particular value.

Figure 2-93
WebDB Enum
Inspector

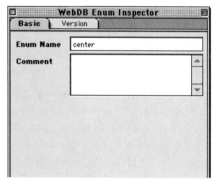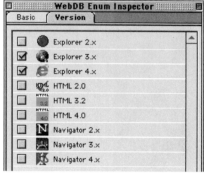

WebDB Character Inspector

On the Web Database's Characters tab, select a character (listed in bold) to bring up the WebDB Character Inspector (see Figure 2-94). The name is listed in the active Name field, while its HTML equivalent is listed in the inactive field to its right. A brief description of the character is included in the Comment field.

The ISO fields display the character's ISO decimal and hexadecimal (base 16) code, while the Mac fields (which display on both Windows and Mac) display the numeric and byte codes for Mac OS encodings, as well as the local symbol for that character.

Check Write to create a value that gets written for this character that's different from the name. We haven't yet seen an instance of this, but it must crop up from time to time.

A large preview of the character is rendered at the bottom of the inspector.

Figure 2-94
Web Database
Character
Inspector

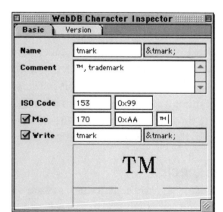

Cascading Style Sheets

Cascading Style Sheets (CSS) can control the typeface characteristics, position, border, and other attributes of a selection or block of text in an HTML document. However, GoLive has two distinct ways to access and use CSS.

- In the Style Sheet Editor, accessed by clicking the stairstep icon in the Layout Editor, you can create and define styles that you apply to text ranges and paragraphs in an HTML file.

- In the CSS tab of the Web Database, you can examine and create browser sets that control how GoLive simulates the previews of different browsers on different platforms in the Layout Preview. (This tab also affects what browsers show up in the Version tab of the WebDB inspectors for tags, attributes, and enumerations, for configuring the HTML Source Editor's syntax checking.)

Both the Style Sheet Editor and the CSS tab use the same inspectors for creating or changing individual styles: collections of characteristics that control the display of a selection and use central management, so changing the style changes the appearance of all selections to which that style was assigned.

There are a few inspectors specific to the CSS tab and the Style Sheet Editor that are broken out below; the CSS Selector Inspector is common to both (see Figure 2-95).

Figure 2-95
Getting to the
WebDB CSS
inspectors

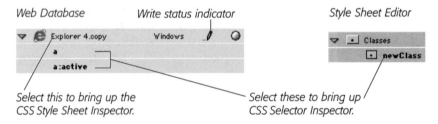

Web Database's CSS Tab

In the CSS tab of the Web Database, select a style sheet grouping (such as the Windows version of Internet Explorer 4.0). The CSS Style Sheet Inspector that comes up has all of its fields dimmed because the built-in browser sets that GoLive provides are locked and cannot be modified. You can create new sets by selecting an existing set and clicking the Duplicate button in the CSS toolbar; this creates a new set with a pencil icon to the right, signifying that you can modify the set.

CSS Style Sheet Inspector

The CSS Style Sheet Inspector displays general information about the set on the Basic tab (including name and operating system), as well as a Comment text field for a brief description (see Figure 2-96).

Figure 2-96
CSS Style
Sheet
Inspector

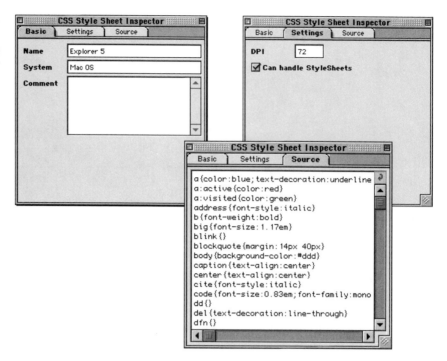

The Settings tab displays the assigned screen resolution for the selected system, which controls how it previews pixel-based settings in the CSS Selector Inspector. It also indicates whether or not it can handle style sheets.

The Source tab lists the selectors and properties for every tag a browser might display. This tab shows essentially the contents of a browser set in brief.

Style Sheets Editor

The Style Sheets Editor appears when you click the stairstepped icon in the Layout Editor. It's discussed in depth in Chapter 26, *Cascading Style Sheets*. Selecting any style in the editor brings up the CSS Selector Inspector, discussed below. The one inspector unique to the editor handles externally linked style sheets.

External Stylesheet Inspector

In the Style Sheets Editor, click the External tab and select an outside style sheet source, or create a new item by clicking the New Item or Duplicate buttons in the Style Sheet Toolbar (see Figure 2-97). Modify or enter a new style sheet location using the URL field's tools. Click the Open button to open the style sheet document for editing, and click either directional arrow buttons to move the item up or down in the list to change the cascading order.

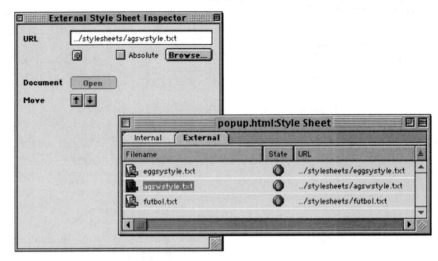

Figure 2-97
CSS External
Style Sheet
Inspector

CSS Selector Inspector

To view or edit the attributes of a specific style in either the Style Sheet Editor or the CSS tab, select a style name (in bold) listed underneath the style sheet group, which brings up the eight-tab CSS Selector Inspector.

The following illustrations, Figures 2-98 to 2-105, show an example of setting up a new style using each of the eight tabs.

Figure 2-98
CSS Selector
Inspector's
Basic tab

Figure 2-99
CSS Selector
Inspector's Font
Properties tab

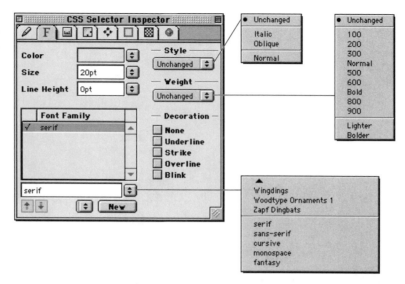

Figure 2-100
CSS Selector
Inspector's Text
Properties tab

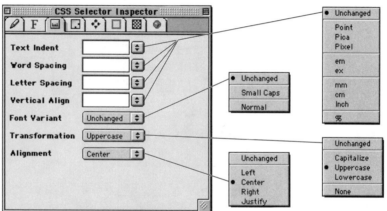

Figure 2-101
CSS Selector
Inspector's Box
Properties tab

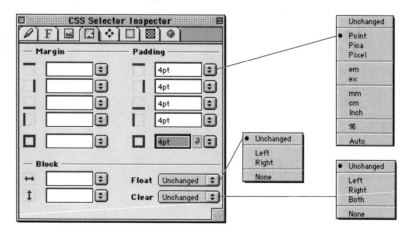

Figure 2-102
CSS Selector
Inspector's
Positioning
Properties tab

Figure 2-103
CSS Selector
Inspector's
Border
Properties tab

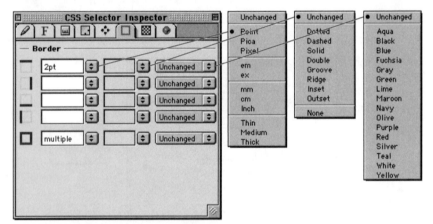

Figure 2-104
CSS Selector
Inspector's
Background
Properties tab

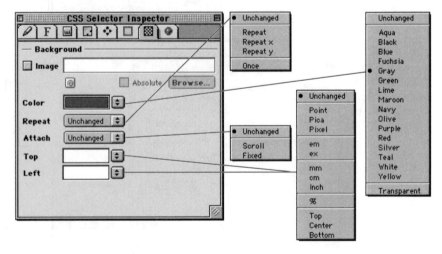

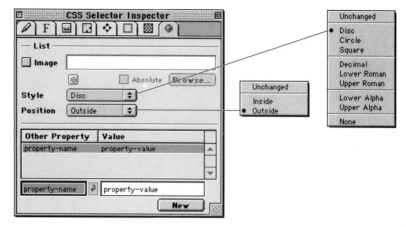

Figure 2-105
CSS Selector
Inspector's List
and Other
Properties tab

Zat is Not My Dog!

The Inspector palette is powerful, multifaceted, deep, and omnipresent. However, you should now have a grasp on its many manifestations, and can take this information and control more of GoLive's inner workings.

In the next chapter, we move on to the rest of the pieces that make GoLive tick: *Palettes and Parts*, covering the other things that float, click, and slide.

CHAPTER 3

Palettes and Parts

After the first two chapters, your head might be swimming a bit from everything that's been thrown at you. This chapter turns down the volume a little, giving you a visual reference guide to the supporting parts and pieces that make GoLive's engine hum along. Here's what's covered:

- Starting with the Palette, each tag icon is broken out with references to information about specific inspectors that control the attributes of the tag, as well as what chapter further details how GoLive works with the code.

- The various flavors of the contextual Toolbar are covered, with references to each button's function, and what causes each Toolbar to appear .

- While the eight tabs—or nine tabs, depending on your platform—of the Color Palette are covered extensively in Chapter 9, *Color*, each tab of the Color Palette is referenced here.

- And finally, get an introduction to the editors and windows that control GoLive's advanced features, including the JavaScript Editor, Timeline Editor, Track Editor, and Style Sheet window.

The Palette

The Palette is the WYSIWYG heart of GoLive. While seeming a little cumbersome at first—especially for those of us who pine for keyboard shortcuts—dragging and dropping tag icons onto a page quickly becomes second nature.

The Basic Tab

If you're designing pages, you spend most of your GoLive time with the Palette's Basic tab open. In it, you find an arsenal of the most often used page layout tag icons (see Table 3-1). These can be inserted by dragging and dropping or by double-clicking the icon with the Document window set to the Layout Editor or HTML Source Editor.

Table 3-1
Basic tab
icons

Palette Icon	Icon Name	Chapter Detail
	Layout Grid	Chapter 12
	Layout Text Box	Chapter 12
	Floating Box	Chapter 12
	Table	Chapter 10
	Image	Chapter 8
	Plug-in	Chapter 28
	Java Applet	Chapter 28
*	ActiveX	Chapter 28
	Horizontal Rule	
	Horizontal Spacer	
	JavaScript	Chapter 23
	Marquee	
	Comment	
	Anchor	
	Line Break	
	Tag and End Tag	

* Both Mac and Windows icons depicted, respectively

The Forms Tab

Like the tag icons from the Basic tab, you can insert Forms tags into either the Layout Editor or HTML Source Editor (see Table 3-2 for the complete list). For complete details on configuring forms in GoLive, see Chapter 13, *Forms*.

Table 3-2	Palette Tag	Tag Name
Forms tab icons		Form
		End Form
		Submit Button
		Reset Button
		Button
		Input Image
		Label
		Text Field
		Password
		Text Area
		Check Box
		Radio Button
		Popup
		List Box
		File Browser
		Hidden
		Key Generator
		Field Set

The Head Tab

The tag icons found in the Palette's Head tab help you control the background workings of a page, from keywords and description of the page to refresh rate and scripts you can create to, say, sniff for the version of a browser viewing the page (see Table 3-3). Unlike the tag icons available in the previous two Palette tabs, these icons can only be placed into the Head section of the Document window's Layout Editor. These HTML tags are further explored in Chapter 6, *Page Overview*.

Table 3-3	Palette Tag	Tag Name
Head tab icons	⟨𝒫⟩	IsIndex
	⟨URL⟩	Base
	⟨≣⟩	Keywords
	⟨✛⟩	Link
	⟨META⟩	Meta Tag
	⟨☼⟩	Refresh
	⟨?⟩ ⟨/?⟩	Tag and End Tag
	⟨♀⟩	Comment
	⟨◉⟩	Script

The Frames Tab

The Palette's Frames tab diverges slightly from the way the previous three tabs work. Rather than dragging icons that represent HTML tags into a page, you drag icon representations of frame layouts into the Document window's Frame Editor.

Tip: It's a Drag You cannot double-click a Frameset icon to place it within the Frame Editor; it must be dragged in.

See Figure 3-1 for a visual representation of all the layout options you have at your disposal. For everything you ever wanted to know about frames (and a little more), see Chapter 11, *Frames*.

Figure 3-1
Frames tab
icons and
examples

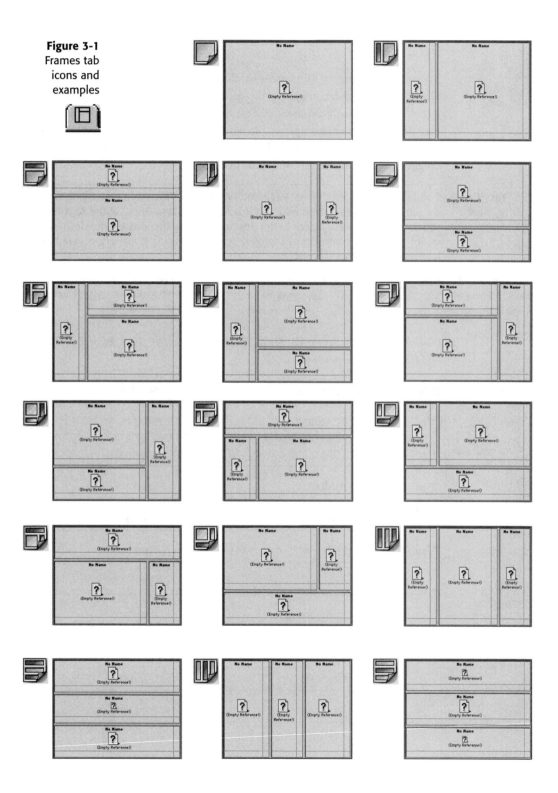

Site Tab

Taking a break from the Document window, we move to the basic controls for the Site window, which let you group files and collections of color references and external Web and email references. You can either drag or double-click these icons to place them into their appropriate Site window tabs (listed in Table 3-4). If you try to add an icon to a tab where it doesn't belong, it either returns to the Palette (if dragged) or an error sounds (if double-clicked).

Tip: It's a Drag, Part 2   If you double-click the Generic Page icon while in the Files tab, a new, blank, untitled default GoLive page is created in a folder entitled "New Files" at the root level of your site (see Figure 3-2). For better positioning, drag the icon to your desired folder. For even more control of new pages, think about using stationery, covered in the following "Site Extras Tab" section.

Figure 3-2
Adding a generic page

GoLive adds a warning icon to remind you that nothing currently exists on this page.

More information. See Part 3, *Sites*, especially Chapter 16, *Files, Folders, and Links*, and Chapter 17, *Sitewide Sets*.

Table 3-4
Site tab icons

Palette Tag	Tag Name	Site Tab
	Generic Page	Files
	URL	External
	Address	External
	Color	Colors
	Font Set	Font Sets
	Folder	Files
	URL Group	External
	Address Group	External
	Color Group	Colors
	Font Set Group	Font Sets

Site Extras Tab

The Palette's Site Extras tab is two-tiered, housing your collection of HTML stationery and GoLive Components, both of which can also be accessed by opening up the Extra tab of the Site window. If you're confused as to what the difference is between these two items, here's a quick refresher:

- Stationery files are template pages that allow you to create a consistent layout for use throughout your site. When you open a stationery file from the Stationeries folder in the Site window's Extra tab, you are prompted to open either the original file for editing, or create a new, unnamed page using that file's contents.

- Component files are HTML source files that can include one item (such as an image) or a collection of HTML code—including page-defining tags like Body —which can then be inserted into individual pages. If a component is modified, all pages including that component are automatically updated.

You shift between component and stationery views via the popup menu at the bottom of the Palette. To insert a component, you *could* insert a Component icon from the Palette's CyberObjects tab, then use the Component Inspector to link to a file in your Site window. But as long as you have a collection of files in the Components folder, simply drag the component's icon into an open HTML page.

To add a new page to your site based on a stationery file's layout, drag its icon into a desired folder in the Site window, where you are prompted to type a name in the file's highlighted name area. (GoLive prevents you from adding stationery files to a page or component files to a site.)

To modify an existing stationery or component file, you must open it from within the Site window's Extra tab; you cannot double-click the Palette icon. See Figure 3-3 for more on stationeries and components.

Tip: Customizing Icons

If you save a file into either the Stationeries or Components folders, or drag files from the desktop into either of those folders, then look at the Extras tab of the Palette, you see that the files are represented by generic file icons (GoLive icons on the Mac and Explorer icons on Windows). However, you can change this icon to a thumbnail shot of the file's content by opening the file from the Site window, modifying it (even just adding a space and deleting it), and saving it. The icon immediately changes in the Palette.

Tip: It's a Drag, Part 3

You cannot double-click a stationery or component file to insert it; it must be dragged to a location in its respective window.

More information. See "CyberObjects" in Chapter 2, *The Inspector*, for details on the Component Inspector. See Chapter 21, *Site Specials*, for further details on creating and managing stationery and component files.

Figure 3-3
Site Extras tab

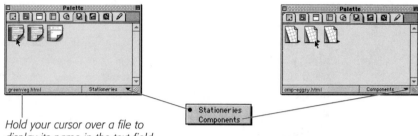

*Hold your cursor over a file to
display its name in the text field
at the bottom of the Palette.*

*Files in the Components folder that don't
have the .html or .htm extension (like
super.txt) do not appear in the Palette, while
files that don't appear with a stationery file
icon in the Stationeries folder do appear in
the Palette (like greenveg_more.html).*

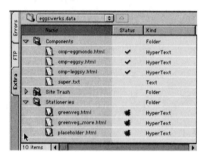

*All files in the Stationeries folder, no matter
what icon appears, act like stationery,
prompting you to choose between
modifying the original file and creating a
new page when it is opened from within
the Stationeries folder. (Windows and Mac
dialogs differ.)*

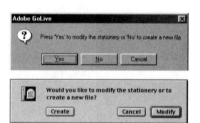

CyberObjects Tab

You can find the whole range of GoLive's special Actions and Action-like objects
(including the Component tag icon) collected under this tab, from a date and time
stamp to a URL list popup menu. See Table 3-5 for a list of CyberObjects and where
in the Layout Editor they can be placed (either in the Head or body section).

**Tip: It's a
Drag, Part 4**   You can double-click the CyberObject icons that go into the body section of the
Document window, but you must drag the Head Action and Browser Switch icons
into the Head section.

More information. See Chapter 25, *Actions,* for more on CyberObjects.

Table 3-5	**Palette Tag**	**Tag Name**	**Page Location**
CyberObject tab icons		Date & Time	Body
		Button Image	Body
		Component	Body
		URL Popup	Body
		Inline Action	Body
		Head Action	Head
		Browser Switch	Head

QuickTime Tab

To add tracks to QuickTime movie and sound files, from music and sound to text and links, drag a QuickTime Track icon into the Track Editor (no double-clicking). The track appears at the bottom of the track list on the left side of the editor.

More information. See Chapter 28, *Plug-ins and Media*, for more on editing QuickTime files.

Table 3-6	**Palette Tag**	**Tag Name**
QuickTime tab icons		Video Track
		Filter Track
		Sprite Track
		Sound Track
		Music Track
		HREF Track
		Chapter Track
		Text Track

Custom Tab

You can add any commonly used image or plug-in media file to the Custom tab by dragging it from any page into the tab where a thumbnail of the object appears. GoLive doesn't allow you to drag files directly from the Site window into the Custom tab (see Figure 3-4).

Figure 3-4
Custom tab

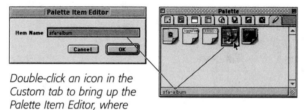

Place your cursor over the Custom tab item to display its name in the text field at the bottom of the Palette.

Double-click an icon in the Custom tab to bring up the Palette Item Editor, where you can name the item.

Place your cursor over the thumbnail and GoLive displays "No Name" in the lower left corner of the Palette. To give the object a name, double-click the thumbnail to bring up the Palette Item Editor; type the object's name in the Item Name field and click OK. The object in the Custom tab references the file originally referenced in the page that the object was dragged from (got that?), so it doesn't need to be placed into a special folder (a lá components).

So, you're probably wondering to yourself, how is this really different from a component? For one thing, Custom tab objects are limited to object files—no text allowed. Components, on the other hand, can be made up entirely of text—even text only—because the file that is being referenced by the GoLive page is actually another HTML file. Further, custom objects don't automatically update themselves wherever they appear in a site when they're modified; components do. To update custom objects, you have to open every page on which they appear, make any change, and save them.

The Color Palette

Press Command-3 (Mac) or Alt-3 (Windows) to open the Color Palette, from which you can select colors and shades of gray to add to items on your page, including text, table cells, and page backgrounds. To add color to an item, select a color from one of the Color Palette's tabs and drag a color swatch from the Preview Pane to the desired location, such as highlighted text on a page or a color field on an inspector.

You have up to eight tabs to choose your color from on the Mac and up to nine in Windows, each of which allows you to manipulate, select, and store colors just a little differently.

Color Palette Basics

The first four tabs (RGB, CMYK, Grayscale, and Indexed Colors tabs; on Windows, the HSV tab is also added) allow you to manipulate sliders or type in values to come up with color combinations (see Figure 3-5). If you turn the Percent button on (so that it is checked in Windows or appears depressed on the Mac), you switch from a numeric range of 256 color steps to a percentage range. (And yes, despite what the manual says, you can choose to display values in percentages in Windows.)

On the Apple/Windows Colors tab, you can select from a fixed set of 256 system colors using an eyedropper cursor icon. The Real Web Colors tab allows you to use the eyedropper, as well as choose from a list of values, which include a color swatch and hexadecimal value. The Web Named Colors tab drops the palette scheme and allows you to choose from a list of colors either by name or hex value.

Tip: Tabbing Through Fields   In Windows, not only can you tab from field to field (such as among the R, G, and B fields on the RGB tab), you can also land your cursor into a field's slider. Just click anywhere within the Color Palette and press Tab; you start at the top with the Percent checkbox. When you tab to a slider, press either the left or right arrow to modify the color value by one hexadecimal unit or one percentage point at a time.

Figure 3-5
Color Palette basics

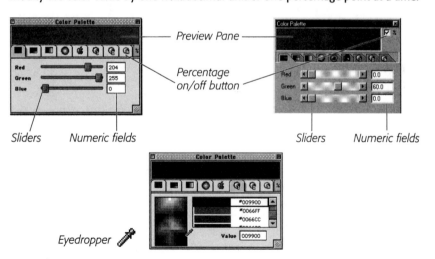

Of course, each tab within the Color Palette is a little different, offering you a slightly different measure of access to finding just the right color.

- The RGB tab allows you to select a color from the red, green, and blue values (see Figure 3-6).

- The CMYK tab allows you to select a color by adjusting the values for cyan, magenta, yellow, and black (see Figure 3-7).

- The Grayscale tab allows you to select a shade of gray (see Figure 3-8).

Figure 3-6
RGB tab

The same color viewed in numeric values (left, in Mac) and percentages (right, in Windows)

Figure 3-7
CMYK tab

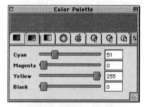

Figure 3-8
Grayscale tab

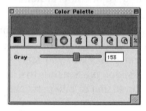

Tip: Turning Colors Gray   After you click the Grayscale tab, the Preview Pane still displays the last color selected from one of the other tabs. To turn that color gray, simply click the slider without moving it.

- The Apple/Windows Colors tab displays five different fixed system color profiles: 256 colors, 16 colors, 16 grays, desktop colors, and a custom palette of colors that you can drop into the 36 available spots (see Figure 3-9).

Tip: Sampling Desktop Colors   On the Apple/Windows Color and Real Web Colors tabs, place your cursor over a color grid to turn your mouse pointer into an eyedropper. Click and hold your mouse, then move your mouse about the screen. The Preview Pane displays any color the eyedropper touches, even items outside of GoLive. To keep a color, select the Custom Palette in the Apple/Windows popup menu and drag a color swatch from the Preview Pane into one of the palette's squares.

- The Windows-only HSV Colors tab allows you to set hue, saturation, and value independently. Set the hue in the outer ring, then set the saturation and value by selecting a point in the interior color square (see Figure 3-10).
- The Indexed Colors tab's color wheel allows you to choose from any color currently available to you from your video hardware. It also includes a Brightness control slider and value input field (see Figure 3-11).

Figure 3-9
Apple/
Windows tab

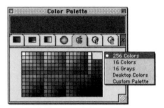

Mac version   *Windows version*

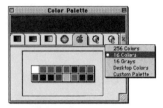

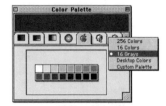

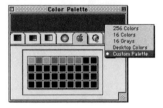

The 34 desktop colors reflect the colors available to the operating system and do not change to reflect different colors chosen for the background desktop.

To add colors to the custom palette, find a color via one of the other Color Palette tabs (such as the Indexed Color tab), return to the Apple/Windows tab's custom palette, and drag a swatch from the Preview Pane to one of the custom squares.

Figure 3-10
Windows HSV
Colors tab

Figure 3-11
Indexed
Colors tab

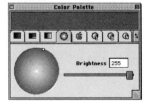

- The Real Web Colors tab (with the Roman numeral I) provides 216 cross-platform, browser-safe colors that don't dither. The Value field displays each color's hexadecimal value (see Figure 3-12).

- The Web Named Colors tab (with the Roman numeral II) displays a collection of colors that can be specified by name, but not all of which are fully browser-safe (see Figure 3-13).

- The Site Colors tab displays the colors collected in the Site window's Colors tab. You must have a Site window open to view its colors (see Figure 3-14).

Figure 3-12
Real Web
Colors tab

Figure 3-13
Web Named
Colors tab

Figure 3-14
Site Colors tab

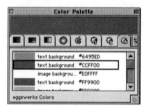

More information. See Chapter 9, *Color*. For details on collecting the colors used by a site, see Chapter 17, *Sitewide Sets*.

The Toolbar

Like the Inspector, GoLive's Toolbar contextually changes to fit the task at hand. But you can breathe a sigh of relief, as it doesn't have quite as many flavors as the Inspector does.

Toolbar Basics

While each toolbar offers a range of different attributes you can tweak, a few items appear on every toolbar.

Link Warnings

Clicking the Link Warnings button highlights broken text and image links on your page with a colored border. This button appears on every toolbar, though it is inactive on toolbars where it's not applicable (such as the Web Database and Stylesheet toolbars). The only toolbar where this button doesn't appear is the Site toolbar, but a Link Warnings icon shows up in the top right corner of a Site window if GoLive detects errors in any of the site's pages.

More information. Find out how to set different link warnings colors in the "General Preferences" section of Chapter 4, *Preferences and Customizing.*

Document/Site Window Toggle

To the right of the Link Warnings button is the Document/Site Window toggle, a popup list of open sites and documents (see Figure 3-15). This works especially well when you have both a Site and one or more Document windows open. With the Document window active, a site icon is displayed; click it to switch directly to the open site file. To return to the last active document, click the icon again, which now displays a document icon. (Clicking this icon only switches you between Site and Document windows, and not between two documents.)

To view a list of all open files, click the down arrow to the right of the icon to display a popup menu with a list of sites and documents (including pages, media files, text files, and style sheet windows).

If you just have a Document window open and no Site window, an inactive document icon is displayed. However, if only a Site window is open, the document icon is active, though clicking it doesn't do any good since there's no Document window open to switch to.

Figure 3-15
Document/Site
Window toggle

Document icon

Site icon

Document list (opened with Site window active, denoted by bullet); site files appear at the bottom of the list on Mac (left), but at the top of the list in Windows (right).

Show in Browser Button

For a true representation of how your pages behave in various browsers, it's wise to use GoLive's browser preview option rather than just relying on the Document window's Layout Preview. Go to the Browsers pane in Preferences to gather a list of browsers found on your hard drive, then check the browser you use most to preview your page designs and assign it as your default browser. If you haven't set up a preview browser (or list of browsers) in Preferences, you are reminded that this information is missing (see Figure 3-16). To rectify this, simply click the Specify button and GoLive automatically opens Preferences.

Figure 3-16
Specify
Browser
warning

Back on the Toolbar, click the Show in Browser button and your page opens in the browser that you checked as your default. If you want to view the page in other browsers within your list, click the down arrow to bring up a popup menu with that list (see Figure 3-17).

The Show in Browser icon takes on the attributes of the browser icon selected as default (such as the Internet Explorer icon). If multiple browsers are selected, GoLive mixes them into an icon mélange.

Figure 3-17
Show in
Browser
buttons

The browser list on the Mac (left) displays default browsers in bold, and a check mark in Windows (right); also note the mixed icon when multiple browsers are selected as default.

Tip: Multiple
Default
Browsers

If, like most of us, you're a bipolar Web designer who needs to check code in both Navigator and Internet Explorer, you can rest at ease and check multiple browsers as your default. When the Browser Switch button is clicked, your page opens in both Navigator and Explorer (each program can only have one version open at a time).

More information. For more on configuring browser sets, see the "Browser Sets" section of Chapter 4, *Preferences and Customizing*.

Text Toolbar

If you work at all with creating or editing pages in GoLive, you see a lot of the Text toolbar. Through it, you can control both the way text looks and the way paragraphs with text and objects act (see Figure 3-18).

Figure 3-18
Text toolbar

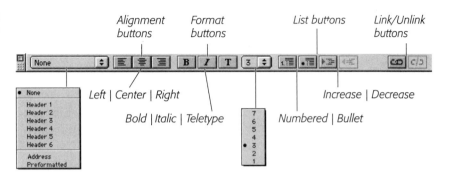

On the macro-text side of things, choosing an HTML header style from the popup menu formats an entire paragraph (all text within a P container tag) as that style. Selecting Address adds italics to the header, while selecting Preformatted formats the header in a monospaced font. For a selected word or range of text, you can choose an HTML text size (1 through 7) and assign basic formatting (bold, italic, and teletype).

For both text and objects (such as images or media files), you can designate a link (or take the link designation away) and assign a list style (numbered or bulleted).

Tip:
Indenting

If you want to indent a paragraph or object without adding a list style, click the Increase List Level button (with the arrow pointing to the right).

More information. See Chapter 7, *Text and Fonts*.

Layout Grid Toolbar

If you add a layout grid to a page while in the Layout Editor, GoLive brings up the Layout Grid toolbar. However, everything within the toolbar is inactive until you add either a layout text box or an object to the grid.

For example, place a layout grid onto a page, then drag an image tag into the grid. The first two fields display its position within the grid structure (32 pixels from the left and 16 pixels from the top), while the second two fields display the object's dimensions (32 by 32 pixels). See Figure 3-19 for this example.

Figure 3-19
Layout Grid
toolbar

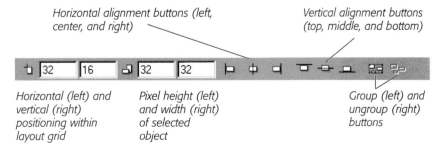

To move an object around the grid, either drag it or use the toolbar's horizontal and vertical positioning buttons. In addition, you can move an object one grid square at a time by pressing your arrow keys.

Add another item to the grid, select the two objects, and move them about as described above. The Group button becomes active in the toolbar (the objects default to ungrouped), and clicking it makes GoLive collect the objects as one group. The total dimensions of the group appears in the height and width fields. This also brings up the Group Inspector, which allows you to choose to keep the contents of this group locked or unlocked. If you choose to lock the items, you can't configure the attributes of each object. However, by choosing unlocked, you can manipulate the group's items individually while still being able to move the group around the grid as one (see Figure 3-20).

Figure 3-20
Layout Grid
Group
Inspector

Locked and unlocked

More information. See Chapter 12, *Layout Grids and Floating Boxes.*

Outline Editor Toolbar

Staying with the Document window, clicking the Outline tab opens the Outline Editor, which in turn brings up the Outline toolbar. The Outline toolbar isn't essential for working in the Outline Editor (as you can drag in tag icons from the Palette), but it can be helpful, especially for such new interface terrain.

From the Toolbar, you can add new tags and new attributes to existing tags, as well as add new containers for text and comments (see Figure 3-21). Click the New Custom Tag button to add a non-HTML tag, such as Active Server Pages (ASP), Extensible Markup Language (XML), or Standard Generalized Markup Language (SGML); the container tag's popup menu allows you to choose from these three options, as well as Unknown. The Toggle Binary button allows you to select whether a tag stands on its own (unary) or requires an end tag (binary).

Figure 3-21
Outline toolbar

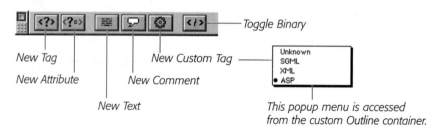

Toggle Binary

New Tag

New Attribute

New Text

New Comment

New Custom Tag

Unknown
SGML
XML
● ASP

This popup menu is accessed from the custom Outline container.

More information. See Chapter 5, *Layout, Source, and Preview,* for details on using GoLive in Outline mode.

Site Toolbar

GoLive relies on the Site toolbar more than others because the program offers fewer keyboard shortcuts to help your fingers do the siting (see Figure 3-22).

Figure 3-22
Site toolbar

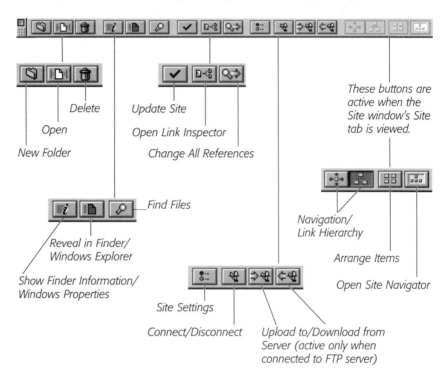

While keyboard shortcuts are few and far between, GoLive does provide many of the Site toolbar's controls at the click of a mouse via a contextual menu (right-clicking in Windows and Control-clicking on the Mac).

For starters, the Site toolbar allows you to do basic maintenance, like adding folders to and deleting items from your site, displaying Mac file information or Windows properties, and opening GoLive's Find dialog box. You can refresh the site to show any files recently saved into the site folder by clicking the Update Site button (checkmark). You can also open the Link Inspector to view what links to and from a page, and change link references to a page by clicking the Change All References button.

When you're ready to transfer files to your Web server, click the Site Settings button to enter your FTP information, then click the Connect button to open up the FTP location. To upload your site from your hard drive, click the Upload to Server button, or click Download from Server if you've made changes on the server and need to update the files stored on your hard drive.

If you're in the Site window's Site tab (where you can view a site map), the last four buttons of the Site toolbar become active. Click either of the first two buttons to toggle between navigational and links views. If Auto Arrange Items is unchecked on the Site View Controller and the map seems a tad messy, click the Arrange Items button to put them in order. If you're viewing a very large site, click the Open Site Navigator button to open a dialog with a smaller thumbnail view of your site, which lets you scan portions of the site with a draggable marquee box.

More information. See Chapter 15, *Site Management.*

Web Database Toolbar

Open the Web Database (Command-4 on the Mac or Control-4 under Windows) and click the HTML tab to bring up the Web Database toolbar (see Figure 3-23). (An inactive Text toolbar appears when the Global tab is selected.) With nothing selected in either Structured (tags organized in subject folders) or Flat (a list of alphabetized tags) view, you can click the New Section button to add another section folder. From there you can add new tags, new attributes to tags, and new values to attributes (using the Enum button). You can also select a tag and copy it (using the Duplicate button), then go in and modify it.

Under the Characters tab, only the New Character and Duplicate buttons are active—which is fine, since that's all you need.

More information. See Chapter 27, *Web Database.*

Figure 3-23
Web Database
toolbar

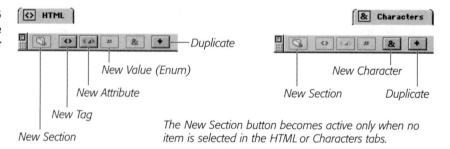

New Value (Enum)

New Attribute

New Tag

New Section

Duplicate

New Character

New Section

Duplicate

The New Section button becomes active only when no item is selected in the HTML or Characters tabs.

Style Sheet Toolbar

To add Cascading Style Sheets to a page, click the stairstepped icon in the Document window's Layout Editor. The Style Sheet Editor opens, and the Toolbar changes to the Style Sheet toolbar. This Toolbar also appears when you open the CSS tab of the Web Database.

Through the Toolbar, you can add classes, tags, and IDs specific to an active page, or link to an outside style sheet (see Figure 3-24).

Figure 3-24
Style Sheet
toolbar

When viewing the Internal tab

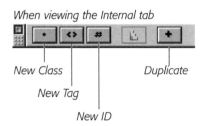

New Class   *Duplicate*

New Tag

New ID

Classes, tags, and IDs are stored in their own areas of the CSS Internal tab.

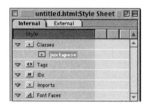

When viewing the External tab

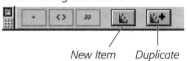

New Item   *Duplicate*

Link outside style sheets from the External tab.

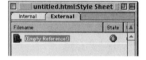

Tip: Style
Sheet
Minutiae

You can't delete an item from the Style Sheet list via the toolbar. To delete a class, tag, or ID, select it from the Internal tab, then choose Clear (Mac) or Delete (Windows) from the Edit Menu, or choose this option from the contextual menu. Additionally, if you create a new item on the External tab, then do something else—like foolishly go back to the Internal tab—it seems that GoLive doesn't permit you to configure the highlighted external item when you come back. Just deselect, and click back to it to bring up the External Style Sheet Inspector again.

More information. See "Style Sheet Editor" in this chapter for more details on adding style sheets to a page. For more on configuring CSS in GoLive, see Chapter 26, *Cascading Style Sheets*, and Chapter 27, *Web Database*.

Advanced Feature Editors and Windows

Four of GoLive's advanced features—Cascading Style Sheets, Dynamic HTML (DHTML) animation, QuickTime editing, and JavaScript—are handled largely through three separate windows (with the help, of course, of several different inspectors). The Style Sheets (CSS), Timeline (DHTML), and JavaScript Editors are accessed by clicking one of the three icons in the top-right corner of the Document window's Layout Editor, while the Track Editor (for QuickTime files) is accessed via the colored film icon in the QuickTime Preview window (see Figure 3-25).

Figure 3-25
Editor icons

JavaScript Editor (coffee bean)

CSS Editor (three steps)

TimeLine Editor (film strip)

Document window's
Layout Editor

Track Editor icon

QuickTime Movie
Viewer

JavaScript Editor

To add a new piece of JavaScript to a page, drag a script tag icon in from the Palette to either the Head section or body of a page, type a name to identify it in the Name field of either the Head Script or Body Script Inspector, and then select the appropriate version of JavaScript from the Language popup menu. Clicking the Edit button opens up the JavaScript Editor in a new window, which is where you type your script or add events and objects from the JavaScript Inspector (see Figure 3-26).

Figure 3-26
JavaScript
editor

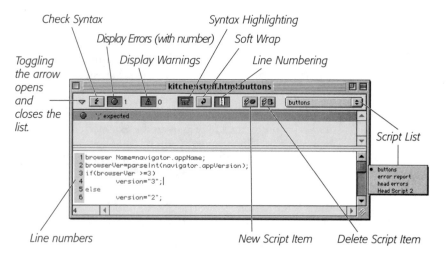

Check Syntax

Display Errors (with number)

Syntax Highlighting

Soft Wrap

Toggling
the arrow
opens
and
closes the
list.

Display Warnings

Line Numbering

Script List

Line numbers

New Script Item

Delete Script Item

Tip: Opening the JavaScript Editor, Part 1   Yes, you can click the coffee bean JavaScript icon to open up the JavaScript Editor; but do it with caution. If you open the editor by clicking the icon without first adding either a Head Script or Body Script tag icon to your page, you are met with a blank, inactive JavaScript Editor. To start a script, click the New Script Item button—no worries, mate. However, GoLive defaults to placing this new script in the Head section of your page (identified by the default "Head Script 1" appearing in the Script List popup menu). Clicking the New Script Item again only produces another Head Script tag.

You can't change the position of a Head Script item to a location within the body by dragging the tag icon in the Layout Editor. You can, however, drag and drop (or copy and paste) a selection of code in the HTML Source Editor or, even easier, a selected container of code in the Outline Editor.

Tip: Opening the JavaScript Editor, Part 2

You can also open the JavaScript Editor by double-clicking either a Head Script or Body Script icon in the Layout Editor.

Move between different scripts in your page by clicking the List Script menu and selecting an item. If you haven't labeled a script—using the Name field in either the Body Script or Head Script Inspectors—GoLive applies generic numeric names to your script, like Head Script 1, Body Script 1, and Body Script 2.

As with the Document window's HTML Source Editor, you can also configure the way GoLive displays code in the JavaScript Editor via the special Toolbar found at the top of the editor. GoLive defaults to coloring different parts of JavaScript (such as keywords, symbols, and operators). To turn off the colors and just display black text, click the Syntax Highlighting button. If you have long lines of code that run off the right side of the Editor, click the Soft Wrap button to wrap lines within the boundary of the editor window. To add numbers to each line of code, click the Line Number button. You can specify the colors for parts of code in the JavaScript item in Preferences, as well as specify font, indent, and printing settings.

To check for errors and warnings of bad syntax within your code, click the Check Syntax button (the one with the lightning bolt), or press Command-K (Mac) or Control-K (Windows). If there are errors in your script, the error log section is opened below the JavaScript Editor toolbar; this area can also be opened and closed by clicking the toggle arrow to the left of the Check Syntax button. A number denoting the number of errors or warnings appears to the right of their respective toolbar buttons. However, no errors or warnings are listed unless those buttons are depressed.

More information. See Chapter 23, *JavaScript*, for more about the JavaScript Editor and related Inspector palettes. For details on configuring JavaScript Editor preferences, see its section in Chapter 4, *Preferences and Customizing*.

Timeline Editor

To add DHTML animations to your page, you must first add a Floating Box icon, then place any kind of HTML content in it. Click the film strip icon in the top right of the Layout Editor to open the Timeline Editor (see Figure 3-27). This displays a single animation track (denoted by the number 1 and an arrow showing

Figure 3-27
Opening the
Timeline Editor

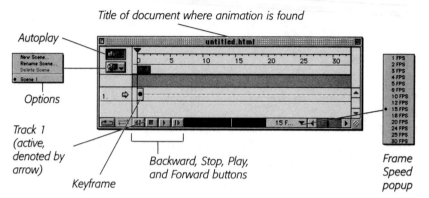

Title of document where animation is found

Autoplay

Options

*Track 1
(active,
denoted by
arrow)*

Keyframe

*Backward, Stop, Play,
and Forward buttons*

*Frame
Speed
popup*

the active track) within a scene and a single keyframe (denoted by the small box surrounding a dot) within the track, placed at the timeline's starting point.

As you've probably picked up, the Timeline Editor uses the metaphor of a film-editing program for its various parts, which break down into three main parts:

- A scene collects all of a page's floating boxes as individual tracks. A page can have multiple scenes involving one or more of the page's floating boxes.

- A track is one floating box, which can then be animated with keyframes.

- A keyframe is one point within the timeline of a track, which denotes a change in property for the floating box (such as a directional change or stacking order).

To add an animated sequence to your page, it's easiest to go back to the floating box in the Layout Editor and drag to the desired points on the page. First, select the floating box, then click the Record button in the Floating Box Inspector. Go back to the Layout Editor, grab the floating box, and drag it to a new location. To add another movement on the page, return to the Floating Box Inspector and repeat the previous steps, clicking Record before each movement.

The points at which you stopped along the path are marked by squares; these correspond to the keyframes that have been added to the track for that floating box in the Timeline Editor (see Figure 3-28).

At the bottom of the Timeline Editor, you can click the Play button to display your animation. You can also view it one frame at a time by clicking the Backward and Forward buttons. The point at which you are in the timeline, viewed at the top of the editor, is displayed in two ways to the right of these buttons: in time format broken down by hours, minutes, seconds, and frames; and in total number of frames. To change the number of frames played each second, select from the range in the Frame Speed popup menu.

To keep your animation playing as long as a page is being viewed, click the Loop button; click the Palindrome button if you want the animation to reverse itself once it reaches the end of its cycle. (For Palindrome to work, you must first click Loop.)

Figure 3-28
Relationship
between Layout
and Timeline
editors

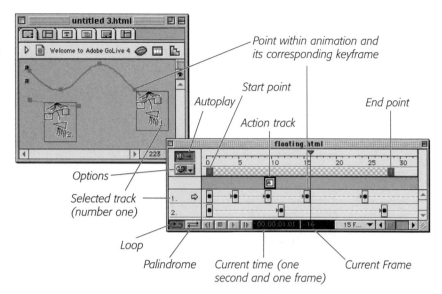

Clicking the Autoplay button, which is on by default, begins the animation as soon as the page is loaded into a browser. However, if this is turned off, the animation can't begin unless an Action is assigned to begin it.

To add an Action, Command-click (Mac) or Control-click (Windows) in the Action Track—the gray track line directly above the editor's first track—to position an Action placeholder at that point. Use the menu in the Action Inspector to select an appropriate Action and configure its attributes. You can also place Actions to trigger at any point within an animation.

Clicking the Options button below Autoplay displays a popup menu that allows you to add a new scene, rename or delete a selected scene, and select from a list of available scenes within a page.

The total length of animation is displayed in the area immediately below the timeline by a yellow band bounded with two red boxes with inset arrows. You cannot increase or decrease an animation's length by moving either of these points. Rather, you have to move the keyframes at the beginning or end of an animation, or create a new keyframe. Command-click (Mac) or Control-click (Windows) within a track to create a new keyframe, or Option-click (Mac) or Alt-click (Windows) on a selected keyframe and release the mouse at a new point to copy the original item.

More information. See Chapter 24, *Animation*, for information about configuring DHTML animations. See Chapter 12, *Layout Grids and Floating Boxes*, for more on configuring individual floating boxes.

Track Editor

Continuing with the movie-editing metaphor, you can use GoLive to edit Quick-
Time movie and sound files—think of it as a mini version of Adobe Premiere.
First, open the QuickTime file by double-clicking the file in the Site window or
double-clicking a plug-in icon where the file is placed within an individual page.
This opens the QuickTime file in a GoLive QuickTime Movie Viewer, which in-
cludes the typical QuickTime toolbar at the bottom. To get to the Track Editor, you
must click the colored movie icon in the top left corner of the QuickTime Movie
Viewer (see Figure 3-29).

Figure 3-29
Track Editor

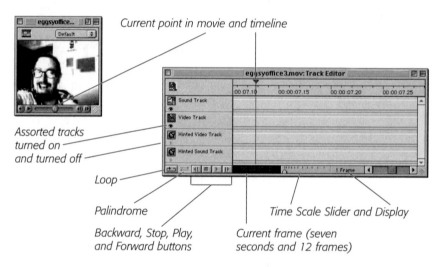

Like the Timeline Editor, a timeline sits at the top of the Track Editor. To
change the measurement amount displayed in the timeline, click and move the
Time Scale Slider at the bottom of the editor; the frame amount appears in the text
box to its right.

**Tip: Timeline
Editor Isn't
the Track
Editor**

If you click the movie icon in the top-right corner of the Layout Editor, you open the
Timeline Editor for DHTML animations. The Track Editor looks very similar to the
Timeline Editor with its time track at the top and play buttons at the bottom. But you
can tell you're on the Track Editor by the QuickTime icon in the top-left corner, as
well as by the individual track icons below it.

**Tip: Return to
QuickTime File**

To return to the QuickTime Movie Viewer, click the Track Editor's QuickTime icon.

**Tip: Moving
to Minute**

Clicking the text box to the right of the Time Scale Slider changes the scale to one-
minute increments.

You can control the playback in the Movie Viewer using the Backward, Stop, Play, and Forward buttons at the bottom of the Editor. Clicking Backward or Forward once moves one frame step at a time. You can also configure a movie to play in a Loop—as well as in a Palindrome—by clicking the buttons to the left of the playback buttons.

Below the various track icons, you see an eye that's either active or inactive, denoting whether that track is available to the viewer. To make a track invisible, click an active eye to make it inactive, and vice versa to make a track visible.

More information. See Chapter 28, *Plug-ins and Media*, for more on editing QuickTime movies, including various media tracks.

Style Sheet Editor

To configure Cascading Style Sheets (CSS) for a particular page, click the stair-stepped icon in the Layout Editor to open the Style Sheet Editor. This is only a collection point for the classes, tags and IDs that you add to your page. The real work is performed through the Style Sheet toolbar, covered earlier in this chapter, which allows you to add items to the Style Sheet Editor, and the CSS Selector Inspector, which allows you to configure individual styles (see Figure 3-30).

If you're not sure what you want to create, here's a quick oversimplification of the three CSS pieces:

- A tag works throughout a page and can change the way all instances of the tag's presentation on that page. For instance, you can set up a CSS tag that displays all H6 tags as 14 point green, bolded Verdana text.

- A class lets you set ranges of text, paragraphs, or sets of paragraphs to a set of character or paragraph formatting independent of any tag.

- An ID is a unique style that can only be assigned once in the document to a range or block of text; it's also independent of any tag.

After deciding the type of style you want to configure for your page, click the New Tag, New Class, or New ID button in the Style Sheet toolbar with the Internal tab of the Style Sheet Editor displayed. A new item is placed under the respective category and the CSS Selector Inspector appears. You can give your style a name in the Name field of the Basics tab, then configure your style using the other tabs.

Tip: Only Classes, not IDs GoLive can only assign classes to text ranges, paragraphs, or blocks. Tags don't need to be assigned, as a browser automatically uses the style for a tag when it displays that tag. GoLive's current release doesn't have built-in tools for assigning IDs; you have to hand edit HTML to add IDs, as explained in Chapter 26, *Cascading Style Sheets*.

Figure 3-30
Cascading
Style Sheet
configuration

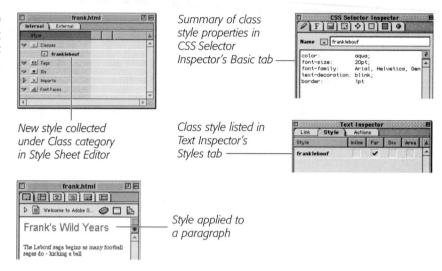

New style collected
under Class category
in Style Sheet Editor

Summary of class
style properties in
CSS Selector
Inspector's Basic tab

Class style listed in
Text Inspector's
Styles tab

Style applied to
a paragraph

To apply a class style to your page, select a range of text, then click the Styles tab of the Text Inspector, which lists the available styles. Check Inline to apply the style to only the selected text within a paragraph, or check Par to apply the style to the entire paragraph. If you check Div, GoLive creates a special container surrounding all the paragraphs or blocks—like list elements or other paragraph-based formats—in your selection, and applies the style to the entire paragraph. Checking Area applies the style to the entire page unless the cursor is in a table cell, in which case it applies just to that cell.

You can also reference style definitions that you've created and collected in a text file. Go to the Style Sheet Editor's External tab, then click the New Item button in the Style Sheet Toolbar. On the External Style Sheet Inspector, navigate to the text file using either the Point & Shoot or Browse buttons.

The file's location is listed under the URL column in the Style Sheet Window's External tab, while its status—good links indicated by a checkmark, broken links by a stop sign—is listed in the State column. If you have a page that references several external style sheets, you can change the order in which they take precedence by selecting a file and moving it up or down the list by clicking one of the two Move arrow buttons (see Figure 3-31).

To edit these styles, open this external file by either double-clicking the file icon in the External tab or selecting a file and clicking the Open button in the External Style Sheet Inspector.

More information. See Chapter 26, *Cascading Style Sheets*. Also see the CSS section of Chapter 2, *The Inspector*.

Figure 3-31
Style Sheet
window's
External tab

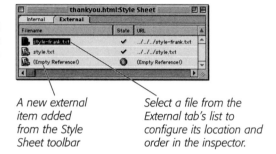

*A new external
item added
from the Style
Sheet toolbar*

*Select a file from the
External tab's list to
configure its location and
order in the inspector.*

*Move style sheets up or
down in the list using
the Move buttons.*

Putting Pieces Together

GoLive's drag-and-drop approach makes it easy to construct sites from individual parts stored in palettes. This organization combined with the WYSIWYG nature of the program allows you to quickly create an enormous amount of sophisticated content—or just place text and images on a page and rapidly format them.

In the next chapter, we tell you how to take all that you've learned up to now and set it to your liking: tweak all the preferences that GoLive provides in order to really maximize your use of the program and get a display that meets your needs.

CHAPTER 4

Preferences and Customizing

So you're humming along—building pages, developing your site, and publishing to the Web—and you're getting the hang of working with your new friend, GoLive. You could continue along this way quite nicely, but perhaps it's time to make a larger commitment to this relationship and deepen the communication and understanding between the two of you—using preferences.

Perhaps this is stretching the relationship metaphor a bit far, but the configurations you set in GoLive's preferences help you work more effectively with GoLive and, in turn, make GoLive that much more efficient in meeting your needs. Within Preferences, GoLive provides you a range of customizing options, from basic interface to usage of GoLive modules to designating network proxy servers.

This chapter covers each section within the Preferences dialog, as well as the Site settings, and global HTML formatting options found in the Web Database.

Preferences Basics

To get to Preferences, press Command-Y (Mac) or Control-Y (Windows), or select Preferences from the Edit menu. Preferences displays a list of panes for each major setting area on the left side of the window. Those with a toggle arrow (Mac) or plus sign (Windows) to their left have additional preference sections. To reveal and hide those items, simply click the arrow or plus/minus signs.

Tip: Navigating Preferences   You can use the up and down arrow keys to navigate through the menu on the left side. To open or close an item that has other items below it (such as General), press Command-right/left arrow on the Mac, or Windows key-right/left arrow on Windows. Press a letter key (such as B) to go to an item starting with that letter, but it can be a little persnickety about that.

On the Mac, your preference settings are written to a file named "CyberStudio Preferences" (a leftover reference to Adobe GoLive's previous incarnation) and placed in the System Folder's Preferences folder. In Windows, the preferences file (PrefFile.prf) is placed in the GoLive application folder.

After setting any preferences during a session with GoLive, you must quit the program for them to be guaranteed to be retained. If for some reason GoLive up and "unexpectedly quits" on you (i.e., crashes) or you do a forced quit (Command-Option-Escape on the Mac or Control-Alt-Delete in Windows), any preferences made during that session do not show up the next time you open GoLive.

Tip: Negating Preferences   If you are having problems with GoLive crashing, or if you just want to start from scratch, first quit GoLive, then go to the folder location on your system that holds the Preferences file and drag it to either Trash (Mac) or the Recycle Bin (Windows). When you start GoLive again, your preferences are set to the program's default settings.

Tip: Swapping Preferences   If you're sharing GoLive with someone who requires different settings (such as for networking) or you just have distinct ways of working, you can easily swap in and out each other's customized preference files. Set up a workflow system with your GoLive partners where, after quitting the application, you drag the preference file out of its system-designated home to a special user folder. Whomever opens GoLive next either gets the default settings or can drag in their own customized preference file before opening the program.

General Preferences

Open Preferences for the first time and GoLive deposits you at the top in the General pane which sets a variety of standard program behavior.

When you open the program, GoLive defaults to opening a blank, new document. If you want to change this, select either Show Open Dialog (allowing you to navigate to a file automatically) or Do Nothing (to open no document windows, your previous set of open palettes) from the At Launch menu; the default setting is Create New Document.

If you want the Document window to open in a mode other than the Layout Editor (such as the Outline Editor), select your desired tab in the Default Mode popup menu. Remember that in Windows you don't have the option of selecting the Mac-only Frame Preview (see Figure 4-1).

To open a specific file each time you create a new document in GoLive (Command-N on the Mac, Control-N under Windows, or New from the File menu), check the New Document box, then click the Select button and navigate to the desired file. If you uncheck this option later, then decide that wasn't such a good idea, GoLive retains the location of the file as an inactive entry in the file field.

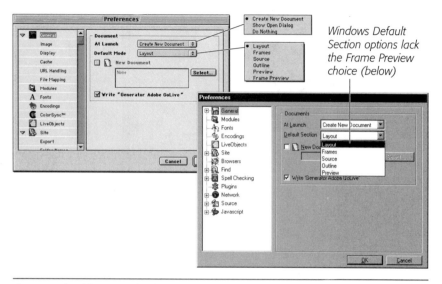

Figure 4-1
General
settings

*Windows Default
Section options lack
the Frame Preview
choice (below)*

**Tip:
Designating
Stationeries**

If you work with a specific design structure for new pages in your site, designate a stationery file as your default new file.

GoLive also defaults to inserting a Meta tag which tells the world GoLive 4 created the page. Here's the code's text, found in the Head section of the page (but you can only turn it off via this preference setting):

```
<meta name="generator" content="Adobe GoLive 4">
```

If you don't want to add this to your page, simply uncheck Write "Generator Adobe GoLive".

Image

Reveal the other general preference items by clicking the arrow (Mac) or the plus sign (Windows) to the left of the General pane, then click Image (see Figure 4-2).

With GoLive's drag and drop support, you can drag an image from an open file (such as in Photoshop) or from a page in a Web browser and drop it into an open GoLive page. That image preview is then saved as a temporary browser-compatible image file (with a generic numerical name, such as image7106732.jpg). Under Picture Import, you can select a folder where these collected images reside. GoLive defaults to placing these images in the Import Images folder within the main GoLive application folder.

**Tip: Importing
Images in
Windows**

Dragging images from Internet Explorer into a GoLive document does not place a temporary image file into the Import Images folder. Rather, GoLive references the image found in the Windows folder's Temporary Internet Files folder. To import an image into GoLive's Import Images folder successfully, right-click on the browser

Figure 4-2
Image settings

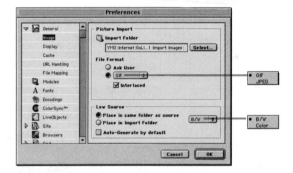

image and select Copy from the contextual menu. Then return to the GoLive document, right-click at your desired insertion point, and select Paste.

Also, you can't just drag a linked image from IE, and it seems rather impossible to drag any image from Navigator. For both of these instances, you must use the copy and paste method.

Under File Format, select the browser-compatible file format to use when saving dragged and dropped images (either GIF or JPEG).

Tip: Adding Format   If you choose PNG from the Modules pane, discussed later, it also appears in the File Format popup menu list.

With GIF and PNG, you can check Interlaced, which starts rendering a pixilated image in the browser and gradually improves its resolution as the entire file is delivered to the browser cache. This option increases the file's size slightly. With JPEG, you can check Progressive (which acts like Interlaced for GIF and PNG), as well as your desired compression level from the popup menu. On the Mac, you can also check Use QuickTime, which uses QuickTime's JPEG encoding algorithm instead of Adobe's (see Figure 4-3).

Figure 4-3
File format
options

GIF options   JPEG options for the Mac (Use Quick-   PNG options
                  Time not an option for Windows)

If you check the Ask User option, you are met with an Import Image dialog box, which allows you to navigate to a desired directory folder and choose the format of the file. This is handy, as it allows you to give the file a coherent name (instead of something like "Image-1276465113.jpg"); however it does take away a bit of control over the formatting of the file. For instance, if you choose JPEG, GoLive automatically saves the file as a progressive JPEG, and you don't know which level of compression is selected. In addition, this import/save dialog doesn't contain the nifty GoLive Save button that lets you choose to go directly to either the site's Root, Stationeries, or Components folders (see Figure 4-4).

If you want to generate lowsource versions of images placed into GoLive pages, you can choose to store those in either the same folder as the original image or into the folder designated as the Import Image location. Choose black and white or color in the popup menu. If you want GoLive to automatically generate these low-resolution images, check that option. Remember that you can also create lowsource images via the Image Inspector Basic tab.

Figure 4-4
Image file
saving options

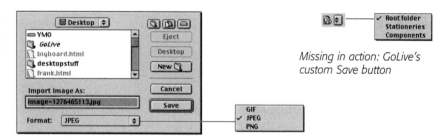

Missing in action: GoLive's custom Save button

Display

Click the Displays settings under the General pane to configure how link warnings and resize buttons on images are shown.

Under Marking, click the color field to the right of either Styles or Link Warnings to bring up the Color Picker (Mac) or the Color dialog box (Windows) to choose a new color. (Despite the GoLive manual's insistence that you can drag colors in from the Color Palette, you can't; you have to rely on these two operating system color sources.) The Link Warnings color is displayed when Show Link Warnings is checked in the Layout View Controller and broken links are discovered in a page. The Styles color is displayed when you select an item from either the Mark Style or Mark Tag popup menu in the same Controller. In the Frame Border popup menu, select a weight for the line that surrounds the style, tag, or broken link.

Under Sideknobs, you can choose how resize handles are displayed; they appear at the bottom, corner, and right side of HTML objects. Select a size from the popup menu, a color using the Color Picker or Color dialog box, and choose between 2D and 3D buttons. If you select 2D knobs, the color is not displayed (see Figure 4-5).

On the Mac, GoLive provides two additional preference options that support Mac OS 8.5 and later. Checking Appearance Theme Savvy enables Golive's support for the Appearance Manager, while checking Use Navigation Services enables OS 8.5 and later's Navigation Services in Open and Save dialog boxes.

Figure 4-5
Display
settings

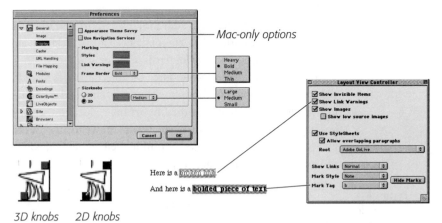

— *Mac-only options*

3D knobs   2D knobs

Here is a [link text]
And here is a **bolded piece of text**

*Link warning (top) and tag/style marking when selected in
Layout View Controller*

More information. See Appendix A, *Macintosh Issues and Extras*, for details on
GoLive's support for these two features.

Cache (Mac)

When we first saw the Cache preference, under the General pane, we thought we
had the chance to tweak GoLive's performance on the Mac. (Cache is not available
in Windows preferences.) Here you would choose to enable GoLive to store intermediate image files in a designated cache folder—recommended if you are working with image-intensive pages to boost performance.

   We're always enthused to find ways of speeding things up, so you can imagine
our disappointment when we discovered, after talking with Adobe, that the Cache
setting actually does nothing! For technical reasons that we aren't privvy to, the
feature has been disabled within GoLive, although the settings in the Preferences
window remain. If you want to play with the settings anyway, we won't stop you—
but GoLive's performance won't be affected by the changes (see Figure 4-6).

Figure 4-6
GoLive's
interface for
the disabled
Cache settings

URL Handling

Click URL Handling under the General pane to configure a couple of basic URLisms.

Select the Check URLs Case Sensitive option to allow GoLive to treat internal URLs as if capitalization counts. On Unix and under Windows, two files named identically with different capitalization (like "ag.html" and "Ag.html") are treated the same; however, on the Mac, capitalization is retained, but the Macintosh can't distinguish between two identically named files with different case.

If you want GoLive to add "mailto" automatically into front of email addresses typed in a URL field, check Auto Add "mailto" to Addresses.

To change all links to absolute URLs (in reference to the base URL of the site) rather than relative (which uses the current page as the reference point), check Make New Links Absolute.

Checking Cut URLs After This [sic] Characters allows you to trim the way that URLs with arguments attached to them are displayed. A URL can include information that gets passed to a server, generally after a question mark to mark the start of the data part of the URL; GoLive distinguishes URLs from one another by the entire URL unless you check this box.

The URL Filter area allows you to set patterns, like file extensions or directory paths, that GoLive treats as special files; these are ignored when the program creates a list of missing linked files and other errors. The filter allows you to keep GoLive from wanting to find CGI scripts, for instance, that aren't stored on your local hard drive; we typically add /cgi-bin/ to the list.

To change which files GoLive considers to be missing, click the New button and type a file extension or directory pattern (like .pdf or /pdfs/) in the URL Filter text field. Any file or folder that matches this pattern has its icon replaced with a gear to indicate that it's a special file (see Figure 4-7).

Figure 4-7
URL Handling
settings

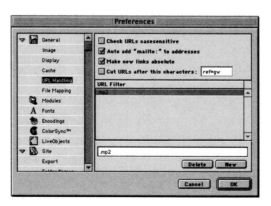

Assigning a URL filter changes icons of all instances of a file format to the gear icon.

After you make changes to some of these items and click OK, GoLive brings up a dialog which asks whether you want to update your site to reflect the changes you've made. Clicking OK to that prompt causes GoLive to revise your currently open site to reflect the new settings.

File Mapping

To view and edit files not directly supported by GoLive—like media files that require plug-ins, such as MP3 audio or RealVideo files—you can double-click their icons in the Site Window (or their plug-in tag icons in a page) to open the file in its native application—assuming, of course, that you have that application installed. You can edit GoLive's list of file formats and the applications that open them in File Mapping under the General pane.

GoLive defaults to checking Enable File Open in Other Applications, which allows you to open files via double-clicking. If this is unchecked and you try to open a plug-in file, you receive an error message telling you that GoLive can't open it (see Figure 4-8).

Figure 4-8
File Mapping
error

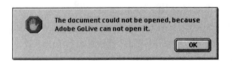

If you want to modify the configuration for an existing file format, go through GoLive's default file mapping list and select your desired file format extension (or suffix, as GoLive refers to it). The file format suffix appears inactive in the text field at the far left below the file list, but the Open With popup menu and Mime Type and Kind text fields are active and editable. (Once you make an edit in one of these areas, the Suffix field becomes active.)

To specify a native application to handle a file (from either Default or GoLive), choose Browse from the popup menu to bring up an Open dialog box, within which you can navigate to the desired application. Note that if you make a modification to an existing file type, a bullet appears to the right of the item listed in the Open With column denoting that you have made a change.

To create a new file type, click the New button, then type its suffix, assign how the file should be opened via the popup menu, and type the appropriate file information in the Mime Type and Kind fields (see Figure 4-9).

Tip: Deleting
File Formats
GoLive doesn't allow a ready means by which you can delete an item from its file mapping list. The Delete button remains inactive as long as an entry hasn't been edited. If you do want to delete an entry, select it from the list, make a modification in the popup menu or in either the Mime Type or Kind text field, and the Delete button becomes active for you to click.

Figure 4-9
File Mapping
settings

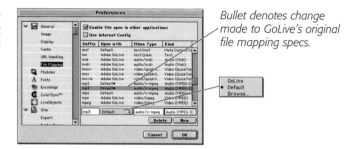

Bullet denotes change
made to GoLive's original
file mapping specs.

On the Mac, you can check the Internet Config option to let this utility handle all file mapping information. In addition, you can also import Internet Config file mapping information into GoLive.

More information. See Chapter 14, *Page Specials*, for a full explanation of this feature; consult Appendix A, *Macintosh Issues and Extras*, for details on using Internet Config file-mapping settings.

GoLive Modules

You can control GoLive's application functionality via the Modules pane. Installed into the Modules folder within the GoLive application folder, they work much like Mac OS extensions: you can turn them on and off to increase responsiveness and memory requirements for GoLive. If you make a change to the Modules list in Preferences, you must quit and then restart GoLive to make the changes take effect.

Say, for instance, that you decide you can do without the Document window's Outline Editor, as you really only use the Layout and HTML Source Editors to build your pages. Click the Modules pane, and scroll down the list to find the HTMLOutline Module. (In Windows, the word "Module" is lopped off the list item title.) To learn more about this module, click the Show Item Information toggle arrow below the list. This reveals the size of the module, as well as its version number and when it was last modified. You can also read a brief description of what the module does for GoLive in the text box to the right.

If after digesting this information you decide you really want to do away with the Outline Editor tab, uncheck the HTMLOutline Module in the list; GoLive then reminds you that you must quit the program and restart it for this action to take effect (see Figure 4-10).

AIAT Module (Mac). Activates Apple Information Access Toolkit (AIAT), which gives you the ability to simulate Internet search engine queries. Checking this option adds the Search in Site Index tab to the Find dialog and allows you to find all

Figure 4-10
Modules
settings

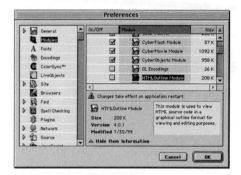

instances of a word or phrase within a site's pages for index-based search capability of an entire Web site (see Figure 4-11). See Appendix A, *Macintosh Issues and Extras* for more details.

Figure 4-11
AIAT search
capabilities

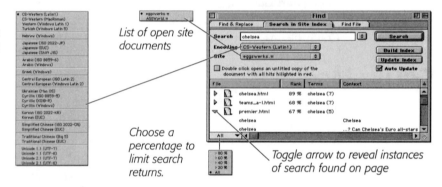

List of open site documents

Choose a percentage to limit search returns.

Toggle arrow to reveal instances of search found on page

CJK (Windows). Accesses Asian text encodings for Windows (much the same as the GL Encodings module does for the Mac).

Color Palette. Displays GoLive's integrated Color Palette and allows for dragging and dropping color swatches. If unchecked, the Color Palette isn't available and you have to rely on the Color Picker (Mac) or the Colors dialog box (Windows) for choosing colors.

CyberFlash. Maintains links embedded in Shockwave Flash files.

CyberMovie. Used for the editing of HREF Tracks in QuickTime Movies, as well as making it possible to add filters for video effects and preview movies.

CyberObjects. Used for editing DHTML animations and floating objects. If unchecked, the Palette's CyberObjects tab disappears, as does the Timetrack Editor icon from the Layout Editor.

GL Encodings (Mac). Accesses Asian text encodings on the Mac (much the same as the CJK module does for Windows).

HTML Outline. Allows you to view and edit HTML source code in the HTML Outline Editor's graphical format. If unchecked, the HTML Outline Editor tab isn't available.

IE Extension. Allows you to use source code specific to Internet Explorer (such as the marquee and ActiveX control tags). If unchecked, these IE tag icons don't appear in the Palette's Basic tab.

JavaScript Editor (Windows). Allows Windows users to work with JavaScript and access the JavaScript Editor. If this is unchecked, the JavaScript Editor coffee bean icon doesn't appear in the Layout Editor.

MacOS Encodings (Mac). Accesses the Text Encoding Converters (TEC) built into the Mac OS .

Modules Manager. Allows you to enable or disable GoLive's collection of modules. It is checked by default and appears in the module list as inactive so you can't turn it off.

Network. Used to support a File Transfer Protocol (FTP) connection. If unchecked, the FTP tab in the Site window's Extra tab isn't available, and all FTP fields in the Site Settings dialog (accessed via the Site toolbar) are inactive.

OpenRecent (Mac). Provides access to documents (pages, site documents, and media files) most recently opened. If unchecked, the Open Recent menu item doesn't appear in the Mac's File menu.

PDF. Maintains links embedded in PDF files.

PNG Image Format. Allows you to use images saved in the Portable Network Graphics (PNG) format. If this is unchecked and you try to bring a PNG image into a page, you receive either a broken image icon under Windows or an unsupported image icon on the Mac (see Figure 4-12). In addition, you aren't given the choice to save imported images in PNG format.

Figure 4-12
Unsupported
image file icons

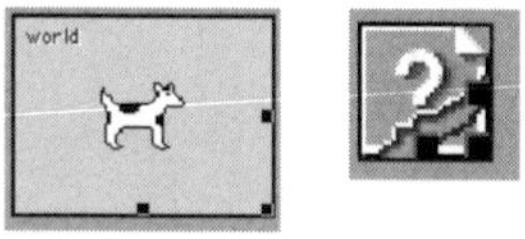

Preview. Allows you to preview the layout of pages and frame sets. If unchecked, the Document window's Layout Preview tab is not available (nor is the Frame Preview tab on the Mac).

Scripting (Mac). Like the Windows JavaScript Editor module, if unchecked, the JavaScript Editor is not available.

Site. Manages Web sites (via the GoLive site file), including all links, images, external URLs, colors, font sets, etc. If unchecked, GoLive doesn't allow you to create or open existing site documents.

Spellchecking. Allows you to check spelling within an individual document or an entire site. If unchecked, the Spellchecking option is removed from the Edit menu.

Standard Encodings (Windows). Accesses the standard ISO and Windows text encodings for Latin, Greek, Cyrillic, Central European, and Baltic scripts.

Web Download (Mac). Allows you to download the entire contents of a Web page, including embedded images. If unchecked, the Web Download option is removed from the Mac's File menu (see Figure 4-13). For details on this feature, see Chapter 14, *Page Specials.*

Figure 4-13
Web
Download

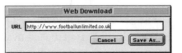

Enter the URL of a page to download with all of its embedded media.

WebObjects. Used for designing components based on Apple's WebObjects technology. If checked, a WebObjects Declaration tab is added to the Document window, as is a WebObjects tab in the Palette (see Figure 4-14). For more on using WebObjects, see Chapter 28, *Plug-Ins and Media.*

Figure 4-14
WebObjects

WebObjects tab in the Palette

WebObjects tab in Document window

Languages and Fonts

If you're working with non-English Web page content, you can set preferences for different language character sets in the Encodings pane. You can also set default display fonts for a range of language encodings.

Fonts

In Fonts settings, you can set the default font that GoLive uses to display text within your documents. Remember that these are not fontset preferences that your audience uses to view your published Web pages; these are interior GoLive-specific font designations.

Click a toggle arrow (Mac) or plus sign (Windows) to the left of a language group to reveal the types of fonts you can set (Proportional, Monospaced, Serif, Sans Serif, Cursive, and Fantasy). Click one of the font selections (such as Proportional) and the Font popup menu at the bottom becomes active. Search through your available system fonts and make a selection; to change the point size, click the Size popup menu and make a selection. On the Mac, GoLive also provides a preview pane when you click the Font Sample toggle arrow (see Figure 4-15).

Figure 4-15
Fonts settings

Click OK and return to a Document window. Content that is typed as GoLive's Default Font—found in the Style menu's Font submenu—is then displayed using the Proportional font.

Encodings

The Encodings section of Preferences allows you to view non-Roman-alphabet characters from outside the standard Western European group (ISOLatin1) in your GoLive pages. Before doing anything with Encodings, make sure you have the proper encodings Modules loaded into your Preferences: the Mac OS Encodings and GL Encodings Module for Mac, or the Standard Encodings and CJK Encodings Modules for Windows.

In the Encodings pane, go through the list and select all language encodings you want to make available to GoLive (see Figure 4-16). Encodings that are not se-lected do not appear in the File menu's Document Encodings submenu.

You can select all encoding subsets for a group (revealed by clicking the group's toggle arrow or plus sign) by checking the group.

Tip: Missing Subsets   If you uncheck certain subsets within a group, GoLive on the Mac denotes that not all subsets are checked by displaying a dash in the group checkbox. Windows, how-ever, doesn't display this dash, so you could be tricked into thinking the entire list of subsets are unchecked.

The Use Charset Info option is checked by default, which tells GoLive to place character set information in the Head section's Meta content tag. If this is un-checked, the Scanning Limit # Characters field becomes inactive; the value in this field tells GoLive how many bytes to search to find encoding and character set in-formation when it opens. To make an encoding subset your default, select it from the list and check Default Encoding; it is then displayed in the list in bold.

Figure 4-16
Encoding settings

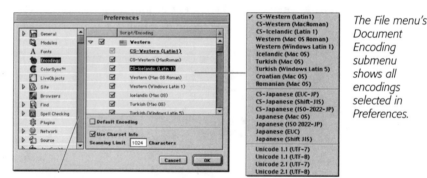

The File menu's Document Encoding submenu shows all encodings selected in Preferences.

The content Meta tag is placed into the Head section when this option is checked:

```
<meta http-equiv="content-type"
content="text/html;charset=iso-8859-1">
```

ColorSync (Mac Only)

On the Mac, you can use Apple's ColorSync color management system (CMS) to display colors within images consistently. This can be done either globally (for all images within GoLive via Preferences), regionally (for all images on a single page via the Page Inspector), or locally (for an individual image via the Image Inspector).

Under ColorSync in Preferences, GoLive defaults to selecting ColorSync as your global CMS. With Display Images Using ColorSync checked, you can also check Use Default RGB Profile If Not Specified, which then uses a color profile built into GoLive when ColorSync is activated but no RGB profile is specified. If Display Images Using ColorSync is unchecked, the Use Default RGB Profile becomes inactive (see Figure 4-17).

More information. See Chapter 8, *Images*.

Figure 4-17
ColorSync
settings

Global ColorSync settings in Preferences (left); ColorSync control panel (right)

Page settings in the Page Inspector

Single image settings in the Image Inspector

LiveObjects

When you bring DHTML objects into a page (from the Palette's CyberObjects tab), GoLive writes the JavaScript for the object in the page's source code by default. If you want to handle code in this way, keep the Write Code in Page option selected in the LiveObjects pane. But if you use components in your pages, you need to choose Import CSScriptLib to write the code for all Actions and other JavaScript features into the CSScriptLib.js script library; it places a reference to this common file in the Head section of each new page.

If you have a site document open, GoLive creates this library file in a new folder at the root level of the site. You can modify both the folder and file names in the Lib Foldername and Lib Filename respectively.

Selecting Import CSScriptLib only shifts this code to the library file for new pages. To move code from existing pages with dynamic components to the library file, you must go into individual page, open the Page Inspector to the HTML tab, check the Import CSS Library radio button, then save the page (see Figure 4-18). Clicking the Rebuild button doesn't perform this task, as you might expect. Instead, Rebuild is used whenever you change the Actions you have loaded into GoLive; clicking the button rebuilds the library file to reflect the new set of Actions.

Figure 4-18
LiveObject
settings

*Making the change
for new pages in
Preferences (left)
and for existing
pages in the Page
Inspector (right)*

More information. See Chapter 23, *JavaScript* and Chapter 25, *Actions*.

Site

The Site pane allows you to configure how GoLive's site management features work, from folder names and the way files are deleted to defining page status and export parameters.

In the Site pane itself, you can configure the following:

- If Check External URLs is checked, GoLive checks links to references outside your site. This requires live Internet access.

- The Reparse Only Changed Files option works in conjunction with site documents. If this is checked when you open a Site window or when you select Reparse from the Site menu, GoLive verifies only those references that were modified since the last check.

- The Reparse Files on Harddisk Rescan forces GoLive to perform a full reparse (opening and checking all HTML in all files in a site) whenever Rescan is selected from the Site menu.

- Checking Spring-Loaded Folders allows you to open a closed site folder and display its contents when dragging a Point & Shoot lasso, links, or files on top of the desired folder for a few seconds. If this is unchecked, you can hold the Point & Shoot lasso over a folder, but it only expands the contents below the folder. (Despite what the manual says, this option works for Windows, too, and is even more crucial there. If unchecked, you can't access files contained within the site folder when dragging a Point & Shoot lasso.)

- Checking Ask Before Deleting Objects forces GoLive to prompt you before you delete objects off a page using Clear from the Edit menu or the Delete key.

- If you check Create URL Mappings for Alias Folders, GoLive builds a mapping between any aliases or shortcuts in the site folder and external sites. This allows you to create manageable links between several sites that each have their own site file and folder, but all exist on local hard drives or volumes.

Under the When Removing Files section, you can choose to move files to Go-Live's site trash (which saves the files within the site data folder) or move deleted files directly to Trash (Mac) or the Recycle Bin (Windows). If Show Warnings is checked, you receive a gentle reminder about the action you're about to perform (see Figure 4-19).

Figure 4-19
Site settings

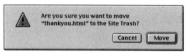

This warning dialog appears when deleting files if Show Warning is checked.

Tip: Deleting   To delete files, select a file or range of files (by shift-clicking), then click the Delete button on the Site toolbar. You can also use the contextual menu by Control-clicking and choosing Clear (Mac) or right-clicking and choosing Delete (Windows). On the Mac, you can also select a file and press Command-Delete.

More information. See Chapter 15, *Site Management*; Chapter 16, *Files, Folders, and Links*; and Chapter 21, *Site Specials*.

Export

If you need to configure your Web site to fit a special folder structure (such as a flat directory structure), want to strip out all unnecessary tags and extra space, or are using a feature like URL Mapping that needs to rewrite URLs before files are up-loaded, you can export a site to another folder fully cleaned up and ready to go. Before exporting, go to the Export pane, and tweak the following (see Figure 4-20):

- Under Hierarchy, choose As In Site to mirror the current directory structure (GoLive's default). Checking Separate Pages and Media creates two to three folders: one for HTML pages (Pages) and one for image and media files (Media). A third folder called Other gets created if you have any externally ref-erenced files that need to be copied in. Checking Flat strips away the site's sub-folders and exports all files into one folder.

- Checking Folder and Pages under Honor Publish State exports directory group and individual files according to the option selected in the Publish popup menu of the Folder or File Inspector.

Figure 4-20
Site Export
settings

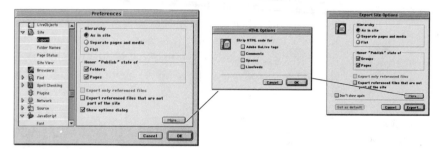

With Show Options Dialog checked in Export Preferences (above left), the Export options are mirrored in the Export Site Options dialog (above). Clicking the More button on either Preferences or Export Site Options reveals options for cleaning up HTML code.

Checking Folders and Pages under Honor Publish State exports directory groups and files according to their selected option in the Publish popup menu in either the Folder or File Inspector (bottom left).

- If you check Export Referenced Files…, GoLive exports all files referenced by your site's pages that aren't part of the site document. The Export Only Referenced Files option remains inactive unless you uncheck either of the Honor Publish State boxes.

- Click the More button to reveal the HTML Options dialog, which allows you to create "pure" HTML by stripping out selected code elements. Checking Adobe GoLive Tags removes program-specific tags. Check Comments to delete all comments. Checking Spaces or Linefeeds removes white space (tabs and spaces) and returns at the end of lines, respectively.

- Check Show Options Dialog to reveal a dialog box that mirrors the options listed on the Export pane—one more way to make sure you're exporting correctly. If you make changes on the Export Site Options dialog and want to make those permanent, click the Save As Default Button; the Export pane then reflects those changes.

More information. See Chapter 18, *Staging and Synchronizing Sites,* and Chapter 21, *Site Specials.*

Folder Names

The Export Folder Names section of the Site pane's Folder Names settings works in conjunction with the Export section, allowing you to name those folders that you export files to (see Figure 4-21). The Generic Pages section, however, works

Figure 4-21
Site Folder
Names
preferences

with basic file and directory information for your site. Here you can enter a custom HTML suffix in the Extension field (for instance, choosing .htm instead of .html), type default names for newly created folders in the Folder Name field, and name your default home page (welcome.htm instead of index.html).

Page Status

You can add another layer of identification to the files collected in your site by creating a set of color-coded page status entries. In Page Status settings under the Site pane, click the New Status button to add an item to the list. In the highlighted text field, type a name for this status item, then click the color field to the left and choose a color from the Color Picker (Mac) or Color dialog box (Windows). To do away with a status, select it from the list and click the Delete Status button.

To assign a status to a file, go to an open Site window and select any file (page, image, media, text, etc.). In the File Inspector, go to the Page tab and select from the Status menu, which gives you the option to assign No Status (default) or one of the status items you set up (see Figure 4-22). You can view objects with their status label in the Site map in the Display tab of the Site View Controller.

Figure 4-22
Page Status
settings

 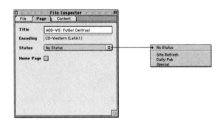

Tip: Status versus Labels If you're working on the Mac, you have another option for assigning a name and color to a file: Finder labels. In the File Inspector's File tab, the Label popup menu mirrors the label names and colors assigned in the Finder. (To modify these, see Appendix A, *Macintosh Issues and Extras*.) You can assign a label to a file in the Site window and the file icon changes to the color set up in the Finder's Preferences; you can also view by Finder label in the Site tab (see Figure 4-23).

Figure 4-23
Mac Finder
labels

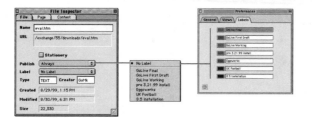

More information. See Chapter 19, *Site Maps*, and Appendix A, *Macintosh Issues and Extras*.

Site View

To change the colors displayed in the Site window's Site tab for items such as the lines representing links between files, click Site View under the Site pane. Here you can modify the colors that represent navigation and link lines, file name type, and the Site tab's background. Click a color field to bring up your system's color utility and select your desired color. Reset the colors to the original GoLive settings by clicking the Default Settings button (see Figure 4-24).

Tip: Setting Colors First   If you modified the Site View colors in Preferences, then checked your handiwork in an existing site, you would be disappointed. The changes made in Preferences only affect the colors displayed in sites you create after that point, and do not affect existing sites. To change the Site View colors in an existing site, go to the Site View Controller's Color tab and select your colors by dragging color swatches from GoLive's Color Palette into the color fields.

Figure 4-24
Site View
settings

For existing sites, make changes in the Site View Controller's Color tab.

Previewing in Web Browsers

GoLive's Layout Preview feature gives you a decent, quick 'n' dirty look at how your page looks when actually viewed in a browser. However, to get a more precise look at how your page elements are represented, click the Show in Browser button from the Toolbar. GoLive then opens the page (or a page selected from the Site window) in a browser or browsers designated in the Browsers pane.

If you click the Show in Browser button without first designating a browser, you receive an error dialog box reminding you of this fact. Simply click the Specify button to open up the Browser preferences.

To gather a list of all browsers found on your system, click the Find All button. After GoLive searches your hard drive, a list appears in the pane above. To remove a browser from the list, select it and click the Remove button. To add a new browser after you've found your original set, click the Add button and navigate to that browser application.

Check a browser that you want to set as your default. After exiting Preferences by clicking OK, clicking the Show in Browser button opens the browser (if it's not already open) and previews your selected page. If you want to preview a page in another browser in the list not designated as default, click and hold the Show in Browser button to reveal the entire list of browsers found on your hard drive, then choose your desired browser. Additionally, if you didn't check a default browser and you click the Show in Browser button, GoLive reminds you that you didn't set this option with the previous error dialog (see Figure 4-25).

Figure 4-25
Browser
settings

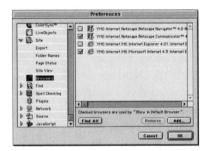 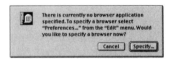

If you click the Show In Browser button and don't specify a browser or set of browsers as your default, GoLive reminds you with this dialog (above).

Tip: Setting
Multiple
Browsers

To get a feel for how a page behaves in different browsers (i.e., Navigator versus Explorer), check a version of each different browser flavor in Preferences. Then, when you click the Show in Browser button, your page automatically opens in each application. Be careful, though, not to check multiple versions of the same browser (such as Navigator 4 and 4.5), as you typically can open only one version at a time.

Document Editing

GoLive provides two text-based tools to help you make changes to documents inside and throughout your site. The Find feature allows you to perform searches as well as make replacements both in an individual file and across all the files within a site; the Spell Checking feature checks spelling on individual pages and across a site, and can keep a list of custom spellings.

Find

To set general Find preferences, go to the Find panel (see Figure 4-26). Keep the Hide "Find" Window If Match Is Found option unchecked if you want to keep the Find dialog open after performing your search. Checking this closes the Find dialog as soon as your search item is located, but does not close it if nothing is found.

You can search across a site for items in a file's source code by checking Source Mode under the Find dialog's Find in Files section or by selecting Source Editor from the Treat Files As In menu under Windows. When an item is found, GoLive opens the page to the highlighted item in the Document window's Source Editor. In Preferences, you can choose to search only Web pages (Use Only HTML Files) or all Web pages and associated style sheets (Use HTML and Text Files).

Under the Find pane's Regular Expr. settings, you can set up a list of wildcard search options for GoLive to use as prefabricated searches when using regular-expression pattern matching. Wildcard searching uses special characters to represent one or more characters in a search string. For example, "Frank L[a-z]+" finds all instances of "Frank L" that are then followed by any combination of lower case letters (from "Frank Lebeouf" to "Frank Langella"). The "[a-z]" designates the range of lower-case letters you want to find, while the plus sign tells GoLive to find one or more occurrences of the characters contained within the two brackets.

GoLive comes with several built-in patterns. To create a new pattern, click the New button and type a descriptive name for this item in the highlighted Name field. In the Expression field, type what you want to search for, such as any number that follows the word "GoLive" or a common change you make across your site. If

Figure 4-26
Find settings

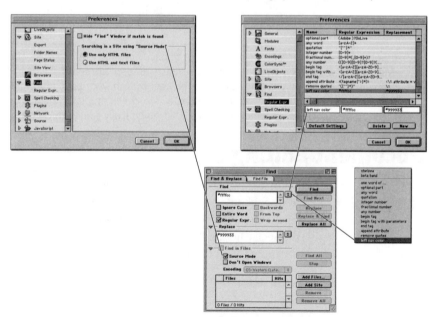

you plan on using the Replace feature as well, enter the word or string that replaces the found text in the Replacement field. After exiting Preferences, open up the Find dialog, click the popup menu button to the right of Find, and select the item you just created from the list.

More information. To learn more about GoLive's Find feature, see Chapter 14, *Page Specials* (basic Find on page); Chapter 21, *Site Specials* (sitewide Find); and Chapter 22, *Advanced Features* (regular expressions).

Spell Checking

When checking spelling on GoLive pages, you can store unrecognized words in a personal dictionary by pressing the Learn button. To edit this customized collection, go to the Spelling pane, select a word from the list, and make your edit in the text field below the list pane (see Figure 4-27). Choose All Languages from the popup menu above the list pane to have words in the list appear across the spectrum of languages, or create a customized list for an individual language.

As with the Find feature, GoLive also provides a Regular Expr. section under spelling where you can create a list of wildcard spelling strings for GoLive to ignore. GoLive's built-in list includes a pattern for normal URLs (like ftp and http) to keep them from popping up left and right while you attempt to check spelling.

More information. To learn more about using GoLive's Spell Checking feature, see Chapter 14, *Page Specials.*

Figure 4-27
Spelling
settings

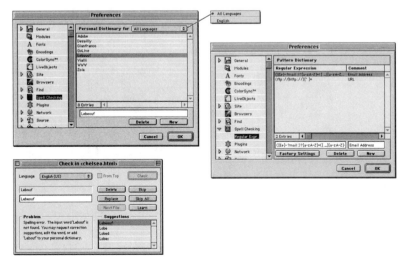

Plug-ins

GoLive works with media files (like QuickTime, Flash, etc.) in much the same way that Web browsers do, with plug-ins that handle the media's playback stored in the Plug-ins folder within the GoLive application folder. If you place a media file into a page without including the plug-in, you can't preview the file directly in GoLive.

Tip: Adding Plug-ins   Remember that if you make any additions to the GoLive Plug-ins folder, they don't show up in the Plug-ins pane (nor can they be used by media files inserted into GoLive pages) until you quit and run the program again.

Under the Plug-ins pane, you find a collection of media players placed into the Plug-ins folder listed with the MIME type, the player that handles this type, and the file name extension that triggers GoLive to use this plug-in player. Below the list pane, you can make modifications to these fields, as well as choose another plug-in player that can handle that file type (if one is available). You can also designate whether GoLive should or should not play the file when previewed.

To add a new item, click the New button and enter a valid MIME type. If an appropriate plug-in player already resides within the Plug-ins folder, GoLive assigns that in the popup menu. Type the file suffix in the Extensions field, then any comments in the Info field (see Figure 4-28).

More Information. See Chapter 28, *Plug-ins and Media*.

Figure 4-28
Plug-ins settings

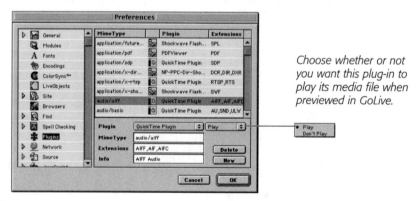

Choose whether or not you want this plug-in to play its media file when previewed in GoLive.

Network

In the Network pane, you can set up basic connectivity (see Figure 4-29). If your ISP or network requires that you connect via a proxy server (for filtering or security reasons), check either the Use FTP Proxy or Use HTTP Proxy options and fill in the server address and Port number below. If you need to jump over a firewall (metaphorically, of course) or are having other problems connecting to an FTP

Figure 4-29
Network
settings

Figure 4-29
Network
settings

server, check Use Passive Mode (PASV) to initiate a connection from GoLive rather than requesting that a server connect back to you, which is the unchecked default behavior. Check Keep Connections Alive to continue to ping the Web via your Internet connection so it doesn't close down due to lack of activity. Keep Use ISO 8859-1 Translation checked to use the Latin1 character encoding set which covers the majority of Western European languages.

On Windows, you can check Resolve Links, but it doesn't have a documented function. (This reminds us of when National Public Radio's All Things Considered program called Dave Berry and got his answering machine. The message was, "If you'd like to press 1, press 1. If you'd like to press 2, press 2…" And so on.)

On the Mac, you can choose either to use the network settings from Internet Config, or from the Internet control panel if you're using System 8.5 and above; see Appendix A, *Macintosh Issues and Extras* for details on Internet Config.

FTP Servers

You can collect a list of frequently used FTP addresses under the Network pane's FTP Servers settings (see Figure 4-30). Click the New button, then type the address in the highlighted Server text field (where GoLive places a generic "ftp.company. com" placeholder). If your FTP location goes deeper than the main server address, type its directory after the forward slash in the Directory text field. Leave the Username field blank if the FTP server accepts anonymous users; otherwise type in your required name .

Figure 4-30
FTP Server
settings

GoLive adds entries to these settings from the FTP Upload & Download feature (in the File menu) or the site FTP settings. In both locations, you can select Add Server to List, and GoLive adds it to the FTP settings. From both locations, you can select any server setup listed in FTP settings to fill in the FTP server fields automatically.

Up-/Download (Mac Only)

On the Mac you can designate a particular application to open specified file types downloaded from FTP locations (or using Web Download under the File menu) through the Network pane's Up-/Download settings (see Figure 4-31). This specification is needed for the Mac, as its system relies on a four-character code embedded inside a file to identify its file type and creator, and files downloaded from Windows or Unix servers don't include this information.

Figure 4-31
Up-/Download
settings

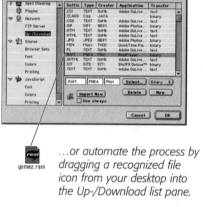

Adding the .ram extension for RealPlayer application files

Check file type and creator codes in Internet Config or the Internet control panel (below) in Mac OS 8.5 and higher...

...or automate the process by dragging a recognized file icon from your desktop into the Up-/Download list pane.

To add a new file type, click the New button and a new item is added to the list. Type the file extension in capital letters beginning with a period in the Suffix field; for instance, enter .ram for RealPlayer media files. Press Tab to go to the Type field and type the necessary information; for .ram files, the Type is PNRA. Click the Select button and navigate to the application on your hard drive that you want to open up this type of file.

After clicking OK, the Creator field is filled in for you; for .ram files, the creator code is PNst. In the Transfer popup menu to the right, choose whether this file should be downloaded as a text or binary file. To find the necessary file information, you can open Internet Config (or the Internet control panel) and check for the individual file extensions under File Mapping.

**Tip: Dragging
File Types** If you don't want to go through the hassle of researching file ty,e and creator codes, there is an easier way. Just drag an example of your desired file type from the Desktop into the list pane in the Up-/Download preferences and all required information (Type, Creator, Application, and Transfer) are automatically filled in.

You can also import file information from Internet Config or check the Use Always box to bring those mappings directly into the Up-/Download settings.

More information. To learn more about GoLive's networking, see Chapter 18, *Staging and Synchronizing Sites.* For more on using the Web Download feature and Up-/Download settings, see Appendix A, *Macintosh Issues and Extras.*

Code Appearance

The Source and JavaScript panes let you control how your code appears in the Document window and JavaScript Editor, respectively, from colors for specific pieces of code to font appearance. Additionally, you can turn on and off drag-and-drop support and configure how the code appears when printed. In Source, you can also configure browser sets to act as a base for syntax checking of HTML.

Source

Click Source to set the general source code preferences, the top three of which control certain behavior within GoLive (see Figure 4-32). To turn off drag and drop support, uncheck Enable Dragging of Marked Text. Uncheck Relaxed Checking if plan to use uppercase characters in your code. If Do Not Mark Unknown Attributes as Errors is unchecked, GoLive's Source Editor syntax checker marks non-HTML tags and unknown attributes as errors.

The next section controls how code is displayed in the Source Editor, and includes a preview window to show you an example of what you've just modified.

Figure 4-32
Source settings

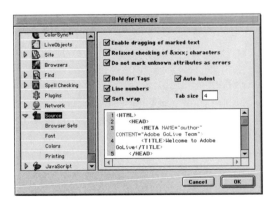

GoLive defaults to checking Bold for Tags and Auto Indent. To play around with the size of this indent, type a value in the Tab Size field. If you want to add line numbers or make your code soft wrap (so that long lines don't run off the right side of the window), check those options.

Browser Sets

The Source pane's Browser Sets settings control code specifications that the HTML Source Editor's syntax checker uses to find errors and warnings (see Figure 4-33). For instance, the default choice of Netscape & IE 3, 4 (denoted by a bullet) checks your code against the combined specifications for Netscape Navigator and those two versions of Microsoft Internet Explorer. However, if you're designing pages for an audience that still uses older browsers (such as Navigator 2.0), you want to check for errors against those specifications. These sets are found in the Source Editor's Browser Compatibility popup menu, which allows you to check your code against any of the sets you've created in this Preferences section.

Figure 4-33
Browser Set
settings

Browser sets configured in Preferences appear in the Source Editor's Browser Compatibility popup menu.

To modify an existing set, select it in the list, then check the browsers or HTML standard you want to include in that set. To create a new set, click the New button, type a name in the text field, then check the browsers or HTML standards you want to include in the set.

More Information. See Chapter 5, *Layout, Source & Preview,* and Chapter 27, *Web Database.*

Font

In the Source pane's Font settings, you choose a font found on your system to display code in the Source Editor (see Figure 4-34). Click the Name popup menu to select from your list of available fonts, and then select a point size from the Size popup menu. If you want all code to appear bold, check that option. Checking Condense shortens the space between letters, while Extend adds space.

Figure 4-34
Source pane's
Font settings

Getting fancy with your code font.

Color

The top section of the Source pane's Color settings allows you to choose your default view option when you open the Source Editor (see Figure 4-35). Choosing No Syntax Highlighting displays all text in your default font color, while choosing Detailed assigns different colors to each of a plethora of code syntax, from HTML attributes to special characters. Choosing Media & Links only colors entire tags for images, plug-in files, and links, while choosing URLs highlights only the link reference in hypertext and image tags.

You can set the colors for the various items in the color fields below. The color you choose in the Text color field is displayed for all page content; or, it's the color used if no syntax highlighting is selected.

Figure 4-35
Source pane's
Colors settings

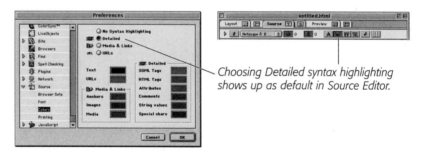

Choosing Detailed syntax highlighting shows up as default in Source Editor.

Printing

Under the Source pane's Printing settings, you can configure how your source gets output to a printer (see Figure 4-36). Check Printer Specific Settings to have the options below take effect, such as the different colored syntax highlighting, bold typeface for tags, and line numbers along the left side of the page. (Some of these options only have real effect on a color printer, but black-and-white printers can simulate colors as grays.)

Check Use Special Font for Printing to use a specific font style with your printed pages. Here you can set an available font, its size, and whether it's printed as bold, condensed, or extended.

Figure 4-36
Source pane's
Printing
settings

JavaScript

The preferences for how the JavaScript Editor displays and prints codes is nearly
identical to the HTML Source Editor preferences; however, it lacks a section for
determining which JavaScript version the syntax checker uses (see Figure 4-37).
(The browser-specific version of JavaScript is determined in the JavaScript
Inspector's Language menu.)

Tip: Where's
JavaScript?
If you open Preferences and don't see the JavaScript section at the bottom of the
right pane, don't panic. You probably just turned off the JavaScript Editor in Modules.
To return those preferences to the list, check JavaScript in Modules, then quit and
run GoLive to bring them back.

More information. See Chapter 23, *JavaScript*.

Figure 4-37
JavaScript
settings

JavaScript general preferences

Font preferences

Color preferences

Printing preferences

Site Settings

While the Site section in Preferences affect how GoLive works with site documents as a whole, the Site Settings dialog configures preferences for individual sites. Bring up Site Settings by pressing Command-Option-Y (Mac) or Alt-Control-Y (Windows), selecting Settings from the Site menu, or clicking the Site Settings button (see Figure 4-38).

Figure 4-38
Site Settings

Site Settings button

The General pane that opens first features just one setting: the home page for the current site. To change which page is designated as the root of the site's hierarchy, use the Point & Shoot button to navigate to the file in the open Site window. To see which file you currently have selected as home, click Show and GoLive displays its location in the Site window (see Figure 4-39).

Figure 4-39
General
settings

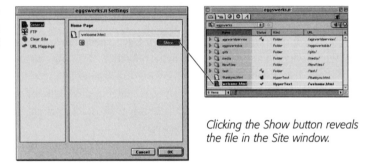

*Clicking the Show button reveals
the file in the Site window.*

In the FTP pane, configure the information for the server you upload your site to via the FTP tab in the Files tab's split-pane view. Some of the same information appears here as under the Network pane in Preferences (see Figure 4-40).

Figure 4-40
FTP settings

Note that GoLive seems to ignore settings originally made in Network preferences. For instance, if you checked Use Passive Mode under the Network pane's settings in the Preference's dialog box, that option isn't checked in Site settings, nor are Upload options such as Honor Publish State or Upload Referenced Files.

The Clear Site pane mirrors the options you can configure in the Clear Site feature, which can be opened by selecting Clear Site from the Site menu when you have a site document open. Here you can determine how to clean out or update all the tabs in a site at once or individually (see Figure 4-41).

Figure 4-41
Clear Site settings

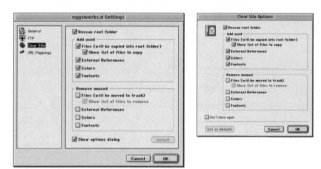

To update your site properly, you must check Rescan Root Folder. Checking Files under Add Used copies all items referenced by a site's pages stored outside the site folder *into* the site folder. Checking External References, Colors, and Fontsets collects those items into their respective tabs in the Site window under New Files folders. Check the options under Remove Unused to get rid of orphaned or unused pages, URLs, colors, and fontsets.

If you are managing a Web site that crosses a number of servers or directory folders, you can configure those settings in the URL Mapping section of Site Settings (see Figure 4-42). Learn much, much more about URL mapping between sites and server in Chapter 21, *Site Specials*.

Figure 4-42
URL Mapping settings

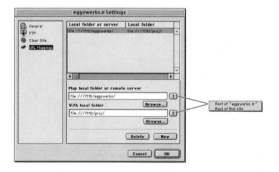

Web Database

To set preferences for the Web Database, open it up by selecting it from the Special menu or pressing Command-4 (Mac) or Control-4 (Windows).

Global Tab

The Global tab contains settings for configuring the way HTML gets formatted in all subsequently created or modified pages; the results can be viewed in the HTML Source Editor or by opening the HTML page in any text editor (see Figure 4-43). The tab controls these features:

Figure 4-43
Global HTML
formatting
settings

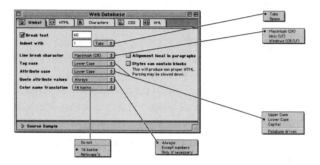

- Where lines break, if at all, by inserting extra returns (Break Text and the field to its right)
- Indentation for nested code levels (Indent With and the field and popup menu to its right); you can choose spaces or tabs
- Which characters to insert to create line breaks based on platform (Line Break Character menu)
- Capitalization of tags and attributes (Tag Case, Attribute Case)
- Whether attributes have quotation marks placed around them (Quote Attribute Values).
- What color names to use in the HTML, if any (Color Name Translation)
- Whether alignment gets embedded in each paragraph or GoLive writes a surrounding CENTER tag (Alignment Local in Paragraphs)
- Whether font formatting and similar styles can span more than one block, like a paragraph or list entry (Styles Can Contain Blocks)

To see how you are affecting the display of code, click the Source Sample toggle arrow at the bottom of the Mac Web Database or check Source Sample on Windows.

More information. The Web Database is covered in Chapter 27, *Web Database*.

CSS Tab

Use the CSS tab to configure basic style sheet settings, the most important being the Use Style Sheets option. If this is unchecked, GoLive doesn't allow you to use Cascading Style Sheets.

In the Default Unit popup menu, select a unit of measurement (Point, Pica, Pixel, En, Ex, Millimeter, Centimeter, Inch, or Percent) to use as the default measurement in the CSS Selector Inspector.

In the Output popup menu, designate how style sheet source code should be formatted; choose from Compressed, Compact, Nice, and three levels of Pretty.

More information. See Chapter 26, *Cascading Style Sheets.*

Preferential Treatment

Tuning up GoLive's preferences before starting to work can save you endless hours and frustration. Discovering hidden preferences you've forgotten or never known about that can help color-code your text or produce better output can be a great surprise and pleasure. Many folks leave settings the very end, but we've discovered that setting up the program right—detailing it to your needs—is like tuning a piano before you sit down to play: the results are always better.

CHAPTER 5

Layout, Source, and Preview

We've covered a lot of ground so far—palettes, inspectors, toolbars, preferences, JavaScript and QuickTime Editors, site documents, FTP settings…whew. But it's time we take a look at the the Document window, the engine at the heart of Web page creation in GoLive.

The Document window brings together all the different elements necessary to create a page. You drag icons from the Palette into it; you bring up JavaScript, CSS, and DHTML editors; you add keywords and a description to the Head section; and, of course, you add images, text, tables, and other page items to create your final piece.

So let's take a spin through the nerve center of page production.

Document Window Basics

At the top of each Document window are tabs for GoLive's different modes of editing and previewing, each of which allows you to view your page in a different manner: Layout Editor, Frame Editor, HTML Source Editor, HTML Outline Editor, Layout Preview, and the Mac-only Frame Preview (see Figure 5-1). When you first launch GoLive, the Document window defaults to Layout Editor; you can change this preference under the General pane's Documents settings in the Preferences dialog box to open in any of the five or six modes.

If you collapse the Document window on the Mac to a width of 311 pixels or fewer, the Layout, Source, and Preview tabs are represented only by icons (the Frame Editor and Frame Preview tabs are normally represented only by icons). In Windows, all tabs are iconized and named, and do not collapse when minimizing the Document window.

Figure 5-1
Document
window tabs

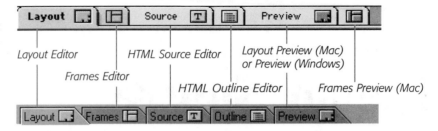

Tip: Double-Clicking Mode Tabs   If you double-click one of the mode tabs on the Mac, they all roll up underneath the document's titlebar (see Figure 5-2). You're not saving a whole heck of a lot of screen space, but it could be helpful in a pinch. To bring them back, click the bottom edge of the tabs, which is flush with the title bar. Also, if you get annoyed with Adobe's Hot Help boxes that appear when you move your cursor over an item, you can turn them off by selecting Hide Hot Help from the Help menu. If you're using Windows, move along, nothing to see here.

Figure 5-2
Collapsing
Document
window (Mac)

Collapsed horizontally   *Collapsed vertically*

You can adjust the window's size by selecting an option from the Change Window Size menu at its bottom right (see Figure 5-3). The bulleted value at the bottom of the list is the window's current width. The list gives you six options, from 50 to 780 pixels, but it does not allow you to type in another value. GoLive defaults to a 580-pixel window size, which is its suggested setting for a 14-inch monitor.

However, you can drag your window to a desired width and height, then select Window Settings from the popup menu, where you are met with the Window Settings dialog box. With HTML Windows checked, click OK, and be sure to save

Figure 5-3
Setting default
Window
Settings

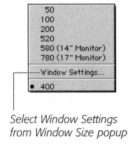

*Select Window Settings
from Window Size popup*

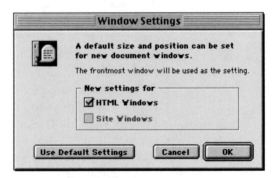

If you don't have a Site window open, the Site Windows option is inactive. Otherwise, checking the box sets the window size preference for every Document window subsequently opened in that site.

the current document (otherwise this change is lost). From here on out, every document opened (new and old) opens at both this pixel width and height. To return to GoLive's default of 580 pixels wide, select Window Settings and click the Use Default Settings button. Note that the Window Size popup menu is not available in source or outline editors, nor is it available in the Preview tab in Windows.

Tip: Maximum Width	If you're designing for both Mac and Windows, which most designers must, consider using 520 pixels as your default window rather than 580. For reasons we've never determined, a Macintosh and Windows box both displaying a resolution of 800 by 600 pixels don't have the same horizontal screen territory available. On a Mac, a site designed for 580 pixels wide and displayed at 800 by 600 forces a user to scroll left and right, which—unless a specific effect is intended—we find just annoying.

Layout Editor

The Layout Editor is where you will likely spend the most time when developing content for individual pages. (Of course, if you're an old-school hand-coder who can't "see" a page without a panoply of tags and attributes, there's the HTML Source Editor, which is detailed in the next section.) But the Layout Editor is not an island! With help from the Palette's collection of HTML tags, you can build the layout of a page visually and tweak tag attributes via the various Inspector palettes. Then, for text content, GoLive gives you a few choices to accomplish your formatting tasks. With a piece of selected text, you can:

- Choose items found in the Format and Style menus
- Click a button on the Text toolbar, which mirrors the majority of menu options
- Press one of a collection of keyboard shortcuts, which mirror the majority of both menu and toolbar options (see Tables 5-1 and 5-2)

The Layout Editor has a number of icons on the bar below the Document window's tabs (see Figure 5-4). If you click the arrow at the far left of the bar, the Head section opens up below, which is where you can configure items that contain information about the page, such as keywords and a page refresh. You find icons for these tags under the Head tab of the Palette (the third tab in).

Tip: Opening the Head Section	If you don't have the Head section already open, you can drag an icon from the Palette's Head tab and place it over the toggle arrow for a second. The Head section then opens for you to place the tag.

Moving to the right, clicking the Page icon calls up the Page Inspector. This inspector allows you to configure a page's basic attributes, including page title, background and link colors, and a designated ColorSync profile. You could also click

Table 5-1 Style menu keyboard shortcuts	**Action**	**Mac**	**Windows**
	Plain Text	Command-Shift-P	Control-Shift-P
	Bold	Command-Shift-B	Control-Shift-B
	Italic	Command-Shift-I	Control-Shift-I
	Underline	Command-Shift-U	Control-Shift-U
	Strikeout	Command-Shift-A	Control-Shift-A
	Superscript	Command-Shift-+ (plus)	
	Subscript	Command-Shift-- (minus)	
	Teletype	Command-Shift-T	Control-Shift-T
	Edit Font Sets	Command-Option-F	Control-Alt-F

Table 5-2 Format menu keyboard shortcuts	**Action**	**Mac**	**Windows**
	No Header	Option-Shift-0	Control-Alt-Shift-0
	Header 1	Option-Shift-1	Control-Alt-Shift-1
	Header 2	Option-Shift-2	Control-Alt-Shift-2
	Header 3	Option-Shift-3	Control-Alt-Shift-3
	Header 4	Option-Shift-4	Control-Alt-Shift-4
	Header 5	Option-Shift-5	Control-Alt-Shift-5
	Header 6	Option-Shift-6	Control-Alt-Shift-6
	Align Left	Command-Shift-G	Control-Shift-G
	Align Center	Command-Shift-M	Control-Shift-M
	Align Right	Command-Shift-R	Control-Shift-R
	Default Numbered List	Command-Shift-3	
	Default Unnumbered List	Command-U	Control-U
	Increase List Level	Command-+ (plus)	
	Decrease List Level	Command-- (minus)	

Figure 5-4
The Layout
Editor

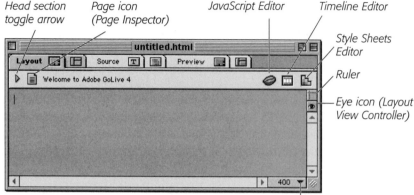

Head section toggle arrow   *Page icon (Page Inspector)*   *JavaScript Editor*   *Timeline Editor*

Style Sheets Editor

Ruler

Eye icon (Layout View Controller)

Window Size popup menu

the default "Welcome to Adobe GoLive 4.0" text to the right of the Page icon to re-name your page's title, bypassing the Page Inspector. When finished typing, press Return, Enter, or Tab to accept the change.

More information. For an illustration of the text formatting buttons, see the "Text Toolbar" section of Chapter 3, *Palettes and Parts*. Learn more about the Page In-spector in the "Document Layout Inspectors" section of Chapter 2, *The Inspector*.

Layout Editor Advanced Features

At the far right of the Document Window are icons for GoLive's advanced func-tions: JavaScript, Dynamic HTML animation, and Cascading Style Sheets (which are detailed in Chapter 3, *Palettes and Parts*, and in their own chapters in Part 4, *Advanced*). In addition, you can also view and measure against vertical and hori-zontal rulers as well as highlight different aspects of your page (from bad links to individual HTML tags) using the Layout View Controller.

JavaScript. Clicking the coffee-bean icon opens both the JavaScript Editor and the JavaScript Inspector. To create JavaScripts for your page, you use these items in tandem. To begin writing a script, click the New Script Item button and start typ-ing the script in the main window area. You can have scripts in either the Head section or body of your HTML document. (See Chapter 23, *JavaScript*, for more information on using JavaScript in GoLive.)

Timeline Editor. Clicking the filmstrip icon brings up the Timeline Editor, where you can configure DHTML-based animations. (QuickTime movies are edited with a similar-looking interface, but it's not identical; see Chapter 28, *Plug-ins and Media*.) The Timeline Editor allows you to arrange objects in sequences over peri-ods of time using DHTML (see Chapter 24, *Animation*).

Cascading Style Sheets. Clicking the stairstepped icon opens up the Style Sheets Editor, from which you can add text and paragraph styles to a page using the Cascading Style Sheets (CSS) specification. The Toolbar changes to the CSS toolbar, from which you can add styles (see Chapter 26, *Cascading Style Sheets*).

Rulers. Click the Ruler button in the top-right corner—the icon looks like the corner of a grid—and a pair of horizontal and vertical rulers appear in the main window set to pixel measurements (see Figure 5-5). If you are editing a table cell, the ruler recalculates its horizontal and vertical zero settings to match the cell. To get rid of the ruler, simply click the Ruler button again.

Figure 5-5
All hail the Ruler!

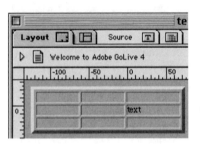

The ruler resets its zero point to the left border of a cell when editing a table.

Layout View Controller. Clicking the eye icon opens the Layout View Controller, which is where you can configure how GoLive looks and acts as you work in the Layout Editor (see Figure 5-6). (This Controller is detailed in full in "Document Layout Inspectors" in Chapter 2, *The Inspector*).

Unchecking Show Invisible Items causes GoLive to hide line breaks and tag icons on the page. You can also press Command-I (Mac) or Control-I (Windows) to hide and show invisible items, or select the item under the Edit menu.

Figure 5-6
Layout View Controller

Click the eye icon to bring up Layout View Controller.

Checking Show Link Warnings activates the "green bug" Link Warnings icon in the Text Toolbar.

A thick border appears around images and text links when Link Warnings is checked (or selected from the Toolbar).

Link Warnings.

A generic image icon appears in image tag placeholders when Show Images is unchecked.

If you check the Show Link Warnings box, GoLive displays a colored border surrounding all links and images with an empty or invalid reference. Pressing Command-Shift-L (Mac) or Control-Shift-L (Windows), or selecting the item from the Edit menu, also turns link warnings on and off. Additionally, you can click the Link Warnings button in the Toolbar (represented by a green bug) to turn the warnings on and off. (If you check the box on the Layout View Controller, the toolbar button becomes depressed.)

If you uncheck the Show Images box, images disappear from your page, with only the border, a generic image icon, and any Alt text remaining.

For more information about configuring the Style Sheet options at the bottom of the Layout View Controller, see Chapter 26, *Cascading Style Sheets.*

Frame Editor

At the top of the Document window, click the Frame Editor tab. GoLive displays a window chock full of nothing but a reminder in the middle that there are "No Frames." To add a frame configuration to your page, click the Palette's Frames tab and select one of the many pre-designed frame sets. (The icons give you an idea of the basic layout of the frame set.) Drag the icon of your desired set into the Document Window; double-clicking the icon doesn't work (see Figure 5-7).

The Document Window is then filled with the layout of the frame set, with an Empty Reference icon in each frame indicating that it needs to be linked to an HTML page. The Frame Set Inspector also pops up and allows you to configure orientation (either horizontal or vertical) and borders (size, color, and framing).

Click within one of the individual frames, and the Frame Set Inspector changes to the Frame Inspector (see Figure 5-8). (If you want to return to the Frame Set Inspector, click a frame border.) Here you can specify the frame's size—choosing either Pixel or Percent from the popup menu to the right of the Size field—as well as its name.

Figure 5-7
Frame Editor
and Frames
tab of the
Palette

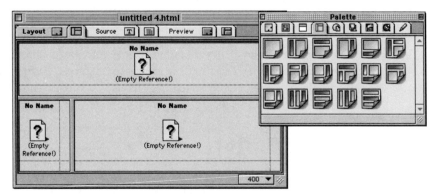

Figure 5-8
Frame
Inspectors

Frame Set Inspector

Frame Inspector

To select a content file for the frame, type in the name and directory location of the file or click the Browse button and navigate to the file. If you are adding a content file from a site file, you can use the Point and Shoot navigation button or drag and drop a file from the Site window.

To preview the frame's content, click the Preview Frame button on the Frame Inspector; toggle it back off to turn off the preview. On the Frame Set Inspector, you can also preview all frames by clicking its Preview button. Or, you can preview by selecting the Frame Preview tab at the top of the Document Window.

To edit a frame's content, double-click the frame to open the referenced file. To change the size of a frame, click and drag a border. To change a frame's location on the page, click a frame and drag it over the another frame, which turns gray.

If you want to add another frame to the mix, choose an icon from the Frames tab of the Palette and drag it into the Document Window. The layout is modified according to the frameset that was added.

Tip: Layout Editor Reflects Frame Changes

If you return to the Layout Editor after placing your frame set, notice that the Page icon has changed to indicate that frames have indeed been added (see Figure 5-9). Clicking the icon still calls up the Page Inspector for you to configure link colors, etc. You can type text and add material into the Layout Editor, but if you have content files selected for the frames, whatever you add is placed into a Noframes tag and is not visible in the browser.

Figure 5-9
Framed page

The Page icon in the Layout Editor changes to indicate a frameset has been added to the Frames Editor.

More information. For a full rasher (British for "whole buncha") of frame examples and how they relate to their icons, see Chapter 3, *Palettes and Parts*. For the skinny on frames and frame sets, see Chapter 11, *Frames*. Also see "Creating a New Site" in Chapter 1, *Getting Started*, for details on configuring a site.

HTML Source Editor

Click the Source tab at the top of the Document Window to view the HTML source code for your page. Here you can edit your HTML as you would in any other text editor. You get no help from the Inspector, but you can add icons from the Palette's Basic, Forms, and CyberObjects tabs to insert placeholders. If you try to add a tag icon from another tab (say the Keyword tag icon from the Head tab, even dragging it into the Head section), GoLive just ignores the action.

You can also make text selections and click items in the Toolbar—except lists and indents—or select them from menus and have the HTML applied to those selections. If you have nothing selected, then no code is inserted. Selecting Undo after applying code to a selection removes just the HTML code which closes the inserted tag, such as </FONT> at the end of a font size or text color format.

The row of buttons just below the Source tab is where you control how your source code appears, as well as how you check for errors in your HTML (see Figure 5-10). GoLive defaults to indenting the code and differentiating the various pieces with colored syntax highlighting (black for text, blue for HTML tags, red for URLs, etc.). You can modify how codes are displayed by clicking the various buttons, or configure the default display in Preferences under the Source icon.

Syntax errors. To check for errors in the HTML code, select the browser range from the Browser compatibility menu. Choosing a browsing range lets you see how a given browser reacts to tags you're using. GoLive defaults to three browser sets: Netscape and Internet Explorer 3 and 4; IE 2-4; and Netscape 2-4.

Next, click the Check Syntax button, and the HTML error log opens directly below. (You can also press Command-Option-K (Mac) or Control-Alt-K (Windows), or select the item from the Special menu.) With Display Errors and Display Warnings turned on, you see a list of what goes haywire for the selected browser set. The number of errors and warnings appears in the counter to the right of the Display Warnings button. (If these buttons are toggled off when the Check Syntax button is clicked, you don't see a list of errors and warnings, but they are detected and enumerated by the counter to the right of the buttons.) Click an error or warning and the window jumps to the offending item and highlights the code.

Figure 5-10
HTML Source
Editor menu

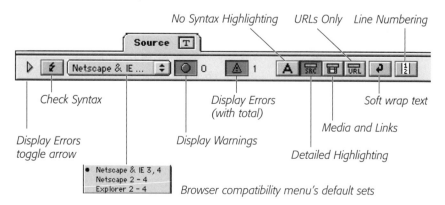

Browser compatibility menu's default sets

When you check a page's syntax, GoLive uses HTML tag information stored in the Web Database to determine whether any given bit of HTML should be identified as an error or with a warning. So if you have a custom tag that's not in the Web Database (or simply misspelled a tag), you receive a warning that GoLive doesn't recognize the tag. GoLive also warns you about the contents of attributes based on how they should work with different browsers. A few examples:

- When Netscape & IE 3,4 is selected, the Size attribute for the HR tag in Figure 5-11 shows up as a warning that it is not supported (even though those browsers do indeed support it). Although the HR tag is marked as supported by all browser and HTML versions in the Web Database—found by selecting the tag, then clicking the Version tab of the WebDB Tag Inspector—the attribute is checked only for Explorer 4.x and HTML 4.0.

- Also in Figure 5-11, note that the attribute's value is marked as an error. This is due to the attribute's value being set to Number in the WebDB Tag Inspector's Value Type popup menu.

- What's the difference between and error and a warning? That's a good question, and one that GoLive doesn't really help to define. With the <TITLE> tag misspelled as <TTLE>, you might expect to get an error (see Figure 5-12). Instead, the misspelled tag provokes just a warning. However, an error appears for its closing tag, </TITLE>, because GoLive can't detect a matching start tag.

To check syntax for other browser versions, select another set from the menu, then click the Check Syntax button to display those warnings. New browser sets can be created and configured in Preferences under the HTML Source Editor.

Figure 5-11
Checking
syntax, part 1

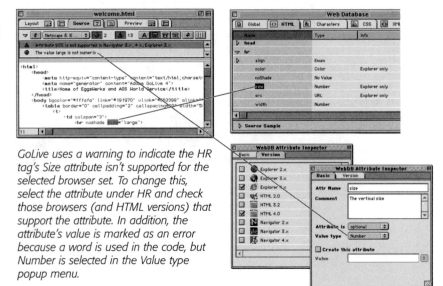

GoLive uses a warning to indicate the HR tag's Size attribute isn't supported for the selected browser set. To change this, select the attribute under HR and check those browsers (and HTML versions) that support the attribute. In addition, the attribute's value is marked as an error because a word is used in the code, but Number is selected in the Value type popup menu.

Figure 5-12
Checking
syntax, part 2

The misspelled Title tag causes GoLive to display a warning, but its correctly spelled closing tag causes an error because the corresponding opening tag wasn't found.

Appearance. You can control the appearance of code in the HTML Source Editor via the syntax control buttons. By default, GoLive colors HTML by category, with black for text, blue for HTML tags, red for URLs, etc. But there are four options total, only one of which can be selected at a time. The other three options are:

- Set your code to black text by clicking the Turn Syntax Highlighting Off button.

- Highlight just links and pieces of media (images, QuickTime files, etc.) by clicking the Hilight Media & Links button

- Highlight links only by clicking the Hilight URLs button

By the way, GoLive uses the "hilight" spelling for those last two buttons on the Mac side. (Oh those crazy, left-brain Mac programmers!)

To keep your code from running off the side of the page, click the Soft Wrap button; this option keeps lines from extending beyond the current width of the window, but it doesn't create a "hard" wrap by inserting a carriage return character. Click the Display Line Numbers button, and the line numbers that show up in syntax checking also appear along the left edge of the window.

More information. For a refresher on creating new browser compatibility settings, as well as setting syntax appearance, see the "Source" section of Chapter 4, *Preferences and Customizing*. For details on the Web Database, see Chapter 27, *Web Database*.

HTML Outline Editor

Click the next tab to the right of the Source tab and you open the HTML Outline Editor. At first, you might wonder what alternate dimension you just stepped into. You're met with a collection of hierarchical "container tags" that can be collapsed by clicking the toggle arrow to the right of the bubbled tag handle. For instance, if you click the toggle arrow of the Head container tag, you close up all the code associated with the Head tag appearing indented below it, plus the closing Head tag. Meanwhile, the Body tag still is visible. To close up the containers for the entire page, click the toggle arrow on the HTML container (see Figure 5-13).

The objective of working in Outline mode is to configure code using a container metaphor. Each tag may have several attributes itself; it may also contain other tags and text. All the values attached to any tag are accessed through popup

Figure 5-13
Viewing code
in the HTML
Outline Editor

*An image and accompanying
text added in Layout Editor...*

...then viewed in HTML Source Editor...

```
<body>
<img height="53" width="39" src="file:///YMO/gifs/eggsy.gif">
Welcome to the AGS World Service!
</body>
```

...then viewed in HTML Outline Editor...

Click gray show/hide attributes arrow to add attributes to tag.

Click exterior
toggle arrow to
expand/collapse
container.

Click interior toggle arrow to
expand/collapse attributes.

BGCOLOR
attribute
preview

Drag-and-drop
handle

Vertical line
connecting
beginning/
closing tags

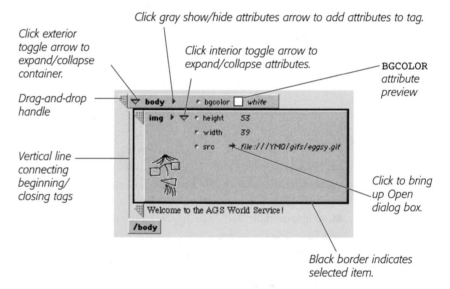

Click to bring
up Open
dialog box.

Black border indicates
selected item.

menus on the containers. You probably won't find yourself writing code in this view. Take a look at simply adding a graphic and a piece of text in Layout mode, in Source mode, then in Outline mode.

It's a bit daunting, but the HTML Outline Editor can be very helpful for moving around large sections of code (by grabbing the handle of a container tag and dragging it to a desired spot), as well as for beginning coders who can have the benefit of using the popup menus of a container tag to see what attributes can be used with that particular tag. Some programmers also favor an object model where they know exactly what they're getting into so they're not just typing, but actually manipulating elements.

Say you wanted to add an alignment attribute to this IMG tag. Click and hold the show/hide attributes arrow (the smaller gray arrow to the right of the HTML tag; not to be confused with the larger, outlined toggle arrow to the immediate right) to bring up a popup menu of available attributes, and select Align (see Figure 5-14).

Figure 5-14
Modifying code in HTML Outline Mode

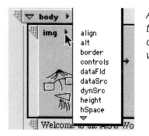

Adding an attribute to the IMG tag (left), then adding the attributes value (right)

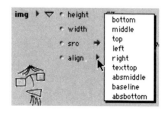

The Align attribute would then be added to the tag container's list of attributes, from which you can click the gray arrow to its right and call up another popup list, this time of the available values for the attribute.

You could also click the space to the right of the gray arrow and type the attribute's value. If you've typed the value name incorrectly, the Outline Editor doesn't warn you that you've made a syntax error. The only way to check errors is to return to the Source tab and run the Syntax Checker (see Figure 5-15).

Figure 5-15
Checking code in HTML Source Editor

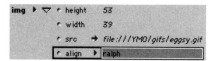

The HTML Outline Editor doesn't tell you when you've made a coding error. You have to return to the HTML Source Editor to check for syntax errors.

HTML Outline Editor (above) and
HTML Source Editor (below)

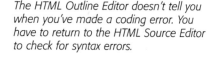

The Toolbar has contextually changed to become the Source toolbar, from which you can insert tags, attributes into tags, text, comments, and custom tags (for XML, ASP, etc.).

You can also access these Source toolbar items from the Special menu, or through keyboard shortcuts (see Table 5-3).

Most HTML tags are binary, meaning that the tags enclose attributes and file information within a container (sound familiar?) bounded by a beginning and a closing tag. Some tags (such as Img) don't require a closing tag, and are called unary tags. (There are also a few tags, such as P, that can operate either way.) Clicking the Binary/Unary toggle button adds a closing tag to tag that doesn't nec-

Table 5-3	Palette	Mac	Windows
Outline keyboard shortcuts	New HTML Tag	Command-Shift-K	Control-Shift-K
	New HTML Text	Command-Shift-T	Control-Shift-T
	New HTML Comment	Command-Shift-C	Control-Shift-C
	New Custom Tag	Command-Shift-N	Control-Shift-N
	New HTML Attribute	Command-Shift-A	Control-Shift-A
	Toggle Binary	Command-Shift-B	Control-Shift-B

essarily require a closing tag. For example, click a P tag to select it (a black boundary surrounds the tag), then click the Binary/Unary toggle button from the Toolbar, and a closing tag is added directly below the selected tag.

More information. Review the Outline toolbar buttons in Chapter 3, *Palettes and Parts.* For more on creating custom tags, see Chapter 27, *Web Database.*

Layout Preview and Frame Preview

To see how your work previews in a browser and test your links, click the Layout Preview tab (sometimes called just the Preview tab in Windows). GoLive's previewing capabilities give you a close approximation of how your page's layout behaves when viewed by your audience.

GoLive doesn't preview JavaScript effects coded into a page. However, if you've placed plug-in players into the Plug-ins folder found in the GoLive application folder, you can see a page's plug-in files previewed. If not, preview the page in an external browser that does include the plug-in.

Tip: I Can Preview Clearly Now   If you aren't seeing the Layout Preview tab, it's probably because the module isn't loaded. Go to the Modules pane in Preferences and make sure that the Preview Module is checked, then quit and start the program.

Moving the mouse over a link turns your cursor into a pointing hand, denoting that the link is indeed hot. Click a link to an internal page (one that is housed on your hard drive) and that page opens. However, if you click a link to an external URL, you receive an error message (see Figure 5-16).

Since GoLive's previewing feature is limited, it's best to use the actual external browsers your audience might use to preview your pages. After setting up a list of available browsers found on your hard drive in Preferences, click the arrow to the right of the Toolbar's Show in Browser button (available in just about every contextual toolbar) to reveal the list. If you just click the button, your page opens in

Figure 5-16
Clicking
external links
in Layout
Preview

Clicking an external URL in any preview tab causes an error.

the default browser(s). You can also preview a page in your default browser(s) by pressing Command-T on the Mac or Control-T under Windows (or accessing this item, as well as your browser list, from the Special menu).

As in the Layout Editor, use the popup menu at the bottom right corner to adjust the size of the window as well as set the default size for opened documents.

Tip:
Previewing
Using CSS
Root

When using the Layout Preview mode on the Mac, the inspector becomes the Document Layout Controller (a close cousin to the Layout View Controller, accessed by clicking the eye button on the Layout Editor). Make sure Use Style Sheets is checked, then click the Root popup menu to reveal a list of browsers (see Figure 5-16). Selecting an item from the list (which is based on the default style sheets found in the CSS tab of the Web Database) allows you to see how different browser versions from different platforms render your pages. For instance, select one of the Windows options (such as Explorer 4) and notice how font size and space between

Figure 5-16
Previewing
different
browser sets in
a preview tab

Selecting a browser from the
Root menu to preview pages in
different browser simulations; the Root menu options reflect the browser sets found in the CSS tab of the Web Database. The text in the IE 4 for Windows simulation (below left) is very large compared to the Adobe GoLive default (middle) and Mac IE 4 simulation (right). Also, note that just a little extra space is added between P tags in the Mac IE 4 example compared to the GoLive default.

Windows IE 4   *Adobe GoLive default*   *Mac IE 4*

paragraphs grow. You can make this same selection from the Layout View Controller when in Layout Editor mode; however, it doesn't carry through when you move to Layout Preview.

Unfortunately, this tip doesn't fully work for Windows users. While the Document Layout Controller isn't available from any preview tab, you can still access the Root popup menu via the Layout View Controller when in the Layout Editor and preview browser behavior there.

Frame Preview. If you're designing a page with frames and using a Mac, you need to click the Frame Preview tab to preview the page. If you haven't built frames and click the Frame Preview tab, GoLive reminds you that you have no frames. Windows users need not worry about this as the Preview tab handles both non-framed and framed pages. (Unlike in Layout Preview mode, the Document Layout Controller does not appear.)

More information. For a reminder of how to configure settings for viewing pages in external browsers, see the "Browser Sets" section of Chapter 4, *Preferences and Customizing*. See Chapter 27, *Web Database* for more on setting up style sheets.

Turn the Page

There you have it—the program in a nutshell. With the knowledge of how every part of GoLive works, you're ready to make pages. The next part of the book, *Pages*, covers how to use all of the different kinds of HTML and GoLive objects that you can put on a page, as well as more tips on using GoLive tools coupled with real-world production tips to make page creation simpler, more reliable, and more efficient.

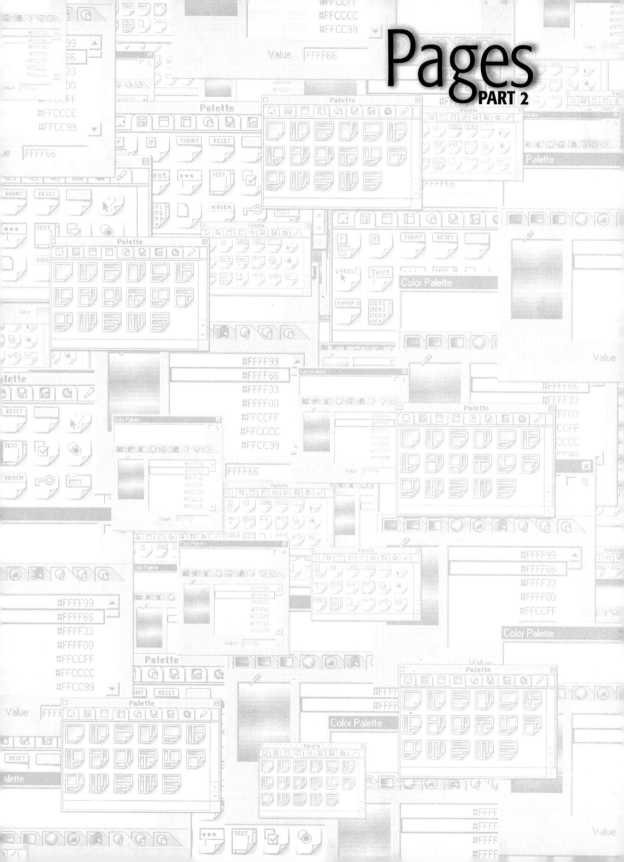

Pages
PART 2

CHAPTER 6

Page Overview

The basic unit of the Web is the page: a set of text, graphics, and other items that comprise the contents of a browser window. In this part of the book, we provide a comprehensive overview of all page-based activities you can perform in GoLive.

In this chapter, we identify all the elements that appear in or affect the Head part of a Web page, or the part that contains information about the page. The rest of this section is devoted to the items that appear in the body of the page, or the actual contents, including text and fonts, images, and color.

Page Structure

An HTML page is broken into two major areas: the head and the body. GoLive mirrors this structure by creating a graphically-oriented Head section in which items that aren't displayed but contain information about the page are dragged into and manipulated; and a body section, in which the contents of the page itself are added to, stored, and edited.

Head Section

The Head section could be seen as the control center for the page. Inside the Head container, HTML pages store all the information necessary to display a page. This can be as little as a Title tag or as complex as dozens of JavaScripts, CSS styles, and Meta tags describing the page's contents.

Since a browser reads and interprets the Head section of a page before it starts on the body of the page, anything that affects that body, like scripts, generally need to get stored in the Head section.

Several kinds of objects wind up in the Head section in HTML and in GoLive.

- **Title.** The name that appears in the browser window's titlebar.
- **Base.** The Base tag identifies a static URL that gets used as the root of any relative link on the page. This overrides the current location of the page within its site, which typically gets used to determine relative links.
- **Meta tags.** Meta tags contain information about the contents of the document, including a description of the content, keywords derived from the page, and so on.
- **Link tags.** Links are a special kind of tag that create a relationship between the page they appear on and other pages or objects. For instance, you can embed fonts in a Web page using Netscape's TrueDoc system via a Link tag to connect to the font file elsewhere on your site or on the Internet. (Note how these differ from hypertext links which don't contain information about the kind of link they are, but simply point to another location.)
- **Scripts.** JavaScript, Jscript, VBScript, and other scripting languages generally—though not exclusively—put all of their scripts in the Head section. (See Chapter 23, *JavaScript*, for more on where to locate JavaScript code and why to use the Head Script or Body Script icons.)
- **Cascading Style Sheets (CSS).** CSS enables advanced typographic control and the ability to position elements precisely on a page, See Chapter 26, *Cascading Style Sheets.*

Tip: Other Head Tab Tags The Head tab of the Palette also holds the Isindex, Tag, Close Tag, and Comment tag, which are fully described in Chapter 2, *The Inspector*, and Chapter 3, *Palettes and Parts*.

Body Section

The other chapters in this part of the book are devoted to specific parts of creating items in the body of the page.

- **Text and Fonts:** everything about specifying typographic characteristics, using typefaces, and structuring paragraphs
- **Images:** inserting and manipulating images, creating image maps; using Color-Sync (Mac only)
- **Color:** managing all the tabs in the voluminous Color Palette
- **Tables:** the ins and outs of creating tables
- **Frames:** how to use GoLive's Frame icons, Frame Editor, and Layout Preview or Frame Preview to create frames that work

- **Layout Grids and Floating Boxes:** all your questions answered about two GoLive-specific features that manipulate HTML or CSS for exact page positioning of objects

- **Forms:** an explanation of form elements, structuring forms, and integrating with a server

- **Page Specials:** spellchecking, Web downloading, file mapping, an other primarily page-based features

Base

The Base tag lets you change the local context in which relative links get interpreted (see sidebar, "It's All Relative"). Drag the Base tag into the Head section, and the Base Inspector lets you set the reference (see Figure 6-1). Check the Base box and choose a location to which relative links are appended.

Checking Write Base Always Absolute ensures that all references are written back to the root of the site, or the starting slash after the server name for your site.

Figure 6-1
Setting Base
URL via the
Base Inspector

Meta

Meta tags allow you to specify information about the page on which the tag appears, such as a description of its content or keywords that describe the content. You can code numerous Meta tags by hand, and GoLive provides the framework for that. However, GoLive also prefabricates two kinds of commonly used Meta tags.

Plain Meta Tag

Drag the Meta icon from the Head tab into the Head section, and GoLive brings up the Meta Inspector. You can set the Meta tag through the popup menu to either Name or HTTP-Equivalent. Names are used for information about the page; HTTP-Equivalent is used for simulating header information that accompanies a Web page when it's sent by a server to a browser.

In the field beneath the popup menu, enter the Meta tag's title, such as "description". In the Content text area below that, enter the contents of the tag, such as a description of the page.

A great explanation of a variety of available Meta tags and their specifications can be found at http://www.webdeveloper.com/html/html_metatags.html (see Figure 6-2).

Figure 6-2
Meta tags in
Layout Editor
and HTML
Source Editor

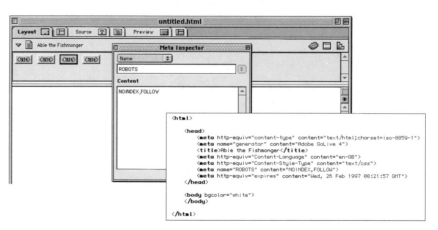

It's All Relative

HTML pages use two different ways of linking to other resources: fully qualified "absolute" links and relative links. We explain this distinction in great depth in the "Absolute versus Relative" sidebar in Chapter 16, *Files, Folders, and Links*, but here's a sneak preview.

Fully qualified absolute links (as opposed to GoLive's Absolute) require a resource type, a server name, and a file location. For instance, a file link might look like:

```
http://www.necoffee.com/flavor/syrup/
doubletall.html
```

The "http" is the resource type (Web protocol), the server is www.necoffee.com, and the file location includes the whole path after the server: /flavor/syrup/doubletall.html.

A relative link requires the context of the page on which it appears to navigate to the resource, which has to be stored locally. So if you're viewing a page that's located at

```
http://www.necoffee.com/flavor/syrup/
doubletall.html
```

and you put a relative reference to the page of

```
snickerdoodle.html
```

a Web browser constructs a full reference of

```
http://www.necoffee.com/flavor/syrup/
snickerdoodle.html
```

If you need to navigate to a higher folder, use two dots plus a slash to signify "up one folder level." So a relative link up two levels from doubletall.html of

```
../../decaf/notenough/whybother.html
```

causes a browser to construct a link of

```
http://www.necoffee.com/decaf/
notenough.html
```

Refresh

The Refresh tag lets you set the time before which the browser loads another page in place of the one on which the Refresh tag appears. It can even be the same page if you're providing updated information that changes every few seconds or minutes, and the user can just leave the page open, like a traffic status page.

The Refresh Inspector sports only a few settings (see Figure 6-3). You can set the delay before the page reloads; it can be set to zero for an instant redirection to another page. You can either choose This Document or specify another page to load.

Figure 6-3
Refresh
Inspector

Keywords

A well-produced page includes keywords in a Meta tag. Internet search engines consult Meta tags, in part, to construct their indexes and place those pages in order of precedence on their results pages.

The GoLive Keywords tag offers a straightforward approach to inserting them (see Figure 6-4). The Keywords Inspector lets you enter, but not re-order, any keywords. If you want to re-order keywords, switch to the HTML Source Editor, change the order of keywords, and return to the Layout Editor to view the changes in the Keywords Inspector. The order of keywords may effect the ranking in some Internet search engines, but the truth is unknown.

Tip: Search
Secrets
We recommend you reach Danny Sullivan's Search Engine Watch (http://www. searchenginewatch.com) for the best information on the subject.

Link

The Link tag lets you create relationships between the current document and other documents on a site or on the Internet. Typically, you use this tag for two purposes:

- To connect the contents of external CSS style sheets, as described in Chapter 26, *Cascading Style Sheets*. There's no reason to code this kind of Link tag by hand, as GoLive has a built-in linking feature that automatically creates the right Link tag code. (In fact, if you create one of these by hand coding, GoLive

Figure 6-4
Keywords
Inspector

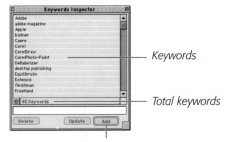

Keywords

Total keywords

Enter new keywords and click Add

"takes it over"—that is, it removes it from the Head section's graphical display and shows the file in the External tab of the Style Sheet Editor.)

- To reference fonts that get retrieved by a 4.0 or later Netscape browser or Internet Explorer running an ActiveX object and are rendered to display type in a browser window. (Internet Explorer uses a different method to link in fonts as part of the CSS specification; see Chapter 26 for more on that, as well.)

The Link Inspector—not to be confused with the one that shows links in the Site window—lets you enter the appropriate attributes depending on the kind of link. However, few common uses for this tag currently exist.

If you'd like more information on what values you can use with the Link tag, see http://www.w3.org/TR/1998/REC-html40-19980424/struct/links.html#edef-LINK. It's a little dense, but it's the best resource available.

Head and Shoulders

When someone is said to have "a good head on their shoulders," it's usually a compliment to their intelligence. Although the head section in HTML is important, we think you'll agree that on the Web the body is much more important. Call us superficial, but the next several chapters concentrate on building a better body—which, in the long run, makes people realize that you're the one with the good head on your shoulders.

CHAPTER 7
Text and Fonts

Despite the flash and glitter of images on the Web, and despite the maxim of a picture equaling a thousand words, text forms the majority of what your eyes spend their time perusing on a page. But text has received the least amount of hype and attention. While advances in sound, animation, and image compression have transformed the look and experience of the online world, most of the Web's words are still viewed in browsers' default fonts. Like the flashing "12:00" display on millions of VCRs, 12-point Times is the modern user option that never gets changed. (Most people don't even know they *can* change it.)

Granted, things could be much worse. Anyone raised on the green- or amber-on-black block letters of early computers may think that just having fonts with serifs and letterspacing is a quantum leap towards greater legibility. In HTML, we can specify a fairly broad range of type styles: bold, italic, underline, strikethrough, paragraph alignment, bulleted lists, and more. But only recently have we been able to apply attributes such as different fonts, variable type sizes, and colors—and even then it was a chore to code the necessary tags in HTML.

In GoLive, you can set specific visual formatting like bold or italic, as well as structural definitions like Code, Pre, and heading styles. How these appear is defined by the defaults in each browser, some of which can be modified by users. GoLive also offers tools for managing fontsets—or designer-specified sets of fonts for a browser to display type in—to broaden compatibility among browsers.

Tip: More on Text in GoLive   This chapter explains how to manipulate and style text. Chapter 12, *Layout Grids and Floating Boxes*, covers GoLive's positioning controls for text and objects on a page. Cascading Style Sheets, which represent a huge leap in text control, but only for the recent browsers, are covered in Chapter 26, *Cascading Style Sheets*.

Entering Text

After installing GoLive for the first time on our systems, one of the first things we did to test the program was type a few lines of gibberish into the Layout Editor, then preview the file in a Web browser. You can type directly into the Layout Editor as if it were a dedicated word processor, copy and paste text from another program, or drag text from an open application directly into GoLive.

Paragraphs and Line Breaks

As you type or edit text, two types of line breaks—methods of starting text on the next line at the margin—are available. Following the word-processing convention, GoLive formats text in paragraphs by default. Pressing Return (Mac) or Enter (Windows) inserts a paragraph break, which on the Web signals that extra vertical space is added following the end of the paragraph.

If you'd rather not let Web browsers determine how much space belongs after each paragraph, you can insert line breaks by pressing Shift-Return (Mac) or Shift-Enter (Windows). If you're feeling particularly mouse-happy, you can also double-click the Line Break icon in the Basic tab of the Palette, or drag it to the desired location in your document. Some designers use multiple line breaks to separate paragraphs in order to maintain more control over how much space appears before and after their paragraphs (see Figure 7-1).

Figure 7-1
Paragraph and line breaks

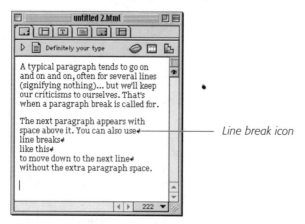

Line break icon

Tip: Pasting Text Corrects HTML Entities   If you copy and paste text from an outside source into the Layout Editor, GoLive automatically converts some nonstandard text elements into their HTML entities. For example, an ampersand (&) becomes "&", the copyright symbol (©) turns into "©", and accented letters like the "e" in "café" is transformed into "café". This helps ensure that readers don't see strange characters when their browsers hit those elements in the HTML source code. (See "Characters Tab" in Chapter 27, *Web Database*, for a discussion of entities.)

Navigating Text

With so many words on the Web, you need effective ways of navigating them all, whether you're traversing a couple paragraphs or several screens' worth of text. This may seem like a basic point, but, like designing a Web page, you'd be surprised at the difference good navigation makes.

Navigating with the Mouse

The easiest method to move around is to use your mouse to place the text-insertion point where you want to type or edit. Double-clicking selects a single word; triple-clicking selects a line, and quadruple-clicking selects an entire paragraph. If you right-click in Windows, or Control-click on a Macintosh, a contextual menu appears with the option to Select All. (Typing Command-A on a Mac or Control-A under Windows also selects all text and objects on a page.)

GoLive supports drag-and-drop editing, so you can select a block of text, then drag the selection to a new location—even onto another open page window. To make a quick copy of a text range, hold down Option (Mac) or Control (Windows) while you move it (see Figure 7-2).

Tip: Make Macintosh Text Clippings

Not only can you drag text blocks to other documents within GoLive or other open applications, you can also create a text clipping on the Macintosh by dragging text to the Desktop. This can be handy if you need to use a block of text frequently, but don't want to set up a GoLive Component. Dragging text from the HTML Source Editor works the same way.

Figure 7-2
Drag-copying
text selections

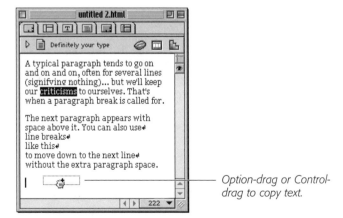

Option-drag or Control-drag to copy text.

Navigating with the Keyboard

You may not always want to reach for the mouse when you're typing, so it's important to know how to get around via the keyboard using the arrow keys and modifiers. Table 7-1 lists the results of the possible key combinations. Holding down Shift when performing any of the following actions selects the text range from the cursor's starting position.

	Arrow Key	Macintosh	Windows	Result
Table 7-1 Modify your keys to success	Up	none, Command, or Option	none, Alt, or Control	moves cursor up one line
	Down	none, Command, or Option	none, Alt, or Control	moves cursor down one line
	Left	none	none	moves cursor one character to the left
	Left	Option	Control	moves cursor one word* to the left
	Left	Command	Alt	moves cursor to beginning of line
	Right	Option	Control	moves cursor one word* to the right
	Right	Command	Alt	moves cursor to end of line**

* The cursor jumps between the beginnings and ends of words when using Option, rather than just the beginnings.

** The exception is when a line ends with a line break, rather than a full paragraph character, in which case the cursor is placed at the beginning of the next line.

Tip:
Navigating
Without
Moving

Pressing the Home, End, Page Up, and Page Down keys changes what's displayed in the Layout Editor, but doesn't move your cursor to those locations. If you want your cursor to appear at the end of the document, for instance, you must either move it with the arrow keys or scroll to the end and click where the cursor should appear.

On the other hand, this method of navigation makes it easier to locate your cursor if you've scrolled elsewhere on the page: just press one of the arrow keys to force GoLive to display the cursor. If the page structure makes it difficult to see the cursor by itself, press Shift plus an arrow key to spot the newly-highlighted text.

Formatting Text

Before launching into the specifics of styling text on a Web page, we need to take a step back and explain the difference between structural formatting and styled-text formatting. Although GoLive, for the most part, treats the variations as general text formatting, the underlying distinction between the two helps you understand why some formats, like bold and strong, seem to produce the same visual results, and to give you a taste of what's to come as Web formatting matures.

A Brief History of Formatted HTML Text

The Web wasn't necessarily intended to be a designer's playground. HTML provided a convenient framework for displaying information in a more readable format, featuring text styles and inline images (and, of course, connected pages using hyperlinks), that could be read on any computer with a Web browser.

Since there was no guarantee that someone reading your document had the same typefaces or support for styled text, such as offered in a word processor, HTML was devised as a set of tags defining a document's structure rather than the specifics of its appearance. (This is the theory behind Extended Markup Language, or XML, which provides an even more generic structure.) Structuring tags also circumvented the need to support several proprietary file formats; HTML files are plain text, readable by nearly every computer system from PalmPilot to Unix workstation to IBM mainframe.

So, for example, instead of creating a headline in 36-point Franklin Gothic type, the relevant text was simply tagged as a headline, letting the browser format it to the program's settings for what a headline should be—in most cases, this meant bold type set two to three times larger than the body text. This structural approach provides more flexibility when sharing information because it identifies sections of a document—such as headlines, quotations, and code examples—as objects, not as text with local formatting applied.

Unfortunately, structure tended to drive designers nuts in early implementations of HTML, because designers are accustomed to specifying exactly how something will look. That's why HTML also allows styled-text formatting, letting you display text in italics, or underlined, or in a monospaced font without assigning a structural classification to it.

As HTML has evolved over the years, this type of local formatting has lost favor with the architects of the HTML spec at the World Wide Web Consortium (W3C). The HTML 4.0 specification, while calling for backwards compatibility with the formatting introduced in earlier versions of the specification, now recommends styling text using Cascading Style Sheets (CSS). Although in the long run this may prove to be the better implementation, especially in terms of being able to more easily update a site's appearance, sometimes we just want to make a word italic and move on to the next element on the page.

Text Styles

GoLive currently supports text styling in a number of ways, available either from the Text toolbar or the Style menu and applied to any highlighted text in the Layout Editor. Styles can also be combined with one another. Table 7-2 displays the basic styled text options.

Table 7-2	Text Style	Example
Text styles	Plain Text	Typefaces by Josef Stylin'
	Bold	**Typefaces by Josef Stylin'**
	Italic	*Typefaces by Josef Stylin'*
	Underline	Typefaces by Josef Stylin'
	Strikeout	~~Typefaces by Josef Stylin'~~
	Superscript	Typefaces by ᴶᵒˢᵉᶠ ˢᵗʸˡⁱⁿ'
	Subscript	Typefaces by Josef Stylin'
	Teletype*	Typefaces by Josef Stylin'
	Blink	(see next tip)
	Nobreak**	

* Teletype is a method of applying local formatting to display text in a monospaced font.

** Nobreak lets you specify that the highlighted text not wrap to the next line if it's being displayed in a narrow browser window, a table cell, or when placed beside an aligned image.

Tip: Don't Blink The blink format was introduced by Netscape and quickly became one of the most derided tags ever, since not everyone wants to be repeatedly flashed by text. GoLive does not display the blink effect in either the Layout Editor or the Layout Preview; you have to open the page in a Netscape browser to see it in action. Although we have seen an occasional clever use of blink (it convincingly reproduces a word processor's flashing cursor), we don't recommend its continued use.

Tip: Mix and Match Styles You don't have to pick just one text style or text structure tag; feel free to mix and match them as you wish. If your style soup gets to be too murky, simply select Plain Text from the Style menu, Plain Structure from the Structure submenu, or both.

Text Structure

The Structure submenu of GoLive's Style menu lists the structural formatting options, which are also applied to any highlighted text. Unlike the text styles above, the appearance of text formatted with these tags depends on how a browser is configured to display them. Structural definitions tend to identify the kind of content rather than the formatting that should be applied to them; for instance, "quotation" instead of "italic."

Structural definitions are helpful when using Cascading Style Sheets as well; for example, you could specify that text marked as Emphasis appear not only in italics, but colored red and slightly larger than the rest of the text (see Chapter 26,

Cascading Style Sheets). The descriptions in Table 7-3 note GoLive's display as well as the common appearance in Web browsers (though they may differ among products, platforms, and versions).

Table 7-3
Structural
styles

Structure	Appearance
Plain Structure	The default style offers no frills
Emphasis	Text appears in italics
Strong	Text appears in bold
Quotation	Text appear in italics
Sample	Text appears in a monospaced font
Definition	A truly structural tag, the text doesn't change its appearance in GoLive
Variable	Text appears in italics
Code	Text appears in a monospaced font
Keyboard	Text appears in a monospaced font

Paragraph Formatting

In addition to formatting snippets of highlighted text, HTML includes the ability to choose a format that gets applied to an entire paragraph. Unlike text styles, you cannot mix and match paragraph formats.

Headings. Web browsers include built-in definitions for six heading levels. Structurally, headings act as classifications whose appearances can be easily manipulated with Cascading Style Sheets; stylistically, headings often pack an obvious "this is clearly a headline" punch to your text. You can apply headings from the Format menu or the Paragraph Format menu on the Text toolbar (see Figure 7-3).

Figure 7-3
Heading
formats

In addition to appearing in different sizes and styles, headings automatically include space after the text.

Preformatted. Preformatted text disobeys a few laws of HTML for the sake of making things easier for Web authors. Normally, Web browsers ignore line breaks and multiple spaces in an HTML file, relying on paragraph and other vertical markers—like the end of a list—to identify paragraphs and other blocks of text that should be separated vertically. Preformatted text instead reproduces the text exactly as it appears in the HTML, in a monospaced font including any hard returns, even without paragraph or line break tags (see Figure 7-4). Preformatted text works well when showing longer code samples or content, like bracketed text, that would normally require HTML entities to display properly.

Figure 7-4
Preformatted
text

The line breaks of the preformatted section (within the PRE tags in the HTML Source Editor) are applied, whereas the line breaks in the paragraph below are ignored by GoLive and Web browsers.

Address. This format is used for addresses or other contact information that automatic indexing programs look for when scanning your Web site. GoLive and most browsers display the text in italics.

Text Alignment

Most of the text we read in Western European languages is aligned to the left edge of a page or column, but that doesn't mean there isn't room for a little nonconformity here and there; and GoLive handles all kinds of text encodings, so multiple alignment styles can be handy for that purpose.

In addition to left-side alignment, GoLive can center or right-align paragraphs: click the desired alignment button on the Text toolbar or choose from the Alignment submenu of the Format menu. To return to the paragraph's default alignment, either select Default Alignment from the Alignment submenu or click a highlighted alignment button to deactivate it (see Figure 7-5).

Figure 7-5
Text alignment
using the
Toolbar

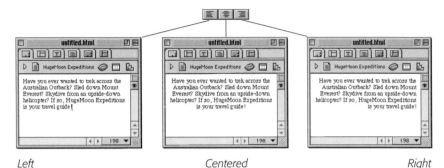

Left   *Centered*   *Right*

Alignment Overrides. Paragraph alignment is only one of several methods GoLive offers for aligning elements. Paragraph alignment is much different than image alignment, which wraps text around the image (see Chapter 8, *Images*). You can also align text within a table cell by setting the cell's alignment attribute (see Chapter 10, *Tables*). And, as you might expect, the various alignments can be combined depending on the layout you're aiming for. In this case, it's good to know how the alignments interact with each other, and which ones override the others.

In general, paragraph alignment dominates. If you enter text within a table cell and set its paragraph alignment to Right, the text remains aligned right even if the table cell's horizontal alignment is set to Left or Center. When setting image or table alignment for purposes of wrapping text, however, you can get both effects simultaneously. An image with its Alignment set to Left, but placed at the front of a paragraph that's been aligned right, sticks to the left of the screen while the wrapped text appears beside it aligned right (see Figure 7-6).

Figure 7-6
Alignment
overrides

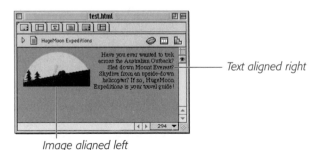

Text aligned right

Image aligned left

Block indent. Although not technically an alignment attribute, GoLive supports block indentation of paragraphs, which simply indents the paragraph using HTML's Blockquote tag. From the Alignment submenu of the Format menu, choose Increase Block Indent or Decrease Block Indent, depending on how far you want to indent the text. Unlike using an unnumbered list to indent a paragraph (see

"Unnumbered List" later in this chapter), Block Indent brings the paragraph's margins in from both the left and right sides (see Figure 7-7).

Figure 7-7
Block indent

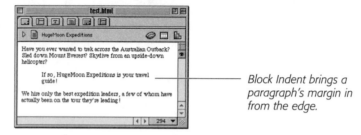

Block Indent brings a paragraph's margin in from the edge.

Text Size

Text size in HTML isn't expressed in points, as it is most everywhere else on your computer, because HTML doesn't understand descriptions like 10-point Times. In order to make the Web more accessible, text size is expressed structurally, not styl-

GoLive Is in Charge of Font Size Tags

From GoLive's perspective, text is always sized using the absolute method, unless you employ CSS to specify text sizes in points, pixels, or some other absolute unit. Even if you manually change the font sizes in the HTML Source Editor to relative values, GoLive changes them back to absolute values when it reparses the page. (To make GoLive reparse, switch to the Layout Editor and make some minor change before switching back to the HTML Source Editor.) We're not exactly sure why GoLive insists on absolute values, since that puts a rock through the notion of being able to control a page's HTML code using GoLive.

The implications of this action can ripple across your pages, depending on the functionality you're shooting for. Some people use the Basefont tag to force a browser to use a different size other than its default as the starting point for resizing on a page. In practical terms, this allows them to specify a size smaller than normal for Windows users, whose text tends to display larger than on Mac-

intosh systems (see the sidebar "Why Windows Web Pages Have Tiny Text" for more information on platform text differences). Unfortunately, GoLive strips out the Basefont tag and adjusts the page's other text sizes accordingly. (It's for our benefit that it does this—of course! But a switch to turn off this behavior would be nice, too.)

HTML also supports two additional text size tags, Big and Small, which change the current size by one increment. These, too, are changed to Font tag Size attributes.

The only workaround is to add Noedit tags to ensure that GoLive doesn't mess with the text. An example would be:

```
<NOEDIT><BASEFONT="2"></NOEDIT>
```

This becomes unwieldy in the Layout Editor, which no longer displays the text the way you want it—defeating at least part of the idea of visual Web page editing. But at least it leaves your code intact.

istically, based on the text-size settings in most Web browsers. This way, it doesn't matter how large your monitor is, or whether you're viewing it at its maximum resolution—the text on a Web page is almost guaranteed to be readable.

Choose from seven sizes by using the Relative Font Size popup menu on the Toolbar, or the Size submenu under the Style menu; the default text size is three (see Figure 7-8).

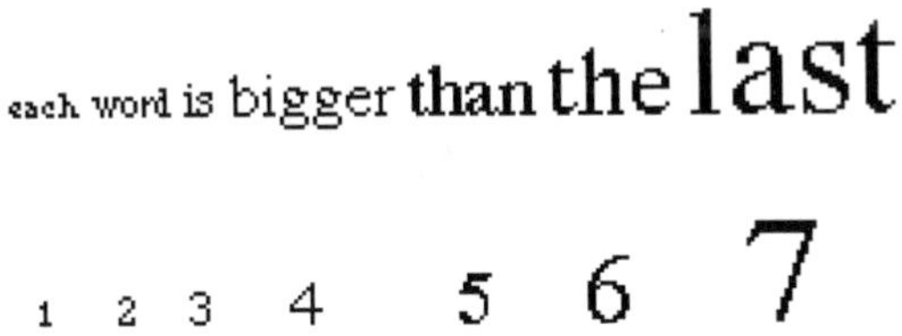

Figure 7-8
Text sizes

each word is bigger than the last

1 2 3 4 5 6 7

Absolute versus relative text sizes in HTML. There are two ways to express font size within HTML. Absolute sizing specifies a number on the 1-7 scale; relative sizing tells the browser to use a size that's equal to a number more or less than the browser's default font size.

In reality, each method is somewhat relative, since there's no way outside of using CSS to define a specific point size (or even a specific number of pixels tall). So, if you've set your browser to display a larger font size by default (like the "large" option in Internet Explorer, or a larger point size in Netscape Navigator's preferences), the browser is always computing the correct size based on those settings. In the code, however, the difference is plain: absolute sizes are referenced by their number, while relative sizes look like this:

```
<FONT SIZE="+2">
```

Glancing at the results in most browsers, there seems to be no difference. Assuming that a browser is using "3" as the default, specifying a size of "+2" or "5" achieves the same results. The difference comes when the user selects a new browser default font size. In this case, assuming the new default is "4," the absolute size of "5" still renders text at what the browser knows to be a size of "5". The relative size comes out at "6" instead, being two more than the default size (see Figure 7-9).

Figure 7-9
Absolute and relative text sizes

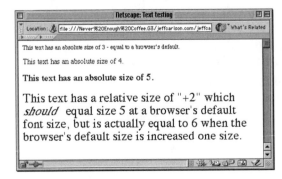

Why Windows Web Pages Have Tiny Text

by Geoff Duncan, Technical Editor,
TidBITS *(http://www.tidbits.com/)*

Most Macintosh users have encountered Web pages with unbearably tiny text. If you haven't, spend a few minutes browsing Microsoft's Web site (http://www.microsoft.com/windows/)—especially pages devoted to Windows itself—where it's not uncommon for Mac users to see text one to four pixels in height.

This phenomenon isn't limited to the Web. Do all Windows users have some sort of telescopic vision that makes text appear larger to them?

Why, yes. They do.

Making points. The confusion begins with a unit almost everyone uses: the point. People use points every day, choosing a 12-point font for a letter, or a 36-point font for a headline. But do you know what a point is?

Many people tell you that a point is $1/72$-inch. That's correct, but only for the imaging systems used in most computers (including Apple's QuickDraw and Adobe's PostScript). Outside of a computer, the definition of a point varies between different measurement systems, none of which put a point precisely equal to $1/72$-inch.

For the purposes of understanding why text on Windows Web pages often looks too small on a Macintosh, you can do the same thing your computer does: assume there are 72 points to an inch.

Not your type. When you refer to text of a particular point size, you're describing the height of the text, rather than its width or the dimensions of a particular character (or glyph) in a typeface. So, if there are 72 points to an inch, you might think 72-point characters would be one inch in height—

but you'd almost always be wrong. The maximum height of text is measured from the top of a typeface's highest ascender (generally a lowercase d or l, or a capital letter) to the bottom of the face's lowest descender (usually a lowercase j or y). Most glyphs in a typeface use only a portion of this total height and thus are less than one inch in height at 72 points.

With that in mind, how does a computer use this information to display text on a monitor?

Let's say you're writing a novel, and you set your chapter titles in 18 point text. First, the computer needs to know how tall 18 points is. Since the computer believes there are 72 points in an inch, this is easy: 18 points is $18/72$-inch, or exactly one-quarter inch. The computer then proceeds to draw text on your screen that's one-quarter-inch high.

This is where the universe gets strange. Your computer thinks of your monitor as a Cartesian grid made up of pixels or "dots." To a computer, your display is so many pixels wide by so many pixels tall, and everything on your screen is drawn using pixels. Thus, the physical resolution of your display can be expressed in pixels per inch (ppi) or, more commonly, dots per inch (dpi).

To draw 18-point text that's one-quarter inch in height, your computer needs to know how many pixels fit into a quarter inch. To find out, you'd think your computer would talk to your display about its physical resolution—but you'd be wrong. Instead, your computer makes a patent, nearly pathological *assumption* about how many pixels fit into an inch, regardless of your monitor size, resolution, or anything else.

If you use a Mac, your computer always assumes your monitor displays 72 pixels per inch, or 72 dpi. If you use Windows, your computer most often assumes your monitor displays 96 pixels per inch (96 dpi), but if you're using "large fonts" Windows assumes it can display 120 pixels per inch (120 dpi). These assumptions mean a Macintosh uses 18 pixels to render 18-point text, a Windows system typically uses 24 pixels, a Unix system typically uses between 19 and 25 pixels, and a Windows system using a large fonts setting uses 30 pixels.

Size does matter. This leads to the answer to our $20 question: why text on Web pages designed for Windows users often looks tiny on a Mac. Say your computer's display—or Web browser's window—measures 640 by 480 pixels. Leaving aside menu bars, title bars, and other screen clutter, the Mac can display 40 lines of 12-point text in that area (with solid leading, meaning there's no extra space between the lines).

Under the same conditions, Windows displays a mere 32 lines of text; since Windows uses more pixels to draw its text, less text fits in the same area (see Figure 7-10). Thus, Windows-based Web designers often specify small font sizes to jam more text into a fixed area, and Macintosh users get a double whammy: text that was already displaying using fewer pixels on a Macintosh screen is further reduced in size, even to the point where the text is illegible to even those with the best eyesight.

The fundamental issue is that the computer is trying to map a physical measurement—the point—to a display device with unknown physical characteristics. A standard computer monitor is basically an analog projection system: although its geometry can be adjusted to varying degrees, the monitor itself has no idea how many pixels it's showing over a particular physical distance.

Thus, in terms of raw pixels, most Windows users see text that's 33 percent larger than text on a Macintosh—from a Macintosh point of view, Windows users do, in fact, see text with telescopic vision. When you view the results on a single display where all pixels are the same size, the differences range from noticeable to dramatic. The Windows text is huge, or the Mac text is tiny—take your pick.

[This sidebar was adapted from a longer article first published in TidBITS #467/15-Feb-97, copyright 1998 TidBITS Electronic Publishing. To read the entire article, go to http://db.tidbits.com/getbits.acgi?tbart=05284]

Figure 7-10
Text size differences between Mac and Windows

Both screens viewed in Internet Explorer with the text size set to Medium.

If you prefer to use relative sizes, follow the steps below to change the settings in GoLive's powerful Web Database.

1. Open the Web Database by selecting it from the Special menu, or pressing Command-4 (Mac) or Control-4 (Windows).

2. Switch to the HTML tab, and expand the Inline Styles section.

3. Select the "font" entry (don't expand it, just highlight it).

4. Check the Write Font Sizes Relative box.

Lists and Indents

Without the margin and indent features of a word processor, formatting list material would be a frustrating endeavor. Fortunately, GoLive supports and previews HTML's list features, making it easy to create not only typical lists of items, but also to use lists for presentation purposes.

Numbered List. To create a list that includes numbers before each paragraph, highlight the text and click the Numbered List button on the Toolbar, or select Default Numbered List from the List submenu of the Format menu. You can choose which style of numbering you want displayed by choosing the other options from the same menu (see Figure 7-11).

Tip: No Need to Select All Text

Since lists are a paragraph (or block) setting, you don't need to make sure every character in a paragraph is selected before applying the list level commands. As long as a portion of the paragraph is selected, the entire block between returns is formatted in the list style.

Unnumbered List. If your list isn't dependent on numbering, create an unnumbered list by clicking the Unnumbered List button on the Toolbar or selecting Default Unnumbered List from the List submenu of the format menu. In this case, you can choose among bullets, circles, or squares.

Figure 7-11
List types

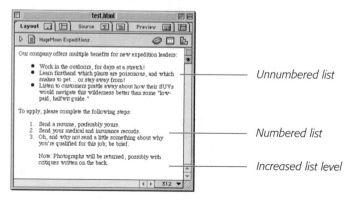

Unnumbered list

Numbered list

Increased list level

Tip: CSS
Bullets With CSS, you can specify a wider variety of bullets for unnumbered lists, including images you specify yourself. However, no browser we know of supports this very cool design feature yet.

Increasing and decreasing list levels. One advantage to using lists is that you don't have to precede each item with a number or bullet; a list can just as easily serve as an indented margin for the selected range of text. Click the Increase List Level button on the Toolbar or select it from the Format menu's List submenu to push the text horizontally to the right. The Decrease List Level button and menu item move the text back toward the left margin.

Tip:
Removing
Bullets or
Numbers You'd think that turning a list back into regular text would be a matter of clicking the Numbered List or Unnumbered List buttons to toggle the setting, but that's not the case. To rid your text of bullets or numbering, use Decrease List Level instead.

Term and Definition. Harking back to its academic origins, HTML includes the capability to define terms and definitions (structural formatting). Select part of a paragraph and choose Term from the List submenu of the Format menu to tag it as a term; the appearance doesn't change in the Layout Editor. To create a definition for the term, select the text and choose Definition from the same menu. This action formats the text indented from the left margin without the vertical space imposed by normal paragraphs (see Figure 7-12).

Figure 7-12
Terms and
definitions

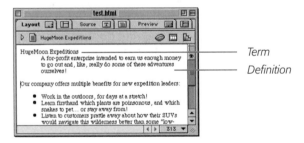

Indenting using horizontal spacers. Another method of indenting text is the use of HTML-defined spacers called Horizontal Spacers in GoLive. Despite their name, these spacers are not limited to being just horizontal.

Tip: Spacers
are Netscape
Only The downside to spacers is that they're currently only recognized by Netscape browsers, limiting their usefulness across a broad range of viewers.

Double-click the Horizontal Spacer icon from the Basic tab of the Palette, or drag it to the Layout Editor to add a spacer. You can specify its width in the Spacer Inspector to create a single line indent by changing the value in the Width field or stretching the spacer element by its object handle. A spacer also can be set to

Vertical, which fills the length of the text and offers a variable height value; or Block, which creates a rectangular space that can be aligned like an image (see Figure 7-13).

Figure 7-13
Horizontal
Spacer tag

Spacers work in Netscape browsers, above, but not in Internet Explorer, right.

Text Color

A page's default text color can be set in the Page Inspector, but there are times when you may want to apply local color formatting within the body text.

Applying text color. To color a range of text, first select it in the Layout Editor, then choose a color from one of the Color Palette's tabs. Drag the color swatch from the preview pane and drop it anywhere on the selected text to apply the new color (see Figure 7-14).

Be sure to select your text before coloring it; if you drag a swatch to the Layout Editor with nothing selected, GoLive just inserts the word "Color" with that color applied to the text.

If you're editing text in the HTML Source Editor and don't know the hex value of a specific color, dropping a color swatch in your text inserts the following code, which you can use in a FONT tag:

```
COLOR="[hex value]"
```

Tip: When Adding "Color" Is Helpful

A common user frustration with GoLive is dragging a color swatch from the Color Palette and dropping it on the page without any text selected (or missing the selected text due to poor reflexes, cats jumping onto the computer, etc.). However, inserting the word "Color" in a selected color can actually come in handy. If you don't currently have active text, but want to establish a page's colors, drag swatches to wherever you like. Then, simply double-click the word "Color" and paste or type the intended text. This avoids having to select text ranges, jump to the Color Palette, then jump back to the page with a color in tow.

Removing text color. If you decide that colors just aren't working visually within your text, highlight the colored area and select Remove Color from the Style menu to return to the page's default text color.

Figure 7-14
Coloring text

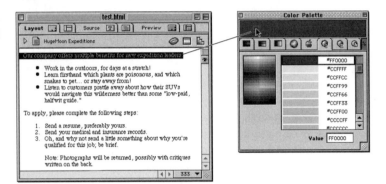

Using Fonts

A welcome change in modern Web browsers is the ability to specify typefaces other than the limited selection used in a browser's preferences. Just as color and text formatting can affect the tone and presentation of your text, using different fonts adds to the character of Web pages. Font support also allows you to use faces such as Verdana or Georgia that were created specifically for onscreen reading.

The downside to using fonts in your Web documents is there's no guarantee that everyone viewing your page has the font you've specified installed on their system. However, this doesn't turn out to be too much of a downside (maybe it's more of a slightly-vertically-declined plane?) because of the flexible way HTML handles font selection.

Specifying Fonts

Before leaping into how GoLive handles font selection, we quickly need to explain how Web browsers treat fonts. As with text size, typefaces are defined using the Font tag, which tells the browser which font to use for the text that follows it. But if the viewer's computer doesn't have that face installed, they see only the default text—still acceptable, but misses the mark on communicating the designer's vision. That's why designers typically define *several* fonts in the Font tag, separated by commas; a Web browser looks at the first font listed, and uses it if it's installed. If it's not installed, the browser moves on to the next font, then the next, and the next, until either a match is found or the list ends, at which point the default font comes back into play. For greater compatibility, designers choose fonts that are more likely to be installed on users' machines, such as the faces used by the operating system. In HTML, the code looks something like this:

```
<FONT face="Helvetica, Arial, sans serif">
```

In this example, most browsers and platforms are accounted for: Helvetica ships with the Mac OS, Arial is a default Windows font, and "sans serif" is a general descriptor that tells the browser to use whichever font has been set up for sans-serif use in its preferences.

GoLive recognizes the fonts in these types of groupings, called "fontsets," in order to present the most compatible front to its Web pages.

Applying fontsets. That said, styling text in a particular font is an easy task: select a font by going to the Style menu, then navigate to the Font submenu. The active fontsets are noted only by the name of the first font in the set, but the backup font options get applied as well (see Figure 7-15).

Figure 7-15
Applying
a fontset

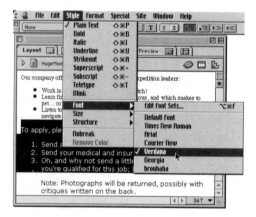

Editing Fontsets

GoLive is preconfigured with three common fontsets that all but ensure that any viewer sees the fonts displayed. Although they work well, we have enough typographical sense behind our eyeballs to want to customize the fontsets and use other typefaces (see the sidebar, "Seen Onscreen").

**Tip: Local,
Global, and
Sitewide
Fontsets**

GoLive tracks three kinds of fontsets: local to the page, global to the program (any page opened in the program), and specific to a site. Both global and local fontsets show up above a dividing line in the Font submenu; site-specific sets show up below that line. We discuss working with global fontsets in Chapter 2, *The Inspector*; site fontsets are covered in Chapter 17, *Sitewide Sets*.

Font Set Editor. To edit or create fontsets, choose Edit Font Sets from the Font submenu of the Style menu. Specify either default fontsets (or global fontsets), which appear on the Font list in every GoLive document, or page sets, which are used only for the frontmost open document. Click a set in the Font Sets pane at left to view its contents in the Font Names pane to the right (see Figure 7-16).

Figure 7-16
Editing
fontsets

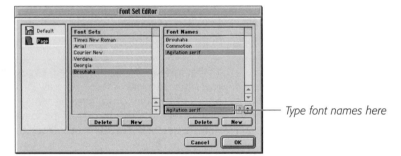

Type font names here

To create a new, empty fontset, click the New button at left. A new font (appropriately named "New Font") appears at right. Type the name of the font you want to use, then press Enter; since that's the first font in the new set, the set takes its name. If you want to add more fonts, simply click the New button beneath the Font Names pane and type their names in the field below. You can also click the popup menu to the right of the field and select fonts that are currently installed on your system.

Seen Onscreen

Most of the fonts installed on your computer herald from a long history of printed typography. Being able to view on your computer screen close approximations of what a typeface would look like when printed was one of the strengths behind early desktop publishing. The problem is, those fonts were designed with print in mind, and aren't necessarily designed to be read in great quantity onscreen.

With the popularity of CD-ROM-based multimedia and the Web, typographers are devoting more efforts to making fonts that read better onscreen—some of which may never see the printed page. After a bit of trial and error, we've become partial to a handful of faces that we use when de-

signing for (and browsing) the Web, reading email every day, and using word processors. Favorite faces include Microsoft's free fonts Verdana and Georgia; Adobe and Bitstream's Minion Web and Myriad Web; and Apple's venerable New York and occasionally even Geneva.

Each of these feature, on average, a taller x-height (the vertical measurement of a lower-case letters), roomier letterspacing, and a pixel-level attention to detail that avoids misshapen or overly jagged letters. If you've been suffering with Times all this time, try a font that's been designed expressly for onscreen reading; the difference is an eye-opener (and an eye-saver).

When you're finished, click OK. As far as we can tell, you can enter as many fonts as you like, or stick with only one. With your fontsets created, apply them from the Font menu as normal.

Tip: Careful Typing Produces Better Typography	When you type the names in the Font Names field, it doesn't matter whether you have these fonts installed on your system, or whether the fonts exist at all. GoLive assumes that you know what you're typing, and accepts it. If you make a spelling mistake or typo, such as "New Yurk" instead of "New York," a Web browser looks for New Yurk, then moves on to the next font in the list.
Tip: Default and Page Sets Don't Mingle	If you want to create a set that appears in both the current page and GoLive's fontset defaults, you have to create the set twice. There's no way to create one and then duplicate it to the other except by hand. Also, creating a new default set doesn't make it appear in the page set, even though by definition the page becomes subordinate to the default; you must quit and relaunch GoLive for it to show up.
Tip: Make Your Fonts Available	If you're worried someone may not possess the font you have in mind for your page, consider using one that is freely accessible. Microsoft has made several fonts, such as Verdana, Georgia, and Trebuchet, available as free downloads from its Web site at http://www.micosoft.com/typography/; they're also now added when you install a recent version of Internet Explorer or Outlook Express. The downloads are fairly small, so your viewers can install them easily and return to your site later to get the full effect of what you've designed.
Tip: Where There's a Will-Harris…	If you want to know anything or everything about fonts and the Web, consult the digital font guru Daniel Will-Harris's Web site at http://www.will-harris.com. Dan was one of Glenn's first Web hosting clients back in 1994, but we're not biased. Dan's Esperfonto project, his numerous columns, and other interesting items (pickles? chocolate sauce?) at his site, are worth a long, involved look.

Zapfing Early Internet Explorer Users

The Font tag's Face attribute made its first appearance in Internet Explorer, which—at the time, not so long ago—was a small player and the object of scorn and laughter by millions of loyal Netscape Navigator users. (Who now find themselves in a surprisingly shrunken minority.) Once they found out they could specify any font on a person's system, some pages began showing up filled with unreadable characters: they had set a Face attribute at the beginning of the text so that the iconographic fonts Zapf Dingbats and Wingdings were displayed. Netscape users were unaffected, because their browsers didn't display fonts other than the ones specified in the preferences. Of course, this is now irrelevant since modern Web browsers recognize the Font tag…but sometimes it's good to know where you came from, isn't it?

You Look Simply… Fontastic

Text on the Web used to be about as exciting as the endless columns of copy on old-time newspapers: it seemed to go on and on and on, without offering any pizzazz. What most people don't realize is that a lot of hard work went into making those newspaper columns as readable as possible—legibility wasn't sacrificed, just a bit of excitement. The Web, finally, is reaching the point where legibility and control can co-exist, and the presentation of type can be just as interesting as the snazziest graphics.

CHAPTER 8
Images

The Web existed before it could handle images, but it wasn't considered very exciting. To make it more useful, the early Web browser engineers threw in the ability to display poor resolution, limited-color-range images at excruciatingly low speeds and—presto—the commercial Web was suddenly hot property. Folks began banging down the doors to be let in, no matter how slow it was.

Combining images with text on the same page also marked the beginning of wide-scale online publishing and opened the field for graphic designers to make an impact. You can only simulate graphics with text for just so long.

Before visual page editors existed, adding images to a page with hand coding was a laborious process. GoLive, in contrast, lets you add images by dragging them from the desktop or Site window, or by browsing local hard drives and other resources.

Once an image is on a page, you can assign attributes like alignment and spacing via the Image Inspector, letting you immediately see how the changes appear on the page.

Image Formats

Before the Web, bigger seemed better: larger images had more resolution, and image formats that were *lossless*—that is, preserved all the data and color variation in an image—were always better. But the Web has shaken things up. The relatively small amount of bandwidth available to most Web users gets overwhelmed by the size of most uncompressed, full-resolution, high-fidelity color images. Obviously, some kind of accommodation has to be made.

To that end, two image formats, GIF and JPEG, rose to the top. GIF was the first format that the earliest graphical Web browser Mosaic supported, and for better or for worse, we're stuck with it. JPEG, on the other hand, offers some superior tradeoffs for quality of an image versus its size, and as more users' system can handle displaying a few thousand or more colors on their monitors at once, its use has really taken off. PNG, a third format designed from the ground up to meet the needs of Web users, offers a variety of tradeoffs among compression, color palette, and image quality. Although PNG has found some takers, many browsers can't display PNG images.

GoLive doesn't have the ability to edit images directly—otherwise, why would we all have so many megabytes of Adobe Photoshop or CorelDraw sitting on our systems?—but it's helpful to know the advantages and limitations of each format to get the best performance out of your pages.

GIF. Images saved as GIF (Graphics Interchange Format, pronounced "jiff") files are the universal language of the Web, with all browsers in all versions displaying almost all kinds of GIFs. The GIF format compresses data in two ways: first, by reducing the number of colors in the image to a palette of no more than 256 different colors, meaning that color takes less space to store; and second, by analyzing patterns of repeated color and replacing them with tokens that take up much less space (see Figure 8-1). Line art, like logos or simple drawings, work best when saved as GIF files.

GIFs also support two extra features, both of which are useful for Web page design. You can set a transparent color in a GIF so that the background shows through, allowing you to simulate layering an image over other images or a background. And you can include multiple frames in a single GIF to provide simple animation; many Web ad banners use GIFs to cycle through a message.

JPEG. For images that are more "photographic" in nature, turn to JPEG (Joint Photographic Experts Group, the body that came up with the specification). JPEG is a *lossy* compression format, meaning that the algorithm that creates the JPEG

Figure 8-1
GIF image

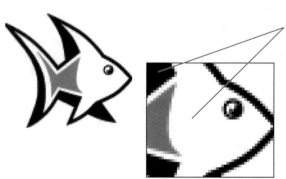

Large areas of solid color, combined with a low number of colors in the image, make logos and line-art excellent candidates for the GIF format.

is a *lossy* compression format, meaning that the algorithm that creates the JPEG throws away information when creating the compressed image file. The JPEG algorithm can provide more or less faithful color and image quality on a sliding scale from most faithful, in which the most accurate representation of the image is created at about a 2 to 1 ratio, to least faithful, in which visible artifacts in the image show, including pixelization, but the ratio can be as high as 100 to 1. JPEG uses a perceptual system so that the least important color distinctions are removed first; it also has built-in compression to further reduce the amount of space the final data takes up.

Although it sounds like the end result would resemble a patchwork of pixels, JPEGs can be surprisingly accurate to the original image while being drastically reduced in file size (see Figure 8-2). JPEG images don't support transparency or animation, however.

Figure 8-2
JPEG image

JPEG compression actually degrades the quality of your image (compare the original at left to the JPEG version at right), but does so in a way that is barely detectable to most viewers depending on the level of compression.

PNG. The newcomer to the graphics world is PNG (Portable Network Graphics), pronounced "ping." PNG images compress slightly better than GIF images (anywhere from five to 25 percent improvement), and feature alpha-channel transparency like Photoshop's (providing more options than GIF's one-bit transparency), gamma correction, and improved interlacing for faster perceived downloading. PNG offers completely faithful image reproduction in which no color or quality is lost; or, you can use a GIF-like palette to reduce the colors to 256 or fewer.

The problem, so far, is that PNG has yet to be fully adopted by the major Web browsers. Netscape Communicator, for example, can view inline PNG graphics, but doesn't support alpha-channel transparency as of this writing. And at least 25 percent of browsers still in general use can't display PNG images in any form. There's little doubt that PNG will be the wave of the future; it offers too many features that designers would love to take advantage of. Adoption of the format will take some time, however. For a more detailed look at the PNG specification, see http://www.cdrom.com/pub/png/png.html.

Tip: Patent Medicine   The PNG format arose for a reason in addition to building a format specifically for the Web: patent payments. Both GIF and JPEG are encumbered with patent licensing and payment issues that make it virtually impossible to release entirely free, non-problematic versions of source code for programs that create and/or read GIF and JPEG images. PNG is purposely designed to use only public-domain algorithms and requires no licensing fees for any part of its system.

Inserting Images

Like most page elements in GoLive, inserting an image is a simple drag-and-drop operation. Drag the Image icon from the Basics tab of the Palette to a location on the Layout Editor; you can also double-click the Image icon to insert an image placeholder.

If you're in the HTML Source Editor, you can also drag or double-click the Image icon to insert the appropriate HTML code into the document. All of these actions insert a blank image placeholder sized to match the icon's dimensions (32 pixels square).

Enter the pathname of the image you want to use in the Source field of the Image Inspector's Basic tab, click the Browse button to locate the file, or use the Point & Shoot tool to specify a source image (see Figure 8-3).

Figure 8-3
Inserting images

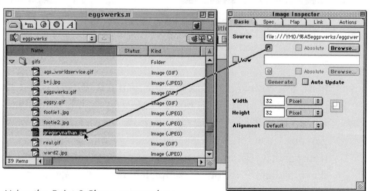

Using the Point & Shoot approach to grab an image from the Site window

If you already know which graphic file you want to use, you can drag it from the Desktop or the Site window to the Layout Editor. Unlike inserting an image placeholder, however, dragging an image file directly to the HTML Source Editor creates a link to the file, not the code required to display the image.

Drag-and-Drop Importing

When we're in the middle of planning a site, we create hundreds of sample pages and images to test our ideas and their iterations. Before having GoLive at hand, testing and development meant lots of time in Photoshop converting all our graphics—even the scrap ones we knew weren't going to be final production images—to GIF or JPEG format just to view them in a Web browser. As you might expect, that took time, even after automating the process as much as we could with Photoshop Actions.

But now we have software that understands the different stages of workflow. GoLive lets you import any PICT, TIFF, or BMP (a Windows bitmap format) image file directly into the Layout Editor: simply press Command-Option (Mac) or Control-Alt (Windows) as you drag. You can also drag an image from an open Photoshop document without using a key combination.

Depending on your image settings in GoLive's preferences (see below), the file is converted to a temporary GIF, JPEG, or PNG file. The image isn't production-quality—you won't want to upload it to your site for use—but it's certainly good enough for roughing out your ideas. Plus, you don't have to switch gears and do the image conversion yourself, but rather stick with the task at hand.

Tip: Merge Layers in Photoshop for Import

It's a rare day when we don't have Photoshop and GoLive open simultaneously, so it's great to drag from one to the other to create test images. Be aware, though, that when you drag from Photoshop, only the active layer of a multi-layered image is imported into GoLive (see Figure 8-4).

If you need the composite image, be sure to merge the layers before dragging; you can always select Undo in Photoshop to get your layers back, or, since you were no doubt smart enough to save your file before merging, select Revert to go to the last saved version. Any transparent pixels in Photoshop are changed to white during import, and only the size of the active image (not the entire canvas) is copied into the GoLive document.

Figure 8-4
Dragging active layer

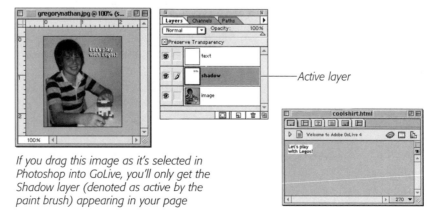

If you drag this image as it's selected in Photoshop into GoLive, you'll only get the Shadow layer (denoted as active by the paint brush) appearing in your page

The converted files are stored in the Import Images folder, which is located in the same folder as your GoLive application; they're given names like "image-1275542589.gif". You can choose to control whether they are imported as GIF, JPEG, or PNG files by opening GoLive's Preferences window and choosing a format from the File Format options in the General pane's Image settings. Or, you can click the Ask User button to be prompted each time you import a file. (See Chapter 4, *Preferences and Customizing.*)

Tip: Import Images Files Aren't Uploaded	Converted files usually aren't high-quality versions of the originals, but there's another reason you don't want to rely on them as final images on your page: Files in the Import Images folder aren't recognized if you're uploading your site using GoLive's Upload to Server function (Chapter 18, *Staging and Synchronizing Sites*). You should create final versions by the time the site goes live, but if you're staging draft pages on a Web server for a client, you need to manually move the temporary files to another location where GoLive recognizes them as valid files the next time you upload the site. For this reason, we like to employ the Ask User setting in GoLive's image preferences to specify a folder in our site's directory. (We usually name that location something like "tempgifs" to keep them separate from the final files.) Alternately, you can change the location of the import folder in the preferences, but that can get hairy if you're working on multiple sites concurrently.
Tip: Clean Up Leftover Image Placeholders	When you have image preferences set to Ask User and then import an image using drag and drop, be sure to delete the image placeholder icon that was created to store the image if you decide to cancel the operation. Otherwise, you wind up with an orphaned image placeholder that's not connected to any object.

Image Attributes

Control over the display of images has rapidly become one of the factors that sets the newer browsers apart from the older ones. The newest HTML specifications and the newest extra features in browsers offer a huge number of settings that let you better control the appearance of an image. Some options have been around since practically the beginning of the visual Web; others are more recent. A few features are dedicated to improving how quickly or crisply browsers display images.

Width and height. It's our shared opinion that every Web page should include the height and width tags for every image; fortunately, GoLive offers this feature by default when an image is placed or imported. Providing width and height measurements to browsers helps speed up page loading because the browser doesn't have to retrieve images to know their size, which speeds up the page's display.

Tip:
Dimensions
in Files
GIF, JPEG, and PNG image file formats all list their dimensions in the first few characters of the data that comprises the file. But the browser still has to retrieve part or all of the file before it grabs that information if you don't specify width and height.

GoLive automatically pulls the height and width values from each image when placed on the page and displays the information on the Basic tab of the Image Inspector. If you really don't want the values to appear, select Image from the Height and Width popup menus, and GoLive leaves the fields blank.

Tip: Other
Dimensions
If you edit the height and width that GoLive fills in for the image, a browser resizes the image to fit the dimensions you specified. See "Resizing Images," below.

Border. HTML provides a method for drawing borders around images, but we guess that 90 percent of border usage is to apply a setting of "0" to help suppress the ugly blue line that shows up around linked graphics by default when no border is specified (see "Linking Images" later in this chapter). If you want a border of greater than zero to appear, enter a number in the Border field to specify the border's width in pixels (see Figure 8-5). If the image is linked, the border displays as the page's link color; otherwise, it shows up as the page's text color. (See Chapter 2, *The Inspector*, for how to set a page's link and text colors.)

Alt. The Alt attribute holds text that gets displayed before images load on a page or when the user doesn't want to or can't load images. In GoLive, you set the Alt attribute through the Alt Text field, located on the Spec. tab of the Image Inspector.

The Alt text is usually a description of the image that should load in its place, giving the viewer a quick preview of what's to appear while waiting for the rest of the graphics and text to load (see Figure 8-5). Adding Alt tags to your images also

Figure 8-5
Image
Inspector Spec.
settings

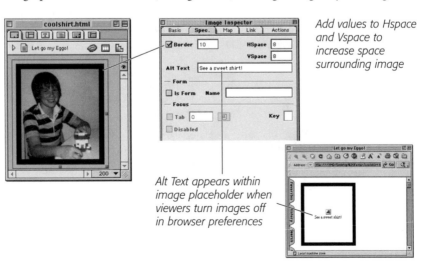

Add values to Hspace and Vspace to increase space surrounding image

Alt Text appears within image placeholder when viewers turn images off in browser preferences

makes your page more accessible for those text-only Web warriors who surf with images turned off or in the pure text Lynx browser for Unix (we know several people who prefer to surf the Web this way, especially on slower modem connections). It's also a great aid to the visually impaired who require non-graphical elements to navigate a page.

Hspace and Vspace. These attributes define the space, in pixels, that pads the image from surrounding text or other items; Hspace adds space both to the left and right of an image, while Vspace adds it to the top and bottom (see Figure 8-5). The two corresponding fields are found in the Spec. tab. Padding an image comes in handy when wrapping text around an image, so the text and the picture aren't crammed against each other.

Tip: Padding with Pixels Because the Hspace and Vspace options add space to both directions of an image, not just either side, we prefer using a transparent GIF to the right of a flush-left image, or to the left of a flush-right one. This allows us to space just in one direction and leave the other flush with the margin.

Lowsource Images

Speed is everything when it comes to Web graphics. You want your viewer to see the page as fast as possible, but not everyone has a fast connection to the Internet—yet. And although you can optimize most graphics down to a small number of bytes, some images just end up large enough that it's going to take time for most users to download and display them.

One perceptual trick to get around this dilemma is to offer sneak-peek versions of your graphics that are small enough to download quickly, but take up the same space and contain the same image as the higher resolution graphic (see Figure 8-6). Typically, these "lowsource" images (defined in HTML as "lowsrc") are black and white to keep the file size smaller; sometimes the lowsource is a 1-bit

Figure 8-6
Generating
lowsource
images

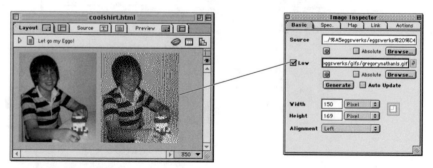

*Original image (left) and generated
lowsource image (right)*

GIF, while the full-resolution image is a 24-bit color JPG. The browser shows the smaller image first, and then displays the higher-resolution image on top of it when it's done loading. (Or, if it's a progressively saved image, as it starts to load.)

If you've created your own lowsource image, click the Low box in the Image Inspector's Basic tab to specify the file.

Tip: Use Any Image as Lowsource   Although the purpose of using lowsource images is to load a preview version of a graphic quickly, you actually can specify any graphic as a lowsource image. Some designers have used this to create some beautiful and surprising effects.

Generating lowsource images. GoLive can generate a lowsource image for you when you click the Generate button.

By default, the lowsource image GoLive creates is a black-and-white GIF that exists in the same directory as the original image. In GoLive's preferences, you can choose to save lowsource files in the Import Images folder—but see "Tip: Import Images Files Aren't Uploaded," earlier in this chapter, before you do. You can also set whether the preview image is rendered in black and white or color. If you check the Auto-Generate by Default box, GoLive creates lowsource images for every graphic you place on your pages.

Tip: Clever Color Previews   GoLive features a clever way to create color lowsource images. Since GIFs compress best when they have a limited number of colors, black and white images are great because they feature only two. What GoLive does for color images is reduce the color palette; it also shrinks the image down to half the size of the original, thereby reducing the number of pixels in the file. When displayed at the same size as the original, you get a rough preview that's still in color, but also loads quickly.

Tip: Animated GIF Lowsource   GoLive generates a lowsource GIF of any image you throw at it, even animated GIFs. However, only the first frame of the animation is rendered as the lowsource, not the full series of frames.

Resizing Images

As you should expect from a visual editor, GoLive supports resizing any images you place on a page. You can stretch, squash, or proportionally resize them to your heart's content.

However, we suggest thinking twice before publishing a page with images that have been resized in GoLive (or any visual editor, for that matter). The problem with resizing is that Web browsers generally don't display resized images very well because they're trying to compensate for the graphic's new size based on the limited amount of information available in the original. Also, a browser is not Photoshop: it doesn't have the algorithms and tools inside it to provide the kind of resampling and smoothing that a photo-editing program can.

Resized images, though not horrible, do tend to appear blocky or have misplaced pixels—a trained Web designer can usually spot immediately if the height and width values in the HTML don't match the intrinsic dimensions of the graphic. Plus, you're asking the browser to do extra work, which can slow its rendering time, making viewers wait a bit longer to see a full page. For finished pages, it's always better to resize the original in a true image editor, then save it as a new file (like "doggy_sm.gif").

Tip: Resize While Designing

We don't want to make a blanket statement that resizing in GoLive is a bad tool. Like the feature for importing images using drag and drop, resizing images is good for mocking up pages during development; it allows you to experiment with different image sizes and placement on the page without having to create multiple resized versions. Just remember to create a final image that matches the final specifications you choose.

Resizing in the Image Inspector. To change the dimensions of an image, enter new values in the Width and Height fields in the Basics tab. When the values don't match the graphic's actual measurements, a resize warning icon appears in a corner of the image (see Figure 8-7). Clicking the resize icon to the right of the fields returns the image back to its original dimensions and proportion.

Figure 8-7
Resizing images

Resize warning icon appears in image…

…and resize warning button becomes active in Image Inspector

You can also choose to express the dimensions in percentages by selecting Percent from the popup menus to the right of the Height and Width fields. Be aware, however, that you're not specifying a percentage of the original image size, but a percentage of the *page*. So, an image with a width set to 100 percent would fill the width of the entire window when viewed in a Web browser (see Figure 8-8).

If you'd rather not include the size values at all, select Image from the popup menus to remove the values and return the image to its actual dimensions.

Resizing using object handles. Dragging an image's object handles also resizes the image, allowing you to change the size manually without using the Image Inspector's

Figure 8-8
Choosing percent for width and height

Choosing Percent in the Width and Height popup menus causes the image to resize in relation to the size of the browser window when viewed.

numeric values. To resize the image proportionally, press the Shift key while dragging. Pressing the Control key lets you preview the image dynamically as it resizes, rather than displaying a bounding box to indicate the dimensions (see Figure 8-9).

If you've opted to resize the image using percentage values, you can't use object handles to manipulate the graphic.

Aligning Images

As with text, you can specify how an image is aligned on the page. However, image alignment offers more than just the ability to push a picture to one side of the screen or the other; text can wrap around aligned images.

Unlike placing images in a page-layout program, images on the Web are treated as if they were just another character or element. (They were originally called "in-line images," which fell out of fashion some time ago.) In fact, before browsers featured object alignment, pictures would display at the beginning, end, or sometimes

Figure 8-9
Dynamically resizing images

Dragging resize handle (left) displays only bounding box; Control-dragging the handle (right) dynamically resizes image in document.

in the middle of a line of text—resulting in uneven line spacing to compensate for the height of the graphics. So when you're specifying an image's alignment, what you're doing is telling a Web browser how the image should display in relation to the line of text where it's contained.

Tip: Place Images at the Front of the Line

You can put an image anywhere you like, but we prefer to position them at the beginning of a line or paragraph of text. If you're using left or right alignment (see below), text wrapping is much more consistent than if the image appears at the end of a paragraph. Keep in mind that a Web browser reads the page the same as you read text—left to right, top to bottom—and formats it accordingly.

With an image selected, choose one of the following options from the Basic tab's Alignment menu.

Left, Right. These are the most commonly used alignment settings, and it's plain to see why: text and other elements wrap around an image, making the best use of space and generally presenting a more professional look to the page (see Figure 8-10). Unlike the rest of the alignment options, left and right alignment can change the location of the image itself. Depending on the size of your image, the wrapping can be unflattering, so watch out for odd results. If several pictures are left-aligned without much text between them, an awkward stairstepping effect happens (see Figure 8-12 later in this chapter).

Figure 8-10
Aligning images

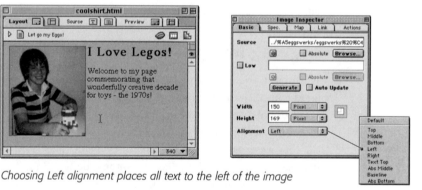

Choosing Left alignment places all text to the left of the image

Tip: Easy Margin Control Using Alignment

If you don't like the various ways HTML indents text (such as block indent or un-numbered lists as described in Chapter 7, *Text and Fonts*), you can control the size of a text margin by placing an aligned image to the left of it. Insert a transparent GIF at the beginning of the text section, and specify its height to be large enough to span the depth of the text; make its width the distance you want from the edge of the page's true margin. Then, set the image's alignment to Left or Right and watch the text snap into place. This won't work in all circumstances, since text sizes can vary widely among browsers and platforms, but it's often a simpler method than building tables or using other means.

Top, Middle, Bottom. Not surprisingly, these settings place text at the top, in the middle, or at the bottom of the image. That's fine for single lines of text, but if your graphic appears at the beginning of a paragraph, only the first line is affected; the rest of the paragraph in that case falls below the image (see Figure 8-11).

Figure 8-11
Top, Middle and Bottom alignment

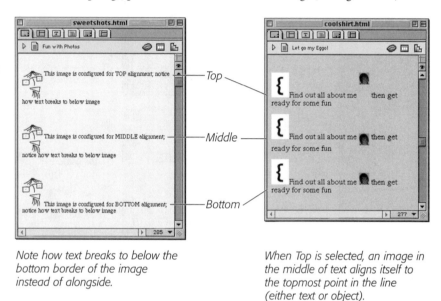

Note how text breaks to below the bottom border of the image instead of alongside.

When Top is selected, an image in the middle of text aligns itself to the topmost point in the line (either text or object).

Depending on the height of the line, however, these settings can position an image above or below the text surrounding it. For example, if the line of text includes a large image that increases the line height, placing a smaller image on the same line and setting its alignment to Top would align the tops of both images, lifting the second image high above the text (see Figure 8-12).

Text Top, Baseline. Images aligned to Text Top or Baseline stick to the height of the text, regardless of the text's line height (see Figure 8-13)

Figure 8-12
Stairstepping effect

With little accompanying text, series of images with left alignment bunch together

Abs Middle, Abs Bottom. This pair of alignment settings positions text and other elements at the absolute middle or bottom in relation to the aligned image, which may not necessarily be based on the midpoint of the text's height. This is often useful when centering graphic bullet images to text lines (see Figure 8-13).

Figure 8-13
Text Top, Abs
Middle, and
Two Bottoms

Text Top

Bottom

Abs Middle

Abs Bottom

Linking Images

Images can stand out from their surroundings in more effective ways than text. Also, most navigation systems tend to use images as buttons or other elements. So you frequently find yourself turning an image into a hypertext button, which, when clicked, works just like a text link. Any image can be turned into a link with a minimum of fuss.

With an image selected, select New Link from the Special menu, click the New Link button on the Toolbar, or click the New Link button in the Link tab of the Image Inspector. Then specify the link's destination using Point & Shoot navigation, clicking Browse and locating the file, or by entering the file's pathname in the URL field. If you want, enter the link's title text and a target for the link. By default, linked images appear with a three-pixel border to signify that a link exists. To remove the border, specify a border value of zero on the Spec tab of the Image Inspector.

Tip: Auto-Set Border to Zero

Unless you like having ugly blue boxes surround your linked images, be sure to set the image's Border setting to zero. The problem is, that means setting the value each time you place an image in GoLive. We hate repetition, which is why we were happy to discover another handy use for GoLive's Web Database feature (also see Chapter 27, *Web Database*). See "Image Link Border to Zero" in that chapter for instructions on resetting the border default for a new image link to anything you choose.

Imagemaps

One of the differences between the Web and full-screen multimedia development tools is that the Web doesn't let you define any area on the screen as a link, where most multimedia programs use the whole screen as an interface. However, the Web does let you turn images (which could take up an entire screen) into an analogue of multimedia by letting you define one, several, or dozens of areas on an image that each have separate links and other image properties.

These definable areas are called imagemaps; they've been around since near the dawn of the Web, and they're one of the most common tools to use with a site navigation strip or graphical interface on the Web.

You can define the regions in an imagemap using a variety of shapes, including rectangles, circles, and polygons. Each region's exact pixel coordinates at each point on the shape (or the oval's center point and width and height) are stored in the HTML file. When a Web browser is told that an image is acting as an imagemap, the browser examines the pixel location of where a user clicks, and loads the corresponding URL for that region.

Tip: Client-Side and Server-Side   In the olden days, imagemaps required a server to process the user's clicks—the imagemap's region file resided on a server and a special program there, often called htimage, handled the translation. These were called server-side imagemaps, as opposed to in-the-HTML client-side imagemaps. If you find old HTML files that still reference a server script, consult Chapter 20, *Importing a Site*, which offers a section on refurbishing drab old sites.

Before GoLive and other visual editors, building imagemaps required a third-party mapping program, or a great deal of patience and graph paper to calculate each region's coordinates by hand. Now, creating an imagemap is a matter of switching tabs in the Image Inspector. With an image selected, click the Map tab and check the Use Map box (see Figure 8-14). GoLive creates a name for the map based on the filename, but you may want to change the name to something that doesn't sound like the name of a future android's serial number.

To link a portion of an imagemap, use the region tools to highlight an area for the link and enter the destination address in the Map tab's URL field. The other fields for that region act the same as if you were defining a single image link.

Figure 8-14
Image Inspector's Map tab

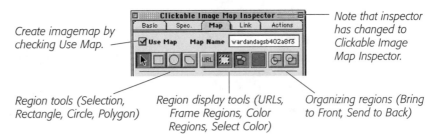

Create imagemap by checking Use Map.

Note that inspector has changed to Clickable Image Map Inspector.

Region tools (Selection, Rectangle, Circle, Polygon)

Region display tools (URLs, Frame Regions, Color Regions, Select Color)

Organizing regions (Bring to Front, Send to Back)

Tip: Grab Imagemaps by Their Edges If the Is Map box is checked, GoLive won't let you grab or move the image as you normally would. The internal area is reserved for the imagemap tools, which take over when your cursor is in that region. So, to select the image, click on its edge (the cursor changes into a gloved hand), then move or resize the image as normal.

Region Tools

The region tools are used to define and select areas in your image that lead to other URLs.

Selection tool. An all-purpose pointer, the Selection tool is used to select, move, and resize imagemap regions.

Rectangle and circle tools. Use these tools to create simple rectangular or circular regions (see Figure 8-15). Don't worry if the shapes you create aren't pixel-perfect; since imagemap areas aren't visible on the Web, they only need to cover the approximate area where you want the viewer to click to follow a link. The Circle tool creates only proportional circles, not ovals.

Tip: Windows Highlights Actually, the only time you might see imagemaps appear on the Web is when you tab through a page using Windows Internet Explorer or Netscape Navigator. Because Windows uses the Tab key to move from each link or field to the next, even the shapes on an imagemap can show up. We've seen some scary maps on occasion, but it's not quite like letting your slip show.

Polygon tool. For regions that don't fit nicely into the rectangular or circular molds, the polygon tool provides a highly flexible way to build custom-shaped link fields. With the Polygon tool selected, click to create a series of points connected by straight line segments around the area; GoLive automatically closes the selection, so you won't have any open-ended polygon fields (see Figure 8-15).

When you're finished defining the region, select one of the other region tools to deselect the polygon. If you then click the polygon with the Selection tool, the object is selected as a grouped object, which you can resize. If you resize the image, the regions scale in proportion.

Figure 8-15
Rectangle, Circle, and Polygon map tools

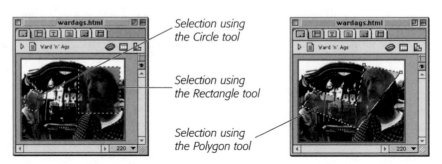

Selection using the Circle tool

Selection using the Rectangle tool

Selection using the Polygon tool

If you want to edit the shape's individual points, double-click the region with the selection tool to activate the polygon's defining points. After modifying them, click outside the shape or select another region tool to deselect it again. Once you've created a polygon, you cannot add new points or remove existing points.

Tip: Adding Points in HTML

If you're really desperate not to start from scratch, you can insert extra point coordinates in the HTML. A point in a polygon requires two values: the x and y coordinates, which are listed in the code that defines the shape, as in this example:

```
<area href="poly_gone.html"
coords="102,189,64,160,115,103,150,179" shape="polygon">
```

Each pair of numbers represents one point, which means there are four points to this polygon. To add another, get the location values of the new point (open the image in Photoshop and use the Info palette to indicate where your cursor is), then add them to the list, x before y.

Tip: The Hidden Polygon Point

Every polygon you create in an imagemap actually contains one more point than the number you specified. To test this, check the Is Map box for an image, then draw a triangle with the Polygon tool by clicking the mouse three times, one for each corner. Now, with the Selection tool, double-click the polygon to edit its point locations, and move the triangle's first point—now you have a four-sided polygon. The "hidden" point is actually the shape's end point.

Tip: Complex Polygons Increase File Size

If you're fanatical about keeping your HTML files as small as possible so they load quickly, try not to use too many complex polygons in an imagemap. Unlike rectangles and circles, which require only a few pixel coordinates, each point of a polygon must be defined in the HTML (see Figure 8-16). Granted, we're talking about text, which loads much faster compared to almost everything else on the Web; but the less work the browser has to do, the faster the page loads and responds.

Region Display Tools

GoLive makes it easy to identify and control the appearance of imagemap regions while you're working in the Layout Editor.

Display URLs. For a quick reference of where the region's link takes viewers, the Display URLs button shows the link or links' contents on top of the appropriate area of the mapped image.

Figure 8-16
Polygon code

Frame regions. Clicking this button displays a dotted line around region edges.

Color regions. With this button selected, regions are filled with a color to make them even easier to find. Colored regions are semi-transparent so you can still see the images beneath them (see Figure 8-17).

Select color. Everyone has their own color favorites. If a hot pink region color clashes too much with your page's ochre-colored background, feel free to select a new color for the region highlight. The color you select applies to all regions; you can't color-code different regions with different colors (though that would be a neat feature in a future version of GoLive).

Figure 8-17
Region
display tools

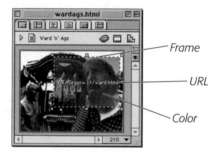

Frame

URL

Color

Organizing Regions

GoLive also includes two buttons for changing the layer order of imagemap regions. If you wind up with overlapping regions and you don't want to redraw boundaries, you can use the Bring Region to Front or Send Region to Back buttons to get the right one on top.

Tip:
Reordering
Directives

Although layered regions aren't really a function of HTML imagemaps, Web browsers do read the imagemap directives (the lists of shapes and coordinates) in the order they appear in the file. So a directive coming earlier than another is the equivalent of being a higher layer. When you use Bring Region to Front or Send Region to Back, GoLive shuffles the HTML; very neat.

Tip: Storing
Other Links

Another use of imagemap layers in GoLive would be a quick method of rotating links for the same image that change often. You could set them up all at once, then bring inactive links to the front when the need arises. It does bulk up your HTML and it does slow down an imagemap's processing time in a browser when a user clicks, so don't go hog wild.

ColorSync (Macintosh Only)

If you work with more than one computer system, you can see that what you view on one screen may not be exactly the same as what you view on another. Monitor brands and hardware differ, software treats imaging differently depending on the company and the platform. Apple's answer to this is ColorSync, a system that attempts to make images appear as the designer intended no matter which combination of hardware and software is being used.

For ColorSync to work in GoLive, make sure the Display Images Using ColorSync box is checked in the ColorSync section of GoLive's preferences.

Tip: ColorSync Installation in Mac OS — You need to have ColorSync installed on your Macintosh; some versions of Mac OS didn't install it by default (or you might have chosen not to install it). You can install it typically off the latest CD-ROM you have with your system, but we recommend getting the most up-to-date version. So unless you recently set up or purchased your computer, go to Apple's ColorSync section at http://www.apple.com/colorsync/, and find the latest version of the software there.

ColorSync Profiles. This feat of color management magic is accomplished through the use of ColorSync Profiles, sets of data that describe how your monitor, scanner, digital camera, or other device "sees" color. These characterizations generally rely on feeding color into them and using a colorimeter to measure their output values so that their subjective notion of color can be compared to an absolute, physical property of color.

Tip: Roll Your Own Profiles — If you don't have a profile set up for your monitor, go to the Monitors and Sound control panel and click the Calibrate button. Follow the instructions on each screen, then name your custom profile (see Figure 8-18). This isn't as perfect as using a color meter with a suction cup on your monitor, but it can take you a surprisingly high degree closer to what images should objectively look like on your screen.

Figure 8-18
Creating a
ColorSync
profile

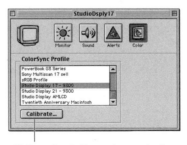 

Clicking the Calibrate button in the Monitors and Sound control panel starts the Monitor Calibration Assistant.

Tip: Great Idea, Minimal Support

We like the possibilities that ColorSync offers, but currently there's very little support for it on the Web; at this writing, only Internet Explorer 4.5 for Macintosh can display an image with a ColorSync profile applied. Apple promises to release a Windows version of ColorSync, but Microsoft allegedly isn't very happy about this—though there is no global CMS solution in Windows currently available.

In GoLive, you can apply a ColorSync profile to an image by switching to the Link tab of the Image Inspector, and clicking the Profile button in the ColorSync section. Use the Browse button to locate the profile that represents your hardware configuration.

From here you can also choose to use GoLive's built-in profile or not use it at all by selecting Default or None, respectively.

Tip: Embedded ColorSync Profiles

Photoshop 5.0 and later support the ability to embed a ColorSync profile into an image when saving it. If a profile already exists within the image file, it's name appears in the Embedded field.

Page-wide implementation. You can specify profiles for every image on your page, but since it's more likely you'll set the same profile each time, GoLive has a way to apply a single profile to an entire page. Click the Page icon in the Layout Editor, then switch to the ColorSync tab of the Page Inspector to link to a profile.

Tip: Copy Profiles to Your Site Folder

To make an externally-referenced profile work, you need to upload it to your Web site along with the HTML and image files that use it. So although you can link to a profile located in the ColorSync Profiles folder within the System Folder, it doesn't get uploaded to the site, and therefore isn't referenced.

Imagine Great Images

It's not an understatement to say that inline images turned the Web from an interesting way to share information into a new designers' medium. GoLive makes it easy to add images to your Web pages, freeing you to spend your time making great images.

CHAPTER 9
Color

We've each taken our fair share of art and design courses throughout school and beyond. Littered amid that history of paper, canvas, brushes, and charcoal lie dozens, even hundreds, of mostly-squeezed paint tubes covering the full visible-color spectrum (and maybe even some ultraviolet and infrared colors too). Although we were taught that color is actually the perception of light interacting with a surface, our stained-hands-on experience told us that color was usually a combination of pigments that eventually swirled into a brownish muck at the center of our palettes.

Today, most of our color usage has returned to the realm of light, with trillions of photons projected daily to ignite pixels with specific hues on our screens. Coming up with a certain color on the Web is a matter of combining numerical values, not watercolors or oils, but that doesn't mean you have to suppress your inner fingerpainter. GoLive's color capabilities let you easily choose the tone you want, or experiment with several different ones.

In fact, the robustness of GoLive's color features continues to surprise us: not only does it offer a palette of the 216 "Web safe" colors for use on the Web, it includes resources for defining colors in RGB, CMYK, and HLS color spaces, long the bastions of print publishing. And as you'd expect, GoLive makes working with color incredibly easy, with most operations requiring a simple drag and drop of a color swatch.

Tip: The Slightly Misleading ColorSync Name GoLive supports Apple's ColorSync technology on the Macintosh, which is an effort to make the colors viewed on one computer setup appear the same on other, dissimilar, machines. However, ColorSync deals with synchronizing the color of images, not HTML-based color found in objects like table cells or text. So, see Chapter 8, *Images*, for more information about this unique approach to providing a consistent viewing experience.

Color on the Web

Color is a subjective thing; for example, the paint in Jeff's living room is perceived as cream by some people and slightly pink by others (cream is the intended perception). Depending on the lighting, the time of day, the colors of objects in the same field of vision, and dozens of other factors, one color can take on multiple appearances. The same is true on the Web, where we must deal with hundreds of different monitor types and calibration settings, plus the default color values of different browsers and operating systems.

We also have to deal with color in a historical context. Although these days you can buy a fully-loaded PC system for less than $1,000, it was only a few years ago when even moderate-quality hardware was expensive. We didn't have 17-inch

A Bit About Bits

Everything in computing is represented, at its foundation, in bits. You're probably more familiar with massive amount of bits counted as bytes (each of which contains eight bits), kilobytes, megabytes, gigabytes, and upward. A bit is the smallest increment of binary data, and can have a value of 1 (on) or 0 (off). When we talk about monitors and screen resolution, we sometimes express it in bits, like 8-bit color, which represents 256 colors (see Table-9-1). This may sound overly geeky when all you want is to make a table cell purple, but understanding this fundamental unit of measurement makes it easier to mix-and-match color values in the Color Palette.

Bit Depth	Math	Total Colors	Also Known As...
1	$1+1$ or 2^1	2	
2	2^2	4	
3	2^3	8	
4	2^4	16	
5	2^5	32	
6	2^6	64	
7	2^7	128	
8	2^8	256	
15	2^{15}	32,768	Thousands of colors (older Macs)
16	2^{16}	65,536	Thousands of colors (newer Macs)
24	2^{24}	16,777,200	High color, millions of colors

Table 9-1 Deep bits

monitors that displayed millions of colors, because the horsepower and memory requirements to drive them were affordable only to very wealthy corporations. As a result, many of today's Web standards are based on the state of computing when those standards were first created.

The field of color management has slowly evolved with the technology in order to work toward color's holy grail: everyone seeing the same color. We're not there yet, but we are getting closer.

Color Between Platforms

One of the frustrations of Web designers is that Macintosh and Windows operating systems use different bases for displaying color. This is especially evident in images, but carries over to background and text colors as well because the two systems feature different gamma defaults. Gamma is a representation of how the same input value, like a specific percentage of black defined in software, gets displayed as the output in a given physical system, like a monitor or printer. Due to the ways in which the two operating systems translate color values for display at the software level, colors tend to be lighter on a Macintosh, or darker under Windows, depending on your point of view.

Tip:
Adjusting and Simulating Gamma

You can tweak gamma settings on both platforms to varying degrees by using the Adobe Gamma control panel that ships with Photoshop 5 and later for both platforms (see Figure 9-1). This control panel allows you to simulate Windows gamma on a Mac more effectively than the reverse. Also, Adobe ImageReady (Mac and Windows) features a gamma simulator for the opposite platform when previewing images (see Figure 9-2).

Figure 9-1
Adobe Gamma

The Adobe Gamma control panel is used to aid hardware calibration, but you can also use it to simulate Windows or Mac gamma levels.

The Web-safe color palette. Color also differs among platforms because the engineers who built color into each system's operating system chose slightly different color values to use for each default color palette. Of the 256 colors available in an

Figure 9-2
Simulated
gamma using
ImageReady

An image viewed on a Macintosh...   *... appears darker under Windows*

8-bit color system, 216 of them match up across all platforms, including Mac, Windows, and typical Unix interfaces. This is what's commonly called the *Web-safe*, or sometimes browser-safe, color palette (see Figure 9-3). Using colors from this palette makes it more likely that what you see on your screen looks the same on another computer system, even if that system has old equipment or is set to a low bit depth.

Keeping this information in mind can help avoid problems later on, and underscores the point that you should be sure to test your pages on as many platforms as possible.

Figure 9-3
Web-safe
color palette

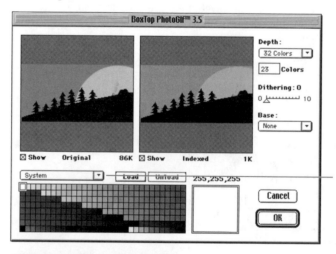

The Web-safe color palette, unlike your computer's system palette, is usually associated with Web images, as shown here. But the colors apply just as well to page backgrounds, table cells, etc. (which is admittedly difficult to show here in grayscale).

Choosing the Web-safe color palette (in this case referred to as the Netscape color palette) offers fewer total colors to work with, but increases the chance that colors display the same on all platforms.

Applying Colors

Normally, we would make a point of explaining all the options available before telling you how to implement a feature. But in this case, applying colors is so easy we wanted to give away the how-to first. The section following this one, "Selecting Colors," offers the skinny on how best to find the color you're looking for.

To bring up the Color Palette—if it's not visible—select Color Palette from the Window menu (Mac) or from the View menu (Windows). You can also click any color field in an inspector.

GoLive lets you apply colors to text, tables, layout text boxes, floating boxes, frame borders, and just about anything else that contains a color field in its inspector. From one of the color tabs, select a color to load into the Preview pane, then drag a color swatch from that pane to an object's color field (see Figure 9-4). If you're using the Real Web Colors, Web Named Colors, or Site Colors tabs, you can drag the swatch directly from the color list in each tab.

Some items allow color to be applied directly, rather than through the Inspector palette. You can drop a color swatch on a highlighted selection of text, for example, or drop directly onto a floating box or layout text box. If you try to drop a color onto an area of text that isn't highlighted, however, GoLive inserts the word "Color" styled with the color you specified (see Chapter 7, *Text and Fonts*).

Figure 9-4
Applying color

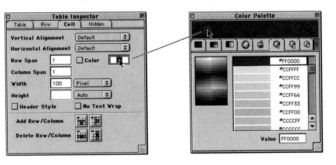

Drag from the Preview pane to an inspector's Color field.

Tip: Drag to Select a Background Color

To change the background color of a page, you normally must drag a color swatch onto the appropriate field in the Page Inspector. However, a shortcut is to drag a color swatch directly onto the Page icon in the Document window's Layout Editor. This action can't be undone via Undo.

Tip: Applying Text Color Without the Text

Ever the inquisitive types, we tried dropping color swatches on everything to see what would happen, including images and table borders. Unfortunately, we weren't able to apply table background colors without using the color field in the Table Inspector, nor turn photos of pets and family members hot pink. We did discover that dropping a swatch onto an object that doesn't directly react to the color actually adds a font color to that area. So, any text written immediately following an image appears in that color. You never know until you try is our motto (for today, anyway).

Applying Colors in Other Editors

Although setting colors in the Layout Editor is the easiest and most visual approach, GoLive offers a couple interesting color uses in the HTML Source Editor and the HTML Outline Editor.

HTML Source Editor. You can't apply a color to objects while editing their HTML code, but you can use the Color Palette to help you grab the right hexadecimal values that define colors. If you drag a color swatch anywhere in the HTML Source Editor, GoLive inserts

```
COLOR="[color value]"
```

at the point where you dropped the swatch. This way, you can set up a tag (like a font definition or table cell, for example), then insert the color you want without having to look up the hex value.

HTML Outline Editor. Drop a color swatch onto the color attribute of a tag to change it. This can be especially useful for setting attributes that aren't directly supported in the Layout Editor, such as a table's border color (see Chapter 10, *Tables*, for information on editing tables and cells).

Selecting Colors

It's great to select color by eye in a visual editor rather than imagining color while looking up and then typing hexadecimal values; it's another reason we like working in a WYSIWYG editor. Now all we have to do is click on the Color Palette and not even worry about what the color's numeric values are. (Of course, you could simulate the Color Palette by buying a Web-safe color poster listing hex, RGB, and named values, and hang it near your desk...which we admit to having done before GoLive appeared.)

But which color palette to click? GoLive includes eight different tabs on the Color Palette—nine, if you're using Windows—that each offer a different way of selecting colors. (See Chapter 3, *Palettes and Parts*, for a visual overview of each.)

Tip: The Color Palette's Color Palette? Before you begin to think we're repeating ourselves, we just wanted to point out the difference between Color Palette (capitalized) and color palette (not capitalized). The Color Palette is the floating window where GoLive's color controls are located. A color palette is the portion of a tab on the Color Palette where the actual colors are located. This is an example of how real-world metaphors can get confusing in the computer world: a physical palette is what we use to hold and mix colors on, but the notion of a digital palette that can hold other things (like commands, text fields, etc.) works well when describing the floating windows. Now, before you begin to think we're repeating ourselves, we just wanted to point out...

The Value of Color Values

If the Web were a box of Crayons, there would be a lot of confused kids. Although we would look at a color and call it "red," computers need a numeric definition of what constitutes red. With the exception of the Real World Colors tab, the values in the Color Palette tabs are expressed either as digits, percentages, or in hexadecimal notation.

Digits. Colors are defined using an 8-bit scale, which gets its roots from the amount of information required to draw a colored pixel onscreen (see the sidebar "A Bit about Bits," earlier in this chapter). Values range from 0 (none of the color) to 255 (all of the color), for a total of 256; mixing different colors this way gives you a full spectrum of color (see Figure 9-5).

Percentages. Clicking the Percentage on/off button switches the value display to percentages in the RGB, CMYK, Grayscale, and Indexed Color tabs. Printers mix percentage amounts of inks to arrive at a desired color, and the technique has migrated to the digital realm as well. (We won't even begin to address additive versus subtractive color here; if you're interested, a book like *Real World Photoshop 5* can tell you more than enough about the topic.)

Hexadecimal notation. When it comes down to adding color to HTML code, the values end up in hexadecimal, or base 16, notation, which is just a more compact and neat way to specify the color value. GoLive's great color strength is that you don't need to mess with hexadecimal; choose a color visually, and GoLive supplies the correct hex value. Then again, if you know the hex value but not its color, type the code into the Value field to see its match.

Figure 9-5
Color notation

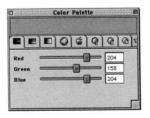

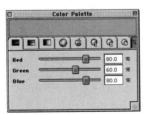

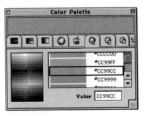

The same color expressed in digits, percentages, and hexadecimal notation.

GoLive's Color Palette Tabs

With the Color Palette displayed, clicking the tabs brings up the following palettes.

RGB. The RGB tab selects colors using mixtures of red, green, and blue, which is the combination that monitors use to display color. Technically, everything you're looking at onscreen is being represented in RGB.

CMYK. If you're trying to match a color from a printed color swatch, enter its values in the CMYK tab. Cyan, magenta, yellow, and black (represented by K, since B would stand for blue) are the four ink colors used in process-color printing.

Grayscale. Classic like old movies and early television, the grayscale tab can display up to 256 levels of gray.

Indexed Color. The Indexed Color tab lets you choose your color using a combination of brightness, selected using the slider, and the range of colors that can be displayed on your existing monitor and screen depth. For example, if your screen is set to display 256 colors, or 8-bit color, you see more dithering (where the computer pairs different-colored pixels in an attempt to approximate the color) than if you were viewing at a resolution of thousands of colors, or 16-bit color.

Tip: Slider Slickness

The RGB, CMYK, and Grayscale tabs feature sliders as well as numeric fields for defining a color. Click and hold the slider knob to change the color amounts. If you're using the Windows version of GoLive, you can tab to the knobs and adjust the levels using the left and right arrow keys. On both platforms, if you click a slider's path, the value increases or decreases 10 percent, depending on which side you click.

Apple and Windows Colors. These tabs, available on their respective platforms, present the built-in 256-color system palettes. From the popup menu on these tabs, you can also choose to display a reduced palette of 16 colors or 16 grays, desktop colors (the ones the system reserves for its own use), or a custom palette of colors you can drag from the Preview Pane (see Chapter 3, *Palettes and Parts*).

HSV (Windows only). GoLive for Windows also includes the HSV tab, which displays colors based on their hue, saturation, and value. Some people find this to be a quicker and more visual way to nab the color they're looking for. Note that the RGB values are also shown here, but always in digits—the Percentage toggle doesn't affect this tab.

Real Web Colors. Honestly, this is the tab we keep open 90 percent of the time we use GoLive. It offers an overview of the colors available as well as a scrolling list (with hex labels) showing larger swatches of the colors. But the main reason is that the Real Web Colors tab displays only the 216 Web-safe color palette. Sticking to this ensures that our colors are viewable on any system; there's nothing worse than spending a lot of effort choosing the perfect color, only to realize it looks like garbage on other computers.

Web Named Colors. Some days, we'd like to give it all up and become the people who name colors—did they hire these folks away from mail-order catalogs (aubergine? periwinkle? almondine?). The Web Named Colors displays a list of colors that Web browsers recognize by name (so in the HTML, "#FFDAB9" is actually substituted with "PeachPuff"). Despite the often creative naming schemes, the downside is that not all the colors in this tab display the same on all browsers.

Site Colors. The Site Colors tab simply reflects the contents of whatever colors are present in the Colors tab of the Site window when a site file is open. You cannot add colors to this tab, only use it as a quick reference to select colors that you've already set up for a site. The name of the current site reflected in the tab is displayed in the lower left corner of the Color Palette. See Chapter 17, *Sitewide Sets*, for information on how to create and store site colors.

Tip: Select a Color from Anywhere on the Screen	Frequently, we have an image or other element that contains the exact color we want to use on our page. Instead of trying to match it to a value in one of the Color Palette tabs, you can grab the value directly. Switch to the Apple/Windows (depending on your machine), or Real Web Colors tab, then click within the color proxy to the left of the tab, but keep the mouse button pressed. Now, feel free to roam the

Why So Much Color?

As we mentioned at the beginning of this chapter, there are only 216 Web-safe colors. In most cases, you want your site to be available to the most possible viewers, which is why most designers stick to the Web-safe color palette. So why does GoLive include support for color spaces that don't necessarily show up on the Web, like CMYK?

We can think of a few reasons. Hopefully, there will come a day when we're not all limited by the number of colors that can be displayed safely, so GoLive has the functionality required to scale up when needed. Virtually all the tens of millions of machines shipping in the last couple years have

video display cards that show thousands or millions (16- or 24-bit) of colors on a monitor, but there are still many millions more older machines that don't that are still being phased out and upgraded. So that day isn't decades off—it's a year or two away.

Second, if you're working with a group that you can identify as having more modern equipment or if you're designing for a corporate intranet in which you know that everyone's machine is capable of more than the Internet mean, you can use the full breadth of color.

eyedropper cursor over any part of your screen, even the menu bar or applications that are visible behind GoLive. When you release the mouse button, the color beneath the eyedropper is loaded into the Preview pane.

The Art of Color

In some respects, GoLive has made color a more complex issue than in other Web design applications. With as many as nine color palettes available, selecting the right hue or background shade can be almost overwhelming. *Almost.* In reality, the simplicity of applying colors to Web objects overcomes the number of methods for selecting those colors. It's almost enough to make us hang up our paints and brushes for good. Almost.

CHAPTER 10
Tables

The Web hasn't always been a designer's medium. As we mentioned in Chapter 7, *Text and Fonts*, HTML is a *structural* formatting language, which shows anyone with a browser the same information regardless of their choice of font, type style, or screen size. However, this flexibility became a problem when representing tabular information—like spreadsheet results. Netscape soon introduced HTML tables, which became the tool of choice to display this kind of data in structurally defined rows and columns.

We've spent enough time around graphic designers (and each other) to know that designers not only appreciate useful tools, they also like to discover new uses for those tools that the tool makers never dreamed about. Needless to say, it wasn't long before the Web's first designers turned the tables on tables. Now the unassuming HTML table has become one of the most reliable and flexible tools used by Web designers. With tables, you can build a framework that controls where elements appear, paint in colors without using images, and add variety to your pages.

The "traditional" cost of wielding this tool has been complexity. Even veteran HTML coders can be found glued to their computer screens deciphering which tags belong to which table cell (and trying to find the one errant tag that's preventing the table from being drawn at all in some browsers). Fortunately, GoLive's table tools make it easy to create, edit, and bend tables to your will in ways that barely resemble a standard table—and with a minimum amount of direct code wrangling.

Creating a Table

If you've ever used a spreadsheet application like Microsoft Excel, tables are a familiar sight. No matter how you stretch, shift, or align them, tables always exist as rectangular blocks of *cells* (see Figure 10-1). Because of this structure, cells naturally fall into *rows* (horizontal, left-to-right) and *columns* (vertical, top-to-bottom). As you'll see, tables are highly configurable. They can contain column headings and captions, nest within other tables, and be manipulated in a variety of ways. You can specify the size and the number of cells, the amount of space between their edges and contents, the width of their border, their alignment, and, as they say, much, much more.

Building a New Table

To take advantage of these features, you first need to create a table, a quick and painless process. From the Basic tab of the Palette, drag and drop the Table icon on your page; you can also double-click the icon to insert a table at your current text insertion point on the page. A perfectly useful three-column by three-row table appears (see Figure 10-2).

To start entering information, click inside a cell—not on its border—and begin typing. Or, drag page elements from the Palette, such as images or forms, or items from any of the tabs in the Site window; consider each cell to be a microcos-

Working around the Table Default

Having tables spring full-formed into the world is a wonderful thing, especially if you've ever spent time writing them by hand. (We'll go into how the underlying code works later in this chapter.) But sometimes you don't want to apply GoLive's default table attributes, which have these specifications every time: three columns, three rows, a width of 200 pixels, border set to 4, cell spacing set to zero, and cell padding set to 2. Although huge chunks of GoLive are configurable (see Chapter 27, *Web Database* to appreciate the full ramifications of this statement), there's no way to change the default values of a new table.

Why would you want to change GoLive's table defaults? Perhaps you know that every table throughout your site will have five columns, or

you need a white background color every time. Whatever the reason, you'll be happy to know that you have choices beyond a 3-by-3 default table.

The secret is the Custom tab in the Palette, which can hold any object you create on an HTML page except for simple text selections (see Chapter 3, *Palettes and Parts*). Create a new table and apply your settings. Highlight it by positioning your cursor to the right or left of the table and selecting it as you would select any other character or image. Grab the selection (your cursor turns into a grabber hand) and drag it to the Custom tab of the Palette (see Figure 10-3). Double-click your new icon to give it a descriptive name. You can then drag and drop the icon onto any page, instead of dropping the standard Table icon.

Figure 10-1
Elements in a
table

Options for the Schleswig-Holstein Wedding Reception ——— *Caption*

——— *Headings*

	Fish	Vegetarian	Fowl	Red Meat
A	Faux Snapper		Chicken	Beef Tenderloin
B	Halibut	Paprikash	Duck	Veal Medallions
C	Salmon		Duck	Sirloin of Beef
D	Perch	California Roll	Goose	Ribs
E		Spana Kopita	Quail	Tongue

——— *Individual cell*

Row spanning   *Column spanning*

Figure 10-2
Default table

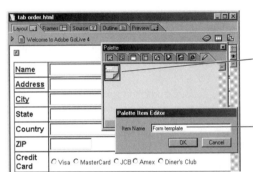

Three rows

Three columns

Figure 10-3
Adding a table
as a custom
palette item

The table was dragged into the tab

*Double-clicking the item allows you
to give it a name*

Where's the Column Tab?

It's like one of those "What's missing from this scene?" tests. The Table Inspector contains tabs for Table, Row, and Cell (and Hidden, but that's a special case, and it mangles this analogy). Why not a tab for Column?

The reason hearkens back to ye olde days of code: HTML allows you to specify the settings for a row because cells are defined as elements that exist within rows. Tables are built sequentially left-to-right, then top-to-bottom.

As a browser reads HTML that constructs a table, it's working much like an old-fashioned typewriter. It reads an enclosing TABLE tag followed by a row tag, followed by individual cell tags. It puts each new cell to the right of the previous cell until it reaches an end-of-row tag. It then moves down to the next row starting at the same left margin, and builds cell-by-cell across. (see Figure 10-4, built from the following HTML).

```
<TABLE>
<TR>
    <TD>Left Cell, Row 1</TD>
    <TD>Right Cell, Row 1</TD>
</TR>
<TR>
    <TD>Left Cell, Row 2</TD>
    <TD>Right Cell, Row 2</TD>
</TR>
</TABLE>
```

Figure 10-4
Left to right

Left Cell, Row 1	Right Cell, Row 1
Left Cell, Row 2	Right Cell, Row 2

mic Web page. You've just accomplished in a few seconds what formerly took hand coders several minutes to set up.

With a basic table in place, you can now begin to modify most of its attributes from within GoLive's Table Inspector tabs. Virtually all of these attributes display correctly in all current Web browsers.

Tip: HTML 4.0 and Tables	The HTML 4.0 specification offers additional table attributes, but GoLive doesn't support them visually. See Elizabeth Castro's book, *HTML 4 for the World Wide Web*.

Border. You can specify a table's border thickness in pixels by changing the value in the Border field of the Table Inspector's Table tab. GoLive's default border setting is four pixels, which is quite large for most table uses—likely set high for visibility when you're working on a complex page. However, it does help to illustrate how browsers render borders. Instead of flat lines, table borders are shaded to simulate a raised, beveled look. The higher the border setting, the larger the "picture frame" appears (see Figure 10-5).

Figure 10-5
Table borders

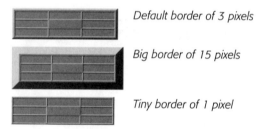

Default border of 3 pixels

Big border of 15 pixels

Tiny border of 1 pixel

Provide the Numbers—the Correct Numbers

When a Web browser encounters table code that's missing width values, it has to read in and examine the HTML code for the entire table to determine its dimensions before drawing it. For large tables, that can take a long time.

(When we both upgraded to newer computers last year, we were pleasantly surprised that many Web pages displayed much quicker—a result of the faster processors parsing table-heavy pages, even on the same slow modem connections.)

To help make your pages load faster, be sure to include table and cell widths when you specify your table settings.

But even those specifications can introduce problems if your math happens to be more art than science. Although GoLive does its best to make sure your numbers add up correctly, it relies on you to get your figures straight. For example, create a new table that's 400 pixels wide. Now select the top cells in each row and specify widths for each so that the numbers don't add up to 400 (let's say 75, 10, and 35). The table retains its width, but also retains the values you assigned, which only add up to 120 pixels (see Figure 10-6).

Most browsers are forgiving enough to approximate the widths. But we've seen unexpected results when the numbers don't add up.

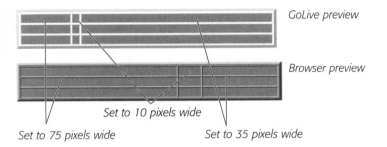

Figure 10-6
Bad table
math

GoLive preview

Browser preview

Set to 10 pixels wide

Set to 75 pixels wide   Set to 35 pixels wide

If you don't want borders to appear at all, set the border value to zero. GoLive displays invisible borders using gray lines. (If you don't see them, make sure you have Show Invisible Items active in the Edit menu.) Note that the value you assign in the Border field applies only to the border surrounding the table, not to the borders of the cells inside, unless the value is set to zero.

Width and Height. The Width and Height fields control the size of tables, rows, and cells in their respective tabs in the Table Inspector. Rows, however, can only have their height set, not their width.

There are three ways of controlling width and height, all of which are found in the popup menus that accompany the fields.

- Auto: The default setting tells the Web browser to take the current window's width and height, add in the contents of the cells, and figure out how wide and tall to make each cell and the entire table. Auto is often good for tables that don't require specific dimensions, as the browser tries to ensure that everything fits.

- Pixel: Enter a number to specify the number of pixels wide or tall a table or cell should be. If your table is part of a page's structure, you'll most likely want to use pixels (see "Tables as Structure," later in the chapter).

- Percent: Because not all Web browser windows share the same dimensions, you can set a table to take up a percentage of the space in a browser window, or set a cell to use a certain percentage of the table's dimensions. You can choose numbers higher than 100 to force a table off the edge of the screen, if you want, but why?

Tip:
Specifying
Column
Widths

It's a good idea to include table and cell widths to help speed up the display of your Web pages, but you don't have to get carried away. A table column always stretches to fit the width of the widest cell, pulling the other cells in the column with it. So don't feel obliged to set the width for every cell in your table. Specifying the width of just one cell in a column saves you a little time, and streamlines your code. When you click another cell in that column, GoLive displays the correct value in the Width field.

Cell spacing and cell padding. The Cell Space field in the Table tab (called cell spacing in HTML) controls the thickness in pixels of a table's internal cell borders.

The Cell Pad field (called cell padding in HTML) controls the indent on all four sides of a cell from the cell and table borders (see Figure 10-7).

Figure 10-7
Cell Pad and
Cell Space

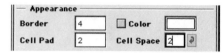

Configuring cell padding and cell spacing in the Table Inspector

Cell spacing and cell padding accomplish similar tasks: they both add breathing room to the cells' contents. However, in the case of colored backgrounds in table cells (see "Addings Colors to Tables," later in this chapter), the difference can be drastic. Suppose you're using different colors for different cells, and have applied a separate color to the entire table. If you set the Cell Pad amount to zero, your text gets crammed right against the cell's edges; by contrast, a larger value adds space around the cell's contents to better offset the text (see Figure 10-8).

Figure 10-8
Offsetting text
with cell
padding

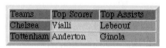 

Cell padding set to 0 (left) and 4 (right)

Using a higher Cell Space value adds space between cells, but has its own pitfalls. In the example table above, the background color of the table shows through the wider cell borders in Internet Explorer (see Figure 10-9). Under Netscape's browsers, however, the larger cell borders become transparent, leaving you with multiple cell islands separated by the Web page's background color or image (see Figure 10-10).

Figure 10-9
Cell spacing
border colors
in Explorer

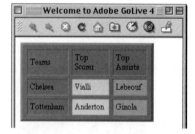

Figure 10-10
Cell spacing
border colors
in Navigator

Since cell spacing and cell padding are table-wide values—you can't set them for individual cells—it's easy to experiment with different combinations and view the results immediately.

Tip:
Sometimes
Math Is Hard

Cell spacing and cell padding have a tendency to confuse a table's Width value. When you increase cell spacing or cell padding, you're adding pixels that increase the overall width and height of the table (see Figure 10-11). However, the table Width field remains the same, and doesn't reflect the increased width.

Unless you want to watch other elements on your page crowded out by swelling tables, factor in the cell padding and cell spacing amounts into the table width value. For example, if your 200-pixel table with a border set to 0 contains two columns that are both 100 pixels wide, but you want a cell spacing of 10 pixels, you would need to add a total of 30 pixels to the table width: 10 each for the left and right edges, plus 10 for the border separating the two cells (see Figure 10-12).

Figure 10-11
No added width with cell padding and cell spacing

Note that only the interior spacing changes, not the overall width of a table, when configuring these two attributes

Cell padding   *Cell spacing*

Figure 10-12
Adding width to compensate for cell spacing

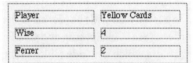

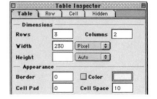

Add to the table's width the amount of Cell Space (10 pixels here) for the left and right edges and for each border separating the table's columns (in this case, adding up to 30 extra pixels)

Header style. With a cell selected, check Header Style in the Cell tab to center the cell's contents and apply bold formatting to its text (see Figure 10-13). Although you could just as easily apply bold to the text and specify the cell's alignment to get the same effect (see below), the table header style is treated as a unique element in HTML—another example of structural formatting versus visual formatting.

You generally use table headers for column or row headings at the top or left of a table, but you can apply the style to any cell. You can also apply local formatting on top of the table header style.

Figure 10-13
Applying
Header Style
to a table cell

Why use the header style? It's stylistically neater to identify the table's headings with a tag devoted to that task, but it doesn't make much difference in a user's appreciation of the table.

No Text Wrap. A table column always stretches to fit the width of the widest cell, as we pointed out earlier. But in most cases, that stretching applies only to the width of the longest word in a cell. By default, text within cells wraps to the next line. If you want a cell's text to remain on one line, check the No Text Wrap box in the Cell tab.

Background color. Applying colored backgrounds within tables adds color to a page without having to download images, speeding up a page's load time. You can apply color to entire tables, rows in a table, individual cells, or all three, by clicking the Color checkbox located on the Table, Row, or Cell tabs in the Table Inspector. Clicking the color field beside the checkbox displays the Color Palette (if it's not already visible). Select a color from the Color Palette—which is covered in greater detail in "Adding Color to Tables," later in this chapter—and drag it to the color field in the Table Inspector to apply the color.

A table color is applied to the entire table. In the Layout Editor, cell colors stop at the edges of their cells, so in a table with wide border sizes, the page's background color shows through the borders. (See "Cell Spacing and Cell Padding," earlier.)

Cell colors override row colors which override table colors, so you can specify all three and use that hierarchy to determine which color a cell will ultimately be. For instance, you might want to use an overall table background to contrast with the page's background color, and alternate colors in every other row to make the contents easier to read. Specific cells might be in yet another color to highlight certain facts or figures (see Figure 10-14).

Tip: Fill Cells to Show Their Colors   Even if you've applied a color to a table cell, you won't see the color unless the cell has something in it. In otherwise empty cells, insert a non-breaking space to solve the problem: Option-spacebar on the Macintosh, or Shift-spacebar under Windows.

Alignment. Tables support two types of alignment: the alignment of the table itself, which forces other elements to wrap around it, and alignment of the contents of table cells.

Figure 10-14
Coloring parts
of a table

Team	Win	Draw	Lose	Points
Bob	2	1	0	7
Futbol Centraal	1	2	0	5
Toxic Avengers	0	3	0	3

Setting the color for entire table

Team	Win	Draw	Lose	Points
Bob	2	1	0	7
Futbol Centraal	1	2	0	5
Toxic Avengers	0	3	0	3

Specifying colors for different rows

Team	Win	Draw	Lose	Points
Bob	2	1	0	7
Futbol Centraal	1	2	0	5
Toxic Avengers	0	3	0	3

Specifying color for specific cell

With the table selected, select either Left or Right from the Alignment popup menu in the Table tab. Just as with images, the text that follows wraps around the table. Unlike images, however, you can't control how much space appears between the edge of the table and its surrounding items.

Controlling the alignment within cells offers much more flexibility (see Figure 10-15). When you select a cell, you can access both Vertical and Horizontal alignment menus on the Cell tab. Contents can be set vertically to Top, Middle, or Bottom, while the horizontal options include the expected Left, Right, and Center.

Figure 10-15
Vertical and
horizontal
alignment

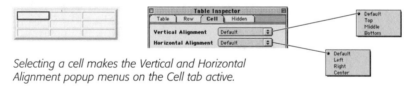

Selecting a cell makes the Vertical and Horizontal Alignment popup menus on the Cell tab active.

You can also apply the same settings to each cell within a row by switching to the Row tab and making your choices. This is a quicker method of applying the settings across multiple cells. If the Row and Cell alignment settings contradict each other, Cell settings override Row settings.

All the alignment popup menus also include Default as an option, which applies the settings found in Table 10-1.

Tip: Check Paragraph Alignment

Paragraph formatting surrounding a table also affects its alignment on the page. If the paragraph is set to be right-aligned, for example, the table hugs the right side of the page, even though you haven't specified any table alignment within the Table tab.

This applies even if your table isn't embedded in a paragraph. If you had set text alignment, delete the text, and replace it with the table, it's likely that the alignment settings could still exist.

Select the table by highlighting it as you would a character, and check the alignment buttons on GoLive's toolbar. The table alignment settings are as much about controlling how elements wrap around the table as they are about pushing elements to the left or right sides of the pages.

Table 10-1
Default table alignment settings

Attribute	Setting
Table	Left*
Row, vertical	Middle
Row, horizontal	Left
Cell, vertical	Middle
Cell, horizontal	Left

* Naturally, alignment can vary depending on your Web browser's settings, providing yet another reason why testing on a variety of platforms and browsers is essential.

Caption. A table can also optionally contain a caption. With the table selected, check the Caption box on the Table tab, then choose whether the caption appears above or below the table (see Figure 10-16). A space appears where you can place your cursor and begin typing. Just as with regular text, you can apply local formatting (font face, size, color, etc.), but it always appears centered in GoLive.

Figure 10-16
Table caption

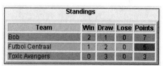

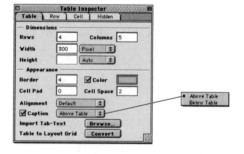

Checking Caption places a text field above or below the table.

Tip: Aligning Captions   Here's yet another example of how different browsers choose to interpret HTML. When you choose either Above or Below from the Caption popup menu, GoLive places an `ALIGN=TOP` or `ALIGN=BOTTOM` attribute in the Caption tag. If you don't want your caption to be aligned in the center of your table, and you're using Internet Explorer, you can substitute Left or Right in the Align attribute. However, this only applies to the caption's default positioning, which is above the table; if you choose to put the caption below the table, it is automatically centered. If you're using Netscape, the point is moot, since the browser only supports top and bottom alignment.

When you select the table, the caption is selected as well. This symbiosis is great if you need to reposition the table, but it can be dangerous if you decide to detach the caption. Be sure to copy and paste the text in the body of your page, because the text gets deleted if you uncheck the Caption box.

Hidden. By now you've probably noticed the intriguingly-named Hidden tab in the Table Inspector. Clicking the tab with any part of a table selected shows you the geometry of your table (see Figure 10-17). This can be especially helpful when working on a complex table when you need to see its structure without the clutter of its contents. Individual cells that are selected appear with a bolder outline. Unfortunately, you can't select cells by clicking them in the Hidden tab, a simple touch that we'd love to see incorporated into later versions of GoLive.

Figure 10-17
Table
Inspector's
Hidden tab

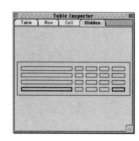

The selected cells in the table are displayed in the Table Inspector's Hidden tab.

The primary use of the Hidden tab, surprisingly, is to reveal objects or comments that have been placed between cells. Such items appear as blue dots. You can't add them directly in GoLive's Layout Editor, but you can insert them in the HTML Source Editor. Although we'll talk more about the underlying HTML for tables later, try this: view the HTML Source Editor and locate the code for a table cell. It looks like this:

```
<TD>Let me out of this cell!</td>
```

In front of the opening <TD> tag, insert a comment:

```
<!-- Begin whining plea for freedom -->
```

Return to the Layout Editor, select the table, and click the Hidden tab (see Figure 10-18).

When you click the blue dot, the table on your page is temporarily replaced by whatever appears between the cells; in this case, it's a Comment icon that displays "Begin whining plea for freedom" in the Comment Inspector when you select it. To return to the view of the table, deselect the blue dot by clicking anywhere else on the tab.

Figure 10-18
Detecting
hidden table
code

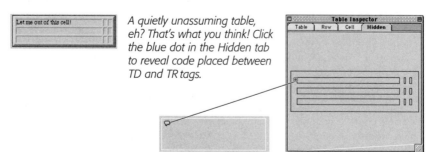

A quietly unassuming table, eh? That's what you think! Click the blue dot in the Hidden tab to reveal code placed between TD and TR tags.

The Fine Art of Table Selection

Despite the painstaking care taken to develop any software program, there are always bits—even in a 4.0 software release—that make you feel more like a Swiss watchmaker instead of a designer: some task that requires intense concentration and focus to get just right. A little slip and that there watch don't tell time too well no more. In GoLive, selecting tables takes a good eye and a steady hand too, especially in a complicated or nested table.

Every good lesson has a fundamental key idea, and here's the one that transforms table selection from random guesswork to precision selecting: it's not *how* you use your mouse, but *where* you use it. Being a visual Web editor, GoLive takes a spatial approach to table selection, so the position of your cursor on the table determines what's going to happen when you click the mouse button. The cursor also changes shape depending on the table region it's pointing at.

Tip: No Undo for Accidental Table Resizing A bit of a warning: if you accidentally resize the table when trying to select a part of it, you can't undo the changes you make. Your only hope to restore a table, a cell, or a row to its original measurements is to revert to a saved copy of the HTML file.

Selecting the Contents of a Cell

It's likely that you'll want to start entering information into your table first thing, so click in the middle of a cell to place your text cursor within it. The cursor becomes an I-beam or text insertion cursor (see Figure 10-19), which you can use to type text or provide a target for placing other elements such as graphics.

Figure 10-19 Selection and insertion cursors

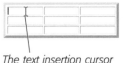  

The text insertion cursor   *The cell selection arrow*   *The table selection hand*

Tip: Can't Get a Cursor to Appear You may find yourself unable to get a text-insertion tool to appear when you click at the top of a large cell (see Figure 10-20). That's because the default setting for a newly created cell is to center text top to bottom within the cell. When you click at the top, GoLive doesn't associate that action with text because there's no text at the top.

You can solve this one of two ways: set the table cell's vertical alignment to Top (see later in this chapter); or, if clicking in the top of the field doesn't bring up an I-beam, click in the middle of the field.

Tip: Selecting All Contents Within a Cell Typically, choosing Select All would seem to select everything on your page. But the engineers at Adobe get extra credit for making GoLive smart about selecting items within a cell. With your text cursor active within a cell, choose Select All from the Edit menu and you highlight objects and text *within that cell only*.

Figure 10-20
Accessing text
tool in large
cells

If at first you don't succeed, click within the middle area of a larger cell to acquire the text-insertion tool, or select a Top vertical alignment for the cell

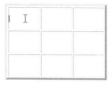

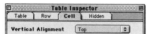

We use Select All within cells constantly, especially when we want to copy the contents of one cell (including font, color, and size attributes) and paste them into another.

Tip: Use Tab Tables can be particularly mouse-intensive items in GoLive. Give your wrists a break
to Move by using the Tab key to move among cells, left to right, then down to the next row.
Between Pressing Shift-Tab reverses the direction.
Cells

Selecting an Entire Table

Move the cursor to either the top or left side of a table and you'll notice that the arrow becomes a grabber hand (which looks a lot like the glove of a particularly famous cartoon mouse). Clicking the table in this state selects the table and displays the Table tab in the Table Inspector. If you continue to hold on, you can drag and drop the entire table to another location on the page, in another open window, or into the Custom tab of the Palette.

You can also place the cursor at the right edge of the table to select it. However, if the table's width is set in pixels, the cursor becomes a dark blue icon with arrows pointing left and right. This is technically the tool for manually adjusting the table's width, but as long as you just click and don't drag, the cursor still just selects the table. The cursor remains an arrow if the Table's width is set to Auto or Percent.

You can also select a table by highlighting it as you would a block of text, or by placing the text cursor at the left or right side of the table and pressing Shift with

Setting Type Characteristics for All Cells in a Table

You thought by the heading of this sidebar that we were going to reveal a feature you thought you'd overlooked in GoLive: a way to select a bunch of cells and apply text formatting, such as font or color, to all the contents of the selected cells. Although there are some attributes that you can apply with multiple cells selected, like font size, others are not available, like font color (see "Applying

Formatting to Multiple Cells" later in this chapter).

But we do have a workaround: a method of setting characteristics for all the members of a table at once using GoLive's Find feature and regular expression find and replace. It's a bit too involved to introduce here, as we have to explain regular expressions first. See Chapter 22, *Advanced Features*, for an example of setting parameters this way.

either the left arrow or right arrow key. Unfortunately, this only selects the table as an object on the page, like text or an image. You need to click the top or left edges of a table to be able to bring up the Table Inspector and access GoLive's table-editing features.

Selecting a Cell

You'll probably spend more time selecting individual cells than other table elements because cells are where most of a table's formatting happens. Position your cursor over a cell's bottom border or its right border (making sure the pointer is not an I-beam), and click. The cursor in this case doesn't change.

If the table's width is set in pixels and the cursor turns into the dark blue resizing cursor when you're attempting to select the rightmost cell, you've moved too far to the right, and clicking here selects the entire table instead.

With a cell selected, you can return to editing its contents by pressing the Return key. This can come in handy if a cell is so small that you can't get the mouse's I-beam cursor to appear; simply select the cell and hit Return.

Tip: Increase Cell Spacing for Easier Cell Selection If you're having trouble positioning your cursor to select cells, it's okay to cheat a little. Increase the Cell Space value in the Table tab while you're editing, which gives you larger borders between cells; anything higher than 10 works nicely. GoLive considers the border between cells part of the cell, so your pointer doesn't even have to be touching the edge of the cell to select it. When you're finished editing, just restore the previous Cell Space value. (Since it's a table-wide setting, you only have to change it once.)

Tip: Use the Hidden Tab in Complex Tables Sometimes tables just don't end up as nice and clean as they begin. If you have several cells, or cells that are unusually small, positioning your cursor to select one cell instead of its neighbor can be a difference of only a few pixels. Click the Hidden tab on the Table Inspector to view a structural representation of the table. Selected cells appear with bold outlines. Although you can't use the Hidden tab as a proxy to select cells—we're holding out for this feature in a future version—it can make it much easier to see where your mouse clicks are landing.

Tip: Table Editing Through Cell Selection When you select a cell, the Cell tab automatically comes up in the Table Inspector. But it can be helpful to remember that although the cell is the primary item selected, you can also make changes to values that affect the whole table. If you switch to the Table tab or the Row tab, you don't need to deselect the cell and reselect the table or row to edit those attributes.

Selecting Multiple Cells

The ability to select more than one cell and apply settings to them all is one of the great benefits of using GoLive instead of hand-coding HTML table tags. Hold down the Shift key when selecting cells to select multiple, non-contiguous cells. With one or more cells selected, you can also choose Select All from the Edit menu or the contextual menu (or press Command-A on a Mac or Control-A under Windows) to select all the cells.

With multiple cells selected, a few items on the Cell tab become inaccessible. You can't add or delete rows or columns (see "Editing Tables," later in this chapter), and you can't specify cell widths or heights, though you can change whether the values are set to Pixel, Percent, or Auto.

If some settings conflict, such as cell alignment, the affected popup menus become blank. If you then choose an option from the same affected menu, it resets all cells selected to that popup choice. Leaving it alone preserves the original settings.

Selecting a Row or Column

Holding down the Shift key while the cursor is at the top or left edge of a table changes the cursor to a blue arrow pointing right. Clicking the left edge selects all the cells in the nearest row; clicking the top edge selects all the cells in the nearest column.

This technique also works for inverting a cell selection. If one or more cells are already selected in a row or column, Shift-clicking the top or left edge deselects those cells and selects the others.

Nesting Tables

You can place whole tables within the cells of a surrounding table, commonly referred to as *nesting*. This is often done when a page's overall structure is defined by a table, and a standard table needs to be displayed on the page (see "Tables as Structure," later in this chapter). The problem sometimes is that selecting individual cells from within nested tables can be difficult if the tables' borders run against each other.

Fortunately, GoLive has implemented a nice keyboard shortcut to get around the problem. Select a cell and then press Control-Return (Mac or Windows) to select the cell's parent table. If that table is nested within another table cell, then that (grandparent?) cell is selected (see Figure 10-21). You can repeat this process for as many levels as it takes to get to the top of the table hierarchy.

Tip: Quick Cell Selection Without Leaving the Keyboard
If your text cursor is within a cell, you can use Control-Return to select the cell and bring up the Table Inspector. If we're typing with both hands on the keyboard, it can be a pain to grab the mouse, locate the cursor's position, maneuver the pointer to an edge of the cell, and finally click to select it. This way, one Control-Return keyboard action saves us four steps, some unnecessary hand-flailing, and a bit of brainpower too!

Figure 10-21
Nested tables

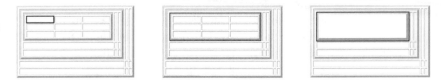

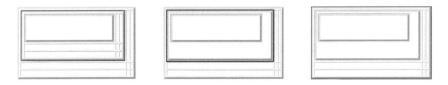

Starting with a single selected cell, press Control-Return to select the cell's table, again to select the cell where that table is nested, again to select that cell's entire table, and so on, and so on…

Editing Tables

It's highly unlikely that every table you create needs to look like the default you get when creating a new table. Using the flexible table editing tools in GoLive, you can resize a table's dimensions, add and remove cells, and "span" cells over others to customize the table's appearance.

Resizing Cells and Tables

There are two methods of resizing table elements. With the table or a cell highlighted, you can input pixel or percentage values into the Width or Height fields in the Table, Row, or Cell tabs. If you already know the table's dimensions, this is the best way to set specific values.

Sometimes, though, you don't have the math worked out, or you just want to begin with a boring old table and see how you can mold and stretch it into a close approximation of the masterpiece in your head. This is where the second method comes in: manipulating table dimensions by dragging the table's borders. In some cases, you can resize elements by simply clicking and dragging; other capabilities require the use of a modifier key, like Command or Control, as you click and drag.

As we mentioned earlier, in "Selecting a Cell," the results from manually resizing tables and cells depend on whether the Width and Height values are set to Pixel, Percent, or Auto. If the cells' width attributes are set to Auto, you can squish and stretch as much as you want; if you've previously specified pixel widths for the cells, the table's dimensions are constrained to accommodate those settings. Also, remember that cells never shrink narrower than their contents, so the longest word in a cell defines that cell's (and column's) minimum width.

The following rules apply when manually resizing (see Figure 10-22).

Figure 10-22
Dragging to
resize tables
and cells

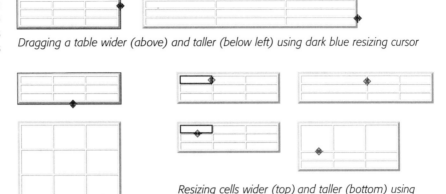

Dragging a table wider (above) and taller (below left) using dark blue resizing cursor

Resizing cells wider (top) and taller (bottom) using light blue resizing cursor

Table width. Position your cursor at the table's far right edge until it becomes a *dark blue* resize cursor (a left-and-right arrow icon) to change the width of an entire table. Clicking and dragging lets you expand or compress the width; GoLive automatically adjusts the internal cell widths to maintain their individual settings.

If your table and cells are set to Auto widths, however, the dark blue resize cursor doesn't appear. Hold down the Option (Mac) or Alt (Windows) key when the pointer is in the right edge region to invoke the resizing control. When you click and drag, your table's Width setting automatically switches to Pixel.

Table height. Similar to setting Table Width, position the cursor at the lowest edge of the table until it becomes a *dark blue* resize cursor (in this case an up-down arrow), then click and drag to adjust the height. Also, like table width, you may need to hold down the Option or Alt key to invoke the resize control if the table's height is set to Auto, which changes the setting to Pixel.

Cell width. Follow the same basic procedure when resizing table cells. If a cell is set up to be measured in pixels, you see a *light blue* resize cursor appear; if not, press Option or Alt when you drag. You can only adjust cell widths from the right border.

Cell height. Position your cursor at the bottom of a cell. If you don't see the *light blue* resize cursor, press Option or Alt and then drag to change the height.

Tip: "Live" Resizing Display   Normally, GoLive displays only a dotted outline to indicate the table's or cell's dimensions as you drag them to a new width or height. However, GoLive can also actively redraw the table with all its attributes (such as cell spacing, background colors, etc.). Under Windows, hold down the Control key as you drag. On the Mac, hold down both the Control and Option keys; the pointer becomes the contextual menu cursor, even though a contextual menu doesn't appear.

Adding and Deleting Cell Rows and Columns

You can attack the problem of adding and deleting cells in three ways: using the Table Inspector, dragging table borders with command keys held down (adding cells only), or using keyboard shortcuts. However, these methods don't all produce the same results. Knowing what to expect saves you time and hopefully prevents you from unintentionally deleting table data, as GoLive happily dispenses with the contents of deleted rows or columns without warning you.

Tip: Add and Delete Apply to Rows and Columns It's important to mention here that these add and delete functions only apply to rows and columns. If you're trying to remove a single cell within a table so that another cell expands to take its place, what you really want to do is hide that cell using the spanning techniques mentioned later in "Cell Spanning."

Adding and deleting using the Table Inspector. If you've just created a new table and know the number of rows and columns it needs, enter those numbers in the Rows and Columns fields of the Table tab. New columns are added to the right of existing columns, while new rows are appended to the bottom of the table. Enter a number smaller than the current number of rows or columns to remove cells from the right side or bottom of the table. You can change these figures at any time.

At the bottom of the Cell tab in the Table Inspector are four buttons for adding and deleting rows. They are only active when a single cell is selected, even if you're removing a column and have only cells in that column selected. Clicking the Delete Row or Delete Column button deletes whichever row or column contains the selected cell.

Clicking the Add Row/Column buttons adds a row or column, but with one essential twist: new rows appear *above* the row containing the selected cell, while new columns appear to the *left* of the selection—the opposite of adding rows and tables using the fields in the Table tab (see Figure 10-23). This subtle difference makes it possible to control how existing cells shift within the table, bypassing the need for a lot of cutting and pasting of cell contents.

Adding by dragging table borders. As a rule, we like to avoid making frequent trips to the Table Inspector, which is why we like the capability of adding rows and columns by dragging their borders. This only works on the table as a whole (you can't drag a cell border in the middle of the table and expect a new column to appear there), but it's a great way to expand a table quickly and easily. (Unfortunately, you can't delete rows or columns using this method, though it's a feature we'd like to see.)

Position your cursor on the table's right edge (for adding columns) or the bottom edge (for adding rows), just as if you're going to resize the table. With the Command key (Macintosh) or the Control-Shift keys (Windows) held down, drag

Figure 10-23
Adding rows
and columns

Original table with selected cell

After clicking Add Row and Add Column button in Cell tab of Table Inspector

After increasing row and column count to 5 in the Table tab of Table Inspector

the table's border. A plus sign (+) appears on the arrow cursor, and dotted outlines representing new cells appear. The new "ghost" cells match the width or height of the rightmost or bottom cell, so drag out at least that amount for the new cells to appear. Continue to drag until you've added as many columns or rows as you'd like, then release the mouse button.

Adding and deleting using keyboard shortcuts. As you've no doubt guessed, we love keyboard shortcuts. You can quickly add or delete rows and columns using the keys described in Table 10-2.

Table 10-2
Keyboard
shortcuts for
adding and
deleting

Action	Numeric Keypad or Standalone Key	Standard Keyboard
Add a row	* (asterisk)	Shift-8
Add a column	+ (plus sign)	Shift-= (equals sign)
Delete a row	Shift-Del	Shift-Delete (Mac) or Control-Shift-Delete (Windows)
Delete a column	Del	Delete (Mac) or Control-Delete (Windows)

Cell Spanning

Even if you're really using a table to display tabular information instead of as a formatting element, it's rare that you'll want to maintain an even grid of cells. There are times when a cell's contents need to fit across the two cells below it, for example, or you want an image to run down the length of the table. *Cell spanning* enables you to instruct one cell to extend or span, like a bridge, across other cells (see Figure 10-24).

Figure 10-24
Cell spanning

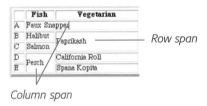

Row span

Column span

Cell spanning follows the same directional principle as table cells, operating from left to right, top to bottom. So, select a cell that is either to the left or the top of the cell that's going to be overtaken by the span. With the cell highlighted, go to the Table Inspector and enter the number of cells it covers in the Row Span or Column Span field of the Cell tab. Alternately, you can hold down the Shift key and press the right arrow or down arrow key to apply the span; pressing Shift and the left or up arrow removes the span.

When dealing with cells that are part of a column or row span, think of that area as a single cell (the upper left one in the spanned section) that has simply grown to hide the other spanned cells. The cells that are "hidden" behind the spanned cell aren't affected by changes applied to them (such as when you select a column by Shift-clicking at the top of the column). There is no way to select a cell that is "hidden" by a span (we were hoping that's what the Hidden tab was for, but it's not—at least not yet).

A Hidden Problem? Count Those Columns!

You can wind up in an unsolvable rut if you miscount the number of columns in your table when setting column spans. GoLive and Internet Explorer use a different algorithm than Netscape Navigator in interpreting column spans, so a table can look fine previewed in GoLive and IE, and terrible (for no clear and obvious reason) in Navigator.

The problem lies in the fact that you can't specify the number of columns as part of an HTML table. The browser has to determine the columns by reading the entire table and looking for the row that contains the most cells. It then uses this number to compute and display cells that span columns.

Navigator isn't forgiving, and if you have more column spans than actual cells, it inserts extra, weird space into each row. Explorer and GoLive, on the other hand, count column spans as part of the overall cell count and still render the table cor-

rectly, ignoring the missing column.

You can find out if you're suffering from this problem by using the Hidden tab in the Table Inspector. Click each cell across a row and count all column spans in the Cell tab of the Table Inspector, even cells that have a 1 in the Column Span field. Now click the Hidden tab and count the number of cells it displays in its preview geometry. If the column spans exceed the preview, this is your problem.

You can quickly fix this problem by changing all your excess column spans to lower values. A new column suddenly appears as you do this, which you can then delete using methods previously mentioned. Now you can readjust column spans, if necessary. Generally, this solves the whole problem and makes Navigator behave (oh, be*have*!).

Tip: Inserting Oversized Contents into Spanned Cells

A cell resizes to fit its contents; a graphic or set of text too large to fit into a cell's existing dimensions causes it to grow. If you plan to use cell spanning to accommodate a large graphic or text, it might be easier to apply the dimensions before inserting the element to avoid throwing off any preset values in the surrounding cells.

Adding Color to Tables

Originally, the only method for adding color to a Web page was by specifying its background color or image, or by adding other images to the layout. When you start adding colorful images, as we're all too aware of on the Web these days, your download times begin to crawl under the weight of all those pixels. The emergence of colored table cells offered a refreshing change: visual variety without loading a single image! Even better, applying colors to tables in GoLive is a simple matter of dragging and dropping swatches from the Color Palette—with only a few oddities to watch out for.

The Table, Row, and Cell tabs in the Table Inspector each contain a Color field, plus a checkbox for activating or deactivating the color. If the Color Palette is not visible, clicking the Color field displays it, and, if there's a color in the field, drops that color into the preview pane of the Color Palette. (See Chapter 9, *Color*, for more about color in GoLive.)

Applying a Cell or Row Color

With a cell or group of cells selected, choose a color from the Color Palette and drag it to the Color field in the Row or Cell tab. Dropping the color in the field automatically checks the Color box if it wasn't already selected, and applies the color. Once a color has been loaded into the Color field, you can check or uncheck the Color box to apply or remove the color without erasing it.

Cell colors override row colors, so if you apply a different color to a cell within that row, the cell's color is displayed (see Figure 10-25). Unchecking the Color box in the Cell tab reverts the cell's color to the row color.

Applying a Table Color

Like setting a background color for your page, you can specify a background color for an entire table. Follow the same procedure for applying a color as above, but drop it onto the Color field in the Table tab.

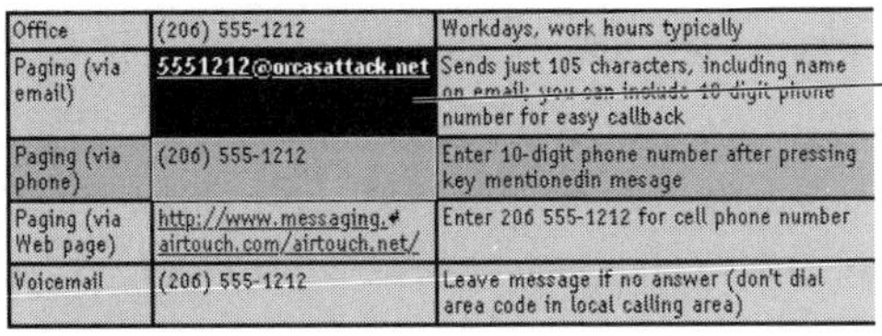

Office	(206) 555-1212	Workdays, work hours typically
Paging (via email)	5551212@orcasattack.net	Sends just 105 characters, including name on email; you can include 10-digit phone number for easy callback
Paging (via phone)	(206) 555-1212	Enter 10-digit phone number after pressing key mentionedin mesage
Paging (via Web page)	http://www.messaging.airtouch.com/airtouch.net/	Enter 206 555-1212 for cell phone number
Voicemail	(206) 555-1212	Leave message if no answer (don't dial area code in local calling area)

Rows set to alternating colors while one cell set to its own color

Figure 10-25 Cell color overrides row colors which overrides table background

As we mentioned in "Cell Spacing and Cell Padding," earlier in the chapter, Web browsers don't display table colors consistently. GoLive's Layout Editor displays only the table's cells filled with the background color, not the space occupied by its borders (increase the Cell Pad and Cell Space values to see a vivid example of this). When you view the table in Netscape Navigator, the borders are transparent and reveal bits of a page's background color or image; but if you look at it in Internet Explorer, the table color is applied to the entire table, borders included (see Figure 10-26). Also remember that the color won't show up at all in cells which are completely empty. See the tip "Fill Cells to Show Their Colors" earlier in the chapter. Also, individual cell colors, as well as row colors, override the table color.

Tip: Nest Tables to Create Colored Borders	You can't specify a table's border color in GoLive without editing the HTML tags directly, but there is a way to create colored borders. Build a table containing only one cell, set the Border value to zero, and apply your desired border color to the entire table. Then, create a new table within the cell, sized smaller than the first depending on how thick you want the colored border to be. Set this table's background color so that the back table doesn't show through. Not only do you have more control over the border effect, the result is more consistent than current HTML implementations in 4.0 browsers (especially in terms of border size and line weight).

A Bad Idea Gone Even Badder

We mentioned at the outset of this chapter that you can use tables to paint without images—clearly a catchy overstatement used to grab your interest, right? Well, you'd be surprised. Most table and cell coloring is used as a backdrop to text or other elements on a page. But a recent April Fool's joke proved that you can also use tables to reproduce images, pixel-for-pixel.

Every Web image is made up of rows and columns of colored pixels, aligned in a rectangular grid. Sound familiar? For the April 1, 1998 issue of the electronic journal TidBITS, Jeff wondered if it would be possible to reproduce an image by substituting colored pixels with colored table cells, thereby eliminating the need to load an image at all.

Travis Anton of BoxTop Software (http://www.boxtopsoft.com/) took the idea one step further and created PhotoHTML, a fully-functional Photoshop plug-in that converts images into HTML tables (see Figure 10-27).The only graphic used is an invisible spacer GIF to make sure that each cell is populated to make the background color display in all browsers.

As with too many brilliant ideas, alas, PhotoHTML has one major flaw: the code required to reproduce even a small image in table format winds up being larger than the graphic it replaced! And if the pseudo-image is large, most browsers either tend to take a long time to parse and render the code, or choke on it entirely. Designers, *please* don't try this at home! (Unless you *really* want to, in which case it can be downloaded from the *Real World Adobe GoLive 4* Web site.)

Warning: a really good way to crash GoLive is to open PhotoHTML files larger than about 50K; GoLive really tries to open it, but it *kinna handle it, cap'n!*

Figure 10-26
Background
show-through

In a table with exaggerated cell spacing, it's clear how Internet Explorer (left) shows the table's background color, while Netscape Navigator (right) shows the background image through the interstices

Figure 10-27
An image as a
table via
PhotoHTML

The original (left) turned into a table with PhotoHTML and opened in GoLive (middle); cell spacing added for cool, new age effect (right)

**Tip: Don't
Drag Colors
to the Cell
Itself**

You can only apply a cell color using the Color field in one of the Table Inspector's tabs. If you drag a swatch from the Color Palette to the table itself, GoLive thinks you're specifying a text color and inserts the text "Color" in your target cell, conveniently set to the swatch color. Hopefully, future versions of GoLive will apply a cell color when a cell is selected to make the process even more intuitive than it already is.

Importing Table Content

So far, we've been concentrating on building and editing tables from the ground up. Often, however, we need to build a table from preexisting data, such as a spreadsheet. Although it's possible to create a table and then type the values into the cells, GoLive's Import Tab-Text feature is much more efficient.

GoLive reads and parses delimited text files, which simply means that each cell of spreadsheet information is separated by a specific character. You can import files delimited by tabs, spaces, semicolons, or commas into GoLive. If you haven't done so already, open your spreadsheet and save it as a text-only delimited file.

Tabular data almost always comes from a spreadsheet program, but that doesn't mean you have to go out and buy Microsoft Excel for this purpose. The delimited format can be created in any word processor or text editor, and can be easily exported from most database programs, like Microsoft Access and FileMaker Pro. What's important is that the data lives in a text-only file.

Tip: Choosing the Right Delimiter	The point of a delimiter is to pick a character that doesn't get used for any other purpose in the file in question unless it's enclosed with two sets of quotation marks. The quotation marks denote that everything between them is data.

So if you use tabs, spaces, semicolons, and commas throughout your data, make sure and set up your output so quotation marks surround all cell data. (Some programs do this by default, like FileMaker Pro.)

We often use tabs as delimiters because most spreadsheet and database programs don't let you enter the tab character as data; we can be sure it's unique.

Now, switch to GoLive and create a new table. Don't worry about specifying the number of rows or columns; GoLive automatically generates the cells it needs. Select the table and click the Import Tab-Text button labeled Browse in the Table tab. When prompted for the file, be sure to specify the type of delimiter from the Col. Separator popup menu before clicking OK or Open.

Tip: Importing with a Cell Selected	It's quicker to select the table as a whole, which displays the Table tab in the Table Inspector, then click the Import Tab-Text button. However, the process also works if you have one or more cells in the table selected. Switch from the Cell tab to the Table tab and click the Browse button; the incoming data automatically begins at the upper-left cell of your table, no matter which cell was selected when you began.

Tip: Don't Span Cells Before Importing	GoLive's table import feature lets you start with a default 3-by-3 table and changes its dimensions to accommodate the imported information. However, if you've applied cell spanning to the table before importing, those cells remain spanned, possibly throwing off the cell order of your incoming data.

Tip: Importing into a Populated Table	If you want to merge two sets of tabular data into one table, you're better off using your spreadsheet or a word-processing program to paste the text of the second table after the first. You *can* import delimited data into a table that already contains data, but the results are less than desirable. GoLive starts filling the table from the upper-left cell, even if it's occupied. You won't actually lose your original data, but it is forced to coexist with the new information, resulting in cells containing both.

Importing into Nested Tables

Earlier in the chapter we mentioned that you could nest tables within tables, and you can do the same with nested tables based on imported data. After you build a table, simply create a new table within one of the parent table's cells and click the Browse button on the Table tab.

Applying Formatting to Multiple Cells

Since we can select multiple cells, it makes sense that we should be able to set formatting on those selected cells. Unfortunately, some attributes work across multiple selections while others don't. Table 10-4 lists how much control you have with more than one cell selected.

	Can Change	Cannot Change
Table 10-4 Multiple formatting hits and misses	Cell color	Font color
	Fontset	List formatting
	Cell alignment	Text alignment
	No text wrap	Nobreak style
	Font style (bold, italic, etc.)	
	Header style	
	Remove font color	

Tables as Structure

Web browsers were created to suit the user, who could specify his or her own fonts and sizes and expect that the text would wrap to fit any browser window size. Unfortunately, this had the side effect of driving some graphic designers completely insane, because they had such limited control over the visual presentation. From a graphic design standpoint, the original approach was akin to making every printed brochure a letter-sized sheet of white paper with Courier text.

But when HTML tables appeared, designers realized that they didn't have to be restricted to traditional tabular data. Instead, tables can provide the framework necessary to invite all sorts of design flexibility. We know designers who start every page by creating a table enclosing its contents. With a table as the structure of your page, you can specify columns or sidebars or special areas for navigation graphics.

Fixed versus Percentage Measurements

If you know the dimensions of your design, you can specify fixed pixel widths to establish—and retain—the design's measurements, regardless of the size of the browser window. This enables you to control where images and other elements are placed. Instead of working on a sliding, unpredictable layout, you've created a framework which has predictable results.

Using tables doesn't mean you lose the ability to create a page that adapts to the viewer's screen. A fixed-width table that occupies the first 500 pixels of a window may look fine in most browsers, but can get lost amid the expanse of a window opened to its fullest on a large monitor. (Similarly, the right edge of your layout gets cut out of smaller windows.) In times like this, consider tailoring your design to use percentage widths instead; you still maintain control over where objects load, but the cells expand or contract to make the best use of the available space (see "Width and Height" earlier in the chapter).

Tip: Create Structural Templates	If you've created a design that relies on the same underlying table structure, or frequently-used structures like navigation bars, speed up your work by using the Custom tab of the Palette. Create a blank table with the dimensions you need (including any static elements such as logos, etc.), then drag it to the Custom tab. When you create a new GoLive document, simply drag that table template to your page to start building its contents.
Tip: Stitching Together Split Images	If you're using a larger image that's been split into smaller ones, placing these smaller sections into a table ensures that they don't drift apart in some layouts. Create a table cell for each section, setting each cell's alignment so that the images get pushed together; for example, in a 2-by-2 table, the upper-left corner's horizontal alignment would be set to Right while its vertical alignment would be set to Bottom. Make sure that the cell padding, cell spacing, and border values are set to zero to remove spaces introduced by those attributes. (Programs that slice-and-dice for you, like Adobe ImageReady, Photoshop 5.5, or Macromedia Fireworks automatically create a table structure like this for you.)

Building Forms Using Tables

Forms are notoriously tricky to lay out on a page, since the size of text fields and other form elements vary widely among browsers and platforms. Building your form with table cells, however, imposes a structure that helps keep your forms visually consistent (see Figure 10-28).

Place item labels in the first cell in a row, and then put form elements like text fields or checkboxes into their own cells to the right on the same row. This lines up the left edges of all your fields, making the form easier to follow and enter data into.

You can use cell alignment settings balance text which describes or names a field or set of fields, and the form entry fields themselves. We often set the vertical alignment to Middle to offset font size and automatic leading discrepancies, especially when placing checkboxes or radio buttons beside text.

Figure 10-28
Form embedded in a table

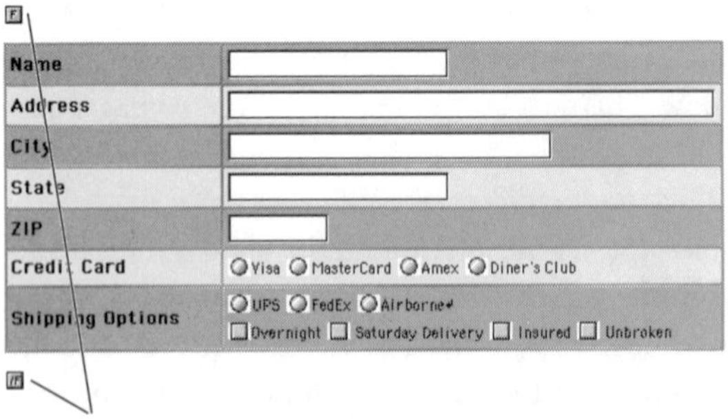

To make it clear where the form begins and ends, we like to keep the Form tag and End Form tag outside the table itself, although there's no technical requirement for that.

Converting Tables to Layout Grids

Perhaps you're using GoLive to edit an existing site with a table-based structure, or maybe you've decided that the extra elements your client wants to add to his site would be better off created with one of GoLive's layout grids. Whatever the reason, you don't have to throw away your previous tables and start over.

Select a table, then click the Table to Layout Grid button (labeled Convert). The dimensions of the table change to a layout grid. Images and other objects in the table remain in the same places; cells containing text become layout textboxes (see Figure 10-29). Unfortunately, GoLive offers no easy method of converting a grid back into a table. Its unfortunate because in the underlying HTML, grids *are* tables—just highly complicated ones. (For more on working with layout grids, see Chapter 12, *Layout Grids and Floating Boxes.*)

Figure 10-29
Table turned
into layout grid

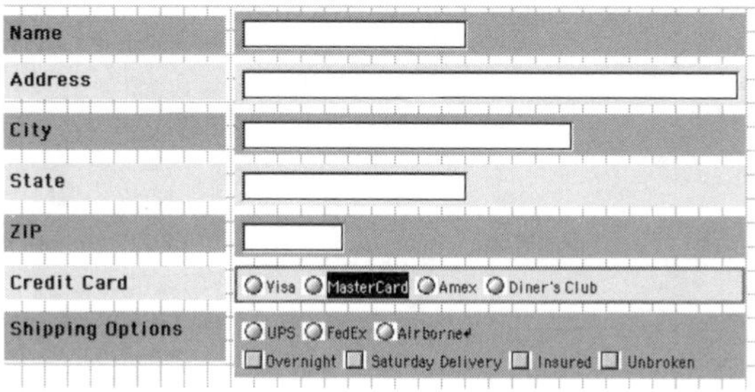

This simple form was turned into a layout grid, transforming each cell into a layout text box, each of which can hold any kind of HTML content, not just text.

Turning Layout Grids Into Tables

Although there's no built-in support for converting layout grids into tables, that doesn't mean it's impossible. Grids don't exist in HTML, which means GoLive is performing a clever hack to create a complex table at the source code level that responds according to its grid features.

Click a layout grid to select it, then uncheck the Show checkboxes. Switch to the HTML Source Editor and locate the beginning of the grid, which looks something like this:

```
<table cool width="394" height="305"
border="0" cellpadding="0" cellspac-
ing="0" gridx="16" gridy="16" bgcol-
or="#ffffcc">
```

Looks familiar, doesn't it? To turn the grid into a genuine table, remove the attribute "cool". When you switch back to the Layout Editor, you'll see a standard table, which you can edit and clean up using GoLive's table tools. It's not exactly beautiful, but it could mean a lot less work required to manipulate the information.

Once you've performed this change, it's unlikely you can switch the table back to a grid without performing major surgery. Make sure and save the page (or back it up) before trying this out.

Ubiquitous Tables

Whether they're displaying complex tabular data or providing the skeletal structure of an entire page, tables have evolved into a tool that very few designers can live without. It might take you a little time to learn the subtleties of creating and modifying tables in GoLive, especially to get the hang of selecting individual cells. But the time you save later is well worth suffering that initial burst of feature-shock.

Frames

In the physical world, windows serve a specific purpose: the clear glass allows us to enjoy the sunshine and look outside without actually having to *go* outside (an important distinction if you've ever lived in a sunny, but cold, climate). The window's frame usually acts as a border for the stuff that's happening outside—the window's "content." You can change the size and shape of the window, but the content remains the same.

Now picture a church or cathedral—preferably something older, gothic, European. There are lots of windows, all made of glass, but the multicolored panes stretching to the ceiling take on a completely different purpose. Each window is something to look *at*, not through, and its different panes tell their own stories—content existing for ages.

In the digital world, we usually employ one window through which to view a section of the Internet. That Web browser window frequently changes shape and position on our screens, and occasionally joins other similar browser windows when we're "multitasking." But essentially, the window is a single pane of clear glass looking outside at the Web.

At least it was until Netscape introduced the concept of *frames*. Like the stained-glass cathedral window, frames allow you to split a browser window into multiple sections. They can simultaneously display different parts of the Web, different parts of your site, or even act as graphical interface elements.

Frames versus Framesets

Looking at a framed page in a Web browser, it's easy to see what's happening on the surface: within your browser's window, the separate panes are set to display different pieces of information, even including other Web sites that weren't necessarily built with frames in mind. The structure beneath the surface, though, can be a bit confusing at first, especially if you're accustomed to building non-framed Web pages (see Figure 11-2).

Frameset. To create a framed set of pages, first create an HTML document that contains one or more *framesets:* HTML code that contains the geometry of the frames in the browser window, or their absolute location and dimensions of each frame. Framesets also contain any properties specific to each frame, such as its border width and border color. The frameset references individual HTML files that make up the contents of the framed page. The name of the HTML file containing the framesets is what appears in a browser's Address or Location field when the framed page loads. In GoLive, the document you create and save in the Frame Editor contains one or more framesets. In fact, when GoLive creates a frameset that contains both horizontal and vertical frames, it's actually placing a pair of nested framesets (see "Creating Nested Framesets" later in this chapter for more information).

Frame. The window panes created by the frameset are the frames themselves, and contain the external HTML files referenced by the frameset. In GoLive, you can specify each frame's size and name, whether or not its scrollbars are visible, and if

Keep Your Framesets and Frames Separate

Indulge us if we repeat an important point: the contents of a Web page can be displayed within a frame, but the Web page must be a separate entity from the frameset. Fortunately (or unfortunately, if you don't like crashing programs), a self-reference problem in GoLive illustrates this point beautifully.

Suppose you've been working on a page in GoLive's Layout Editor, and realize midway into editing it that the page would work better in frames.

The *right* thing to do would be to save and close the existing file, create a new GoLive document, and start over by building your frameset. The current file would then be referenced by this new frameset, and life in GoLiveLand would be sunny all the time.

However, the logical, intuitive action—if you hadn't worked much with frames in GoLive—

would be to click on the Frame Editor, drag over a frame icon, and start creating a frameset.

The next logical act would be to reference the page you were just working on in the Layout Editor by using Point & Shoot to select it from the Files tab, as the source of one of the frames.

If you now were to switch to Frame Preview, you'd instigate a self-referencing loop that can't be broken without forcibly quitting GoLive (press Option-Command-Esc on the Macintosh and click Force Quit, or Control-Alt-Delete under Windows and select End Task when prompted); in Windows, it's sometimes possible to click on another view to break out of the loop...Ouch!

Remember: Create framed pages from scratch, not by starting in the Layout Editor and switching to the Frame Editor.

Figure 11-1
Framed page
in browser

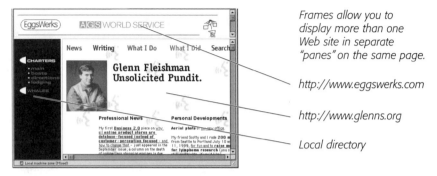

*Frames allow you to
display more than one
Web site in separate
"panes" on the same page.*

http://www.eggswerks.com

http://www.glenns.org

Local directory

Figure 11-2
GoLive's
Frame Editor

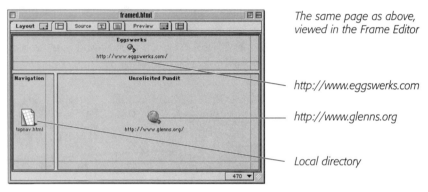

*The same page as above,
viewed in the Frame Editor*

http://www.eggswerks.com

http://www.glenns.org

Local directory

the user can resize the frame borders manually by dragging them. These attributes are all defined within the frameset file, not the HTML files that make up the frames' contents (see "Creating Frames" below to configure these settings). With Web frames, you're pointing at separate HTML files that comprise the frame's content. At first, this may seem like an awkward solution, what with having to pull together several files to create one Web page, but it's clean and it works. (Also see the sidebar, "Keep Your Framesets and Frames Separate.")

Do You *Really* Need to Use Frames?

Before you start going frame-happy, determine if you really need to use frames on your site. Most of the frame examples we've seen while cruising the Web really don't require frames; a much simpler Web page can do just as well. Frames in current browser versions are more stable than their earlier incarnation, so they tend to be more reliable (some browsers had a tendency to crash if you even mentioned the word "frames" within earshot

of the computer). But frames also introduce a layer of complexity to a site that, in many cases, is completely unnecessary. This isn't to say that frames should be avoided; we just don't like seeing people struggling through unnecessary amounts of work when a simpler solution is at hand.

Use the site's content and your own design sense to determine if frames are appropriate.

Creating Frames

GoLive's frame-creation tools are some of the best we've seen, and make setting up frames no more difficult than the steps we've covered so far to build basic pages.

Building and Populating a Frameset

GoLive includes 16 preset frameset layouts, accessible from the Frames tab of the Palette, plus one Frame icon for adding individual frames to existing framesets. To create a new frameset, click the Frame Editor tab in the document window, choose a layout icon from the Palette, then drag it to the Frame Editor (see Figure 11-3). If you drag the single Frame icon onto a blank document, the file automatically turns into a frameset. Don't worry if the layout doesn't initially reflect the structure you're trying to build; you can easily manipulate the frames later.

Figure 11-3
Dragging frame layout icons

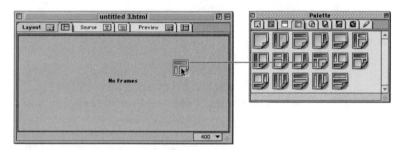

Tip: Single Frame Icon versus Other Frameset Icons
It could be argued that GoLive's Frames tab really only contains one tool, despite the presence of 17 icons. The single Frame icon, in the upper-left corner, is used to create individual frames in the Frame Editor; wherever you drop it on a page, GoLive automatically builds or edits framesets to accommodate the new frame. The other 16 icons are really just templates whose structure could easily be rebuilt by repeatedly dragging the single Frame icon to the page. This is another example of why we love using GoLive: dragging one or two icons saves a huge amount of time compared with writing the frameset code by hand.

Clicking anywhere within a frame selects it and displays the Frame Inspector, which controls settings for individual frames. To select a frameset instead, click a border separating the frames; this displays the Frameset Inspector, which handles global frame options and values.

Tip: Frameset or Empty GoLive Document?
If you view an existing HTML file in GoLive through the Layout Editor and discover no content on the page, don't be alarmed. It could just be a frameset. To make a quick determination, look at the document's Page icon (see Figure 11-4). A frameset file displays a frame icon; regular HTML files feature a regular page icon design with horizontal lines.

Figure 11-4
Two flavors of
the Page icon

Page icon as seen in the Layout Editor   *Page icon indicating a framed page*

Tip:
Identifying
the Frameset
Icons

The Frameset icons have been designed to easily tell the relative size and place-ments of frame borders you're likely to end up with when you drag them onto the Frame Editor. However, the last four icons seem redundant; the only differences among the two vertical frames and the two horizontal frames is their color scheme. Or is it? Figure 11-5 illustrates what you should expect when you drag them to your document.

Figure 11-5
Identifying
the four
"redundant"
frame icons

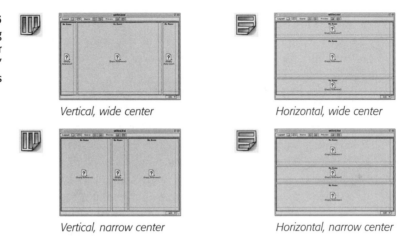

Vertical, wide center   *Horizontal, wide center*

Vertical, narrow center   *Horizontal, narrow center*

Adding and deleting frames. If you want to create a framed page that has a dif-ferent look or a different number of frames than the prefabricated icons in the Frame tab of the Palette, drag the single Frame icon from the Palette to the loca-tion you want to insert a new frame.

Dragging this icon onto an existing horizontal frame generally splits it into two vertical frames. Likewise, dragging it onto a vertical frame usually splits it into two horizontal ones (see Figure 11-6).

Tip:
Controlling
How New
Frames Are
Inserted

Dragging the single Frame icon from the Frames palette creates a new frame in your layout, but which orientation? In our semi-scientific testing—meaning we repeatedly created new frames until we were sick of it—dropping the icon most anywhere in a single-frame frameset created a new vertical frame to the right of the existing frame. However, dropping the icon directly on top of the existing frame's icon, or near the bottom of that frame, caused a new horizontal frame to appear below it. When more than a few frames existed on the page, new frames usually appeared vertically. Fortunately, moving frames into new positions is a simple matter of dragging the frame, so the inconsistency of GoLive's Frame icon shouldn't cause you to lose sleep.

Figure 11-6
Adding frames
with the single
Frame icon

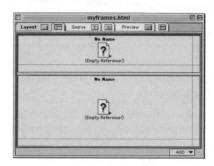
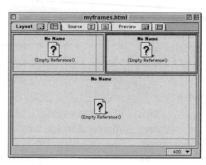

*Original frameset layout
dragged in from the Palette...*

*...and after adding single
frame icon to top frame*

If you make too many new frames, delete them one by one by clicking within each frame's borders to select it, and then pressing the Delete key. You can't select multiple frames and delete them at once.

Creating Nested Framesets

Like tables, you can nest framesets within frames. As mentioned earlier, when Go-Live creates a frameset that contains both horizontal and vertical frames, it's actually creating a pair of nested framesets (see Figure 11-7). Simply drag a new Frameset icon from the Palette into an existing frame. The existing frame doesn't act as a container, the way a table cell holds a nested table; instead, the frame resizes to accommodate the new incoming frameset. For example, suppose you have a frameset containing two horizontal frames. If you drag one of the two-framed frameset icons from the palette, you'll end up with four separate frames, not three. You can select a nested frameset by clicking one of its frame borders; a dark outline indicates the current selection.

Figure 11-7
Natural nested
framesets

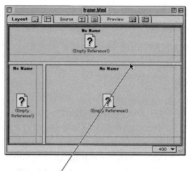
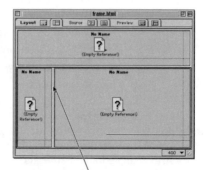

*Clicking the horizontal divider
highlights the page's master
frameset, indicated by a bold box
surrounding the frameset.*

*However, clicking the vertical divider
reveals that the bottom two panes
belong to their own frameset, which
is therefore nested within the master
frameset.*

Using the Noframe Version of a Frameset

Frames aren't for everyone nor everyone's browsers. Some browsers feature the option to not view frames, while other, mostly older, browsers don't recognize frame coding at all. Users in these situations typically would see a blank page when encountering a frameset.

Fortunately, GoLive automatically adds the simple Noframe tag to every framed document. With Noframe in the HTML, the browsers mentioned above ignore the frameset code and display the content included within the Body tags.

In most cases you can add a line or two of text explaining that the viewer has happened upon a framed page. But you can also build a full page that echoes the contents of the frames and leads the user either to the pages that load within the frames (see below), or to alternate pages set up specifically for folks who can't or won't view frames. This way, your pages' content is available to everyone in one form or another.

Use the Layout Editor to build the Noframe page, just as you would a normal document, without worrying about it interfering with your frames (see Figure 11-8). To preview the page in GoLive for Macintosh, switch to the Layout Preview.

Figure 11-8
Noframe page

People who can't view frames see the Noframe page, which you build in GoLive's Layout Editor.

If you're running the Windows version, you can't preview the Noframe page because Windows uses an embedded version of Microsoft Internet Explorer to preview pages. Internet Explorer supports frames, which is why Adobe doesn't provide a non-framed preview tab. You just have to rely on the Layout Editor's view as the preview.

Tip: Previewing Noframe Pages on Windows

You could install an old version of Netscape Navigator or Internet Explorer that doesn't support frames and preview your Noframe content in that browser. However, older browsers have their own sets of problems when used with newer operating systems, especially when you're running, say, IE 3 and IE 5 on the same machine. Consult http://www.zdnet.com/swlib/topics/browsers.html for information on downloading older browsers archived at that site.

Tip: Provide a Link to Unframed Pages

It's good Web etiquette to give the viewer a choice between framed or unframed pages by providing a link in one of your frames that leads to an unframed version of the site. Perhaps visitors won't see the full brilliance of your design, but at least they won't click away in search of someone else's brilliance.

Specifying the Contents of a Frame

With a basic frameset built, it's time to populate the frames within it. There are three methods for linking frames in a framed page to HTML files (see Figure 11-9).

Drag and drop existing files. From either the desktop or an open Site window, drag an HTML file's icon to the desired frame. You can also grab the page icon from an open document and drop it onto a frame.

Point & Shoot. Here is another area where GoLive's Point & Shoot tool comes in handy. With your cursor placed anywhere within a frame, hold down the Command key (Mac) or Alt key (Windows) and drag from the frame to the file you want to use in the Files tab of the Site window. You can also "shoot" at the Page icon of an open file. The Frame Inspector's Point & Shoot button works too.

Tip: Point & Shoot for Anchored Links	If you're using the Macintosh version of GoLive, you can display a specific section of an HTML file, other than its beginning, within a frame. Open the HTML file and use Point & Shoot to direct your cursor to that location on the page to create a new anchored link. Similarly, you can direct your cursor to an anchored link within a file being displayed in the Site window (indicated by a gray anchor icon beside the link).

Figure 11-9
Methods of populating frames

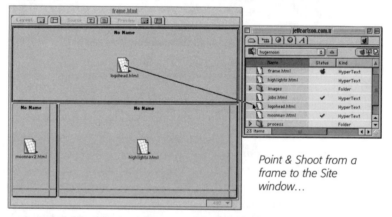

Point & Shoot from a frame to the Site window...

...drag and drop a file from the Site window...

...or type the filename in the Frame Inspector's URL field.

Enter a path in the URL field. When a frame is selected, type the path name of the frame's source file into the Frame Inspector's URL field, or click the Browse button to search for the file. This path can be a pointer to a file on your hard disk, or a page that exists elsewhere on the Web, in which case a globe icon appears within the frame.

Previewing Framed Content

The Frame Editor makes it easy to see which files appear in each frame, but displaying just the file icons is contrary to the whole idea of creating Web pages visually. Two options are available for seeing what your frameset looks like in a real browser.

Frame Preview window. If you're running the Macintosh version of GoLive, click the Frame Preview icon in the document window to get a fairly accurate representation of what the framed page will look like in a Web browser.

The Windows version uses only one Preview window. If the document contains framesets, the frames are previewed. Only local files are displayed, so any external URLs referenced in the Frame Inspector's URL field remain blank, even if you have an active Internet connection. You cannot edit the frames in the Frame Preview window (see Figure 11-10).

Figure 11-10
Previewing a
framed page

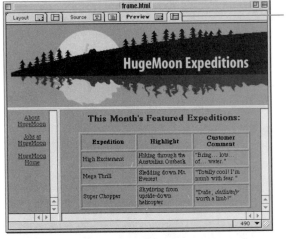

On the Mac, click the Frame Preview tab.

GoLive for Windows displays framed pages in the standard Preview tab.

Frameset and frame previews in the Frame Editor (Macintosh only). As you're working in the Frame Editor, you can opt to display the contents of the entire frameset or just individual frames to get an idea of how the frames interact with one another. You can't edit the referenced HTML files directly, but previewing them helps to establish the overall look of the frameset.

Click a frame border to bring up the Frameset Inspector, then click the Preview Set button. Each frame containing a local file displays the page's contents. Clicking the Stop Preview button reverts back to the default file icon view (see Figure 11-11).

To view only the contents of selected frames, select one and click the Preview button on the Frame Inspector. Click the button again to stop previewing.

Figure 11-11
Previewing individual frames

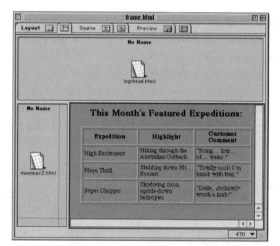

Click here to preview the contents of the selected frame.

Editing Frames

Real-world objects only go so far when used as computer-interface metaphors, and this is where the idea of the stained-glass window begins to break down. Unlike

The Mystery of the Macintosh GoLive Preview Set

The Frame and Frameset inspectors contain a bit of mystery; they're both full of buttons that appear to duplicate other features. But the choice to use VCR-style buttons stumps us.

In the Frame Inspector, clicking the Preview button causes it to appear "pressed" while previewing is active. In the Frameset Inspector, how-

ever, the same functionality requires two buttons: Preview Set, which resembles a "play" button, and Stop Preview, which looks like a "stop" button. Neither button appears pressed when active. Hopefully, consistency and simplicity will improve in a future version.

solid windows made of glass and lead, framesets feature the ability to move panes around easily, allow users to stretch their dimensions, load information in specific frames, and more.

Editing the contents of a frame. Rare is the occasion when all the HTML files you place into frames are in perfect shape. Invariably, something must change; when it does, simply double-click the frame to open its associated HTML file in a new window. GoLive adds a nice touch to this action: the new window appears the same size as your frame, in roughly the same location. You can open all your frame content files this way and work on them as if they were in a virtual frameset (see Figure 11-12).

Figure 11-12
Editing frame
contents

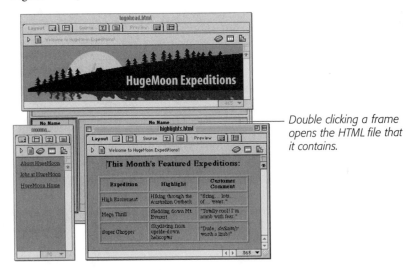

Double clicking a frame
opens the HTML file that
it contains.

Tip: Frames and Search Engines   Frames can often confuse search engines, because the content of your frameset file doesn't actually include the content of the framed page. If you've put a lot of time and effort into including descriptive Meta tags in your files, your work may be ignored by search engine robots which look only at the frameset information. So, be sure to put your Meta tag information in the frameset file as well.

Moving and Resizing Frames

Moving frames and framesets is fairly intuitive: click within a frame to select it, then drag the selection to where you would like the frame to appear. However, you can only move individual frames within their parent framesets. If you want a frame to appear in a separate nested frameset, use the Frame icon to add a new frame where you'd like to move an existing one, make sure it's pointing to the same

HTML source file, then delete the old frame (see Figure 11-13). To move an entire frameset, Control-click and drag the frameset's border.

Resizing a frame is also easy, provided you're aware of how GoLive handles the settings that regulate frame size. When you build a frameset by dragging the single Frame icon from the Frames palette, the Size attribute in the Frame Inspector is set to Scale, which simply balances the size automatically with other frames in its row or column. In this case, although you can grab the divider and drag a ghosted version of it, the size won't actually change.

To make the size change permanent, you must first set the Size option either to Pixels or Percent, depending on whether you want to set the size in absolute or relative terms. You can either drag the frame border to set the size, or you can enter values directly into the Size field. Switching back to Scale re-balances the frames.

If you build your frameset by dragging a prefab Frameset icon from the Frames menu, you can just drag the borders to resize the frames, because at least one frame's Size attribute is set to either Pixels or Percent.

Figure 11-13
"Moving" a frame into another frameset

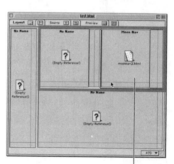

We want to move the Moon Nav frame into the left column frameset, but Moon Nav will only move within its own frameset.

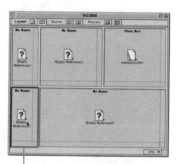

Use the single Frame icon from the Palette to create a new frame within the left column frameset.

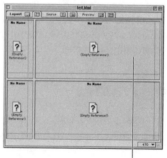

Delete the old Moon Nav frame.

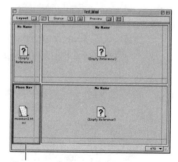

Rename the new frame to Moon Nav and set its source as the original HTML file.

Tip: Awkward Inspector Display When Resizing

To resize a frame, you need to click the frame's border. To select a frameset, you need to click the frame's border. Spot any similarities? Unlike resizing table cells, you can't resize a frame and view its exact pixel or percentage dimensions as you drag its border, because the Frameset Inspector appears in place of the Frame Inspector as soon as you release the mouse button. So, if you're shooting for a specific height or width for your frame, it's better to enter that value in the Frame Inspector's Size field.

Tip: Balancing the Scales

Web browsers like balance, because it means they don't have to work as hard to interpret the dimensions of a page. If you specify a frame's height or width in pixels or percentages, make sure at least one more frame in that row or column has its size set to Scale.

Controlling users' resizing options. Not all the frame settings are intended to control the page from the designer's side. A unique frames feature is the ability for users to resize their frames within Web browsers. Checking the Resize Frames box in the Frame Inspector gives users this option, and puts a small indented circle in the middle of the frame's border (see Figure 11-14). GoLive assumes that you want absolute control over your frame sizes, so this option is turned off by default.

Figure 11-14
Resizable frame indicator

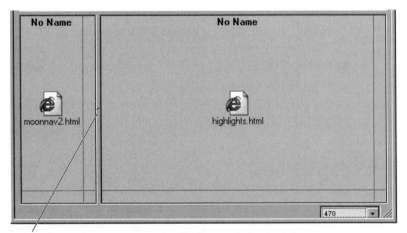

This indicates that users can resize the frame within a Web browser.

You can also control whether or not a frame's scrollbars are displayed in the browser. If the contents of the frame exceed the size of the window, browsers automatically show horizontal or vertical scrollbars. But you can force them to remain hidden by setting Scrolling to No. Similarly, choosing Yes draws scrollbars (even if they're inactive) every time. Since scrollbars in most browsers tend to take up a lot of space, especially in smaller frames, this feature can be useful for controlling a frame's appearance as well as its functionality. The Auto setting leaves the decision to draw the bars to the browser (see Figure 11-15).

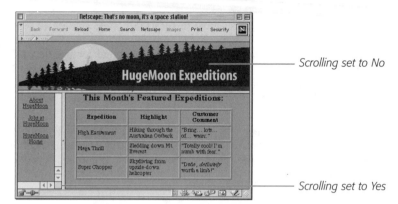

Figure 11-15
Controlling
scroll bar
appearance

———— *Scrolling set to No*

———— *Scrolling set to Yes*

Frame Borders

Frame borders can be part of how you navigate or interpret a page, and they can be modified in a few ways to control their effect and display. Click a border to bring up the Frameset Inspector, where you can change the following options.

BorderSize. GoLive assigns borders with a default thickness of six pixels—big enough to grab and manipulate, but not so large that they become obnoxious. Checking the BorderSize box lets you enter a pixel size to change the border's thickness. Often, designers set frame borders to zero so that the page doesn't blatantly look like it's been split into frames (see Figure 11-16). One downside is that zero-pixel borders cannot be dragged to resize frames in most browsers, even if the Resize Frame box is checked.

Border Skirmishes

If you play around with frame borders in GoLive, you'll discover that you can apply different attributes to separate borders within nested framesets. For example, a vertical border at left could be dark green, while a horizontal border at right could be bright yellow, and sized at 20 pixels.

What you see in your browser is a different matter; the programs we tested all favored one setting over another. But which settings override others? Logically, it would make sense that the parent frameset would win out, but experience proves otherwise. In the example above, the bright yellow border wins out in Netscape Communicator, despite being the child frameset. The two border colors draw correctly under Internet Explorer 4.0 for Windows, but don't display at all in IE for the Macintosh. When it comes to border sizes, though, it's the parent that instructs the child. Setting the left border to zero above applies that thickness to the right-hand border as well.

As with too many aspects of HTML, the final results vary depending on which browser and platform you're using. Until the mythical day comes when all browsers treat HTML the same, you're better off testing your pages' effects with as many variations as you can get your hands on.

Figure 11-16
Invisible frame
borders

With borders set to zero, the page receives a more uniform look. Frames whose content exceeds the frame size display scrollbars—the only indication on this page that frames are being used.

BorderColor. If a border's size is set larger than zero, you can apply a color to it. Check the BorderColor box, then drag a swatch from the Color Palette to its color field. Unlike table colors, where dropping a swatch onto a color field automatically checks the Color box, you must first check BorderColor, then select a color.

BorderFrame. The BorderFrame setting is a bit confusing on the surface, and requires a brief dip into the HTML being used in the page. Some settings, like table border sizes, are only set numerically; telling a browser to render a table with a border of zero effectively produces a borderless table. In the case of frame borders, two triggers come into play: the numeric size, and also an on/off toggle for displaying the border. In HTML, the Frameborder tag can have a value of "1" or "Yes" to indicate that a border is visible, or "0" or "No" to hide the border.

Therefore, if you really want your borders hidden, you need to set GoLive's BorderSize to zero *and* specify that the BorderFrame is set to No. This also applies to border colors; if you specify a border color but BorderFrame is set to No, the color doesn't display (though in some browsers, a larger-sized BorderSize setting causes that much space to be filled with the browser's default background color).

Tip: Using Frames as Layout Elements

A good way to avoid some of the unpredictability of how browsers display frame borders is to circumvent the border settings altogether. If you want a thick black border separating two vertical frames, for example, you could set the border's size to 10, its color to black, and make sure that BorderFrame is set to Yes.

Or, you could create a frameset containing three frames, with the borders hidden. The left and right frames hold the page's contents, as you would have done with a two-frame frameset. Then specify that the middle frame's width is 10, and use a source HTML file that contains nothing but a background color of black. You've cut down the number of variables at work, and you can also reuse that black-background page in other framesets.

Naming and Targeting Frames

We've covered the structure of frames and framesets, and how to manipulate their appearance. Moving still further away from our stained glass metaphor, frames are designed to interact with one another so that all of them in combination work together as a whole on the page. To use a common example, if you're using a vertical frame to the left as a navigation bar, clicking a link should change the contents of a main content frame to the right. To accomplish this, you have to identify each frame with a unique name; otherwise, the link's destination page is likely to override your frameset and fill the entire window.

When you create a new frameset, each frame is titled "No Name" in the Frame Inspector's Name field. Whenever we build framed pages, one of the first things we do is name the frames to prevent confusion later in the process: simply type in a new name and press Return.

Creating frame links. Linking to a frame is essentially the same as linking to a file (see Chapter 1, *Getting Started*), only in this case, you must specify a name to go along with the link's source. This is why naming frames is so important.

To start, open a frame's HTML file by double-clicking the frame. For purposes of explanation, let's assume that you want to create a link in the left-most frame, titled "left-nav," that displays a new page as the contents of the bottom right frame, titled "right-main" (see Figure 11-17). Perform the following steps to create the link.

1. Select the text or image to be linked, and choose New Link from the Special menu.

2. On the Link tab of the Text or Image Inspector, enter the link's destination in the URL field by typing the filename or using the Point & Shoot tool.

3. Specify the intended frame by entering its name in the Target field. If your frameset file is still open, the popup menu at right includes the names of all frames at the top of the list. In our example, use "right-main" as the target.

4. Be sure to save the content file.

Now, when you click the link, your browser first looks for a frame with that name before loading the page. If one is found, the contents are loaded into that frame.

Tip: Point & Shoot Can Kill Mac Targets

If you've already established a link within a file that points to a named frame as its target, think twice before using the Point & Shoot keyboard shortcut under the Mac version of GoLive. Normally, holding down Command enables you to click and drag from a text selection to the Site window to create a new link. Unfortunately, changing an existing link using this technique erases the name specified in the Target field. The Point & Shoot tool located in the Link Inspector, however, retains the target name.

Figure 11-17
Targeting
frames

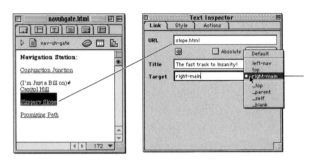

*The names of the
frames in the active
document are displayed
in the Target popup
menu.*

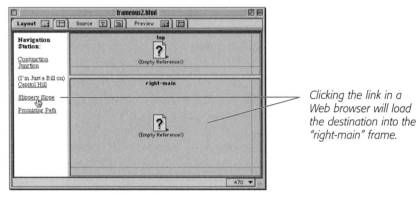

*Clicking the link in a
Web browser will load
the destination into the
"right-main" frame.*

**Tip: Multiple
Open
Frameset
Files**

When you have more than one frameset file open, the Target popup menu lists all the names available. If your frames share the same names across several files, close the frameset files that you're not using to make sure the link is pointing to the correct frame.

**Tip:
Renaming
Frames**

If you rename a frame, you run the risk of breaking the links to it. GoLive's ability to manage links automatically throughout a site is great, but unfortunately the feature doesn't extend to target names as far as we can tell. The good news is that you can easily use the search and replace tool to find the old frame name and replace it with the new name across all the files within your site (see Chapter 21, *Site Specials*).

Special built-In targets. The Target popup menu also features four targets that let you direct the contents of a link without using a specific frame name.

- **_top** directs your browser to load the targeted page into the existing window, overriding the frameset.

- **_self** replaces the contents of the frame containing the link with the targeted page.

- **_blank** loads the targeted page into a new browser window.

- **_parent** acts like _top, but is applied when you have nested framesets, loading the contents into the parent frameset.

Are You Game for Frames?

Over the last few years, we've grown accustomed to looking *at* the Web on our computers, though it's more accurate to say that we look *through* our computers to glimpse the Web. With frames, you can multiply that view dramatically, using the same screen space to display and interact with more of the Web.

CHAPTER 12

Layout Grids and Floating Boxes

From the dawn of time—1994—designers have had but one ambition: the ability to place text *precisely where they wanted it* on a Web page. GoLive supports two major solutions to this goal, although both have their own sets of drawbacks and considerations.

GoLive's layout grids are actually complex arrays of table cells carefully spaced and controlled so that they force type to appear in specific positions based on the table formatting. Floating boxes are GoLive's way of packaging a feature from Cascading Style Sheets (CSS) in which you can specify the absolute position of a block of HTML on a page (see Table 12-1).

Tip: You Can Never Go Home (Page) Again
Both features produce incredibly complex HTML that can't really be edited by hand. Once you start using layout grids and floating boxes, you can't easily go back, as the HTML contains coordinates and/or a vast number of tags for spacing. A graphical interface becomes a necessity to hide the numbers and complexity.

We've grouped grids and floating boxes together in this chapter because their function is the same: specifying the position of elements on a page, rather than allowing HTML to wrap and warp text and images to fit its own built-in vision.

In some ways, both features subvert HTML, which is a way to specify things generically enough that a given set of HTML code can display on multiple machines in different ways without losing the general look and feel. But more importantly, both features offer designers at least a glimpse of the Way Things Should Be, in which page creators can design something that can match their vision and have it appear much more similar on many users' machines.

Table 12-1
Grids versus
floating boxes

Feature	Grids	Floating Boxes
HTML basis	Table cells and special tags	Standard CSS
Browser support	Table complexity requires 3.0 or higher major browser	Only 4.0 and higher major browsers that are CSS1 compliant for positioning tags
Positioning units	In units as small as one pixel, which is the only available measurement unit	In any increment of any absolute units, such as whole pixels, fractions of an inch, etc.
Arbitrary positioning anywhere on page	No, grids are inserted into normal HTML flow; objects on grids can be placed	Yes, floating boxes can be positioned precisely anywhere on a page
Animation	No	Yes, used with JavaScript as the basis of DHTML animation
HTML beauty	Pretty dense, impossible to hand edit, proprietary GoLive tags	Compact and straightforward, but all coordinate-based so still quite difficult to hand edit
Overlapping objects	No, each grid is its own object on the page in the HTML flow	Yes, each floating box has its own layer setting which allows transparency and overlap between any number of boxes
Contain the other	Grids can't contain floating boxes except inside Layout Text Boxes	Floating boxes can contain grids (as well as any HTML)
What can be put on or in them	Every kind of HTML object except text, which requires a special Layout Text Box; the Layout Text Box, however, can hold floating boxes and all other kinds of HTML, including other grids	No limitations; like a mini-HTML page

Tip: When to Use Positioning

We've found most sites that need exact positioning are using a variety of rich media: lots of rendered type and graphics, special effects, plug-in-based media, and so forth. For a simpler site that contains mostly HTML-formatted text and a few images, a layout grid or a floating box or two might involve more stress on the user's browser than is needed for practical use.

Let's start with grids, which rely on the simpler aspects of table formatting, before proceding to floating boxes, which require some introduction to CSS. (Tables are covered in full in Chapter 10, *Tables*, while CSS is discussed in Chapter 26, *Cascading Style Sheets*.)

Layout Grids

Layout grids use a graph-paper metaphor for locating items on a page (see Figure 12-1). You can set a grid to rigidly lock all items dragged on it to the defined grid lines, or you can disable that control for either or both horizontal and vertical directions and freely drag objects around.

Figure 12-1
Text and objects on a layout grid

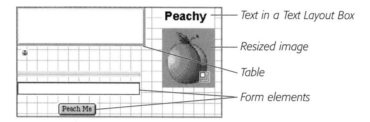

Getting started couldn't be simpler. From the Basic tab of the Palette drag a Layout Grid onto an HTML page (see Figure 12-2). GoLive inserts a 200-by-200 pixel grid as a default with 16-pixels-square grid spacing. This also brings up the Layout Grid Inspector and adds layout items to the Toolbar.

Handling the Grid

Grids have a set of properties including dimensions, color, and alignment that can be set or edited through dragging or through the Layout Grid Inspector.

Location. The Layout Grid Inspector doesn't allow you to change the location of a grid because grids are inserted into the flow of HTML itself. If you want to move a

Browser Compatibility

Grids use table tags and elements, and therefore require browsers newer than Netscape 2.0. But because of the intensity and quantity of table elements GoLive uses to make a grid, 3.0 browsers and higher are really required.

Floating boxes, because they rely on CSS properties, only work with 4.0 browsers and higher.

Both features may work differently on different platforms and releases of the same browser because of the juryrigging that make this work.

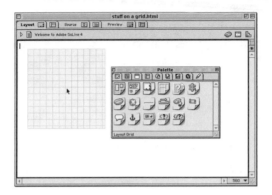

Figure 12-2
Dragging in a
layout grid

grid, you can select it and drag it to a new location, or cut and paste the entire grid. However, you can't exactly position the grid on a box in an arbitrary location; you must use a floating box to achieve that.

Grid elements. Grid units are preset at 16 pixels in both directions, but you can modify these through the Layout Grid Inspector. If you uncheck Snap for either or both directions, objects can be dragged to any spot on a grid regardless of the grid lines. Unchecking Visible for either or both directions removes the grid lines display.

Resizing. You can resize the grid by dragging handles on the left, bottom, or right sides of the layout grid, or by specifying new values in the Layout Grid. The grid always grows or shrinks on the right and bottom edges.

Holding down the Shift key while dragging keeps the grid proportionate. Adding the Control key on both Mac and Windows provides an interactive display.

You can't resize a grid smaller than the width of the largest object's right or bottom edge.

Optimizing. Clicking Optimize in the Layout Grid Inspector resizes the box to the furthest right and bottom edges of objects contained in the grid (see Figure 12-3).

Behind the Grid

Grids make use of some non-standard HTML that GoLive uses to create the grid preview correctly and to locate objects in the table cells it uses to comprise the grid.

For instance, in the Table tag, GoLive identifies the table as a component of a grid by inserting multiple attributes such as Cool and Gridx. These tags are ignored by browsers, which are supposed to interpret only HTML tags and attributes that they know.

Other items include Spacer, a filler tag used to indicate the kind of space to insert in a row and Xpos, an attribute of TD (table cell) which defines the absolute horizontal position of an item in pixels.

Figure 12-3
Optimizing the
layout grid

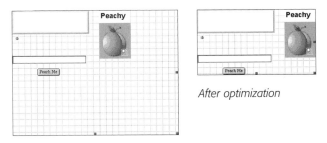

After optimization

Before optimization

Alignment. A grid can be aligned by default (to the uppermost and leftmost location available), or to the left or right.

Background color. A background color can be set for the entire layout grid by clicking the color swatch to bring up the Color Palette and dragging a swatch onto it, which automatically checks the Color box.

Grid Objects

Any HTML object from any tab on the Palette can be dragged directly onto a layout grid. GoLive shows a bounding box of the item as you drag it around so you can see how big an area it can take and to which grid lines it snaps if Snap is set for either direction.

Text can only be added by inserting a Layout Text Box, which can contain any kind of HTML object itself, including layout grids and floating boxes. Layout Text Boxes have their own Inspector which allows you to set a separate background color in the text box.

Tip: Indecent Nesting You can nest a floating box with a layout grid inside a Layout Text Box inside a layout grid (see Figure 12-4). Only a higher power knows exactly how any given browser would react to this abomination, however.

Figure 12-4
Nesting layout
grids inside
floating boxes
ad infinitum

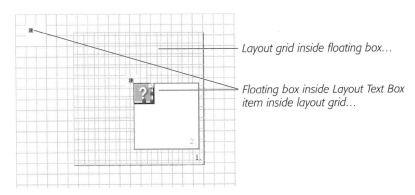

Layout grid inside floating box...

Floating box inside Layout Text Box item inside layout grid...

Moving. After an object is placed, it can be dragged around a layout grid. If you drag it near the edge, the bounding box for the item stops previewing if its left or top edge goes too far right or down (see Figure 12-5).

You can move objects from the keyboard by selecting the object and using the arrow keys. Pressing Control-Alt (Windows) or Option (Mac) plus an arrow key moves objects in one-pixel increments if Snap is checked. Press those keys when Snap is unchecked to move objects in grid increments.

The Toolbar also shows the coordinates of an object on the grid; you can enter new values to move the object (see Figure 12-6).

Resizing. Objects on a layout grid can be resized by grabbing their control handles and dragging (see Figure 12-7). You can also enter values into the width and height fields in the Toolbar.

If you want to resize objects to be the same size, select the object that serves as your model for size, then select any other objects on the grid. Click the Same Size button in the Multiselection Inspector's Alignment tab, and all the objects are now identical to the first one selected (see Figure 12-8).

Behind the Box

Floating boxes use a somewhat more elegant and simple approach for inserting a precisely positioned item on screen. (This explanation requires some knowledge of CSS, which you can acquire from Chapter 26, *Cascading Style Sheets*.)

First, all the material that appears in the floating box is inserted in the HTML using a Div (division) container. The Div tag is used just for CSS to help divvy up areas of a site into self-contained blocks. Each floating box is assigned a unique identifier in the Div tag.

Next, the positioning and other characteristics of the box are written to the page's style sheet as an individual style that has the corresponding unique identifier.

For instance, if we named a box "bingle," in the head part of the page in the style declaration, you might have

```
#bingle { position: absolute; top:
17px; left: 24px; width: 100px;
height: 100px; visibility: visible }
```

The box itself would be represented in the HTML as

```
<div id="bingle">Whole lot of shakin'
goin' on</div>
```

Dragging or reshaping the floating box or changing specifications in the Floating Box Inspector cause the style #bingle to be rewritten. Editing the contents of bingle changes the material in the Div container labeled bingle.

It's surprisingly straightforward, but again, not something you generally want to manage by hand.

(We've noticed that if you create a CSS unique identifier that has block properties—like position, margin, or border—GoLive turns it into a floating box. You can demonstrate this by switching to the HTML Source Editor and back to Layout Editor, or closing and opening the document. Back in Layout Editor, the paragraph or range of text now appears as a floating box. Nothing to be done about this; it's almost a feature!)

Figure 12-5
Dragging an
object off the
layout grid

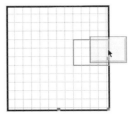

*The bounding box displays
only while the object is on
the grid (left); the layout
grid's highlight and the
object's bounding box
disappear when it leaves the
grid (right).*

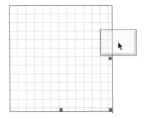

Figure 12-6
An object's
coordinates in
the Toolbar

Figure 12-7
Resizing an
object in a
layout grid

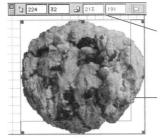

*Dimensions change as you
drag the resize handles*

Resize cursor

Figure 12-8
An object's
coordinates in
the Toolbar

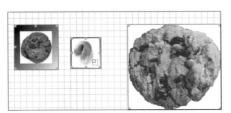

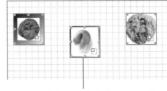

*After resizing with fortune cookie
selected as the model image*

Before resizing

Aligning. If you select two or more objects, you can use the alignment features in the Multiselection Inspector's Alignment tab or in the Toolbar (see Figure 12-9). The vertical and horizontal alignment buttons move the selected objects as a group without changing their position relative to one another. You can align top, middle, or bottom, and left, center, and right by clicking the appropriate buttons.

Distributing. With three or more objects selected, the Special tab of the Multiselection Inspector provides options for scattering or reshuffling the objects in your selection.

Figure 12-9
Alignment
options

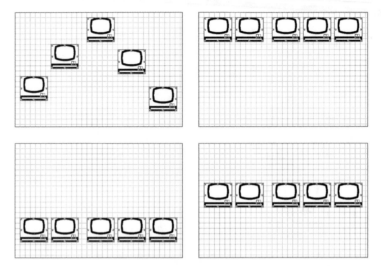

*Random (top left), align top edges (top right), align bottom edges
(bottom left), align middles (bottom right)*

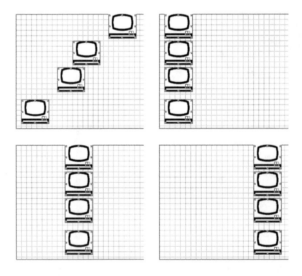

*Random (top left), align
left edges (top right), align
centers (bottom left), align
right edges (bottom right)*

Both horizontal and vertical options are broken into Offset and Distribute categories. Choosing Offset allows you to specify a distance that each object is offset from the next. So, clicking align by object's borders with Offset chosen spaces each object's top and bottom or left or right edges apart from each other by the Offset value (see Figure 12-10). (All the buttons below Offset and Distribute gray out if you choose an Offset value too large to work in the layout grid with the objects you have selected.) Choosing Distribute spaces the objects by the farthest left and right or top and bottom objects in the selection (see Figure 12-11).

Figure 12-10
Offset by
objects'
borders

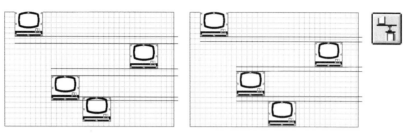

Random vertical spacing

Vertical spacing between items adjusted to a uniform 15 pixels

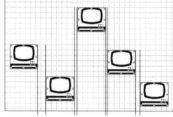
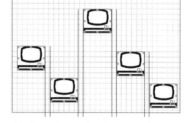

Random horizontal spacing

Horizontal spacing between items adjusted to uniform 15 pixels

Figure 12-11
Distribute

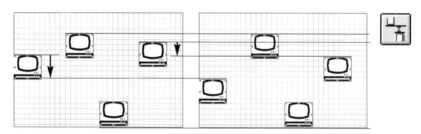

Random vertical spacing

Vertical spacing distributed between objects; top and bottom objects stay put

Horizontal choices are align by center, align by left edge, align by right edge, and by adjacent left and right edges. Vertical choices are align by top, align by middle, align by bottom, and by adjacent top and bottom edges.

Grouping. You can select multiple objects and click the Group button in the Toolbar to turn them into a single larger object (see Figure 12-12). The Group Inspector lets you lock a group in its current location; it also reveals how many items are in a group.

Select the group and click Ungroup to turn them back into individual objects.

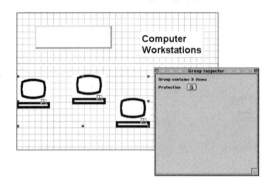

Figure 12-12
Grouped
object and
Group
Inspector

Floating Boxes

Floating boxes have many of the same properties as layout grids, but they offer two distinct advantages and one distinct drawback.

The advantages? You can put a floating box *anywhere* on a page; you're not limited to inserting it into a position forced by the sequence of HTML. And the amount of code to make a floating box appear is simpler and more standardized, meaning less strain on the browser which creates a greater chance of it looking like you expected.

The only real disadvantage is that only version 4.0 and later of Netscape Navigator and Microsoft Internet Explorer can handle floating boxes because the features rely on CSS. People without 4.0 or later browsers (or the Opera browser's 5.0 or later release) see lumps of material scattered around the screen. So take heed of your audience before committing to floating boxes.

Inserting a Floating Box icon. Creating a new floating box is just as easy as adding a layout grid: drag a Floating Box icon from the Basic tab of the Palette onto an HTML page (see Figure 12-13). GoLive inserts a small yellow placeholder that's labeled SB. This placeholder indicates the spot in the HTML source where the contents of the floating box are inserted. However, the placeholder's location doesn't affect the positioning of the contents of the box on the page.

Figure 12-13
Dragging in a
Floating Box
icon

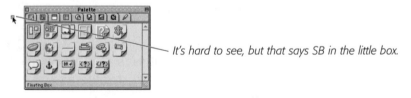

It's hard to see, but that says SB in the little box.

Tip: German Lesson   Why SB for a floating box? The German for floating box would be something like Schwebende Büchse: SB. GoLive's original developers were (and many still are) based in Hamburg, Germany.

Adding objects. You can drag any kind of object or type into the floating box. If you drag in objects larger than the box, the box's size increases to fit them (see Figure 12-14).

Figure 12-14
Floating box
resize

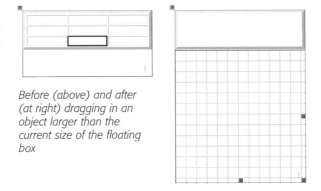

Before (above) and after (at right) dragging in an object larger than the current size of the floating box

Resizing. Floating boxes can be resized by using the mouse, exactly as with layout grids. When you mouse over any of the three control handles on the bottom, right, or lower-right corner, the cursor changes into an arrowhead (see Figure 12-15). Dragging resizes the box.

Adding the Shift key constrains the resizing to the proportions of the existing box. Adding the Control key (both Mac and Windows) provides a live preview as you drag.

Figure 12-15
Resizing the
floating box

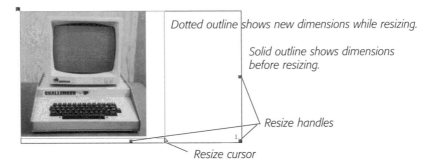

Dotted outline shows new dimensions while resizing.

Solid outline shows dimensions before resizing.

Resize handles

Resize cursor

Moving. If you mouse over any of the four borders of a floating box, the cursor changes to a left-pointing gloved hand (see Figure 12-16). This indicates you can drag the box. A box can be dragged anywhere on the page.

Floating Box Inspector

The Floating Box Inspector offers several controls to further extend a floating box.

Figure 12-16
Floating box
movement
cursor

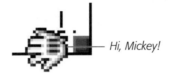

— *Hi, Mickey!*

Coordinates and size. The inspector, of course, allows you to set the left and top origin position of the box in pixels. But you can also change the box's dimensions in pixels, as a percentage of the browser window, or as an automatic resize to fill the necessary space.

If you change the Width or Height fields to Auto or Percent, the appropriate control handles disappear, so you can't drag that dimension any more but must set it through the Floating Box Inspector.

Tip: Auto Width, Height   Selecting Auto for Width appears to resize a floating box from its current coordinates to the full width of the browser window. However, setting Height to Auto resizes the box to only the depth necessary to fit the objects it contains.

Name. You can name each floating box to better identify it in the Floating Box Controller (see below). But it's also useful and pretty necessary to name them when creating animations; see Chapter 24, *Animation.*

Depth of layer. Floating boxes may overlap one another, and you control their stacking order by entering a value into the Depth field, which is called the Z-Index field in CSS (Z being the top-to-bottom dimension in a coordinate system).

The higher the number, the closer to the top the floating box, um, floats (see Figure 12-17). Numbers do not have to be sequential; you can assign numbers 7, 21, and 50 to three boxes, and that still places them in order from bottom to top (or most occluded to least).

Figure 12-17
Layering
floating boxes

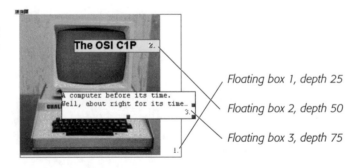

Floating box 1, depth 25

Floating box 2, depth 50

Floating box 3, depth 75

Visibility. You can hide the contents of the floating box both in the Layout Editor and in a browser window by unchecking the Visible box. (This setting interacts in interesting ways with the Floating Box Controller, described below.)

Color. A floating box's background color may be set by dragging a swatch into the Color field. Dragging the swatch in also checks the Color box.

Background image. Floating boxes are like mini-HTML pages, and can have their own tiled background images (see Figure 12-18). You set the background image for a floating box exactly as you would for an HTML page: browse or Point & Shoot to find an image.

Figure 12-18
Background in
a floating box

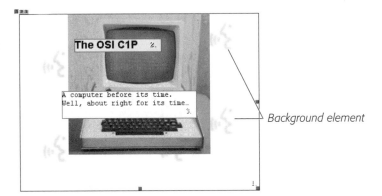

Background element

Animation Settings. A whole chunk of the Floating Box Inspector is labeled Animation and has features that relate to using floating boxes in Dynamic HTML (DHTML) animation. We address this advanced feature at length in Chapter 24, *Animation*. None of these options affect using floating boxes for absolute positioning on a page.

Floating Box Controller

If you have a number of overlapping floating boxes, you may need to invoke the Floating Box Controller from the Windows menu (Mac) or View menu (Windows) to help manage which boxes are displayed, or which are editable to better manipulate or modify them (see Figure 12-19).

Each floating box on a page shows up in the Floating Box Controller with the name assigned to it in the Floating Box Inspector; you can change these names at any time through the inspector.

The Floating Box Controller features just two settings: visible and editable. Clicking the eye icon next to a layer hides both the box and its contents. Clicking the pencil icon renders the box immobile and its contents uneditable.

The Visible checkbox in the Floating Box Inspector and the eye and pencil controls in the Floating Box Controller interact in a complex enough fashion that they need a table to explain them all (see Table 12-2). Generally, you use the Visible

Figure 12-19
Floating Box
Controller

Table 12-2
Checking or
unchecking
Visible with
Floating Box
Controller
options

State	Action	New State	What's Visible
Visible checked Eye black	Uncheck Visible	Eye and pencil dim	Box remains but its contents are hidden
Visible unchecked Pencil either black or dimmed, Eye dimmed	Click eye	Eye turns red	Box and contents both visible
Visible unchecked Eye red	Click eye	Eye changes back to black, dims	Box and contents both hidden
Visible checked Eye black	Click eye	Eye turns red, dims, and pencil dims	Box and contents both hidden
Visible checked Eye black Pencil black	Uncheck and recheck Visible	Eyeball and pencil both dim, then both turn black	Box and contents both visible

checkbox to control the object's display in a browser *and* the Layout Editor and Layout Preview, while the eye icon controls a floating box's display *only* in GoLive.

You Control the Vertical, You Control the Horizontal

Layout grids may have already seen their time come and go—it was just a few years ago that they were all the rage. Adobe wisely included the feature, as it is backwards compatible with older browsers. But, our luck with getting them to work on a wide variety of commonly used browsers is low; there's always some element that runs five feet deep on a page or just doesn't go to the right part of the screen.

We've seen the future in floating boxes, but there's still time to wait as the user community gradually upgrades its way through older browsers to the 4.0 and later releases that fully support the sophisticated options available with CSS, including absolute page positioning.

For the time being, we urge restraint and careful choices before running it up the flagpole and discovering that no one's saluting—because no one can see the flagpole.

CHAPTER 13
Forms

The Web gets called an interactive medium, but without adding multimedia plug-ins like Shockwave or writing form-verifying JavaScripts, you can only directly interact with a Web page in two ways: by clicking on a link, or by filling out and submitting a form. Everything else is just reading.

We all know what a link is, but what exactly is a form? Although we typically think of a form as a set of text fields to fill out, it is actually a defined section of a Web page, much like a table. A form includes fields to type into or menus to select items from and it may also have buttons that submit and reset the contents. A form can be as simple as a single button or as complex as an e-commerce checkout page, on which you enter your shipping information and credit card number. You can even plug in some JavaScript and make a form more intelligent in processing what's being entered into it—see Chapter 23, *JavaScript*.

When a user clicks a Submit button in a form, the Web browser sends the contents of the form to a specified server script or program. The server processes and acts on this information in some fashion; it might store the form's contents in a database, send e-mail with its details, or deliver a custom page that depends on values selected in the form. The server, after processing the form, typically hands back a Web page to the browser, though it could also provide a file to download, a RealAudio file to play, or something more complex.

GoLive lets you create all the parts of a form with drag-and-drop simplicity. You have to tweak almost every element you drag into place—by adding settings, resizing fields, or typing in precise sequences of data or directory paths provided by your Webmaster or system administrator—but GoLive's management of the process lets you create complex forms without much fuss.

If you open a page with existing forms, GoLive will display all its parts using its own symbols, and all elements will be just as editable as if you'd created the page using GoLive's tools.

GoLive's Preview window gives a reasonable indication of the appearance of form elements, but if you try to type or select items, the preview is less exact. It's much better to test forms in actual browsers, especially since different browsers offer different support and display of the various form elements.

Parts of a Form

GoLive supports all standard form elements and attributes, using the Form tab of the Palette and various form element inspectors to insert and set up a form. GoLive also lets you use new form features from HTML 4.0 that are not supported by all browsers.

A form comprises two parts: an enclosing container and a set of fields. The container is made by using a Form tag to open the form and a corresponding /Form tag to close it. You can have as many forms on a page as you like, each in its own Form container.

The fields may be any of a dozen or so types of input elements, including fields and buttons, discussed in "Input Elements," later in this chapter.

Tip: Form Elements and JavaScript	GoLive offers support for adding JavaScript "handlers" to form elements; these provide actions based on selecting items in a list, checking a box, or submitting a form. These handlers have to be entered through the JavaScript Inspector's Event tab, explained in Chapter 23, *JavaScript*.
Tip: Where to Find Form Pieces	All the pieces to create forms are found in the Forms tab of the Palette (see Figure 13-1). Any item referenced below as something you can drag into place must be dragged from this palette; or, you can double-click the item to have it inserted wherever your cursor is in the text. See Chapter 3, *Palettes and Parts*, for a blow-out illustration of this palette.

Front-End, Not Back-End

It's important to remember that GoLive only helps you set up the part of the form which constitutes the data entry, or "front-end." It doesn't provide any help in dealing with the server's handling of the form, or the "back-end" processing, where data is manipulated.

For reference, we provide a bit of code in perl in a sidebar at the end of this chapter, which you can use to help test your forms. However, you'll still have to work with a developer, a Web site that offers form processing as a service, or prepackaged software to handle form submission.

Figure 13-1
Forms tab of
the Palette

**Tip: Using
Tables for
Forms**

The GoLive manual wisely suggests dropping your form elements into a table, other-wise you can't line up text and fields. You can see some examples of setting up form elements in a table in "Building Forms Using Tables" in Chapter 10, *Tables*.

Form Container

To set up a form, first drag a Form icon to your page (see Figure 13-2). You should also, for a proper form and good form (sorry), drag over an End Form icon. All your input tags, described below, get inserted between these two placeholders.

Figure 13-2
Dragging a
Form icon to
your HTML
page

**Tip: Close
Form New to
CyberStudio
Users**

If you were a CyberStudio 3 user, you'll note that the End Form icon is new. In CyberStudio 3, the </FORM> tag was implied and inserted automatically; if you wanted to move its location, you needed to edit the HTML in the HTML Source Editor to move the tag. In GoLive 4, you both open and close a form.

**Tip: Auto End
Form**

If you switch to HTML Source Editor without inserting an End Form icon, GoLive does it for you.

**Tip: No End
Form
Inspector**

The End Form placeholder has no inspector corresponding to it, as it consists of just </FORM> in HTML.

With the Inspector palette displayed, clicking a Form placeholder brings up the Form Inspector (see Figure 13-3), which includes five items you can set.

Name. Naming a form isn't required; in fact, all your forms can have the same name. But if you want to use JavaScript to modify or interact with a form, it's a good idea to name each form differently and, probably, descriptively (see Chapter 23, *JavaScript*).

Action. When a user clicks a submit button, their browser bundles up the data they've entered and sends it as part of a regular request to the Web server. But the

Figure 13-3
The Form
Inspector

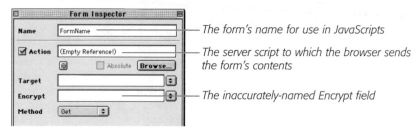

— The form's name for use in JavaScripts

— The server script to which the browser sends
the form's contents

— The inaccurately-named Encrypt field

browser needs to know what script to request to pass the information to, and this is what the Action field provides.

The Action field typically specifies the location of a script or program that's accessed on the same Web server on which the form is located—but not always.

If the processor exists on the same machine, you would generally enter a full path from the root of the server, such as */cgi-bin/form-process*, and then check the Absolute box in the Form Inspector. (See Chapter 16, *Files, Folders, and Links*, for an explanation of absolute and relative links.) You can also browse to find a script to link to, or use the Point & Shoot tool, but typically you'll type in a path provided by your system administrator or Webmaster.

If the program is located on another machine, you need to enter a full Web address starting with *http://*.

**Tip: Avoiding
mailto: as an
Action**

It's possible to make a form's action be a mailto: link, but we warn against that. Unless the user's browser is correctly configured to send mail, it won't work; the user gets an error. Even if it will work, most browsers pop up a security dialog box warning that the form is being sent via email. It's much more reliable to use a script, even one that just emails you the form contents, as that will work 99.99 percent of the time.

Target. With framesets, you can use this popup to target the returned page (see Chapter 11, *Frames*). The popup menu to the right of the Target field includes four standard target destinations.

- **_top** loads the page within the current window, but independent of the current frameset

- **_parent** loads the page within the frame containing the current frameset when you're using nested framesets

- **_self** loads the return page within the same frame as the form

- **_blank** works independently of frames, opening a new browser window to load the return page

Encrypt. This field is named incorrectly; it should be called Encoding, which is what it controls. A Web browser has to turn any "illegal" characters in a form—

certain text and non-text characters that can't be sent through standard Web protocols—into representations that can be sent. It encodes these characters in one of two ways, available from a popup menu next to the field.

The default encoding is the same as "application/x-www-form-urlencoded". If you've seen text like "%2E" in a URL, then you were looking at part of that encoding; the % sign means that the two characters that follow are the hexadecimal (base 16) number for the ASCII character code. In this case, 2E is the code for the equals sign (=).

The other method of encoding, "multipart/form-data", gets used to transmit files to a Web server correctly by identifying where they start and end (we cover this a bit later in the chapter).

GoLive provides a field here to enter another value in case a new method is developed, but we haven't seen any yet.

Method. You can have a Web browser send data to a server by one of two methods: GET or POST. The GET method sends form data as part of a standard file request to a server. The browser appends all the data to the end of the file request for the script you specified in the Action field.

The problem with GET is twofold. First, you expose all your information in the URL, which can look ugly and might display passwords or other private information on screen or in a browser's cache or history file. Second, GET requests are limited to less than 256 characters on some browsers, so form data could be truncated.

The solution is to use POST, which is appropriate in almost every case. With a POST request, the browser still asks the server to process the data with a specific script, but it sends the form data as a separate stream of text, hidden from the user, and with no apparent limit with newer browsers. (We did have problems with Netscape 1.0, but none since.)

Input Elements

With your form all set up and ready to submit, you need to add elements that a user can type data into or select values from. If you've ever worked with FileMaker Pro or Microsoft Access, many of these terms, types, and concepts will be familiar to you.

Input elements may contain preset data, like months of a year in a popup menu, or they may require a user to enter data from scratch, like their last name. HTML provides for several kinds of input elements tailored to each of these needs. We've divided them into similar categories.

To access settings for each type of element, drag them into an HTML page, make sure the Inspector palette is displayed, and select the item to bring up the appropriate Inspector. There are inspectors, of course, for every kind of element.

Text Fields

Text fields allow users to enter any arbitrary set of characters, like someone's name, email address, or credit card number. If you want the field to appear with a value already filled in or selected, enter it in Content.

The number of characters shown onscreen is set via Visible; you can also drag the handle on the right side of the field to resize interactively. Unfortunately, each browser interprets width slightly differently, so there's absolutely no guarantee that setting Content to "10" will allow for only one or as many as 10 characters to be visible onscreen. Setting the field size with Visible doesn't constrain the user from exceeding that length. You can limit overall characters in a field by entering the maximum number in Max.

HTML lets you hide the contents of a field as a user enters it by using a password field. GoLive supports this feature with the Is Password Field checkbox. You can drag a Text field or a Password field separately from the Forms palette, or you can change your mind later, using the checkbox.

Tip: Password Isn't Encryption If you use the Password field, be aware that it's not really secure. All a Password field does is prevent someone from reading a password as someone types it by substituting bullets or dots for the typed characters. The value in a Password field is not encrypted when it's sent to a server; it's sent in plain text, so it could be intercepted or logged in some fashion, though that's unlikely. Many sites use a Password field combined with a secure server as the right mix of caution and protection.

Text Area

For longer text entry, like user comments on a feedback form, use the Text Area field. You can roughly control the dimensions of a Text Area field by specifying its width in characters in the Columns field, and its height in lines of text in the Rows

Naming Elements

All input elements share one attribute: Name. When a form is submitted to a server, the name identifies which field a value came from. Because of this, you should name elements carefully. Sometimes scripts require highly specific names for different fields, and a Webmaster may need to tell you exactly what to name each item.

If you're using JavaScript for form verification (discussed in Chapter 23, *JavaScript*), your JavaScript will most likely address each element by the name you provide. Radio buttons are the one exception to this rule, as they share a group name that identifies members. But you still have to choose that group name. See "Choices," below.

field, or by dragging on its control handles. However, as with text fields, every browser interprets these dimensions differently.

You can set text to wrap automatically to the next line as a user types or pastes it in by setting Wrap to Virtual or Physical. Setting Wrap to Off turns off automatic line wrapping, so text just keeps running off the left margin as a user types (see Figure 13-4 for the differences).

Figure 13-4
The Wrap attribute interpreted by different browsers and platforms

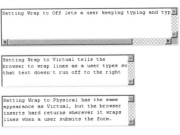

Mac Internet Explorer 4.5, Windows Internet Explorer 5.0, and Windows Netscape Navigator 4.6 all interpret Wrap settings the same, correct way.

Mac Netscape Navigator 4.6 wraps text with Wrap set to Off, which is incorrect.

Bad Wrap

Wrap is a funny attribute. Neither the HTML 3.2 or 4.0 specifications support it as a facet of Textarea, so it's not an official part of HTML. Netscape introduced it in Navigator 2.0 using the terms Off, Soft, and Hard, according to Web-Reference.com (http://www.webreference.com/).

A Soft wrap automatically breaks text at the end of a line onscreen, but the line breaks aren't sent as part of the form submission to the server. A Hard wrap inserts line break characters wherever the text wraps onscreen when submitting the form.

Internet Explorer used to use the terms Virtual and Physical to mean Soft and Hard, but according to Microsoft's developer resource site, the browser now uses Soft and Hard.

The developers of GoLive went with the new In-

ternet Explorer terminology, but if you examine the settings in the Web Database for Textarea you'll see that GoLive shows this tag as having Netscape 2, 3, and 4 compatibility only (see Chapter 27, *Web Database*). This is correct in that Netscape supported wrapping back as early as 2.0, but incorrect in terms of terminology and current support.

Windows Navigator and Internet Explorer as well as the Mac version of Internet Explorer correctly use GoLive's Wrap settings; Netscape Navigator for Macintosh ignores the Off setting.

For consistency with the newest terms and settings, you could also edit the HTML directly, and change Wrap to be set to Soft or Hard. Or, if you're overly ambitious, you can edit your Web Database to use Hard and Soft.

Tip: Wrap on Mac, Visible on Windows GoLive's interface designers decided to rename this attribute as Visible in the Windows version of GoLive to match the text field's property. However, "Wrap" is the actual attribute name, so we use that as the popup menu name here to avoid some confusion.

If you leave Wrap set to Default, Netscape Navigator interprets this as Off, while Internet Explorer automatically wraps.

The Data field works just like Content for text fields; you can prefill a value here to be displayed whenever the user retrieves the page, but the user can type over it.

Lists

Forms can have preset lists of items to choose from in two formats: a popup menu or a scrolling list (called a "list box" by GoLive). The main difference between the two styles is that you can only make a single selection from a popup menu, while a scrolling list can have multiple selections; the HTML is the same for both objects.

You can drag either a Popup or List Box icon from the Forms palette into a form and use the Inspector palette to change one into the other (see Figure 13-5). Browsers typically display a popup menu or dropdown list when Rows is set to 1 and Multiple Selection is unchecked. If either attribute is different (more than one row or multiple selections allowed), browsers tend to display a scrolling list. GoLive honors this behavior in its previews. With Multiple Selection checked, a user can choose more than one item from the list by holding down the Command key on a Mac or the Control key under Windows and clicking on different items.

Figure 13-5
Popup menus and scrolling lists

Mac Internet Explorer 4.5

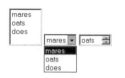

Windows Internet Explorer 5.0

Popup menus and scrolling lists display differently in each browser depending on how many rows are displayed and whether Multiple Selection is checked.

The settings are, from left to right in both illustrations: multiple selection, show four rows; no multiple selection, show one row; and multiple selection, show one row. (One row is empty in each example.)

GoLive automatically inserts three placeholder items in the list of items when you create a Popup or List Box element. You can create an indefinably large number of items for a list. The text in Label shows up on the Web page; the text for Value represents what's sent to the server if that option is chosen.

To preselect an item, select it, click the checkbox at the bottom, and it will be highlighted in a list or displayed in a popup menu. If you preselect more than one item without having Multiple Selection checked, GoLive allows it, though it's "illegal" HTML, and browsers won't know quite what to make of it.

Tip: Editing Lists in Source
Sometimes we find it easier to edit list elements in Source view because GoLive's editor doesn't have the ability to rearrange items. If you first select the list, and then click the Source tab in your page window, the HTML for the list is highlighted. You can then drag and drop items to rearrange their order, or copy and paste to insert new items (see Figure 13-6). When you click the Layout tab, you'll see all your work reflected in the Inspector palette.

Figure 13-6
Rearranging popup menu values by cutting and pasting HTML

Enter values directly into the Form Popup Inspector to create the elements in a popup menu or scrolling list.

To rearrange them, select the item in the Layout Editor and switch to the HTML Source Editor tab.

Select and cut the entire line containing the element you want to rearrange, and paste the line into the correct new order.

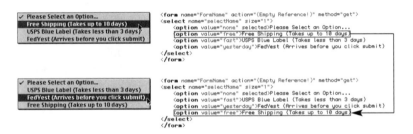

Tip: Label in GoLive Isn't Label in HTML
What GoLive calls the Label in the List Item Editor is actually the Value attribute in HTML. This is confusing, as HTML 4.0 has a new attribute for the items in a list called Label which allows you to specify a label to appear instead of text if you're using the new hierarchical menu feature described in "HTML 4.0 Features," later in the chapter. This is only an issue if you want to hand code this new feature—which GoLive doesn't yet support—and get confused about what attributes are named.

Choices

When designing a form, you often want to present information that the user can simply check or click to choose. HTML provides checkboxes, which offer a binary checked/unchecked choice, and radio buttons, which work like a single selection popup menu in that only one item from the set may be selected.

Both objects have a Value attribute, which is what the browser sends to a server when a form is submitted and the checkbox or radio button is selected. You can precheck or preselect these elements by checking Selected.

Checkboxes are all standalone elements, but radio buttons are created in sets with at least two members. (A single radio button makes no sense, as one member of a group must always be selected, and a single-member group can't have its button turned off.)

You can create a radio button set by dragging a Radio Button icon from the Forms palette onto a page and bringing up the Form Radio Button Inspector. Entering any text for Group creates a new group which is automatically added to the popup menu next to the Group field. For the next button you create, you can select the group from the popup menu.

Tip: Radio Button Group Fails to Display

In the Mac version of GoLive, we've noticed that after creating a new radio button and entering a name in the Group field, this newly created group doesn't always show up for other radio buttons. If this happens, save the page, close it, and reopen it.

Tip: Mass Button Production

If you know you're going to have several radio buttons belonging to a set, start by creating one and giving it a group name and value. Highlight the button, copy it, then paste however many you need. All of them will already be set to the correct group, avoiding multiple trips to the Group popup menu.

Laying out checkboxes and radio buttons requires some extra work in spacing. You want to prevent the label for the button or box from being confused with one on the right or left. We often insert non-breaking spaces (Option-space or Alt-space, or " " in HTML) to better distance one button from the next (see Figure 13-7).

Figure 13-7
Non-breaking spaces for button legibility

If you use the Label element, described under "HTML 4.0 Features," below, you can associate a bit of text which, when clicked, also selects a radio button or checks a box.

Standard Buttons

HTML forms originally used one of two buttons to perform actions: a submit button would send a form to the server; a reset button causes the browser to empty all the fields and change the form back to its default state. Submit Button and Reset Button icons can be dragged directly from the Forms palette onto an HTML page. Selecting either button with the Inspector palette open brings up the Form Button Inspector.

You can convert a Submit Button into a Reset Button by clicking the appropriate radio button in The Form Button Inspector. The Normal option invokes an

HTML 4.0 kind of button which has no built-in behavior; we explain how to use it under "HTML 4.0 Features," below.

If you check the Label box, you can change the text that appears inside the button from Submit and Reset to anything you wish. We often change Submit to "Send the Form" and Reset to "Erase All Entries."

You can also use a custom image as a submit button by dragging the Input Image icon onto an HTML page. This item can only be used to submit, not reset. GoLive presents you with a full array of image options in the Form Image Inspector, but most browsers don't support image maps or other special attributes for this kind of image.

Tip: Easily Change an Existing Image to a Submit Button	GoLive offers two image icons in the Palette, depending on the context, but they're exactly the same. The only functional difference between the Image icon on the Basic tab of the Palette and the Input Image icon on the Forms tab of the Palette is that the latter automatically marks the Is Form checkbox on the Spec tab in the Inspector. So if you already have an image on your page that you want to use as a submit button, simply check the Is Form box instead of deleting the existing image and dragging the Input Image icon from the Forms tab.

Hidden

Some server programs require a bit of extra identifying data to be sent along with a form, that the user shouldn't be able to see or modify. To include this information, use a Hidden input tag. GoLive represents hidden items with a small H, which, when selected, activates the Form Hidden Inspector.

Set the Name and Value as instructed by a system administrator. Often, a hidden field is inserted as a placeholder in a template that a server program uses to insert identifying data.

Upload Files

When you need to let users upload files via a Web page, you can use the File Browser element. When a user clicks the Browse button, the user's browser displays a file dialog that lets them choose a file. The file they choose is inserted into the field portion of the element; you can use the Visible field or drag on the control handle to display more or fewer characters of the file name.

When the user clicks a submit button, the browser transmits the file as part of the form data. You must set Encryption (encoding, really) to "multipart/form-data" in the Form Inspector, as described above, for file upload to work. The server also must be configured to interpret the file data.

Key Generator

GoLive includes the Key Generator icon to be thorough, but nowhere on the Net can we find a sensible, non-hyper-technical explanation for this Netscape-specific tag. (Most explanations bemoan the fact that there's no explanation.) What we did find describes its use as part of a method of using public and private key cryptography through a Web interface. If you think this applies to you, read the two very dense paragraphs at Netscape's page on the subject: *http://developer.netscape.com:80/docs/manuals/htmlguid/tags10.htm#1615503*.

HTML 4.0 Features

Forms haven't changed much since the early years of HTML, but the HTML 4.0 specification, a guideline to implementing standardized advanced HTML features, includes some nice refinements and new tags that help create forms which are easier to use and more visually appealing. Only some of these features are currently supported in either Internet Explorer or Navigator in their 4.0 releases. Because of this, if you use any of these elements or elaborations, you're potentially limiting your audience.

We discuss all the 4.0 elements, as if they actually work, for the purposes of describing how to use them and their intended function. We're relying heavily on a combination of how GoLive encodes the specification, how existing browsers display it, and what the actual 4.0 specification states. But we suggest that you:

- Carefully read WebReference.com's explanation of HTML 4.0 features in Netscape Navigator and Internet Explorer (http://www.webreference.com/dev/html4nsie/forms.html) to figure out whether the specific set of features you want to use are supported by the browsers you want to apply them to.

- Test your forms in your anticipated users' most typical browsers to ensure that, at best, they look the way you want, and, at worst, new things don't display but also don't disrupt the page.

Most of the HTML 4.0 features that relate to existing elements are grouped in the Focus section of various Forms inspectors. Some features are new elements that provide new capabilities.

Focus and Field Modifiers

Focus refers to which field or element is currently being edited or selected. On the Macintosh, focus is less clear, so to speak, because the Macintosh interface doesn't highlight checkboxes, buttons, and other similar elements, only fields that you can type into. But under Windows and Unix, any item that's being manipulated—like a checkbox being selected—gets highlighted in some manner and has the focus put on it (see Figure 13-8). GoLive lets you apply focus settings to most fields that allow input. The kinds of focus are broken into discrete settings.

Figure 13-8
Focus on fields

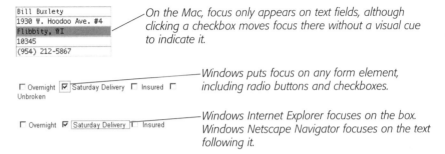

On the Mac, focus only appears on text fields, although clicking a checkbox moves focus there without a visual cue to indicate it.

Windows puts focus on any form element, including radio buttons and checkboxes.

Windows Internet Explorer focuses on the box. Windows Netscape Navigator focuses on the text following it.

Tabbing Chains

You can help a user logically fill out a form by letting them press the Tab key to jump through fields in a specified order. This is especially useful when using tables and forms together, as the default tab order might run from left to right across columns while the items occur in more logical order (like name, address, city, state, zip) from top to bottom.

GoLive offers two ways to set the tab order. You can select an item, check the Tab box in its inspector, and number the item in the order you want it to appear (see Figure 13-9). The tab numbers have to follow one another in ever increasing order, but don't have to be the next higher number. So whether you number tabs 10, 15, 20, 25 or 1, 2, 3, 4, both work the same way. This can be handy if you plan to insert fields later and want to leave a gap in numbers so you don't have to renumber the entire form.

You can also use a more point-and-click method of ordering tabs, either by selecting Start Tabulator Indexing from the Special menu, or by clicking the icon to the right of the Tab field in a form inspector. If an item has already been assigned a number, that number appears adjacent to the item in a yellow box; otherwise, a question mark is displayed. As you click from item to item, the current number is assigned to that element, and the counter increases.

Clicking the icon in the inspector again or selecting Stop Tabulator Indexing from the Special menu turns off the tab-order display and brings everything back to normal.

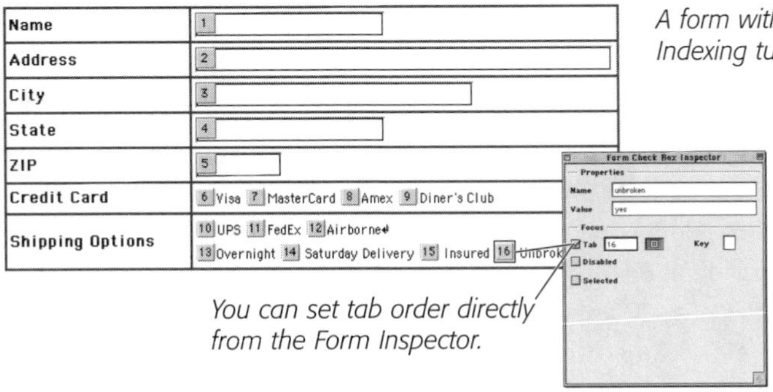

Figure 13-9
Tab order

A form with Tabulator Indexing turned on

You can set tab order directly from the Form Inspector.

Tip: Tab Numbering Bug Whenever you have tabulator indexing turned on, every click increments the tab order counter, whether you click on an item that already has a number or just click anywhere on a page. However, the gap between numbers doesn't affect tab order. So each time a user presses Tab, the browser determines the next highest numbered field, and moves focus there.

Read-only

Checking Read-only in fields that support this attribute causes compatible browsers to display the field, and any content you pre-filled, but does not allow modification. This might be useful for showing the user information in the same manner as the rest of a form and implying that it's being submitted as part of the form data.

Disabled

Checking Disabled makes a field act just like a read-only element. Since JavaScript can turn the disabled status of a field on or off, programmers might want to use the Disabled checkbox to keep certain fields inaccessible, and then activate them based on a user's actions.

For instance, if you provide a user login where a radio button allows users to choose between logging in and changing their password, you might want the new password field to be disabled unless the user clicks the correct radio button (see Figure 13-10).

1. On your HTML page, name the Change Password checkbox "changepass" and click Disabled in its inspector.

2. Click the JavaScript coffee bean button, bring up the JavaScript Inspector (if it's not already visible), then click on the Events tab.

3. Expand the view under document, your form name (FormName by default), and the checkbox that you've named changepass.

4. Select OnClick and enter "NewPass()" in the Event Code field.

HTML 4.0 Resources

Of the myriad books about HTML that burden bookstore shelves, we have consistently recommended one title as the best HTML reference you can buy. *HTML 4 for the World Wide Web: Visual QuickStart Guide*, by Elizabeth Castro (Peachpit Press, ISBN 0-201-69696-7) offers easy-to-understand information about the current specification.

You can also read the W3C's technical final draft section on forms online (http://www.w3.org/TR/ REC-html40/interact/forms.html).

If you want to see what's technically different between HTML 3.2 and 4.0, see the W3C's list of changes (http://www.w3.org/TR/REC-html40/ap-pendix/changes.html#h-A.1.9).

WebReference.com provides an excellent guide that outlines which form features are supported in which browsers (http://www.webreference.com /dev/html4nsie/forms.html).

Figure 13-10
Setting up a
way to toggle
a disabled
field

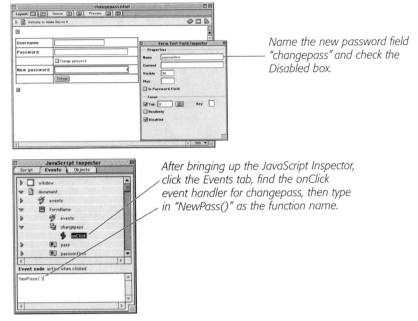

*Name the new password field
"changepass" and check the
Disabled box.*

*After bringing up the JavaScript Inspector,
click the Events tab, find the onClick
event handler for changepass, then type
in "NewPass()" as the function name.*

5. Click the new Head Script button in the JavaScript Editor and enter this as its
    contents:

```
function NewPass () {
  if (document.forms[0].changepass.value == "yes") {
      document.forms[0].passconfirm.disabled = false;
  } else {
      document.forms[0].passconfirm.disabled = true;
  }
}
```

Keystrokes

Users can move to a specific field or element by pressing a keystroke combination
if you assign a letter in the Key field. On the Mac, a user types Command plus that
key; under Windows, Alt plus that key. If you use this shortcut, you need to mention it alongside the element, as there's no other indication.

Keep in mind that on a Mac, most alphabetic Command key combinations are
already assigned, so this feature doesn't provide much utility.

New Buttons

Standard HTML forms can have buttons that submit and/or reset a form, or an
image that serves as a submit button. HTML 4.0 extends the standard button and
adds a new, rich media button.

If you drag a Submit or Reset icon to your page and click Normal in the Form Button Inspector, you're actually turning the button into an HTML 4.0 button—the underlying HTML changes the button to a, well, "button" type of button. This kind of button has no action associated with it, like submit or reset; it can be used with JavaScript to trigger actions to better simulate an interactive user interface.

The rich media button is simply called Button in the Forms palette. This kind of button supports content inside its frame, which includes anything you can express in HTML, including images or even QuickTime movies. This button can be set via the Form Button Inspector to work as a submit or reset button, or like the Normal button described just above.

Better Labeling and Grouping

HTML 4.0 provides a couple nice interface subtleties that make an HTML form look more like a program's dialog box—more familiar and easier to use at the same time.

List Hierarchies

In a popup menu, items are all displayed at the same depth—flat. HTML 4.0 adds tags and attributes to lists that make it possible to code submenus without losing legible display in previous browsers. GoLive lacks support for these two features, resulting in the need for hand coding (see Figure 13-11).

The Optgroup tag allows you to group a list of elements into submenus. Label becomes the submenu name. <OPTGROUP> can have a number of elements, and is then closed with its mate, </OPTGROUP>.

The Label attribute for Option gets displayed as the submenu item, while the Name's value is sent as form data if that item is selected. In older browsers, the text following the Option tag gets displayed, and the Label attribute and Optgroup tags are ignored.

Label

A label is a piece of text that may be associated with a given field, such as a checkbox or radio button. Clicking the text has the same effect as clicking the field, bringing the focus to that field, or, in the case of a button, selecting or checking it.

GoLive uses Point & Shoot linking to create the association between a legend and its object. If you bring up the Form Label Inspector, you can point-and-shoot onto the element you want. Later, pressing the Show button draws a line to the associated object.

The value that GoLive automatically creates for the Reference field is best left alone, as it requires hand tweaking the associated field's HTML in Source view if you want to change the reference name.

Figure 13-11
OPTGROUP tag

```
<SELECT name="Shipping">
<OPTGROUP label="UPS">
<OPTION label="UPS Ground"
value="UPS Ground">UPS Ground
Shipping (3-10 days)
<OPTION label="UPS 2-day"
value="UPS 2-day">UPS Blue Label (2
days)
<OPTION label="UPS overnight"
value="UPS overnight">UPS Red Label
(overnight)
</OPTGROUP>
<OPTGROUP label="US Postal
Service">
<OPTION label="USPS First Class"
value="USPS First Class">USPS First
Class (3 to 7 days)
<OPTION label="USPS Priority Mail"
value="USPS Priority Mail">USPS
```

```
Priority Mail (2 to 3 days)
<OPTION label="USPS Express Mail"
value="USPS Express Mail">USPS
Express Mail (1 to 2 days)
</OPTGROUP>
<OPTGROUP label="FedEx">
<OPTION label="FedEx Two-Day"
value="FedEx Two-Day">FedEx Two-Day
(afternoon following next day)
<OPTION label="FedEx Standard"
value="FedEx Standard">FedEx
Standard (next business day after-
noon)
<OPTION label="FedEx Priority"
value="FedEx Priority">FedEx
Priority (next business day morn-
ing)
</OPTGROUP>
</SELECT>
```

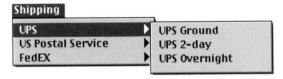

The HTML above would produce something like the menu at left in a fully HTML 4.0 compliant browser, which is yet to appear.

Tip: Pointing Out the Wrong Place GoLive has a problem with pointing the legend to the right place if you associate it with an identically named field on the page. GoLive points to the first instance of the field's name, rather than to the one you've chosen. Even renaming the correct field doesn't seem to help; it just keeps pointing to the wrong field.

Fieldset and Legend

You can group elements together into nifty boxed sets, just like GoLive does in its Inspector palettes, by using the Fieldset icon. Dragging this icon over creates two different HTML tags: the Fieldset tag groups the set of items; the Legend tag provides the label for the set.

Unchecking Use Legend removes the text and deletes the tag. You can also position the legend, although GoLive only previews left, center, and right positioning.

CGI and Forms

Forms get processed by a Web server through the Common Gateway Interface (CGI), a method by which a browser sends data requiring a script to process it, and then the server hands off this data to a separate program. That program performs whatever manipulations it requires and hands off a Web page to the server; finally, the server feeds the Web page out to the browser.

Form a Line

Since forms make up a significant portion of the Web's interactivity, the importance of getting them right is paramount. GoLive's approach to forms makes them easy to construct, maintain, and modify, and in the process you'll find that it helps you make them good-looking as well.

A Script to Test Forms

This isn't a programming book, so we're not going to reveal the secrets of creating the server scripts necessary to process forms via CGI. These scripts vary greatly by platform and server setup. You may not even have access to write or install programs on your site's Web server.

However, we want to give you a little help, as testing forms can be mystifying. If you are using a Web server on which you can run scripts and the perl scripting language is installed, you can enter and run the following script. (This script is also found at http://realworldgolive.com/simplecgi.txt.)

Enter everything exactly as seen here, remembering to use straight, not curly, typographer's quotes. The first line requires the path to your system's copy of perl; under Unix, you can enter "whereis perl" and replace "/usr/local/bin/perl" (the first line) with the results.

This script, when called via the Action attribute in a form that a Web browser submits, simply produces an alphabetical list of all the field names and values submitted by the form. This gives you a chance to run a test and make sure the values are being transmitted properly.

We also have a copy of this script running at the Real World GoLive Web site (http://realworldgolive.com/cgi-bin/simplecgi), which you are welcome to use as well. Just enter the URL above in the Form Inspector for your Form placeholder.

```perl
#!/usr/local/bin/perl
if ($ENV{'REQUEST_METHOD'} eq "GET") {
  $in = $ENV{'QUERY_STRING'};
} elsif ($ENV{'REQUEST_METHOD'} eq "POST")
{
  read(STDIN, $in, $ENV{'CONTENT_LENGTH'});
}
@in = split(/&/,$in);
foreach (@in) {
  s/\+/ /g;
  local($key, $val) = split(/=/,2);
  $key =~ s/%(..)/pack("c",hex($1))/ge;
  $val =~ s/%(..)/pack("c",hex($1))/ge;
  $in{$key} .= " and " if
(defined($in{$key}));
  $in{$key} .= $val;
}
print "Content-type: text/html\n\n";
print "<HEAD>\n<TITLE>Results of form
</TITLE></HEAD>\n<BODY BGCOLOR=\"#FFFFFF\">
\n<TABLE BORDER=\"1\" CELLSPACING=\"2\">
<TR><TH VALIGN=\"TOP\" ALIGN=\"LEFT\">Field
name</TH>\n<TH VALIGN=\"TOP\" ALIGN=
\"LEFT\">Value</TH></TR>\n";

foreach (sort { $a cmp $b } keys %in) {
  print "<TR><TD VALIGN=\"TOP\"
ALIGN=\"LEFT\">$_</TD>";
  print "<TD VALIGN=\"TOP\"
ALIGN=\"LEFT\">$in{$_} </TD></TR>";
}
print "</TABLE></BODY>\n";
exit 1;
```

CHAPTER 14

Page Specials

Although you'd think we'd covered every possible page feature in this part of the book, there are still a few items defying categorization that help you in creating and managing pages. These include page-based searching as well as search and replace, a preview of a page's download time, and a couple of tweakier issues that affect how files get opened and downloaded within GoLive.

Find

For longer pages or pages on which you need to change the same element multiple times, consider using the Find feature found under the Edit menu, or invoked by pressing Command-F on the Mac or Control-F under Windows (see Figure 14-1).

Find offers some simple and powerful controls for locating items on a page.

Find field. Enter the text you want to find here. The Find field keeps track of your most recent searches, so you can "replay" them by selecting from the popup menu next to the Find field.

Ignore Case. Checking this box ignores the capitalization both in what you've entered and what's on the page. So searching for "EaRtH" matches earth, EARTH, Earth, and eArTh.

Entire Word. This option limits the find to whole words, which are defined as characters between white space like returns, spaces, and tabs.

Figure 14-1
Find dialog
box's Find &
Replace tab

Mac and Windows Find & Replace tabs are almost identical

Regular Expr. GoLive offers the very powerful option of using regular-expression pattern matching to specify wildcard patterns to find (and replace) items in text. This feature is involved enough that we've given it its own section in Chapter 22, *Advanced Features.*

Backwards, From Top, From Bottom. If you check Backwards, GoLive searches from the current point in the text to the start of the document. Checking From Top searches from the start of the document to the bottom. If you check Backwards, From Top becomes From Bottom; checking From Bottom searches from the end of the document backwards to the start.

Find button. Click Find to find the first instance of the text in the Find field.

Find Next button. Finds the next instance.

Replace

Finding isn't just enough: the utility of the Find & Replace tab is, of course, being able to replace items wherever they occur on a page or in just selected instances. Click the expand triangle next to the word Replace at the bottom of the Find dialog box to open the Replace field if it's not already expanded. As with the Find field, recently used Replace entries are in the popup menu to the right of the field.

Replace button. Click this button to replace the current instance.

Replace & Find button. This button performs the replace operation, and then does the equivalent of Find Next.

Replace All. It's dangerous, but tempting, and generally useful—clicking Replace All changes all instances in the document that it finds. Just in case, make sure you have a backup copy of the file before replacing all.

Tip: Find in Files   You can also perform sitewide find and replace, which we cover in Chapter 21, *Site Specials*.

Spellchecking

Spellchecking is the best thing ever to hit comptures. Computres. Computers. But it requires human intelligence to operate successfully. GoLive's spellchecking offers most of the standard features found in Microsoft Word and other applications.

You can spellcheck an entire document or a single page; the controls are almost identical. If you want to spellcheck a site, you need to have the Site window as the frontmost window when you select Spellchecking from the Edit menu; otherwise, bring the page you want to check to the fore (see Figure 14-2).

Figure 14-2
Spellchecking

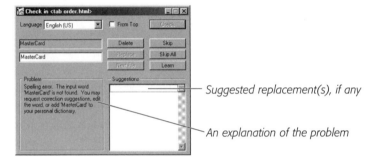

Suggested replacement(s), if any

An explanation of the problem

Language. Select a language from your installed dictionaries if the default doesn't match the language of the page.

Tip: World-wide Spell-checking   Because GoLive was designed for an international audience, you can spellcheck for any of the languages you have installed. GoLive supports dictionaries for most Western European languages, although the US distribution appears to come with just the US English and UK English ones. GoLive's dictionaries for US and UK English appear to be the only ones available as of this writing.

From Top. Check this option to examine the entire page; otherwise, the spellchecking starts at the text-insertion point.

Checking

Click the Check button to start spellchecking. GoLive displays each word it finds misspelled just below the Language menu. If it suggests a replacement, it puts it in the field below that, which can be edited, or you can enter a word when it offers no suggestions. If you prefer a suggestion that's not the spellchecker's top choice, click it to have it automatically inserted.

GoLive catches both spelling errors and a few other problems, such as repeated words or miscapitalized entries. It explains its rationale for catching the word in the Problem area.

The other options are controlled via buttons.

Delete. GoLive deletes the word from the page where the misspelling was found.

Skip. This skips just the current instance of the word.

Skip All. GoLive remembers this word and skips all subsequent instances of it.

Replace. The program inserts the word you've entered or GoLive suggested into the text.

Learn. GoLive adds the word to its exception dictionary, which you can edit via the Preferences dialog box's Spell Checking pane.

Next File. This option is only available when you're spellchecking a site, and it allows you to force GoLive to move to the next file, even if the current file hasn't been completely checked.

Skipping

GoLive has a neat and (to our knowledge) unique method of allowing you skip certain kinds of text using regular expressions. You can set up the program to avoid spellchecking patterns that use the regular expression wildcard matching that's discussed at length in Chapter 22, *Advanced Features*, in the context of the Find feature.

In the Regular Expr. settings under the Spell Checking pane of the Preferences dialog box, GoLive has two preprogrammed expressions: one for email addresses and another for URLs that start with ftp or http (see Figure 14-3).

Figure 14-3
Regular
expression
skipping
patterns

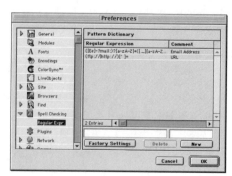

If you wanted to have GoLive not check any proper nouns, for instance, you could add:

```
[A-Z][\-a-zA-Z0-9]+
```

Document Statistics

You usually have to wait until a page is fully designed and created to test how long it might take for an average user to download, images and all. Fortunately, GoLive offers the Document Statistics feature, which can provide a total size for the all the content on the page, a word and character count, and an estimate for download time at different speeds (see Figure 14-4).

Figure 14-4
Document
Statistics
feature

GoLive doesn't take into account real-world issues in its estimates, however, like latency. Latency is the amount of time it takes to get data from point A to point B, not how fast it's moving. An analogy would be a stream of cars that get stopped on a slow stretch of road between two exits on a highway: they might travel 60 mph before and after the slow stretch, but it still takes each car a while to get through the bottleneck.

Go Live also doesn't account for Net slowdowns and platform and browser overhead (how long they take to deal with content once it's arrived). For instance, a page with eight images that's only 20K total would take 21 seconds to download at 9600 bits per second (bps), according to GoLive. However, most browsers are configured to download only four items at a time. Plus, a 9600-bps modem has high latency, meaning that it takes a while to get data gushing through the pipe. The slower the connection, generally the higher the latency, slowing down the whole process.

So for up to 28,800 bps, we'd multiply GoLive's estimate by three for real-world purposes; up to ISDN, we'd multiply by two. For T1 and T3, the estimates are useful for pages with lots of multimedia, but the mechanisms by which data gets sent across the Net seems to limit it to an effective throttle of about 400 kilobits per second (kbps) maximum, or one-fourth of a T1 line. (FTP can be much faster, but the Web seems to max out lower.)

Web Download

Web Download is a special, standalone feature that lets you type in any Web page location starting with http://, and have GoLive download the page, as well as any images or other objects that appear on the page (see Figure 14-5). (The exception is anything referenced in JavaScript or other scripting languages; it only downloads media mentioned in HTML.)

Figure 14-5
Web
Download

GoLive opens a page with the same title, but all of the images are stored in the Import Images folder in the GoLive application folder. You can edit and save this page with its new image references, and then upload it back to the server. However, doing so usually breaks all of the links on the page, as they have been rewritten to reflect the local storage location of the downloaded images.

Tip:
Relocating
Imported
Images

You can specify another location for imported images in the Preferences dialog box under Image settings in the General pane. See Chapter 8, *Images*, and Chapter 4, *Preferences and Customizing*.

If you use the FTP Upload & Download feature described in Chapter 18, *Staging and Synchronizing Sites*, double-clicking a page in that window brings up a page in the exact manner as using Web Download. The difference is that with FTP Upload & Download, you must have access to a server; with Web Download, you need merely enter a URL.

Tip:
Unethical
Behavior

It would be easy to grab any page for any purpose anywhere on the Net using this feature. However, it's important to recall that all material on the Net is copyrighted regardless of whether it states so or not. In fact, unless it states explicitly that it's *not copyrighted* (i.e., the author has placed the material into the public domain), international copyright law says that the very act of creation implies a copyright that's defensible. So despite the fact that you *can* download material at will, it doesn't mean you should.

File Mapping

Most kinds of documents can be viewed or edited by more than one application. In its File Mapping settings, GoLive maintains a list of document types and the programs that can handle working with them so that you can open files directly by double clicking them inside GoLive just as you could from the Windows or Macintosh Desktop.

File Mapping is found in the General pane of the Preferences dialog box on both Macintosh and Windows (see Figure 14-6). File Mapping reveals the defaults that Adobe built into the program, including the notion that GoLive itself can open a whole variety of files for editing. For instance, if you have the QuickTime Module installed (it's called CyberMovie), GoLive "knows" it can open and edit AIFF sound files, QuickTime ".mov" (movie) files, and other video and sound formats.

To enable File Mapping, make sure that Enable File Open in Other Applications is checked. If it's unchecked, double-clicking or selecting a file and choosing Open from the File menu has no effect for file types that GoLive can't directly open.

Figure 14-6
File Mapping
settings

Mac settings with
Internet Config enabled

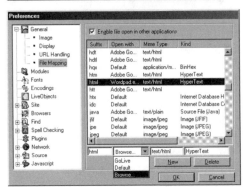

Windows settings

GoLive relies on the bit at the end of a file following a dot—the extension—the same way that Windows does. For instance, a PDF file is named "folderol.pdf" while an HTML file could be named "snooker.html" or "scrabble.htm" (either .html or .htm).

The structure of File Mapping is pretty straightforward, and it's identical for Mac and Windows.

Tip: Using
File Mapping
in Files Tab

We discuss how File Mapping affects opening files in the Site window's Files tab in Chapter 16, *Files, Folders, and Links*, where it's more contextually appropriate. For now, we want to concentrate on how to edit and manage the settings.

Tip: Internet Config (Mac)
Internet Config is a program that, among other things, maintains a list of file types and programs associated with them for use in programs like GoLive. If you check Use Internet Config, any preferences you've changed in GoLive are overwritten. For more on using Internet Config, see Appendix A, *Macintosh Issues and Extras*.

Suffix. The Suffix column lists the file type's extension.

Open With. Open With lists the application that should open the file if double-clicked. The Default setting means that GoLive relies on its mappings or information stored in the file, but you can change Default to a specific program to override this.

MIME Type. MIME Type defines the kind of data it is, something that's necessary for feeding out content over the Internet. Under Windows, GoLive uses MIME Type for FTP Up-/Download operations.

Kind. Kind is a text description created by Adobe identifying the variety of content.

Modifying Settings

File Mapping allows all of its settings to be changed by clicking the line containing the settings and entering new values in the fields. For instance, if you want to map PDF files to be opened in Adobe Acrobat, you'd click the line starting pdf, and select Adobe Acrobat from the Open With menu.

New Items

You might find it necessary to add extensions for files you regularly work with that GoLive doesn't currently list or that aren't available. Adding extensions is extremely simple. Click the New button. Enter the extension, choose an application to open the file from the Open With menu, enter the MIME type (if you know it), and type a description in the Kind field. Click OK.

Methods of Opening

There are several methods of opening a file (see Figure 14-7).

- Right-click (Windows) or Control-click (Mac) an object on the page or a file in the Site window, and select Open in "Program Name" or Open in Adobe GoLive from the menu.

- Double-click the item on a page or in the Site window's Files or Site tab.

- Select the item in the Site window's Files or Site tab and select Launch File from the Site window's In Finder (Mac) or In Explorer (Windows) menu.

Figure 14-7
Different ways
of opening
a file

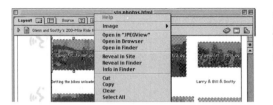

Right-clicking on an item on a page on the Mac; the Image submenu, not shown, has the same six options as just below it.

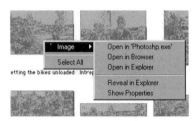

Under Windows, the Image submenu contains all of the open and reveal options.

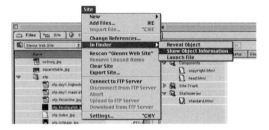

Selecting an item in the Site window and choosing from the Site menu's In Finder submenu; this is the same under Windows, except it reads "In Explorer".

Open Files

With File Mapping on, trying to open or launch an item has a different effect depending on what characteristics we or the program's developers assigned to the file.

No extension or an extension that's not listed. If the file lacks an extension or has one that GoLive doesn't list in File Mapping, GoLive for Windows brings up the Open With dialog box that presents likely suspects for being able to open the program—if there's no extension, it's possible that Windows would list a very large number of applications (see Figure 14-8).

Figure 14-8
Windows
Open With
dialog box

On the Macintosh, GoLive's behavior depends on whether you have a file translator installed; this translator exists in many incarnations over many system versions; you can buy commercial versions that support more file types than the built-in Apple-provided one. If you have anything in your Control Panels folder called EasyOpen or File Exchange and it's set to ask you about files it doesn't know how to open, double clicking an unmapped file in GoLive brings up a dialog box which prompts you to choose an appropriate application (see Figure 14-9). As on Windows, the Mac might present a list of dozens or even hundreds of applications.

Figure 14-9
Macintosh File
Exchange
dialog box

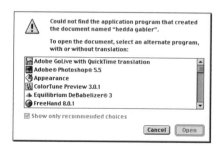

Listed extension. For file types that have an extension listed, the information for that type affects the options GoLive presents. If you use the contextual menu to select an option, GoLive shows Open in Adobe GoLive if the extension is mapped to Adobe GoLive or if GoLive knows that it can open that file type even if it's mapped to another program. The menu also shows Open in "Program Name" if anything but GoLive has been mapped to the extension (see Figure 14-7, above).

If the application that's been mapped to the extension doesn't exist, despite the fact that it's listed, GoLive shows an error stating that the document can't be opened with the specified program. In that case, your best solution is to edit the program listed to another application you do have available.

Now That We're on the Same Page...

At this point you've probably learned more about Web page creation in a short amount of time than most of us absorbed in the same amount of time hand coding HTML. That's the magic of using GoLive—plenty of the Web workings behind the scenes remain behind the scenes, allowing you to focus more energy on design than on code.

But you haven't reached the end (if you have, go get a new copy of this book, because there should be several hundred more pages following this one!). If you want to put your pages together into a collection of pages, GoLive can offer you an entirely new set of options: its site-management features. The next part of this book, *Sites*, is devoted to just that.

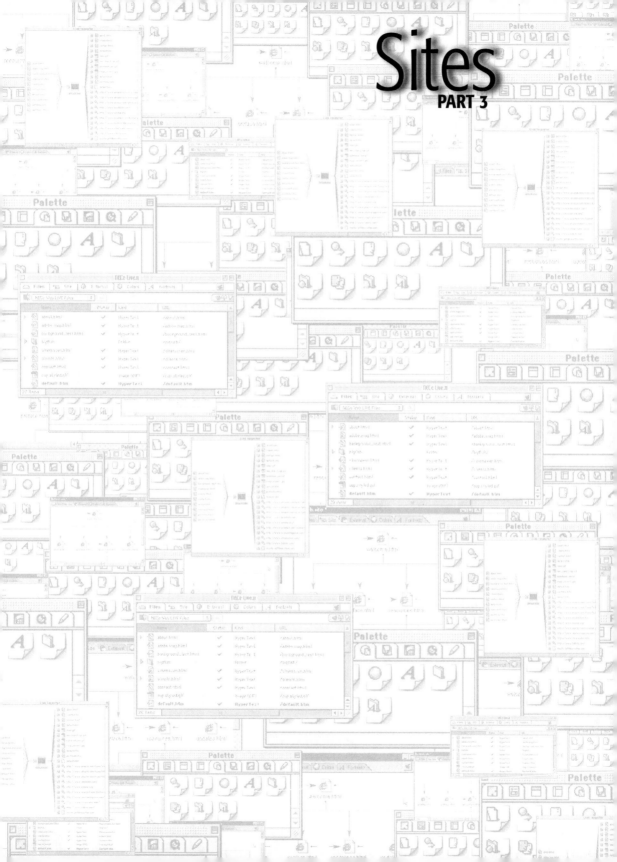

Sites
PART 3

CHAPTER 15
Site Management

Most of the Web sites you create wind up growing organically, not according to a logical plan. Although you may start with guidelines, a design scheme, and a site map, it's impossible to predict exactly how the branches of your site might extend beyond your initial plans.

That's where site management steps in; it helps you apply order after chaos intrudes. Or, you can use it to fend off entropy by making all your changes through a structure that keeps track of all the details for you.

Many Web site tasks make you feel more like an assembly-line robot than a human being; you're making the same changes over and over again. By using site management, you avoid tedious repetition, and throw frequent, brain-numbing tasks at the computer—which it seems to enjoy.

GoLive offers extensive-site management features that let you create, update, and debug a site through a simple interface. You use dragging and dropping and popup menus to accomplish most tasks.

GoLive also lets you easily see the scope of what you're creating or changing. For nearly every kind of item—a color, a link, an image, and so on—you can see every reference to it in the site. When looking through the site map, you can visualize the relationship between various parts of the site. And, with a few mouse clicks or drags, you can incrementally update part of a site or radically revise everything.

This chapter covers how GoLive deals with a site: where all the parts live, what commands are available, and how the program divides different aspects of site management into sections. It also examines the specifics of working with all the tools outlined here.

If you find yourself needing a review, or you want to get a visual breakout of every element, flip back to Part 1, *GoLive Basics*, in which the interfaces, elements, palettes, toolbars, and menus are fully annotated.

Setting Up a Site

Before you can start taking advantage of GoLive's site-management features, you have to create a site file. You either create a new, blank site; or import a directory's worth of files from your local hard disk or through access to an FTP server.

Making a New Site

If you select the Blank item from the New Site submenu in the File menu, or type Command-Option-N, GoLive prompts you for a site name. On the Mac, GoLive likes to include a dot and the pi (π) symbol at the end of the file name to help distinguish the site file. Under Windows, it adds ".site" to the site file name.

GoLive gives you the option of creating a new folder to house the site file and its associated folders. We recommend creating the folder for cleanliness' sake; GoLive names it "New Site ƒ" by default on the Macintosh and "NewSite folder" under Windows.

If you don't specify a new name, GoLive creates a site file named "New File.π" (Mac) or "New File.site" (Windows), and two folders named New Site and New Site.data (see Figure 15-1).

Figure 15-1
Folder
organization

Site folder ——————

—————— Site file

GoLive's site data

Importing a Site

If you already have a site created, or in progress, that you want to bring under GoLive management, the program lets you import your current working site into a new GoLive site file. You can import a site whether it is stored locally (on your hard drive or on the local network) or somewhere on the Net (in a place you can access via FTP).

Tip: Help on
Importing a
Site

Making imported sites sing can be a more difficult task depending on the size and age of the site. This process includes rooting out dead files, bad links, old imagemaps, and many other examples of rot. We devote an entire chapter to this surprisingly typical task, Chapter 20, *Importing a Site*.

GoLive offers two import commands corresponding to bringing in local and remote sites.

Import Site from Folder. Select the Import Site from Folder option from the New Site submenu and GoLive brings up a dialog box prompting you for your existing site's folder location and for you to specify a home page inside that location.

Click the Browse button under Please Select an Existing Site Folder to Create a New Site, and use the standard file selection dialog box to find your existing folder. GoLive creates its own site files and folders, explained below, at the same level as your existing site folder. You may want to create a new folder that contains just the existing site before importing into GoLive to prevent new items from mingling with other files and folders.

The home page should be the first page a user retrieves when they type in your URL without a page selected, such as http://realworldgolive.com. We discuss making the decision about what your home page is in Chapter 16, *Files, Folders, and Links*. GoLive considers the home page as the root of all navigation and links.

Import Site from FTP. After choosing Import Site from FTP from the New Site submenu, GoLive prompts you with its typical FTP connection dialog, described at length in Chapter 18, *Staging and Synchronizing Sites*. (Refer to Chapter 18 if you don't know all the values to enter into this area.)

In this case, GoLive asks you to select the destination folder into which it is going to download your site. We suggest you create a new folder that contains GoLive's own files and data, then create another new folder inside of that to store your actual site files.

You can create this new folder by checking Create Folder in Import Site from FTP in Windows; on the Mac, you first must go to the Desktop to create the nested folders.

When you click the Browse button under "Please Select the Home Page on the Remote Server," GoLive connects to the FTP server using the settings you provided. You can browse the remote directories and files to find the home page.

Site Folders

When you create a new site or import an existing site, GoLive creates three items on your local hard drive: the site file, the site folder, and the site data folder (see Figure 15-1, above).

Site file. The site file contains the database of items found on the site—a list of HTML files, images, and other documents, and their internal references; the database of external links; a list of colors and fontsets; and all your local preferences. It also contains any customization done to a site map.

The site file can be saved after changes are made to any of the attributes that are part of it. Its save-to-disk behavior is a little odd. If you quit without saving changes to the site, GoLive saves changes to the site file but doesn't warn or ask you about saving changes. However, you can select Save after any changes are made.

Tip: Saving the Site File Regularly

There is no auto-save feature for the site file until you quit the program, and you could easily spend hours working in GoLive without a save—which we don't recommend. Since the site file contains all the above-mentioned items, you'll lose any information not contained in the Web site itself that you may have manipulated.

For instance, if you create folders to organize your links in the External tab and unceremoniously crash, those folders will not appear when you reboot; the links will still be intact if they're present in the site's individual HTML files, but not if you created them from scratch in order to add them to pages.

The site file, when opened in GoLive, becomes the Site window described above. The site itself—the actual files listed in the Files tab—gets stored in the site folder.

Site folder. This folder contains all the files that comprise your Web site: HTML pages, media files, and other objects, including JavaScript libraries and CSS documents. It is essentially a local, identical representation of your remote Web site, with all files, directories, and links intact. You can also keep files in the site folder that you don't upload to the Web site. We discuss how to prevent files from being uploaded in Chapter 16, *Files, Folders, and Links,* and Chapter 18, *Staging and Synchronizing Sites.* (You can run into trouble here with references to files, like aliases, symbolic links, and shortcuts; we also discuss solutions for that in Chapter 18.)

When you import a site, locate your site folder down a directory level so that the site file and folders aren't lumped with other files (see Figure 15-2).

Figure 15-2
Nesting the site folder

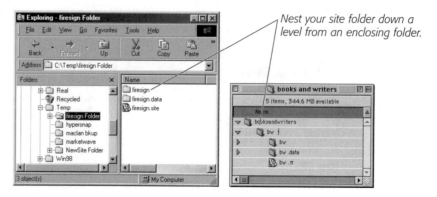

Nest your site folder down a level from an enclosing folder.

Site data folder. The site data folder gets named just like your site folder, with ".data" appended; for instance, if your site folder is called "bobsite", the site data folder is called "bobsite.data". It holds the GoLive miscellany: stationery, components—even trash, as a temporary holding bin before you empty it (see Chapter 16, *Files, Folders, and Links*).

   In the Site window's Files tab, you can open the split-pane view (to the right on the Macintosh or below under Windows) and click on the Extras tab (see Figure 15-3). The items in this tab correspond exactly to the items in the site data folder.

Figure 15-3
Extra tab

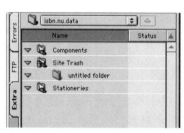

Macintosh and Windows split-pane views of the Extra tab

Site Window

GoLive organizes a site into five categories inside a Site window (see Figure 15-4). The Site window contains five tabs, each of which handles a specific aspect of site management.

   The five tabs in the Site window—Files, Site, External, Colors, and Fontsets—divide into three categories.

- **References and files:** the Files and External tabs help you manage HTML files, folders and directories containing items, media and other files, e-mail addresses users can click on, and any external URLs.

Figure 15-4
Site window

- **Site map:** the Site tab offers a graphical and outline view of the relationship among all the elements in a site; it also allows you to prototype sites and add links by dragging and dropping.

- **HTML attributes:** the Colors and Fontsets tabs provide a central location to view these attributes applied to text and other items anywhere in a site.

By centralizing all this management into one window, it's a simple task to view all the elements by category in a site. For instance, you can find out which colors have been used for a site that may have been created elsewhere and imported into GoLive; or, you can change a reference to another location on the Net with a single Point & Shoot action.

References and Files

The Files tab in GoLive shows all the files that comprise the site and are stored on your local hard drive, whether they are HTML files, GIF images, or other media files.

The Files tab manages all references made inside HTML files that point to other objects on your site, such as other HTML pages, GIF and JPEG images, Shockwave presentations, and PDFs. We talk about the Files tab in Chapter 16, *Files, Folders, and Links.*

If you click the split-pane button in the Files tab (Macintosh) or the expand triangle at the bottom of the Files tab (Windows), you can also examine errors, stationery, items thrown in the GoLive trash, and components (see Chapter 21, *Site Specials*), and access an FTP file list displaying the contents of remote FTP servers (see Figure 15-5). The FTP tab lets you manage uploads and downloads to your Web site (see Chapter 18, *Staging and Synchronizing Sites*).

Figure 15-5
FTP server tab
in the Site
window

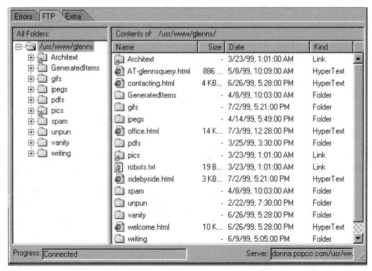

The External tab shows all references to URLs that reference external Web pages or other objects like public FTP servers and downloadable PDFs. Any item inside an HTML hyperlink that starts with a resource identifier link, like http://, ftp://, or mailto:, gets extracted and turned into an object you can manage in the External tab. We examine the External tab in Chapter 16, *Files, Folders, and Links*.

GoLive 4 added to CyberStudio 3's site management controls the tremendous ability to handle links embedded in several kinds of media files: QuickTime, Acrobat PDF (Portable Document Format), and Flash files. This media file management means that you can update URLs and internal references to files on the site without having to go back to the source program and data and recreate a new media file. We also cover this process in Chapter 16, *Files, Folders, and Links*.

Site Map

The Site tab offers a chance to glimpse the internal organization of a site in a two-dimensional framework. GoLive lets you see this organization using a couple different views—one by links, the other by navigation—and even lets you create an entire site by building links visually (see Figure 15-6).

Figure 15-6
Site tab

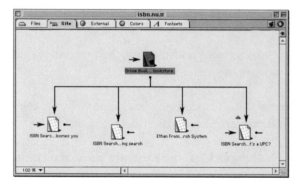

The site map helps you visualize whether a site is navigationally organized too wide or too deep. You can also correct links or redirect them using the Link Inspector with the site map. For more detail, see Chapter 19, *Site Maps*.

HTML Attributes

The Colors and Fontsets tabs land in the same bucket because both tabs let you view a summary of a single HTML attribute. The Color attribute is found in many different HTML tags, including those for table cells, page backgrounds, and individual text ranges. (See Chapter 9, *Color*, for more detail.)

The Fontsets tab shows a summary of the contents of the Font tag's Face attribute. This is plain text containing a list of fonts in order of preference from left to right that the page designer would like the viewer's browser to display a range of text. (See Chapter 7, *Text and Fonts*, for a deeper explanation.)

The Colors and Fontsets tabs both offer tools to create and name specific uses of colors or fontsets, and extract a list of all those items used in a site. However, the tabs don't allow you a quick method for changing colors or fontsets throughout your Web site. In Chapter 17, *Sitewide Sets*, we'll explain more about each tab and discuss multiple methods of simulating site management for these two attributes using Find & Replace.

Site Preferences

GoLive offers a few application-wide site preferences that affect your current site and new sites created later. These are all found in the Edit menu, under Preferences, by clicking the Site icon and the triangle or plus sign next to it.

Most of these preferences are described in detail in other chapters, which we'll indicate below.

Site

The Site preferences panel controls most checking and parsing behavior; that is, how and when GoLive checks files and URLs.

Check External URLs. Checking this box causes GoLive to confirm whether external URLs still exist. See Chapter 16, *Files, Folders, and Links*.

Reparse Only Changed Files, and Reparse Files on Hard Disk Rescan. These two options control how often GoLive checks the source HTML to see if changes were made that it hadn't tracked internally. See Chapter 16, *Files, Folders, and Links*.

Spring-Loaded Folders. If this option is checked on the Macintosh, folders automatically open when you drag files over them or use the Point & Shoot tool and hover over them. Under Windows, this option lets you display the contents of folders in the Explorer pane of the Files tab by dragging or using Point & Shoot; you can also expand folders to show nested folders.

Ask Before Deleting Objects. If this isn't checked, you can delete items with impunity without any warnings. Danger, danger, Will Robinson!

Create URL Mappings for Alias Folders. URL mappings are a highly powerful, yet confusing feature for splitting content over multiple Web sites, which we provide some step-by-step clarification on in Chapter 21, *Site Specials*.

When Removing Files. These radio buttons allow you to select which Trash to move deleted files to: the internal one in the site data folder handled by GoLive, or the system's Trash folder (Macintosh) or Recycle Bin (Windows). Unchecking Show Warning moves files when you delete them without any comment. These options are covered in depth in Chapter 21, *Site Specials*.

Other Site Preference Tabs

The Export preferences are covered in Chapter 21, *Site Specials*; Page Status in Chapter 16, *Files, Folders, and Links*; and Site View in Chapter 19, *Site Maps*. The Export Folder Names field in the Folder Names settings is also handled in Chapter 21, *Site Specials*.

The Generic Pages options control what GoLive calls new items and folders when you create new pages in the Site tab. The Extension field controls the suffix for HTML files. On Windows machines, that's often set to .htm, although GoLive defaults to .html even in its Windows version. The Folder Name field is used only when you create new pages through the Site tab's Navigation Hierarchy. If you create a blank site, GoLive uses the Home Page Name to set the default home page.

Site Menu, Palette, and Toolbar

GoLive often has different methods of displaying the same object or feature in the different locations within the program that allow you to insert that object or access that feature. The same item might be labeled and shown three different ways in the Site menu, palette, and toolbar. And two features are found only in the Site toolbar.

The Site menu is comprehensive, but many items overlap in the palette and toolbar. The Site toolbar displays by default. The Site tab of the Palette can be accessed by selecting the Palette under the Window menu (Mac) or View menu (Windows) ; or, by pressing Command-2 (Mac) or Alt-2 (Windows). Click the Site tab (see Figure 15-7).

Figure 15-7
Site tab of the
Palette

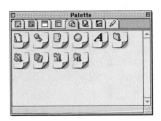

Tip: Site Tab, Site Tab There are two Site tabs in GoLive; the Site window has a Site tab that shows a site map, and the Palette has a Site tab that contains icons of items you can create in the tabs of the Site window.

The Site menu and toolbar gray-out choices that aren't available for the tab you have selected; the menu items may change their contents as well. The Site tab of the Palette lets you drag objects that aren't applicable, but when you release them, they snap back to the palette; if they're appropriate, the whole tab highlights on its edges, just like dragging files into a folder on the Desktop. The Site tab of the Palette only contains items corresponding to the New submenu.

Because we run down all the toolbar's options in Chapter 3, *Palettes and Parts*, we won't recapitulate them. Here are all the site-specific commands found on the Site menu, toolbar, and tab of the Palette.

New Group, Page, URL, Address, Color, Font Set. The Site menu's New submenu creates all the objects you need in each tab. The submenu only shows appropriate objects for the tab you're viewing. The Site tab doesn't allow you to insert anything, but the other four tabs allow you to create objects (see Table 15-1).

Table 15-1
Site window tabs and corresponding objects

Tab	New object
Files page	
External	URL or address
Color color	
Fontsets	fontset

If you want to group any items in any of the tabs except Site, you insert a folder. In the Files tab, this creates a new directory into which you can drag files. In the External tab, you can group by URL or address; the Colors and Fontsets tabs each have their own folder type as well.

You can insert the appropriate folder for the tab you're in by selecting Group from the New submenu or clicking the New Folder button in the Site toolbar. (Clicking the New Folder button always creates a new URL Group in External.)

The Site tab in the Palette contains 10 icons: the first five correspond to the five objects; the next five to the five kinds of group folders.

Add. If you add files through this menu item, GoLive copies your selection to your site folder. We'll cover this in more depth in Chapter 16, *Files, Folders, and Links*.

Import File. This item is available only in the External tab, and can be used to import bookmark files from Web browsers. See Chapter 16, *Files, Folders, and Links*.

Change Reference. Selecting this option from the menu or clicking the Change Reference button in the toolbar brings up a Change References dialog box that allows you to change all instances of an internal or external link. We cover this in Chapter 16, *Files, Folders, and Links.*

In Finder/In Explorer: Reveal Object, Show Object Information, Launch File. When a file is selected in either the Files or Site tab, this menu becomes available. The corresponding items in the toolbar are ordered by launch, show info, and reveal, and aren't all grouped together (see Figure 15-8).

Figure 15-8
Toolbar icons
for objects

— *Reveal Object*

Launch File   *Show Object Information*

Reveal Object switches you to the Desktop, opens the folder containing the file, and selects it. Show Object Information repeats that action, but brings up the information window in the Desktop (Info on the Mac or Properties in Windows).

Launch File opens the file with the application it was created in. You can change the application through various means, including changing the creator code on the Mac, editing the Registry in Windows, or updating File Mapping in GoLive on either platform. Because File Mapping is more of a page-based feature, we provided some guidelines to modifying its settings in Chapter 14, *Page Specials*; there's a few Mac-specific tips in Appendix A, *Macintosh Issues and Extras.*

Rescan, Get…Used, Remove Unused…, Clear Site. Depending on which tab you're in, the first two of these menu items change names. In the Files tab, selecting Rescan checks the site folder on the local hard drive, and updates the Files tab to reflect its current state; the Remove… item is grayed out. Holding down the Option or Alt key changes Rescan to Reparse All, and causes GoLive to rebuild its database of links from the source HTML of your pages. This option is necessary when hand-editing HTML files or using the Find feature to change HTML. (We give you more information on this subject in Chapter 16, *Files, Folders, and Links*, and Chapter 20, *Importing a Site.*)

In the External, Colors, and Fontsets tabs, the menu items change to Get (References, Colors, Fontsets) Used and Remove Unused (References, Colors, Fontsets). These tabs have to be refreshed by hand by selecting the Get…Used menu item.

If you delete URLs, addresses, colors, or fontsets from pages in your site, they persist in the appropriate tab after you've added them; or, if you create new objects and don't apply them to pages, they remain. Selecting Remove Unused… deletes any item that isn't used somewhere in the site.

Get…Used and Remove Unused… for the External tab are covered in Chapter 16, *Files, Folders, and Links*; and for the Colors and Fontsets tab in Chapter 17, *Sitewide Sets*.

Clear Site offers the same kind of functionality as Remove Unused…, but it allows you to remove all kinds of unused objects at the same time with some selectable options. This is covered in Chapter 21, *Site Specials*.

Export Site. Export Site creates an exact duplicate of your site folder while allowing you to remove GoLive-specific tags, remove extra white space, and/or reorganize the site's hierarchy. See Chapter 21, *Site Specials*, for all the options.

Connect to Server, Disconnect from Server, Abort, Upload to Server, Download From Server. These commands all relate to connecting and transferring files to and from the FTP server which holds your remote Web site. The Site toolbar uses a single button that toggles between connect and disconnect, and separate buttons for uploading and downloading (see Figure 15-9). The FTP features get full coverage in Chapter 18, *Staging and Synchronizing Sites*.

Figure 15-9
FTP controls in
Site toolbar

— *Download from Server*

——————— *Upload to Server*

Connect/Disconnect to Server

Settings. The Settings item corresponds to items specific to your site (see Figure 15-10). There are other settings for site behavior that are global—they affect any site you open after changing them. (See Chapter 4, *Preferences and Customizing*.)

Figure 15-10
Site settings

The General setting contains only the name of the home page for the site. Different servers allow you to set the home page name, some by default, others by choice. You can change your home page here by browsing or using the Point & Shoot button. You can also change it by clicking on any page in the Files tab, bringing up the File Inspector's Page tab, and clicking Home Page.

Clear Site controls the settings for that command; see just above and in Chapter 21, *Site Specials*, for more.

FTP settings reflect any choices you made in setting up an FTP server and location specific to this site. See Chapter 18, *Staging and Synchronizing Sites*.

URL Mappings controls a very complex set of behaviors that allows you to split your Web site among multiple remote locations. We cover this with some examples in Chapter 21, *Site Specials.*

Site Navigator palette and Arrange Items. The toolbar has two buttons that aren't reproduced anywhere else: the Site Navigator palette and Arrange Items buttons. (See Chapter 19, *Site Maps,* for more on both features.)

If you have the Site tab selected in the Site window, clicking the Site Navigator Palette button brings up—surprise, surprise!—the Site Navigator palette. There's no other way to get there (see Figure 15-11).

Figure 15-11
Site Navigator
palette

Clicking this button in the Site toolbar is the only way to display the Site Navigator palette.

The Arrange Items button cleans up a site map viewed through the Link Hierarchy in the Site tab after you've turned off Auto Arrange Items and made changes by dragging items around.

Set Your Sights

With the big picture in mind, let's set our sights on setting up sites, and walk through the details of each aspect of creating, maintaining, and updating sites using GoLive.

Files, Folders, and Links

The heart of GoLive's superlative site management is its ability to manage, display, and update links between files in a site it administers, as well as that site's links to items elsewhere on the Web. The Site window may have five tabs, but the Files tab and the External tab are where you spend the vast majority of your time.

Keeping track of file names and locations is a thankless and tedious task that's at the core of site management. It's one of those deeds that, if performed poorly, can take vast amounts of time to get back on track. Without a program like GoLive handling those details, many Webmasters and site producers (and their staff) spend way too much time writing notes on slips of paper and taping them to their monitors. Ultimately, the Post-It Note forest overwhelms the visible area of the screen, and that's when site-management software is way overdue.

When you create any site, you're really creating a set of relationships between resources. Some of these resources may be files stored at the Web site, like HTML pages and GIF images; others may be documents stored elsewhere on the Web or on an intranet, like a PDF file containing a form a user can print out, or a simple Web page with more information on a subject.

Whenever a Web browser retrieves a page or file, it's fundamentally the same process regardless of whether that file is linked from another page on the same Web site, or if it's linked from a site in Turkey. The user's Web browser still has to go out on the Internet, make a connection to the site, negotiate the file's transfer, and download it.

GoLive cleverly recognizes these similarities by providing management tools for local files that reflect the contents of your Web site as well as a view into all of the "external" resources your site links to elsewhere on the Web.

Files Inside GoLive

Ordinary documents on the Macintosh or Windows desktop don't have much intelligence. That is to say, on their own, they might have an icon and a file extension or file type that identifies them to the operating system. But unless they're opened by an application, the desktop can't peer inside those files and tell you what's what. However, when those same files are viewed through the Files tab in GoLive, they exhibit lots of smarts, revealing links and other object relationships.

The Files tab mimics the display of files and folders in the Mac OS Desktop or in My Computer under Windows 95 and later. Files can be moved up and down folder levels, renamed, and deleted.

GoLive maintains a hidden database in the site file stored on your local hard drive that contains every link and image reference in all HTML files. If you have the right GoLive Modules loaded, any external URLs used in QuickTime movies, Flash objects, and Acrobat PDF (Portable Document Format) files are also put into this database (see Chapter 4, *Preferences and Customizing*, and Chapter 22, *Advanced Features*, for more on modules).

Because every link and image is managed by this database, whenever you act on a file, GoLive prompts you to update all references to that file, and then it updates its own internal list.

For instance, let's say while building a site you put all of the images at a single folder level, the main level of your site. This is pretty typical for a small site that unexpectedly gets bigger. You may suddenly find yourself with hundreds of files at the main level and want to reorganize.

But because of how GoLive tracks references, you can just drag and drop to your heart's content. In this case, you could create a folder named "images" in the Files tab, and drag all your image files into it (see Figure 16-1). GoLive would then prompt you to change all of the HTML and media files that contained links pointing to those images. Clicking OK would allow GoLive to rewrite the links, move the files, and everything on the site would remain working and correctly linked into place.

Working with Files in a Site

At the simplest level, opening the Site window brings up the Files tab showing the list of files already in the site; if you started from scratch, the Files tab is empty except for a blank home page (see Figure 16-2).

Root Location

The root of a site is the same as your site folder. When you create a new link within a page, and check the Absolute box below the URL field in the inspector, the URL is displayed with the full path based on the site folder—even if the link is in the

Figure 16-1
Reorganizing
files in the
Files tab via
drag and drop

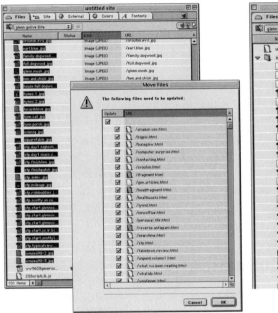

Select and drag images in a flat layout into the images folder, and GoLive prompts you to rewrite all of the HTML and media pages that link to these images

Images in their new location

Figure 16-2
An empty Site
window

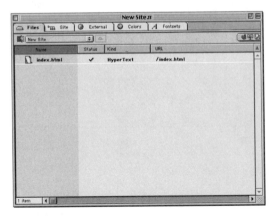

same current directory. For example, suppose you're working in a file called "hobbes.html" located in the "comics" folder. Linking to a file in the same folder would normally display just the file name in the URL field of the inspector. However, with Absolute checked, the URL would show: "/comics/calvin.html". In traditional computer parlance, "root" refers to the base level of your hard drive, like "C:" in Windows or the "Macintosh HD" (or whatever you may have renamed it) on the Mac; GoLive is smart enough to treat your site file's directory as the root for its Web site. See the sidebar, "Absolute versus Relative," for a more detailed explanation. The Macintosh and Windows versions of GoLive have different graphic displays of the root level (see Figure 16-3).

Macintosh. In the upper left of the Files tab on a Mac, GoLive displays a Mac OS icon and a popup menu showing the name of the current root folder. You can view this menu to see where on the local hard drive the root is located, but all of the levels above the current one are grayed out and inaccessible.

Windows. Windows uses the Windows Explorer style of file navigation to handle the display of folders. The root of the site is shown directly below the label "All Folders:"; folders in the site are shown with dotted lines connecting them from the root folder.

File Information

Each file and folder is shown with its name, its status (links are all working, links broken, etc.), its Kind (document, folder, HTML file), and the URL showing the file's location in the site from the root of the site.

Figure 16-3
Macintosh and
Windows
views of the
site's root

The Mac version of GoLive shows the entire path from the hard drive down to the site folder; every level is inactive except for the root (and below).

Windows shows just the root on down in the Explorer.

Table 16-1
Absolute and
relative
references

Type of link	User is at...
Relative	http://www.etaoin.com/shrdlu/welcome.html
Relative folder	http://www.etaoin.com/shrdlu/welcome.html
GoLive Absolute	http://www.etaoin.com/pdevil/welcome.html
Relative with ".."	http://www.etaoin.com/pdevil/welcome.html
Real absolute	http://www.etaoin.com/pdevil/dvorak.html

Tip: Typing to Select Typing the first few letters of a file name selects the file in the list. Under Windows, you can press Tab and Shift-Tab to switch between the File Explorer's folder and files list, and select a file or folder by typing the first few letters. On the Macintosh, the first letters of what you type show up in the item count box at the lower left corner of the Site window.

Absolute versus Relative

All references in GoLive, whether they're hypertext links or media links, fall into one of two categories (see Table 16-1):

- Absolute: the entire URL is specified, including what's called a "scheme": http, ftp, file, etc., like http://www.bootyc.com/foo/bar/path.html or ftp://ftp.windbagx.com/mish/e/gas/nonsense.pdf
- Relative: just the part containing a filename or a path to a filename is included, like "bar/path.html" where "bar" is a folder

A relative reference uses the context of where you are within a site to generate the rest of the link. If I'm at http://www.bootyc.com/foo/welcome.html, the relative URL above treats "bar" as a folder without having to know about the enclosing "foo" folder, and path.html as a file in that folder.

GoLive mixes up the issue by calling a certain kind of relative URL "Absolute," counter to the HTML specification that defined these terms. Version 4 of GoLive added an Absolute checkbox in all Inspectors and dialogs in which a file path can be specified. This checkbox doesn't turn the file reference into a true, absolute URL (sometimes known as a fully qualified URL); rather, it provides the entire path from the root of the Web site down to the file.

So in the above example, if we made path.html into a GoLive Absolute reference, the URL would turn into

```
/foo/bar/path.html
```

This kind of reference always works on a given server, no matter where in the directory the linking file is located. Using GoLive Absolute references makes your files somewhat more portable without adding too much of a management burden, as GoLive can cope with its own form of Absolute reference as well as any kind of relative link to a file on the site. It can also easily rewrite Absolute links into relative ones by using Change Reference, described later in this chapter.

You can force GoLive to make all new links Absolute ones by checking New Links Absolute in the URL Handling settings of the General pane in the Preferences dialog box.

Link in HREF is…	User winds up at…
letterpress.html	http://www.etaoin.com/shrdlu/letterpress.html
oldstyle/numerals.html	http://www.etaoin.com/shrdlu/oldstyle/numerals.html
/shrdlu/welcome.html	http://www.etaoin.com/shrdlu/welcome.html
../shrdlu/welcome.html	http://www.etaoin.com/shrdlu/welcome.html
http://www.qwerty.com/welcome.html	http://www.qwerty.com/welcome.html

Viewing Folder Contents

Double-clicking a folder or selecting it in the Windows Explorer folder pane expands it to fill the Files tab (see Figure 16-4). However, on the Mac, you can click the expand triangle to show nested items inside folders in the same view (see Figure 16-5).

Figure 16-4
Windows
Explorer

Figure 16-5
Macintosh
expanded
folder view

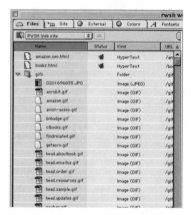

Revealing and Opening Files and Folders

With a file or folder selected, you can manipulate a file in various ways, from revealing its enclosing folder on the Desktop, to duplicating it, to opening it in the application that created it.

Tip:
Accessing
Options

Most of these options are accessible through both the Edit and Site menu's In Finder or In Explorer submenu, and under slightly different names as a contextual selection by right-clicking under Windows or Control-clicking on the Mac (see Figure 16-6). They are also paralleled in the Site toolbar just like most of the buttons to the left of the Connect to Server button.

The In Finder (Mac) or In Explorer (Windows) submenu in the Site menu offers three options for most items: Reveal Object, Show Object Information, and

Figure 16-6
The many
ways of
opening

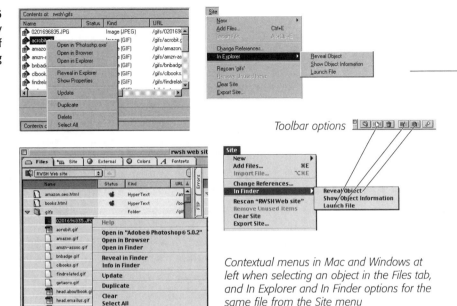

Toolbar options

*Contextual menus in Mac and Windows at
left when selecting an object in the Files tab,
and In Explorer and In Finder options for the
same file from the Site menu*

Launch File; these options are available only for single selections. (These items were
discussed briefly in the previous chapter; here's the fuller explanation of all three.)

The Edit menu makes available Clear, Duplicate, and Select All for files and
folders. The Site toolbar offers a final option, Update, available only in the Toolbar
and in the contextual menu. Clear and Duplicate work on multiple selections;
Select All and Update don't require any selection to work.

Reveal Object. Selecting this command opens the item's enclosing folder in the
Desktop with the item selected in it (see Figure 16-7). The contextual menu reads
Reveal in Finder (Mac) or Reveal in Explorer (Windows).

Figure 16-7
Revealing
objects on
Desktop

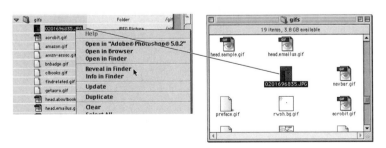

Show Object Information. This option brings up the Information window on the
Macintosh or the Properties window under Windows showing the file system
characteristics and values, such as modification date, file size, and so forth. GoLive

has inspectors that do much the same; see "File Inspector," later in this chapter. This option is called Info in Finder (Mac) or Show Properties (Windows) in the contextual menu.

Launch File. The most complex option is Launch File, as it relies on quite a bit of underlying detail to work correctly.

Selecting Launch File or double-clicking a file opens the file in the application specified in the File Mapping settings of the General pane in the Preferences dialog box. This is a sufficiently complex subject, so we devoted a whole section to it in Chapter 14, *Page Specials*. In brief, you can set GoLive to open certain kinds of files and choose applications (or use defaults) to open others. (If there's no program set, different options control what program or dialog box appears when you double-click the file.)

Using the contextual menu shows two to four options: Open in Adobe GoLive (if it's a file type GoLive has built-in support for), Open in "Program Name" (if another program is listed in File Mapping), Open in Browser (GoLive opens the file in the default browsers), and Open in Finder or Open in Explorer (GoLive launches the file from the Desktop). For file types GoLive doesn't support and no program is specified for, the Open in Adobe GoLive and Open in "Program Name" options are both omitted.

Status Icons

The Files tabs shares with the External and Site tabs a set of status icons which indicate the state of a file's links (see Figure 16-8).

Folders can also have status icons attached with one of the icons next to an expand arrow showing that the folder contains files with links that are broken, has empty files, or has files that should be in the folder but are missing (also see Figure 16-8).

Checkmark. All of the item's links are up to date and GoLive knows where the actual file is on the local hard disk.

Green bug. A page's links to some items are missing. (Clicking the green bug or Link Warnings icon at the top of any Web page highlights all the broken links on the page with a colored outline;

see Chapter 5, *Layout, Source, and Preview*, for more about this topic.)

Yield sign. The page is empty; typically, it was created from a template or through the Site tab.

Stop sign. In the Files or Site tab, the file is missing; it also shows up in the Missing Files folder in the Errors tab (see "Errors," later in this chapter). In the External tab, the URL has been tested and failed.

Question mark. This icon gets attached to a file when GoLive can't find the actual item on the local hard drive. It typically shows up in the Errors tab.

Crossed-out folder. This icon, which symbolizes orphaned files—ones that aren't stored in the site folder but are referenced by the site—helps you troubleshoot before uploading a site to a server.

Figure 16-8
Status icons

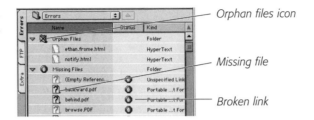

Orphan files icon

Missing file

Broken link

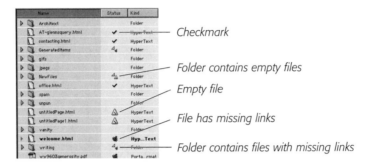

Checkmark

Folder contains empty files

Empty file

File has missing links

Folder contains files with missing links

Tip: Creator Overridden by GoLive (Mac)

The Site window's Files tab displays the files as the Macintosh Finder sees them, which means you may see different icons for files of the same type. The most common example on our systems is a mixture of HTML files that show icons for GoLive and the text editor BBEdit (the icons are just a reflection of what program that file has been associated with in the file's internal Creator flag). If you were to double-click them in the Finder, the program associated with the icon opens the file. But within GoLive's Site window, the File Mapping setting overrides the file's Finder flag every time. This way, you don't have to worry about accidentally launching a different program for the same type of file.

Tip: Setting an Alternate HTML Editor

File Mapping and contextual selection is especially useful for setting an alternate HTML editor on the Mac. If you set up a program for the .htm and .html extensions in File Mapping settings, GoLive still "knows" it can open the files, so double-clicking them opens the files with those extensions in GoLive. However, Control-clicking on the Mac reveals the Open in "Other HTML Editor" option, which allows you to more easily access that editor.

Tip: Opening Problems (Mac)

We had a small problem when upgrading to GoLive 4.0.1 for Macintosh where GoLive would no longer open files when double-clicked in the Files tab. It turns out that our Desktop database wasn't updated when we installed the update.

We found two solutions: first, rebuild the Desktop database, which you do by holding down Command-Option as the Mac starts up. When the MacOS asks if you want to rebuild your Desktop, click OK. The other solution involves the File Mapping settings. We changed the setting for .htm and .html to be Adobe GoLive instead of Default, and this worked as well.

Clear. Selecting Clear prompts GoLive to ask if you want to delete the selected file or files.

Duplicate. The selected item or items are duplicated.

Select All. All items in the Files tab are selected. Pressing Command-A (Mac) or Control-A (Windows) accomplishes the same thing.

Update. Update checks for any new content and adds or deletes files that have been changed on the Desktop (as opposed to changed through the Files tab, discussed below). If you have a site subfolder filling the Files view or have a folder selected while contextually selecting, only that folder's contents are updated.

Inspectors

The Files tab features two inspectors that help you examine and modify the properties of files and folders: the File Inspector and the Folder Inspector. For HTML files, there are three tabs in the File Inspector: Basic, Page, and Content; for media files, just the Basic and Content pages appear. (This is different for certain special kinds of rich media; see Chapter 28, *Plug-ins and Media.*)

Basics. The File tab of the File Inspector is almost identical to the Folder Inspector's only display (see Figure 16-9). The Name field allows you to change the file's or folder's name.

Tip: **Changing** **Names**	You can also change the name of an item by clicking on the name portion in the file list and waiting for it to highlight, then editing or typing over it. GoLive prompts you to rewrite any links pointing to that item after you press Return or Enter.

Aliases and Shortcuts

Most platforms let you create pointers to files that serve as proxies for them: the Macintosh uses aliases and Windows uses shortcuts (see Figure 16-10). However, GoLive treats both kinds of pointers as plain files, showing the File Inspector's Basic and Content tabs when an alias or shortcut is selected.

GoLive lets you map aliases to other sites if you've split your content among multiple Web servers; and it supports, to some extent, links that are used on Web servers to point to content elsewhere on your Web site.

But support remains a bit tricky to sort out, and we'd recommend not using aliases unless you need to use URL Mapping, described in Chapter 21, *Site Specials.* We also provide a much fuller explanation of how links and pointers work in uploading and downloading sotes in "Aliases, Shortcuts, and Symbolic Links" in Chapter 18, *Staging and Synchronizing Sites.*

Figure 16-9
Basic items in
File tab of File
Inspector

Figure 16-10
Shortcuts and
aliases

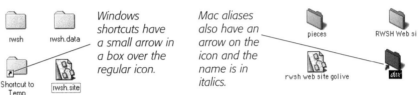

The URL field, which can't be edited, shows the location of the file or folder relative to the site's root.

The Publish menu allows you to choose under what circumstances a file or folder gets uploaded to a Web server when you use the built-in FTP features of GoLive. (See Chapter 18, *Staging and Synchronizing Sites*, for an in-depth discussion of this option and how it interacts with other GoLive preferences.)

The Created and Modified fields, which can't be edited, show the date and time of the file's creation and last changes.

The Size field appears only in the File Inspector, and simply shows the size of the file in bytes.

The Stationery checkbox, Label menu, and Type and Creator fields only appear in the File Inspector on the Macintosh; for a discussion of them, see Appendix A, *Macintosh Issues and Extras*, as they don't affect how you work with files or folders.

Page tab. The Name field shows the page's title, which you can edit here without opening the file. (Otherwise, you have to open the page and either enter the new title next to the Page icon or via the Page Inspector.)

The file's encoding is listed in an uneditable box; you have to open the file and save it as another name to change its encoding.

The Status field lets you set a GoLive-only tag to help sort or view items in the Site tab (see Chapter 19, *Site Maps*).

The Home Page checkbox lets you change the root page for your site—the page from which all the hierarchical links are mapped for uploading referenced files or creating a site map. However, you can't simply uncheck the box with the home page selected. Instead, select the page you *want to become* your new home page, and check the box there; that box turns bold in the Files tab, and the other page's Home Page box becomes unchecked. (You can also reset your home page via the Site Settings, discussed in Chapter 15, *Site Management.*)

Content tab. A preview of the content of the file appears here if GoLive knows how to preview it (see Figure 16-11). For HTML files, GoLive must already have opened, modified, and saved the file for a thumbnail to show up. For other media, the appropriate module must be loaded. For instance, without the CyberMovie Module loaded, QuickTime movies and sound files don't preview in this tab (see "Modules" in Chapter 22, *Advanced Features.*)

Figure 16-11
Content
previews

Adding Files to the Site

GoLive lets you add content to the Files tab in several ways, making it convenient to use whatever method you prefer. The methods include:

- Using the Add Files menu item under the Site menu
- Dragging and dropping from the Desktop into the Files tab
- Creating new, blank files to fill with content
- Using Stationery to create new pages
- Copying them from the Desktop into the Web site folder, bypassing GoLive

Tip:
Analyzing
Added Files
When files are added in the first two methods, GoLive scans them for links and adds those relationships to the site file. If you add files to the Web site folder on the Desktop, you have to go through a few more steps, described below, to hook in the content of the files.

Add Files. The only method to add files to your site from within GoLive is to select Add Files from the Site menu. The dialog box allows you to navigate to any location reachable through the file dialog box and add files to the list by selecting them and clicking Add (see Figure 16-12).

Figure 6-12
Adding files

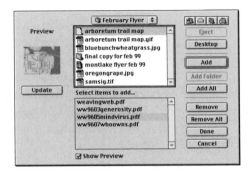

Clicking Add Folder adds the folder's contents to the list, including nested subfolders; clicking Add All adds the entire current contents of the file browser's display, including all nested subfolders. You can individually remove items by selecting them and clicking Remove, or delete your entire selection of files by clicking Remove All.

Clicking Done copies all the items, wherever they are, to the site folder; the files appear immediately in the Files tab and are located in the site folder unless you're viewing the contents of a subfolder, in which case they're copied into that folder. Clicking Cancel is the equivalent of clicking Remove All and Done: the end result is no action taken.

Dragging into Files tab. Sometimes, it's just easier to find what you need on the Desktop, select it, and drag it into the Files tab. GoLive is perfectly content to let you act this way; in fact, it's just as good as using the Add Files option. (We applaud the developers for not straitjacketing users by giving them just one method!)

Before dragging items into the Files tab, it's a good idea to arrange the window so that you can see the area you're dragging into when you're on the Desktop. If you want to nest the items inside a folder—that is, not put them at the root level of the site—it's a good idea to open that folder (Mac) or select it from the Explorer (Windows) so that it's the only thing in the Files tab (see Figure 16-13).

Figure 16-13
Dragging files
into an open
folder

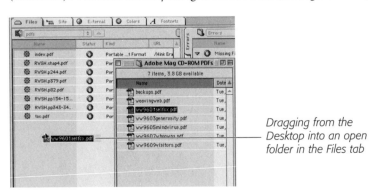

Dragging from the Desktop into an open folder in the Files tab

Items you drag are immediately copied to the site folder and appear in the Files tab. If any of the files are HTML or media files that have embedded links in them, GoLive brings up the Copy Files dialog box and notifies you that the links need to be updated (see Figure 16-14). Generally, you click OK. Clicking Cancel halts the copy, so if you want to copy the files without updating links, uncheck the boxes for those files (or the box at the top for all files), and then click OK.

Figure 16-14
Updating links
in added files

Dragging into the Desktop folder. Although we think it a bit uncouth, you can bypass GoLive altogether and copy or move files directly into the site folder on the Desktop. The problem with the direct route is that when you return to GoLive, it doesn't know the files have been added. See "Tuning Up," later in this chapter, on how to get GoLive to add these files and folders.

Adding empty files. When you're prototyping a site to build out content, it can be useful to add empty files that will eventually have real content. Using the Site tab, you can add templates or absolutely blank pages with link placeholders (pending links) to other items in the site. (See Chapter 19, *Site Maps*, for the details on prototyping.)

You can also drag a Generic Page icon directly from the Palette's Site tab; GoLive creates an untitled page with a yield icon in the status column. If you double click the Generic Page icon, the program creates a New Pages folder (if it doesn't already exist) and adds the untitled files inside it.

Adding stationery. GoLive lets you create templates in the form of stationery, which are stored in a special folder in the split-pane view of the Files tab. We discuss stationery at some length in Chapter 21, *Site Specials*.

Moving Files

Because GoLive tracks every link in and to every file, moving and reorganizing items in a site is a cinch. You can select any file, folder, or set of items, and drag them to a new location; GoLive prompts you with a dialog asking you which files should have their links rewritten to reflect these new locations. This list includes files you're moving as well as any files that have links to the items you're moving.

Unless you have a specific reason not to, you should click OK, so that GoLive updates the links; otherwise, links get broken, and GoLive reports missing and orphaned files (see "Errors," later in this chapter).

Creating Links

It's also a snap to add links in GoLive, because it can be done entirely by using Point & Shoot navigation or by dragging and dropping links. Of course, you can also actually type links into a field in most cases.

There's also a method of creating placeholder links in the Site tab that we discuss briefly here.

Point & Shoot

GoLive's Point & Shoot navigation lets you simply drag from any link field or from certain selected items directly onto the object you want to link. It's as simple as that. Although you can use Point & Shoot on individual pages to make anchors—specific locations on a page to jump to—it's most powerfully employed in creating hypertext links and links to media files.

Tip: More on Point & Shoot
We devote a section in Chapter 1, *Getting Started*, to the Point & Shoot tool with all its ins and outs. If you're having any trouble using it, consult that chapter for more information.

Tip: External Linking
Everything described in this section that works for local links in your site functions just as well for external URLs found in the External tab. See "External Links," later in this chapter.

Point & Shoot button. The most common use of Point & Shoot is via the URL field in the Image Inspector's Link tab and Text Inspector's Basic tab, although the field and tool are found in the Map tab of the Image Inspector for individual mapped areas, and numerous other places in the program (see Figure 16-15).

To use Point & Shoot, drag the icon onto the Site window, bringing that window to the front after a few seconds delay. If you drag on top of the Files, Site, or External tabs, GoLive switches to that tab, and then you can drag to items in those locations.

Figure 16-15
Some of the many appearances of Point & Shoot navigation

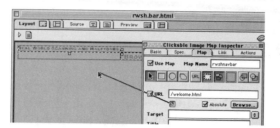

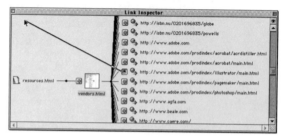

Point & Shoot navigation in the Map tab of the Image Inspector, the Link tab of the Text Inspector, and for each of the links in the Link Inspector

If you drag on top of a folder, after a slight pause, GoLive opens the folder to reveal its contents. Dragging over the folder up a level icon (Mac) or onto the Folder Explorer (Windows) lets you move up folder levels as well.

Tip: Spring Loaded (Mac)   On the Mac, you can disable the ability to drag onto folders and tabs to open them by unchecking Spring Loaded Folders in the Site pane of the Preferences dialog box. We prefer keeping this feature active as it allows us to easily move items around without positioning everything perfectly first.

When you hover over a linkable object, like an HTML file or external link, the item highlights (see Figure 16-16). If you release the Point & Shoot tool's link line on top of that item, the link is added into the URL field.

Hunt the Wumpus

One of the best ways to use Change References is to clean up older HTML pages that might have a variety of references to the same file. We recommend one method in Chapter 20, *Importing a Site*, that our friends at Adobe thought involved too many steps. They suggested a simpler alternative for some cases: use Change References and type in all the old references one at a time in the top field, while leaving the bottom field set to your new value. For instance, if we want a whole variety of files to point to /foobar/sniggle.html, we might search for these three URLs:

```
http://www.snark.com/foobar/sniggle.html
/home/users/wumpus/foobar/sniggle.html
~wumpus/foobar/sniggle.html
```

Then we could replace those, one at a time, with the new location. This works sitewide and cleans up the management task of having lots of different URLs that point to the same file.

Figure 16-16
Adding a link
via Point &
Shoot

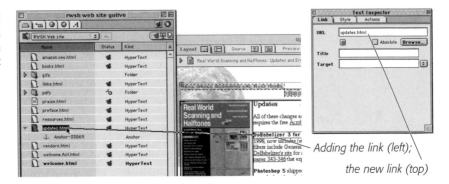

Adding the link (left);
the new link (top)

If you release the mouse button on top of the wrong kind of item—for instance, a fontset in the Fontsets tab—or if you release it without having anything selected, the line snaps back like a broken rubber band. Hey, no one can accuse us of not liking good eye-candy! (We'd like to show this effect in a figure, but it's a system-level animation, so try it on your own.)

Point & Shoot shortcut. With any text selected on a HTML page, holding down the Command key (Mac) or Alt key (Windows) turns the cursor into a Point & Shoot tool (see Figure 16-17). You can drag from that text onto any kind of object or tab as described above to complete the link.

Figure 16-17
Point & Shoot
shortcut

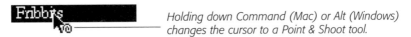

Holding down Command (Mac) or Alt (Windows)
changes the cursor to a Point & Shoot tool.

If you drag to a location on the same HTML page or on another open HTML page, GoLive creates an anchor link pointing to that exact location on the page. Clicking that link takes the user directly to that spot.

Dragging Links

Although it's not quite as elegant, you can drag a file or folder from the Files tab directly into an HTML page. Wherever you release the mouse, the item's name is inserted, and it's automatically linked back to the source. You can then rename the link.

Typing Links

You'd hardly believe it in a WYSIWYG program like GoLive, but you really can just type in links in the URL field instead of using Point & Shoot or drag and drop. Of course, that's about as déclassé as paying with green paper at the supermarket these days (you should see the looks we get). It's almost always better to use Point & Shoot because it constructs the links perfectly. But you can certainly type in a filename in the same folder, an Absolute-style path, or a URL for a file location elsewhere.

**Tip: Movin'
On Up!** GoLive follows the Web convention for relative links, so if you want to refer to a file up a folder level from where the linking file is located, you insert two dots and a slash (../); this means "go up a folder level." For instance, if you want to link to wonder-bro.html which is located two levels higher in the "jerry" folder, you'd use a link like

```
../../jerry/wonderbro.html
```

Pending Links

In the Site tab, you can add pending links, or placeholders where links should be added, by dragging files on top of other files. By creating these in-process links, you can later go back and turn the pending links into actual ones by inserting items on the page and adding the links to them.

For instance, when you're prototyping a site, you might know that page A needs links to pages B, C, and D, but the navigational elements that will link to B, C, and D aren't yet created. After you create those elements, you can go to the Pending tab of the Page Inspector and connect the items with the pages they point to. Chapter 19, *Site Maps*, covers this subject in great detail.

Modifying and Examining Links

The features for looking at existing links and modifying them are equally as strong as the tools for creating links. For examining links, GoLive offers the powerful Link Inspector; for modifying existing links, you can use either the Link Inspector or the Change References feature.

**Tip: Hand
Editing Links** As with creating links, you can hand enter new links in the URL field of an Inspector.

Link Inspector

The Link Inspector is your best friend in managing a site. It can show all the in-bound connections to a given file and—for HTML and media files that have embedded URLs—all the other items the file connects to (see Figure 16-18).

The Link Inspector is comprised of two main parts: its window and its controller. (The Link View Controller is thoroughly covered in Chapter 2, *The Inspector*, so we don't reiterate it all here.)

Invoke the Link Inspector by selecting it from the Windows menu (Mac) or View menu (Windows), or by pressing Command-5 (Mac) or Alt-4 (Windows). Clicking the eye icon on its upper right brings up the Link View Controller.

Selecting any file in the Files tab or Site tab creates a display in the Link Inspector of all the inbound and outbound links relating to that file. Use the Link View Controller to specify whether the inspector should show inbound or outbound links at all, and, if so, which kinds of outbound links to display. Filter out external links and other types to help clarify the outbound links.

Figure 16-18
Link Inspector

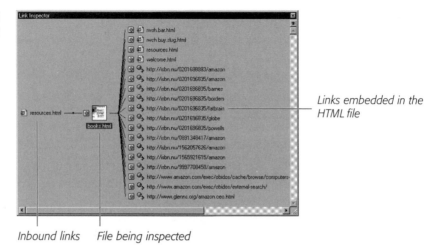

Links embedded in the
HTML file

Inbound links   File being inspected

Selecting the file at the center brings up the File Inspector. Selecting one of the linked-to or linked-from objects makes that object the star, putting it in the central position of the Link Inspector.

Any item that is linked to, including the selected item if it has any inbound links, has a Point & Shoot icon next to it. Using Point & Shoot from the Link Inspector, you can redirect the link that points at that object to any other object. This allows you, for instance, to update an old external link on a page by viewing it in the Link Inspector, and just dragging the Point & Shoot link line onto the External tab and on top of the correct new external link. (You can also click the Change References button or select that from the Site menu, and the current item in the center of the Link Inspector is entered into Change All References To.)

This feature is especially useful for troubleshooting errors. Select the file with an error from the Errors tab in the split-pane view of the Files tab, and the Link Inspector displays all the files that point to the missing or broken item. Use the Point & Shoot icon to reconnect the error icon to the correct item, and GoLive rebuilds the links. Voilá!

Change References

The Change References feature allows you to change a reference throughout a site to another reference. It even works within the Link Inspector. Bring up the Change References dialog box by selecting it from the Site menu or clicking its button in the Site toolbar.

With an item selected in the Files, Site, or External tab or with an item showing at the center of the Link Inspector, selecting Change References brings up the dialog box with the Change All References To field prefilled with the selected item (see Figure 16-19). That field is uneditable if an item was selected when you chose Change References.

Figure 16-19
Change
References
dialog box

With nothing selected and nothing in the Link Inspector, bringing up the dialog box allows you to type, browse, or Point & Shoot a value for the Change All References To field. In either case, you can navigate the replacement value for the Into References To field.

Tip: To and To Let's be clear: Although both the from and to fields of the Change References dialog box use the preposition "to," the top field (Change All References To) means "from the current setting" and the bottom field (Into References To) means "to this new setting."

Change References, like most site features, is undoable, so be sure to make a backup first.

If you want to ensure that everything's normal after using Change References, use Reparse All as described under "Tuning Up," next.

Tuning Up

After you've done quite a bit of work in the Files tab, it could seem, well, a bit out of sort. Generally, GoLive tracks all the elements in a site, but if you've clicked Cancel here and unchecked a box there, and edited your HTML in a text editor way over there, some of your links and files might need a bit of cleaning.

GoLive offers a few tools for helping out in that department. Here are three tips for cleaning up missing files or deleted files, updating problems, and missing thumbnails. (We offer more tips under "Errors," later in this chapter.)

Rescanning site

If you've added content by dragging it into the Web site folder on the Desktop or otherwise manipulated files without using GoLive, you need to rescan the site. Rescanning forces GoLive to re-examine all of the items in the folders that comprise the site.

Select Rescan from the Site menu; the current site name is inserted after Rescan in the menu. If you've selected a folder's contents so that it fills the file list, the Rescan menu item appends that folder's name (see Figure 16-20).

Tip: Update It appears that clicking the Update button, selecting Update from a contextual menu,
vs. Rescan or selecting Rescan from the Site menu all rescan the site for new or deleted files.

Figure 16-20
Rescan

Rescan site (left) and folder (right)

Tip: PDF Problem (Mac only) Mac OS 8.6 introduced an odd problem that could cause crashes in version 4.0 of GoLive due to bad font resources. Apple released a fix that corrected its end of the problem, and Adobe later released GoLive 4.0.1, which separately took care of the problem. (By the way, If you ran the Apple fix before running the GoLive 4.0.1 updater for Mac, you need to reinstall GoLive 4.0 from its original disks or installer before running the 4.0.1 updater.). Password-protected PDFs can also cause a crash.

However, if you still get crashes when rescanning a site that has had PDF content added to it, check that you're running 4.0.1 or later. If you are, run the font resource repair program. See http://realworldgolive.com/macos86.html for links to utilities and updates.

Reparse All

If you've been a little naughty and worked on raw HTML in another editor than GoLive's HTML Source Editor, GoLive isn't up to speed on the contents of that file. You have two choices:

- You can open any files you've edited elsewhere, make a small change (like typing and erasing a space character), and then save it

- Hold down the Option key (Mac) or Alt key (Windows) and select Reparse All from the Site menu

Reparse All walks through all of the HTML on the site and recreates the invisible GoLive database of links and other information.

Tip: Reparse Changed If you check Reparse Only Changed files in the Site pane of the Preferences dialog box, GoLive checks the modification date of the file against its record of the last time it dealt with the file. If the modification date is more recent, only then does it reparse the file. We're not sure why you'd want to turn this off.

Tip: Reparse While Rescanning If you check Reparse on Hard Disk Rescan in the Preferences dialog box's Site pane, then Rescan and Reparse All have the same functionality.

Creating Thumbnails

GoLive automatically makes thumbnails of HTML pages after you've modified them at least once in the program and saved those changes. These thumbnails are used in the Content tab of the File Inspector as well as in one of many possible views in the Site tab.

However, if you've brought in HTML from other sources, GoLive hasn't had the opportunity to create a preview for the file. Press Command-Option (Mac) or Control-Alt (Windows) and then select Create Thumbnails from the Site menu; it only appears when these keys are depressed.

For larger sites, creating thumbnails can take some time, as GoLive has to open every page, internally render a preview, save the preview, and move on. GoLive puts up a progress bar to show you how far it's gotten on larger sites.

Tip: Image Thumbnails

Create Thumbnails has no effect on images. If you want previews of images in the Content tab, make sure the appropriate file format modules are turned on in the Modules pane of the Preferences dialog box (see Chapter 22, *Advanced Features*).

To get thumbnail previews in the Site tab when viewing items as icons on the Mac, you need to enable the thumbnail feature in Photoshop or a similar program so that it makes thumbnails when you save files (see Figure 16-21). You can use a batch process in Photoshop or Equilibrium DeBabelizer to open and resave all of your images with thumbnails if it helps you create a better site map (see Figure 16-22).

Figure 16-21
Creating previews in Photoshop

— *Preview settings*

Figure 16-22
Batch processing in DeBabelizer

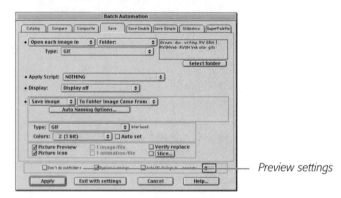

— *Preview settings*

External Links

So far, we've been talking mostly about links from resources that are all located on your hard drive and in your Site window. But many sites contain extensive links to other Web resources; others may simply have a few scattered URLs throughout the site. Managing these resources can be eased with a couple of GoLive features while using the same controls for adding and modifying external links as those you use for internal links.

Two of the biggest problems in keeping a site fresh and functional are tracking when those links go bad, and changing them throughout the site when the original reference changes. GoLive automates both features in the External tab.

Let's walk through managing link objects, editing the values stored in them, and then discuss link validation.

Link Objects

When you import a site, GoLive automatically generates a list of external references (see Figure 16-23). The External tab shows both "external" URLs—links to other sites referenced from your site—as well as any email addresses that you can click on as links (ones you specified using "mailto:").

Figure 16-23
External tab

When there's more than one link with the same domain or host name, GoLive adds a number to the object's name.

Grouping. If you have a large number of external references, you might want to group them by category for easier viewing. With the External tab active, click the New Folder button in the Toolbar, name the folder, and then drag and drop your external URLs and email links into them.

You can also drag in a URL Group or Address Group folder from the Site tab of the Palette. If you select a group, the Group Inspector appears, allowing you to change the icon for the group; the functionality is identical whether you chose URLs, Addresses, New URLs, or New Addresses.

Updating. If you've added or removed external URLs or email addresses from your site after importing or creating it, you can select either Get References Used from the Site menu to update the External tab, or Remove Unused References to delete entries you are no longer using anywhere in the site.

GoLive adds new addresses and URLs to the first groups it finds tagged as New for that category; if no such group exists, GoLive creates it.

If you use Remove Unused References and you've created items in the External tab that haven't been added to pages in the site, those items are removed from the tab and can't be restored.

Creating. It's easy enough to create links from scratch. Drag an Address (for email) or URL icon into the External tab, or double click either icon.

Renaming. You can name the link objects anything you want. They are named, by default, with part of the hostname after "www.", or for names like "store.apple. com", with the start of the name. For multiple URLs with similar names, the program adds a number following the name (see Figure 16-23, above).

Managing Links

Each URL or email address in the External tab consists of two parts: the name that GoLive or you assign to it (which appears in the Name column of the tab), and the actual URL or address (which appears in the URL column).

Importing Bookmarks from Browsers

For those of you who have accumulated a massive number of links in your Web browser, GoLive offers a quick way to turn those links into entries in the External tab: the Import menu item in the Site menu. Adobe has set up GoLive with the link format styles for Netscape Navigator's bookmarks file and Internet Explorer's favorites file—as well as Netscape's mail client address book format for email addresses—so that all you need to do is select Import and navigate to your bookmarks or favorites file. GoLive can even preserve the folder structure, if you've applied one (see Figure 16-24).

On the Mac, both browsers store their bookmarks in the System Folder's Preferences folder. Internet Explorer has its items in the Explorer folder in a file called "Favorites.html". Netscape Navigator keeps its links in the Netscape Users folder, generally under a user's name in that folder; the file is called "Bookmarks.html".

Under Windows, Netscape and Microsoft store their information in very different places. Netscape stores its "Bookmarks.html" file in Program Files\Netscape\Users\ and then under the individual user's name (which might be just you). Internet Explorer places its favorites as individual files in the Windows, Win32, or Win98 directory, depending on whether you're running Windows 95, NT, or 98, respectively. The files are loose in the Favorites folder.

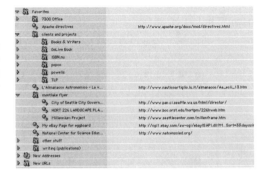

Figure 16-24
Imported
bookmarks
using same
folder structure
as in browser

GoLive tracks the URL or address so that each one is unique in the site, regardless of the name assigned to it. The URL or address is centrally managed so that changing it in the External tab changes it wherever it appears throughout the site.

You can modify the values for URLs that aren't referenced in the site (ones you've created from scratch to insert later), as well as ones that have links to them using a few methods.

Tip: Link Inspecting URLs The Link Inspector works just as well on URLs as it does on files. Select an item from the External tab and bring up the Link Inspector to see all the files that reference that URL (see Figure 16-25).

Figure 16-25
Link Inspector
showing links
to a URL

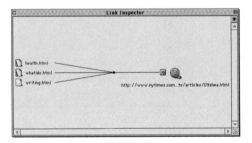

Reference Inspector. The Reference Inspector appears when you select either a URL or an email address in the External tab. It allows you to change the name of the object or the URL or address the object represents. The Edit button allows you to bring up a dialog box for more easily editing longer Web locations.

If you edit the URL field and press Return, Enter, or Tab, GoLive brings up the Change Reference dialog box letting you know and approve which files need to be rewritten to reflect the new URL. If you only change certain pages, instead of accepting all of the ones that GoLive proposes, it leaves the original link in place (with the files you chose not to modify still pointing to it), and then creates a new External object with your new value; the files you chose to change now point to it.

Let's say you have 10 links that all point to a certain external Web page. Then you decide half the links should point to a different page on the site. You can edit that first link in the Reference Inspector and then choose only the five pages you want to change to the new URL from the Change Reference dialog box. GoLive creates a new URL entry and changes five pages to point to it (see Figure 16-26).

Figure 16-26
Splitting one
URL into two

 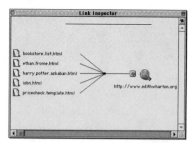

*The original URL
has five files
pointing to it.*

*Edit the URL but only
check three of the five
files to have the
reference rewritten.*

*GoLive creates the new object with its three references, but also
leaves the original one in place with the two unchanged references.*

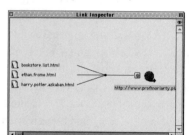 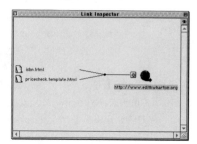

URLs are often way too long to fit in the URL field of the External Inspector (see
Figure 16-27). Clicking the Edit button brings up a dialog box that allows you to see
the entire URL and edit it much more easily.

Figure 16-27
Using the Edit
URL dialog box

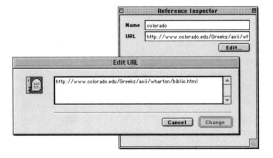

Change Reference. You can select an item in the External tab and bring up the
Change Reference dialog box to choose which reference to point to. This is pretty
similar to using the Reference Inspector, but a clearer way to see what you're doing
(see the confusing similar "Change References" section, earlier in this chapter).

Point & Shoot. You can use Point & Shoot in the Link Inspector or Change
References dialog box to link to a new URL or address.

Checking Links

GoLive can automatically check whether external links still exist, or whether
they've become "cobwebs"—links that no longer bring up pages or sites that no
longer exist.

Choose Preferences from the Edit menu, select the Site icon, and then select
the Check External Links option (see Figure 16-28). Now every time you view the
External tab in an editing session, GoLive tests each link, displaying a stop sign for
bad links (version 3.1.1 displayed a check mark for good links, but version 4.0
marks only the bad ones).

Figure 16-28
External link
validation
preference

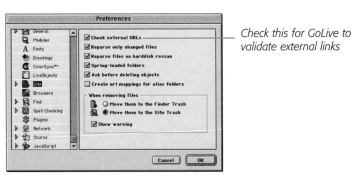

*Check this for GoLive to
validate external links*

If you have a number of links, the checking can take a while, so you may not see problems immediately; Adobe recommends increasing the memory allotted to GoLive for Macintosh to help avoid problems with larger sites.

If you have a slow connection to the Net, GoLive doesn't take much longer to test links than on a fast connection, because it only has to send a tiny amount of information to validate the link.

Tip: Memory Full! (Mac) When we have a site file open in GoLive for Macintosh and check the Check External Links preference, we immediately get two messages. First, "Memory is running low"; we click OK and are then told, "Memory full!" at which point GoLive quits. Checking the preference before opening a Site window prevents GoLive from displaying this error, but it doesn't appear that GoLive then checks links.

Tip: No Action! (Windows) Under Windows, if we check the Check External Links option, it appears to do nothing. There's no feedback.

Tip: Bypass GoLive Validation GoLive's built-in tool for checking external links is not robust, reliable, or configurable enough for a production-quality job. A simple site Glenn set up as a self-promotion and personal Web site has over 500 links. GoLive isn't very happy with it—it crashes, chokes, or marks links as bad when they're just redirects to other sites. Unfortunately, we haven't found a tool that does the job any better. The one tool we preferred was discontinued in 1997. We're still looking for a link validation solution we like.

Extras

The Files tab features a few extras that relate to site management in the split-pane view of the Files tab. The split pane appears to the side on the Macintosh and at the bottom on Windows (see Figure 16-29).

The two tabs of great interest are the Errors tab, where you can review all errors that GoLive has found with missing files or orphaned files, and the Site Trash folder in the Extras tab, where you handle the detritus of the site as you speed it on its way to Davy Jones's locker or other nether regions.

Tip: Other Split-Pane Items FTP is covered in Chapter 18, *Staging and Synchronizing Sites*, while stationery and components are both dealt with in Chapter 21, *Site Specials*.

Errors

GoLive uses the Errors tab to show problems where files are located—or are not located—on the site. Open the split-pane view by pressing the Aspect Control icon (that's what Adobe labeled it in the keyboard shortcuts card, so that's what we're calling it), and click the Errors tab. GoLive lists two kinds of errors there:

Figure 16-29
Split-pane
view under
Mac and
Windows

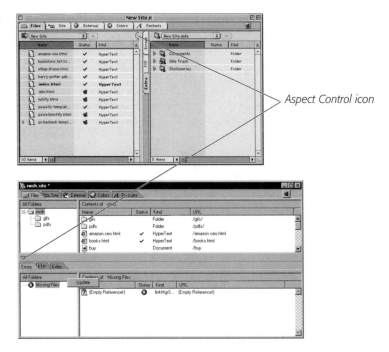

Aspect Control icon

- Missing files, where GoLive can't find the file referred to by a link that's supposed to be in the local site folder

- Orphaned files, where the file referred to is located outside of the site folder on the local hard drive

If you want to see where either kind of file is located, you need to scroll or expand the Errors tab to view the URL column, which shows where GoLive thinks the file should be (for missing files) or where on the hard drive the file is located (for orphaned files).

You have several options for fixing both kinds of errors.

Missing Files

Selecting a file with a question mark next to its name in the Missing Files folder brings up the Error Inspector. You can browse, Point & Shoot, or type in a new name to fix the error (see Figure 16-30). You can also bring up the Link Inspector, and use Point & Shoot to specify a replacement file or relink to the correct file on your site.

There's even a third option: select Change References from the Site menu and use that interface, described earlier in the chapter, to update the link.

Tip: Shortcut for Editing Long URLs You can also click a file in the Errors tab to see its URL displayed in the Error Inspector. However, if the URL is too long to fit into the URL field, Option-click (Mac) or Control-click (Windows) to bring up the Edit URL dialog box, which features a larger text field to see the entire URL.

If you need more information about what link has gone bad, you can use the Link Inspector to find files that reference the link. Open one of those files, click the

Figure 16-30
Fixing errors

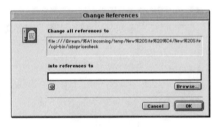

Fixing the error at left using the Error Inspector, Change References, and the Link Inspector

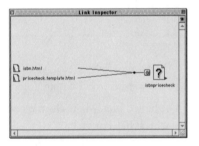

Omitting Certain Files

Sometimes with large PDFs, we don't store the file in the local site folder, just on the Web server, because we don't want GoLive to re-upload or re-download the file—it's easier to manage on our own. However, not putting in local copies of the files causes GoLive to put every one of them in the Missing Files category of the Errors tab (see Figure 16-31). But there's a way out.

GoLive has a feature called URL Handling (not to be confused with File Mapping or URL Mapping) that lets you specify patterns in file names or folder names to ignore any related errors.

For our PDF omission, we go to the Preferences dialog box, and under the General pane, find the URL Handling settings. We add ".pdf" as an item, click OK, and then are prompted (if we have a site file open) to decide whether to apply those changes to all open sites. The answer is usually yes.

By mapping .pdf, the whole list of missing files disappears from the Errors tab making it easier to understand exactly what's gone wrong with the site. We often map "/cgi-bin/" as well, because the scripts referenced inside GoLive are typically not stored in the local folder, but are on the Web server in that special directory.

Figure 16-31
URL Handling

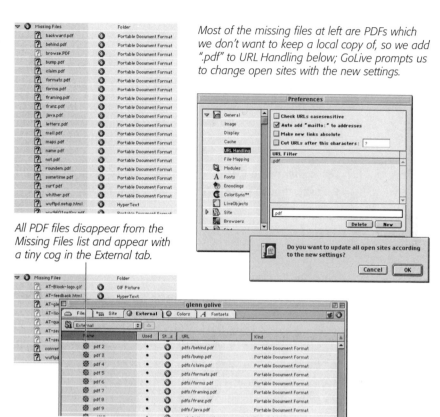

Most of the missing files at left are PDFs which we don't want to keep a local copy of, so we add ".pdf" to URL Handling below; GoLive prompts us to change open sites with the new settings.

All PDF files disappear from the Missing Files list and appear with a tiny cog in the External tab.

Link Warnings icon, and then you can troll through the page to find what was linking to the missing file. (This is often easier than trying to figure out what a file named "oc8989aa.html" is supposed to contain.)

Orphaned Files

Orphaned files are located outside the site folder, and may contain content that you've collected from other sources. However, before you upload the site, you need to make sure that GoLive has incorporated that file so that it gets properly referenced on the Web—otherwise, users would get an error when they clicked the link to the orphaned item.

You can choose one of four approaches to correct orphaned files.

Copy them locally. If you simply drag the orphaned file icon into any location in the files list side of the Files tab, GoLive makes a local copy of the file and links it in.

Clear Site. The Clear Site feature, discussed in Chapter 21, *Site Specials*, has an option that allows you to copy any external files (into the "New Files" folder in the site) to correct this problem wherever it appears. It's equivalent to selecting all of the orphaned files and dragged them over, but much simpler.

Export Site. You can hold off dealing with this problem until you're ready to transfer the site, and use the Export Site feature which makes a copy of your site. As one of the options, you can specify Export Referenced Files That Are Not Part of the Site; see Chapter 21, *Site Specials*, for the full explanation of this feature.

Leave them alone. This only works if you're willing to have broken links on your Web site, though we expect you're probably not.

Trash

When you delete a file from the Files tab or Site tab of the Site window, GoLive offers a number of configurable options for disposing of that file.

You can have the program toss the file in the Desktop trash (the Mac Trash icon or the Windows Recycle Bin); or, you can keep the trash a little closer by using GoLive's built-in Site Trash folder in the Extras tab of the split-pane (see Figure 16-32). The option of where the deleted files go is set through the Preferences dialog box in the Site pane. If you select Move Them to the Finder Trash (Mac) or Recycle Bin (Windows), GoLive immediately moves files into that location; if you select the other (default) option, Move Them to the Site Trash, the items are stored in the site data folder's Trash folder.

Figure 16-32
Site Trash

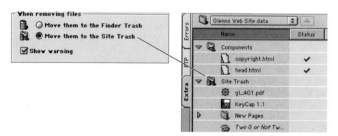

If you uncheck the Show Warning box, files you delete are moved without comment to the appropriate trash. If you are using the Site Trash, right-click (Windows) or Control-click (Mac) the Site Trash folder in the Extras tab, and select Empty Trash from the menu. This doesn't actually empty the trash, but rather moves it to the Desktop trash.

The safety mechanisms built into deletion are noteworthy, as they give you two to four options to say no or recover items before they're gone for good. (Of course, you made a backup, right?)

Managing Media Links

When GoLive 4 was announced, one of the features that made many media-inten-sive users stand up and take notice was the support for managing URLs embedded inside QuickTime movies, PDF documents, and Flash files. The excitement arose in part because editing the URLs in these documents in the past required the ap-plication that created it; with Flash, the source files were needed and the presenta-tion had to be recompiled.

GoLive's management for these three media types is set through three mod-ules: CyberMovie Module for QuickTime, PDF Module for PDFs, and CyberFlash Module for Flash. You can enable or disable these modules separately through the Module pane of the Preferences dialog box depending on what media you typical-ly use (see Chapter 22, *Advanced Features*).

Tip: Other Media Links	Although GoLive handles these three formats with aplomb, it doesn't manage links embedded in JavaScripts, Java applets, ActiveX controls, external CSS style sheets, and other file types.
Tip: More on Formats	For more information on the QuickTime, PDF, and Flash formats, see Chapter 28, *Plug-ins and Media*.

For all three kinds of media, bringing up the Link Inspector shows the rela-tionship between all the links embedded in the media files and where they point (see Figure 16-33). You can use the Link Inspector's Point & Shoot button to relink any files that are missing or that you want to change.

Figure 16-33
Emedded Web
links in a PDF

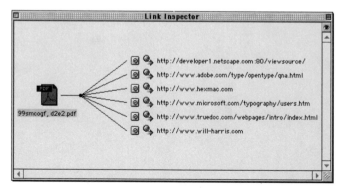

QuickTime offers an additional tool for editing URLs. Open the QuickTime movie, click the film icon in the upper left corner, and select the HREF Track in the Film Editor. You can now directly edit any URLs embedded in the movie through the HREF Track Inspector (see Figure 16-34).

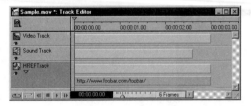

Figure 16-34
Editing URLs in
QuickTime
movies inside
GoLive

Single File Ahead

Link management is GoLive's single most powerful feature; with control of it, you can maintain sites of hundreds, thousands, or even several thousand pages without breaking a sweat—though you might make the argument for a faster machine despite GoLive's agility. Even the best program needs a little help from the processor.

CHAPTER 17
Sitewide Sets

Consistency may be the hobgoblin of little minds—if you believe Ralph Waldo Emerson—but it's a necessary trait for designers. Keeping track of all the fiddly little bits is the foundation of good Web design.

HTML's built-in color and font support may put the lie to Mr. Emerson. As we noted back in Chapter 7, *Text and Fonts*, and Chapter 9, *Colors*, each appearance of a color or set of fonts stands on its own as a separate occurrence. Keeping track of and updating these elements once occupied vast amounts of time for Web page designers and production folks, as they carried out innumerable manual search-and-replaces or used text processors to handle many files.

GoLive provides a central location in the Site window for structuring and viewing fontset and color usage. However, it lacks a site-management feature to allow changes you make in the Colors and Fontsets tabs to be applied throughout the site. (You can bypass site-management limitations in this regard by using Cascading Style Sheets, but only with more advanced browsers; see the sidebar, "Style Sheets for Pages and Sites," below)

The strength of GoLive's colors and fontsets features is the ability to help you deal with handling complex, seemingly arbitrary sets of names and numbers without resorting to pencil, paper, and hand-keying new values everywhere they appear. Our old habit of keeping several pieces of paper with scrawled hex color values is finally waning, thanks to GoLive.

In this chapter, we review how GoLive approaches centralizing the listing of colors and fontsets, how to create new items inside the respective tabs, and some workarounds and solutions for using the Find feature in conjunction with the Colors and Fontsets tab.

Creating and Editing

Colors and fontsets each have a dedicated tab in the Site window called, surprisingly enough, Colors and Fontsets. You can use these tabs to view, update, and create colors and fontsets.

Both tabs offer similar features, so we'll try to avoid redundancy when explaining them.

Tip: Font Space Sets It's not just you—GoLive sometimes calls fontsets "fontsets," "font sets," or "fonts," depending on where in the program you are. Whenever you're selecting a range of text and applying a type choice, you're using a fontset, whether the set has one member in it or a dozen.

Creating

Let's start with the basics: making new entries in the Colors and Fontsets tab. You can also group entries into subcategories or hierarchies in each tab.

New Entries

GoLive offers several ways to create new entries. Whichever method you select creates a new entry called "untitled font set" or "untitled color". If you create several new entries, GoLive adds a number to the subsequent items, as in "untitled color 2".

Tip: Select the Right Tab GoLive adds some contextual sensibilities to your actions, so make sure you have the Colors or Fontsets tab selected when you need to work with colors and fontsets. If you click the Group icon in the Toolbar, for instance, it creates the appropriate kind of new group depending on which tab is selected. Likewise, only the correct options for the tab you've selected get displayed in the Site menu's New submenu.

Style Sheets for Pages and Sites

As you may know, you can centralize all of your font choices and color usage with a page-based or external style sheet using Cascading Style Sheets (CSS). CSS allows you to centralize specifications into a single location in an HTML page or a separate style sheet file, then use those specs repeatedly through pages, in a site, or even across the Internet. However, CSS support is limited to version 4.0 and later browsers from Microsoft and Netscape, and, to some extent, from other vendors. Also, CSS is not implemented consistently everywhere.

We devote Chapter 26, *Cascading Style Sheets*, to the appropriate occasions to use CSS, and how to use it within GoLive. In the current chapter, we provide solutions for working with about 95 percent of currently used browsers; CSS, on the other hand, works with perhaps 60 to 75 percent of visitors' software at this writing, depending on the kind of audience for a given site. CSS also has drawbacks in reliability and consistency that we discuss in Chapter 26.

You can create new colors and fontsets in five ways.

- From the Site menu, select Color or Font Set from the New submenu.

- From the Site tab of the Palette, drag a Color or Font Set icon into the tab, or double-click the icon.

- Drag a color swatch from the Color Palette directly into the Colors tab (see Figure 17-1).

Figure 17-1
Dragging color
swatch into
Colors tab

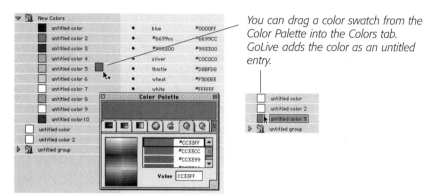

You can drag a color swatch from the Color Palette into the Colors tab. GoLive adds the color as an untitled entry.

- Create a new color or fontset on any page in the site, return to the appropriate tab, and select Get Fontsets Used or Get Colors Used (see "Extracting," below).

- Drag colors or fontsets from one Site window to another; you can select items from one site and drag them into the appropriate tab of the other site.

You might create a set of colors from scratch in the Colors tab that you're going to use throughout a site, name it distinctly, and then apply it as needed. This is easier than specifying a color each time, or letting GoLive name a color generi-cally—with "untitled"—after you create it (see "Applying," below).

New Groups

A group in the Colors or Fontsets tab is simply an enclosing folder that you can name. You can nest groups as deep as you like, putting folder inside folder inside folder. Creating groups can be useful when you're trying to map out where fontsets or colors are used in different parts of the site, but this is not a feature we com-monly find ourselves using.

GoLive automatically creates a group called New Fonts or New Colors if you've manipulated or deleted entries and then selected Get Fontsets Used or Get Colors used (see "Extracting," below).

You can create new groups in three ways.

- Under the Site menu, select Group from the New submenu.

- From the Site tab of the Palette, drag a Font Set Group or Color Group, or double-click either Group's icon.
- Click the Group icon on the Toolbar.

Once you've created a group, you can drag any other items from the tab into that group. If you try to drag an item into a group that already contains an item with the same name, GoLive asks you if you want to replace the existing item.

Extracting

GoLive maintains an internal list of fontsets and colors in the site file, in the same way it tracks external references and internal links. However, it doesn't automatically update the Colors and Fontsets tab to display all those items.

When you've made changes to any pages in a site and want to view the current list of active fontsets and colors, select Get Colors Used or Get Fontsets Used from the Site menu. GoLive updates the list to add any items not already present. If you're starting from scratch with no colors or fontsets listed, GoLive adds them all, and names them just as if you were creating them from scratch: "untitled color", "untitled color 2", and so on; the name can vary by platform.

If you import a site into GoLive, the program automatically scans the site for colors, fontsets, links, and external references, and populates all of the tabs in the Site window with "untitled" entries.

GoLive doesn't track colors and fontsets by name, so renaming an item won't cause GoLive to insert another entry in the Fontsets or Colors tab.

GoLive uses the contents of a color or fontset—its stored value, like "Arial,Helvetica,Geneva"—to determine whether or not every fontset in the site is already listed. If you edit the value of an object, selecting Get Fontsets Used or Get Colors Used creates a new copy of the object with the original value extracted from the site.

You can also use the Clear Site item in the Site menu, which bundles together a number of site maintenance features in one swell foop; we discuss Clear Site in depth in Chapter 21, *Site Specials*.

Viewing

You can see which fontsets and colors are in use after extracting or creating them by selecting the appropriate tab.

For fontsets, GoLive shows the name, whether it's in use in the site, and the full list of fonts in that set.

For colors, GoLive displays the name, whether it's used in the site, the HTML code for the color, the hexadecimal value, and whether it's a Web safe color or not. (For more on these details, see Chapter 9, *Colors*.)

Link Inspector. Although GoLive lacks global style sheet features for colors and fontsets, you can use the Link Inspector to see on which pages these objects are used. Selecting a color or fontset with the Link Inspector displayed shows all HTML files that contain that color or fontset (see Figure 17-2).

Figure 17-2
Link Inspector
view of links to
a color

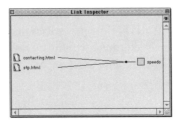

Editing

Editing colors and fontsets is simple; it's done through an item-specific inspector in which you can rename the object or change its value. You can also change the name of a fontset or color by clicking its current name in the Fontsets or Colors tab. The item highlights when it's editable, so you can type in a new name or edit the existing one.

Tip:
Renaming
Colors and
Fontsets

We recommend that you rename colors and fontsets to be more descriptive and mnemonic (like "main table cell background color") instead of generic (like "untitled color 17"). GoLive won't touch the name unless you edit its value, so it's a good way to identify for what purpose the color or fontset is intended.

Fontsets. We introduced the Font Set Editor back in Chapter 7, *Text and Fonts*, and explained its shortcomings and odd design. You would think that in editing fontsets in the Fontsets tab you would use the same editor, wouldn't you? Unfortunately, no; we have to introduce yet another inspector, the Font Set Inspector.

The Font Set Inspector works just like the Font Set Editor and has the same limitations; it's presented in an Inspector palette format. (See Chapter 7, *Text and Fonts* for tips on using the Font Set Editor to avoid repetition.)

The only real difference between the editor and inspector lies in the name. The Font Set Editor calls a fontset by the name of the first font in its list; the Font Set Inspector uses the name GoLive gave it, or the set name you provided in the Fontsets tab.

Colors. The Color Inspector has just two values: the name and a color swatch. You can drag new colors from any tab of the Color Palette onto the swatch in the Color Inspector.

Applying

The Fontsets and Colors tabs aren't just useful for seeing what's going on in a site; they can also be used as a source for applying fontsets and colors to items on a page. GoLive doesn't bring windows to the front when you're dragging these items onto selections, so you have to play windows (not Windows) gymnastics to display the tab in the background and the HTML page's selection in the foreground. Carefully drag an object from the background without releasing the mouse button, hover over the selected text or the color swatch in an inspector, and then release (see Figure 17-3).

Figure 17-3
Dragging colors and fontsets onto pages

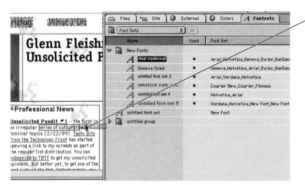

You can drag items from the Colors or Fontsets tabs if you arrange windows so that the area of the Web page you want to drag onto is visible.

Fontsets. You can apply fontsets by dragging a set from the Fontsets tab onto an HTML page, or by selecting one from the Style menu's Font item.

If you have a range of text selected, you can drag a fontset onto the selected text, and the fontset is applied (see Figure 17-4). If you drag the fontset anywhere else on a page, GoLive inserts some text identical to the fontset's name; that text has the fontset applied to it, as well. (see Figure 17-5).

With or without any text selected, you can choose a fontset from the Font item's submenu under the Style menu; fontsets listed below the second dividing line are all found in the Fontsets tab (see Figure 17-6).

Site fontsets also show up in the popup menus for font specifications when you're creating Cascading Style Sheets; see Chapter 26, *Cascading Style Sheets*, for more on this facet of fontsets.

Colors. Colors may be applied through many methods. You can

- Drag a color from the Colors tab onto the Color field in any inspector.

- Drag a color onto an HTML page, where GoLive inserts the text "Color" set to that color.

- Drag a color onto a selection on an HTML page, where GoLive sets the selection to that color.

Figure 17-4
Dragging a
fontset onto a
selected range
of text

Select some text in the Layout Editor.

Drag a fontset onto the text.

The fontset is now applied.

Figure 17-5
Dragging a
fontset onto a
page with no
text selection

If you drag onto a page without a text selection, the name of the fontset is inserted.

Figure 17-6
Font menu

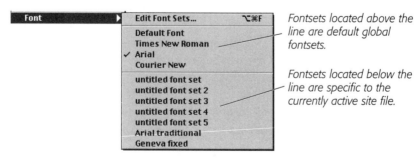

Fontsets located above the line are default global fontsets.

Fontsets located below the line are specific to the currently active site file.

- Select the color from the Color palette's far right tab, the Site Colors tab, and apply it as you would any other color.

The Site Colors tab displays the name of the current site file in the lower left corner (see Figure 17-7).

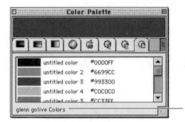

Current site name + Colors

Removing Unused

If you want to clean out a cluttered Fontsets or Colors tab after *completing* a site, select Remove Unused Colors or Removed Unused Fontsets from the Site menu.

If a color or fontset you created from scratch in the two tabs has not yet been applied to text or to another object somewhere in the site, you don't want to use this command. Remove Unused deletes every color or fontset that GoLive doesn't find applied to an object somewhere in the site. If you created those elements to use later, you would have to recreate them.

You can also use the Clear Site command, mentioned above, and described in depth in Chapter 21, Site Specials, to remove unused fontsets, colors, links, and other doodads, all at the same time.

Making Sitewide Changes

Since GoLive doesn't provide fontset and color management, you have to use workarounds to create the results you want. GoLive does let you create and name fontsets and colors, so as long as you never change your mind or your design, you don't need to know these tricks. (Since that's never happened to us in our experience, you certainly need to know these tricks.)

Adding. We suggest that if you want to apply fontsets to ranges of text, you use the standard creation and apply process noted above. There's no simple or even complex way to apply text to certain categories of type (the one exception being the contents of table cells).

Placeholders. One option for making a site manageable is to start out by using a placeholder. Instead of specifying real font names in your fontsets, call them "fontset-a", "fontset-b", and so forth. This won't preview badly, as all browsers ignore these unknown fonts and use their default typefaces to display the text.

When you've figured out which fonts you really want to use, you can employ sitewide find and replace, described below, to change all instances of your placeholders with real fontset names.

Changing. The most typical need for site management is to make a global change that harmonizes all instances of a given item. For instance, let's say you're using two fontsets, "Arial,Helvetica,Geneva" and "Geneva,Arial,Helvetica". You decide the latter is more appropriate for your needs than the former, so you want to simply change all instances of "Arial,Helvetica,Geneva" into "Geneva,Arial,Helvetica".

Another case might involve several different fontsets, all of which you want to simplify into a single fontset that's consistent throughout the site.

Sitewide Find and Replace

To make a sitewide change in a fontset or color, you need to use the Find feature in the Edit menu (see Figure 17-8). Since Find is irreversible, make a backup copy of your site as described in Chapter 15, *Site Management*, before proceeding.

1. Select Find from the Edit menu.

2. Click the Find & Replace tab.

3. Click the arrow to expand Replace and Find in Files.

4. Click the Add Site button.

4a. If you only need to make these changes on particular pages, click the Add Files button and select just the pages you want to change.

Figure 17-8
Find & Replace
settings for
sitewide
change

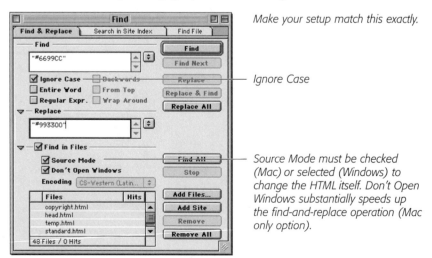

Make your setup match this exactly.

Ignore Case

Source Mode must be checked (Mac) or selected (Windows) to change the HTML itself. Don't Open Windows substantially speeds up the find-and-replace operation (Mac only option).

5. In the Find field, enter the value you're looking to replace. You can find this in the Colors tab in the column labeled Value, and in the Fontsets tab in the column labeled Font Set. Type this exactly as it appears, preceded by an equals sign and a quotation mark, and followed by a quotation mark.

6. In the Replace field, enter your replacement value, discerned in the same manner. If you are replacing the item with something new, not found in the site, create the new value first so you can copy its exact appearance.

7. Make sure your settings match those in the figure: Ignore Case checked, Entire Word and Regular Expression unchecked, and Source Mode and Don't Open Windows checked. (Source Mode allows you to find and replace text in HTML instead of text as formatted in the Layout Editor, while Don't Open Windows—a Mac-only option—speeds the process up substantially.)

8. Click Replace All. Magically, it's all done.

Color Me Fontsettable

Fontsets and colors may get a little out of hand, but with some elbow grease they're still manageable—just not site manageable. A hobgoblin may not be man's best friend, but it does keep a Web site under control.

CHAPTER 18
Staging and Synchronizing Sites

Trapeze artists may perform their best work without a net, but Webmasters typically work both with the Net and with a net to prevent errors in their work from becoming immediately apparent to their Web site's next visitor.

When you're modifying a site, you're making changes on a local copy stored on your computer's hard drive or a local area network (LAN). Any changes you make have to be synchronized with the remote Web server. Remote, in this case, means any machine other than the one you're working on, whether it's down the hall or across the planet.

If your Web site server is located on a LAN, you might be able to copy your files to it through a Windows NT shared volume, Samba, an AppleShare file server, NetWare, NFS, or many other programs with trademarked names. However, most site-management software, GoLive included, doesn't offer tools for synchronizing over a LAN because each kind of network sports its own peculiarities; plus, files may become unreadable or strangely modified after being transferred from one platform to another, like Mac to Windows.

Instead, the standard method of transferring documents is via File Transfer Protocol, or FTP. Running on everything from ancient mainframes, old minicomputers, recent PCs, and futuristic PDAs, FTP is one of the most independent transfer methods available. (If we ever get the ability to store information in chips within our heads, it's even-odds that FTP will be one way we send files to it.)

GoLive has two ways to access remote file systems using FTP. The method you'll probably use the most is embedded inside the Site window's Files tab, and helps you synchronize content between your local copy and remote Web site. The other implementation is a general purpose FTP client, for when you just need to retrieve files via FTP without synchronizing with a GoLive site.

We cover both methods, and describe some of the pitfalls and tricks of dealing with storing your files out there in the ether.

Tip: FTP Server at Your Service We're assuming that you already have access to an FTP server through which you modify your Web site's files. If you don't, it might be wise to get that set up and return later, as FTP can be obscure even when illustrated. It's wise to cultivate a good relationship with your ISP or webmaster, since they control the final steps before your site goes live.

How FTP Works

FTP gets used to transfer files between two machines, a server (which controls the file transfer) and a client (which initiates sending or receiving files). The FTP protocol defines the method of performing file transfers.

On one end, you have an FTP server, which is a piece of software that mediates access to files found on its hard drives or network. The FTP server lets you log in, tracks your actions, and handles the transfer of files and other details. The FTP server also protects the machine on which it runs from unauthorized access, so users can't go messing with files that don't belong to them.

On the other side of the exchange is an FTP client, which runs on your computer. The FTP client talks to the server in a special language that's part of the FTP protocol and allows them to understand each other. Fortunately, this language is hidden from view most of the time. It usually shows up in error messages, but you don't need to know it to understand what's going on.

FTP clients can be pretty stripped-down, requiring some obscure typed commands, as with the Unix "ftp" command or the similar program found in Windows 98 and NT as ftp.exe (in Windows\System). But FTP clients can also be highly graphical, hiding all the low-level FTP client/server commands entirely from view. Some FTP clients for Mac and Windows—like Anarchie Pro for Mac and WS_FTP for Windows—let you access remote files through an interface that looks just like the Macintosh or Windows Desktop.

Most of what an FTP client accomplishes is sending and receiving files; ditto for the FTP server. The built-in GoLive FTP client handles that part fine, but it also offers limited control of lower-level settings that control file access.

GoLive's FTP Clients

GoLive's two different methods of working with FTP may seem redundant on the surface, but both offer distinct advantages. The Site window's FTP client, accessed through the Files tab, gets stored as a setting for a site and adds the ability to synchronize the site's content on your local hard drive with the files and directories on a remote Web site via FTP. The standalone client, on the other hand, lets you easily connect to any FTP server to which you have been granted access. Since we often find ourselves uploading and downloading files, the standalone client can often save us the trouble of launching a separate FTP application. To access the standalone FTP client, type Command-Shift-F, or select FTP Upload & Download from the File menu (see Figure 18-1).

Figure 18-1
GoLive's
standalone
FTP client

You can access the Site window's FTP client by first clicking on the Files tab, then clicking the FTP tab in the window's split-pane view. If the split-pane view is not currently displayed, bringing it up varies by platform. On the Mac, click the icon bar in the upper right of the tab, and then click the vertical tab labeled FTP (see Figure 18-2). In Windows, click the triangle at the bottom of the Site window to expand the view, and then click the horizontal FTP tab (also see Figure 18-2). The settings for connecting to a server are typed-in directly in the standalone client or can be selected from a popup menu discussed below.

The Site window's FTP settings are displayed by selecting the Settings item from the Site menu (see Figure 18-3), or by clicking the Settings button on the Site

Figure 18-2
Displaying the
Site window's
FTP pane

Click this icon bar on the Macintosh…

…or this triangle under Windows.

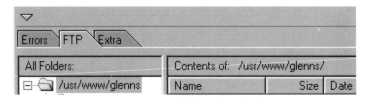

Figure 18-3
FTP pane in
Site settings

toolbar. If you click the Connect/Disconnect to Server button on the Site toolbar without entering settings, you are presented with the Settings dialog box set to the FTP pane.

Setting Up a Connection

To connect to any FTP site, you typically need three pieces of information: the FTP server name in Internet form, a username, and a password. You may also have to specify a path to a directory.

The Site window's FTP client offers a couple of additional advanced options for connecting to more recalcitrant FTP servers, or connecting if you're located behind a firewall or proxy server.

Server

The server is the machine that's running FTP software that you connect to in order to change content on your Web site. You need to enter its full name, like "ftp-www.earthlink.net". If you get a DNS error or a "server not found" error, double-check the address.

Username and Password

A system administrator or ISP should have given you a username or account name and password when you were set up with FTP access. These are typically the same ones you use for email. If you don't have these or get an error when using them, it's time to check back with whomever operates your site's systems.

The username and password allow an FTP server to determine if you have permission to create new files, overwrite old ones, create directories, and perform other file-related tasks (see sidebar, "May I, Please?").

Tip: You Need an Account

Not all FTP servers require a username or password; some repositories of files offer anonymous FTP access, where you log in as "anonymous" using your e-mail address as a password. However, it's extremely unlikely that you would ever be interacting with Web site content without an account controlling access to the files.

If you check the Save Password box in the Site FTP client, you can enter your password in the Password field, and never be asked for it again.

Tip: Tabbing over the Port Field

In the Site FTP client, it's easy to tab from the Username field right into the Port field and start typing your password if you forget to check the Password box. We find ourselves making this error all the time. The default value for Port is 21, so if you simply erase what you just typed into that field, the FTP client stops working. Re-enter 21 for Port, and you'll be back to normal.

If you don't check Save Password, you'll be prompted during each session for the password the first time you try to connect to the FTP server. After you enter it once, you can connect, disconnect, and reconnect without re-entering it. Closing the Site window or quitting GoLive resets this information, and you'll have to enter the password again on your next use.

Tip: Don't Save Your Password

We don't recommend you check Save Password on a machine that's not physically secure. That is, if your machine is used in an environment where others have ready access to it, you're better off entering the password each time. Leaving the password on the machine allows anyone to connect to your live Web site and make changes, including—depending on how the server is configured—deleting all your files. (For many people, this isn't an issue unless you work in a college dorm, have really serious enemies in your company, or have a three-year-old who likes computers.)

Directory

The FTP Directory is the path from the root or top level of the FTP server to the folder where your Web site files live. This pathway often bears little or no resemblance to the URL for your Web site. FTP servers can be configured to hide most directories from users, only letting them have access to a fraction of the remote files and folders for added security.

Most of the time, you can just enter your account name and password, leaving Directory blank, and the FTP server automatically brings up the directory for the account. With the standalone FTP client, GoLive fills in the Directory field with the location that the FTP server puts you in; in the Site FTP client, the popup location menu gets changed to that directory (see Figure 18-4).

If you need to enter a directory name, you'll have to ask the system administrator or Webmaster for the path; it's rarely intuitive, and there's no standard location for where files are found.

Keep in mind that GoLive requires that you enter all paths in the default FTP/Unix format. Each directory is separated by a forward slash (/), even if the remote server is running some flavor of Windows or runs on a Mac. So a Windows NT file path like C:\inetpub\wwwroot\site1\html\ would get entered as /inetpub/wwwroot/site1/html/ in an FTP path.

Figure 18-4
Marching
along the path
to your Web
server

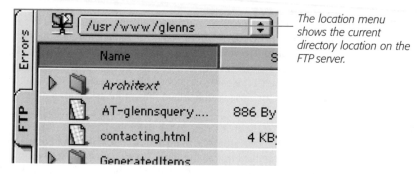

The location menu
shows the current
directory location on the
FTP server.

Advanced Settings

The Site FTP client offers additional options that can help you connect to an FTP server that dislikes the standard methods. FTP works over TCP/IP, the language of the Internet. TCP/IP uses ports, which are like pigeonholes for mail delivery, to address traffic, with each kind of service (Web, FTP, telnet) having a standard port that handles that protocol.

FTP service is always initiated from a client to a server via port 21; all FTP servers, by default, expect a note in that slot to initiate an FTP session. Some FTP servers are configured to listen on a different port, however, and you can enter a new value into the Port field.

FTP service uses a variety of ports to handle a session after that first request. The FTP server essentially replies to that note by initiating another connection on a different port. But some local network administrators, for security reasons or just bloodymindedness, may not allow traffic from outside your local network to connect back in.

The Use Passive Mode checkbox allows you to run an FTP session in which the FTP client initiates all traffic. This prevents you from being blocked. You can set this as an application-wide default in the Edit menu's Preferences dialog, under Network (see Figure 18-5).

Figure 18-5
Use Passive
Mode
checkbox in
Network
Preferences

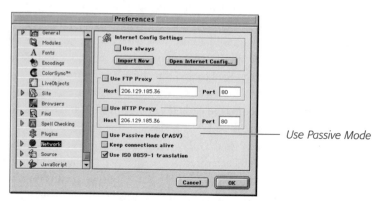

Use Passive Mode

You shouldn't have to change the port or use a passive connection unless you're told by a system administrator or by your ISP or remote Web service provider. See "Troubleshooting," later in this chapter, for advice on this and other problematic connections.

Presets or "Favorites"

You can preset the server, username, and directory in GoLive's preferences (choose Preferences from the Edit menu), under Network: FTP Server (see Figure 18-6). Entering settings for your "favorite" FTP servers makes it easier to later access them through the popup menu on both the standalone and site FTP clients (see Figure 18-7).

Figure 18-6
FTP favorites
preferences

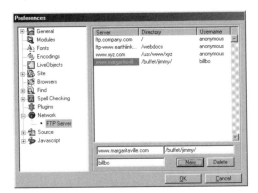

Figure 18-7
Selecting and
adding items
to the FTP
favorites
popup menu

Selecting Add Current Server adds the current settings to the favorites popup menu.

ISPs and Directories

Most ISPs configure their FTP servers so that you don't have to type a long and obscure pathway into the Directory field; they just drop you into the right location automatically. Some ISPs set up their internal directories so that it appears to you as if your Web site directory is the only directory that the FTP server can reach.

For instance, if you use Earthlink's Web service, which comes with their standard subscriber accounts, you connect to ftp-www.earthlink.net. If you enter your user name and password, the Earthlink FTP server drops you into the /webdocs directory. This directory is unique to your account, and you can't access other directories.

You can also add items in either FTP client by entering your server information and then selecting Add Current Server from the presets popup menu (also in Figure 18-7).

Connecting to the Server

Once you've set up all your parameters, connecting and disconnecting to an FTP server is merely a matter of clicking a button or selecting a menu item.

FTP servers won't let you stay connected indefinitely, but GoLive doesn't provide a warning when the FTP server has booted you off. Most FTP servers disconnect after 10 or 20 minutes of idle time; others may disconnect after hours. If you try to act on files in the FTP window after a disconnect, GoLive displays the error message, "Unexpected Disconnect".

Proxy

Your network administrator may tell you that you have to use a "proxy server" to access FTP and Web servers outside of your local network. If so, you need to set this in the Edit menu's Settings item under Network. Check the Use FTP Proxy box and enter the values for Host and Port provided by the administrator (see Figure 18-5, a couple pages earlier).

If you're using Internet Config for your settings on a Macintosh and need to configure an FTP proxy, see Appendix A, *Macintosh Issues and Extras.*

Connecting

To connect, simply click the Connect button for the standalone client; or, for the Site client, click the Connect/Disconnect button on the Site toolbar or select Connect to Server from the Site menu. You can also Control-click (Mac) or right-click (Windows) either the standalone client or the Site's FTP pane and choose Connect from the contextual menu that appears.

If you get an error on connecting that isn't something obvious like "incorrect password," check out "Troubleshooting," later in this chapter.

Disconnecting

To disconnect, click the Disconnect button for the standalone client; or, for the Site client, click the Connect/Disconnect button on the Site toolbar, or select Disconnect from Server from the Site menu. Disconnect is also available on the contextual menu that appears when you Control-click (Mac) or right-click (Windows) either window.

Abort

You can abort during the connection process by clicking Abort in the standalone client, or selecting Abort from the Site menu for the Site client. You can also press

Command-period on a Macintosh, or the Esc key under Windows, to stop the process. (Abort is also used to stop other FTP behavior in progress.)

File Handling

Now that you've connected to a server through either GoLive client, you can man-handle the FTP directory's contents as much as you want—within the constraints set by the system administrator or Webmaster, of course.

FTP servers can separate out several different kinds of file changes. For instance, an FTP server treats deleting, overwriting, creating, and renaming a file as different activities, and can limit different users to varying activities.

The FTP server's configuration for your account establishes how you can act. You may be able to upload files to certain directories of the Web site, for example, but not others. It might let you delete files in one folder, but not in another.

All of these parameters get defined by the system administrator or Webmaster, so you have to consult with them to apply parameter changes. If you're running your own FTP server, however, you control the means of access, and need only fiddle with settings to make sure you have enough permission to carry out your tasks (see the sidebar, "May I, Please?" later in this chapter).

With the FTP client window open, you can now examine and manipulate files, folders, and links (see the sidebar, "Aliases, Symbolic Links, and Shortcuts").

Status

A status field at the bottom of the Site FTP client and the top of the standalone FTP client shows how GoLive is currently interacting with the FTP server. This field is unlabeled on the Mac and called Progress in Windows. The messages include, "Connecting…", "Connected", "Downloading Files", and other standard behavior. At any point while the status field shows an action in progress, you can click the Abort button or select Abort from the Site menu to cancel the operation.

Selection

If there's no selection, the FTP clients show you the number of items in the current window. This appears at the bottom of both clients.

Live Editing

When you double-click any file in the FTP file list, GoLive downloads it to a temporary files location, nesting it inside folders that exactly match the directories in the path to that file via the FTP server. GoLive also retrieves any graphics necessary to make the page display correctly. (In fact, it's identical to using the Web Download feature under the File menu; see Chapter 14, *Page Specials*.)

After making any changes to this file, selecting Save will re-upload it to the same location you downloaded from. The danger with editing files in this manner is that image links are incorrectly rewritten to point to the temporary location; you can keep an eye out for this by using the Link Inspector to see the Media file links from the page (see Chapter 3, *Palettes and Parts*).

Live editing works with both FTP clients, and it's a neat trick. It combines the advantages of local editing with immediate updating. If you edit a file this way that's part of a site, you can use the Download From Site feature to get the latest version to replace the local hard drive's copy of the file, or just drag the file over to the local files side of the Files tab (see below for more on both options).

Adding or Uploading

You can add files and folders from the Desktop or the Files tab by dragging them into the FTP client window. Neither FTP client warns you about overwriting files on the FTP server, however. The more sensible way to add files is to use the synchronization features, described later in "Synchronizing." If you don't have permission to create or overwrite files, you get an appropriate error when you attempt it.

Unfortunately, you can't drag aliases or shortcuts into the FTP window and have them appropriately point to another file (see sidebar, "Aliases, Symbolic Links, and Shortcuts"). A system admin with direct access to the Web server filesystem has to create pointers, whether in Unix or any other operating system.

Downloading

Any file or folder can be downloaded to your local hard drive by dragging it onto the Desktop or into any open Site window, regardless of which GoLive FTP client you're using. If you drag a folder, all the contents are recursively copied.

If you drag an item into the Files tab of the Site window, and an item with the same name already exists, you'll be asked whether you want to replace it.

When you drag a pointer or link (see sidebar, "Aliases, Symbolic Links, and Shortcuts") from the FTP window onto the Desktop or into the Files tab, GoLive copies the file that the link on the Web server points to, rather than making a local alias or shortcut to the item. If the link points to a folder, it copies its entire contents.

Creating Folders

In the standalone FTP client, you click the folder icon next to the Directory field to create a folder. The default name is "untitled_folder" on the Mac and "newuntitledfolder1" under Windows.

If you have a folder selected when you click the icon, it nests the new folder inside the old one. GoLive automatically selects the folder you've just created, so you need to click elsewhere in the FTP window if you want to create additional empty folders to avoid nesting them.

Additional folders get named starting with "untitled_folder 2" on the Mac and "newuntitledfolder2" under Windows.

Tip: Problem Adding Multiple Folders on Certain FTP Servers

If you don't rename the folder and attempt to add another one on certain FTP servers, the FTP clients on the Mac give you an error stating that the folder has an illegal character in it. Rename "untitled_folder" to anything else, and then it works. This happens because GoLive for Macintosh tries to create a space in the second and subsequent folder names; some servers don't allow spaces in file and folder names.

Moving

You can drag any file in an FTP window and move it to any folder depth. GoLive doesn't offer the same spring-loaded folder action in FTP windows as it does in all tabs and windows on the Macintosh, so you will have to click on the Mac folder-expansion triangle or use the Windows folder explorer to display a nested folder or file.

Technically, FTP servers don't support moving a file. GoLive is actually copying the file to the new location and then deleting it from the old location. Because of FTP restrictions, you may not always be able to move files.

Renaming

You can rename a file in either FTP client by clicking on the file's name. The file's title will become highlighted, and you can type in a new name. If you don't have renaming permissions on the FTP server, GoLive displays an error.

Tip: Don't Rename or Move Files on the FTP Server

Renaming or moving items on the FTP server is dangerous, because GoLive won't rewrite references to those items as it does when you rename or move files or folders in the filesystem part of the Files tab. You should only rename or move items on the server when you're trying to fix a problem or move a file or folder to a different name so that you can copy a different version of it to the Web site.

Deleting

Deleting files on the FTP server requires specific permission. If you don't have permission, GoLive displays an error. If you do have permission, GoLive asks you, "Do you really want to delete the selected item(s)?"

Tip: You Can't Revert after Deleting

You cannot revert after deleting a file off the server like you can when you delete a file out of the Files tab, so make sure you're doing the right thing before you click OK. One strategy we've found useful is dragging outdated files into a folder called, predictably enough, "old.files". We occasionally go through that folder and toss old items, but having them available for a while ensures that we don't lose any work in case we need to go back a few revisions to restore data.

FTP Inspectors

For viewing detailed properties of items accessed via FTP, GoLive provides three FTP inspectors, one each for pointers, files, and folders. (If you don't know what a pointer is, see the sidebar, "Aliases, Shortcuts, and Symbolic Links.") These inspectors are named FTP Link, FTP File, and FTP Folder, respectively, in GoLive 4.0.1 (see Figure 18-8). (In Windows GoLive 4.0, they were named Remote instead of FTP.)

The inspectors collect details about the items and present them through a consistent interface regardless of whether you're accessing a Macintosh, Windows, Unix, or even BeOS FTP server on the other end.

All three inspectors show the modification date of the item, if available, and the URL to reach the item via FTP (also see the sidebar, "Do You Have the Time?"). You can't copy and paste the URL; it's just there for reference.

They also show the permissions "map": who may read, write, and execute the file, folder, or link (see the sidebar, "May I, Please?"). Changing the set of permissions requires you to click the Set Rights button. For folders, you can also change all permissions for every file and folder inside of it, no matter how many levels deep those files and folders are nested, by checking the Recursive box.

Figure 18-8
Windows and
Mac versions
of the three
FTP inspectors

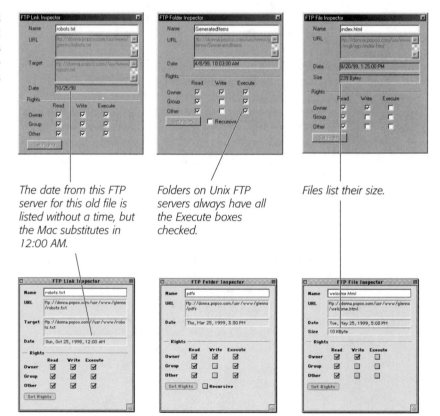

The date from this FTP server for this old file is listed without a time, but the Mac substitutes in 12:00 AM.

Folders on Unix FTP servers always have all the Execute boxes checked.

Files list their size.

Depending on how the FTP server is set up, you may not be able to change permissions at all. If you can't and you need to, there's no way to change this in GoLive. You'll need to ask the system administrator responsible for the server to add "chmod" and perhaps "umask" support. (If they don't know what this means, you may just be out of luck.)

Tip: Why Execute Is Checked on Folders	You may wonder why all Web site folders accessed through a Unix FTP server have Execute checked for all three kinds of users. It's an obscure but important attribute; folders that contain items which everyone everywhere can access (whether as read-only or as modifiable items) must be set as executable. It's just one of those things that doesn't make specific sense on the surface, but is required for low-level FTP operations. So don't just uncheck Execute and click Set Rights because it looks wrong, as that will bar all access to the folder.

The FTP Link Inspector also shows the object pointed to in the Pointer field in the form of a URL. The FTP File Inspector reveals the file size of the selected document.

You can change an item's name on the FTP server by changing it in the appropriate FTP inspector or by clicking the file name and typing a new one. However, making a change in this manner won't rewrite links from other files that point to it.

Aliases, Symbolic Links, and Shortcuts

Your mother may have told you that pointing isn't polite, but it is efficient. Every major operating system lets you create multiple pointers to the same document, program, or folder so that you don't have to make multiple copies of the thing itself.

Apple added *aliases* to Macintosh System 7 so that users could, for instance, put links to their most common programs and documents in a single place, or get to a specific deeply-nested folder without opening window after window. Microsoft added the same functionality in Windows 95 through *shortcuts*. Unix has pretty much always had *symbolic links*.

What's the difference between aliases, shortcuts, and symbolic links? Not much. They all point to an actual resource and can be moved around and still retain their link to that resource. But they only occupy a few bytes and they don't duplicate the contents of the resource.

The biggest difficulty you'll find with pointers is that GoLive, in its 4.0 incarnation at least, always downloads everything found underneath a pointer. That is, you can't set it to only download the pointer itself, which would logically turn it into an alias or shortcut depending on whether you're running GoLive on a Mac or under Windows.

When you attempt to upload an alias or shortcut, GoLive turns it into a plain text file on the FTP server, which doesn't serve much of a purpose either; or, it may balk at uploading it at all, saying, "not a plain file."

The FTP protocol won't allow you to make pointers; you have to get a system administrator to make them on the Web site filesystem.

We provide some strategies for dealing with both shortcomings in "Synchronizing."

Synchronizing

GoLive includes a simple set of controls for keeping your local copy of the content and the remote Web site content consistent and up to date. These features let you synchronize in either direction, and offer some control over what gets uploaded from the local version of the Web site. (Note that synchronization only works with the Site FTP client.)

If you use the Upload feature, only files on your local hard drive modified more recently than those on the FTP server are uploaded. The Download feature, conversely, only downloads files from the FTP server that are newer. (The timing issue may be problematic, though; see the sidebar, "Do You Have the Time?")

GoLive doesn't actually compare the contents of the local and remote files; it just looks at their dates and times. This means that if you've edited both the file on the FTP server and in your local copy of the site, GoLive won't harmonize the differences and merge the file. You'll have to do that yourself, using Microsoft Word's Merge Documents feature or other software.

May I, Please?

Every computer that lets users access its files remotely has a built-in set of policies that control which users can access and modify files. These policies are called file permissions, and correspond to settings attached to each file (Windows and Unix) or directory (Mac, Windows, and Unix).

For users who haven't had to deal with remote files over a network, file permissions can be intimidating. The Macintosh and Windows systems generally let you read, write, delete, and overwrite all of the files on the local drive; you can lock files in different ways on both with a little effort. But when you share your files or access shared files, there has to be some intermediation so that any user passing by can't destroy your Web site.

File permissions define who owns a particular file or directory, what group (if any) may have special access to it, and how the rest of the world can interact with it. The owner, the group, and the world can each have separate permissions set for access. The owner and groups are typically set up by user accounts on a system; the owner is a login name for a particular user, while a group contains any number of users and/or other groups, depending on the operating system.

Each platform has slightly different ideas about permissions, but the Mac is most restrictive when used as an FTP server. Unlike Windows NT and Unix, the Mac OS can't set file permissions for individual files, only for directories (see Table 18-1). GoLive maps this behavior by showing group read and write permissions checked for any file you select and view with the FTP File Inspector. If you try to change the settings and click Set Rights, you get an error: "FTP Error: 404, Parameter Not Accepted."

Unix, on the other hand, not only allows control over all files, but it even uses these access controls to restrict who changes what files when you're working on a keyboard connected directly to the machine.

Operating System	What They Call...			Folder only
GoLive calls it:	*Owner*	*Group*	*Other*	*n/a*
Macintosh	User	Group	Everyone	yes
Windows 98	*	*	*	yes
Windows NT	User	Group	Everybody	no
Unix	User	Group	World	no

Table 18-1
Permission categories by platform

*Windows 98 supports password-based file sharing and permissions, but FTP servers running under Windows 98 may map different permissions settings onto files and folders.

Getting Set to Synchronize

Before you upload files for the first time, you'll want to check the settings for the Site FTP client. Click the Site Settings button or select Settings from the Site menu, and then click FTP.

Upload Settings

The two checkboxes for Honor Publish State and the Upload Referenced Files Only checkbox represent just *two* separate methods of deciding what to upload, even though you can check or uncheck all *three* of them independently (see Figure 18-9). These options are more about deciding what *not* to upload than deciding what gets uploaded.

Tip: Setting Publish State
Every file, folder, and link has a "publish state," which directs GoLive whether or not to upload the object in a file synchronization. You set this state via the Publish popup menu in the File and Group inspectors (see Figure 18-9).

Figure 18-9
Upload options and setting the Publish state

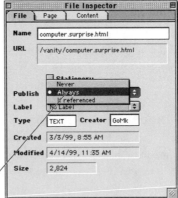

The Publish state is set for each item via the File or Group Inspector.

The Honor Publish State checkboxes mediate whether pages and folders that have Publish set to Never or If Referenced get uploaded. The interaction of options is confusing enough that we list them all in Table 18-2.

The bottom line is, if you check Honor Publish State for Pages or Groups (files and folders), GoLive relies on the Publish flag set for each item, which is set to Always by default. These choices apply only when the file is newer than the corresponding item on the FTP server.

- If the flag is set to Always, it always uploads the item.

- If the flag is set to Never, the item (and its contents, if it's a Group or folder) isn't uploaded.

- If it's a file and it's set to If Referenced, GoLive uploads it only if the item appears in the link hierarchy; that is, if the item gets referenced from any link that descends from the home page you've defined. You can view the link hierarchy in the Site tab (see Chapter 19, *Site Maps*).

Do You Have the Time?

When you synchronize files using GoLive, you may think you're dealing with absolute time; the files are modified at an exact moment locally or on a Web site, and GoLive just compares those numbers.

Unfortunately, it's more complex. We didn't realize the extent of this problem until we started researching it for this book. And, frankly, it's a mess, partly because of the FTP protocol's lack of precision about time.

FTP Time Isn't Your Time. It may come as a surprise that much of the time on the Internet is regulated by time zones. Your email client, for example, makes a quick calculation based on the difference between the time and location a message is sent, and your current time and location.

As a general rule, however, FTP servers don't send the time zone they're in as part of a file listing, nor do they send the seconds after the minute for file modifications. For files older than one year, FTP servers send just the date and year of the file's last modification. (Some FTP software sends more, but the most commonly used Unix servers don't.)

Also, there's no guarantee that the FTP server machine's clock is actually set to atomic time or any other close approximation, and the FTP protocol doesn't include a provision for it to send its current time of day and time zone.

What this adds up to is that if you're working in Oregon and your files are stored on a server in New York, you have a three-hour difference in the modification dates for your files the moment you copy them from your local hard drive to the remote FTP server. The local modification date and time aren't sent as part of the FTP protocol, either.

So, if I modify a file at 10:22:07 a.m. PDT and copy it to New York over the Internet, assuming the system clock is set right, the modification date on the file server will immediately be set to 1:22:00 p.m. EDT. But the server sends this time as part of the file's listing as just "1:22".

Some servers are set up with a little less-than-attentive care, and they might be set by default to Greenwich Mean Time (GMT), which is eight hours later than Pacific time, and is often the default setting for new Unix servers.

- If it's a folder, and Publish is set to If Not Empty, and the folder has any contents, GoLive creates the folder on the FTP server if one doesn't already exist. However, this option only matters if all the items inside the folder wouldn't upload on their own. GoLive creates any necessary folders for enclosed items that get uploaded.

- If you check Pages or Groups under Honor Publish State, the Upload Referenced Files Only setting is ignored. It should be grayed out, but it isn't; this appears to be an interface problem. (In the Upload Options dialog box, it is correctly grayed out.)

With Honor Publish State's settings off and Upload Referenced Files Only checked, GoLive only uploads newer files that are in the link hierarchy as described just above. If a new file is in a folder that doesn't exist on the FTP server, this option automatically creates that folder.

GoLive's Clever Hack. GoLive has a clever workaround. In the Site file, it caches the local modification date for any files you copy over to an FTP server during an open connection to the server. So when you copy a file, the time and date you see in the FTP client show as identical to the local file's modification timestamp.

However, if you disconnect and reconnect to the server, close the Site window, or quit GoLive and reopen it, time gets out of joint: the cached value that matches the local file's timestamp is no longer displayed. According to Adobe's technical support staff, the offset is still stored in the Site file, but you can't access or see this information.

If you try to synchronize after this, your local file will appear to be older than the server file in the Pacific to Eastern time zone case above. However, if GoLive correctly uploaded and stored the time offset, you're still okay.

Even more subtle is when your files and your server are in the same time zone, but the server's system clock is off, a typical occurrence. Again, GoLive caches the local hard disk modification time, but if the clocks are a few minutes apart, you can run into some baffling problems when using synchronization if you edit and upload a file repeatedly over a few minutes.

The time displayed and the actual time may appear to be off and GoLive may refuse to synchronize certain files without providing a clear reason in the inspectors.

Room for Improvement. We've suggested to Adobe that they expose the offset settings that GoLive caches and stores to better allow users to understand what the modification time really is. We'd like to see two features added to the program: 1. The ability to set a time zone for the FTP server as part of the FTP settings available in the Site menu's Settings item. 2. The ability to view, store, and change a clock offset by having GoLive write a test file to the FTP server and retrieve the timestamp. It already performs an action similar to our second suggestion, but you can't access or change that information.

These two features would resolve the above problem almost entirely.

	Page/folder state	File is reffed	Setting checked	Item gets uploaded?
Table 18-2 Which newer items uploaded based on Publish state and Upload settings	Any state	Yes	Upload Ref Files	Yes
	Any state	No	Upload Ref Files	No
	Always	Yes or no	Honor Publish State	Yes
	Always	Yes or no	None	Yes
	If Referenced	Yes	Honor Publish State	Yes
	If Referenced	No	Honor Publish State	No
	If Referenced	Yes or no	None	Yes
	If Not Empty	Yes or no	Honor Publish State	If it has contents
	Never	Yes or no	Honor Publish State	No
	Never	Yes or no	None	Yes

Tip: Upload Options Ignored — In the release version of 4.0 and 4.0.1 for Mac, no matter what setting was chosen for Honor Publish State or Upload Referenced Files Only, GoLive always honored the Publish flag.

Show Options Dialog

Checking Show Options Dialog brings up choices almost identical to the Upload section of FTP Settings. The Upload Options dialog box also lets you set whatever changes you make as the new FTP Settings by clicking Set Defaults.

Tip: Upload Settings Don't Appear (Windows) — As recently as the 4.0.1 release of GoLive for Windows, no matter what options you set in the Settings dialog, the Upload Options dialog box has everything checked. If you uncheck the Honor Publish State checkboxes as well as Upload Referenced Files Only, the Upload Options box has them all checked. If you uncheck the Honor Publish state boxes, even though Upload Referenced Files is grayed out and can't be unchecked (another bug), it acts as if it's unchecked.

If you check Don't Show Again, this disables the Show Options Dialog setting. We recommend disabling this dialog unless you frequently need to change whether or not you're honoring the Publish state.

Show List of Files to Upload

When either uploading or downloading files, having this option checked shows a list of all the files that are affected. You can then deselect individual files by unchecking them. Folders aren't listed separately, but as part of the path of files being uploaded.

On a Mac, you can select or unselect all items in the list by checking or unchecking the box at the very top (see Figure 18-10). Under Windows, you can

Figure 18-10
Choosing files
to download
by checking or
unchecking on
the Macintosh

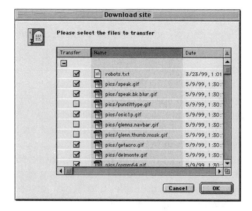

Figure 18-10
Choosing files
to download
by checking or
unchecking on
the Macintosh

select all items (press Control-A or choose Select All from the Edit menu) and check any box in the list (see also Figure 18-11). This will check or uncheck all items.

We always leave this option on so we can make sure the right files have been swept up in the net.

Figure 18-11
Control-
clicking to
toggle multiple
files for
download
under
Windows

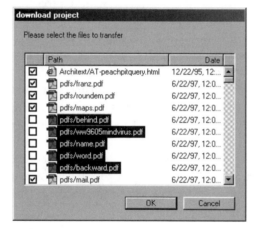

Uploading

To upload the latest versions of files in the Files tab, connect to the FTP server and click the Upload to Server button in the Site toolbar, or select Upload to Server from the Site menu.

GoLive then presents you with the Upload Options dialog box, followed by the file list, as described above.

First Time

The first time you transfer a site to a remote server, you can select Upload to Server, and GoLive will transfer all of the files and create all of the directories, essentially initializing the site.

Choosing Files

It's a good idea to choose to upload all files, as GoLive usually figures out which ones are the right ones. If you upload some and not others, you face the problem that some of your links won't work on the live site.

Tip: Upload Overload

Sometimes GoLive for Macintosh appears to want to upload all of the files from your local copy, even when they're not newer than those accessed via FTP. This can happen if the folder that contains your site gets manipulated on the Desktop, or for other reasons we haven't yet pinned down.

Whatever the cause, GoLive's notion of which files need to be uploaded gets reset. The unfortunate solution is to let GoLive have its way, and upload all the files it wants. Otherwise, you cannot use the Upload to Server feature to identify specific files after that; it always wants to upload all of them.

Out of Sync Uploads

If you delete or reorganize your content locally, GoLive can't track these changes and upload them. This means that if you remove a file in the Files tab, it won't be automatically removed from the FTP server when you synchronize.

Similarly, if you move content around, such as moving all your images from the root level of the Web site to their own folder, GoLive doesn't reshuffle them per your new local arrangement on the FTP server. Instead, it treats the new folder as a new object, and wants to upload it and all the contents.

To fix this problem, you have to delete, rename, or move the corresponding files on the server. Or, you can delete all of the items affected, and use the upload feature to reinstall a clean copy. This latter solution is easier.

If you need to create new pointers, delete old ones, or move existing ones via GoLive—well, you can't. The FTP protocol, as we noted earlier, doesn't have a provision for coping with pointers. You have to ask your system administrator to make these changes on the server itself. (If the system admin is someone other than yourself, ask politely.)

Tip: Mirror Upload Site

To avoid problems that sometimes happen when taking content live, we suggest that (if possible) you set up a mirror or "staging" site for help with synchronizing. You can use this location to test the upload and make sure everything worked right. You can then use a standalone FTP program to copy the files to the real Web site.

It's possible to set up a staging site to test new content by having a directory pointed to by a separate Web server. Or, you can even nest your test inside a folder on your main Web site. It may sound like a bit of extra work now, but trust us: experience has taught us the value of mirroring sites in progress.

Uploading to Multiple Servers

Updating a site that's split between multiple servers can be tricky, and may involve the use of the URL mapping feature. We discuss this feature and its implications in Chapter 21, *Site Specials*.

Exporting

Instead of using the Upload to Server feature, you can use Export Site from the Site menu, and then copy the resulting folder over using a standalone FTP program or the GoLive standalone client. See Chapter 21, *Site Specials*, for more details.

Downloading

There are occasions when you have to edit a file on the Web server itself, rather than editing files locally and uploading them. Or, a server might be generating automatic files for you that you need to retrieve.

By clicking Download from Server in the Site toolbar or selecting that item from the Site menu, you can download all files from the server that were modified more recently than the local copies (see the earlier sidebar, "Do You Have the Time?"). GoLive also downloads any folders and files which aren't found in the local copy of the site.

Tip: Over-writing the Home Page	In order to overwrite the page you chose as your home page (see Chapter 16, *Folders, Files, and Links*), you must use the Download from Server feature. There are messy workarounds involving renaming the file locally, selecting a new home page, and so forth, but it's not worth the hassle.

Avoiding Links

The Download from Server feature tries to download everything that's not present in the local copy, including links or pointers (see the sidebar, "Alias, Symbolic Links, and Shortcuts"). We haven't figured out a workaround that prevents this behavior, and it can generate an awfully long list of files to review.

The solution, if you have a lot of links or many files nested underneath them, is either to drag specific files you need from the FTP pane to the Files pane or to uncheck inappropriate items from the files list that appears when you use Download From Server.

Out of Sync Downloads

As noted above, under "Uploads," GoLive doesn't synchronize file deletions or moves between local and remote copies. So if you have some orphan files on the Web site, the Download from Server command will try to download these files, as there are no local copies. Either delete these from the Web site, move them, or uncheck them from the files list displayed after you select the command.

Troubleshooting

Some common problems with FTP that GoLive can't control might plague you. Here's the symptoms and what you can tell a system administrator to do to fix it.

GoLive passes through FTP errors that the FTP server reports. Many of these are semi-opaque, and provide little information for troubleshooting the problem.

For a list of all FTP error codes, see the following page at our Web site for reference: http://www.realworldgolive.com/ftpcodes.html. This list is abstracted from the FTP protocol description. A system administrator may want the specific code, so the more information you can provide, the better.

Connection

Connecting to a server should be straightforward, but there are enough variables to complicate the process.

Wrong username or password. If you enter the wrong username or password, GoLive should tell you specifically that either the username or password is incorrect. If you think you're using the right information, confirm it with the system admin. We've found that a typical cause for a wrong username or password is incorrect capitalization. Often, it's critical to type a username or password exactly, with the same caps and lower case, as what's provided to you. It's also easy to hit the Caps Lock key by accident, as you can't see what you're typing when you enter the password.

Wrong host name. If you enter the hostname incorrectly you should get a DNS error, which means that the domain name you entered with that particular machine or host name doesn't have an Internet address. Double check the information provided and contact the system admin if it persists.

No response from server. The first time you try to connect to a server, if you don't get a response in a reasonable period of time, it might be that the server is down or not reachable from your Internet location. If this persists, contact the system admin with the dates and times you tried to connect.

User not authorized. Systems often have to be configured to allow users to access them via FTP. Your account may be properly set up, but when you try to connect you get "530: Login failed: user not authorized." The system admin will need to double check his or her settings for your account to confirm you have access.

GoLive can't support server. From your perspective as a user, the FTP server's operating system and type of software are invisible. However, there are dozens (maybe hundreds) of different FTP server software packages, and GoLive only supports the most popular for Unix, Linux, Windows 98/NT, and Macintosh.

The GoLive manual doesn't provide a list of supported servers, but you may get no error—and no connection—when it encounters one that uses a different format from the established standards.

File List

After GoLive connects to the server, it should quickly display a list of items in the directory you've connected to. If you don't get this list, the problem could be one of the following three situations.

Permission problem. The account's directory isn't set up to allow you "read" access, meaning that you can't see the files in them. The system admin must make system changes to make this work for you.

Proxy server or network interference. Networks with firewalls, proxies, or other intermediaries might require you to check Use Passive Mode in order to make an FTP connection work. In these cases, you might be able to connect to the server, but it won't download or upload files, and it might not be able to send a file list.

Unknown mystery. Sometimes on the Macintosh, we find that we just can't use FTP any more. Connections get made, but no file lists are ever transferred. Rebooting the Mac through a normal restart from the Finder usually fixes the problem. We haven't found an explanation for this behavior.

Can't Access Directory or Upload

You may find that there are areas of a site you can't reach via FTP, or certain directories won't allow you to upload files. Both of these problems are permission related, and require the system administrator to change permissions to allow you or your group read, write, and/or execute permission to the appropriate directories.

Upload directive. Additionally, if you can't upload, many FTP servers require a separate "upload" directive that allows a user to login and upload to specific directories. If the directory isn't specified in that directive, the user can't add, overwrite, delete, or rename files.

Web site is inaccessible. You may find that Web surfers can't reach files on your Web site. GoLive allows you to change file permissions as long as the FTP server is configured to let you change them. If users can't reach your Web site, make sure the files you've added are set, under the FTP File or FTP Link Inspector, to Read for Other. For folders, both Read and Execute must be checked for others.

If you click Set Rights and get an error, then you will need the system admin to make the permissions changes for you.

For Macintosh servers, you only need to set folder permissions via the FTP Folder Inspector to Read and Execute, as files lack separate permission controls.

Locked and (Up)loaded

With a mastery of FTP staging and synchronizing in hand, you'll keep your site up to date with a minimum of effort and maximum of aplomb.

It's important to remember that even experienced Internet hands find themselves flummoxed facing FTP on occasion, as the number of potential problems in correctly setting up FTP access on a server can be manifold.

However, a good network or system administrator can make your part of the job easy: figuring out what goes where and when it needs to get put there.

CHAPTER 19

Site Maps

Web sites spring links like a leaky bucket, making your head spin from the already overwhelming task of tracking the relationships among pages. Sites can also quickly grow beyond our capability to easily visualize their full extent.

The Web site development process should start with a picture of the interrelationship of the parts of a site. Some designers will produce extensive maps showing each level of a site and how navigational links take a user from place to place. But after a site is built, you often can't match the map to the real Web site. When a site starts getting edited on a hands-on, daily basis, logic may fall apart.

A number of standalone software programs provide post-facto mapping, taking a Web site and building a picture of its navigation or link structure. GoLive has this feature built right in. The program's designers considered it important enough to devote a tab to it in the Site window.

GoLive's Site tab lets you view a site's structure with options to control which items are included in the display. You can see just HTML files, or every item on a site; you can see files that have links to them, or files that are orphaned. If you're really ambitious, you can even create new pages and insert link placeholders (*pending* links) within the Site tab by dragging, dropping, and clicking. If you like working this way, you could actually create or prototype a whole Web site.

Tip: Site Tab not Site Window
GoLive's nomenclature—its naming of things—shows a slight lack of, um, differentiation. The Site tab really should be named the "Site Map" tab, but, apparently for brevity's sake, it's named just "Site." We always make a distinction among the site file (the file on the hard drive that holds site information and preferences), the Site window (the full window on-screen that contains all the tabs), and the Site tab (the site map view).

Tip: Parents, GoLive uses a fairly standard practice in Web design of naming pages "parents" that
Children, and are above other pages in a hierarchy; the pages below parents are their "children."
Siblings "Siblings" are pages down a level in the hierarchy from a parent that are all linked
from the same parent.

Viewing versus Building

The Site tab shows you a two-dimensional picture of the relationship among
pages, images, Web sites, and other objects on your Web site based on internal
links, external references, placed images, and certain kinds of media files, like
PDFs. It also displays the full range of linking and visual features, helping you get
more than just a mental image of the relationships of one file to another, or one
part of a site to another (see Figure 19-1).

Figure 19-1
The visual
panoply of the
Site tab and
associated
palettes and
inspectors

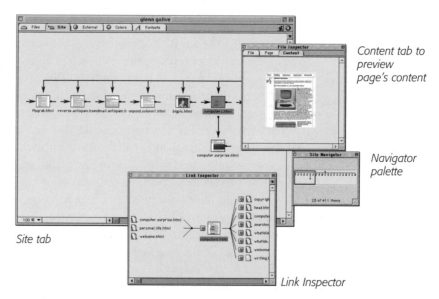

*Content tab to
preview
page's content*

*Navigator
palette*

Site tab

Link Inspector

You can use the Site tab in two significant ways: to view a site's parts and their
relationships (as well as customizing the display and rearranging items for better
output or visual organization); and to create pending links and new pages as part
of prototyping, building, or extending a site. Each hierarchy is color coded, so you
can identify which view you're displaying without having to use an inspector. By
default, the Link Hierarchy is blue and the Navigation Hierarchy is green.

Link Hierarchy. The default method of viewing a site map is according to its hierarchy of links, which appears when you click the Site tab in the Site window. You
see that the Link Hierarchy option in the Site View Controller's Arrange tab is se-

lected; also, the Link Hierarchy button on the Site toolbar is pressed. With Link Hierarchy selected, you're limited to viewing and rearranging items without any effect on the underlying files or current or pending links between items.

Navigation Hierarchy. To build or modify a site, select Navigation Hierarchy in the Arrange tab, or click the Navigation Hierarchy button in the Site toolbar. In this mode, you get all the same features as in Link Hierarchy, with the added ability—as configured through the Site View Controller—to drag and drop new pages and create link placeholders or pending links that identify links to add later.

The next section covers both the Link Hierarchy and the overlapping features in Navigation Hierarchy. "Prototyping and Modifying," later in this chapter, examines all the options and features specific to the Navigation Hierarchy.

Viewing and Organizing

If you already have pages built in your site, when you click the Site tab, GoLive displays a simple default site map . As you make changes to your site or as you build your site in other tabs, the site map is automatically updated to reflect this.

Moving around

The site map works like a big canvas, similar to the canvas or pasteboard found in desktop publishing programs. You generally see only a fraction of the canvas at a given time (depending on the size of your window and the complexity of the site). GoLive provides several tools you can use to pan and zoom around the site map.

Zoom menu. The Zoom menu, located at the lower-left corner of the Site tab, allows you to select a magnification amount; the default is 100 percent, where thumbnail previews are displayed at 72 dpi.

The Zoom menu offers preset enlargement and reduction factors: 10, 20, 50, 80, 100, 150 (see Figure 19-2). You can also select Fit Site in Window, and GoLive reduces the site map to very tiny proportions to accommodate the window size. The Zoom menu displays the currently selected percentage.

Figure 19-2
Zoom menu

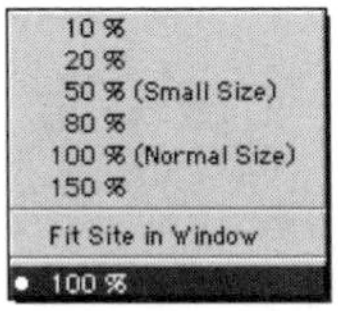

Tip: Zoom for Layout not Thumbnails

Most of the view percentages outside of 100 percent don't scale well, but the Site tab is more about organization and layout than about previewing. The page thumbnails GoLive creates are sized for 72 dpi at 100 percent view in the Site tab, and are pixilated at larger sizes. The type and link arrows become gigantic at large and small sizes. It's possible to use these other views for reference, although we prefer to set the scale to 100 percent and use the Site Navigator, described below, to show us the site's structure.

Magnifying glass. Holding down the Control key (Mac) or the Shift key (Windows) turns the cursor into a magnifying glass to enlarge the site map. You can click to increase magnification by the Zoom menu preset amounts. You can also drag to create a marquee and select an area, and GoLive zooms to the closest preset magnification.

Tip: 300 Percent View

If you drag over a small area with the magnifying glass, covering only a few pixels, GoLive jumps up to 300 percent—an option not offered in the Zoom menu.

If you hold down both the Control and Option keys (Mac) or Shift and Alt keys (Windows), the cursor displays a minus sign in the magnifying glass, and lets you zoom out to preset amounts.

Drag. You can drag the contents of the site map around its window by holding down the Command key (Mac) or the Control and Shift keys (Windows). This feature gives you the feel of reaching through a physical window to move a piece of paper around to view the part you want.

Site Navigator palette. For true ease in panning around the site map, invoke the Site Navigator palette. The only way to bring up this palette is by clicking the Site Navigator button on the Site toolbar (see Figure 19-3). (This icon's appearance differs in the Mac and Windows versions of GoLive, but its function is the same.)

The Site Navigator gives you a thumbnail of the entire site, with a marquee which you drag to control the currently visible section of the site map. When you drag the marquee, the window scrolls as you drag; or just click points on the site

Figure 19-3
Site Navigator palette

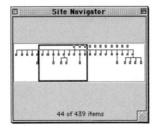

thumbnail, and the Site tab instantly shows that area of the site map in the visible window. The palette is resizable; you can make it absurdly large (see Figure 19-4).

The Site Navigator also shows you the number of elements in the site's File and External tabs, and how many of those are currently displayed.

Figure 19-4
Unintended
use of Site
Navigator
palette

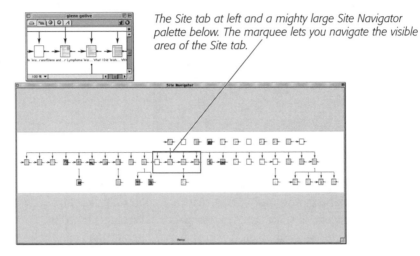

The Site tab at left and a mighty large Site Navigator palette below. The marquee lets you navigate the visible area of the Site tab.

Examining Links

Viewing a site's files and objects is only half the picture; the real benefit of a site map is viewing the relationships among objects. GoLive offers some powerful help in using the site map as a portal into the structure of the site.

Adobe calls the horizontal arrow pointing at an object from the left its Incoming Link, and the horizontal knob exiting from the right its Outgoing Link (see Figure 19-5). (Together, Adobe refers to them as *Side-Knots*, although this term isn't used in the program itself.) These two items provide your main interface for examining links in the Site tab.

Figure 19-5
Side-Knots

Incoming Link ➡️   *Outgoing Link*

Did leish.... Wh'Whe

The Link Inspector acts as a vital part of all site-management features involving relationships among elements in the site. In the Site tab, clicking a page's Incoming or Outgoing Link brings up the Link Inspector with that page as the focus (see Figure 19-6). You can use Point & Shoot selection from the Link Inspector to link if you want to change existing links to point at other objects in the Site tab. (Or, you can drag the Point & Shoot link line onto the Files tab and change an existing link to point to any file in that tab.)

Figure 19-6
Bringing up
the Link
Inspector

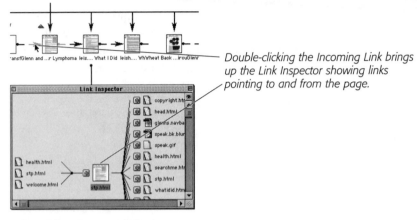

Double-clicking the Incoming Link brings up the Link Inspector showing links pointing to and from the page.

Viewing Connections

Hovering over a page's Incoming Link makes it dim to a tint of its current color. The Outgoing Link graphics for every page on the site which point to that page also dim to easily visualize their relationships (see Figure 19-7). The opposite is also true: hovering over a page's Outgoing Link dims it and all the related Incoming Links on the site that the Outgoing Link points to (see Figure 19-8).

Figure 19-7
Dimming
Outgoing Links
by pointing to
an Incoming
Link

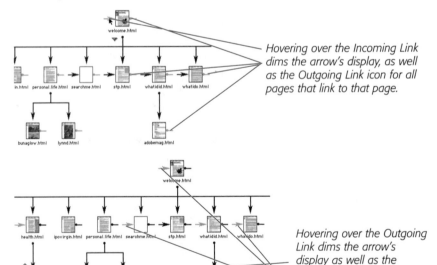

Hovering over the Incoming Link dims the arrow's display, as well as the Outgoing Link icon for all pages that link to that page.

Figure 19-8
Dimming
Incoming Links
by pointing to
an Outgoing
Link

Hovering over the Outgoing Link dims the arrow's display as well as the Incoming Link for all pages that are linked by that page.

If you click the icon of an HTML page, the links from all other pages that have Incoming or Outgoing Links pointing to, or linked from, that page turn black (see Figure 19-9). The link lines belonging to pages one level up within the hierarchy turn black as well. You can select multiple HTML pages, and have all link lines and link graphics highlight in black.

Figure 19-9
Link lines turn
black to show
relationships

Clicking an HTML file turns black all the Outgoing Links pointing to the file, as well as the link lines from the parent page in the hierarchy.

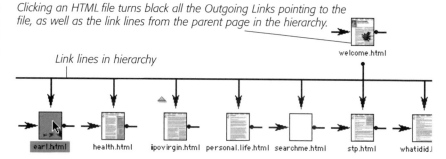

Expanding and Collapsing Hierarchies

To better examine subsections of a site's hierarchy, you can expand or collapse everything above or below a given page. As you hover over a page, an up-pointing and/or down-pointing triangle fades in. (The fade effect, while kind of nifty, is just for show and doesn't affect how you interact with it.)

Clicking an up-pointing triangle collapses all pages at the same level (sibling pages) and above the current level (parent pages), and makes the current page icon look like a stack of pages (see Figure 19-10). Clicking a down-pointing triangle collapses all the pages below the current page, and also creates a page stack of the HTML previews (see Figure 19-11).

**Tip: Collapse
to Print**

When you want to print just selected portions of the site map, collapse the hierarchies that don't need to appear on the printout.

Figure 19-10
Collapsing the
whole
hierarchy

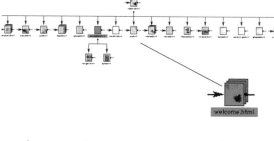

An entire Web site hierarchy can collapse to a single file by clicking a down-pointing triangle.

Figure 19-11
Expanding
collapsed
sections

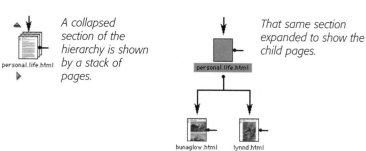

A collapsed section of the hierarchy is shown by a stack of pages.

That same section expanded to show the child pages.

Missing Links and Other Indicators

The site map uses the same symbols as the Files tab to show errors or problems in HTML files. If a page has a green bug on it, for instance, there's a missing link on the page. A yellow yield sign means that the page has just been created and has no contents.

Tip: False Alarms The stop sign icon—which means that GoLive can no longer find a file in the same site that another site page links to—sometimes shows up where it shouldn't when you collapse hierarchies in the Site tab. We've seen it when collapsing a view where the pages below the parent page are just fine (see Figure 19-12).

Figure 19-12
Errors where none exist in child pages

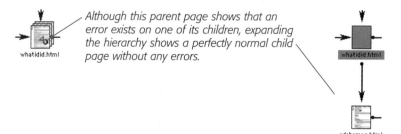

Although this parent page shows that an error exists on one of its children, expanding the hierarchy shows a perfectly normal child page without any errors.

Editing and Accessing Items

The site map provides some shortcuts for editing and opening items, whether they're HTML files or other objects in your site.

Thumbnails. Many items have previews that display in the Content tab of their inspector, such as HTML pages and the File Inspector. Whenever you save an HTML file from within GoLive, the program generates a small thumbnail.

Strangely, in the Site tab, if you have Show Items as Thumbnails selected in the Site View Controller's Display tab (see below), GoLive only displays HTML page previews, not image previews. If you choose Icons instead, then the image previews are displayed for files in which a thumbnail has been saved in an image-editing program like Adobe Photoshop (see Figure 19-13).

Tip: Creating Thumbnails If your site contains pages that have never been edited by GoLive and are imported from other sites or programs, you can generate thumbnails for the entire site by switching to the Files tab and pressing Command-Option (Mac) or Control-Alt (Windows). A menu item labeled Create Thumbnails appears only when you have these keys depressed (see Figure 19-14). Select it, and GoLive opens and saves every HTML file on the site.

If this menu item doesn't appear when you press these keys, make sure you have the file list selected in the Files tab. (If you had previously clicked the Errors, Extras, or FTP tabs, or selected any item in those tabs, GoLive doesn't consider the files list selected, and some options are grayed out.)

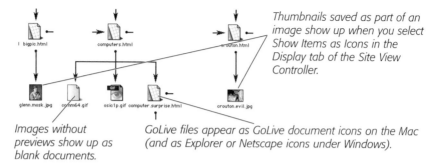

Figure 19-13
Image
thumbnails
with Show
Items as Icons
selected

Thumbnails saved as part of an image show up when you select Show Items as Icons in the Display tab of the Site View Controller.

Images without previews show up as blank documents.

GoLive files appear as GoLive document icons on the Mac (and as Explorer or Netscape icons under Windows).

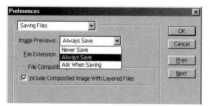 

In the Saving Files Preferences in Photo-shop, you can set the program to create Image Previews automatically. If you select Ask When Saving, the Save Thumbnails box in the Save As dialog can be checked or unchecked.

Figure 19-14
The Create
Thumbnails
menu item

Tip: Updating
Thumbnails
on Windows

After you create thumbnails or save a changed page, Windows doesn't appear to always automatically update thumbnails in the Site tab. To force GoLive for Windows to update this display, switch to Link Hierarchy in the Arrange tab of the Site View Controller and click New From Links at the bottom. (Don't do this in Navigation Hierarchy if you've added new links or pages through the Site tab.)

Editing items. Edit the name of a file or the title of any object in the Site tab by clicking its name in the Site tab. The name is highlighted and you can type over it or edit it. When you make changes to the name displayed in the Site tab, GoLive treats the change just as if you made it in the Files tab or External tab. The program prompts you to confirm the changes to links on every page affected by the edit.

You can edit the names of any objects you display in the Site tab, including URLs if you choose to display them in the site map (see "Customizing the Site Map," below). However, when you edit the name of a URL in the Site tab that's longer than 31 characters, GoLive incorrectly tells you that you can't name files with more than 31 characters on the Macintosh. This error shouldn't be generated for URLs, which are not files. You have to use the External tab to edit URLs, instead of this visual approach.

If you have Item Label set to Page Title in the Site View Controller's Display tab (see below), clicking the file's title field below its icon lets you edit the HTML page title instead.

Opening and working with files. Double-clicking a file in the Site tab opens it. If it's an HTML file, it opens in GoLive. For other files, the preferences you set take precedence for controlling which applications open which files (see Chapter 22, *Advanced Features.*)

You can apply the commands located under the Site menu's In Finder (Mac) or In Explorer (Windows) submenus—such as displaying information about a file or revealing the file's location within your hard disk's hierarchy—to any file you select in the Site tab, not just HTML pages. Under Windows, these options are also available by right-clicking the file and choosing from the popup menu. You can also use the Change References item, or the Point & Shoot icon in the Link Inspector, to redirect files and links, including pointing at files in the site map itself.

Deleting files. If you press the Delete key, the selected file or files are thrown into whichever trash you specified (see "Trash," Chapter 16, *Files, Folders, and Links*). You can also right-click an item under Windows and choose Delete from the popup menu, or select Clear from the Edit menu on either platform. (GoLive warns you about deleting files, but if you have multiple items selected, all of them are thrown into the trash, and you have sort the trash to restore their locations.)

If you choose to use GoLive's Trash in the Extras tab, which is the program's default, you can drag any item you trash back to where it belongs in the Files tab.

Customizing the Site Map

All the attributes of the Site tab are set through the Site View Controller, which is really an inspector with four tabs (see Figure 19-15). You can access the Site View Controller by clicking the eyeball in the upper right of the Site tab, or by bringing up the Inspector palette and clicking an empty area in the site map background.

The Site View Controller offers a myriad of options, like most of the inspectors in GoLive. Only one checkbox is unavailable to the Link Hierarchy view, noted below; all the other features work equally well for the Link Hierarchy and the Navigation Hierarchy.

Figure 19-15
The Site View
Controller

All four of the tabs—Arrange, Filter, Display, and Color—control which items are displayed and how they appear. The Arrange tab also includes controls for creating a table of contents and rebuilding the Navigation Hierarchy. Instead of walking through the tabs, we've grouped their options thematically to discuss the different features you can access through them.

Structure

The default site map shows a two-dimensional outline of pages and other objects and the links among them. As mentioned earlier in this chapter, you can set this view in the Arrange tab to either the Link Hierarchy (for viewing) or the Navigation Hierarchy (for prototyping or adding links).

Tip:
Switching
Between
Hierarchies

It's quicker to switch between the two hierarchy styles by clicking the Link Hierarchy or Navigation Hierarchy button in the Site toolbar.

However, the Display tab offers a different take on both views. Select Site View (the default) or Outline as the Display option. Selecting Outline turns the site map into something akin to the Files tab's linear display of files (see Figure 19-16). Each level of links is represented by an indent, with a triangle (Mac) or a plus sign (Windows) that expands or collapses the list of items underneath. You can press Option when clicking the expansion symbol to expand or collapse all levels on the Mac; this doesn't work under Windows.

Figure 19-16
Site map
viewed as
Outline

The outline view is a much more convenient way to examine URLs and image links because of its list format. This view makes it possible to display the entire URL at once.

Tip: Can't Rearrange Order (Mac) Although the Mac version of GoLive in Outline view has standard column headers and the ascending/descending order button in the upper-right, GoLive has disabled all these elements because this view is intended as a site outline, not a file sorter.

Content

GoLive considers a site as a collection of everything found in the Files and External tabs, but you don't see all of them in the default view setup of the site map. To minimize the visual confusion that would result from displaying *everything* (unless you're using a 40-inch gas-plasma monitor), GoLive's Filter tab on the Site View Controller controls which items actually show up in the site map.

Filtering. The Filter tab lets you select to display any combination of six categories:

- **HTML files:** any pages on your site
- **Media Files:** images, PDFs, QuickTime movies, or anything linked to a page that's not HTML
- **Folders:** any item referenced as a folder or directory; this doesn't include folders that are just part of a path to get to files
- **URLs:** everything listed in the External tab as a URL
- **Addresses:** all e-mail addresses listed in the External tab
- **Missing Files:** files that GoLive lists in the site but can't find on the local drive

You can further filter the file display by selecting either If Reachable or If Unreachable under the Reachable from Homepage heading (unchecking both empties the window!).

Using Filter helps you see all the relationships on segments of the site, and allows you to print out relationships in more detailed chunks, especially in Outline view.

Item label. When displaying pages, you can set whether the pages display their filename or their title by selecting either Page Title or File Name under Item Label in the Display tab.

Expanding and collapsing. We mentioned earlier in the chapter how to collapse and expand levels of the site map through clicking the up-pointing and down-pointing triangles. If these triangles get in your way when prototyping a site or re-arranging items, you can suppress them by unchecking the wordy Use "Hide & Show" Live Button box in the Arrange tab.

Incoming and outgoing links. In the same location, you can turn off display of the Incoming and Outgoing Link graphics by unchecking Show Side-Knots.

Table of contents. Finally, if you want to summarize all the content on your site, in hierarchical form, in an HTML page for reference or to adapt as a page on the site, use the Create T.o.C. Page feature in the Arrange tab of the Site View Controller. If you're viewing the site map as the Navigation Hierarchy, the button is labeled From Navigation, and creates a map based on pending and real links. In the Link Hierarchy, the button says From Links and uses the current links to create the table of contents. Unfortunately, there's no way to customize the creation of this page or have GoLive update a modified page.

Aesthetics

GoLive offers enormous control over the aesthetics of site maps; this can help considerably when printing a site map out to a color printer, or just trying to make relationships more readable.

Auto Arrange Items. The primary control for arranging items is the Auto Arrange Items checkbox in the Arrange tab. If you have Auto Arrange Items checked, all the objects in the Site tab lock to a grid. You can also check Stagger Items, which offsets every other item by a small amount (see Figure 19-17).

Figure 19-17
Staggered
items

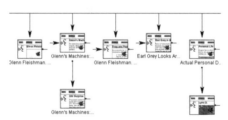

Unchecking this option allows you to drag objects around in the site map to your heart's content. GoLive automatically redraws link lines to wherever you put an object. Checking Auto Arrange Items immediately resets the location of all objects (see Figure 19-18). You can also click the Arrange Items button in the Site toolbar to restore the default arrangement of the site map.

Item display. The Display tab provides controls over the appearance of objects and the link lines between them.

The Show Items As heading offers four options (see Figure 19-19):

- **Icons:** the icons for objects as seen in the Desktop, including image previews if they were saved with previews from an image-editing program. The filename or title gets displayed beneath the icon.

Figure 19-18
Auto arranging

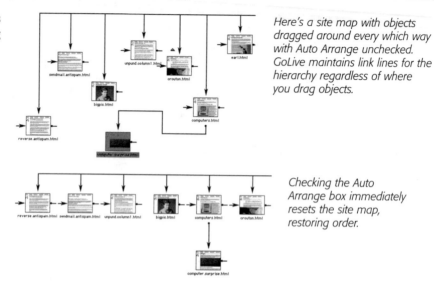

Here's a site map with objects dragged around every which way with Auto Arrange unchecked. GoLive maintains link lines for the hierarchy regardless of where you drag objects.

Checking the Auto Arrange box immediately resets the site map, restoring order.

- **Frames:** a graduated-fill box with the filename or title inside of it.

- **Thumbnails:** a small rectangle containing HTML page thumbnails, if available, with filename or title below the box (see earlier in this chapter on creating thumbnails).

- **TV Screen:** for those raised on television, this provides a comforting rounded-corner box that contains the filename or title.

Figure 19-19
Show Items As
options

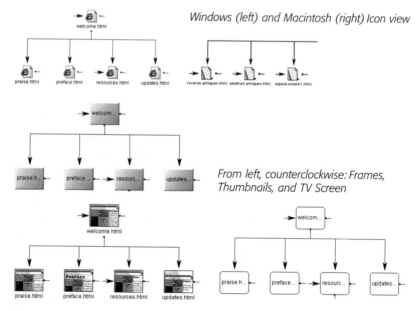

Windows (left) and Macintosh (right) Icon view

From left, counterclockwise: Frames, Thumbnails, and TV Screen

Item spacing. You can control the spacing of items by entering pixel values for the 100 percent view in the Horiz. and Vert. fields under Grid Spacing. The size of frames, TV screens, and thumbnails are all fair game using the Width and Height fields under Frame Size.

Link lines. GoLive also offers three kinds of link lines: a brace-like curve, a diagonal line, and a right-angle line. We prefer the latter for its angular clarity; it's the default, shown throughout this chapter. The other two types are shown in Figure 19-20.

Figure 19-20
Link line styles

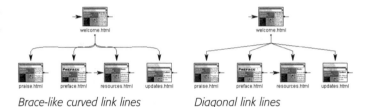

Brace-like curved link lines   *Diagonal link lines*

Connection colors. In the Color tab, you can set the color display for Navigation Curves and Link Curves (link lines in the Navigation Hierarchy and the Link Hierarchy), text, and the background color. Again, this can help in printing a legible or nice-looking site map on a color printer, or when you're making onscreen presentations or even Web pages out of the site map.

Item colors. The Item Color division in the Color tab sets the color of individual items when viewed as Frames or TV Screen in the site map.

 If you choose Finder Label on the Macintosh, whatever color you've set for the icon on the Desktop becomes the color for that item in the site map; this is the default on the Macintosh (see Figure 19-21).

 You can also set Item Color to Status Label or Monochrome, the only two options available for Windows; Status Label is the default for Windows.

Figure 19-21
Labeling files
in the Finder

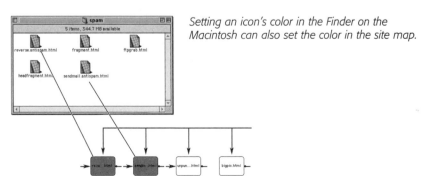

Setting an icon's color in the Finder on the Macintosh can also set the color in the site map.

Status labels are special colors and names you set up in Preferences under the Edit menu, under the Site preference's Page Status. You can assign a Status to HTML pages only through the File Inspector's Page tab (see Figure 19-22).

Monochrome sets all icons to the same color.

Figure 19-22
Setting Status
labels

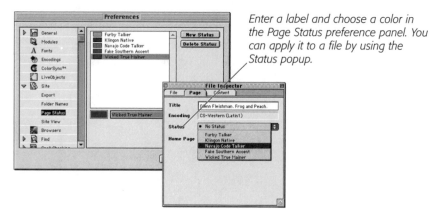

Enter a label and choose a color in the Page Status preference panel. You can apply it to a file by using the Status popup.

Navigation Controls

If you're using the Navigation Hierarchy to create or modify pages and links in the Site tab, then you'll be concerned with two more items in the Site View Controller's Arrange tab.

The Use "Create New Page" Live Button checkbox turns on or off the display of new page icons around an existing page. (These buttons are described under "Prototyping and Modifying," below.)

After adding links and pages in the Navigation Hierarchy, you can remove all your changes by pressing the New From Site button at the bottom of the tab. This button is called From Links or From Navigation under Windows, depending on the hierarchy you're viewing.

Printing

It seems that printing a site map was not a top priority for GoLive's developers, as there are no options, and the printed output is not great. When you print from the Site tab, GoLive essentially prints out a screen grab, tiling the onscreen map onto several pages.

You cannot control tiling, nor preview the results. Lines around objects scale to be hairline thin or monstrously large. Whichever colors you choose in the Colors tab of the Site View Controller get used in the printing process, whether you're creating Acrobat PDFs or printing to a color output device.

Tip: Print at
100%

The best output we get is at 100-percent view. The type looks reasonable, and the thumbnails or other graphics display without too much pixelization.

Tip: Print to PDF	You can print your site map to a PDF file and then open it in Adobe Illustrator to tweak the previews and type for better visual allure.
Tip: Printing the Outline View	The Outline View fares best when printing, as it's mostly text in formatted lines. You can use Page Setup to rotate a page sideways (landscape) to fit longer columns of text along the length of the page.

Customizing page headers and footers (Mac). GoLive for Macintosh has settings in the Page Setup dialog box that allow you to customize the text that appears on the top and bottom of each page (see Figure 19-23). (As of 4.0.1 for Windows, these options were not available, although Windows previews output.) GoLive offers choices for the left, middle, and right of the header and footer:

- **Date:** the current date

- **Title:** the site file's name

- **Username:** Whatever name is entered in File Sharing (Macintosh)

- **Page Number**

You can also set whether a line is printed below the header and above the footer.

Figure 19-23
Header and footer options for printing

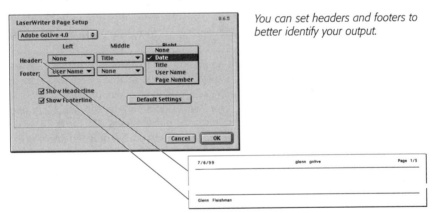

You can set headers and footers to better identify your output.

Prototyping and Modifying

Confession time: At first we didn't know what to do with GoLive's features for building a Web site from within the Site window. Blatant featuritis, we said. But after working with it, we discovered that GoLive's Navigation Hierarchy offers a powerful *prototyping* tool that can also be used to extend and modify an existing site. With Navigation Hierarchy selected in the Site View Controller's Arrange tab, you can create placeholders for new links and add new pages by dragging and dropping. You can also add external Web page references, e-mail addresses, and media files (like images) using the same method.

After you've added link placeholders, use the Pending tab in the Page Inspector to make the new connections inside the HTML pages. The Pending tab provides a variety of visual clues that help you arrange links and pages in the correct order.

With this tool, you may consider throwing out your pencils and graph paper in favor of building initial site maps from within GoLive.

Tip: New from Site Resets Any Changes If you make changes to a site map, you can reset it back to its original condition on the Macintosh by clicking the New from Site button in the Site View Controller's Arrange tab. This resets all changes you've made to the structure of the site.

Under Windows, this button's name is either From Links or From Navigation, depending on which hierarchy you're viewing. The former resets the Link Hierarchy's display; the latter deletes any new links or pages from the Navigation Hierarchy.

Adding Links

The process of adding link placeholders to HTML and media files in your site, external Web references, and e-mail addresses, is as simple as dragging and dropping.

Because this method works visually, you have to display the kind of object to which you want to create a new pending reference. Using the Filter tab of the Site View Controller, explained above, make sure that both HTML pages and any other kind of object to which you want to create a pending link are checked.

Tip: Displaying Not Yet Linked Objects If you're trying to add a pending link to an object that isn't currently referenced anywhere on the site—a URL you added in the External tab, for instance—you must check If Unreachable in the Filter tab to make it display in the site map.

Adding pending links works differently in the Site View and the Outline View. Whichever view you use to add placeholders, GoLive displays dotted lines to show links that don't already exist to objects you've dragged into places (see Figure 19-24).

Figure 19-24
Pending links

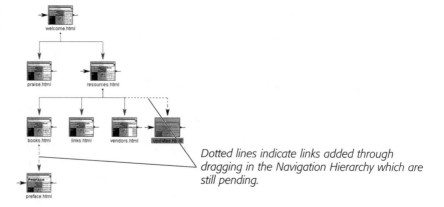

Dotted lines indicate links added through dragging in the Navigation Hierarchy which are still pending.

**Tip: Existing
Links Show
Solid Lines**

If you drag a page so that it's in a different position in the hierarchy but it has an existing relationship in that new location as a parent, sibling, or child, the link line stays solid, even though the link is added to the pending list.

Site View. To add a pending link in the Site View, simply drag an object into the proximity of the target HTML page's icon. You can drag the object onto one of four directions around the icon: top, bottom, left, or right (see Figure 19-25). Each of those directions corresponds to a position in the hierarchy relative to the HTML page you're dragging onto:

- **Top:** parent

- **Bottom:** child

- **Left:** previous sibling (as in a sequence of pages)

- **Right:** next sibling (as in a sequence of pages)

Figure 19-25
Dragging new
links into place

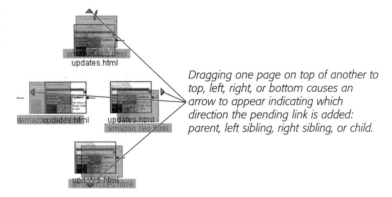

Dragging one page on top of another to top, left, right, or bottom causes an arrow to appear indicating which direction the pending link is added: parent, left sibling, right sibling, or child.

**Tip: Sibling
Directions**

Siblings' directions, left and right, are arbitrary unless your siblings indicate a sequence of pages. For instance, many sites organize their help pages so that the start of a sequence of pages is reachable from a parent page, and then you walk through one page to the next by clicking a next or previous button that's part of the site's navigation. In these cases, organizing siblings from left to right makes perfect sense.

**Tip: The
Home Page
is Special**

You can't add parent or sibling pages to the page you've defined as your site's home page; it always has to be the root of the site.

Outline View. In the outline view, drag the object to which you want to create a pending link, such as another page, into the space just below an HTML page. GoLive displays a right-pointing triangle and a dotted line to indicate the position where the pending link to the object will be inserted (see Figure 19-26).

- If you drag directly onto the HTML page's icon, the triangle stays at the same indent level as the page; this makes a sibling link.

Figure 19-26
Creating links
in Outline view

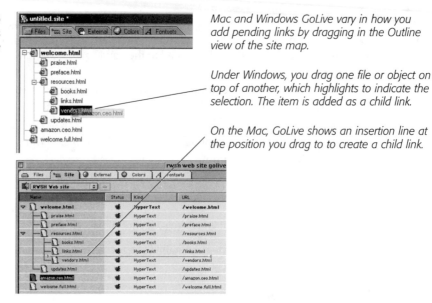

Mac and Windows GoLive vary in how you add pending links by dragging in the Outline view of the site map.

Under Windows, you drag one file or object on top of another, which highlights to indicate the selection. The item is added as a child link.

On the Mac, GoLive shows an insertion line at the position you drag to to create a child link.

- If you drag to the right of the icon, the triangle indents a fixed space; this makes a pending child link. Dragging above an HTML page makes it a "left sibling;" below, a "right sibling." (See "Tip: Sibling Directions," above.)

- You make pending parent links only by dragging onto an HTML file a level higher than the one to which you're adding a link placeholder.

Adding Pages

The Navigation Hierarchy mode also lets you add entirely new pages to a site via the Site tab. You can add generic blank pages, along with links to and from them, or you can use stationery items to add your own templates.

New pages that have been added but not yet opened, modified, and saved have a yellow yield sign on them in the Site tab and in the Status column of the Files tab.

Blank pages. To add blank pages, you need to have the Use "Create New Page" Live Button checked in the Arrange tab of the Site View Controller. Now, when you hover around an existing page in the Site View, little page icons pop into view. Clicking one creates a new page with a parent, child, or sibling link, depending on the direction you clicked in; see "Adding Links," above, for more on directional selection.

You can't add pages using this method in the Outline view.

Blank pages are added, by default, into the New Pages folder at the root of your site. You can change this name and the default extension (.html) in Preferences under the Edit menu; choose the Folder Names preference under the Site heading.

Stationery. Adding stationery is just as simple. Bring up the Palette and select the Stationery/Components tab. Drag a piece of stationery out of the palette and onto one of the directions around an HTML page. The stationery gets inserted. Clicking a New Page button in the Site View around that new stationery page inserts that same stationery file.

Working with Pending Links and New Files

After adding new links and pages, you need to use a separate interface to access those pending items. This interface is the Pending tab in the Page Inspector.

In either the Files tab or Site tab, double-click an HTML file to open it. Click the Page icon at the top of the page and bring up the Inspector palette, which is now called the Page Inspector. Click the Pending tab.

The Pending tab shows a list of all existing links to HTML and media pages stored locally on the hard drive. It also displays any pending links to other objects on the site, external Web references, and e-mail addresses (see Figure 19-27).

The Pending tab has four columns:

- **Name:** the link's name. In the case of URLs and e-mail, GoLive lists the full link, even when you've named the object in the Externals tab.

- **Pending:** a blue arrow means that the link has been added in the Navigation Hierarchy but hasn't yet been added to the page.

- **Nav:** a visual cue to indicate in which direction this link is from the current page within the site hierarchy. That is, a link to the home page would always have a green arrow pointing up to it, indicating that it was above the current page. (The current GoLive manual doesn't explain the Nav column, so we assume it was a late addition to the program.)

- **URL:** the full path on the local hard drive to internal links or media files; the full URL for e-mail addresses and external references.

Figure 19-27
Pending tab

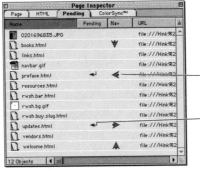

The Pending tab shows all links on the page, as well as those that have been added in the Site tab through the Navigation Hierarchy but haven't yet been added to the page.

— Navigation cues, indicating parent, left and right siblings, and child links.

— This arrow means the link is pending.

Putting Pending Links on Pages

You add objects from the Pending tab onto a page in one of three methods. After applying any of these three methods, the pending icon disappears from that object in the Pending tab (see Figure 19-28). External references and e-mail addresses are removed from the list after they're added to the page.

Figure 19-28
Dragging a
pending link
onto a page

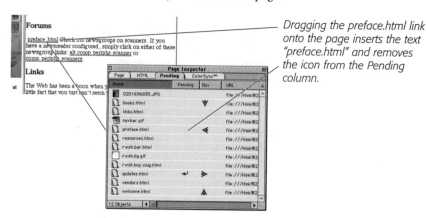

Dragging the preface.html link onto the page inserts the text "preface.html" and removes the icon from the Pending column.

Dragging. Drag the link from the Pending tab onto the page. If the link isn't an image, GoLive creates a hyperlink using the text as the display name of the object in the Pending tab. If the link is an image, GoLive inserts it.

Selection. First, select text to be linked on the page. Second, click the Page icon at the top of the Document window. Third, drag any kind of item, except an image, from the Pending tab onto the selected text. This turns it into a hyperlink to the pending item. (If you drag an image, GoLive deselects the text and inserts the image.)

Site map or Files tab. You can drag items from the site map or out of the Files tab onto an HTML page. This isn't the most efficient method, nor does it directly use the Pending tab, but it does remove the pending status once you've dragged the object over.

Setting Up New Pages

New pages created through the Navigation Hierarchy are bereft of contents unless you've dragged stationery over to create new pages. In either case, when you're ready to link the files into the site, use the Pending tab, described above, to add links.

However, you probably want to move the page to an appropriate location, as well. We recommend first adding all your pending links and objects, and then dragging the page in the Files tab to its permanent location. GoLive automatically prompts you about all references that need to be rewritten for that page's move, just as when you move any object in the Files tab.

Once you add links or any content to a new page and then save it, the yellow yield sign icon disappears in the site map and Files tab.

The Big Picture

When Web sites get big (and even the simplest ones tend to grow faster than expected), you need some way of wrangling the entire beast, not just its individual pages. The Site tab lets you look at your Web site as a totality instead of scattered items and objects. Having the big picture can help you structure and restructure a site to have more utility. It definitely makes a handy tool for debugging errors and building something that your users can more easily navigate and comprehend.

Importing a Site

If we had chapter subtitles in this book, this chapter's would be "This Old Site." Much like the popular home-fix-it show *This Old House*, this chapter aims to take a perfectly serviceable site that's fallen on hard times, clean it up without radically changing its character, and bring it into the modern age.

Some sites that we've worked on started their lives *way back* in 1995 and have accumulated years of the equivalent of soot and creosote build-up, with ancient tags and old HTML hacks lingering in the crevices of Web pages. GoLive is an excellent chimney sweep of old sites, brushing away the grime.

Updating an old site isn't quite as easy as just opening it up in GoLive and creating a site window. In addition to creating the right options in GoLive, you may want to take the opportunity to reorganize the site's files, delete old and orphaned material, clean up outdated or incorrect references, and toss out bad HTML. You'll also probably want to ditch server-side imagemaps, an outdated method of using images to navigate that adds latency to a Web site.

The best time to approach a site renovation is when you first start, nailing all the problems and making all the corrections in an orgy of find-and-replace actions. You'll be surprised by how much renovation you can do in only a few hours.

Importing

Importing a site is straightforward, but you can save yourself some extra labor and make the process of updating the site easier if you follow this procedure. Let's assume a site is about artichoke growing, and that the site file name is "artichoke.site" (see Figure 20-1).

Figure 20-1
Setting up
import folders

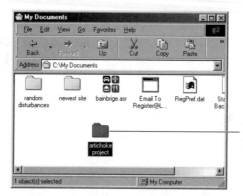

*This folder contains the original copy
of your site as a backup, and the new,
imported copy of the site that you
work on in GoLive.*

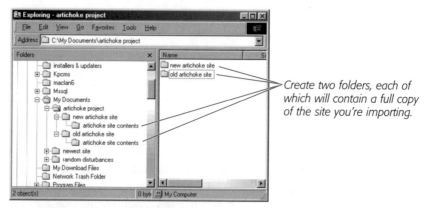

*Create two folders, each of
which will contain a full copy
of the site you're importing.*

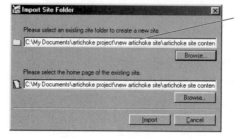

*Select the copy of your site that you
have placed in the new site folder.*

1. Create a folder on your local hard drive called "artichoke project".

2. Create two folders inside this folder: one called "new artichoke site", the other called "old artichoke site".

3. Download or copy your old site into a folder called "artichoke site contents" and copy into both the new and old site folders. The intention of this is to keep a backup handy.

4. Open GoLive and select Import from Folder from the File menu's New Site submenu.

5. Select the folder containing the site inside the "new artichoke site" folder. Don't create a new folder, as you've already nested folders correctly.

6. Select your site's existing home page (you can change this later as part of your renovations, if you need to).

7. Click OK. GoLive will now build the site file. For larger sites, this can take some time, and may require you to allocate extra memory to GoLive under the Mac OS. (See Chapter 1, *Getting Started*.)

Many site cleanup changes we're going to suggest are not reversible. So, as we suggested in Chapter 15, *Site Management*, you should make backups of your current site folder as you work, to avoid having to return to the beginning after you've made significant progress. Whenever you do a large sitewide change using Find and Replace, for instance, we'd recommend making another site copy just beforehand.

Cleaning

Back in the bad, old days, when everyone was writing HTML by hand in NotePad or SimpleText—some people still do, by the way—we wrote some pretty ugly code. Part of the problem was consistency; if you're writing by hand, it's easy to forget elements or do the same thing in a different way each time. Part of the problem was a lack of rigor by the browsers; you could omit quotation marks around attribute values in HTML tags and Netscape would forgive you.

It wasn't until the release of Internet Explorer (IE) for Windows 2.0 that we discovered how bad a job we'd done. IE was much less forgiving, violating the edict of the Internet: "Be conservative in what you do, liberal in what you accept." However, it was a good wake-up call.

Unfortunately, many older pages never heard the alarm go off and contain lingering, terrible, inconsistent code—especially in tables—that can cause unexpected errors in different versions of different browsers.

We have a multistep approach to surmounting these HTML problems by identifying each kind of problem and solving it using Find & Replace. (If you're not comfortable or familiar with GoLive's Find & Replace command, we recommend you read up on it in the next chapter, *Site Specials*, before proceeding.)

For each of these examples, we'll provide the code to put into the Find & Replace fields. You should select Add Site before making these changes so that they're made consistently across an entire site (see Figure 20-2 for setup guidelines).

Tip: **Mandatory** **Reparse All**	When you've completed any or all the suggestions in the rest of this chapter, hold down the Option key (Mac) or Alt key (Windows) and select Reparse All from the Site menu. This forces GoLive to re-read all the HTML files and rebuild its internal database of links.

Figure 20-2
Find & Replace
options

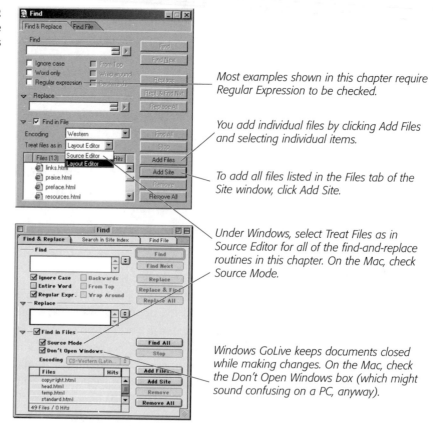

Most examples shown in this chapter require Regular Expression to be checked.

You add individual files by clicking Add Files and selecting individual items.

To add all files listed in the Files tab of the Site window, click Add Site.

Under Windows, select Treat Files as in Source Editor for all of the find-and-replace routines in this chapter. On the Mac, check Source Mode.

Windows GoLive keeps documents closed while making changes. On the Mac, check the Don't Open Windows box (which might sound confusing on a PC, anyway).

Attributes Without Quotations

Early Web browsers didn't always require quotation marks around attributes in an HTML tag to interpret the tag correctly. This can lead to confusion when modern browsers read the URL, as certain characters should be surrounded by quotation marks to make it clear that they are part of a value.

Tip: What's an HTML Attribute? An attribute is any element that follows the tag's name. For instance, in the expression `<img src="/images/joplin.jpg" border="0">`, both border and src are attributes of img. The quotation marks follow the equals sign and fully enclose their values. Attributes always have a space preceding them, though some of them don't have values, like the checked attribute for a form checkbox.

There are two ways to fix this problem. The first is to bring up Web Database from the Special menu, and in the Global tab set Quote Attribute Values to Always. In the Find dialog box, click Add Site, and in the Find *and* Replace fields, enter a period. This forces GoLive to open and modify every file, which also forces it to rewrite the HTML according to the Web Database's settings.

The second method doesn't force the rewriting of every page, but it is a bit more involved. This method uses regular expression pattern-matching in the Find feature, described in more depth in Chapter 22, *Advanced Features* (see Figure 20-3).

This operation finds every instance of a space followed by any text not containing a space or equals sign, followed by an equals sign. The part after the equals sign must not contain a quotation mark, a space, or a close HTML symbol (>).

Check	Regular Expr.
Find	`(\s[^= ]+=)([^" >]*)`
Replace	`\1"\2"`
Click	Replace All

The only place this feature might cause problems is if you have text in your site that looks like the pattern. Consider a statement like, "You must remember that when x=y, the resultant formula gets changed to q=2xy." The above routine would make the first statement be "x="y"" and the second "q="2xy"".

Figure 20-3
Fixing missing quotation marks

Before

```
<img align=bottom src=gifs/ban-
nerd.gif width=470 height=141>
```

After

```
<img align="bottom"
src="gifs/bannerd.gif"
width="470" height="141">
```

Fully Qualified HTTP References

Due to some faulty thinking on the part of some early browsers and our ever-fallible minds, many hypertext references and image source tags in the olden days used the entire site name to reference the object.

That is, we'd write a fully qualified reference like:

```
<a href="http://www.foobard.org/foobard/pages/woof.html">
```

instead of using a relative reference, which would make the site portable and easier to work with, like:

```
<a href="/foobard/pages/woof.html">
```

or even, if the user were viewing another page in the /foobard/pages directory:

```
<a href="woof.html">
```

Using a fully qualified reference means that if you relocate elements, the entire Web site, or even the folder level, you have to rewrite every reference in the site.

GoLive extracts all references like this and lists them in the Externals tab. Unfortunately, you can't change an external link into an internal one; GoLive generates a specific error rather than accomplishing the task. But you can use Find & Replace to do it for you.

In this next method, we use what GoLive calls Absolute links, which are actually relative links that specify the root of the Web site (for more on this distinction, read the sidebar "Absolute Versus Relative" in Chapter 16, *Files, Folders, and Links*). If you move files around in GoLive's Site window that are referenced via GoLive Absolute links, GoLive will rewrite them just like it would any standard relative link.

In the example above, our absolute URL is http://www.foobard.org/foobard/ pages/ to reach items on the site; our GoLive replacement URL is just /foobard/ pages/ to get to the same location (see Figure 20-4). The following Find & Replace action takes care of the problem.

Uncheck	Regular Expr.
Find	`="http://www.foobard.org/foobard/pages/`
Replace	`="/foobard/pages/`
Click	Replace All

Figure 20-4
Full URL replacement

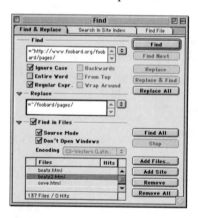

Before

```
<LI>For answers to your jousting
questions, visit with <a href=
"http://www.foobard.org/
foobard/pages/oustingexperts.
htm">Jousting with the
Experts</a>.<LI>Feel like
browsing? Check out our
searchable <a href="http://
www.foobard.org/foobard/pages/
calendar/joustsearch.cgi">
Jousting Event Calendar</a>.
```

After

```
<LI>For answers to your jousting questions, visit with <a
href="/foobard/pages/joustingexperts.htm">Jousting with the
Experts</a>. <LI>Feel like browsing?  Check out our
searchable <a href="/foobard/pages/calendar/joustsearch.cgi">
Jousting Event Calendar</a>.
```

Subsite Paths

Some early Web servers required an extra directory in the front of the path to your files, so that to get to files for www.ishkabibble.com, your URLs would all look like

```
http://www.ishkabibble.com/ishkabibble/
```

Most servers lack this limitation, and, in fact, we've had to add automatic redirects on the sites we work on so that the server rewrites URLs on the fly to remove this subsite path information. This adds time to processing a Web transaction.

If you no longer need this part of the path, you can easily remove it after following the above steps to clean up quotation marks and full references. Put in your own path for "subsitepath" below, and this will replace all instances (see Figure 20-5).

Uncheck	Regular Expr.
Find	=\"/subsitepath/
Replace	=\"/
Click	Replace All

Figure 20-5
Subsite path
replacement

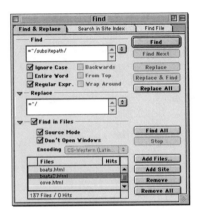

Before

```
<LI>For answers to your jousting
questions, visit with <a href="
/foobard/pages/joustingexperts.
htm">Jousting with the Experts
</a>.<LI>Feel like browsing?
Check out our searchable <a
href="/foobard/pages/calendar/
joustsearch.cgi">Jousting Event
Calendar</a>.
```

After

```
<LI>For answers to your jousting questions, visit with <a
href="/pages/joustingexperts.htm">Jousting with the Experts
</a>.<LI>Feel like browsing? Check out our searchable <a
href="/pages/calendar/joustsearch.cgi">Jousting Event
Calendar</a>.
```

PageMill Remnant

Just after Adobe shipped PageMill, back in 1995, we started getting reports of a weird attribute that was breaking some weblint (HTML syntax checking) programs. The attribute was NATURALSIZEFLAG. Apparently, PageMill would add this attribute, set to either 0 or 3, for every image source tag in a site.

After some wrangling, it was finally revealed that this attribute was used by PageMill to identify whether an image had been resized within PageMill or not. If it were set to 3, it was still at its original proportions; otherwise it was set to 0.

This was the first well-known instance of HTML code that was proprietary to a given visual page editor. The HTML spec has always stated that any tag or attribute that a browser doesn't understand should be ignored, and Adobe tried to take advantage of that concept. (GoLive inserts a CSOBJ tag to identify components, and occasionally inserts other GoLive-specific information that you can strip if you export the site. Components and Export are both discussed in Chapter 21, *Site Specials*.)

To get rid of this PageMill tag, use the following procedure. This looks for any instance of a space followed by the attribute with the value, surrounded in quotes or not, set to any digit (see Figure 20-6). (Replace _ with a space character.)

Check	Regular Expr.
Find	`_naturalsizeflag="?(\d+)"?`
Replace	*leave empty*
Click	Replace All

Figure 20-6
Naturalsize killer

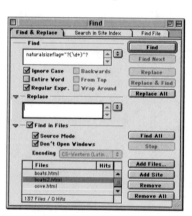

Before

```
<P><CENTER><IMG SRC="gifs/ftwb-
nr.gif" WIDTH="470" HEIGHT="128"
NATURALSIZEFLAG="0" ALIGN="BOT-
TOM"></CENTER>
```

After

```
<P><CENTER><IMG SRC="gifs/ftwb-
nr.gif" WIDTH="470" HEIGHT="128"
ALIGN="BOTTOM"></CENTER>
```

No Background Color or Image

Early HTML lacked any support for a background color or image for a page, so you often find a Body tag all by its lonesome. GoLive doesn't provide a way to set these parameters for a group of pages, so this tip is useful for old and new pages alike (see Figure 20-7).

This will replace any Body tag that contains anything following "body". You can add items like Vlink or other attributes to the basic items listed for Replace below.

Check	Regular Expr.
Find	`<body[^>]*>`

To set all backgrounds to white, no background image:

Replace	`<body bgcolor="#ffffff">`

To set all backgrounds to white with a background image, and with link, text, active, and visited links set to some color:

Replace   `<body bgcolor="#ffffff" background="/gifs/
blur.gif" text="black" link="blue" alink="red" vlink="#ff00ff">`

Figure 20-7
Body clean-up

If you want to leave parts of the Body tag unchanged, and just change the background color to white (#ffffff), for instance, try the following. This method looks for the Body tag followed by any text except a closing angle bracket, followed by the Bgcolor attribute. The first hunk of text is kept, but everything matched after the equals sign is replaced.

```
Find        (<body[^>]* bgcolor=)[^> "]+
Replace     \1#ffffff
```

Improving

There are many things you can do to improve an old Web site and make it more manageable. This includes updating older features to newer ones, extracting repeated elements to centralize them, and reorganizing the site to be easier to manage.

Replacing Imagemaps

Imagemaps, discussed at length in Chapter 8, *Images,* let a designer set up hot areas on an image on which, if a user clicks, their browser gets directed to a new URL assigned to that area.

Imagemaps date back to the graphical Web Stone Age, but at that time they were handled by the server—hence the name "server-side" imagemaps. When a user clicked an image that was defined as an imagemap, the browser sent the coordinates of that click to an imagemap program at the server. The server, using this program, examined an imagemap file that contained sets of areas defined as coordinates. If the click landed in a domain (an area defined by a set of coordinates), the server returned a redirection to a new location; or, if there was a default directive defined and the user clicked an undefined area, the server returned a default URL.

Server-side imagemaps add a transaction with the server, plus the processing time for that transaction, which could add several seconds between a click and the new page appearing. It also adds traffic to your Web server.

With Netscape 2, the idea of client-side imagemaps popped into being, meaning that the entire set of map area coordinates would be embedded in an HTML file, and the browser itself would determine whether a domain was clicked on.

Tip: **Retaining** **Both Sides**	Older Web pages still have the remnants of server-side imagemaps, and it's not a bad idea to retain them, as probably five percent or less of any given Web audience uses browsers old enough that client-side mapping won't work. This gets discussed below, and in Chapter 8, *Images*.

This kind of replacement is often substantially trickier than anything we've talked about in this chapter thus far, as we generally find that old files contain lots of variations on a theme, so a single Find & Replace doesn't work.

Here's the procedure we recommend (see Figure 20-8):

1. Go through many files and identify all the places in which an imagemap is used. Collect these instances in HTML and paste them into a text file for reference. These references will look something like this:

```
<A   HREF="http://www.foobard.com/cgi-bin/htimage/pages/nav.
map"><IMG SRC=" http://www.foobard.com/gifs/nav.gif" BORDER=
"0" ISMAP WIDTH="470" HEIGHT="46" ALIGN="BOTTOM"></A>
```

2. Create a new imagemap inside GoLive for each of your old ones. You could convert the old server-side imagemap to client-side, or create a map that works for both older and newer browsers; typically, this is not necessary.

Tip: **Converting** **Server-Side** **Imagemap** **Files**	Rewriting a server-side imagemap into a client-side imagemap is pretty simple, but we've made it even easier by providing a URL where you can paste code from an old-style imagemap into a text box, press Submit, and have the HTML produced for you. The URL is: *http://realworldgolive.com/convertmaps.html*. Follow the directions on this page and copy and paste the results into the Replace box, as described below.

3. Switch to Source view after you've tweaked the imagemap to your liking in GoLive, and select everything from the first IMG SRC that has the USEMAP attribute in it to the </MAP> at the end. It will look something like this:

```
<img   src="gifs/nav.gif"   alt="bottom   nav   bar"   align=bottom
width="470" height="46" usemap="#bottombar" border="0"><map
name="bottombar"><area href="/" shape="default"><area href=
"/whatcook/whtscook.htm" coords="353,1,467,45" shape="rect">
```

```
<area href="/fresh/fresh.htm" coords="245,2,350,43" shape=
"rect"><area href="/dearsand/drsandy.htm" coords="160,2,242,
45" shape="rect"></map>
```

Paste the code above into a text file as well, as it will serve as your Replace text. (You can also reference an imagemap in an external file; we discuss how to do that in "Imagemaps" in Chapter 8, *Images*.)

4. Go through each of the iterations of the original imagemap and paste each of them in turn in the Find field. In the Replace field, enter something unique, like [[banana]] that won't appear elsewhere in the site.

Figure 20-8
Turning a
server-side
into a
client-side
imagemap

The original image as a server-side imagemap

The image with client-side regions defined using the Map tab of the Image Inspector

Before
```
<A HREF="/cgi-bin/htimage/pages/whalenav. map"><IMG SRC="/
gifs/whalenav.gif" BORDER="0" ISMAP WIDTH="133" HEIGHT="119"
ALIGN="BOTTOM"></A>
```

After
```
<img border="1" height="119" width="133" src="../Exposure
%20001.GIF" usemap="#Exposure%20001b3ac1aef"><map name=
"Exposure%20001b3ac1aef"><area href="/whales.html" coords=
"5,93,92,113" shape="rect"><area href="/lodging.html" coords=
"32,76,99,87" shape="rect"><area href="/directions.html"
coords="32,61,123,72" shape="rect"><area href="/boats.html"
coords="31,50,87,58" shape="rect"><area href="/" coords=
"32,36,79,46" shape="rect"><area href="/charters.html"
coords="7,7,113,28" shape="rect"></map>
```

For large sites with lots of inconsistencies, it can literally take hours to fix all the possible combinations; Glenn spent about two hours on this task for a 1,500 page site that used a variant of the same template—almost, but not quite identical—for every page.

5. Now Find: [[banana]] and drop into Replace the text you extracted in Step 3. Press the Replace All button, and you've magically brought your site into the very late (instead of just late) 20th century.

Instead of pasting in imagemaps that all have to be managed individually, you could also create a component that contains each imagemap and use the technique described next to manage all your imagemaps from a central location.

Turning Repeated Elements into Components

GoLive has a powerful feature called components that lets you reuse snippets of HTML or parts of a page. We discuss this feature extensively in Chapter 21, *Site Specials*. The utility of components is that you can write the HTML once and apply it to every page you want to. Better yet, updating the components automatically rewrites every page on which it's used throughout the site.

Although GoLive wants you to use the drag-and-drop approach to add components to a page, we have a trickier method that lets you replace an old site's template with a GoLive equivalent (see Figure 20-9).

1. Identify a repeating element, like a copyright statement, appearing on each page.

2. Create a component in GoLive, as described in the next chapter, making sure to use the Absolute checkbox for all internal references.

3. Drag this component onto any page.

4. Select the component and switch to HTML Source Editor.

5. The HTML that's highlighted will begin with <CSOBJ...> and end with </CSOBJ>. This is GoLive's internal tracker for that component. Copy that text.

6. In the Find field, use the same technique described under imagemaps above: find every version of the HTML you want to replace with the component, and replace each piece of HTML with [[banana]] or something unique.

7. Put [[banana]] in the Find field, and paste the CSOBJ copy into the Replace field.

Neat trick, eh? Suddenly all your pages are managed with components with very little fuss. Remember to Reparse All, or GoLive will act like an aging relative: "Bobby who?"

Figure 20-9
Rolling your
own
components
for find and
replace

This is the element we want to repeat on every page. Select this material in the Layout Editor, switch to HTML Source Editor, and carefully copy all of its underlying HTML.

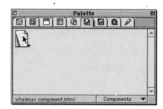

Open a new, blank HTML document and switch to HTML Source Editor. Select all the text and delete it. Paste the recurring element's HTML in, and save the document in the Components folder.

The newly created component now shows up in the Palette and in the Components folder of the Extras tab.

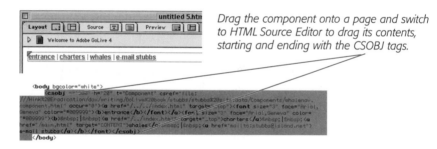

Drag the component onto a page and switch to HTML Source Editor to drag its contents, starting and ending with the CSOBJ tags.

Iterate through all of the variants of the HTML you want to replace with a component, dropping in a placeholder, like [[banana]].

Now paste [[banana]] in the Find field, paste the component's HTML in the Replace field, and hit Replace All.

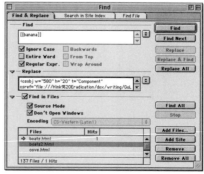

Renaming Files and Reorganizing Structures

Another ancient problem: indecipherable file names. We often named files briefly to match the pre-Windows 95 naming convention from Microsoft of eight-dot-three names: eight characters, a dot, and then three characters. Or, we got lazy, and named files "index1.html", "index2.html", and so on.

When faced with hundreds of files named in this fashion, it can be hard to know where to begin. After following the above steps to clean up your HTML, you can use GoLive's Files tab to rename files to more mnemonic names. As you re-name them, GoLive prompts you to automatically rewrite all occurrences, of course, throughout the site.

A related problem of older sites was a lack of planning for the future. Many sites were created in a flat organizational structure, where you could have hundreds or even thousands of files in a single folder. Again, using GoLive's built-in ability to track internal links, create new folders that divvy up the content and drag-and-drop files into the appropriate subdivision.

Brave New World

It's a marvelous thing to wake up in the morning knowing that your site is humming with HTML 3.2 compatibility, ready to take on the next century of HTML. True, not everything on your pages will take full advantage of the latest and greatest features in HTML, but you can have the sleep of the just when a missing quotation mark doesn't wind up derailing your site.

CHAPTER 21

Site Specials

So far, we've covered site-management features that fit into neat categories, like site maps and fontsets. But GoLive offers so many different controls for working with a site that we have a small pile of items that aren't as readily categorized.

In this chapter, you'll learn about the little things that make GoLive a complete tool for managing a site, from sitewide find and replace to mapping a site onto several remote Web servers.

Sitewide Find and Replace

The Find feature lets you examine usage of given text throughout a site, or make sitewide changes with a click of one button. We cover the basics of the Find feature in Chapter 14, *Page Specials*, and more advanced uses in Chapter 22, *Advanced Features*.

Setting Up Find & Replace

Find is located in the Edit menu, or by pressing Command-F (Mac) or Control-F (Windows). Click the Find & Replace tab, then click the expand control next to the Find in Files checkboxes (see Figure 21-1). The Find & Replace tab now displays controls that allow you to find and replace text in more than one file.

Tip: Find & Replace Not Reversible   Sitewide Find & Replace is not reversible—you cannot revert to previous copies of the files after performing replaces. This is why we suggest that you always make a backup of your site before making significant sitewide changes. Consult Chapter 15, Site Management, for solutions on making backups before proceeding.

Figure 21-1
Finding in site
in the Find &
Replace tab

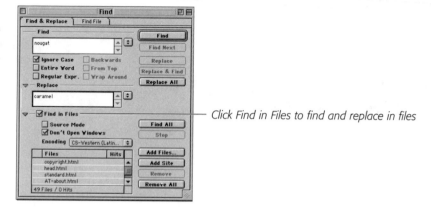

Click Find in Files to find and replace in files

The options below control how files are processed.

Find in Files. Once you add files to the file list, checking this box lets you toggle between finding across many files or finding within the file that's currently open and in the frontmost window.

Source Mode. If Source Mode is checked (Mac) or selected from the Treats Files As In menu (Windows), GoLive examines the underlying HTML of each page. If it's unchecked (Mac) or set to Layout Mode (Windows), the program looks only at the textual content of the pages, ignoring HTML formatting.

Setting GoLive to use Source Mode can be dangerous unless you're searching for highly specific bits of HTML code, such as searches described in the previous chapter, *Importing a Site*, to clean up the HTML in an old site.

Don't Open Windows (Mac only). Sometimes you might need to step through each replacement on each page, in which case you want GoLive to open each page that's being modified. Typically, leaving this box checked makes all the changes happen behind the scenes. This feature doesn't appear in the Windows version of GoLive.

Tip: Floor Show (Mac) Worried that maybe your computer's super-fast processor isn't flexing its muscles adequately? Make it show you the work it's doing. Uncheck Don't Open Windows and click Replace All. Watch as window after window is opened, examined, and shut. It takes an enormous amount of processing power and time and might cause GoLive to run out of memory if it needs to open too many files—but it can be impressive if someone's looking over your shoulder.

Encoding. If your pages use a special encoding for other languages or alphabets and Source Mode is not set, select the correct encoding before performing searches from the Encoding menu.

Using Site-Wide Find & Replace

Your first task is to choose the files you want to search. Either add files one at a time by clicking the Add Files button, or add every HTML file in the frontmost site window by clicking Add Site. You can also drag files from the Find tab into the Find & Replace file list, or drag them from the Desktop into the file list.

Remove files from the list by selecting one or more files and clicking the Remove button. Remove All, naturally, removes all the files from the list. As you add and remove files on the Mac, a counter at the bottom of the file list displays the current number of chosen files; under Windows, GoLive shows the number of files selected at the head of the Files column (see Figure 21-2).

Figure 21-2
Number of
files in list

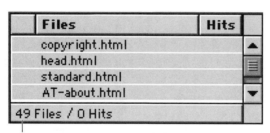

Number of selected files

Finding in Files. Clicking Find All starts the process of scanning through each file. If there's one or more matches on the Find term, the number of matches or hits is displayed next to the file name. On the Mac, a counter at the bottom of the file list is incremented; under Windows, the counter is in the Hits column header. An arrow points to each file as it is processed (see Figure 21-3).

You can also use Find to get the first instance, and Find Next to step through each successive instance of a match; this requires Don't Open Windows to be unchecked on the Macintosh.

Figure 21-3
Processing the
file and num-
ber of matches

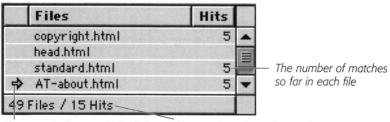

The number of matches
so far in each file

The arrow indicates which file is
currently being worked on

The number of matches so far

Replacing in Files. Click Replace All, sit back, and watch the results. When GoLive is finished, it will provide a summary of the number of instances changed (see Figure 21-4).

Figure 21-4
Number of
replacements

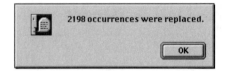

2198 occurrences were replaced.

OK

You can step through changes by clicking the Replace button (which replaces but doesn't find the next instance) or clicking the Replace & Find button (which replaces and then finds the next instance), just as you would in an individual file. (You need to uncheck Don't Open Windows to use this option on the Mac.)

Find Files in Site

For truly large sites, you might prefer an option to navigating up and down folders in order to find a specific file or two. The Find File tab of the Find dialog box allows you to do just this (see Figure 21-5). If you have multiple sites open, you can select the appropriate one from the Find Item in Site window. The menus to the right of Whose let you define the search by Name or URL, and then by whether a file contains, is exactly, begins with, or ends with the text you enter below it. The popup menu to the right of that text field shows the last few searches you've performed.

Figure 21-5
Find files
in site

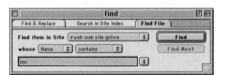

Export Site

While constructing a site, it's easy to wind up with lots of extras as part of the process: extra files that aren't referenced, extra images not found on pages, extra white space characters that help make HTML readable, and so on. Export Site gives you a chance to clean up and simplify without any extra work.

Select Export Site from the Site menu. A dialog box appears with a number of options in multiple categories that allow you to choose how your HTML files are cleaned up, and how the site is structured (see Figure 21-6).

Whichever approach you take, Export Site prompts you to create a new site folder when you click the Export button.

Hierarchy. Since GoLive maintains its own internal database of files and links within a site, there are a couple options for the exported site's structure. The default is to stick with your current structure, but you can also collapse your site in two ways. GoLive automatically rewrites all internal references in the process of exporting.

Figure 21-6
Export Site

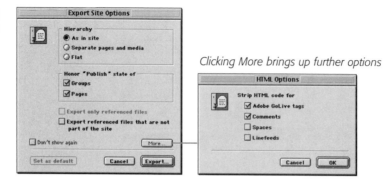

Clicking More brings up further options

If you choose Separate Pages and Media, GoLive puts all HTML files into a folder called Pages; everything else on the site goes into a folder called Media. If you check Export Referenced Files That Are Not Part of the Site, GoLive also creates a folder called Other into which it copies files from outside of your site folder referenced in the site. The home page is placed at the same level as the two folders (see Figure 21-7).

Tip:
Changing
Export Folder
Names

GoLive understands that we all have personal preferences. For example, we tend to store graphics in a folder called "images" in our sites, but we know others who use "gifs" or "graphics" instead. You can set the names of the folders that the Separate Pages and Media option creates through the Preferences item in the Edit menu. Click to expand the Site category, and select Folder Names.

You can also select Flat, in which case all of the files in the site, including the home page, are placed in the same folder (see Figure 21-8).

Publish state and references. In Chapter 18, *Staging and Synchronizing Sites*, we include an extensive discussion of how you can set and use the Publish state on

Figure 21-7
Separate pages
and media
option

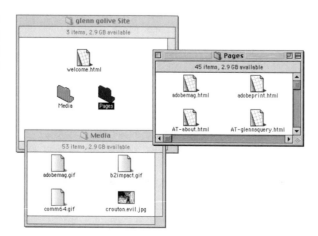

Figure 21-8
Flat option

files to control whether or not they are uploaded to an FTP server when you choose Upload to Server. These same parameters apply here.

If the Publish state of files and folders is set to anything but Always and you check both Groups and Pages under Honor "Publish" State Of, the Publish state limits which files are uploaded.

The Export Only Referenced Files checkbox is grayed out if you check the Honor "Publish" State Of boxes, as the Publish state takes precedence.

You can uncheck both Publish state options, and then check Export Only Referenced Files to export only those files that are part of the site's hierarchy, which can be viewed in the Site tab. If you uncheck this box, all the site's files are exported.

More and HTML Options. Clicking the More button brings up the HTML Options dialog box, which offers some HTML cleaning tools. By checking these items, you can strip out any GoLive-specific tags during export, like those used for inserting components; comments you've added to annotate your page; and extra spaces, tabs, returns, and linefeeds, collectively known as "white space."

HTML doesn't require extra spaces or linefeeds between items, which are put in just for readability (like when you're using the Source Editor to read raw HTML). You can reduce the size of a page by about five percent or more by removing these excess characters. Browsers don't rely on this spacing to display pages correctly.

Tip: The Pre Tag and White Space
The one exception to the "white space" rule is when you're using the Pre tag to format text. The Pre tag, listed as Preformatted in GoLive's Format menu, lets you use the Return or Enter key to signify the end of the line instead of the HTML tags BR and P. GoLive is clever enough to avoid removing these necessary returns.

Tip: Global White Space Settings
The Global tab of the Web Database (found under the Specials menu) lets you set how GoLive formats HTML for all pages created or modified after you change settings. So you can reduce the amount of white space used in your pages on the Global tab and then reformat your site; see Chapter 27, Web Database.

Don't Show Again, Show Options Dialog, and Preferences. As with other dialog boxes in GoLive, checking Don't Show Again allows you to set and use your preferences for exporting a site without accessing the dialog boxes again. You can also set your preferences in the Edit menu's Preferences item with the Export settings under the Site category. The options here are identical to those that come up by default when selecting Export Site. However, there's an additional checkbox labeled Show Options Dialog which you can use to display the export options again after checking Don't Show Again.

Clear Site

Clear Site acts like a gardener: it roots out weeds (unused links, colors, email addresses, and fontsets), while planting seeds (adding files and objects referenced in the site but not in the site folder). You can control Clear Site to a high degree, plucking out just the items that are necessary to keep your site tidy.

Tip: Let's Klar Up This Site When we first saw this command, we thought, "Gee whiz, we'd better not accidentally select this! It'll erase (clear) our site!" It turns out that Clear Site should be called Clean Up Site, as it just tidies up the details. GoLive's German-language origins (as CyberStudio) lend some understanding: it might be a translation subtlety from the German word for clear, "klar," which can mean "clarified" in the sense of, "Is everything clear to you now?"

The Clear Site Options dialog allows you to:

- Rescan the root folder, updating the GoLive site file to reflect any changes you might have made on the Desktop to the files and folders that comprise the local copy of the site. (This is exactly like selecting Rescan from the Site menu or Update from the contextual menu.)

- Add files that are referenced in the site but not located in the site folder, and remove files not referenced in the site but which are located in the site folder.

- Add all elements used in the site that aren't already present, and remove unused ones.

Clear Site lets you turn on and off the add or remove function for each kind of behavior described above on a tab-by-tab basis. That is, you can remove all unused fontsets, but leave unused colors, external references, and unreferenced files.

Clear Site's options for adding and removing files are similar to Export Site, except that with Clear Site they apply to your current working version of the site stored locally—Export applies only to an exported copy.

Add Used files. By checking Files under Add Used, any files not found in the site folder that are referenced in the site are automatically copied into the site folder and all references to them are rewritten. Checking Show List of Files to Copy previews and offers a choice over which files to copy over. (This option corresponds to the Export Site's Export Referenced Files That Are Not Part of the Site checkbox.)

Remove Unused files. You can automatically remove files that aren't used in the hierarchy of files and links descending from your home page by checking Files under Remove Unused. As with adding used files, checking Show List of Files to Remove lets you preview which files are going to be moved to the trash, and selectively change that list.

Add Used and Remove Unused objects. For both the Add Used and Remove Unused areas, GoLive offers items corresponding to three Site window tabs: External, Colors, and Fontsets. These checkboxes correspond exactly to Get …Used and Remove Unused… items under the Site menu in those tabs.

Clear Site preferences. You can set your default preferences for Clear Site in Site Settings, so that when you select Clear Site from the Site menu, the Clear Site Options dialog box reflects these preferences.

If you check Don't Show Again in the Clear Site Options dialog box, you have to go to the Clear Site preferences in Site Settings and check Show Options Dialog.

Templates

Have you found yourself acting somewhat robotic in your Web design and production work, repeating the same activity over and over again with no end in sight (or site)? GoLive offers two site features to relieve tedium caused by a human being having to act like a computer: stationery and components.

Stationery allows you to label and store specific HTML files as templates that you can use as new, blank pages in the Files tab and the Site tab. Components are HTML snippets that you insert in Web pages which are managed from a central location. Changes to the component update all pages on which that component is placed.

Both items are found in similar places in folders, tabs, and palettes because of their similar nature.

Extras tab. The Components and Stationeries folders are nested inside the site data folder. You can reach items in these folders through the Extra tab in the Site window's Files tab. To get to the Extra tab, click the Aspect Control icon in the Files tab. On the Mac, this splits the Files tab into two pieces with vertical tabs; under Windows, this opens up a bottom pane with the tabs along the top.

Saving into the Extras folder. You can save directly into either folder using a special popup menu inside of GoLive's Save As dialog. The popup menu next to the folder name offers an option to save in the Root folder, the Components folder, or the Stationeries folder (see Figure 21-9).

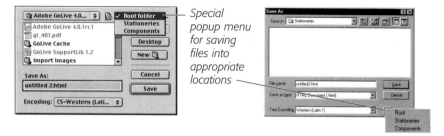

Figure 21-9
Save As special
popup menu

Special
popup menu
for saving
files into
appropriate
locations

Site Extras tab in Palette. Both components and stationery show up in the Palette's Site Extras tab (see Figure 21-10). You can select which of the two you're viewing through a popup menu at the lower right of that tab. Hovering over the item in the Site Extras tab displays the item's name in the lower-left corner of the Palette. Components' icons are tiny previews of their contents.

Figure 21-10
Components
and
Stationeries
folders

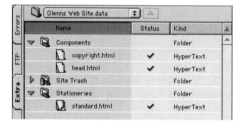

Stationery

Making stationery is straightforward. Create a template file in GoLive that contains all the elements you want on every page, including components (described below). You can turn this page into a piece of stationery by any of these methods:

- Save the file in the Stationeries folder (see above).

- Save the file in the root of the site, and then drag it to the Stationeries folder in the Extras tab. GoLive moves the file, rewrites references, and, on the Mac, changes its icon. (If you Option- or Alt-drag the file, GoLive copies it and turns the copy into stationery.)

- Check the Stationery box in the File Inspector (Mac). (This doesn't move the file, but it does give it stationery properties, which may not be the best idea.)

Stationery setting on Desktop. The Stationery attribute is set at the file level, so you can examine and change this setting on the desktop. On the Mac, select the file and choose Get Info from the File menu.

Using stationery in the Files tab. When you double-click a stationery file in the Stationeries folder, GoLive asks you if want to modify the stationery file itself or create a new document (see Figure 21-11). If you click Create, or if you double-click stationery that's located in the Files tab, the program opens a new, untitled document window with the name "untitled". GoLive adds a number to the document name if you've opened previous new documents during the same session.

Figure 21-11
Prompt when
trying to open
stationery

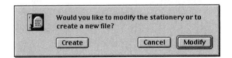

After editing this untitled document, selecting Save or Save As brings up a prompt for a file location and name. After saving the file, it acts just like any another HTML file.

You can also drag stationery from the Site Extras tab of the Palette into the Files tab; GoLive creates a copy of the stationery called "new from" plus the stationery's name.

Tip: Don't Drag Stationery to Files Tab

If you drag stationery from its folder to the Files tab, GoLive moves the stationery file itself, which is not what you want if you mean to create a new document.

Using stationery in the Site tab. In the Site tab, with the view set to Navigation Hierarchy, you can drag stationery either from the Site Extras folder or the Site Extras tab of the Palette on top of existing pages. We cover using stationery in this manner in Chapter 19, *Site Maps*.

Components

Components let you reuse the same piece of HTML over and over again while centrally managing the piece through a single editable file. When you edit the component, every occurrence of that component throughout a site is automatically updated with the new HTML.

Components can be as small as a single piece of text or a tag, or as large as an entire page including all the appropriate page tags, like HEAD (see Figure 21-12). Typically, you'd use components for any kind of element that repeats exactly on every page it appears. You can't use components to insert, for example, a menu bar with section-based rollovers, unless you devise separate components for each section. But if you use one menu bar for the entire site that doesn't identify sections, you can certainly include it.

Figure 21-12
Component
preview and
underlying
code

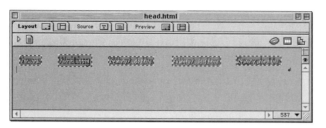

*The preview of a
component*

*The component's raw
HTML, including the
Html, Head, and Body
tags, which GoLive strips
off when it inserts the
component into a page*

**Tip:
Components
and Full
HTML Page
Structure**

Although we prefer to use components as just snippets of HTML without the sur-rounding tag for Html, Body, Title, etc., Adobe tech support recommends structuring components as self-standing pages. For instance, open a page from the Files tab, click the Page icon, and select the HTML tab from the Page Inspector, then click the Settings to Use Page as a Component button. This adds in all the appropriate tags, which GoLive automatically removes when it inserts a component into a page. Adobe prefers this method, as it results in components that can be edited easily and correctly in the Layout Editor.

**Tip: Use
Components
for Copyright
Statement**

The best example we can think of for a component? A copyright statement (see Figure 21-13). Most of the sites we design have a copyright and contact notice at the bottom of every page, no matter how many thousands of pages there are. Using a component for this enables us to modify the date or contact person once and watch 1,000 pages get rewritten on a particularly large site.

Figure 21-13
Copyright as a
component

Copyright ©1999 Never Enough Coffee Creations.
Peachpit Press Visual QuickStart Guide logo and
likeness used with permission.

**Tip:
JavaScript
References
from
Components**

Because components are embedded multiple times, you have to reference all the JavaScript that a component uses through an external link to a JavaScript file rather than embedding every page or embedding in the component itself. In order to do this, every page on which you use a component needs to have a reference to a shared JavaScript file; see Chapter 23, JavaScript, on how to create this reference.

Creating Components

Since components are pure HTML, they can be created in two simple ways.

- In the Layout view in GoLive, create what you want visually, use the Page Inspector's HTML tab to turn the page into a component, and save it in the components folder.

- In the HTML Source Editor in GoLive or in a plain-text editor (think NotePad, SimpleText, or BBEdit), enter the HTML code directly, and save or drag the file into the components folder.

As noted above, you can include all of the foofahroo that a normal HTML page needs, like the Head, Body, Title, and Html tags, but we've found that components work without that information as well.

Using the Page Inspector to make a component. You can turn a page you're viewing in the Layout Editor into a component with the Page Inspector's HTML tab.

1. With the HTML page open and set to the Layout Editor, click the Page icon.

2. Bring up the Page Inspector, and click the HTML tab (see Figure 21-14).

Figure 21-14
HTML tab

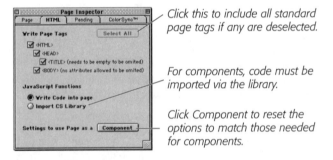

Click this to include all standard page tags if any are deselected.

For components, code must be imported via the library.

Click Component to reset the options to match those needed for components.

Always Use Absolute References

The one real limitation we've run into in creating components is that because they live outside of your site folder, which contains all of the site's pages and media, references to images and other files might show a full path from the root of your hard drive instead of a relative path.

Components, when inserted into a Web page, may continue to show the local reference to an object instead of a relative reference that works when the page is uploaded to a Web site.

We've gotten around this problem (which doesn't happen much in version 4.0) by *always* checking the Absolute box for all references in a component. This makes sure that wherever the component is inserted, the paths to the referenced items work. For each link in the component, bring up the appropriate Inspector palette, and in the Link tab, check the Absolute box. This writes nice, clean HTML that references all files from the root, and never breaks due to a problem with a path.

This was a giant frustration with CyberStudio 3, GoLive 4's predecessor, and many thousands of designers breathed great sighs of relief on seeing the Absolute checkbox for the first time, as it solved long-running problems with managing components successfully.

3. Click the Settings to Use Page as a Component button. If the settings are already correct, the button is grayed out.

4. Note that Import CS Library is selected. This is necessary if you use any GoLive Actions on your page so GoLive doesn't write the JavaScript libraries into the HTML page you're turning into a component; this code wouldn't wind up on the individual pages that the component appears on.

5. Save the page in the Components folder, making sure to end it with .htm or .html, even though you're not going to load it directly onto a site. With an .htm or .html extension, when you open the file, GoLive lets you edit it visually, even though it's a fragment.

Writing raw HTML for a component. If you're familiar with HTML, you can type code directly into the HTML Source Editor or a regular text editor and save it in the Components folder. Or, you can create what you need visually in the Layout Editor, switch to the Source tab, and delete excess HTML.

If you want to edit the component visually, save it with a .htm or .html extension. But if you just want to edit the text of the component, save it without an extension or with a .txt extension; this forces GoLive to open the component in a simple text-editing mode, instead of in a standard page window.

Adding a Component to a Page

GoLive offers a few approaches to adding components to a page. In each case, you drag the component or its placeholder to any insertion point on the page in the Layout Editor.

Tip: Window Overlaps As with other window overlaps, GoLive won't bring the HTML page to the front if you have the Site window displayed on top. So, before you drag the component onto a page, arrange your windows so that the part of the page that you want to drag onto is visible, or the Components folder is reachable so you can drag from it (see Figure 21-15). (Or drag it onto the Toggle Between Windows button on the Toolbar.)

Extra tab. Drag and drop a component from the Components folder in the Extra tab.

Site Extras tab of Palette. With Components selected from the popup menu in the lower right of the Site Extras tab of the Palette, drag a component onto the page.

CyberObjects placeholder. Drag the Component icon from the CyberObjects tab of the Palette. Use Point & Shoot to connect the placeholder to an item in the Components folder of the Extra tab.

Figure 21-15
Dragging component onto a page

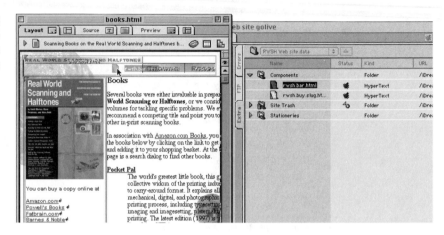

Tip: Why Use CyberObjects Component

At first, we were a little perplexed as to why GoLive includes a Component icon on the CyberObjects tab when all of our components already existed in the nearby Site Extras tab. After all, who needs a blank component?

Designers working within large teams, that's who. On big projects, it's not uncommon for one person to build separate pages that reference an object (like a navigation bar) being built by another team member. Using the CyberObjects Component lets you point to a blank file that will soon become an actual object without having to go back and re-assign the link later. As soon as the component is ready, GoLive can update the entire site to reflect the new element.

Component Code in the Page

Components are inserted distinctively into a page both visually in the Layout Editor and Layout Preview, and textually into the HTML.

Visually, a component appears as a dotted outline around its contents, with a green triangle in the upper left corner (see Figure 21-16).

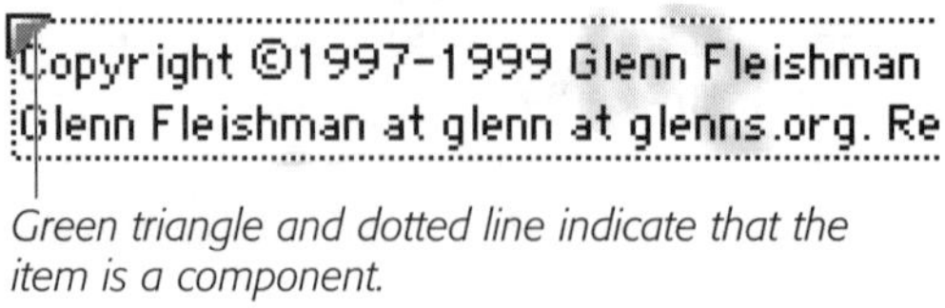

Figure 21-16
Visual indicators of a component in Layout Editor

Copyright ©1997–1999 Glenn Fleishman
Glenn Fleishman at glenn at glenns.org. Re

Green triangle and dotted line indicate that the item is a component.

In the HTML, GoLive inserts CSOBJ, an HTML tag used only by GoLive. This tag's attributes contain the path to the source component file on the local hard drive, as well as dimensions of the component and other details. The full HTML of the component follows with any header tags like Html or Head stripped out, and it ends with a close tag or </CSOBJ> (see Figure 21-17).

(We introduce a neat trick in Chapter 20, *Importing a Site*, that describes how you can fool GoLive into thinking you've inserted components throughout a site

Figure 21-17
HTML for a
component on
a page

```
<p><csobj w="569" h="30" t="Component" csref="../../Glenns%20Web%20Site.
data/Components/copyright.html" occur="0"><font face="Geneva,Helvetica,Arial,Swiss,
SunSans-Regular" size="1">Copyright &copy;1997-1999 Glenn Fleishman except as noted
otherwise. All rights reserved. For permission to reprint, contact Glenn Fleishman at glenn
at glenns.org. Replace the &quot;at&quot; with an @.</font></csobj></p>
```

The CSOBJ container has information used by
GoLive to display and source the component.

using Find & Replace to refurbish an older site—or even a newer one that has repeated elements that aren't components. See "Turning Repeated Elements into
Components," in that chapter.)

Tip: CSOBJ   The CSOBJ tag refers to the previous name of the software, CyberStudio.

Tip: Getting   GoLive inserts a set of CSOBJ tags every time a component appears on a page. Site
Rid of CSOBJ   validators can gag on these tags, and they aren't the prettiest HTML. You can remove
Tags When   them by exporting your site with the CyberStudio Tags box checked (click More in the
Uploading   Export site window). However, the exported site is now sans components, and open-
                        ing it up in GoLive shows the component's text inserted into each page, not a com-
                        ponent reference. (See "Export Site," earlier in this chapter, for more information.)

URL Mappings

The GoLive designers put in an advanced feature for managing Web sites that have
content which may be located on more than one machine, but are linked together.
For instance, a corporate site might have different sites for different products, divi-
sions, or cities, but they could be managed by the same Webmaster or Web team.
Or, you might locate your most commonly updated HTML files on one server behind a slow connection and your larger and less frequently changed image and
media files on another server that offers higher speed retrieval.

GoLive uses URL Mapping to let you set up separate site files for each of these
linked sites, and then connect them together using aliases (Mac) or shortcuts
(Windows). When adding links between these sites, the program correctly sets up
the local links. However, to use URL Mappings correctly, you cannot simply upload your files to a server; you must use the Export Site feature so that GoLive can
correctly rewrite the URLs as they exported.

Tip: Don't   If these descriptions don't match your purposes, stop reading right now. Really, stop.
Read This   This makes our heads hurt to explain, so imagine how you'll feel unless you really
Section   need this feature.

Setting Up URL Mapping

To enable URL Mapping, you need to first locate the two or more site folders that
you want to link together. Create an alias (Mac) or shortcut (Windows) to either

the root level of the site folder, if you need to the entire site, or just create pointers for individual folders as needed. Drag these folders into the appropriate location of each site that needs to relate to the first site (see Figure 21-18).

Figure 21-18
Simplified
notion of
cross-linking
sites using URL
Mapping

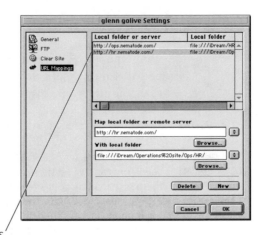

*The Human Resources (HR) site
has an alias from the Operations
(Ops) site and vice-versa which
have been manually mapped to
their fully qualified URLs in settings.*

You can now add URL mappings in Site settings under the URL Mapping pane. Click Browse under Map Local Folder or Remote Server to find the folder for the other site; or, you can enter a fully qualified URL so that when the site is exported, GoLive maps the local alias to its full, correct URL. Under With Local Folder, select the linked folder (such as Ops in the HR site in the figure above) that should be rewritten on export.

Tip: **Automatic** **Addition**	If you check URL Mappings for Alias Folders Map in the Site pane of the Preferences dialog box, GoLive can automatically build mappings for any aliases that you've already added. The program prompts you to update all open sites; click OK to add the mappings to the site's settings.
Tip: **Macintosh** **Crashes**	The 4.0 release of GoLive for Macintosh consistently crashes when we attempt to set up URL mapping. This may be fixed in a subsequent release by the time you read this. However, don't be surprised if following these instructions results in GoLive quitting without warning and without storing any changes you made to preferences.

A Very Special Site

The features described in this chapter are a bag of tricks that you pull out again and again to solve problems or build sites better. Don't mistake this chapter's position for its level of importance.

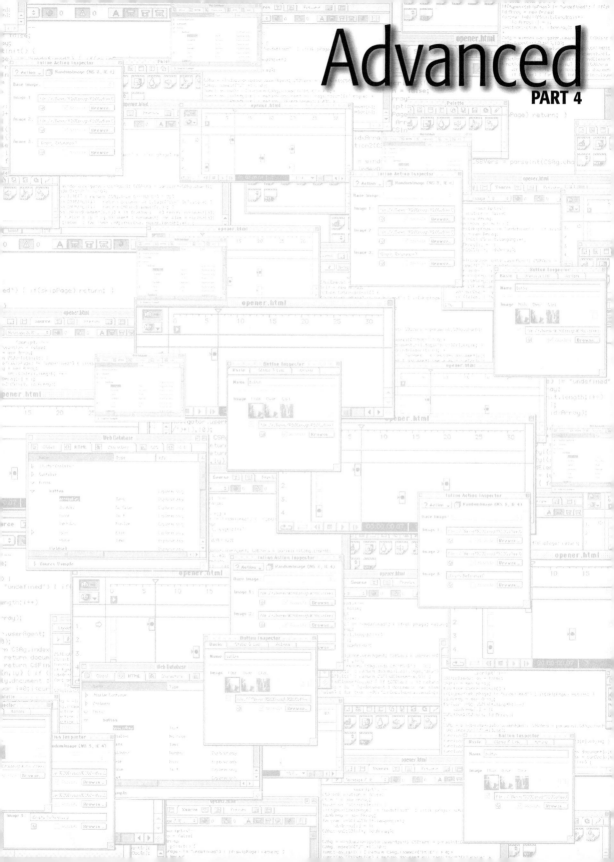

Advanced
PART 4

CHAPTER 22

Advanced Features

GoLive appears to have no end of features, and the more you learn about the program, the more it seems you need—or want—to learn about how to use it more effectively.

In this part of the book, we cover the most difficult-to-learn parts of GoLive, most of which involve a greater knowledge of general Web protocols and standards. GoLive insulates you from the real nitty-gritty, providing a friendly interface that lets you manipulate sophisticated controls behind the scenes. But we'll try both to introduce you to the GoLive approach and to show you what's behind the curtain, so you can twist the dials and knobs yourself.

The chapters that follow provide an introduction and an inside look at:

- **JavaScript:** scripting tips in GoLive's tools

- **Animation:** animating objects on a page with Dynamic HTML

- **Actions:** explain how best to use GoLive's built-in Actions for handling complex coding behavior

- **Web Database:** custom tweaking for more control over underlying HTML and its simulated browser previews when creating pages in GoLive

- **Cascading Style Sheets:** how to create a single, consistent source for text formatting across a page or an entire site

- **Plug-ins and Media:** working with QuickTime, Flash, Acrobat PDF, XML, ASP, and other media types and coding languages within GoLive

Other Advanced Features

This chapter covers a few advanced features that don't fit neatly into other categories, but they certainly go beyond the kinds of tasks that a user doing page layout and site management might encounter on a regular basis.

We cover three advanced features:

- **Regular Expression Find and Replace:** performing complex pattern-based search and replace across a page or site

- **Macros:** shortcuts for inserting longer runs of text into one of three source editors

- **Modules:** managing the extensions or plug-ins that give GoLive some extra oomph or just built-in oomph

Regular Expression Find and Replace

GoLive has a powerful text-handling feature built right into it that's normally found only in the most advanced text editors: regular-expression pattern matching, also called "regexp" for short, and known as "grep" (global regular-expression pattern-matching) in the Unix world.

Regular expressions are wildcard patterns which can match a variety of text that meets their parameters, instead of just an exact run of text. For instance, you could find all tags in an HTML file by specifying a pattern that begins with a less-than sign (<), is followed by any text except a greater-than sign (>), and then ends with a greater-than sign.

The other half of finding is replacing: once you've found a pattern, you can insert parts of what's found in the replacement, so you can make selective changes throughout a document automatically. Let's say that you want to change every instance of bold text in an HTML page to italic text. You could search for <B> followed by any set of text and ending with </B>. You could then replace that everywhere it occurs with <I>, any set of text, </I> with a single command. (You could also break this down into two separate searches, but why do something twice when once is just as easy?)

You activate regular-expression pattern matching by bringing up the Find feature, selecting the Find & Replace tab, and checking the Regular Expr. box (see Figure 22-1).

Tip: Ignore Case Still an Option

Ignore Case still applies to regular expressions, so check or uncheck this as applicable; for HTML tags, you should almost always leave it checked. GoLive creates consistently formatted tags per the Web Database's Global tab setting, so if you're working with a page that hasn't had a GoLive treatment applied—that is, it hasn't been opened, modified, and saved—Ignore Case is even more important.

Figure 22-1
Find & Replace
tab with
Regular Expr.
checked

Tip:
Prefabricated
Expressions GoLive's developers provide a set of prefabricated regular expressions in the Prefer-
ences dialog box's Find pane under Regular Expr. settings (see Figure 22-2). You can
select these items from the popup menus to the right of the Find and Replace fields.
The names that appear in the menus are assigned in the Regular Expr. settings
Name column. You can add your own common expressions here, as well.

Figure 22-2
Find pane's
Regular Expr.
settings

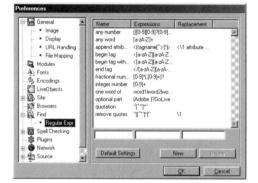

*Items in the
Regular Expr.
settings show up
in the popup
menus to the
right of the Find
and Replace
fields with the
names assigned
to them.*

Find

The Find field with Regular Expr. checked offers more versatility than a standard
search. In the Find field, you can enter any of a series of wildcards that define characters or selections.

Wildcards are one of four types:

- Number of characters to be selected

- Specification of characters or ranges of characters, or a pattern

- Optional selection

- Start or end of line

Reserved Characters

To specify characters that might be part of the following items that have special
meaning ("reserved characters"), you put a backslash or \ in front of them. So, for
instance, if you want to search for "http://www.phlegmatic.com/", you'd enter in
the Find field:

```
http\:\/\/www\.phlegmatic\.com\/
```

This takes a little getting used to, but the missing backslash is almost always the reason for a failed search.

Although < and > and : don't appear to be reserved, we've occasionally found problems searching on them. So just to be on the safe side, we often put a backslash in front of punctuation. GoLive treats backslash plus any character as that character, so adding a backslash doesn't introduce new problems.

Number of Characters

Three symbols control the amount of text selected: the asterisk, the plus sign, and the question mark (*, +, and ?). Let's introduce these first, and then show examples below under "Pattern" where they make more sense.

Asterisk. An asterisk matches *zero* or more instances of the preceding character or characters in a pattern. (The GoLive manual says using this option also keeps the program from showing an error if there's no match.)

Plus sign. A plus sign matches *one* or more instances of the preceding character or characters in a pattern.

Question mark. A question mark makes the preceding character optional. If you precede the question mark with text enclosed in parentheses, the entire text in parentheses is optional.

Pattern

GoLive offers a pretty wide set of character selectors for creating patterns. These include selecting any single character, any character in a specified range or set, any character *not* in a specified range or set, and special selectors that choose all digits, all white space, only returns, and the like.

Period. Entering a period selects any single character. For instance, finding for

```
peters.n
```

matches "peterson" and "petersen" but also "petersbn". To find a run of zero or more instances of any character, you use the very simple expedient of adding an asterisk, as in

```
peters.*
```

which in this example would find "peterson" as well as "petersburg".

Square brackets. You can insert any characters or a range of characters inside square brackets—[and]—to select a range of text that matches only the characters in the square brackets. If you don't put a +, *, or ? after it, it finds just one character that's inside the brackets. Finding for

```
peters[eo]n
```

matches *only* "peterson" or "petersen".

Negative square brackets. If you put a caret (^) at the start of text inside square brackets, GoLive finds only characters that aren't found in the square brackets. This can be useful for trying to find everything up until a terminator. For instance, if you find for

```
<[^>]+>
```

GoLive matches just the interior of a tag. The "[^>]+" means, "match everything *except* a greater-than sign," so the pattern matches everything in the interior until it reaches the closing greater-than sign.

Special matches. GoLive also offers a number of special selectors that correspond to any digit, any white space (tab or space characters), any link break, any tab, and many of their negations (see Table 22-1).

Character	Description
\d	Matches any digit
\D	Matches anything but a digit
\w	Matches any alphabetic character, uppercase or lowercase (i.e., A-Z or a-z)
\W	Matches anything but alphabetic characters
\s	Matches white space, which in GoLive is just tabs or spaces
\S	Matches anything but white space
\r	In the HTML Source Editor, matches line breaks, regardless of platform
\t	In the HTML Source Editor, matches tabs used for indentation
\x00 - \xff	For characters that you can't enter from the keyboard, you can enter their base 16 or hexadecimal value to match them. This is rarely needed in GoLive.

Table 22-1
Special
matches

Optional Selection

GoLive offers two ways to indicate whether a pattern or range of characters is optional when identifying a match.

Vertical bar. The vertical bar or | lets you specify a set of possible matches. For instance, if you wanted to match either the Src or Href attributes in order to change the items they link to, you could find for

```
(HREF|SRC)\=\"
```

You only need to enclose choices in parentheses if there is text before or after the matches that isn't part of what you want to look for. If you wanted to search for Real World Adobe GoLive or Real World Adobe InDesign, you would use parentheses like this

```
Real World Adobe (InDesign|GoLive)
```

Parentheses. If you enclose text in parentheses and follow it by a question mark, the entire bit in parentheses becomes optional. If you want to find any instance of Ezra Stiles College where folks might have forgotten the Ezra, you would search for

```
(Ezra )?Stiles College
```

Start or End of Line

Two special characters help you identify the start or end of a line: the caret (^) for the start of a line or paragraph and the dollar sign ($) for the end of a line or paragraph. The use varies depending on whether you're in the HTML Source Editor (line based) or the Layout Editor (paragraph based) when searching, or whether you have Source Mode checked or selected when using sitewide Find & Replace.

Replace

Finding may be well and good, but *replacing* is what makes regular expression find and replace so very, very cool. You can specify patterns in the Find field that, each time a match is made, can be inserted into the Replace field to change the contents of the matched text or rearrange it.

If you surround something by parentheses in the Find field, you can insert that text in the Replace field by typing a backslash (\) followed by a number indicating that particular set of parentheses' position in the Find field.

For instance, let's say you want to rearrange tags that nest italic inside of bold to have bold nested inside italic. In the Find field, you'd enter

```
\<b\>\<i\>([^\<]*)\<\/i\>\<\/b\>
```

The ([^\<]*) in the Find field indicates that GoLive should capture for each match all text from that point until the next less-than sign.

In the Replace field, you'd put a much simpler response, as the Replace field doesn't require backslashes in front of reserved characters.

```
<i><b>\1</b></i>
```

The backslashed 1 serves as a placeholder for every match of the Find field.

Although GoLive uses parentheses for three purposes, any use of them creates a backslashed reference. So if you're using parentheses to indicate a choice among options, you still have to consider it when counting. For example, changing the start of an absolute reference would look like this in the Find field:

```
(A|IMG) (SRC|HREF)\=\"\~foobar\/
```

In the Replace field, you'd put

```
\1 \2="~hagar/
```

Practical Example

One of the requests we hear all the time is how to change the attributes inside a table, as you can't apply fonts or other features to a table cell. Using regular expressions, you can perform a search-and-replace operation that can work on every cell in a table.

Change all font settings. If you want to replace every font setting for all table cells, use the following.

```
Find: (\<t)(d|h)([^\>]*\>[^<]*)\<font[^\>]*\>
Repl: \1\2\3<font face="Foodle Bold,Scrumptious Light,Skrull">
```

Remove all font settings. To remove all font settings from all table cells:

```
Find: (\<t)(d|h)([^\>]*\>[^<]*)\<font[^\>]*\>
Repl: \1\2\3
Find: \<\/font\>(\<\/t)(d|h)
Repl: \1\2>
```

Add font settings. You can also add font settings to a table that has none.

```
Find: (\<t)(d|h)\>
Repl: \1\2><font face="nickle,loompha,elephant,sans serif">
Find: (\<\/t)(d|h)
Repl: </font>\1\2>
```

Modules

Most publishing and design programs have a plug-in architecture which allows the company that made the program or third parties to extend the program's features, sometimes even transforming the program into an entirely different animal.

Adobe set up the GoLive application with simple core functionality, while most complex features—from reading GIF files to handling site management—can be turned on and off by toggling modules corresponding to the feature.

Tip: More on Modules   A full run-down on each Modules' functionality appears in Chapter 4, *Preferences and Customizing*.

Tip: Third-Party Modules   As of this writing, we haven't seen third-party modules for GoLive, but it's only a matter of time. Because it appears the program has "hooks" for so many of its core functions, a third-party module could add support for new file formats, create a special kind of site map window, or even add more tabs to existing inspectors.

The settings to control which modules load are in the Preferences dialog box in the Modules pane (see Figure 22-3). Clicking the Show Item Information icon brings up a panel that shows information about each module as you select them in turn. Checking or unchecking the box next to a module turns it on or off the next time you quit and run GoLive.

Figure 22-3
Modules pane

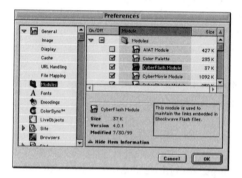

Turning modules off can reduce the amount of memory that GoLive requires and speed up the program. However, it's not ideal to have to turn modules on and off constantly; and, unless you turn off some big chunks, like the Site Module, it may not be worthwhile. Here are a few suggestions of modules you might turn off or on based on your needs.

Default Modules

By default, GoLive loads a core set of standard features. On the Mac, it excludes by default:

- AIAT Module (Internet search engine simulation)
- GL Encodings (Adobe's Mac-based support for Asian language font encoding)
- MacOS Encodings (supports Apple language-encoding modules)

Under Windows, GoLive doesn't load:

- CJK Encodings (Adobe's Windows-based support for Asian language font encoding)
- Standard Encoding (supports other language-encoding modules)

Both platforms exclude by default:

- PNG Image Format (supports reading and writing the PNG image file format)
- WebObjects Module (lets GoLive support the NextStep-based WebObjects coding system)

Media. If you're not planning to edit QuickTime movies or their embedded URLs, you can turn off the CyberMovie Module. Likewise, the CyberFlash Module is needed only for handling Flash objects, and the PDF Module for URLs embedded in PDF files.

AIAT Module. The AIAT Module provides a simulation of how an Internet search engine might index and score pages in your site based on keywords on the pages. See "AIAT" in Appendix A, *Macintosh Issues and Extras.*

PNG Image Format. You only need to turn on the PNG Image Format module on if you expect to use these kinds of images in your site. (For more about this format, see http://realworldgolive.com/png.html.)

WebObjects Module. The WebObjects Module, discussed further in Chapter 28, *Plug-ins and Media*, is only needed if you're using WebObjects to run parts of your Web site. It's nice that GoLive has support for this feature, but it's likely to have an impact for a very small number of users.

Tip: **WebObjects,** **LiveObjects,** **CyberObjects**	These three "Objects" have nothing in common. WebObjects are described above. LiveObjects are called that only once, in the Preferences dialog box, in a panel that sets behavior for the code GoLive writes for Actions. CyberObjects are special nuggets of GoLive-specific code which are inserted by dragging their icons from the CyberObjects tab of the Palette.

Macros

If you spend a lot of time working in one of the three text-editing views—HTML Source Editor, JavaScript Editor, or the WebObjects Editor—you can set up shortcuts or "macros" to insert longer bits of commonly typed text.

Macros have a short name that you type and then press a key combination to transform into the text it's short for. For instance, in the HTML Source Editor, you can type the letter A plus Command-M (Mac) or Control-M (Windows) to insert

```
<A HREF="http://where"></A>
```

with the word "where" highlighted. You can also type "A" and then select Insert Macro from the Special menu.

You can define your own macros by editing the appropriate file in the Text Modules folder in the Modules folder found in the GoLive application's root folder. GoLive has four files in this folder:

- Default.macro holds macros that work in all three editors
- HTML Source.macro for the HTML Source Editor
- JavaScript Source.macro for the JavaScript Editor

- WebObjects Source.macro for those few of you using the WebOjbects declaration editor

Macros consist, one per line, of the macro name and the macro's content surrounded by a unique character or delimiter that defines the start and end of the macro. You can insert marks in the macro that cause text to be highlighted or the cursor to be positioned in a location after GoLive inserts the macro.

For instance, if you wanted to write a macro that would insert a specific fontset in a FONT tag whenever you typed f1, you would enter it into either the HTML Source.macro file or the Default.macro file:

```
f1 «<font face="Geneva,Helvetica,Arial,Swiss,SunSans-Regular"
size="1">»
```

The « and » marks mark the beginning and end of the macro. If you wanted to always type in the SIZE attribute, you'd make a macro like this:

```
f1 «<font face="Geneva,Helvetica,Arial,Swiss,SunSans-Regular"
size="|">»
```

The vertical bar or | indicates that after the macro is inserted, the cursor should be positioned in that location.

The manual devotes several quite exhausive pages to the nomenclature, syntax, and special conditions affecting macros. To avoid too much repetition on a topic covered thoroughly, we suggest you refer to the manual if you think macros would work for you.

Ever Advancing

When someone tells us a particular program fulfills a user's every need, we get skeptical. In the case of GoLive, however, our skepticism has been put aside for the time being. Granted, GoLive probably doesn't do *everything* a designer could want, but it comes pretty darn close.

CHAPTER 23

JavaScript

When you mention the word "programming" to most designers, their eyes glaze over. Programming is something for guys and gals in dark rooms who come into the office at noon or later, and emerge from their hideaways to search for caffeine in the early morning hours. But mention graphical rollovers, form verification, and other nifty tricks that you can do in the browser, and the same designers get excited.

JavaScript, a simple scripting language, can involve programming: defining structured sequences of events that use variable names to control behavior in the browser, adding a lot of low-level, simple interactivity. But GoLive takes a lot of the sting out of JavaScript by providing tools to help make programming simpler, and predefined routines that involve setting values without messing with the underlying code.

In this chapter, we'll talk about the programming part of JavaScript, and how GoLive's tools help you write code and debug it. In the next two chapters, we'll cover GoLive Actions and animation, both of which involve prepackaged JavaScript. Consider this the primer that will help you better understand the whole subject. (If you haven't used JavaScript before, see the sidebar, "Learning JavaScript," before reading this chapter.)

Browser Support

Netscape invented JavaScript (originally calling it "LiveScript" before jumping on the Java bandwagon); it has virtually nothing to do with Java aside from marketing hype. Netscape's browsers all support JavaScript to varying degrees.

Microsoft also found JavaScript to be quite useful, including support for what they call "JScript" since version 3.0 of Internet Explorer. Netscape and Microsoft jointly submitted the JavaScript specification to ECMA, a European technical standards body, to review and maintain as an open standard. You may sometimes run across the strange sounding name "ECMA Script" which refers to the ratified standard version of JavaScript.

Microsoft also employs JavaScript on the server side—in scripts that run remotely on a Web server to carry out tasks—as one of the scripting languages supported by Active Server Pages (ASPs) for server-side scripting. Netscape uses it as well with their server software.

Unfortunately, the JavaScript road has a few potholes to look out for. Although it ostensibly works across browsers (Navigator and Internet Explorer) and across platforms (Mac, Windows, and Unix), different browser versions on different platforms support different versions of JavaScript (see Table 23-1).

And while both Netscape and Microsoft include JavaScript in their browsers, each has added their own extensions to the standardized version. This mandates testing all your JavaScript in as many different browsers as possible to ensure that it actually works. Many times, we've written simple scripts and watched them break on one browser, even as they work on seven others. It is possible for a skilled

Learning JavaScript

This chapter isn't intended to teach you JavaScript, but rather to teach you how to use JavaScript most efficiently in GoLive while taking advantage of GoLive's graphical interface and JavaScript-management features.

If you already know JavaScript, terms like "handler," "procedure," and "variable" shouldn't frighten you. If those terms make you clutch your head and moan, we can recommend some resources for learning JavaScript before getting started.

If you've never touched a programming language before, there are classes and books designed to introduce programming basics using JavaScript's constructs. It's also not a hard language to learn if you've ever written in BASIC, Visual Basic, Fortran, Pascal, or C; you'll pick it up in hours.

JavaScript's popularity has helped create a huge number of excellent books available to help teach yourself the language.

For new users, we recommend *JavaScript for the World Wide Web: Visual QuickStart Guide*, available from—you guessed it!—Peachpit Press. Authors Tom Negrino and Dori Smith assume no previous programming experience on the reader's part. They also include many example scripts that you can use as recipes to put directly into your pages.

Many Web sites also offer excellent tips and tutorials, as well as ready to use cut-and-paste scripts.

Netscape DevEdge: http://devedge.netscape.com/

Web Review: http://www.webreview.com/

Devshed: http://www.devshed.com/

Webreference.com: http://www.webreference.com

You can find links to these sites as well as to buying the book online or from your local bookstore at http://realworldgolive.com/javascript.html.

scripter to write JavaScript code to work around this problem, so that browsers capable of handling the script simply run it while browsers that can't are unaffected.

Using JavaScript in GoLive

If you've decided to take the plunge and learn JavaScript, or if you're already an experienced scripter, you're all set. GoLive provides excellent support for adding scripts to your pages. There are three typical ways to work with JavaScript in GoLive.

*   Using GoLive's built-in JavaScript and DHTML Actions
*   Writing scripts by hand using GoLive's Script Editor
*   Typing scripts directly into the HTML source code

Why Not Actions?

You may be asking yourself, "Why should I slave away writing my scripts by hand if GoLive can do it for me with Actions?" While GoLive's built-in Actions can save

Client-Side versus Server-Side Scripting

You often hear the terms "client-side" and "server-side" bandied about when talk of scripting languages, Java, and Web server CGI (Common Gateway Interface) scripting comes up.

Client-side scripts or programs run on your computer. That is, the script is downloaded—usually as part of the HTML page in the case of JavaScript—and then your machine executes the instructions in the program. Generally, this is as simple as a browser monitoring your mouse movements, so that when your mouse passes over an image, the browser executes a program that swaps out a different image while your mouse is hovering. The advantage of client-side programming is speed and flexibility; your machine doesn't need to contact another computer over the Internet or a company's intranet to carry out a task.

In server-side scripting or programming, the software runs remotely on a server. For instance, when you enter data in a form on a browser and

then click submit, your browser sends all that data to a server. The server runs a program that examines the data and sends a response back to your server. In a case like this, you're sending data that the server processes and stores or performs some action with, like adding your name to a mailing list.

Where this gets confusing is that JavaScript, Java, and other programming languages can be both client-side and server-side, but not simultaneously. Some servers use JavaScript programs (usually found client-side) to process form submissions.

Where the action happens is key. In client-side programs, like JavaScript in HTML, your computer executes the program and produces results locally; with server-side programs, you have to send data to a server, have it run a program, and then get fed the response. Often, the bandwidth required to repeatedly pass basic data between a client and server can overshadow the utility of the software existing on the server's machine.

Table 23-1
Browser
support for
JavaScript

Netscape Navigator browser version	Platform	JavaScript version
2.0	PC & Mac	1.0
3.0	PC & Mac	1.1
4.0+	PC & Mac	1.2

Microsoft Internet Explorer browser version	Platform	Roughly equivalent JavaScript version
3.0	PC	1.0
3.1	Mac	1.1
4.0+	PC & Mac	1.1 plus extensions*

*Each platform features slightly different support for this version of JavaScript.

time by giving you drag-and-drop functionality, there are major advantages to rolling your own scripts.

- JavaScript that is written by hand is almost always smaller and more efficient than that created by GoLive's Actions.

- The built-in Actions don't give you many options for dealing with multiple browsers and platforms.

- While there are many useful Actions, there are many more things you can do with JavaScript if you learn how to write it yourself.

- Actions can respond to many user events, but JavaScript itself responds to many more events, which you may want to call on to trigger scripts.

- The code that Actions create is very complex and difficult to edit by hand. If other people have to update and maintain the site without the benefit of GoLive, the process becomes excruciating. Also, if someone edits the script by hand, GoLive will no longer recognize it as an Action.

What About VBScript and ASPs?

What about other client-side scripting languages like Microsoft's VBScript? While GoLive doesn't offer direct support for adding VBScripts to your pages, it won't overwrite them or change them should you choose to type them in directly.

The same is true for ASP code. ASP code gets inserted directly into HTML pages, but it is executed by the server when the page is run—the code isn't downloaded to the user's machine, just the HTML part of the page.

See Chapter 28, *Plug-ins and Media*, for more about ASP support.

- If a page with GoLive Actions is opened in another visual editor, such as Microsoft FrontPage, the JavaScript may be changed and may no longer work properly.

We cover Actions more thoroughly in Chapter 25, *Actions*, where we show you the best way to use these prefab bits.

Adding JavaScript

If you are a JavaScript Jedi Knight, you can simply click the HTML Source Editor tab of the document window and start typing directly into the raw HTML. However, GoLive's built-in scripting environment offers nice features for both the novice and advanced scriptwriter.

Inserting a Script

You can add JavaScripts to either the head or body part of an HTML page. Generally, you insert them in the head part of the page to ensure they load first and are available when event handlers within the body trigger them.

When you add a script in GoLive, the program handles all the housekeeping tasks for you, like inserting a Script tag and comment tags into the HTML to surround the script.

GoLive offers a Script Editor that lets you enter and modify body and head JavaScripts (see Figure 23-1). The Script Editor has a corresponding JavaScript Inspector, discussed at length in this chapter, which lets you choose JavaScript actions, objects, and versions.

Tip: You Only Need One Script

You can get by with creating a single head script that contains all your JavaScript code. GoLive supports multiple scripts so that you can use different versions of JavaScript in each script, or even different scripting languages, such as Microsoft's Jscript.

Figure 23-1
Script Editor

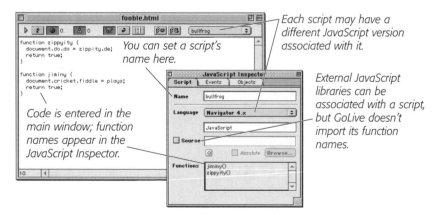

Each script may have a different JavaScript version associated with it.

You can set a script's name here.

Code is entered in the main window; function names appear in the JavaScript Inspector.

External JavaScript libraries can be associated with a script, but GoLive doesn't import its function names.

Adding a head script. Click the JavaScript "coffee bean" button at the top of the Layout Editor, which opens the Script Editor. Click the New Script Item button to add a new head script. GoLive names it "Head Script 1" by default, but you can modify its name in the JavaScript Inspector.

You can also click the Toggle Head Section triangle in the head part of the Layout Editor, select the newly created JavaScript, and use the Head Script Inspector to name it (see Figure 23-2).

Figure 23-2
Head Script
Inspector used
with the Head
Section

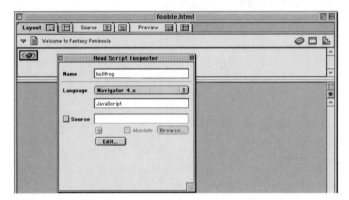

Adding a body script. If, for some reason, you need to insert a JavaScript in the page's body, drag the JavaScript icon from the Basic tab of the Palette and drop it anywhere in the body of your page, but preferably before any event handler that needs to use it. The Inspector palette becomes the Body Script Inspector, and it allows you to name the script and specify a target browser and JavaScript version.

After creating a body script, you can use the Script Editor to edit the script. Select its name from the Select Script menu at the top of the Script Editor (see Figure 23-3).

Choosing a Browser and Language Version

When you create a GoLive head or body script, one of the choices in the corresponding Inspector palette is for Language. The Language menu lists several browser versions. When you choose a browser, GoLive automatically places that browser's version or "flavor" of JavaScript in the text box below the menu and adds the same text to the "Language" attribute of the Script tag. This should prevent a browser that doesn't support the specified level of JavaScript from executing the script.

GoLive tries to help you further by displaying in the JavaScript Inspector's Events and Objects tabs only those items that are supported by the browser version you specified and any later version. So, if you choose to target Navigator 2.0, for example, you don't see the Image object in the object list because that feature was not supported until Navigator 3.0. (See Figure 23-4 for version-specific events.)

Figure 23-3
Editing a body
script

A body script can be edited through the Script Editor by double-clicking it.

The script can be named and controlled through the JavaScript Inspector just like a head script.

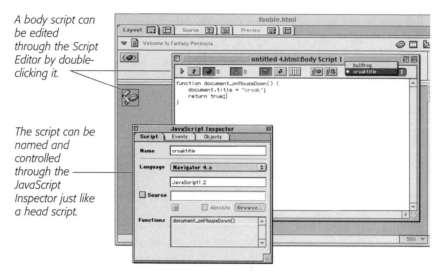

Figure 23-4
Events which
differ by
JavaScript
version

Netscape 3 (JavaScript 1.1) events for a submit button at left; Netscape 4 (JavaScript 1.2) events at right.

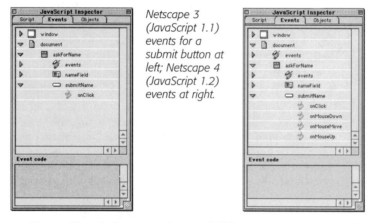

The problem is there are substantial differences among various browsers' definitions of "JavaScript 1.1," or "JScript," especially from platform to platform. And GoLive's method of blocking browsers still allows errors through. If the Script tag says "JavaScript1.2" and the page is viewed in a 3.0 browser, the browser generates a "Function not defined" error when an event handler calls a function, because the browser ignores the head script containing the function, but not the event handler that calls the function.

We prefer adding JavaScript code that checks the browser version and exits without an action, if the browser is too old to do what we want it to. You can force GoLive to write a generic JavaScript language setting by deleting the number following JavaScript in the text field below the Language menu (see Figure 23-5). This will allow all browsers that support any version of JavaScript to use event handlers without error, and your script can decide how to cope with them.

Figure 23-5
Setting
Language to
generic
JavaScript

Delete the 1.2 here to make this script work in any version of JavaScript.

JavaScript Events and the Events Tab

Events are actions initiated by the user or by JavaScript itself that occur in the browser window. This includes a mouse click, the browser loading a page, or even the cursor passing over an object (a "mouseover"). All JavaScripts are triggered by events.

For an event to trigger a script, you add an "event handler" that gets inserted into an HTML tag. The Events tab of the JavaScript Inspector displays a hierarchical list of all the HTML objects on the page that can have event handlers attached to them. Clicking the arrows next to these objects displays all the events they support. Clicking the event lets you enter the name of a JavaScript function in the text box below that gets inserted into the event handler (see Figure 23-6).

Tip: Event Handlers Associate Objects with JavaScripts The event handler associates a given JavaScript function—a self-contained piece of JavaScript—with an action occurring in connection with an object. For instance, you can specify a graphical rollover by attaching a "mouseover" event handler to an image. When a user moves their cursor over the image, this event handler gets triggered, and calls a JavaScript that swaps out the first image with another image.

External JavaScripts

If you're going to use the same JavaScript on more than one page, you can put it in a single file instead of repeating it on each Web page.

Create a text file with ".js" at the end of the file name—the JavaScript extension that Web servers and browsers recognize—and place your JavaScripts in it. You can create your JavaScripts as a head script to use GoLive's JavaScript syntax and editing tools and then copy and paste the contents of it into the .js file. (You can use NotePad or SimpleText to create the .js file.)

To include that JavaScript file, create a new, blank head script in the Script Editor. Set your language and other options in the JavaScript Inspector. Check the Source box and use the Browse dialog or Point-and-Shoot to link to your .js file. GoLive does not show the functions available in this external file; you'll have to make a note of them to enter them into event handlers.

Not all browsers that support JavaScript also support external script files, so be careful to test your pages before creating scripts this way. To bring the script back into the page, copy and paste it from the external file into a blank head script.

Figure 23-6
Events tab

Clicking this event allows you to enter a function under Event Code—in this case, flamingcarrot(x,y)—called when a key is pressed.

You can also drag and drop an event from the Inspector into your code in the Script Editor. GoLive automatically creates a new, empty function, and adds an event handler to the object with a call to the newly created function.

JavaScript Objects and the Objects Tab

JavaScript views the browser window, the page loaded within it, and everything on the page—such as images, links, and form elements—as a collection of objects that it can retrieve information about and manipulate. This group of objects is referred to as the Document Object Model (DOM) and is structured in a hierarchical tree so that individual objects can be targeted by scripts. Think of the object reference as the item's address within the browser's neighborhood.

The Objects tab of the JavaScript Inspector displays a complete catalog of objects supported by the currently targeted browser—displayed in the same hierarchical order as the DOM—including any properties and methods that can be accessed by scripts (see Figure 23-7).

By expanding the list, you can display any specific object on the page and drag and drop it into the Script Editor to add the object reference to your script. You can choose to reference the object by name (if you've given the object a name within the HTML) or by index number, which GoLive displays. The index number changes as you insert or remove objects that appear earlier than the item in the page.

Figure 23-7
Document
Object Model
(DOM)

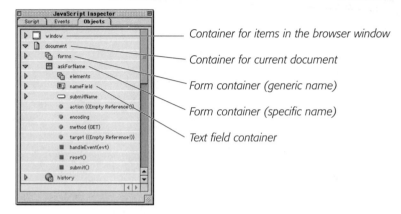

Container for items in the browser window

Container for current document

Form container (generic name)

Form container (specific name)

Text field container

Tip: Naming Form Elements   One reason we suggest naming form elements, like text entry boxes, back in Chapter 13, *Forms*, is to use those names in JavaScript. The mnemonic device of having a name associated with a form element makes it easier to conceptualize how you're working with the element, rather than remember that it is element 12 in the form (see Figure 23-8). Also, if you add or remove form elements, the index number changes; the name stays the same.

Figure 23-8
Form elements
by number
and name

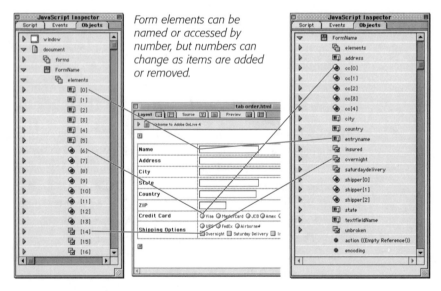

Form elements can be named or accessed by number, but numbers can change as items are added or removed.

Example: The Button Rollover

The best way to illustrate how to take advantage of GoLive's script-editing features is to demonstrate by example. In this case, let's create a version of the popular button highlight or button rollover script. We say "a version" because there are many ways of writing the code to achieve this effect; this is just the way we've found to be most efficient and easy to maintain.

First, click the "coffee-bean" icon at the top of the Layout Editor to open the Script Editor. Click the New Script Item button to create a new head script. This first part of the code preloads the button images so they are stored in the browser's cache, ready to appear instantly. This also stores the images as objects that you can use later within functions.

```
if (document.images){
    buttonOn = new Image()
    buttonOn.src = "images/buttonOver.gif"
    buttonOff = new Image()
    buttonOff.src = "images/button.gif"
}
```

Notice we're enclosing this part of the script within an "if" statement. By testing to see if the "images" object exists for this browser, we can determine if the script will run properly. This is a simpler and more foolproof way of making sure the script is blocked from browsers that can't handle it than actually checking the browser version and platform. We include this object-checking step in the functions below for the same reasons.

Now we create two functions to perform the actual switching of the image: one to highlight the button when the cursor enters the image, and one to switch it back when the cursor leaves. We send the name of the image as an argument to the function and store it in "imageName" so the function knows which image on the page to change. Now, we can use these same two functions for any buttons we want to add later.

```
function highLightOn(imageName){
    if (document.images){
        document [imageName].src = eval(imageName + "On.src")
    }
}

function highLightOff(imageName){
    if (document.images){
        document [imageName].src = eval(imageName +
"Off.src")
    }
}
```

Be sure to click the Check Syntax button at the top of the Script Editor to make sure you haven't left out any brackets or parentheses.

Finally, we need to add the event handlers to the button image to trigger the functions. Click the Events tab of the JavaScript Inspector and find the link object that holds the URL for our button. We use the link object because the actual image object itself doesn't support events. Click the arrow next to the link object and choose "onmouseover". Type the function call in the text area below the event list:

```
hiLightOn('button')
```

Then call our other function from the "onmouseout" event handler in the same way.

```
hiLightOff('button')
```

That's it! Since GoLive's Layout Preview won't actually display the working JavaScript, click the Show in Browser button to see your script in action.

To add more buttons to the page, just preload the graphics for both button states using the same object-naming convention as the first button: button-NameOn and buttonNameOff. Be sure to name the buttons within the HTML, then add the event handlers to call the "highLightOn" and "highLightOff" functions, sending the button name as an argument.

Compare the script we just wrote with the code the GoLive creates to accomplish the same thing via an Action (see Figure 23-9).

As you can see, the handwritten script is much shorter and therefore more efficient, and has the added benefit of working in more browsers while avoiding error messages.

Example: Simple Form Validation

Here's a case in which GoLive Actions lack a trigger that you might commonly use to check what a user has entered in a form before the contents of the form are submitted to the server for processing. This is the "onSubmit" event.

This script checks to make sure the user has filled out a required field before submitting a form. By warning the user before sending the submission to the server, you can save them some time and reduce the load on the server. To keep things simple, we'll use a form with just one field to check (see Figure 23-10).

Syntax Check

The Script Editor Syntax Check is not actually a bug check. Syntax checking confirms that punctuation, spelling, and commands all make sense in the context of the programming language. A misspelled word or a missing parenthesis results in a syntax error.

While a syntax check catches most common mistakes, it won't determine whether a script actually runs in a browser. (There is a deep computer science theory called "the halting problem" that describes why it's hard to write a program that can check another program for whether it will actually run or not; checking for proper syntax is as close as you can get most of the time.)

Remember to test in every browser and platform the visitors of your site might be expected to use. For most sites, this means every version of Navigator and Internet Explorer since 3.0, and the Opera browser latest releases. (Opera is a JavaScript-capable browser that has become ever-more popular among Internet adepts.)

Figure 23-9
GoLive Action
versus
hand coded
JavaScript

The Action code written by GoLive

Handwritten code

Figure 23-10
Simple form

To make objects easier to keep track of, you may want to give the form a name; this way, you can use the name in the script rather than the less descriptive index number.

Like the button rollover example, this script goes in the Head Section of the page. Click the JavaScript coffee bean icon at the top of the Layout Editor to bring up the Script Editor. Click the New Script Item button to create a new header script.

Since this particular script is compatible with any browser that supports even the lowest level of JavaScript, choose Netscape 2.0 as the target browser in the JavaScript Inspector.

Start a new function and give it a name.

```
function nameCheck(){
    if (
```

Use the Objects tab of the JavaScript Inspector to get the object reference for the text field we want to check. Within the Objects list find the form that contains the text field and click the triangles to display the "name" field. Drag and drop the field object "value" reference into the script (see Figure 23-11).

Figure 23-11
Inserting the property into the script

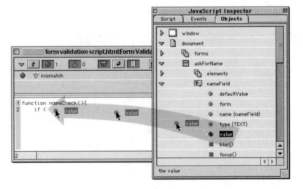

```
function nameCheck(){
    if (document.askForName.nameField.value
```

To check to see if anything has been entered in the "name" field, look to see if the value of the field is empty, indicated by two quotation marks with no space be-

tween them. If nothing has been entered, we pop an alert for the user asking them
to fill in the form. The script also returns "false," which, for the "onSubmit" handler, keeps the browser from sending the contents to the server (see Figure 23-12).

```
function nameCheck(){
    if (document.askForName.nameField.value == ""){
        alert("Please fill in your name before
            submitting the form")
        return false
    }
    return true
}
```

Figure 23-12
Alert on empty
text field when
submitting

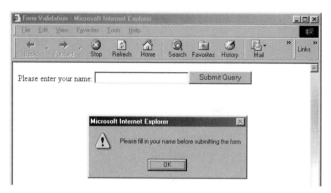

If there is something in the field, the script returns "true," which the browser
interprets as "send the contents of the form to the server for processing."

You now need to add the event handler to call this function. In the Events tab
of the JavaScript Inspector click the triangle next to the form object to display its
events. Select the "onSubmit" event and type in the text window below.

```
return nameCheck()
```

The "return" indicates that we want the function to give us back a true or false
response. If we get "true," the event continues to execute normally; if "false," the
event is terminated and nothing is sent to the server.

One more bit of script you need to add ensures there is nothing in the "name"
field when the page loads. With some browsers, the first field in a form is automatically given a value of "undefined," which cannot be tested for with a script. So, add
another function that makes sure the field is preset to "nothing" (two quotation
marks with no space between them).

```
function setField(){
    document.askForName.nameField.value = ""
}
```

Then, call the function with the onLoad event within the Body tag (which is part of the Window object). As before, this happens in the Events tab of the JavaScript Inspector (see Figure 23-13).

```
setField()
```

Again, use the Syntax Check button to check for errors and test the page in multiple browsers to make sure it works properly.

Figure 23-13
Setting a
function to
prefill a field
with a blank
when the page
loads

The Future of JavaScript

Since JavaScript has proven to be so useful and easy to learn, you can be assured that any effort you put into learning to script will not be wasted. In fact, most Web developers now consider knowing JavaScript to be as essential a skill as knowing HTML itself.

As we take a look at Dynamic HTML—which both browser vendors tout as the future of client-side Web development—in the following chapters, you see that DHTML is really nothing more than JavaScript combined with the positioning capabilities of Cascading Style Sheets. And, as XML becomes more important, JavaScript will be playing a role there, too.

With its wide support and continuing development, JavaScript isn't going away any time soon.

Animation

It's a rare day when Netscape and Microsoft agree on something—anything—so when both companies decided that Dynamic HTML (or DHTML) would be the wave of the future for Web site design, and they incorporated DHTML features into the 4.0 versions of their browsers, most designers took a long, hard look. Unfortunately, most came away somewhat frustrated, disappointed, and confused.

DHTML was supposed to be a simple but powerful way to add certain multimedia features to Web pages that would work across platforms, and wouldn't require plug-ins such as Java, Shockwave, and ActiveX. DHTML would be easy to use; appear and run consistently under Windows, Mac OS, and Unix; and be based on open standards.

But designers' confusion arose from the marketing hype. DHTML sounded like an entirely new animal, when it was actually a patchwork made from many parts, some new and some old. Much like a fax machine was originally the odd union of a slow modem, a cheap scanner, and a bad printer, DHTML joins some new JavaScript features with existing HTML and Cascading Style Sheets positioning to create a whole that is a bit greater than its parts.

This realization brought disappointment. The frustration? There were no tools to easily write the extremely complex sequences of JavaScript that provide exact positioning control over time to move items around or attach animation-like features to a page. Enter GoLive, stage right.

The DHTML Promise

By bringing positioning and scripting together to provide time-based animation controls within the browser, designers have substantially more control over the layout and interactivity of their pages. DHTML lets a designer specify the absolute position of text and images; provides dynamic control over font size, style, leading, and kerning; and allows the animation of elements on the page by moving them along a path or hiding and showing them. You can even change the size and position of the browser window itself.

This sounds wonderful, and it actually is, but as we saw with JavaScript, there's no such thing as smooth sailing when it comes to Web standards.

First of all, DHTML requires a version 4.0 or later browser to work, and (naturally) Microsoft's and Netscape's versions of DHTML are not the same. Much of Netscape's version relies on the proprietary Layer tag extension to HTML, an extension that Microsoft chose not to implement, and the World Wide Web Consortium (W3C) chose not to ratify as a standard. The W3C opted for the absolute positioning already built into the first Cascading Style Sheets (CSS) version, CSS1 (see Chapter 26, *Cascading Style Sheets*).

Tip: Ignoring Netscape's LAYER Tag	GoLive's solution for getting around the cross-browser issue is to ignore the Netscape Layer tag completely and employ CSS Div tags to define independently-layered page elements, which are represented in GoLive as floating boxes (see Chapter 12, *Layout Grids and Floating Boxes*).

Fortunately, both browsers' implementation of DHTML overlap enough that you can often create DHTML that works well in both. GoLive takes advantage of these similarities in its built-in DHTML animation timelines, which is fortunate, since writing DHTML—especially cross-browser animation—can be complex and time consuming.

In Chapter 23, *JavaScript*, we say that writing your own JavaScripts often results in smaller, more efficient pages. However, in the case of DHTML animation, having a WYSIWYG tool that can write the code for you is truly a godsend (and once you take a look at the code required, we're sure you'll agree).

Although the GoLive manual lumps animation and Actions together under the heading of DHTML, we think that there are two distinct kinds of DHTML inside GoLive: animation, in which you're moving objects around a page using floating boxes; and Actions, which are prefab, complex JavaScripts that handle a variety of tasks, like writing a cookie to a browser, or displaying a different image each day of the week.

This chapter covers DHTML animation; Chapter 25 addresses GoLive Actions.

Floating Boxes and Timetracks

GoLive employs two interface elements to let you create and control animation: floating boxes contain the elements you want to animate, and timelines (called Timetracks in GoLive) control their speed and timing.

By placing any content—images, text, form elements, even plug-ins or Java applets—into a floating box, GoLive lets you dynamically control its visibility and its absolute or relative position within the window. You can also animate the box's content by moving it from point to point or along a path.

You can trigger animation automatically when a page loads, set a timer to delay it, run it once, have it loop, or give control to the viewer through mouse clicks and mouseovers. (For a refresher on floating boxes, see Chapter 12, *Layout Grids and Floating Boxes*.)

**Tip: Only 4.0
Browsers
Know
DHTML**

GoLive may do a remarkably good job of dealing with the different implementations of DHTML, but all this slick animation only plays back in the 4.0 and higher browsers. Users with older browsers see nothing. Be sure your audience has a browser advanced enough to display all your hard work before you spend a lot of time and effort building it into all your pages.

Alternatively, you can create two different versions of your pages and use the Browser Switch Action to send viewers to one or the other based on their browser version (see Chapter 25, *Actions*).

Bring up the Timeline Editor by clicking its icon at the top right of the Layout Editor (see Figure 24-1). When you open the Timeline Editor all the floating boxes on the page are automatically listed by number in the order you added them to the page. Each floating box has its own Timetrack which allows you to animate each box independently. An arrow next to a Timetrack indicates which floating box is currently selected.

Figure 24-1
Timeline Editor

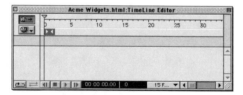

**Tip: Action
Track**

Above standard Timetracks, you'll see a gray bar, which is the Action Track. This Timetrack allows you to choose Actions that are triggered at a given point in time while an animation is playing. The Action Track is explained at the end of this chapter.

The keyframe is the "key" to controlling animation. If you've worked with animation or video-editing applications such as Adobe Premiere or After Effects, or Macromedia Flash or Director, you're already familiar with the concept of keyframes. If you haven't, keyframes may be a little intimidating at first.

A keyframe is a marker on the Timetrack that tells GoLive you want your floating box to be at a certain position on the page at a given time. As you add keyframes and move the box to different locations, GoLive automatically determines the path of the box between keyframes (this is called "tweening" or "interpolation"). The greater the distance between keyframes, the longer it takes the box to move between the two positions. Keyframes can also be used to control more static properties of floating boxes such as visibility and layering order.

Setting Keyframes

Keyframes are set by moving the floating box to a new location and Command-clicking (Mac) or Control-clicking (Windows) the Timetrack at the point in time you want the box to be in that position or option-dragging an existing keyframe to the new time (see Figure 24-2). You can change the settings of a keyframe by selecting it and moving the floating box or by choosing new position, visibility, path shape, and/or relative layer depth settings in the Floating Box Inspector. Also, dragging keyframes closer together or farther apart lets you change the timing between two keyframes in the animation (see Figure 24-3).

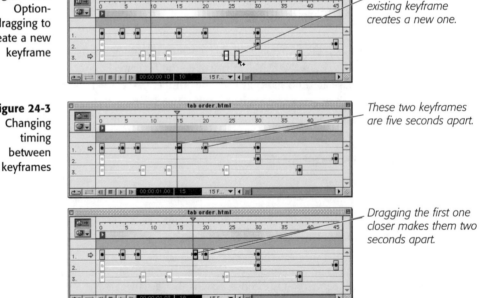

Figure 24-2
Option-dragging to create a new keyframe

Option-dragging an existing keyframe creates a new one.

Figure 24-3
Changing timing between keyframes

These two keyframes are five seconds apart.

Dragging the first one closer makes them two seconds apart.

At the top of the Timeline Editor is a time scale with numbers and tickmarks. Each tickmark indicates a frame of animation. By setting the distance between keyframes you can control the number of frames GoLive generates between the different locations of a floating box, thus controlling the smoothness of the animation. Setting the number of frames per second in the frame rate popup menu at the bottom of the Timeline Editor determines the overall choppiness of the animation; more frames means a smoother performance (see Figure 24-4).

Figure 24-4
Frame rate
menu

1 FPS
2 FPS
3 FPS
4 FPS
5 FPS
8 FPS
10 FPS
12 FPS
15 FPS
18 FPS
20 FPS
24 FPS
25 FPS
30 FPS

Tip: Adding Frames Doesn't Affect File Size Unlike animated GIFs, adding frames to a DHTML animation does not increase the file size of the page by more than literally a few bytes. However, moving images—especially large or multiple images—is very processor intensive. Even if you set the frame rate to 30 frames per second, a viewer using an older computer may only see a choppy animation at 5-10 frames per second. Always try to test animations on a computer that is close to the lowest common denominator of your audience.

Floating boxes—GoLive's way of creating CSS Div tags to identify a section of HTML—are covered extensively in Chapter 8, *Layout Grids and Floating Boxes*, but there are a few controls in the Floating Box Inspector used just for animation.

Depth. The Depth field lets you set the layer of a floating box relative to all other floating boxes on the page: the lower the number you enter, the deeper the layer. A floating box with a depth of 1 appears beneath a floating box with a depth of 2 (see Figure 24-5). Each keyframe associated with a floating box can have its own depth setting. This means that you can animate the depth of layers over time, making objects appear in front of or be obscured by other objects.

Visible. The Visible checkbox determines (what else) the visibility of the floating box at any given time during the animation. As with the Depth setting, each keyframe can have its own visibility setting.

Tip: Start with Invisible Floating Boxes It is a good practice to make invisible while the page loads all the floating boxes that you want to animate, and then start the animation when the page has finished loading using the Play Scene Action set to be triggered OnLoad (see "Triggering Actions" in Chapter 25, *Actions*). This helps the animation run as smoothly as possible.

Type. The Type popup menu allows you to select whether the path originating from the keyframe point is sharp and angular (Linear, the default), smooth (Curve), or jittery and shaky (Random). Of course, each keyframe can have its own Type setting, so your animation path can go from a straight line into a smooth curve into a jitterbug routine (see Figure 24-6).

KeyColor. The KeyColor field lets you change the color of the selected keyframe in the Timeline Editor by dragging a color swatch from the Color palette onto the field.

Figure 24-5
Changing the
depth of
objects

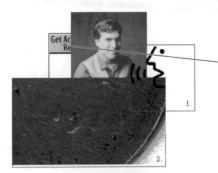

Each of these images is in a separate floating box.

This image has a setting in the Depth field lower than the others.

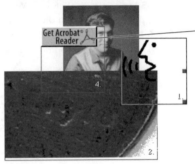

Changing this image's value in the Depth to be higher than all of the other objects places it (and its floating box) on top.

Figure 24-6
Different types
of animation
paths

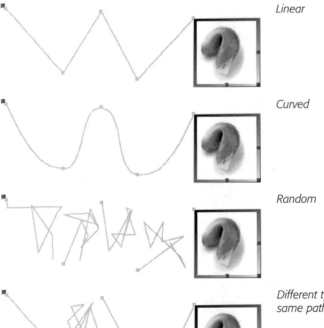

Linear

Curved

Random

Different types mixed on the same path

This feature can help you keep track of which keyframes feature specific events, such as changing layering order or when a floating box enters or exits the page.

Record. The Record button lets you create an animation path and all of its keyframes by dragging the floating box along the path you want it to travel. Position the floating box where you want the animation to begin, click the Record button, and drag the box around the page exactly as you want it to animate (see Figure 24-7). When you're done, click the Record button again to stop recording. The animation path appears in the layout and keyframes show up in the Timeline Editor. After recording, you can adjust a recorded animation just like any other by moving or deleting keyframes or selecting keyframes and moving the floating box.

Figure 24-7
Path using
Record

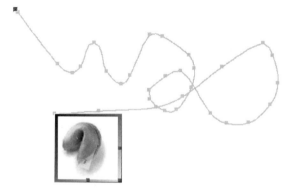

Creating Animations

Building Web elements based on timelines can cause confusion for most "traditional" Web designers, especially if your primary notion of Web time is the long wait while inadequately optimized Web pages load. So, let's run through a few examples.

For our first exercise, we'll create an animation of a company logo flying in from the left and stopping in the upper-right corner of the page. (If you want to follow along with this example, you can download the two logo elements and the HTML page from http://realworldgolive.com/animation.html.)

1. Add a floating box to your layout by dragging over a Floating Box from the Basic tab of the Palette (see Figure 24-8).

2. Drag the logo—either from an image file, the Custom tab of the Palette, or the Files tab—into the floating box. The floating box automatically grows, if necessary, to the dimensions of the image (see Figure 24-9). It doesn't matter where you initially drop the floating box on your page. The position of the top-left corner of the box is always calculated in relation to the upper-left corner of the window.

Figure 24-8
Inserting a
floating box

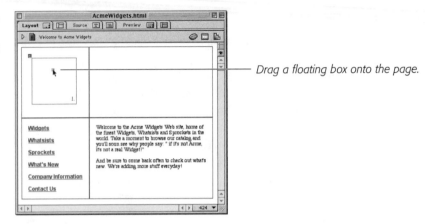

Drag a floating box onto the page.

Figure 24-9
Inserting an
image

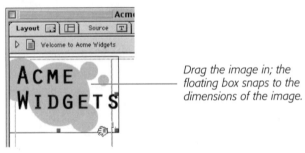

Drag the image in; the
floating box snaps to the
dimensions of the image.

Tip: Floating
Box
Transparency

Since floating boxes are always in front of regular page elements such as text, images, and backgrounds, you may want to make the background of your images in
animated floating boxes transparent for a better effect.

3. Name the floating box to make it easier to track (see Figure 24-10). GoLive au-
tomatically names the floating box "Layer" in the Name field of the Floating
Box Inspector. Enter a new name reflecting its contents; in this case,
"LogoLayer". (GoLive automatically makes the name one word.)

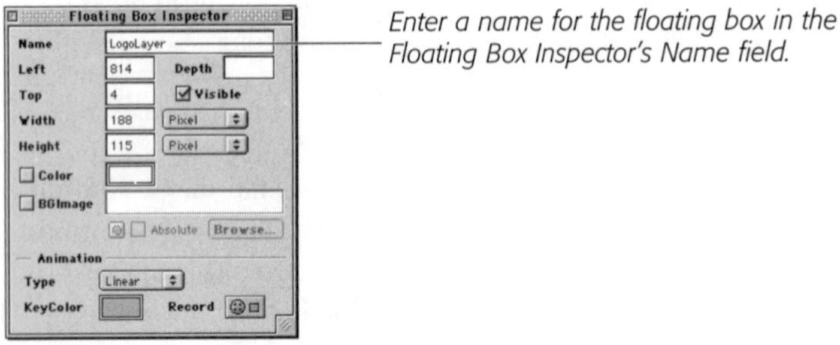

Figure 24-10
Naming a
floating box

Enter a name for the floating box in the
Floating Box Inspector's Name field.

Tip: Selecting the Floating Box

Sometimes it's tricky to know if you've selected a floating box or the image within it. To ensure that you're selecting the floating box, position the cursor so it is hovering over an edge of the box, then click when the cursor changes into a hand (see Figure 24-11). You know you've selected the box if the Inspector palette changes into the Floating Box Inspector. You can also click the small floating box placeholder icon at the upper-left corner of the floating box itself. If you click in the middle of the box, you select its contents, and could accidentally drag the image out of the box.

Figure 24-11
Selecting a floating box

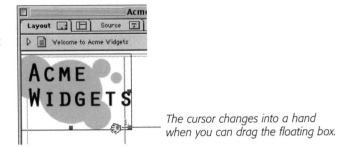

The cursor changes into a hand when you can drag the floating box.

4. Click the Timeline Editor icon at the top of the Layout Editor. This brings up the Timeline Editor with the floating box already included as the first track with the first keyframe inserted and highlighted (see Figure 24-12).

Figure 24-12
Initial Timeline Editor view

First keyframe already inserted and highlighted.

5. Select the first keyframe in the LogoLayer track and position the floating box where you want it to appear in the window at the end of the animation. This approach may seem backwards, but it makes it easier to move the logo in a straight line and have it end up where we want it.

6. To add another keyframe, Command-click (Mac) or Control-click (Windows) anywhere in the LogoLayer track or Option-drag the first keyframe to the point at which you want the animation to end (see Figure 24-13). This creates a keyframe with the logo in exactly the same position as the first keyframe, which is its final position.

7. Move the logo to its starting point. Make sure the first keyframe is selected—it has a bolder outline when selected—and drag the floating box with the logo far enough to the right so it is beyond the monitor size of most of your audience; 1,000 to 1,200 pixels should be plenty (see Figure 24-14). You can track the pixel location in the Left field of the Floating Box Inspector, or you can directly enter a value there.

Figure 24-13
Ending the
animation

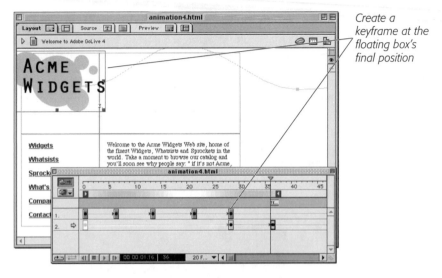

Create a
keyframe at the
floating box's
final position

Figure 24-14
Starting the
animation off
screen

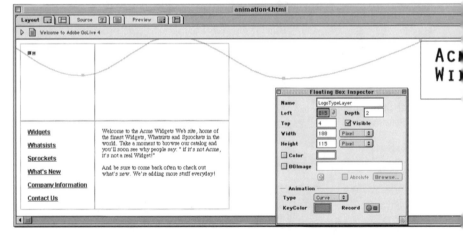

If you move the box by dragging, make sure it's still the same distance from the top of the window as the ending keyframe by clicking each keyframe and checking that each number in the Top field of the Floating Box Inspector is identical.

Tip:
Keyframe
Connectors
in the
Timeline
Editor

You'll note a light gray line in your layout connects the first and second keyframe positions. This is the animation path; the squares at the beginning and end indicate keyframes. When we add more keyframes later on, you'll see that each square on the path corresponds with the box's position at that point in time.

These squares are indicators only and cannot be dragged to edit the keyframe data. You can only change keyframe attributes by dragging keyframes within the Timetrack to change timing, clicking them in the Timetrack and dragging the floating box to a new position, or modifying the values in the Floating Box Inspector.

8. Switch to the Layout Preview tab to preview the animation. To make the movement faster or slower, go back to the Layout Editor (which makes the Timeline Editor reappear) and drag the final keyframe to the left or right; you can also change the Frames per Second setting to change tempo. Experiment until you like the results.

The Time display at the bottom of the Timeline Editor tells you how long your animation is in seconds. Remember, however, that the actual speed and smoothness of the animation depends greatly upon the speed of the viewer's computer.

Tip: Starting Animations after a Page Loads
By default, GoLive sets up an animation to play when your page loads. However, if you uncheck the Play on Load button, you can use an Action to trigger the start of the animation. We cover this later in "Triggering an Action in an Animation."

Throwing Some Curves

To make our animation a little more interesting, let's add some keyframes.

1. Command-click (Mac) or Control-click (Windows) at several points on the Timetrack.

2. Select each of the new keyframes and move the floating box into the new position to create a zigzag effect as the logo moves across the screen (see Figure 24-15).

3. When you preview the animation, the logo follows the new zigzag path. (By first setting up a simple linear animation, it only took a few clicks and mouse movements to dramatically alter the logo's path.)

Figure 24-15
Inserting intermediate keyframes

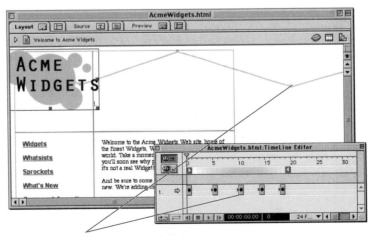

Command-click (Mac) or Control-click (Windows) to add keyframes and then drag the floating box into place.

Changing Multiple Keyframes

By default, GoLive sets each new keyframe with linear motion between it and the next keyframe. To make the animation path curve between two points, instead of following a straight line, select the keyframe and choose Curve from the Type menu in the Floating Box Inspector. You can make the entire path curved, or you can mix curved and linear keyframes. This can have some unexpected results, so you may want to experiment a bit to see what works.

Shift-click each keyframe on the floating box's path or drag a marquee around all of the keyframes, and then select Curve from the Type menu in the Floating Box Inspector. The animation path should now be curvy instead of straight (see Figure 24-16).

Figure 24-16
Curvy path

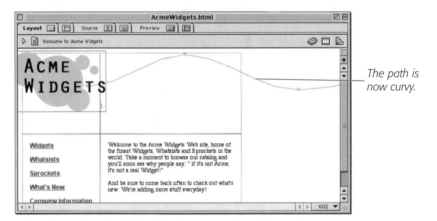

The path is now curvy.

**Tip: Avoid
Random
Motion**   There is another option in the animation menu called Random. This causes the floating box to move in a jittery fashion roughly along the animation path. We don't recommend this feature (unless that's precisely the effect you're looking for) since you really don't have much control over the effect, and we've experienced intermittent browser incompatibilities.

Animating Multiple Elements

Our little logo animation is looking pretty cool now, but what if we want to animate two images independent of each other? To illustrate this, let's split the logo into two graphics: the background shape in one file and the type in another. Each new graphic has a transparent background, so the background rectangles won't cover the images below when we move them (see Figure 24-17).

1. Returning to our original bouncing logo animation, select the original logo graphic and replace it with the image containing just the logo's type. Now we

Figure 24-17
Logo split into
foreground
and
background

Logo foreground

Logo background

have the same animation, but only the logotype bounces into position (see Figure 24-18).

2. To make the background shape drop into position behind the type, add and name a second floating box. This creates a new Timetrack.

3. Both images share the same dimensions and, when placed on top of one another, are registered exactly. The easiest way to align the two elements precisely is to click the last keyframe of the logotype and write down the Left and Top values in the Floating Box Inspector. Then click the first—and only—keyframe of the logo background and type the same values into the two fields (see Figure 24-19).

Figure 24-18
Positioning just
the logo
foreground

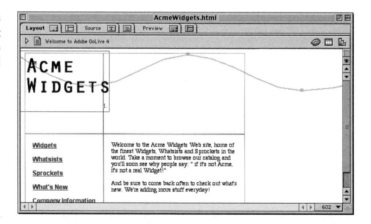

Figure 24-19
Registering
foreground
and
background

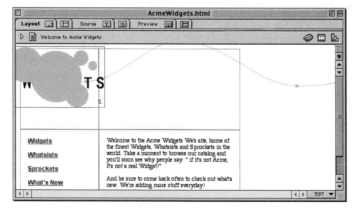

4. Since the background floating box was created last, it is placed in front of the other elements, covering up the logotype box. Move it to the back by setting the Depth value lower than that of the logo box. Remember that each floating box can be its own layer, so a larger Depth value represents a higher layer, also called the Z-Index.

5. Each keyframe can also have its own depth, with the default being the order in which the floating box was created. Make sure the logotype box is always on top. Select all of its keyframes by Shift-clicking them, or dragging a marquee around them, then type 2 into the Depth field.

6. Repeat the procedure to set the logo background's floating box to 1.

Tip: Use Layering to Display Elements   Since keyframes can have independent Depth settings, you can change the depth of a floating box at any time during an animation. This can lead to some interesting effects, such as a moon orbiting a planet using only two graphics and a couple of floating boxes.

Now that the logo background box is behind the logotype, selecting it becomes difficult. This is where the Floating Box controller comes in handy.

1. Choose Floating Box Controller from the Window (Mac) or View (Windows) menu to display a small window listing all the floating boxes on the page by name—another good reason to name your floating boxes mnemonically (see Figure 24-20).

Avoiding Timeline Editor Interface Quirks

There are a few potentially confusing features of the Timeline Editor.

- The direction that the Time Cursor moves—left to right—does not indicate the direction the animated element is moving. For example, in our first animation, the logo moves from right to left while the playback head always moves left to right along the time-elapsed axis.

- The order of the Timetracks in the Timeline Editor does not correspond to the stacking order of the floating boxes, only the order in which they were created. The Floating Box Controller doesn't indicate the stacking order either. The only way to check the stacking order is to select individual keyframes and check the number in the Depth field in the Floating Box Inspector.

- Selecting a keyframe moves the Time Cursor in the Timeline Editor to that keyframe's location, and it selects the floating box that corresponds to it. But the reverse isn't true; selecting a floating box does *not* select any keyframe. If you already have a keyframe selected and then click a floating box, the keyframe remains selected and changes in the Floating Box Inspector corresponding to that keyframe, not the floating box you've clicked.

Figure 24-20
Floating Box
Controller

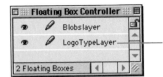

Each layer's name is listed, along with an eyeball to show whether it's visible and a pencil to show whether it's editable.

The Controller identifies the number of floating boxes on the page.

2. Click the eye icon next to the logotype box's name in the Floating Box Controller to make it temporarily invisible, just like Adobe Photoshop's Layers palette. Now we can work with the logo background unencumbered.

Tip:
Invisibility
Applies Only
to GoLive

Making a floating box invisible or locking it in the Floating Box Controller has no effect when the animation is run in a browser. The Controller is just an organizational tool to help you deal with multiple floating boxes while working on the layout or the animation. To control whether a floating box's contents are hidden or shown when a page loads, use the Visible checkbox in the Floating Box Inspector. Also, since each keyframe can have its own Visible setting (just like the Depth setting), you can make a floating box appear and disappear during an animation.

---

3. Add a couple more keyframes to the logo background track to animate it, by Command-clicking (Mac) or Control-clicking (Windows). In this case, because we want it to begin moving after the logotype has stopped, place another keyframe at the same point as the last keyframe of the logotype box.

4. Add one more keyframe about 10 frames later.

5. We want the logo background to begin off the top of the screen, so click the first keyframe and drag its floating box up off the HTML page until it is no longer visible. Make sure that the Left position value is the same as the other keyframes.

6. Drag the second keyframe offscreen to match the first.

7. Make the logotype visible again and preview the animation.

Animation Scenes

What if you want to animate images separately at different times? For example, can you have one element animate when the page loads and another when the user clicks a button? Or, what if, after running our animation, we want to have these same elements move again in an entirely different way on the same page? The answer is "yes," with the use of *animation scenes*.

Think of scenes as somewhat independent Timetracks within the same page that can have a set of shared or separate elements, timing, triggers, and Actions.

With scenes you can have many different animations set up and trigger whenever and however you choose. Let's see how this works by adding a scene to our logo animation.

Setting Up a Second Scene

1. The animation we've already created is called "Scene 1" by default. You can re-name this scene if you choose by selecting Rename Scene from the Scenes menu at the top of the Timeline Editor.

2. Add a new scene by selecting New Scene from the Scenes Menu and give it a name as well, such as "Click Animation". You see a new Timetrack with both floating boxes listed as tracks, but with no keyframes. Our old animation is still there; use the Scenes menu to switch back to see it (see Figure 24-21).

Figure 24-21
Creating a new scene

Our old scene, called LogoScene, is still there.

3. Let's add a little animation that plays when the viewer clicks the logo. To create the animation path this time, we use Record to build a path to match how we move the background image. In Scene 1, select the last keyframe to view both logo graphics in their final positions, then switch back to the Click Animation scene.

4. As before, make the logotype temporarily invisible using the eye icon in the Floating Box Controller.

5. To start recording, select the first keyframe of the logo background track and click the Record button in the Floating Box Inspector.

6. Drag the background floating box to create the animation path; in this case we'll move it in a circle and return it to where it started.

7. Release the floating box to stop recording. GoLive creates a new animation path and a bunch of keyframes (see Figure 24-22).

8. Preview the animation. The Record operation creates normal keyframes, so you can adjust movement or timing just like any other animation.

One adjustment you may want to make is to check the position of the last keyframe to ensure it's the same as the first keyframe, leaving the image back in registration with the logotype. You may also want to delete excess keyframes, as Record creates more than are strictly needed—and the more keyframes, the more browser computation.

Figure 24-22
Recorded path
in new scene

Using an Action to Trigger the Second Scene

Now we have two scenes using the same images that both play when the page loads. This obviously creates a conflict, so we need to make the second scene play when the viewer clicks the logo. To do this, we add an Action to play the scene "onClick" and attach it to the logotype image.

(We add the Action to the logotype and not to the logo background, even though that is the graphic that animates, because the logo background can't be clicked when it's behind the logotype.)

1. Make sure you turn off "Play on Load" for the Click Animation scene at the top of the Timetrack.

2. Select the logotype graphic inside the floating box and add a link to it, but don't worry about linking it to anything. (You can't attach an Action to a floating box, and you have to have a link in order to attach an Action.)

3. Click the Action tab of the Image Inspector and add a Mouse Click trigger.

4. Choose Play Scene from the Multimedia submenu of the Action menu.

5. From the Action configuration options that appear in the inspector, choose Click Animation from the Scenes popup (see Figure 24-23). (Actions are covered in depth in the next chapter, *Actions*.)

6. When you preview the page in a browser you should see the logo animate in the window as before and stop. When you click the logo, the background image should wiggle in a circle back to where it started.

Triggering an Action within an Animation

We've just used an Action to trigger an animation, but you can also use an animation to trigger an Action by using the Action Track, the gray bar at the top of the

Figure 24-23
Selecting an
Action for a
Mouse Click
trigger

Timeline Editor. Assign an Action to a point in time by Command-clicking (Mac) or Control-clicking (Windows) the Action Track at the point in time that you want the Action to be triggered (see Figure 24-24).

To demonstrate, instead of using a Mouse Click to trigger the Click Animation scene, let's make the first scene trigger the next when the first is done playing (see Figure 24-25).

1. Remove the link from the logotype image, which automatically eliminates the Action attached to it.

2. With the Timeline Editor set to display Scene 1, Command-click (Mac) or Control-click (Windows) the Action Track just above the last keyframe of the first scene. The Action Inspector appears.

3. Choose Play Scene from the Actions popup menu under the Multimedia submenu and choose Click Animation from the Scene popup. When the page loads, the first animation sequence runs and then it triggers the second scene automatically.

You can use the Actions track to trigger any of the other Actions as well, such as displaying an alert window at a certain point or playing a sound each time the animation loops.

Figure 24-24
Using the
Action Track

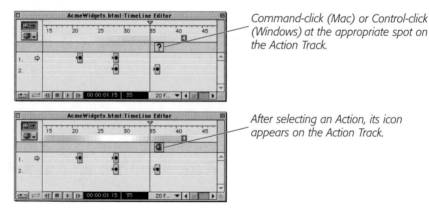

Command-click (Mac) or Control-click (Windows) at the appropriate spot on the Action Track.

After selecting an Action, its icon appears on the Action Track.

Figure 24-25
Triggering a
scene via the
Action Track

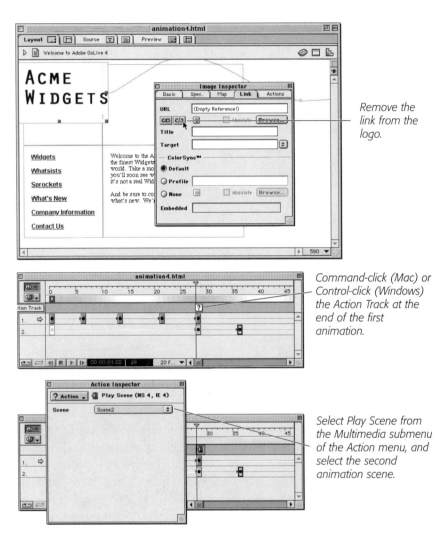

Remove the
link from the
logo.

Command-click (Mac) or
Control-click (Windows)
the Action Track at the
end of the first
animation.

Select Play Scene from
the Multimedia submenu
of the Action menu, and
select the second
animation scene.

The Hard Truth

Just for fun let's take a look at all the code GoLive has been writing in the background for this little animation we've been working with (see Figure 24-26).

Aren't you glad we have a nice, user-friendly visual tool that can write all this for you? Of course, as we said in Chapter 23, *JavaScript*, if you are a savvy scripter, you can write code by hand that is much more compact and efficient. But even if you are savvy enough to hand code, the DHTML animation scripting is complicated enough that the time and effort GoLive saves you is worth the extra overhead.

However, there is another reason we are taking a look at the animation source code. All the code you see has to be downloaded and parsed by the browser before

Figure 24-26
The long, hard
truth of
Actions code.

the page can be displayed, let alone play the animation itself. This translates into a substantially slower browsing experience for your audience, especially if they are using relatively slow modems, older computers, or both.

Although GoLive makes it easy to create DHTML animations, try not to go nuts adding lots of animation all over your pages unless you know that your audience employs a fast network connection. If done in moderation—a little bit here, a little bit there—DHTML animations can add style and impact to your pages.

Actions

Back in the JavaScript chapter, we provided some persuasive reasons why you should hand code your scripts whenever possible. Scripts created "by hand" offer more flexibility and control, and are almost always smaller, more efficient, and carry out their tasks faster. In addition, the scripts generated by GoLive's automated scripting are almost impossible to modify or update without using GoLive; if multiple people are maintaining a site, multiple copies of the software are needed, even if some people don't actually need it for anything else.

But if you're in a hurry and want to assemble prototype pages; if learning anything more complicated than point-and-click might fill your brain with things you don't really want to learn; or if you're in charge of updating your site and you have complete control over which applications to use, then GoLive's built-in JavaScript Actions and CyberObjects make it quick and easy to add functionality and special effects with drag-and-drop ease.

Actions are prefabricated sets of JavaScript and Cascading Style Sheets settings that allow you to just plug in values and let GoLive write and modify the code. Your interface with an Action is through the Actions tab of whichever inspector you're working with. This tab provides you with all the necessary fields and menus to enter numbers, text, or other values specific to each Action.

GoLive comes with a few dozen Actions that encompass a whole range of activities; a few examples include writing a cookie to a user's browser, handling conditions (like "if such-and-such happens, then do this other thing"), and forcing a page to load as the only thing in a window if it finds itself as part of a frameset.

In this chapter, we also talk about CyberObjects, which are like simpler-to-use Actions you insert to include the current date or time, or redirect a user if they're not using a browser you support. CyberObjects also provide GoLive containers for placing Actions in the Head or body section of an HTML page.

Tip: Actions and Browser Compatibility
Most GoLive Actions only work properly in Netscape and Microsoft's 4.0 (or later) browser releases. You can see which browsers each Action is compatible with next to the Action's name in the Action tab. GoLive automatically writes the code so that the JavaScript is hidden from browsers that can't run it. However, this means that users with older browsers see nothing, rather than alternate content which could be displayed if the script were written by an experienced scripter.

The only option GoLive provides for dealing with browser compatibility is a Browser Detection Action that lets you divert users with older browsers to an alternate page. This solution is useful, but it means you must maintain multiple versions for each page containing Actions, adding extra complexity to your site.

Tip: Editing Actions by Hand
If any of the JavaScript code that GoLive Actions creates is modified by hand or by editing the file in another visual editor, GoLive will no longer recognize it as an Action and you won't be able to edit it using the Actions tab of the Inspector palette.

Tip: Installing Actions Plus 1.0
GoLive 4 comes with a free set of extra Actions that the company Adobe bought GoLive from was going to sell as a separate package. Adobe decided to throw in these Actions for free with the 4.0 release, but they're not automatically installed.

On both platforms, the Actions Plus package is added through a separate installer. After running the installer, move the entire folder into a nested location. Find the JScript folder under Modules, and move the Actions Plus folder into the Actions folder (see Figure 25-1). (Later versions of GoLive might allow you to install it in the exact location it belongs in, but as of this writing, you need to relocate the folder.)

CyberObjects

We need to introduce CyberObjects before we talk about GoLive's Actions, as some CyberObjects are needed to use Actions properly. CyberObjects are special GoLive elements that insert or control internal objects (like date- and timestamps), page-based Actions (like inserting an Action into the Head section of an HTML page), and standard Actions. GoLive groups these items together for no particular reason, except that they don't really belong anywhere else, and they are used quite often.

To add these objects to a page, click the CyberObjects tab of the Palette and drag a CyberObject icon into the Layout Editor's body or Head section at the location you want it to appear. The inspector changes to the name of the CyberObject and allows you to set its parameters.

Tip: Testing CyberObjects
Unlike the Actions tab, the CyberObject Inspector does not indicate which browsers the CyberObject works with, so it's critical to test them with multiple browsers.

Internal Objects

GoLive uses two CyberObjects to act as containers for content that the program updates. Neither of them uses JavaScript nor is really an Action.

Figure 25-1
Location of
Actions and
Actions Plus
folders

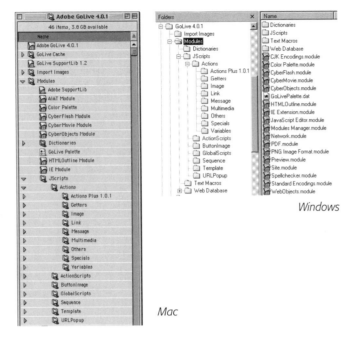

Windows

Mac

Date & Time. Date & Time inserts the current timestamp into a specific location on a page. It's not JavaScript or an Action, but a placeholder that GoLive uses to identify where to insert static text into the HTML each time the page is opened and saved. (No change, other than opening the page, needs to be made for the timestamp to update.)

You can select one of several formats for the date or time, and choose a language/country style from a popup menu (see Figure 25-2).

This CyberObject cannot be accessed or used by other CyberObjects or Actions; it's really just plain text that GoLive itself inserts. When a user views a page with this CyberObject on it, unlike a JavaScript date and time indicator that updates itself, Date & Time is static to the last page saved.

Figure 25-2
Choosing date
and time
formats

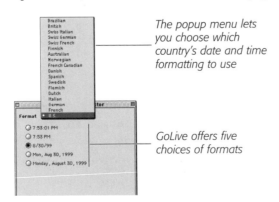

The popup menu lets you choose which country's date and time formatting to use

GoLive offers five choices of formats

**Tip: Weird
Dates and
Times (Mac)** We repeatedly saw a problem in which a string of nonsense characters replaced the date or time for the first three options in the Date & Time Inspector when you selected the same language from its popup menu as your version of Mac OS (such as US English when you're running US English version of Mac OS). The fix for English users was to set the country to any similar language, like British (from the popup menu). This problem was fixed in the 4.0.1 release of GoLive.

Component. The Component CyberObject is a placeholder for inserting a component, a centrally-managed template for a fragment of a page. We cover components and this placeholder thoroughly in Chapter 21, *Site Specials*.

Page Actions

The page-based Action CyberObjects are fully explained later in this chapter under "Triggering Actions." The Inline Action and Action Headitem allow you to insert an Action directly into the Head section or body of a page to trigger Actions based on browser-window activity.

Standard Actions

Browser Switch, Button Image, and URL Popup are essentially identical to any other Action. However, there are limitations to what Actions can support in terms of both previewing and configuration that required these specific Actions to be more heavily integrated into the program itself.

Browser Switch. You can use Browser Switch to detect the browser that loads the page and automatically redirect a user to an alternate page based on their browser, platform, and/or version. If you check the Auto box in the Browser Switch Inspector, GoLive writes the JavaScript code to redirect any browser that can't handle the Actions, animations, or style sheets attached to the current page.

**Tip:
Supporting
Older
Browsers** Browser Switch is the only option to display different content for users with older browsers, if you are not writing JavaScript yourself by hand. Also, 2.0 and older browsers on all platforms ignore the Browser Switch because they don't support the JavaScript necessary to make it work.

Button Image. Button Image is a simple way to create a button that changes its content based on a user action. You can specify the standard image, an image that displays when the user has the cursor over the image, and an image that displays when the user clicks the image. A JavaScript swaps out the image displayed in the browser for another graphic when the specified mouse event occurs.

To use Button Image, create two or three images that have identical dimensions; the browser scales the images to fit if they are not the same dimensions, but this may break the Action in some browsers. You can choose to have this work for mouseovers, mouse clicks, or both. The Button Image Inspector includes three buttons labeled Main, Over, and Click which correspond to the default image, the mouseover image, and the clicked-on image. Click each of these buttons in turn and select the appropriate image (see Figure 25-3).

Figure 25-3
Button
CyberObject
Inspector

The three buttons for Main (no mouse action), Over (when the mouse passes over the image), and Click (when the mouse button is depressed over the image)

You can specify a URL for the button to link to when clicked, or Actions for it to trigger; you can't specify both a regular URL alongside Actions. Button Image also provides a place to enter a message in the Status field of the Inspector palette, that appears at the bottom of the browser window.

You can create these same effects with Actions as well, but since using this one CyberObject can take the place of up to five or six Actions per button it can be much easier to use and set up.

URL Popup. The URL Popup CyberObject provides an easy way to include a popular Web site feature where selecting an item from a popup menu instantly, on releasing the mouse button, loads a new page. You can use the URL Popup Inspector to enter a list of sites, or other pages, on your site. The Detail tab enables you to select whether the new page is loaded in its own new window, or whether it interacts within an existing frameset.

If a user has JavaScript disabled or is using an old browser, selecting an item from the popup menu has no effect; GoLive doesn't include a "Go" button or other submit button coupled with a CGI script that would provide an alternative for older browsers to use this method.

Triggering Actions

Since Actions are made up of JavaScript code, they must be triggered by specific events, such as a mouse click or a page loading. Let's walk through the different categories of event handlers and discuss how to apply them. To apply some of the Actions below, you use items found in the Palette's CyberObjects tab (see Figure 25-4).

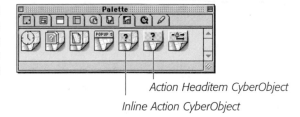

Action Headitem CyberObject

Inline Action CyberObject

Event handlers are attached in one of three general ways: to a page, to text and image links, and to the Timetrack Editor's Action Track. Page-based event handlers trigger Actions from browser-window activity, like loading a page. Text and image link event handlers respond to user activities, such as moving the cursor over an image. Action Track triggers are integrated with the Dynamic HTML (DHTML) Timeline Editor, discussed in Chapter 24, *Animation*. A few JavaScript events available in browsers aren't supported by GoLive.

Page Event Handlers

GoLive offers four ways of triggering Actions to respond to browser-window activity.

- **OnLoad:** when the entire contents of the page have finished loading in the browser window. This is handy for triggering a behavior only when the computer is at rest and has all its resources available.

- **OnUnload:** when the browser begins to access another page. Many adult Web sites use this technique to bring up another window, sometimes in endless succession, to keep users from ever escaping their sites. (Kind of like a Roach Motel with ads for pay-per-view channels.)

- **OnParse:** when the script is read by the browser, but before the rest of the page has loaded. This event handler lets you immediately trigger a behavior, which is useful on longer page loads.

- **OnCall:** when a specific function is called by name. This method allows you to call one function directly from another without nesting function calls.

You can use these events to trigger any arbitrary Action by inserting an Action Headitem or Inline Action from the CyberObjects tab of the Palette.

Drag the Action Headitem to the Head Section of the Layout Editor. In the Action Item Inspector you can choose one of the four events described above, and then select a particular Action and configure it (see Figure 25-5).

If you want to use one of these triggers to insert text into the body of a page, drag an Inline Action into the appropriate location in the page's body. In the Inline Action Inspector, select Document Write from the Action menu's Message submenu (see Figure 25-6); we describe how to configure Document Write in "Message Actions," later in this chapter.

Figure 25-5
Configuring an
Action
Headitem

 — *The four possible triggers you can select from*

Figure 25-6
Configuring an
Inline Action
Inspector

Text and Image Link Event Handlers

Text and Image event handlers are things users do that can be assigned to any range of text, image, or area of an imagemap that has a hyperlink attached to it.

- **Mouse Click:** the mouse button is pressed and released over the object the Action is attached to.

- **Mouse Enter:** the cursor moves over the object the Action is attached to (known as "mouseover" in JavaScript).

- **Mouse Exit:** the cursor leaves the object the Action is attached to (known as "mouseout" in JavaScript).

- **Double Click:** the mouse button is quickly pressed and released twice over the object the Action is attached to.

- **Mouse Down:** when the mouse button is pressed and held over the object the Action is attached to, as if the user were dragging; this is the first half of the Mouse Click.

- **Mouse Up:** when the mouse button, already pressed and held, is released over the object the Action is attached to; this is the second half of the Mouse Click.

- **Key Down:** when any key on the keyboard is pressed.

- **Key Press:** when any key on the keyboard is pressed or held down.

- **Key Up:** when any key on the keyboard is released.

To attach an Action to a linked image, text, or imagemap area, select the object and click the Actions tab of the Inspector palette for that object (see Figure 25-7). A scrolling list of valid events appears under Events. Select the event that is to trig-

Figure 25-7
Assigning an
Action to a link

1. Create a link to an Image

2. Set the border to 0 (zero)

3. Select an Event in the
Actions tab

4. Click + to add an Action

5. Configure the Action

ger the Action and click the "+" button, then choose the Action you want the event to trigger from the Action popup menu and set its options.

You can add multiple events to a link object, and each event can trigger more than one Action. The order that Actions are executed in is set by the order you add them to the event handler. A bullet appears next to each event handler to which an Action is assigned.

Each area on an imagemap can have its own set of event handlers associated with it (see Figure 25-8).

**Tip: Empty
Links for
Actions**   You can get around the limitation of needing a link to assign an Action by linking the text, image, or imagemap region to just #. This tells the browser to link to the current page; when the user clicks the link, the Action is triggered, but a new page isn't loaded. Leaving the link set to "(Empty Reference!)" also works, but causes a link warning.

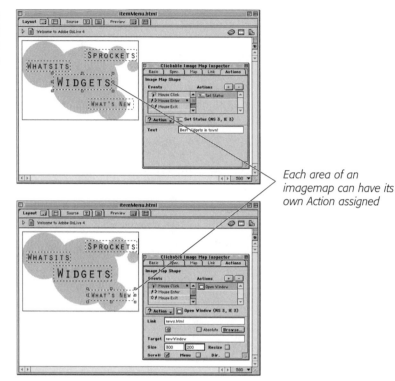

Figure 25-8
Actions and
imagemap
regions

*Each area of an
imagemap can have its
own Action assigned*

Action Track Event Handlers

Actions within an animation are triggered by a timing event controlled by the
Action's position in time on the Action Track in the Timeline Editor. See Chapter
24, *Animation*, for details on triggering Actions within animations.

Unsupported Actions

If you know JavaScript well, you may have noticed that several JavaScript events
are not listed above, including onSubmit, onFocus, onBlur, onChange, onError,
and onSelect. The built-in GoLive Actions don't support these events. If you want
to use them to trigger activities, you have to write the code yourself, inserting the
triggers in the HTML Source Editor.

Configuring Actions

All Actions and their options are configured through the Actions tab; any object that
supports Actions includes this tab in its respective Inspector palette. Each Action has
its own set of text fields, pop-up menus, and buttons which set its parameters.

**Tip: Special
Actions** Some Actions are found only in the CyberObjects tab of the Palette. These CyberObjects are a motley collection of Actions, GoLive features, and placeholders, which we explain in "CyberObjects," earlier in this chapter.

While GoLive makes it easy to apply and configure individual Actions—and the manual does an excellent job explaining the details of every last Action—the tricky part is learning how Actions can interact to combine them to build more complex functionality. The rest of this chapter focuses on this kind of gene splicing.

First, we take a look at all the available Actions, discussing what they do and the best ways to use them. Then, we show examples of using multiple Actions together and setting them up to add some serious capabilities to your pages.

Actions are categorized in GoLive by what they accomplish or the kinds of objects they work with. Getters retrieve something, such as a floating box position or a form value; Link Actions work with links or the contents of pages.

Getters

Getters gather information from the user via HTML forms and store that information in a page-based variable or a browser-stored cookie. Getters also let you detect the position of a floating box within the browser window.

Get Floating Box Position. When triggered by an event, this Action returns the current top-left corner coordinates in pixels of the specified floating box. It can be used with the Condition or Idle Actions to trigger an Action when an animated floating box moves to a certain position.

Get Form Value. Get Form Value retrieves the value or contents of a specific form element (numbers entered in a text box, the chosen item from a pop-up menu, etc.) within a specific form. You can use this Action to retrieve user input to store in a cookie for later use, or to do simple form validation by comparing the form value to a previously-created variable.

Field Entry Indicator

GoLive displays an icon next to many of the fields in an Action tab; click the icon to change the kind of data you enter into the field (see Figure 25-9).

When the red "C" is displayed by default, you must type into the field to set the Action target or value. With some Actions, you can use Point & Shoot to set the value.

When the green question mark is displayed, select an Action from a menu listing all the currently specified Actions. You must first select and configure other Actions before this option is available.

With the blue ball displayed, a menu allows you to select from values that are already defined on the page, such as the name of a form field or variable.

Figure 25-9
Status icons in
the Actions tab

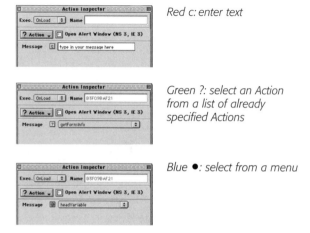

Red c: enter text

*Green ?: select an Action
from a list of already
specified Actions*

Blue ●: select from a menu

Image Actions

The Image Actions let you choose which images are displayed; it also lets you
change them via user events or other Actions.

Preload Image. This Action loads an image into the browser's cache so it can be
displayed quickly when called for by another Action. It's usually used in the Head
section to preload handcoded button rollovers.

Random Image. Random Image randomly switches among three different images.
It can be used to randomize a rollover, or, when placed in-line with the Inline
Action CyberObject and triggered by onParse, it can be used to randomize the
look of the page or the display of banner ads. When it is used to randomly change
an existing image on the page, all three images must have the same dimensions or
the browser distorts the new image to fit the original graphic's area. The base
image must be hyperlinked for the randomizing to work, but this link doesn't have
to connect to anything; you can leave it set to "(Empty Reference!)".

Set Image URL. If you aren't using the Button Image CyberObject, use this Action
to create a classic button rollover effect. You can use this Action with multiple
events—Mouse Enter, Mouse Exit, Mouse Up, Mouse Down, etc.—to create a true
multimedia button. Just remember that each button state must have a corresponding graphic created for it. Use Set Image URL with the Preload Image Action to
make your button image changes more responsive.

   You can use this Action to change any other graphic on the page (not just the
current image) by selecting its name in the Image popup menu. You can do this at
the same time you highlight the button on Mouse Enter, or independently, such as
on Mouse Click.

Link Actions

These Actions control links within a page and the contents of the browser window or frameset.

Go Last Page. This Action reads the browser history—or which pages the user has visited—and sends a user to the one previously viewed, creating a true Back button.

Goto Link. When triggered, this Action sends the user to a specified URL, either local or external. It can be used in the Actions track of an animation to send the user to another page at a specific point in time along the Timetrack.

Navigate History. You can use Navigate History to create a link that takes the user forward or backward within the browser history; it can also jump more than one page at a time.

Open Window. This Action lets you open a new browser window, specify the HTML page to display in the window, specify the name of the window in the title-bar, and declare its size and whether to display scroll bars, menu bar, directory buttons, status bar, tool bar, location field, and resize handles.

Daily Redirect. When you want to direct users to a page based on the day of the week, use Daily Redirect. It can be applied to the header to always display a different page or to a link object to change the link daily.

Daily Image URL. To change an image based on the day of the week, use this Action.

Time Redirect. This action redirects the user to a different HTML page based on the time of day on the user's computer.

Force Frame. If another site attempts to link to an individual page on your site that is normally viewed within a frameset, this Action loads the frameset with the linked page in the correct frame. This Action helps you put a page back into context when a user follows a link to the contents of a frame, such as from a search engine results page. Search engines, like Excite or Lycos, often index the pages that make up a framed page, but you don't want users to load that sub-page without the rest of the framed content. If your site navigation or even a company name exists in its own frame, as is common, the user would have no way to get to the rest of your site.

Kill Frame. If another site attempts to hijack your page and display it within their own frameset, this action reloads the current page in a frameless browser window.

Target Two Frames. This Action allows one link to change pages in two different frames at the same time. For example, if you have a frame that contains a navigation bar listing options as well as a frame that contains some actual content, like one of the items in the navigation bar, you might want to design it so that the navigation bar presents different options when the user moves to a different section of the site. With this Action, the user can click a link and the Action can change both the navigation bar frame and the content frame.

Password. Password allows you to protect pages on your site by using an encrypted password hidden in the JavaScript. Although the password is encrypted, this control doesn't prevent a slightly knowledgeable person from getting past it because JavaScript can be turned off and circumvented.

Target Remote. Used with the Open Window Action, this Action allows a user to click a link in one named window and have changes appear in another named window.

Confirm Link. This Action opens a dialog box with OK and Cancel buttons as well as any message you want to display. If the user clicks OK, the browser continues on to the linked page. This allows you to ask the user a yes or no question, such as, "Are you sure you want to leave this site?" and give them the option of canceling the link.

Message Actions

These Actions let you communicate directly with users through HTML within the page, the text in the status bar, and dialog boxes.

Document Write. Used with the Inline Action CyberObject, this Action allows you to display customized HTML when the page loads. It is used in-line and triggered when parsed because HTML cannot be written to the page once it has finish loading. The HTML displayed may come from a variable, another Action, or text you type yourself.

Open Alert Window. This Action opens a dialog box displaying a message, which the user can dismiss by clicking the OK button. Since every browser displays this dialog box differently, the only control you have over how it looks is the text (see Figure 25-10).

Set Status. The Set Status Action lets you create a message at the bottom of the browser window in the status bar (see Figure 25-11). It's usually used in conjunc-

Figure 25-10
Alert dialog
box in
different
browsers

Mac Netscape Navigator

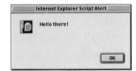

Mac Internet Explorer

Figure 25-11
Status bar

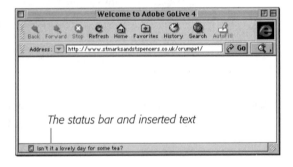

tion with the Mouse Enter event attached to a button to give the visitor a better idea of where the link takes them.

Multimedia Actions

The Multimedia Actions deal with controlling floating boxes and animation (see Chapter 24, *Animation*).

Drag Floating Box. This Action lets a user drag a specified floating box. Unfortunately, the box's outline and contents are not visible while it is being dragged.

Flip Move. When triggered, Flip Move moves a floating box from one absolute position to another; when triggered again, the box moves back to original position.

Move By. When triggered, Move By moves a floating box a specified distance from its last position.

Move To. When triggered, this Action moves a floating box to an absolute position in the browser window from wherever it is on the page.

Play Scene. This Action triggers a DHTML animation timeline.

Play Sound. This Action directs a specified plug-in to play a sound. The plug-in must have the ability to respond to JavaScript; check the plug-in's documentation to discover if it is compatible or not.

ShowHide. ShowHide toggles a floating box's visibility.

Stop Complete. This Action stops all DHTML animation currently running on the page. It's polite to give the viewer the option to stop animation on a page, to keep it from transitioning from entertaining to annoying. Or, you can stop an animation automatically after a certain time has passed using the Condition Action.

Stop Scene. You can choose to stop a specific DHTML animation scene with this Action.

Stop Sound. This Action directs a specified plug-in to stop playing sound. The plug-in must support JavaScript events; see Play Sound above.

Wipe Transition. Wipe Transition lets you use a "wipe" style of transition when hiding or showing a floating box. It's used with the ShowHide Action.

Slide Show. This Action creates a slide show that a user can move through by clicking a button image or text link. All the graphics must have the same dimensions or the browser will distort them to fit the area of the first image.

Slide Show Auto. You can run a slide show through its images automatically using this Action. As with Slide Show, all the graphics must have the same dimensions or the browser distorts them to fit.

Slide Show Auto Stop. You can use this Action along with the Slide Show Auto Action to let the visitor pause and continue the slide show. This Action can be attached to a button image or text link.

Others

The Others Actions mostly act on the browser window itself.

Netscape CSS Fix. A Netscape 4 bug causes pages to lose most of their Cascading Style Sheet (CSS) formatting information when the window is resized. This occurs because Netscape reparses the page's HTML when the window is resized, without taking into account CSS. To be safe you should add Netscape CSS Fix to every page that includes Style Sheets.

Resize Window. This Action changes the size of the current window.

Scroll Down, Scroll Left, Scroll Right, and Scroll Up. This set of Actions scrolls the window down, left, right, or up by an amount in pixels at a speed you specify.

Set BackColor. Set BackColor changes the current window's background color. You can't change the background image using this Action, but you can use a floating box as a background and change it using the Set Image URL Action.

Specials

Action Group. The Action Group is a container that lets you group a set of Actions to be triggered together.

Call Action. If you need to trigger an Action stored in the Head section of the page with the Head Action CyberObject, use Call Action.

Call Function. For hand-coded JavaScripts, use Call Function to trigger a function within a custom-coded JavaScript. This feature allows you to write custom functions using the JavaScript editor for behavior not available in an Action while integrating this custom feature with Actions to speed up the development process.

Condition. This Action tests to see if two floating boxes are intersecting, if a specified key is being pressed, if a certain amount of time has passed, or if a variable matches a value such as true or false. You can trigger one Action if the condition is true and a different Action—or no Action at all—if the condition is false. Using Condition Action with the Get Form Value Action validates form input before sending it off to the server for processing.

Idle. When placed in the Head Section of the Layout Editor, the Idle Action can be set to wait either until two floating boxes are intersecting (usually used with the Drag Floating Box Action) or a specified amount of time has passed. You can specify an Action to trigger when the condition has occurred, as well as an Action to trigger continuously if the condition is false. You can also set the Idle Action to continue even after the condition has been met or stop after the first time it tests true. However, you cannot stop the Idle Action once it is set in motion; you have to wait until after the condition is met and then only if you previously set it to stop. Once stopped, it can be restarted using Call Action.

The Condition Action and the Idle action differ in how they search for behavior to trigger their events. The Condition Action is triggered directly when you test whether something is true or false in the moment; it also covers a wider range of conditions. The Idle Action runs continuously in the background for a limited range of behaviors, and only when a condition is met can it trigger an Action.

Variables

A variable is a container that lets you store text or numbers for use in other Actions. For example, you can ask a visitor what their favorite color is and store it as a variable using the Get Form Value Action. Then you can use that variable to change the background color of the page using the Set Back Color Action. In order to use a variable, you must first create and name it using the Declare Variable Action.

One shortcoming of variables is that the browser can't remember them from page to page; they only work within Actions called on the same page that the variable was created or modified on. The only way around this limitation is to store the variable's value in a cookie, a small bit of text that a Web server or JavaScript can ask a browser to store on the user's hard drive. Cookies can be named and can contain up to 4,096 characters of alphanumeric data (letters, numbers, and punctuation).

You can also assign an expiration date to a cookie, so that you can retrieve the stored value or update it for a fixed period of time. That might be an hour from when you set it, a week later, or even 10 years later (though the odds that someone will be using the same browser in 10 years is too small to measure even with the most advanced computers).

Cookies are stored for a specific site, and a browser reveals a cookie only when it returns to a page at the site for which the cookie was originally stored. Most cookies are set to be available on every page in the site. You update cookies by writing new values to them, which replace any value stored.

Declare Variable. This Action creates a new variable; it can be stored in an existing cookie using Write Cookie.

Init Variable. Set the initial value of a variable with Init Variable.

Read Cookie. Get information stored in a cookie specified by name with Read Cookie.

Set Variable. Store a value in a variable with this Action.

Write Cookie. Write Cookie creates a cookie on the user's computer with a name and expiration time (in hours) that you specify. It also lets you specify to which pages on the site the browser reveals the cookie to; most of the time, you should set this to "/" to let the cookie be revealed on any page on the site.

Visitor Cookie. You can use Visitor Cookie to mark that a user has been to your site. After the first visit, the Action reads the cookie that notes that the user has been there before, and redirects the browser to another page that you choose. This lets you display a welcoming splash screen to first time visitors, and then take them directly to the real main page when they come back.

Delete Cookie. To get rid of a cookie, use Delete Cookie. It sets the cookie's expiration date to the current time.

Combining Actions

Actions don't do much by themselves; creating a variable or retrieving the position of a floating box may be interesting, but it certainly isn't useful unless you apply that information. The trick to unlocking the power of Actions is to create a group that works together to accomplish a task. Here are three examples to get you started thinking about how to use Actions for real-world solutions. (Download the source materials for these examples from http://realworldgolive/actions.html.)

Rotating Banner Ads

Actions used: *Idle/Timeout, Random Image*

This first example randomly changes an image on the page—in this case a banner ad—at set time intervals.

At the top of your example page, place a banner ad that is randomly replaced. For the Actions to work, the image has to have a name; select the image and enter "bannerAd" in the Name field in the Image Inspector's Special tab (see Figure 25-12). The item's name has nothing to do with forms—which is what the section is labeled—but it's where GoLive groups the item.

This Action needs to start running as soon as the page loads, so insert an Action HeadItem from the CyberObjects palette, drop it into the Head section of the layout window, and bring up the Action HeadItem Inspector (see Figure 25-13).

Choose Onload from the Exec menu to trigger the Action as soon as the entire page has downloaded. Select Idle from the Action menu under the Specials submenu. We want the banner to change every 30 seconds, so make sure Exit Idle If Condition Returns "True" is *not* checked, and, in the Condition tab, choose Timeout from the Specials submenu of the Actions menu. There is only one op-

Figure 25-12
Naming the
image

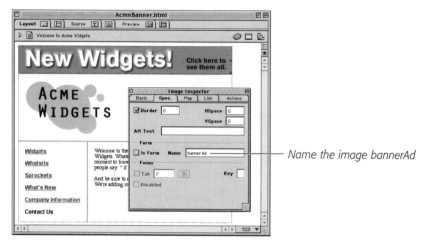

— Name the image bannerAd

Figure 25-13
Adding an
Action
Headitem

Drag an Action Headitem
into the Head section

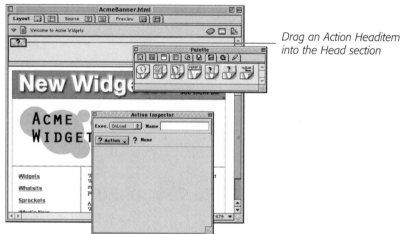

tion to set for Timeout, the length of time to wait in seconds; enter 30 in the Timeout field (see Figure 25-14).

After 30 seconds pass, the Idle Action triggers the Action specified in the True tab. Select the True tab and then choose Random Image from the Image submenu of the Actions menu. Since you named the banner ad earlier, you can select it in the Base Image menu to target it (see Figure 25-15). All that's left to do now is to specify graphics for the three random image slots (see Figure 25-16).

Save the page and preview it in a browser. If all went as planned, the banner should now change to one of three randomly chosen ads every 30 seconds. Because the images are chosen at random, you might see the same one twice in a row; be patient if it doesn't change after 30 seconds (or change the interval to a shorter period to preview the changes).

Figure 25-14
Setting
timeout

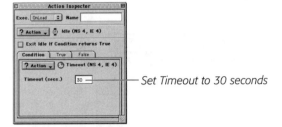

— Set Timeout to 30 seconds

Figure 25-15
Targeting the
banner ad

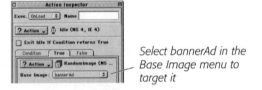

Select bannerAd in the
Base Image menu to
target it

Figure 25-16
Specifying
graphics for
rotation

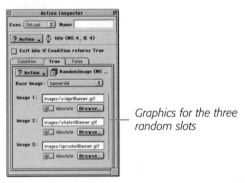

Graphics for the three
random slots

Open a Remote Control Subwindow

Actions used: *Open Window, Target Remote*

This example opens a small subwindow with a menu bar that functions like a remote control, so that when you click a button in the subwindow the browser loads a new page in the main window.

First, create a new page with menu buttons to be linked to other pages on your site. Don't link the buttons just yet (see Figure 25-17).

Add a link or button to your main page layout—for this example, add a text link—that you want visitors to click to open the remote control window (see Figure 25-18). You could also place this Action in the header to automatically open the second window when the page loads.

Select the link and click the Action tab of the Link Inspector. Choose Mouse Click from the Events list and click the Add button. Choose Open Window from the Actions menu's Link submenu. Name the new window "remote" in the Target field and make it 100 by 200 pixels. Uncheck all the display options so that only the status bar is displayed (see Figure 25-19).

Figure 25-17
Creating
remote control
page

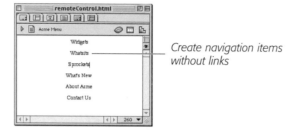

Create navigation items
without links

Figure 25-18
Adding a
remote
control link

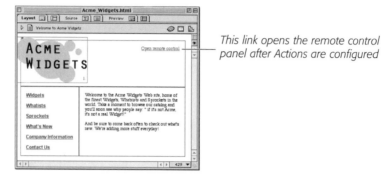

This link opens the remote control
panel after Actions are configured

Figure 25-19
Figure Title

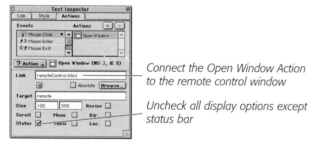

Connect the Open Window Action
to the remote control window

Uncheck all display options except
status bar

Use Point & Shoot navigation or browse to the menu buttons page created earlier to use it as the link page that is displayed in the new window.

Now, to make the buttons in the remote control window functional, open the menu buttons page you created earlier. Select the first button and make it a link. Click the Actions tab of the Image Inspector, add a Mouse Click, and select Target Remote from the Actions menu's Actions Plus 1.0 submenu. (This is one of the Plus Actions, so you have to install the Plus Actions, described earlier in this chapter, before you can use it.)

The Target Remote action automatically targets the original window that opened our new subwindow, so just link to the page we want to display. In this example, we're linking to "widgets.html" (see Figure 25-20). As you can see from the options in the Inspector palette, if the original page contained frames we could also target a frame within that frameset.

Figure 25-20
TargetRemote
from the
Actions Plus
set

*The remote control
targets pages in the
original window using
the TargetRemote Action*

Repeat this last operation with the rest of the menu buttons on the remote control page, then test your new creation in several browsers to see how it works (see Figure 25-21).

Shifting Scripts to an External Library File

If you use Actions, CyberObjects, animations created in the Timeline Editor, or components, you probably employ them on more than one page of your site, especially with popular effects like a mouseover button highlight. Since Actions add a lot of JavaScript code to a page, GoLive offers the option of storing its common JavaScript routines in an external library file that multiple pages in a site can share, without forcing your visitors to download big chunks of script repeatedly.

Pros and Cons of External JavaScript Libraries

You should weigh the pluses and minuses of externalizing your JavaScript code into a library that multiple pages reference.

Benefits:

- Actions and CyberObjects embedded within components won't work properly when viewed in a browser unless you externalize the code using the library.
- Pages load faster since the shared JavaScript only has to download once and it is cached.

Drawbacks:

- GoLive automatically restricts access to the external code to browsers that support JavaScript 1.2 or higher, so even if the Actions you've used are compatible with some 3.0 browsers, the scripts are hidden from them.

- The external file that GoLive creates contains the common code for *every* installed GoLive object that creates JavaScript—Actions, CyberObjects, and animation routines—even if you are only using a single Action. As you may have guessed, this can be huge (as large as 44K if you have all the objects installed); even though it only downloads once, the browser must store it all in memory. This can use up valuable system resources on the visitor's computer.

- Hand editing the code or using another WYSIWYG tool becomes virtually impossible.

Fortunately, the process of externalizing the code is easily reversible, so if you have to, you can bring the JavaScript back into the pages.

Figure 25-21
Window with
remote control

If you choose to do this, GoLive does not move or change any JavaScript that has been added by hand—you have to move that yourself by copying and pasting it into the file that GoLive creates.

To externalize the code of a specific page, bring up the Page Inspector by clicking the Page icon at the top of the Layout Editor, then choose the HTML tab at the top of the Page Inspector. You can select one of two options under JavaScript Functions. The default, Write Code into Page, leaves all the JavaScript in the page. Choosing Import CS Library removes all the Action and CyberObjects scripts from the page, leaving behind only some page-specific parameters and a link to the external code library file. The changes are applied as soon as you save the page.

If you know you want all your code stored externally, you can make Import CS Library the default by selecting Preferences under the Edit menu and clicking LiveObjects. If you have a site open when you change this option, you need to open each existing page and change its Page Inspector setting.

Tip: Rebuild for Actions	The Rebuild button in the LiveObjects pane doesn't rebuild existing pages in a site. It rebuilds the master list of Actions that show up in the Inspector palette's Actions tab after you add a new Action to the appropriate folder.

Building Action-Packed Web Sites

Actions offer enormous help by bundling so many complex features into a few relatively simple-to-use tools. Although actions don't solve every problem or provide an interface to every possible need, they're comprehensive enough to let non-programmers build sophisticated sites, and to let programmers quickly prototype new features without expending the effort to hand code advanced functionality.

Cascading Style Sheets

Early Web designers found frustration in many aspects of HTML's inflexibility. One of the biggest annoyances was having to apply specifications individually to every piece of text to make it look a certain way. Even today, color, font, and style attributes get applied over and over again.

Cascading Style Sheets (CSS) provides a neat end-run around this problem. It allows designers to define their specifications once, in a style sheet, and then apply those specifications to text anywhere on a page or site. Updating the style sheet's specifications changes the appearance of any text tagged with that style sheet the next time the text is viewed in a browser; the text itself is left untouched.

GoLive offers enormous support for virtually every CSS feature, including positioning, font specification, borders, colors, and other, more esoteric, options. GoLive even uses CSS to control floating boxes (see Chapter 12, *Layout Grids and Floating Boxes*), and as part of its Dynamic HTML Animation features described in Chapter 24, *Animation*.

At the end of this chapter, we offer tips for making changes in raw CSS in the HTML Source Editor so you can add codes and features that GoLive does not yet support. If you already understand how style sheets and CSS work, feel free to skip "Style Sheets Backgrounder," and go straight to "Previewing in GoLive."

Tip: CSS1 and CSS2 CSS is a specification proposed by the World Wide Web Consortium (the W3C at http://www.w3c.org) which each Web browser puts its own spin on. The first formal spec was called CSS1, and the latest spec, CSS2, is in wide circulation. Many browsers have picked and chosen from CSS2 features, which we discuss a bit in "Advanced CSS," later in this chapter. GoLive generally provides only CSS1 features, but in cases where the feature described is part of CSS2, we make note of it.

Style Sheets Backgrounder

If you've never used the style sheet features in a word processor or desktop-publishing program, the concept of creating a single definition for text specifications might be foreign. Here's a little background to give you context on their origins and uses.

Ancient Times

Before the digital imaging age, designers could type up a list of specifications—on a typewriter, even—for text they needed typeset for a project, such as a book or brochure. They would write out these "style sheets" defining the font, style, size, paragraph spacing, and other characteristics on a piece of paper with numbers assigned to each style. When a typesetter saw a circled numeral 1, for instance, he or she would refer back to style sheet 1 and carry out its specifications.

This concept carried over into early word processors and page-layout programs (like Microsoft Word and Aldus PageMaker). In every program, the concept is the same: you define the style sheet once in a central location, like a style sheet editor or dialog box, and then select pieces of text and apply a style. The program keeps track of which pieces of text are tagged with which styles.

Changing any part of the style definition updates all occurrences of text tagged with that style in a single document for local styles, or across many documents that link to the same set of external style sheets (see Figure 26-1).

Figure 26-1
Changing
elements of
styles in
QuarkXPress

A chapter of a book set up with styles   *The same text with changes to the styles; the names are the same, but the settings are different*

HTML and Style Sheets

After a few years of wrestling with hand coding type specifications, CSS arrived with a great cheer, as it essentially provides the same kind of control that DTP programs offer over text formatting and style sheets.

CSS defines all the kinds of things you might want to specify for a range of text, including absolute positioning on a page, font specifications, color, lines above and below a paragraph, and so on. You can wrap these specifications into a style sheet that can then be applied to different types of text selections, defined by HTML tags.

You can also base one CSS on another, inheriting all its definitions and adding or changing selected ones. This is where the *cascading* part of CSS comes in, as you can modify style sheets that underlie many other style sheets. The display of the text is based on specifications that cascade through the style sheets, from the first parent style down to the last child, which is actually applied to the text. (CSS also includes user settings and browser defaults as part of this cascade, although not all browsers currently define local settings as CSS styles. This issue is discussed in "Advanced CSS," later in this chapter.)

The main difference between the DTP approach and CSS is that in a page-layout program, changing the style results in predictable, consistent changes every time you view the document, because a single company wrote the style sheet format and the system that previews text on screen. With CSS, as with all HTML-

Simple CSS Coding

CSS has a very simple structure for defining the name of a style sheet and its properties:

```
selector { property: value }
```

The selector is the name of the style, which also defines what text gets selected by it. The property is an attribute, such as font size or width of a rule; the value is, well, the value, defined in units appropriate to the property. (Selectors, properties, and values are described in "Designing Style Sheets," later in this chapter.)

You can have many properties in the same definition, separated by semicolons:

```
EM.figures { color: olive; font-style:
italic; font-variant: small-caps }
```

Because older browsers don't support CSS, GoLive and other programs must hide style code from these older browsers, just as with JavaScript and other scripting languages. GoLive inserts the style information into the head portion of an HTML page. A typical example looks like this:

```
<html>
 <head>
  <title>An Average Page</title>
  <style type="text/css"><!--
   #headings { color: olive;
    font-style : italic;
    font-variant: small-caps }
   h1 { font-family:
    "Times New Roman", Georgia,
    Times; text-indent: 1pt }-->
  </style>
 </head>
<body>
  <h1>How do you solve a problem
  like <span id="headings">
  Maria</span>?</h1>
</body>
</html>
```

based type specs, the browser controls the display. So, depending on the browser, its version, the platform, and certain choices the user might have made, even text defined by a CSS can display differently from browser to browser.

However, it's a large step in the right direction, and it enables a previously impossible level of typographic specification and sophistication that can improve Web site design.

Previewing Style Sheets

The giddy thrill of creating style sheets can give way to a bit of regret if you haven't done a thorough job of reviewing which properties and features work in standard browsers, or haven't tested your style sheets with extensive previewing. So before we show you the GoLive approach to CSS, allow us to offer a few words on planning and previewing your work.

As we suggest often in this book and in this chapter, despite GoLive's generally excellent preview simulations of browsers, there's really no reliable way to tell how a feature—especially a CSS property—works in an actual browser. In this regard, GoLive's failing is in being *too* good. All browsers are "broken" in some regard: a programming mistake or design choice makes combinations of tags work inconsistently; tables are a notable example of broken behavior, in which small, insignificant changes in tags cause a table to work or not.

GoLive implements all its previewing features consistently, using a structured framework, so a feature that works inconsistently in the actual browser shows up correctly in GoLive. (We don't want to be the ones to ask the GoLive developers to purposely break their software; do you?)

Targeting Browsers

Before you ever design a style sheet, you have to make hard decisions about which browsers you plan to support with your site. You face three primary options.

- Support all browsers and use no advanced features. In this case, you can exit this chapter (and this part of the book), since JavaScript, many CSS features, and even frames require you to abandon some part of the audience.

- Support all browsers by providing alternatives to advanced features. You can code CSS into a site that uses all tag selectors (explained later in this chapter) so a browser lacking CSS support can use normal HTML tags, like H1, to display headings and body copy.

- Support only newer, CSS-capable browsers. We don't recommend this option; by mid-1999, fewer than 75 percent of visitors to general consumer Web sites were using browsers that handle a substantial number of CSS properties.

A middle road is to use advanced features as appropriate, but use tag selectors as much as you can. This approach leads to a site that looks just fine in a non-CSS-capable browser, but which could look spectacular (or at least great) in a CSS-compliant browser.

When making these planning decisions, be sure to consult the mother of all compatibility charts, Eric Meyer's CSS Master List from Webreview.com. The latest version at press time appears in this book in Appendix B, *Master List of CSS Compatibility*. (You can retrieve the up-to-the-minute version online at http://web review.com/wr/pub/guides/style/mastergrid.html.)

Previewing in GoLive

GoLive can preview an enormous number of the CSS properties it allows you to set. It also previews some features that you have to hand code. (These distinctions are discussed in more detail later, but it's worth knowing now what these settings do before you launch into building style sheets.)

Use Stylesheets. To get the best preview of CSS effects in GoLive, switch to the Layout Preview tab in any HTML page. Bring up the Document Layout Controller, and check or uncheck the Use Stylesheets box to toggle between viewing the page with and without CSS style sheets.

Root menu. You can simulate different browsers by selecting them from the Root popup menu. These simulations combine the defaults GoLive has encoded for each of the browser versions.

Tip: GoLive's Default Browser Assumptions

If you want to examine GoLive's assumptions about browser defaults, select Web Database from the Special menu and click the CSS tab. Select one of the browsers in the list, and bring up the CSS Style Sheet Inspector. Though you can't edit any of the settings, clicking the Source tab shows you each default that GoLive has set for each tag. This approach lets Adobe easily add new browsers' defaults without recoding the whole program. (For more information, see Chapter 27, *Web Database*.)

Allow Overlapping Paragraphs. Checking Allow Overlapping Paragraphs lets GoLive preview negative margin values, so blocks that may cross each other are correctly displayed.

Mark menus. The Mark Style menu displays any defined classes or IDs; the Mark Tag menu shows the A and BODY tags by default, but also any tags which have been turned into selectors and applied to any text in the document. Selecting an item from either menu highlights its occurrence throughout the document.

Show Links. Selecting Active or Visited previews the look of links while being selected or after being visited. This is nominally a CSS issue because you can also set the active and visited color in the BODY tag (through the Page Inspector's Page tab).

Previewing in Real Browsers

You know you have to do it, but many designers resist: preview your pages in multiple browsers to ensure that the CSS specifications are doing what you hoped and not flowing text off the screen, compressing it beyond legibility, or otherwise impairing the page.

We recommend testing every page of a site on the Macintosh (still at least 15 percent of traffic to most sites) and under Windows in multiple browsers. From our testing, it doesn't seem to matter whether you're running Windows 95, 98, or NT, or Mac OS 8.0, 8.1, 8.5, or 8.6.

The minimally acceptable test bed at this writing includes Windows and Mac machines with few fonts installed (just the defaults, if possible, for best previewing effect) running the last or latest release of:

- Windows

    Internet Explorer 3, 4, and 5

    Netscape Navigator 3, 4, and 4.5

- Macintosh

    Internet Explorer 4, 4.5

    Netscape Navigator 4, 4.6

If newer browsers have appeared, like Navigator 5, add them to the list. If you want to ensure less compatibility or are sure *your* users are running newer browsers, you can omit version 3 on Windows and 4 on Macintosh, leaving six browsers to test instead of 10.

Designing Style Sheets

CSS has two distinct parts: creation and management of the styles themselves, and application of those styles to text ranges. We address the first part in this section, and the second in "Applying Style Sheets," later in this chapter.

GoLive Tools

It's easy to design CSS specifications in GoLive, as the program puts a friendly interface on top of a truly enormous number of choices and specifications. You work primarily with two tools: the Style Sheet Editor and the CSS Selector Inspector.

Both tools let you specify an extensive, seemingly boundless set of CSS specifications; we talk about an end-run around its limitations for certain kinds of special, browser-specific, and advanced tags later in this chapter in "Advanced CSS."

Style Sheet Editor

CSS specifications have their own editor in GoLive, reachable by clicking the Cascading Style Sheets button—the ziggurat-like stairstepped icon at the top right of the Layout Editor. This action opens the Style Sheet Editor, which handles style sheets just for that page.

You can also create a standalone set of style sheets in their own file that can be referenced from one or more HTML files on your site; select New Stylesheet Document from the New Special submenu in the File menu. This is a convenient way to create a site-wide, intranet-wide, or Internet-wide set of shared formatting.

Tip: Internal and External Style Sheets Editors

The difference between the Style Sheet Editor that you use with editing styles located inside an HTML page and the editor that handles external style sheet files is twofold. The name in their respective title bars is different—the page-specific editor has the file name plus ": Style Sheet," while the standalone document displays only its filename—and the page-specific editor has a tab for Internal and External style sheets (see Figure 26-2). Using external style sheets is discussed under "Cascading," later in this chapter. In all other ways, they work identically.

Adding styles. You add styles based on their type (see "Style Sheet Selectors," below) by clicking the New Tag, New ID, and New Class buttons in the CSS Toolbar (see Figure 26-3). Creating a new style brings up the CSS Selector Inspector. New styles are named "newID", "newClass", and "newtag" by default.

Figure 26-2
Internal and External Style Sheet Editors

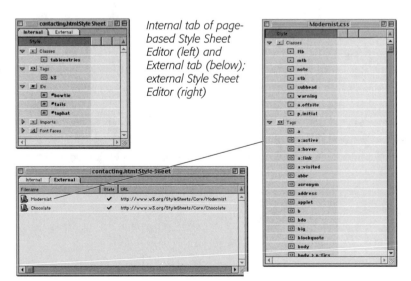

Internal tab of page-based Style Sheet Editor (left) and External tab (below); external Style Sheet Editor (right)

Figure 26-3
Figure Title

New Class | *New ID*   *New External Style Sheet*

New Tag

Naming styles. Styles can be named anything alphanumeric; that is, any name containing just letters and numbers; be sure *not* to include any spaces or other characters. IDs must be preceded by a pound sign, which GoLive requires that you insert (they're not added automatically). Classes require a period before them in the form that they appear in the HTML, but GoLive automatically inserts the period, so don't enter it in the name (see Table 26-1).

Table 26-1
Naming style sheets

Selector	GoLive convention	GoLive name	HTML example
Tag	No brackets	H1	H1 { bold }
Class	No leading period	fridges	.fridges { font-style: italic }
ID	Leading pound-sign	#aquaman	#aquaman { border-top: 1pt dotted aqua }

The style's name is entered in the CSS Selector Inspector's Basics tab in the Name field.

Duplicating existing styles. Select a style in the Style Sheets Editor and click the Duplicate button in the Toolbar to create an exact copy of an existing style.

CSS Resources

Our favorite CSS resource online is WebReference.com's set of tutorials by the incredibly talented youth Stephanos Piperoglou: a Greek native attending an English university writing for Americans (and the rest of the world)! See http://www.webreference.com/html.

You can also read about various aspects of CSS, including troubleshooting and coding tips, in articles written mostly by Eric Meyer on WebReview.com at http://webreview.com/wr/pub/Style_Sheets.

There are a number of books on CSS as well, but unless you're devoting your life to the subject, the online resources probably suffice. If you exhaust them, and find yourself needing more nitty-gritty, more solutions, or more details, scan through the dozen or so CSS titles to see if you can find one appropriate for your work.

If you'd like to wade through a somewhat dry, but thoroughly comprehensive, view of the ideal version of the specification, you can read the actual CSS specification at http://www.w3.org/TR/REC-CSS1. The CSS1 specification is the one currently implemented in some partial form by all the 4.0 browsers. (A newer spec, CSS2, is in progress, and some browsers have already adopted some of its features.)

Deleting styles. Select the style you want to delete, and then select Clear from the Edit menu.

Creating styles that GoLive doesn't support. GoLive allows you to name styles with identifiers that contain extended selections as described in "Style Sheet Selectors" and "Advanced CSS." Generally, these kinds of selectors start with a tag, so create a new tag and, in the Name field of the CSS Selector Inspector, enter the entire selector. (For instance, "H1.extended UL LI" is perfectly legal in GoLive even though the program can't preview its effect.)

Linking external style sheets. Click the External tab and then click the New Item icon, shaped like the stairstepped CSS icon in the CSS Toolbar. This brings up the External Style Sheet Inspector, which lets you choose a file to link to.

If you link more than one external style sheet, you can change its order—and thereby the precedence of the properties of style sheets embedded in the external

Using Import to Link Style Sheets

A different method of linking external style sheets is via the import method, which is not used by GoLive, but which it supports for compatibility.

GoLive's method of linking an external style sheet uses the Link tag, which can also be used for embedding fonts and other external objects. For example:

```
<link href="/shared/standard.css"
rel="styleSheet" type="text/css">
```

This is standard enough, and all the browsers that support CSS also allow you to reference external style sheets with Link. The difference between import and Link is that import statements are embedded inside a style definition.

```
<STYLE><!—
@import url(http://w3c.org/styles/
core-set.css);
--></STYLE>
```

Import's advantage over Link is that because it's nested inside the STYLE tag container, it can import a set of styles that, in turn, import other styles, which themselves can import styles, ad in-

finitum. This lets you create a powerful hierarchy of nested styles for especially complex interlocked sets of documents, such as technical documents that are part of a series of similar, but not identical, documents.

Without the import feature, each page would have to separately use Link to connect to multiple external style sheets. And you'd have to spend some amount of time managing those Link statements, including updating all of them if a single file name changed.

Import statements work like Link statements, in that the order in which they appear in an HTML file controls precedence: the earlier they appear, the lower their precedence; see "Cascading," later in this chapter.

GoLive won't let you create import statements, but if you have a file that contains import statements, GoLive reads the styles and leaves them alone. (It seems like it should display local imported styles in the Import heading in the Style Sheet Editor, but this isn't the case in the current version.)

file—by clicking the up and down Move arrows in the External Style Sheet Inspector. The higher the external style sheet appears in the list, the *lower* its precedence. (For more on this subject, see "Cascading," later in this chapter.)

Clicking the Open button opens the external file for editing using the Style Sheets Editor, as long as it has the appropriate .css extension.

CSS Selector Inspector

Creating a new style through the Style Sheets Editor and selecting it activates the CSS Selector Inspector, your window into the vast specification arena for CSS.

The Basics tab of this inspector allows you to name your style sheet. It also provides a preview of how the actual code of the style sheet definition will appear in your HTML code or external CSS file. A full breakout of each tab of the CSS Selector Inspector is explained in "Style Sheet Specifications," below.

Style Sheet Selectors

CSS groups its style sheets into categories by how they get applied to text. GoLive breaks these out into three categories: tag, class, and ID. Each of these types is a selector: the method by which text in the document is "selected."

You can name these selectors anything that contains just letters and numbers.

Tag. These style sheets apply only to specific HTML tags, like a heading 3 (H3) or teletype (TT) tag, and modify their default appearance as defined by the browser that's displaying the tag. Using tags is the most conservative course, since browsers that don't support CSS use the browser's defaults for the tag; those that support CSS show the extra specifications. You omit the < and > in a tag name.

You can invent tags that browsers ignore—like <PARTYTIME> or <SPAGHETTI>—and apply style sheets to them, but it's better to use the class feature, described next.

Class. Classes are like the French Club in high school: anyone can join the group whether they're a freshman, sophomore, junior, or senior. Ditto with classes: after defining a class, you can plug the class into any kind of tag and the text selected by that tag inherits the properties of that class.

Classes are preceded by a period (such as ".mynewfriend"), but when entering a class name into GoLive, you can omit the period; the program inserts it for you. You can combine tags and classes, and have a class that only applies to a given tag. This can be useful for creating CSS that still works with a non-CSS browser, so that you can use H2, for instance, for similar levels of information, while using the class to format some H2s differently than others.

Tip:
Contextual
Selectors
CSS supports selectors that use nested tags and classes, so you can define something as particular as "an unnumbered list element beneath another unnumbered list element in a paragraph that belongs to the paragraph class 'f1.'" This would be written simply as "P.f1 UL LI UL LI"; pretty elegant, eh? GoLive 4.0 doesn't preview this behavior, but you can name a tag with a contextual selector and GoLive leaves it alone. This subject is discussed in greater depth in "Advanced CSS," later in this chapter.

ID. IDs are uniquely numbered and can be used only once in a document. GoLive currently only lets you define, not apply, IDs; you have to edit the HTML to apply them. When you define an ID, you have to precede its name with a pound sign (#); GoLive won't insert this for you, but the default name for a new ID includes a pound sign. (If you delete the pound sign in the name, GoLive changes the selector to a tag selector.)

Tip: IDs in
External
Style Sheets
If you use external style sheets, everything in every document is uniquely numbered to avoid potentially erratic behavior. (It's possible that some browsers would let you use the same ID for items on different pages, but you would be better off using a class for that kind of shared behavior.)

Style Sheet Specifications

Of the 50 or so properties you can apply to text selections and text blocks using CSS, GoLive lets you specify almost all of them. GoLive previews most, but not all, of the specifications it allows you to select or fill in.

Tip: Preview
in Browsers
for Best
Results
Although GoLive previews many effects, we recommend that you use GoLive just for coding style sheets. Rely on actual browsers to determine whether the effects or styles you're applying actually look the way you want them to.

As mentioned earlier in the chapter, the Web Review summary of features and which browsers support which features is your best resource for determining which features to use to achieve maximum compatibility for the platforms and browsers you expect will visit your pages (see Appendix B, *Master List of CSS Compatibility*).

Character Styles and Paragraph Styles

CSS's inline and block definitions closely match the character and paragraph styles of DTP programs like Adobe InDesign and QuarkXPress. This is a helpful parallel if you've used those programs at all.

Character styles get applied to any range of text,

and typically include just font formatting. Paragraph styles include leading (the vertical space from one line of type to the next), rules (borders around the text), background shades, margins, and vertical space above and below the paragraph (see Figure 26-4).

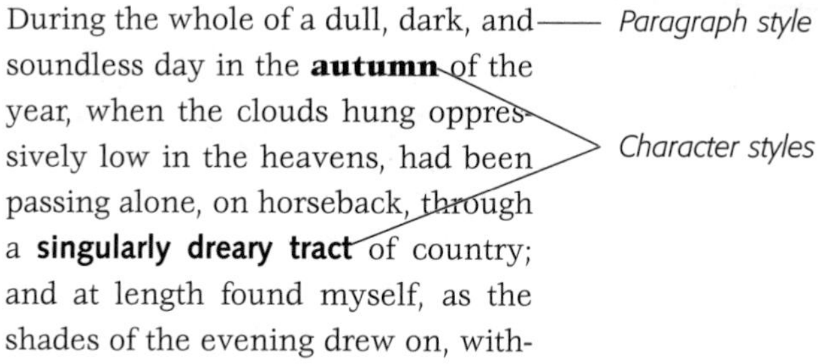

Figure 26-4
Paragraph and
character styles

During the whole of a dull, dark, and—— *Paragraph style*
soundless day in the **autumn** of the
year, when the clouds hung oppres-
sively low in the heavens, had been *Character styles*
passing alone, on horseback, through
a **singularly dreary tract** of country;
and at length found myself, as the
shades of the evening drew on, with-

CSS Model

The characteristics and objects you can set in GoLive range from borders and lines to tiled backgrounds across blocks of text. CSS differentiates between *inline* elements and *block* elements.

An inline element is one that doesn't have a line break before and after it, such as the B (bold) tag. It refers to properties that can affect ranges of text without affecting surrounding formatting.

A block element creates a break in sequence with the text above and below it, such as the P (paragraph) tag.

HTML offers ways to create inline and block elements when using selectors that aren't based on the type of element you want to apply. The Span tag creates an inline range of text; the Div tag creates a block of text.

Because properties know whether they apply to inline or block elements, you can often write a single style that works for both inline and block elements; the block properties are ignored when the style is used with an inline selector.

CSS Specifications

GoLive lets you set most CSS specifications directly through the CSS Selector Inspector. Many of the specs are self-explanatory, such as type size or weight. We've broken the kinds of specs down into major categories for ease of reference.

Tip:
Previewing
the CSS
Definition

GoLive shows the definition of the style sheet as it gets written in the Basics tab; it includes any hand tweaking you've done in the HTML Source Editor. Although you can't edit or copy the text in this preview, it's nice to see all the parameters in one place (see Figure 26-5).

Units

CSS uses several standard units for measuring items, and GoLive supports all these through appropriate popup menus in the CSS Selector Inspector.

Point, pica, inch, cm, and mm. These five units are absolutes. Traditionally, as well as in the CSS specification, there are 12 points to a pica, and six picas to the inch;

Figure 26-5
Text of style
sheet

therefore a point is $\frac{1}{72}$-inch and a pica is $\frac{1}{6}$-inch. Inches are inches. A centimeter (cm) is 10 times a large as a millimeter (mm); there are 2.54 centimeters to an inch.

Tip: GoLive Converts   If you select point, pica, pixel, inch, cm, or mm as your measurement unit and enter a value, you can then select a different unit from the popup menu and GoLive automatically converts one unit into terms of another.

Pixel. You can specify items in absolute pixels, which in every current browser release is identical to a point: 72 pixels to the inch.

Tip: Ideal Pixels   The CSS specification notes that browser developers should consider implementing the pixel measurement using a standard reference pixel so that the same measurement on different monitors would have the same pixel height regardless of the monitor's pitch, or the number of pixels per inch on screen. Most monitors display between 80 and 90 pixels per inch.

Em and ex. An em and an ex are relative measures based on the height of the capital letter M (for em) and the lower-case x (for ex) in the font, style, and type size defined or inherited in the style sheet.

Tip: Em Height Versus Em Width   The em measurement in CSS may confuse typographers and desktop publishers who are used to the traditional definition of an em that dates back to the last century, if not longer: the *width*, not *height*, of a capital letter M. The typographer's name for the CSS em unit would be "cap height," while the ex would be "x-height."

Percentage. If you specify percentage, the question would be, "percentage of *what*?" The percentage is always in terms of another defined unit in the same style sheet, or of an inherited default. Each property that allows percentage as a unit also defines what property the percentage is based on.

In the case of line height, for instance, percentage is based on the text size. If you define H1 as using a font size of 24 points, you can define a line height of 125 percent, which a CSS-compliant browser calculates as 30 points (24 multiplied by 1.25).

Other relative measures (100, XX-Large, Larger). CSS has several relative measures used for font size, line thickness, and other specifications that rely heavily on the browser to figure out what's meant. For instance, you can set a font's size to XX-Large, but a browser has to figure out what the current size is and what's relatively extra-extra large by comparison.

Different browsers map these relative measurements to different aspects, so you're counting on testing and luck to get what you want if you use these kinds of measurements.

Typography. CSS lets you define characteristics of type, including character-specific attributes (font name, color, and size) and paragraph- and range-based settings (line spacing, spacing between letters, and vertical and horizontal alignment). GoLive splits the categories into the CSS Selector Inspector's Font and Text tabs.

Font characteristics are, by their nature, inline properties, while some of the items found in the Text tab have an effect on blocks, like alignment.

Embedding Fonts in GoLive

Beginning with the 4.0 browser releases from Microsoft and Netscape, a designer can now embed actual font outlines into Web pages through one of two methods. Microsoft and Netscape, of course, have different approaches to embedding fonts, pairing Microsoft and Adobe against Netscape and Bitstream (another font foundry); neither method is compatible with the other.

Both methods require using special software to extract font outlines from PostScript or TrueType font files and turn them into a format that a Web browser can download and cache in order to render the type in the browser. Neither method involves any action on the part of the user so long as they are running a browser that supports embedded fonts; if they aren't, they just see the text with whatever other specifications you've applied.

GoLive currently doesn't support either method directly, though we can imagine support being easily added (perhaps encouraged by bundling GoLive with a simple font-embedding tool). In fact, the Style Sheets Editor has an item labeled Font Faces that isn't explained anywhere,

but we can guess its future function.

You can write HTML code coupled with JavaScript that would allow an HTML page to have the correct embedding codes based on which browser is accessing the page. To add the necessary code for Adobe and Microsoft's version of font embedding, use the List & Others tab of the CSS Selector Inspector. Add a property named "font-face" with a value that is the exact name of the embedded font package; the software that creates embeddable fonts can help with this. (The next release of Netscape's and Bitstream's version is supposed to use the same property; it currently uses a Link tag which you can insert via the Link icon in the Palette's Head tab.)

For a full explanation of both methods of embedding, we recommend you read a column Glenn wrote for *Adobe Magazine* on the subject that contains links to several online resources for obtaining free or commercial embedding software, along with tutorials on embedding. We've put the article online at http://realworldgolive/embedding.html.

The same typeface with the same defaults in the same browsers display at varying sizes on different browsers. You can use the absolute pixel measurement to set type to a real size that will always use the same number of pixels, regardless of platform. Set the Size property to a pixel value in the Font tab.

For the world's best explanation of this problem and other solutions, see Geoff Duncan's TidBITS article, "Why Windows Web Pages Have Tiny Text" at http://db.tid-bits.com/getbits.acgi?tbart=05284, which we've excerpted in large part in Chapter 7, *Text and Fonts*.

Borders, fills, and spacing. CSS offers substantial control over the borders and spaces surrounding a block. The CSS model breaks a block down into several areas, each of which has its own control in the Block and Borders tabs of the CSS Selector Inspector (see Figure 26-6).

Figure 26-6
CSS model
and GoLive
controls

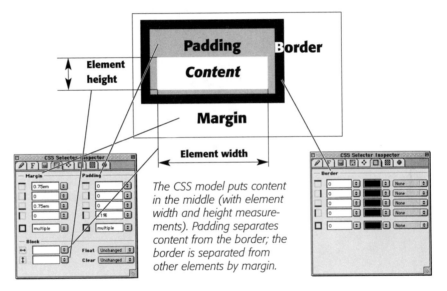

The CSS model puts content in the middle (with element width and height measurements). Padding separates content from the border; the border is separated from other elements by margin.

Two controls are particularly useful for controlling text flow: Float and Clear. Float allows you to set a block as a run-around element, so text flows around it to the right or left. Clear modifies a floating block, so that text to the right or left starts flowing only at the vertical bottom of the box.

The Position tab has two additional block-display features: Overflow and Visibility. The Overflow options set how a block behaves when its contents overflow its container. Visibility allows a block's contents to be hidden or displayed. Both features are part of CSS2, so they may not be supported by many browsers at the moment.

Float and Clear are equivalent to the Align attribute for the Img tag, and the Clear attribute for the P and BR tags.

Positioning. With CSS, you can specify an exact position on a page relative to the upper-left corner of the browser window. Many of the controls in the Position tab are identical, or nearly so, to those in the Floating Box Inspector. The Z-Index field, for instance, corresponds to the Floating Box Inspector's Layer field.

Clipping. Clipping, found in the Position tab, is part of the CSS2 specification, and controls how much overlap is displayed between adjacent, conflicting blocks.

Background. You can control the background of a block or the entire page, including offsetting elements from the upper left. CSS allows you to set a repeating image, just like the Background attribute of the HTML Body tag, but you can also use images and colors to set the background of blocks.

A very cool CSS addition to background is the Attach feature: you can set a background image to be Fixed so that as you scroll down a page, the background is static in the window.

Lists. If you're tired of boring list element bullets, use list specifications to perk up the display, providing better control over the formatting; you can even choose a custom bullet. These specs are set in the List & Others tab.

Other Specifications. GoLive supports adding properties that it currently doesn't offer through its List & Others tab. Click the New button, then enter the property name and its value. This feature doesn't work for properties without values, as it insists on putting a colon at the end of the property name, even when the value is empty.

This is a simple way to add CSS2 properties, as appropriate, without having to code by hand.

Cascading

CSS has a built-in set of hierarchies that control how multiple style sheets, that reference the same selector, interact and produce a specification that is applied against the element.

CSS has two distinct cascades:

- A general-to-specific set of rules that controls how the properties of one selector override those of another selector, preferring the more specific selector.

- A set of rules about precedence based on hierarchy that resolves the interaction of identical selectors in internal, external, and browser-based style sheets.

General to specific. CSS defines selectors in terms of how specific they are; there's even a little formula, with more technical detail than you may ever need to know, that you can use to calculate specificity (see sidebar, "The Specificity Formula").

Generally, a more specific selector overrides properties in a more general selector. So you might define some characteristics for EM, but any properties in EM UL LI (a list element in an unnumbered list set inside an EM tag) override those in EM because they are more specific.

Classes are always more specific than tags, and IDs are the most specific of all. Combining classes, tags, and IDs can create a complex set of overrides. If you start to develop style sheets that require this level of control, we suggest you learn the spec inside and out, especially the specificity formula.

Precedence. More commonly, you'll encounter issues of precedence and hierarchy in how rules get interpreted. In the current CSS model, a browser has built-in style sheets that reflect the browser developer's assumptions. For instance, all the heading styles may be defined using certain fonts that are always found on an operating system.

The browser's styles are overridden by a user's browser preferences (also called the reader's preferences), which represent the next level up in the hierarchy. A user might choose, for instance, to use a font on their system, like Garamond, to display body copy. However, an author's styles—the author being the person who wrote the CSS style sheets in a Web page—override a user's styles except in special cases.

External style sheets have lower precedence than ones embedded in a Web page, and the order in which external style sheets are listed controls their precedence: the earlier it appears (or higher in the HTML document), the *lower* the precedence.

The Specificity Formula

We expect you won't need this information except for complex sets of interlocked documents or style sheets; nonetheless, we're here to serve you, so here goes.

An ID is worth 100. Classes are worth 10 points each. Tag selectors are worth 1 point each. The higher the number, the *higher* the precedence of the selector.

Here are the examples modified from the CSS1 specification:

Tag	ID	Class	Tag	Specificity
LI	0	0	1	1
UL LI	0	0	2	2
UL OL LI	0	0	3	3
LI.red	0	1	1	11
UL OL LI.red	0	1	3	13
#x34y	1	0	0	100

You can adjust this precedence in the External tab of the Style Sheet Editor by selecting an external reference and using the arrows to adjust its position up or down. External style sheets linked via the import command must be edited by hand in the HTML to adjust their order of precedence.

All external style sheets linked using the GoLive method or the Link tag are lower in precedence than any file linked via the import method.

! important. There's one way to assure precedence, which is to use the "! important" override, which GoLive doesn't support or preview. If you insert "! important" after any property's value, that value overrides all other values for that property based on the cascade.

If more than one conflicting style uses "! important" for the same property, the general-to-specific and precedence cascade rules sort out which "! important" is more important.

Tip: In CSS2, Readers Come First	CSS2 uses the important tag to let a reader or user override an author's definitions, the converse of the current version. This lets a reader really have their way when they want it.

Applying Style Sheets

Applying style sheets to text in GoLive is a breeze. Select text—either a range or click in a paragraph, heading, or other grouping—and choose the style you want to apply.

In GoLive 4.0, you can only apply classes to ranges of text. IDs must be hand inserted in the current release, while tags are automatically applied by the browser to any applicable tags.

Applying Classes

GoLive applies classes to text through the Style tab of the Text Inspector. GoLive divides elements into four categories, each of which has its own column heading. Each class, including classes that are subsets of tags, has four checkboxes to the right of its name (see Figure 26-7).

Hovering over a checkbox adds a green plus sign to the cursor; clicking puts a checkmark in the box. To remove the setting, hover over the box again, and notice that the cursor has a red minus sign; click, and the checkmark is removed.

You can apply multiple settings to the same text, checking one or more of the element categories. If you select more than one paragraph at a time or text that has different settings applied, the checkboxes display a hyphen or dash to indicate multiple settings.

Figure 26-7
Applying class
styles

Inline. Inline corresponds exactly to inline elements. GoLive uses the Span tag to insert class selectors used as an inline element. Because the Span tag has no other purpose, it won't cause any other changes to the HTML.

To apply an Inline element, select a range of text before checking the Inline box (see Figure 26-8).

Figure 26-8
Applying an
inline style

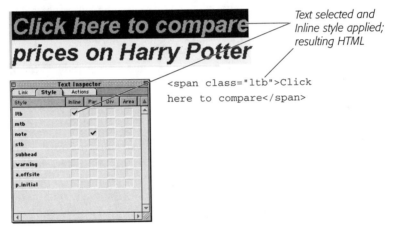

*Text selected and
Inline style applied;
resulting HTML*

```
<span class="ltb">Click
here to compare</span>
```

**Tip: Block
that
Property!**

If you apply a class with block properties set using the Inline checkbox, the CSS spec says that the block properties are supposed to be ignored by the browser. However, as with all CSS properties and principles, each browser may have its own ideas.

Par. The Par element corresponds to the P, or paragraph, HTML tag. You can either place your insertion point anywhere in a paragraph, or select multiple paragraphs before checking the Par box for a class. Each paragraph in the selection becomes its own separate block (see Figure 26-9). This could work well for vertical spacing and other paragraph-specific attributes that affect type flow.

Div. The Par element inserts a Class attribute in *every* paragraph tag in the selection; the Div, or division, element creates just one set of Div tags around the entire set of selected paragraphs or other block units.

Figure 26-9
Par and Div
styles

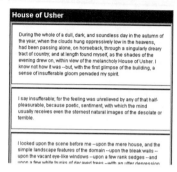

Par checked for selection, applying
block style to each paragraph

Div checked for selection, applying
block style around entire selection

This creates one large block, and block properties, like borders and margins, get applied around the entire division (also see Figure 26-9, above).

Tip: Floating Boxes Took Over My Style!

If you use absolute positioning in a style sheet and apply that style to text with the Div element, when you next switch between HTML Source Editor and Layout Editor or close and open the file, GoLive turns your unsuspecting text into a floating box with its own ID (see Figure 26-10)!

It's unclear whether this is a feature or a bug in the HTML parser, or something entirely different. What we do know is that once your text becomes a floating box, you can apply "local" positioning to it that gets stored as part of the ID definition, not as part of the class definition.

Area. The Area element sets the Class attribute for the Body tag if the text-insertion point is in plain text; the entire page is affected by the Body tag, of course. If the cursor is in a table cell, the Area element affects just the cell, modifying the TD or TH tag for the cell.

Applying IDs

Applying IDs is fairly easy, even though it has to be done by hand. GoLive neither tracks nor allows you to apply them directly, but it does appropriately preview any element with an ID applied.

1. Select the text or block to apply an ID to.

2. Switch to the HTML Source Editor.

3. Omitting the leading pound sign (#) in the name of the ID, apply it to the text in one of two ways:

   a. If the text you want is entirely surrounded by opening and closing HTML tags, insert the ID into the opening tag.

   ```
   <H1 ID="flooby">Town of Flooby Nooby</H1>
   ```

Figure 26-10
Floating box
takeover of
absolute
positioning

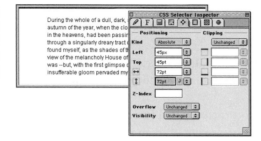

*Absolute positioning applied in a
style to a specific block*

*After switching to HTML Source
Editor and back to Layout Editor,
the block has become a floating
box with the text pasted in*

b. If the text is a range inside a paragraph, use a set of Span tags.

```
The first time I heard of <SPAN ID="flooby">the Town of Flooby
Nooby</SPAN>, I was in the Caspian Sea.
```

c. If you want to create a block covering more than one set of block tags (like
    P or UL), surround the range with a set of Div tags.

```
<DIV ID="flooby">Lots of paraphenalia<P>here to think<P>about.
<P></DIV>
```

4. Switch back to the Layout Editor to preview your IDs.

Advanced CSS

GoLive, in our experience, is the leading bi-platform CSS editor, providing a truly
useful and straightforward interface to CSS complexity.

That said—and this may be hard to believe—there are several features that
GoLive doesn't support and/or preview in the current release. (Adobe promises
additional CSS support in the product manual, and given the quality of the current effort, we can believe that the next release will be quite impressive.)

There are two kinds of features we lump into "Advanced CSS": those that require more detail in the selector part of the CSS (the part that defines which tags,
classes, IDs, or other characters a style sheet gets applied to), and those that are
part of the style sheet definition itself.

Complex Selectors

CSS offers even more specificity and complexity in selectors than available for pre-view and full support in GoLive. You can enter all these selectors in the Name field of the CSS Selector Inspector, even though GoLive won't preview them.

Specificity. Selectors can be nested fairly deeply, so you can specify, for instance, that bold type in a list element of an unnumbered list inside a particular class gets such-and-such properties. You'd write that as:

```
.classname UL LI B
```

That selector won't affect italic formatting in the same nested location. This specificity has a complex set of rules that affect which properties override others; this is explained earlier in the chapter in "Cascading."

Mix-and-match. You can mix tags, selectors, and IDs with amazing aplomb. So, for instance, you can define a selector that affects only the ID #Z27 inside an H1. This would be distinct from ID #Z27 by itself, or ID #Z27 for an unnumbered list element:

```
H1#Z27
#Z27
UL LI#Z27
```

Multiple selectors. All the properties of a selector don't have to appear in the same, single definition, so you can set multiple selectors to have the same property by separating them with commas, and then applying specifics after that.

```
H1, P.barge, EM UL LI LI { font-size: 13 px }
H1 { color: fuchsia }
```

Psuedo-Selectors

The CSS spec provides for what it calls "pseudo-selectors": items that don't really fit the selector mode, but rather directly modify parts of the browser display. This allows the spec to be a little more flexible about certain aspects of the browser in-terface.

Anchor-related. A special class of selectors work with the A or anchor tag: active, link, and visited. These selectors allow you to override the built-in browser behav-ior, which typically turn an active link (one that's being clicked on) purple, a regu-lar link blue, and a visited address red.

Using the syntax A plus a colon plus active, link, or visited, you can specify a variety of inline type effects.

For instance, the following would make all links on a page display in italic regardless of other properties:

```
A:link { font-style: italic }
```

Paragraph-related. CSS defines a few DTP-like characteristics that allow you to provide special treatment on the first character of a paragraph (a drop cap) and the first line of a paragraph.

Use P:first-letter to select the first character, and—surprise!—P:first-line to select the first line.

Browser-Specific Features

Here's a shocker: some browser makers have added features that aren't part of any CSS spec or are currently only supported by a given browser release or platform.

Internet Explorer

Several of the IE-specific tags are cribbed from CSS2, so other browsers may be expected to offer them in time.

A:hover. This selector offers a simple rollover function. Whenever the cursor passes over any hyperlink, the browser changes the type to reflect the properties defined for it. You can even light up the entire area in a different color. (See http://www.webreference.com/dhtml/diner/hover/hover2.html for some incredibly neat examples.)

Display. The display property supports four possible values: none, block, inline, and list-item. None suppresses display—actually deletes it from the screen—of any enclosed HTML. Combined with a relatively simple JavaScript, this property can provide a way to have click-down menus on a single HTML page. Clicking a triangle, for instance, toggles whether the text below that item gets displayed or not.

Cursor. The cursor property changes the shape of the cursor into a specified value when the cursor passes over the item that has the property attached to it. The possible values are quite extensive: hand (the little, um, "famous mouse" hand), crosshair, default (normal cursor), move (four direction cursor), text (the I-beam), wait (watch or hourglass), and help.

There is also a set of "resize" cursors (e-resize, ne-resize, nw-resize, n-resize, se-resize, sw-resize, s-resize, and w-resize) that corresponds to the compass point being used for resizing.

Designing with Style

Repetition is tedious. Repetition is tedious. Repetition is…okay, you get the point. We like using style sheets to avoid tedious repetition of repetitive tedium. It lets us not only control the look of our pages with more specificity, but with remarkably little work as well. For designers working on a Web site in teams, the ability to set central styles that work over an internal network or the Internet can provide a sense of continuity and consistency that many Web sites lack or spend an enormous amount of effort keeping track of.

The caveat is that many millions of people are using browsers that don't support Cascading Style Sheets. However, a well-designed site that uses tag selectors and tag/class selectors can take advantage of GoLive's management, CSS's flexibility, and still look decent on a 3.0 browser.

CHAPTER 27
Web Database

The Web Database is GoLive's unsung hero. It stores all the program's assumptions about how tags work so that as you build pages visually, you get a nice, clean preview. When you switch to the Layout Preview, the browser preview options listed in the Root menu of the Layout View Controller are all based on Web Database settings for each browser.

GoLive uses the Web Database to store all the rules governing tags, including how they are written (their syntax), how they interact with other tags, which browsers they work on, and how they display in the HTML Source Editor.

Other WYSIWYG Web tools have similar embedded properties, but GoLive is unique in building an extensible system that you can access directly as an advanced user. By opening up the behind-the-scenes processes, GoLive gives you the ability to customize how it writes and displays HTML and to add new tags as the HTML standard is updated. This way, you're not beholden to a product's update cycle to add some of the compatibility you need.

The Web Database can also be used:

- To reset some of GoLive's HTML writing defaults

- To define new defaults for some HTML objects that GoLive creates on pages

- As an HTML and character encoding reference

- To add browser dependent, proprietary, or non-standard tags

- To add new special characters or "entities"

- To view examples of special characters

The Web Database Doesn't . . .

GoLive limits the kinds of changes to program behavior you can make by altering elements in the Web Database. You cannot change or add interface items to menus, Inspector palettes, or the Palette. If you add an attribute to an existing tag you don't have access to it through the Inspector palette. However, the new tag or attribute appears as an option in the HTML Outline Editor (see Figure 27-1).

Any new HTML tags or special characters added to the Database aren't previewable by GoLive, either in the Layout Editor or the Layout Preview. Also, GoLive can't automatically detect the browser compatibility of new tags added to the Database, so if you want GoLive to be able to display warnings for the new tags using its HTML syntax checker, you must gather and set compatibility information yourself.

Previewing Output

If you click the expand triangle next to the Source Sample label (Mac) or check the Source Sample box at the bottom of the Web Database window (Windows), you can preview the effects of the changes you make to formatting specifications in the Global and CSS tabs' settings on a sample bit of HTML (see Figure 27-2). The Global tab affects all tags and attributes; the CSS tab controls just the CSS definitions in the Head section of the HTML.

A Word of Warning

While it's commendable that GoLive offers access to its inner workings, this power doesn't come without grave responsibility. Before you dive into the Web Database and begin changing settings with wild abandon, be forewarned that the Web Database's tags closely conform to currently ratified HTML standards. If you alter the tags, their attributes, enumerations, or compatibility settings, GoLive may create non-standard code that displays incorrectly in browsers.

Also, GoLive uses the Web Database when checking your code for errors. If the tags have been changed to non-standard settings, the syntax checker accepts them as correct and may fail to display important warnings.

However, you can easily revert back to factory defaults if you've made changes that don't work

out. Just throw away GoLive's Web Database folder or any of its subfolders after quitting the program. On both Mac and Windows, the folder is found in the GoLive application folder's Modules folder. The next time you run the application, GoLive creates a new database folder with the factory settings.

Don't be fooled by either the Import Old Web Database contextual menu item that appears in the HTML and Characters tabs, or the Import item from the Web Database submenu in the Specials menu. As far as we can tell, neither option is wired to work with the application in the 4.0 release. The Import feature appears to be a way to update the Web Database with more current information, but this capability and the specifications aren't found in the manual or elsewhere.

Figure 27-1
New attributes
available in the
Outline Editor

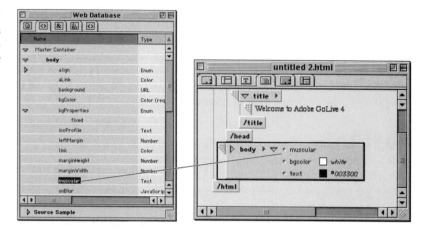

Figure 27-2
Previewing
formatting in
the Source
Sample

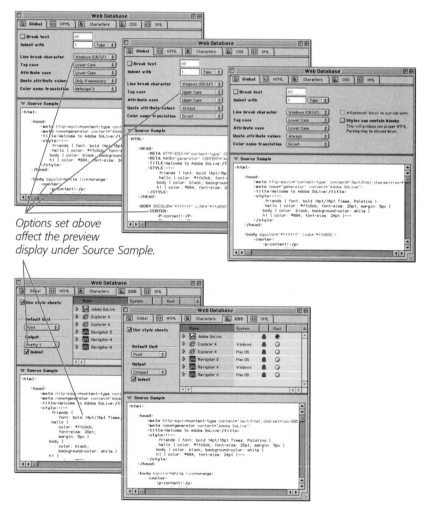

*Options set above
affect the preview
display under Source Sample.*

Tip: Preview-ing (Mac)	In the HTML and Characters tabs, in the Macintosh version, you can drag items into the sample to see how they appear in context to other HTML code (see Figure 27-3).
Tip: Scrolling Source Sam-ple (Mac)	In the Mac version of GoLive 4.0, a bug prevented you from scrolling the sample, but you can drag items into the sample and drag down to scroll the contents of the field. The 4.0.1 update fixes this problem.

Global Tab

When you open the Web Database window for the first time, you see the Global tab. Here, GoLive organizes most of its HTML-writing preferences regardless of whether they're single HTML pages or part of a site (see Figure 27-4). These settings affect the way GoLive writes source HTML code, not how the browser displays the page.

Figure 27-3
Previewing HTML on the Mac

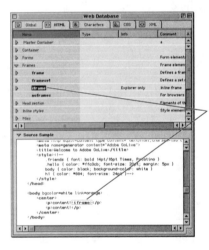

Dragging an item into the Source Sample preview its HTML in context on the Macintosh

Applying Changes Globally

Changes in the Global tab don't affect pages in GoLive retroactively, even though they're program-wide settings. Instead, you have to open each file, make a change to any text in the file, and then save the file for the HTML to be updated.

One workaround we've found is to use the Find feature's Find & Replace tab to find and replace the same item that occurs in every file. Consult Chapter 21, *Site Specials*, for specifics on making sitewide changes using Find & Replace. In brief, put a period in the Find and Replace fields, setting the checkboxes exactly as shown in Figure 27-5. This procedure forces GoLive to open, modify, and save every file in a site, resulting in entirely rewritten HTML.

You need to choose a common character, like the period, in order to force GoLive to modify *every* file. But be certain your Find and Replace fields are identical, or you can mess up all the files in your site. (Make a backup before making this kind of change, as we always recommend.)

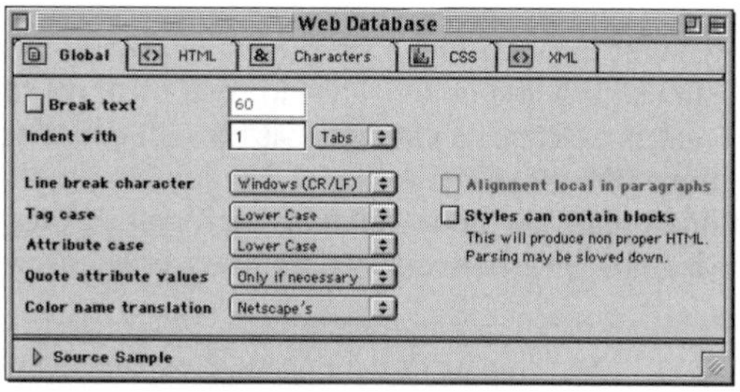

Figure 27-4
Global tab

Figure 27-5
Rewriting trick

HTML Formatting

Most of the settings in the Global tab affect only the appearance of HTML in the HTML Source Editor, to make reading and editing the code easier.

Break Text. Checking this box automatically adds a line break in the HTML after the number of characters you specify. Browsers ignore line breaks, except when used in conjunction with the Pre (preformatted) tag.

Indent With. GoLive "nests" HTML using tabs or spaces to make it more readable by applying a structure based on the blocks and elements. Table rows, for instance, are nested inside Table tags; cells are nested inside rows. You can turn this off by setting the value to 0 (zero), or have GoLive use spaces instead of tabs.

Line Break Character. The line break character is the symbol or symbols that each of the three major platforms—Macintosh, Windows, and Unix—considers a signal for the end of a line. Don't ask why each platform decided on a different symbol; line break envy? GoLive tells you which platform corresponds to which signal as part of the popup values. Using Macintosh line endings puts in a carriage return, or ASCII 13; Unix uses a line feed, ASCII 10, to signal the end; and Windows is gluttonous and uses both.

Tip: Why Switch Line Breaks? If you're creating pages in GoLive for Web serving or editing on another platform—often the case—choose the line-ending style for that platform can avoid a problem where the line break characters can become visible in the local text editor, or are ignored and turn the entire page into a single, way-too-long-to-edit line of text. (FTP should convert line breaks to the destination platform, so this problem may only occur when copying files on a network or onto disks, or emailing them elsewhere.)

Tag Case, Attribute Case. The tag and attribute case affect capitalization. There's no particular technical reason to set them any specific way, as browsers ignore capitalization in tags and attributes. Some people prefer tags to appear in all caps, for example, to distinguish them from the rest of the text. (Older browsers were less forgiving, and this could cause a problem; but that's mostly pre-1996 browsers. Future versions of HTML may require tags to be all lower case, though.)

If you set these options to Database Driven, then whatever values are built into the Web Database's HTML settings set capitalization for tags and attributes.

Quote Attribute Values. This setting adds quotation marks around values like image height and width. For the highest level of compatibility, set this option to Always.

Color Name Translation. GoLive can turn the hexadecimal values used to specify colors into sensible names like "red" and "white." Some browsers recognize only 16 common names, while Netscape has named many more. Although this option makes it easier to identify a color in the HTML code if it's named, you're likely to avoid compatibility snafus if you set this to Do Not. Adobe ImageStyler, for example, choked on named colors when performing a Batch Replace HTML function.

Style Settings

Two settings in the Global tab affect how paragraph-based formatting is written in HTML. We recommend you stick with the defaults and leave both boxes unchecked.

Alignment Local in Paragraphs. This option appears to set whether centered paragraphs use the P tag to control alignment in each paragraph, as in the following code.

```
<P ALIGN="CENTER">text</P>
```

The alternative is to use the Center tag before and after one or more blocks of centered text.

```
<CENTER>text<P>text<P>more text</CENTER>
```

Styles Can Contain Blocks. The cleanest HTML uses paragraph-by-paragraph formatting for text attributes that use the Font tag or other paragraph-based formatting. GoLive can reduce the amount of coding, if you check this option, by putting spanning paragraph formatting across multiple paragraphs.

This method is not the best alternative, as it's not good HTML and some browsers may behave erratically and reset attributes at the beginning of each paragraph regardless of a missing close Font or similar tag.

HTML Tab

The HTML tab organizes all of GoLive's assumptions, preferences, defaults, and compatibility settings for tags—and their legal attributes and attribute values—in one convenient, easy-to-browse location. You can use the HTML tab in three primary ways:

- As a reference to the properties and syntax of existing tags

- To add new tags that Adobe hasn't yet added to GoLive or that the designers chose to exclude to increase compatibility

- To modify some of GoLive's defaults when creating certain new objects

Examining Tags

The HTML tab can organize all the tags and characters logically by where they are used in the page structure or alphabetically by the tags' names. Clicking anywhere in the tab, without making a selection with the WebDB Inspector open, allows you to select Structured (by category) or Flat (all tags listed alphabetically).

Tip: Windows Organization

The Windows version of GoLive uses the Explorer method of showing folders in a pane at the left and its contents in a pane on the right, making it a simple matter to select items and view their properties. This is especially useful in the highly-structured and granular HTML tab (see Figure 27-6).

Figure 27-6
Windows Explorer in the HTML tab

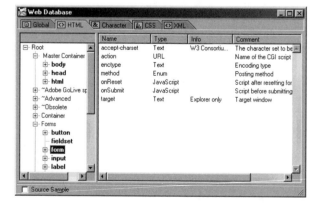

The HTML tab uses several WebDB Inspector palettes that assist with viewing and editing HTML tags. To understand the inspectors, you first need to understand the structure of an HTML tag, whether in GoLive or in the HTML specification.

HTML Syntax and WebDB Inspectors

An HTML tag has a name, like H1 or Img. Each property in a tag, like the height in pixels of an image, is an *attribute*. Each attribute may have *enumerations*, each of which is a legal (or accepted or understood by a browser) value for that particular attribute. For instance, an enumerated attribute for TD (table cell) is align; it can take the values center, char, decimal, justify, left, and right. Most attributes do not have specific enumerations, but can take a required value type, like a color value, number in some unit (pixels, inches, percentage, etc.), or URL (see Figure 27-7).

Figure 27-7
Tag structure

Table attributes

The Table tag's align enumerations

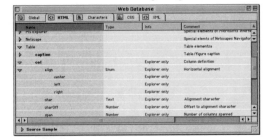

Expanding the view under a tag shows its attributes; expanding enumerations under attributes show the attribute's legal enumerations, when they exist. Using the inspectors, you can view substantial detail about a tag's preview in GoLive, its nature and function in HTML, and how the tag gets structured and interpreted by GoLive.

WebDB Tag Inspector. Selecting a tag from the HTML tab brings up the WebDB Tag Inspector, which includes structure, output preview, and compatibility tabs (see Figure 27-8).

Figure 27-8
WebDB Tag
Inspector

Web Attribute Inspector. If the tag has attributes, expanding the tag (Mac) or selecting the tag in the left pane (Windows) shows the list of attributes. Selecting any attribute brings up the WebDB Attribute Inspector through which the attribute's values are defined, as well as its compatibility and necessity; many attributes are optional (see Figure 27-9).

Figure 27-9
WebDB
Attribute
Inspector

WebDB Enum Inspector. If the attribute has only one set of allowed values—an enumerated list—you can drill down another level and select any enumeration to see the WebDB Enum Inspector, which merely shows its name and compatibility (see Figure 27-10).

Figure 27-10
WebDB Enum
Inspector

Tip: Editing and Adding Values
Later in this chapter, we discuss adding and editing HTML items through the WebDB inspectors. All of those settings in the inspectors that show you the current values can be edited to create new values, tags, attributes, or edit existing settings. (However, GoLive may simply ignore the changes if it's to an item that can't be changed.)

Basic Inspector Settings

The WebDB inspectors' Basic tabs access the most general characteristics of tags, attributes, and enumerations.

Basic tab basics. The Basic tab for each WebDB inspector contains the name of the item and whether it's a tag, attribute, or enumeration. Generally, the Comment field is filled out just for tags, and contains a brief description of the tag's function.

The Tag and Attribute Inspectors offer additional options in their Basic tabs; the Enumeration Inspector has just the Name and Comment fields.

WebDB Tag Inspector. This inspector's Basic tab has three additional items: Structure, Content, and End Tag menus.

The Structure menu defines the tag's nature in terms of its contents. (See Chapter 26, *Cascading Style Sheets*, on the definition of block and inline elements.)

- **Block:** any tag that spans paragraphs or other block elements.
- **Inline Visible:** applies to tags that a browser interprets in order to insert content in their place, like the HL (horizontal line) tag.
- **Inline Invisible:** tags that affect their contents, such as the H1 (heading 1) tag.
- **Inline Container:** can both insert content in their place and contain formatted text or other details. The Applet tag for inserting Java applets is an example of this mixed element.
- **Inline Killer:** used only with the BR tag. The BR (line break) tag is a special case, whether in HTML or in the CSS specification, as it "kills" or ends a line.

The Content menu defines whether GoLive should parse out what it considers extraneous information in a tag. Set to Normal, GoLive cleans up the tag and its contents (if a container) per standard rules.

- The Get All Spaces option preserves extra white space, which is needed in the Pre (preformatted) tag, primarily.
- Core Text leaves the tag and its contents alone to prevent any changes to the syntax of unusual tags. The Noedit tag, for instance, is set to Core Text to prevent GoLive from even attempting to rewrite its HTML.

The End Tag menu corresponds to whether the tag is a container, which requires both an opening and closing tag. Set to None, GoLive doesn't write an end tag; set to Required, it always does.

The two Optional menu items are a matter of fine distinction. Some tags don't require an end tag, but it's useful to insert one for consistency or for some specific browser support. If the End Tag is set to "Optional (Do Not Write)", it means that the person who defined the tag wanted to note it could have an end tag, even though GoLive doesn't write it. "Optional (Write)" is identical to Required in function. (The Attribute option is left as an exercise for the reader, as it is not explained in documentation or through testing.)

WebDB Attribute Inspector. This inspector's Basic tab features three additional items. The Attribute Is menu has three values that fit into two categories. The

Required and Optional settings control whether GoLive writes the tag or not, and whether the syntax checker marks an error if a required attribute is missing. The third option, Alternate, allows an attribute to be missing in raw HTML and not tagged as an error, although GoLive writes the attribute if you create the tag through its interface.

Value Type defines the legal contents of an attribute. The options are relatively self-explanatory. If Enumeration is selected, GoLive has a set of finite possible values for an attribute.

Create This Attribute provides a default value for GoLive to use when inserting the attribute, such as a default border of one for tables. We discuss using this item under "Changing GoLive HTML Defaults," later in this chapter.

Tip: Previewing Attributes with Create This Attribute

Create This Attribute is also useful while creating and editing tags, as it allows you to preview a tag's contents by setting the attribute's value. When you drag and drop the tag into the Source Sample, the tag is fleshed out with both required attributes and any attributes for which you used Create This Attribute.

However, if you've done this as a test for previewing, remember to uncheck the box before leaving the HTML tab to avoid making this your default.

Output Tab

The Output tab appears only in the WebDB Tag Inspector, and controls how GoLive previews a tag in the HTML Source Editor. The tab displays a greeked preview of the HTML formatting.

The Inside and Outside settings are both active if the tag is defined as requiring an end tag. Inside formats the space between the opening and closing tags; Outside formats the space before and after the set of tags.

Setting Inside and Outside to Small provides the simplest formatting, ensuring that each tag is on a line by itself with minimal space before and after. Setting both (or just Inside for standalone tags) to None runs the tags solid in the HTML without any line breaks.

Checking Indent Content indents the tag's contents. For nested blocks of HTML tags, indentation can help aid legibility if the HTML needs to be viewed in its raw state.

Version Tab

The Version tab appears in every WebDB Inspector and reveals the GoLive developers' analysis of which tags, attributes, and enumerations are valid in each browser release and HTML specification.

GoLive uses the settings in the Version tab to allow its HTML syntax checking to interpret correctly whether a given tag, attribute, or enumeration is supported by the browser or browsers against which it is checking. (See "HTML Source Editor" in Chapter 5, *Layout, Source, and Preview*.)

Version settings don't affect how HTML is written in GoLive, nor do they change preferences or settings in browsers loaded on your machine. These settings do correspond exactly with the list of available browsers and specifications shown in the Preferences dialog box's Browser Sets preference under the Source panel.

Major browsers. The browser releases include three generic releases of Internet Explorer and Netscape Navigator each (2.x, 3.x, and 4.x). These are not platform-specific to Mac, Windows, and Unix, despite some differences in implementation in each browser.

HTML specs. GoLive also includes three HTML specifications: HTML 2.0, 3.2, and 4.0. As these specifications tend to either be recommendations for browser developers or documentation of features implemented in earlier browsers, it's more useful as a reference to know which specification a tag appeared in.

As of this writing, the HTML 4.0 spec has not yet been implemented in browsers fully and consistently. The Version tab becomes extremely useful in this case, allowing you to determine whether a tag is supported *only* by HTML 4.0 and not by any of the most popular browsers. It's also a good way to double-check whether you unintentionally used an HTML 4.0 feature in GoLive, which is easy to do.

New browsers and specs. The Version tab only shows major browser and specification releases as of early in 1999. As of press time for this book, GoLive's Web Database hadn't been updated to reflect the Internet Explorer 5.0 release; nor does it differentiate between the 4.0 and 4.5 releases of Internet Explorer for the Mac, or 4.0 and 4.5 versions of Netscape Navigator under Windows and for the Mac.

Can Have Any Attribute. Checking this box suppresses error messages in the syntax checker if attributes exist for a tag that aren't defined in the HTML tab. This is useful for hand-coded HTML that contains nonstandard attributes necessary for particular Web sites or Web server applications.

Adding HTML Tags

Tired of that old, boring HTML? Want to invent some new, exciting HTML? Now you can! Not that it'll work in any browser, but that hasn't stopped anyone yet. But, you might ask, why would I want to add new HTML items?

You may need to add tags to support local uses, like tags used to control database or Web server functionality (but ignored by browsers). Or, you might be relying on a tag or enumeration that none of the major browsers or releases known to GoLive currently support. Or, you might disagree with the GoLive developers' choices about which names or attributes to assign to tags and need to extend the tag's list.

Whatever your reasons, GoLive's Web Database makes adding new HTML characteristics a straightforward process through clicking and selecting items from menus.

Creating New Items

The Web Database toolbar provides the necessary buttons for inserting new HTML items, and offers contextual choices depending on what you have selected. These items are mirrored in the Special menu's Web Database submenu (not to be confused with the Web Database menu item; see Figure 27-11).

Figure 27-11
Web Database
submenu

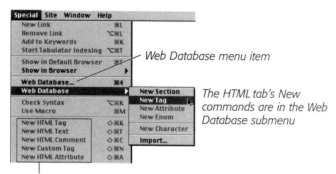

Web Database menu item

The HTML tab's New commands are in the Web Database submenu

These commands work only in the HTML Outline Editor

Once you add any of the below, the appropriate WebDB inspector, including the previously unmentioned WebDB Section Inspector—which we haven't mentioned yet because it's only used to modify section names—allows you to modify any of the settings from the defaults.

New Section. With the HTML tab set to view as Structured, clicking the New Section button creates a new division under which you can organize tags. The WebDB Section Inspector allows you to name the section and describe it (see Figure 27-12).

New Tag. Clicking the New Tag button creates an untitled tag.

New Attribute. With a tag selected, clicking the New Attribute button adds an untitled attribute. You can click this button as many times as you want to create more attributes.

New Enumeration. If you set Value Type in the WebDB Attribute Inspector to Enumeration, the New Enum button activates. Clicking it one or more times creates enumeration entries that correspond to the attribute you selected.

Figure 27-12
Adding a new
section

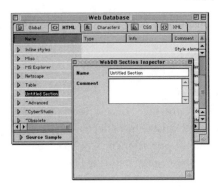

Duplicate. The Duplicate button (also the same as selecting Duplicate from the Edit menu) creates an exact copy of any tag, attribute, or enumeration.

Adding Netscape-Specific Tags

As a practical example, let's add a couple tags that GoLive 4.0 doesn't include in the default Web Database. (These may be added in future releases, but the example is still useful.)

Internet Explorer recognizes a pair of attributes that modify the Body tag so you can specify the offset for a page's contents from the top and left edges of the browser window. IE conveniently names these Topmargin and Leftmargin. These tags aren't available through the Page Inspector, but they are part of the Web Database for the Body tag, and can be added via the HTML Outline Editor.

Netscape Navigator doesn't support these proprietary tags, but starting in version 4.0, Netscape offered its own alternative: the Marginheight and Marginwidth attributes of the Frame tag now also apply to the Body tag to achieve the same result.

Without using the Web Database's HTML tab, you could just type them in by hand in the HTML Source Editor. However, by adding them to the Web Database, you can access these attributes in the Outline view and have their values automatically set to your defaults, thus avoiding potential typing errors. Adding these attributes also means that if you use syntax checking, GoLive accepts these items without complaint.

To add the Marginheight and Marginwidth attributes to the Web Database, expand the contents of the Body tag (see Figure 27-13). Since Marginheight has similar properties to the Topmargin attribute, select Topmargin and click the Duplicate button. GoLive adds a new attribute to the Body tag called "topMargin2".

Select "topMargin2" and, in the WebDB Attribute Inspector, change its name to "marginHeight". You don't need to change the Comment field since it already says "Offset of top margin," unless you want to add something to remind you this is a Netscape-only tag (see Figure 27-14).

Figure 27-13
Creating a
duplicate of
topmargin
attribute

*Select this attribute and then
click the Duplicate button to
create "topMargin2"*

Figure 27-14
New attributes
added to the
Body tag

If you want GoLive to write a value automatically every time you use this attribute, check the Create This Attribute box and enter a value in pixels for the default offset from the top margin.

As a last step, select the Version tab to define browser compatibility so that GoLive's syntax checker gives you the appropriate feedback. Uncheck the boxes next to Explorer 3.x and 4.x, and check the box next to Navigator 4.x.

To create the Marginwidth attribute, complete the above steps by making a copy of Leftmargin, changing its name to "marginWidth", and setting up its compatibility.

Changing GoLive HTML Defaults

As you now understand, GoLive creates HTML tags on pages as objects that are defined in the HTML tab of the Web Database. Changing elements of these objects can change some, but not all, of GoLive's default behavior for inserting new HTML-based items.

Image Link Border to Zero

As an example, let's look at the Img (image) tag. When you add an image to a page and make it a hyperlink, GoLive automatically gives it a border with a width of one pixel. This is the default HTML behavior for this tag.

However, almost all Web designers prefer the default behavior to be to set to no border to prevent an ugly blue link border from appearing. You could manually change the Border field to "0" in the Image Inspector for every image, but why go to all that repetitive trouble? Instead, let's change the Web Database.

Under the HTML tab, expand the Img tag (see Figure 27-15). Select the "border" attribute and bring up the WebDB Attribute Inspector. At the bottom of the Inspector, check Create This Attribute and enter "0" (the numeral zero) in the field below the checkbox.

Figure 27-15
Setting default
for image
border

Outline Editor versus Layout Editor

While the above directions work to change GoLive's default object for the IMG tag, it won't work the same way with all other tags. For example, if you always use white as the background color for all your pages, you'd think you could just make a similar tweak to the Web Database entry for the Body tag.

However, in this case, white becomes the default value only when you insert a background color attribute into the Body tag via the HTML Outline Editor. There's no way to define which attributes appear only in the HTML Outline Editor and which appear as part of an HTML object's default in the Layout Editor.

Characters Tab

HTML itself supports only a limited set of characters and punctuation, and therefore has to use a special method to encode characters that aren't part of that set. It does this using *entities*, or characters given names that are mnemonics for their content. This also frees HTML from relying on the character encoding of a specific platform; no two platforms use the same character code to generate an E with a grave accent over it (è).

A browser interprets the entity and replaces it onscreen with the appropriate character from its local character set. An entity is signalled by an initial ampersand

and terminated by a semicolon; for example, "©" is the code for ©, the copy-right symbol.

HTML displays all the special characters in the Characters tab. This set of char-acters includes most everything in the ISO 8859-1 character set, also known as ISOLatin1 to desktop publishers. The ISO standard reflects standard Roman char-acter sets represented by American and European languages. You can see a list of all entities, ISO 8859-1 and HTML 3.2, at http://www.w3.org/TR/REC-html32.html.

GoLive also includes a few special characters defined as entities as part of the HTML 3.2 specification, like the greater-than sign (>) and less-than sign (<). These are so-called reserved characters; they have a meaning in the syntax of HTML, so if you want to use the actual character, you have to use an entity that represents it.

Organization. GoLive can organize the tab by the character's name or into three categories: Basics, Characters, and General Punctuation. Clicking anywhere in the tab without making a selection brings up the WebDB Inspector from which you can choose Structured (by category) or Flat (alphabetical).

Character details. The Characters tab shows several details about each entity: its name, the character produced, its Mac and ISO 8859-1 character code, and a com-ment that describes the entity.

WebDB Character Inspector. This inspector includes all the information in the general list and provides the hexadecimal values for the ISO and Mac character codes. It also shows a preview of the character that the entity represents. Making the inspector larger creates a larger preview (see Figure 27-16).

Adding Characters

If you're working with non-Western alphabets, you may need to add characters or an entire set into the Characters tab, but it's unlikely you will ever need to add other characters, as new characters need to be supported directly in the browser. Nonetheless, you can easily add new characters to GoLive by selecting New Char-acter from the Web Database submenu of the Specials menu.

Figure 27-16
WebDB
Character
Inspector

Dragging the Inspector palette larger creates a larger character preview

Clicking the New Character button, or selecting New Character from the Web Database menu, creates an untitled entry. Define the character by providing its entity name, which GoLive assumes is the name that gets inserted inside HTML. If you want to name the character differently from its entity value, enter the name in the Name field, and then check the Write box. Enter the entity value in that field, and the preview appears to its right (see Figure 27-17).

Figure 27-17
Setting the
entity's name
separately
from its HTML
value

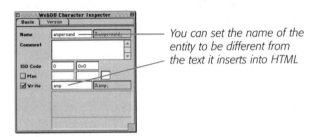

You can set the name of the entity to be different from the text it inserts into HTML

Macintosh-only characters. Both Windows and Mac versions of GoLive show the Macintosh character code for all entities. You can add Mac-only characters with the knowledge that they *won't* show up elsewhere by checking the Mac box and typing a Mac special character in the rightmost box on that line (see Figure 27-18). GoLive generates the appropriate code.

Figure 27-18
Special
Macintosh
characters

Adding sections. If you add new kinds of characters, you might also want to create new sections under which to organize them. Click the New Section button on the Web Database toolbar or select New Section from the Web Database submenu, then use the WebDB Section Inspector to name it and add a comment describing it.

Tweakery. GoLive uses an XML-structured document to store all its entity information. If you wanted, you could add characters directly through this document, called "characters.xml" and found in GoLive's application folder under Modules, Web Database, HTML. However, given that GoLive reads and writes to this document to generate the contents of the Characters tab and to insert entities into HTML, we'd recommend against tweaking the file, unless you're truly insane.

CSS Tab

Contrary to what you might expect, this tab doesn't allow you to define or change CSS properties, like font size. Instead, the CSS Tab has two distinct purposes: to enable Layout Preview to simulate a variety of appearances based on the built-in CSS styles in major browsers, and to set program-wide preferences related to CSS styles.

Browser Preview Settings

The CSS tab provides insight into the way GoLive creates previews of pages in different browsers on different platforms through the Layout Preview's Layout View Controller. On the right of the tab, GoLive lists, by browser/platform pairs, the sets of assumptions that GoLive's designers have encoded about the default CSS browser style sheets for several major browser releases. Consult Chapter 26, *Cascading Style Sheets*, for more information about defining, applying, and previewing CSS styles.

GoLive has six sets of built-in CSS browser style sheets:

- Adobe GoLive: the standard GoLive preview

- Explorer 4, Windows

- Explorer 4, Mac

- Navigator 3, Mac

- Navigator 4, Windows

- Navigator 4, Mac

Tip: Windows GoLive Preview   Because Windows GoLive uses Internet Explorer to provide the Layout Preview, the difference between selecting Adobe GoLive and Explorer 4 from the Root menu of the Layout View Controller is nonexistent.

These browser-based style sheets correspond to items in the Layout View Controller's Root popup menu when you view HTML pages in Layout Preview (see Figure 27-19).

You can change the default for what the Layout View Controller shows as its Root CSS style sheet by selecting the Root radio button next to your preferred browser (see Figure 27-20). Adobe GoLive is the default Root setting.

Settings

Selecting any browser set brings up the CSS Style Sheet Inspector. For built-in styles, you can view, but not edit, settings. The Lock icon provides a visual reminder for these sets; new sets you create have a pencil next to them, showing they're "writable."

Figure 27-19
The Root
menu

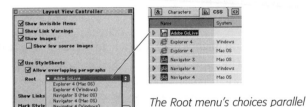

The Root menu's choices parallel
the entries in the CSS tab.

Figure 27-20
Setting the
default root
browser set

The Root radio button
controls the default
browser set in the
Layout View Controller's
Root menu.

Basic tab. The Basic tab displays a browser set's name, operating system, and any comments. These items are all for reference and do not have any bearing on how GoLive creates a preview.

Settings tab. Each browser and platform includes a built-in idea of what the screen density or pixels per inch are. It uses this information to create appropriate sizes of text; we discuss this in depth under "Units" in Chapter 26, *Cascading Style Sheets*. Windows monitors are typically set to 96 dpi, while Mac monitors are set to 72 dpi.

The Can Handle Stylesheets checkbox toggles between whether a browser supports style sheets or not.

Source tab. The Source tab lists all the styles and their properties as they would be inserted into the Head part of an HTML page. This list cannot be edited directly.

Adding New Sets

GoLive offers the flexibility to create new sets or (apparently) to import new sets as they become available. So, if the company writing the Opera browser wanted to ensure better Opera compatibility, they could create an Opera set and GoLive users could import it through the Import item on the Web Database submenu.

To create a new browser set, select any existing browser set and click the Duplicate button in the Web Database toolbar. You can't create a new, empty set, but must duplicate an existing one to do so.

After duplicating a set, use the CSS Style Sheet Inspector to manipulate any of the set-related preferences. To edit individual tags in the set, expand the set's view and select any tag. The familiar CSS Selector Inspector appears, and all the standard options explained in Chapter 26, *Cascading Style Sheets*, are available.

If you need to add new tags, click the New Tag button in the toolbar. To delete tags, select the tag and then choose Clear from the Edit menu.

**Tip: Fooling
Around with
Built-in
Browser
Settings** GoLive has write-protected—hence the lock symbol—these built-in style sheets to prevent changes to core browser previews. However, you can duplicate them and create your own.

If you feel an inherent need to tinker, you can edit the XML-based definitions for this part of the Web Database. This is also a way to bypass the CSS tab to create new browser sets, by writing a new XML document to the specification required.

To edit or add XML, head to the Modules folder in the application folder. Look inside the Web Database folder for the Browser folder. Each CSS set for each browser has its own XML file here.

CSS Settings

Preferences for each different kind of content are found in an area relating to that content. The CSS tab includes several settings that control how CSS styles are used and written in any subsequently created or previewed page.

Use Style Sheets. Unchecking this box disables style sheets throughout GoLive.

Default Unit. When defining or modifying styles in the CSS Selector Inspector, the Default Unit setting controls which default unit to display in the popup menu by default for any CSS property that uses a unit-based measurement.

Output. The Output menu in the CSS tab controls both the Source Sample preview and all HTML output of CSS definitions (see Figure 27-21). As with all HTML, white space is optional in most cases.

The first two Output options, Compressed and Compact are two variations on tight packing. Compressed removes all extraneous spaces; Compact leaves a few in to keep it legible.

Pretty 1, Pretty 2, and Pretty 3 are variations on vertical spacing, indents, and whether the closing bracket appears on a line by itself. Nice is yet another variation on this theme that uses a little less vertical space.

If you uncheck the Indent box, all indents for the Output menu style are measured from a flush left start.

Other Tabs

You might notice an XML or WebObjects tab in the Web Database. These tabs appear by turning Modules on and off; we discuss these extra tags and their corresponding Modules in Chapter 28, *Plug-ins and Media.*

Figure 27-21
CSS formatting
in HTML

Compressed

```
.newclass{color:olive;font-weight:bold;font-size:11px;font-
family:Arial,Geneva;text-align:center}
```

Compact

```
.newclass { color: olive; font-weight: bold; font-size: 11px;
font-family: Arial, Geneva; text-align: center }
```

Pretty 1 & 2 (vertical space varies)

```
.newclass {
   color: olive;
   font-weight: bold;
   font-size: 11px;
   font-family: Arial, Geneva;
   text-align: center }
```

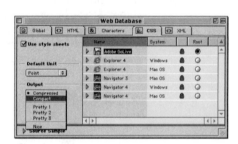

Pretty 3

```
.newclass {
   color: olive;
   font-weight: bold;
   font-size: 11px;
   font-family: Arial, Geneva;
   text-align: center
   }
```

Nice

```
.newclass {
   color:        olive;
   font-weight: bold;
   font-size:    11px;
   font-family: Arial, Geneva;
   text-align:   center }
```

Give It a Try

By giving users access to some of the "guts" of the application, GoLive opens the door to creative and useful customization unavailable in any other programs. Of course, freedom brings responsibility, as abusing the Web Database can backfire on you and cause GoLive to create bad HTML without you necessarily realizing it. But don't be afraid to get under the hood and tinker; you can always revert to factory settings even after disassembling the machine.

Plug-ins and Media

When you're building a multimedia Web site, you can wind up with all sorts of content: Java applets, Flash presentations, Acrobat PDFs, ActiveX objects, and lots of other bits and pieces. GoLive offers support for previewing, inserting, and editing a whole range of rich media and rich formatting languages. In addition, GoLive also offers you the ability to create and edit QuickTime movies directly via the Track Editor.

But first, a word of warning: If you thought you'd escaped the wrath of the Inspector, think again. Like configuring images in GoLive, most of the editing and modifications to embedded media are done almost exclusively through the various and sundry inspectors (hence the decision to focus on them here rather than back in Chapter 2, *The Inspector*).

Netscape-Style Plug-ins

At this point in the history of the Web browser, using browser plug-ins is no big deal. Let's say you come across a page or link that utilizes a plug-in. If you've downloaded and stored the plug-in file within the folder designated by your browser application as the plug-in collection area, then no worries, mate—your browser either plays the media file within the page using the plug-in as a source for the file definition (such as Shockwave) or—as is becoming more and more common—the media is opened in a separate playback application and un-spooled (especially with streaming media, such as the RealPlayer).

GoLive supports any multimedia file supported by either Netscape Navigator or Microsoft Internet Explorer, from QuickTime to Shockwave to VDO to Beatnik. GoLive works in much the same way as a browser. If you've inserted the plug-in file into the Plug-ins folder within the GoLive application folder (see Figure 28-1), you can view your media files using GoLive's Layout Preview. If these plug-in files aren't placed there, then you only see a generic plug-in icon.

Adding plug-ins to GoLive is just as easy as adding them to your browser. Either place them directly into the GoLive Plug-Ins folder via the application's installer, or duplicate the files and move them (Mac) or copy and paste the files (Windows) into the folder. Plug-ins placed into this folder while GoLive is open don't become active until you quit and relaunch the program.

Figure 28-1
Plug-ins folder

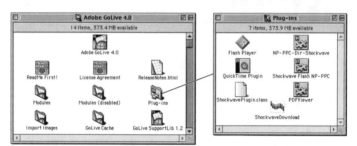

To preview a plug-in file in GoLive, be sure to copy or install the plug-in into this folder.

Why "Netscape Plug-ins?"

The Web browser was not created to be the Swiss Army knife of online publishing programs that it has become. Its initial goal was to combine text with graphics using a set of image file formats that were compressed to jump the low-bandwidth hurdles. It wasn't designed to show movie trailers, air live sports broadcasts, or play celebrity extreme fighting games.

Designers of Web browsers, however, did recognize the need to employ other programs to view certain files the browser couldn't handle. For instance, when a page included a link to a FileMaker database file, that "helper app" could be launched as long as it was defined in the browser preference's MIME file list.

Of course, launching an application takes extra time, sapping the will of the viewer originally interested in the link and making him or her think twice about continuing. To get around this, developers began creating "plug-in" applications that could work directly with the browser to play the media file within the browser window. These smaller applications were stored within a designated spot in the browser's application folder and called upon whenever the browser came across the file format served by the plug-in.

Netscape originated this architecture in Navigator 2.0, and thus begat the reference to "Netscape-style plug-ins." For a while, only Navigator used this plug-in scheme, keeping its name intact. Eventually, Microsoft adopted it for use within Internet Explorer—though the company had tried to steer Web developers toward using ActiveX controls, Microsoft's software standard—and, today, plug-ins are ubiquitous across platforms and browser applications.

The reference to Netscape still lives on in the heart of old-school hacks and developers, but it'll slide away into the sunset at some point, leaving us without this historical marker.

Adding Plug-in Objects

Yes, Shockwave files, Java applets, and ActiveX controls are very different breeds of animals. Yet GoLive groups them together under the same species classification of "objects"—self-contained entities that can be manipulated individually, or collected within a single page (hence the reliance on GoLive's Inspector).

Plug-in Inspector

When you add a multimedia object to a page, GoLive inserts a plug-in placeholder (akin to the Embed tag in HTML). You can add a placeholder directly by dragging the Plug-in icon from the Palette, or you can drag the media file from the Site window or a directory location on your hard drive. If dragged from the Palette, the placeholder icon includes a question mark in the top right corner until you attach a file using any navigation method in the Plug-in Inspector (see Figure 28-2).

Tip:
Recognizing
Plug-in Files,
Part 1

If you drag a file onto a page and it only appears as a text link, you do not have the proper plug-in stored in the GoLive Plug-Ins folder. To rectify this, either add the plug-in to the folder, or use the Plug-in tag icon from the Palette, then navigate to the plug-in.

After finding the source file, the question mark icon disappears and the file's name is placed in the upper left corner of the placeholder. In addition, the generic puzzle icon becomes active instead of dimmed. However, GoLive switches this icon to something more specific (yet still rather generic) for plug-in media that matches items from a list of icons from recognized MIME types (see Figure 28-3).

Figure 28-2
Dragging plug-ins into pages

Placeholder icon dragged onto page from Palette (notice the puzzle icon is faded and a question mark is placed into top right corner, denoting that a file hasn't yet been linked).

Shockwave file dragged onto page is recognized because plug-in is present (note, also, the name of file is added and the puzzle icon looks active).

leftfield.ra ——— *RealAudio file dragged into page is not recognized, however, because plug-in is not loaded into GoLive.*

Tip: A MIME
You Look
Forward to
Seeing

MIME started its life as Multipurpose Internet Mail Extensions, a standard promulgated by a few prominent email gurus (including one of Glenn's idols, Nathaniel Borenstein). MIME was an attempt to bring order to mail attachments, allowing any mail user to encapsulate all kinds of content as parts of an email message and have any MIME-compliant mail reader understand enough about the attachment to, at worst, turn it into a separate file, and at best, decode, play, or display its content.

This standard was useful enough on its own, but the emergence of the Web with lots of operating systems and *lots* of rich media brought MIME to the forefront as a standard that enables all kinds of software—email clients, browsers, FTP software, etc.—to correctly mix, match, and exchange files without losing their essential nature.

Figure 28-3
Plug-in icons

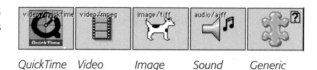

QuickTime   Video   Image   Sound   Generic

The file's URL is entered in the Plug-in Inspector's File field. The inactive Player and Medium fields are pre-filled with what plug-in should play the file, and the type of multimedia file you're linking to, respectively. GoLive gathers this information via the File Mapping settings based on the file's extension (like .wav or .mov); see Chapter 22, *Advanced Features*, for more on File Mapping. If you link to a file without an extension, the field remains blank.

If you need to change the MIME type (or designate one to begin with), check the MIME field to make it active, then select an item from the popup menu button (see Figure 28-4). See Chapter 4, *Preferences and Customizing*, for more information on configuring current and new MIME file types.

Figure 28-4
Plug-in
Inspector's
Basic tab

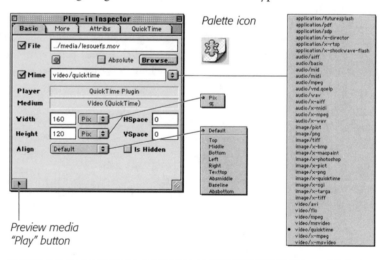

Palette icon

Preview media
"Play" button

Tip:
Recognizing
Plug-in Files,
Part 2

As mentioned before, the question mark icon in the top right corner of the placeholder also disappears once linked to a known file (i.e., one found within your site). However, if you're linking to a URL outside the site, the question mark remains. It only goes away once you check MIME and select the correct file type.

GoLive enters a multimedia file's dimensions into the Width and Height fields. To change dimensions, enter values into either or both of these fields, or drag the placeholder icon by one of the blue handles. Selecting % (percent) from the popup menu for either of these fields resizes the plug-in file depending on the size of a viewer's browser window and relative to the space it inhabits in the page; it also causes the blue handles to disappear on the placeholder icon. To add blank space surrounding the plug-in file, type values in the HSpace and VSpace fields. To align the object on the page, select an option from the Align popup menu.

If you want a multimedia object to play in the background (such as a sound file), check Is Hidden. Note that checking Is Hidden for a visual object defeats the purpose of including it on the page, as it is invisible—but we thought you'd want to know it was possible anyway.

To preview the object while in Layout mode, click the Play button at the bottom left corner of the Plug-in Inspector (which is accessible on all the inspector's tabs). Turn off previewing by clicking the depressed Play button, which brings back the placeholder icon. Preview is also turned off if you click away from the Layout Editor to one of the other modes, then return to the Layout Editor.

More Tab

Click the Plug-in Inspector's More tab to add a name to the object (see Figure 28-5). You can assign a destination link for a page that includes installation instructions by checking Page and entering the URL or navigating to it. The Palette menu configures whether the plug-in appears in the Foreground or Background palette (Windows only). If left as Default, the palette appears in the background.

Figure 28-5
Plug-in
Inspector's
More tab

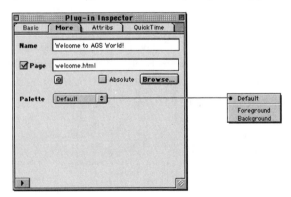

Attribs Tab

The Attribs tab allows you to configure a plug-in's attributes manually. Because of GoLive's close association with QuickTime, the marked attributes found on the QuickTime tab appears in the Attribs tab list. However, if you're working with another form of multimedia plug-in not supported by GoLive (such as Flash), you have to add attributes yourself. (Note that plug-in files not supported by GoLive also have a blank Special tab replacing the QuickTime tab.) Click the New button, type the attribute name in the left Attribute field, then type its value in the right Value field. To modify an attribute, select it from the list and edit either of the two fields. To delete an attribute, select an item from the list and click the Delete button (see Figure 28-6).

Figure 28-6
Plug-in
Inspector's
Attribs and
Special tabs

QuickTime/Audio/Special Tab

As mentioned in the previous section, if a plug-in file is of a variety that GoLive doesn't support directly, the Plug-in Inspector's final tab is a blank Special tab (though it does have a lonely inactive preview button in the bottom left corner). However, GoLive reserves two tabs for a select few file formats: QuickTime and Audio (representing the various sound file varieties, such as AIFF, WAV, etc.).

QuickTime tab. Here's how to set up QuickTime-specific attributes (see Figure 28-7):

- Checking Show Controller (GoLive defaults to leaving this unchecked) reveals the QuickTime playback controls when the plug-in is viewed in a browser. The playback controls add 16 pixels to the height of your object.

- Checking Cache allows the file to be cached by the browser while playing.

Figure 28-7
Plug-in
Inspector's
Attribs and
QuickTime
tabs

- Checking Autoplay allows the file to start playing immediately. Unchecking this option lets the viewer decide when to start playing a file. (Make sure if you uncheck Autoplay to also check Show Controller, or else the file just sits there.)

- If you check Loop, the file repeats itself endlessly. In addition, if you check Palindrome, the file repeats back and forth (i.e., reversing itself when it hits the end; perfect for discovering backward messages in your favorite Beatles songs).

- If Play Every Frame is checked, the browser doesn't take any shortcuts by omitting any frames from your file (a trick used to improve playback).

- Check Link to add a destination URL to the file (adding the location into the Link field, or navigating to the page via Point & Shoot or browsing your hard drive), as well as set a Target (typing the information in the text field or choosing an item from the popup menu).

- Click the Open Movie button to preview the file in a GoLive window. For more information on inspectors you meet when editing QuickTime files, see "QuickTime Inspectors," later in this chapter.

- Set a background color by checking BGcolor and dragging a swatch from the Color palette into the preview field.

- Type a value into the Volume field at which you want the sound to be played back. A value of 100 places the volume slider at the top, while 50 places it in the middle and 0 (zero) places it at the bottom, thus playing no sound. Leaving the Volume field blank produces a default 100-percent QuickTime volume. If you're looking for some Neil Young feedback, you don't get it here; a value greater than 100 just places the volume control at 100 percent.

- Type a value in the Scale field to increase the size of the QuickTime pixels. A value of 1 is the default, while 2 doubles the size, and so on.

After configuring the attributes for a file, click back to the Attribs tab and notice all attributes that were marked are mirrored in the attributes list.

Audio tab. Here's a breakdown of the attributes for audio files (see Figure 28-8):

- Check Is Mastersound to group sounds together using the Nameattribute. In addition, checking this option allows you to spread the controls for a single sound around a page (such as placing the play, stop, and pause buttons in different table cells). If you use this attribute, remember that all sounds in a group must use the Name attribute, and only one sound within the group can have Is Mastersound checked. (This only works with Netscape browsers.)

- Checking Autostart plays the audio as soon as the page begins to load.

- Checking Loop repeats the audio over and over, unless you specify a number of loops in the text field.

Figure 28-8
Plug-in
Inspector's
Audio tab

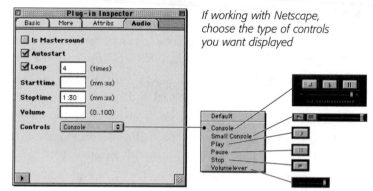

If working with Netscape, choose the type of controls you want displayed

- Type values for Starttime and Stoptime if you want to begin a sound clip at a certain point within the file and stop it at another point. Disregard GoLive's example to the right of each field. The values should be typed in a minute:second:¹⁄₁₀₀-seconds format (i.e., 01:30:05 to start or stop at one minute and thirty-⁵⁄₁₀₀ seconds).

- As with QuickTime files, leave this field blank to default to 100-percent volume, or specify a desired percentage (0 to 100).

- The Controls popup menu allows you to specify a player interface. Console displays the default player interface with stop, play, and pause buttons and a volume lever, while Small Console displays a thinner version with only stop, play, and volume controls. Choosing one of Play, Pause, Stop, or Volumelever displays only that interface item. Note that this is a Netscape-only attribute.

Userdef Inspector (Mac Only)

You can create your own user-defined plug-in or Java applet by creating a definition file filled with the necessary attributes to run the file. The Userdef Inspector is used to set up these attributes, but you have to start out with a little GoLive workaround.

Setting up attributes. In a new, blank GoLive document, drag the Tag icon from the Palette's Basic tab to the Layout Editor, type CS.UD.INTERFACE in the Tagname field, and press Return (notice that the tag placeholder now shows this code). Click on any other display tab, like Layout Preview, in the Document window, then click back to the Layout Editor to find an orange box labeled with the title, "Text". Select the box to bring up the Userdef Inspector (see Figure 28-9). Note that the Userdef workaround only works with the Mac; if you follow the instructions above in Windows, it only results in creating a tag placeholder icon in the Layout Editor with CS.UD.INTERFACE in it.

Figure 28-9
Userdef
Inspector

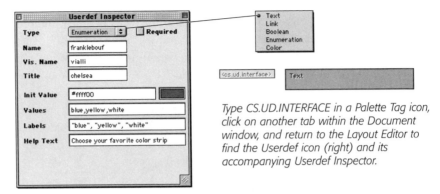

Type CS.UD.INTERFACE in a Palette Tag icon, click on another tab within the Document window, and return to the Layout Editor to find the Userdef icon (right) and its accompanying Userdef Inspector.

In the Type popup menu, choose the type of attribute you want to define. The list includes the following ways to define attributes:

- Text lets attributes use any text content.

- Link lets you define a hyperlink.

- Boolean allows attributes to use two logical states (like yes/no or true/false).

- Enumeration lets you define attributes with multiple options (such as Width, with a choice between Pixel or Percent).

- Color lets you define a color attribute (such as COLOR="#808080").

The chosen option shows up in the top left corner of the Userdef placeholder.

Check Required if a browser needs the attribute you're defining to display the plug-in file. Type a name in the Name field, which appears in the Userdef placeholder icon in the Layout Editor. Type a unique name in the Vis. Name field, then type a title in the Title field. In the Init Value field, type a value that GoLive uses to set the attribute whenever it generates a new instance of the plug-in. You can also drag a swatch from the Color Palette into the color field; its hexadecimal value appears in the text field automatically.

To configure an enumeration, enter the list of values to be used in the Values field, separating items with commas but no spaces. If configuring a boolean attribute, you must type the True item first in the Values field (i.e., "yes,no").

Type a list of descriptive Labels, making sure to separate items with a comma only (unless you enclose each list item in its own set of quotation marks such as "blue," "yellow", "white"). In the Help Text box, write a description of the attribute.

After configuring this attribute, create another by first Option-dragging the Userdef placeholder icon to copy it. Then go through the process of choosing the type of attribute, naming it, assigning it values, and so on.

Saving the definition file. After all necessary attributes have been covered, save the GoLive document as a definition file using the same filename as for the plug-in or Java class, but adding .chasm as the filename extension instead of the typically used extension (such as .dcr or .ram). The file can be saved into the same folder as the unknown media file or Java class, or in either the Modules or Plug-ins subfolders in the GoLive program folder.

Using the definition file. Drag either the Plug-in or Java Applet icon from the Palette to the Layout Editor, then link it to the just-created definition file. GoLive then displays the attributes defined in the file under the Userdef tab of either the Plug-in Inspector or Java Applet Inspector.

Java Applets and ActiveX

Before getting into the nitty gritty of configuring Java and ActiveX in GoLive, let's briefly review what these two pieces of object-oriented media are.

- The Java programming language was developed by Sun Microsystems to be platform independent. Small Java "applets" (which provide a range of functions from groovy animation to database mining) can run on any compatible browser across most platforms. When hooking a Java applet into a GoLive page, look for a file with a .class extension (which compiles Java's bytecode).

- ActiveX, on the other hand, is primarily supported by Windows (despite non-functional checkboxes labeled ActiveX in Internet Explorer for Macintosh), due largely to the fact that it was developed by Microsoft. An outgrowth of Object Linking and Embedding (OLE) technologies, ActiveX "controls" can be inserted into Web pages to enhance formatting and functionality (sounds familiar). The main difference from Java is that ActiveX controls can also be used directly in a wide range of programming languages and applications (including, of course, those created by Microsoft).

GoLive, for the most part, treats these two media objects much like it does plug-ins and images. Simply drag either the Java or ActiveX icon from the Palette into the Layout Editor, and the respective inspector is called up. The Basic tabs of the two inspectors are very similar (see Figure 28-10), save for a few quirks (see the following "Java Applet Specifics" and "ActiveX Specifics" sections).

- In the Base field, type the name and location of the file or navigate to it using Point & Shoot or the Browse button.

- Type values in the Width and Height fields; in the Java Applet Inspector, you can also choose between a fixed pixel or percentage measurement using the popup menus.

- In the HSpace and VSpace fields, you can add blank space (in pixels) surrounding the object; in the ActiveX Inspector, you can also add a border.

Figure 28-10
Basic tabs on
the Mac

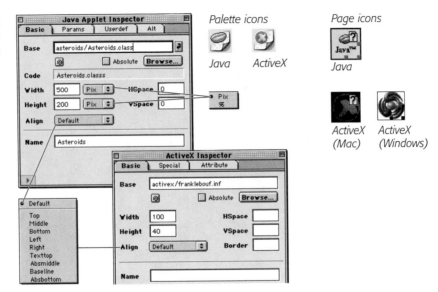

* The Align popup menu offers you the usual attributes for placing your object.
* Type a descriptive name in the Name field.

In GoLive for Windows, you also have the option of importing an existing control found within the Windows System folder. Clicking the Select button brings up the Insert Object dialog, which presents you with a list of available controls and includes a brief description of each (after selecting an item from the list). Click OK and the control becomes a part of your page. Its name is added to the ActiveX Inspector in the space below the Name field and its attributes are listed in the Attributes tab (see Figure 28-11).

In addition, the Java Applet Inspector displays the name of the applet in the inactive Code field, and provides a Preview button in the bottom left corner of each tab (allowing you to test the applet without leaving the Layout Editor).

You can modify these objects further by adding attributes to Java applets using the Param tab of the Java Applet Inspector and the Attribute tab of the ActiveX Inspector. Click the New button, then type the name of the attribute in the Name field and its value in the Value field. Make sure to click New when you add an attribute to avoid typing over the attribute you just set (see Figure 28-12).

The additional tabs of the two inspectors allow you to configure the attributes for each object even further.

Java Applet Specifics

If you created a Java applet with a definition file (using the Userdef trick described in the previous section), click the Userdef tab to display the attributes you set up using the Userdef Inspector. The Userdef tab does not appear in GoLive for Windows.

Figure 28-11
Windows
ActiveX
Inspector

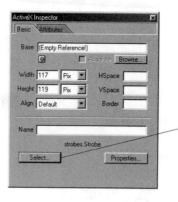
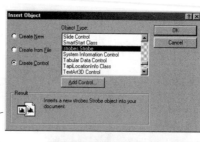

Figure 28-11
Windows
ActiveX
Inspector

With the Windows ActiveX Inspector, you can reference a control using the Base navigation options. You can also click the Select button to bring up the Insert Object dialog, which presents a list of controls stored within the Windows system. Note that the control's file name appears below the Name field. The control's attributes are then filled in automatically (right).

Figure 28-12
Adding
attributes to
ActiveX and
Java Inspectors

In the Alt Text field of the Alt tab, you can add a plain text message that displays when loading an applet has been disabled by a browser (see Figure 28-13).

To format a rich HTML message (which displays when Java is not supported by a viewer's browser), check Show Alternative HTML and a text box appears within the Java Applet placeholder. Click within the box and either type or paste your code or drag tag icons in from the Palette. If you click on another tab within GoLive, then return to the Layout Editor, the Java Applet placeholder returns to its normal icon. Check the Show Alternative HTML again to display the work you've already done, then add more if needed (see Figure 28-14).

Figure 28-13
Java Applet
Inspector's
Userdef and
Alt tabs

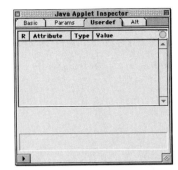

Figure 28-14
Displaying
alternative
HTML for Java

*Normal Java
Applet tag icon*

*Java Applet tag
icon with Show
Alternative HTML
checked*

**Tip:
Streamlining
Alt Text**

If you want to add alternative text to your Java applets, you should come up with one piece of text you can use for all applets—because that's all GoLive seems to allow you to use. If you add text to the Alt Text field in one applet, the same text appears in that field in other applets, even for those that reside on other pages within your site. If you try to delete the text from one applet, they all lose their alt text. Kind of frustrating, but (looking on the bright side) it can help you come up with a single message to send to viewers who have disabled Java.

ActiveX Specifics

The ActiveX Inspector for the Mac also features a Special tab, from which you can configure the following (see Figure 28-15):

- Enter a URL in the Data field for a data file that is accessible by the control.
- In the Linktype field, specify the link the control should use when sending data to its target application.

Figure 28-15
ActiveX
Inspector's
Special tab

- In the Target field, type the application that runs the control
- In the Standby field, type a status message that displays while the control loads

Note that although you can add ActiveX controls while working on the Mac, you can't preview the controls in GoLive.

XML

XML (or eXtensible Markup Language) is the greatest thing since spacially divided grain-based baked food products—or so its proponents maintain. XML is a human-readable, machine-understandable, general syntax for describing hierarchical data that lets users define and tag discrete categories of information using simple text labels, very much like HTML.

Huh?

In other words, XML is customizable (i.e., "extensible") code that looks and reads like you do, but there's no implication built into the format that describes how the data should look. Instead, it just describes what the data consists of. For instance, <H3> in HTML always means a heading level 3, and virtually all browsers interpret it as such—it has a fixed meaning that defines both the content and its display. Whereas, in XML, you might define a headline in some fashion, like <BOOKTITLE>, but that definition wouldn't inherently describe its output, just that the enclosed information was, in thise case, a book's title. (It could also be the name of a type of flower, because the tag's name is entirely arbitrary; but it's not likely.)

Instead of relying on (and conforming to) the fixed code of HTML from which each browser or other interpreting software has to decipher what P and A HREF mean, you could create your own XML language (or "vocabulary") that describes the data that's being presented (rather than telling the browser how to present it). Thus, a file might start:

```
<booktitle>Real World Scanning and Halftones</booktitle>
<price currency=us>29.95</price>
<pagecount>464</pagecount>
```

The idea is that a database can write this kind of output using agreed-upon names for items. Any kind of information could be structured using tags, and any kind of display program (a browser or word processor) or interpreter (like a database or a price-comparison engine or whatever) would be able to process or display information in a document using definitions identical to those in the program that created the document.

This function allows many different programs to access the same data without using proprietary formats, making it easier to exchange rich information across systems and to reuse the same information in many different places without rewriting it for each purpose.

It also means that more advanced browsers or other systems could read HTML files and use embedded XML tags that describe the actual data in those files to provide better kinds of information, or a wider variety of displays. For instance, all bookstores could use a shared vocabulary for describing book content like price, name, authors, and so on. A price-comparison engine could be built into a browser that would extract this information without a lot of tedious pattern recognition—it would just see <price> and go from there.

To create your own XML language, you would create a Document Type Definition (DTD) which defines the elements, structure, and behavior for this vocabulary. (In fact, HTML is redefined as XML in the form of a DTD.)

Tip: More XML Information   We really can't teach you XML in a few pages, but you're probably dying to know more about it, right? The World Wide Web Consortium (W3C) offers extensive documentation, examples, and other information at its Web site at http://www.w3.org/. A great starting point for learning about XML is http://www.w3.org/XML/1999/XML-in-10-points.

XML in GoLive

So how does XML work with GoLive? Well, though it doesn't exactly support XML, GoLive does allow it to be used without a hassle.

In the Web Database, click the XML tab to view available XML tags and definitions. The structure of inspectors associated with this tab is similar to the HTML and Characters tabs. Click the DTD group file (indicated by a GoLive document icon) to reveal the XML DTDInspector; toggle the directory arrow to open up a list of elements. Select a bold element to view the XML DTDElement Inspector, then go one more level down, select an attribute and view the XML DTDAttribute Inspector (see Figure 28-16). You can see this file structure mirrored in the XML's Adobe GoLive folder (CyberStudio folder in Windows), housed within the GoLive program's Modules folder. Open the Compiled DTD folder to find two files:

Figure 28-16
XML Tabs file structure and attribute inspector

XML tab of Web Database

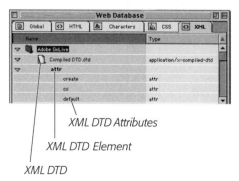

XML DTD Attributes

XML DTD Element

XML DTD

Selecting an attribute displays the XML DTD Attribute Inspector

Compiled DTD.cdtd (which lists all tag elements and attributes) and Compiled DTD.dtd (which condenses the .cdtd list and is used as the XML vocabulary file).

Click the Compiled DTD.dtd file icon in the Web Database to learn an interesting little fact about GoLive and XML: the Web Database, which defines GoLive's code parameters for HTML, XML, CSS, is written in XML (see Figure 28-17). Very clever, Mr. Bond!

Figure 28-17
XML DTD
Inspector

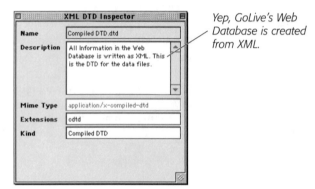

Yep, GoLive's Web Database is created from XML.

The Web Database Toolbar is inactive while in the XML tab; you must instead use contextual menus by either Control-clicking (Mac) or right-clicking (Windows), or use the Web Database options under the Special menu. You can't make an addition to one of the three GoLive XML DTDs (though you can Clear or Delete an item), but you can bring in your own DTD by choosing Import DTD (see Figure 28-18). GoLive automatically deposits this file (formatted as text) in the Imported folder. Note that you can't import a .cdtd file—only .dtd files; when imported, GoLive extracts the condensed information from the .dtd file and creates a companion .cdtd file.

Figure 28-18
Importing XML
DTD file

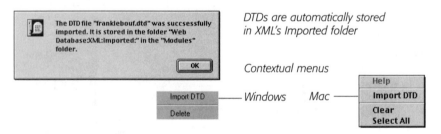

DTDs are automatically stored in XML's Imported folder

Contextual menus

Windows   Mac

XML DTD Inspector

In the Web Database, click one of the DTD files; this causes the XML DTD Inspector to display general information about this vocabulary file (as seen in Figure 28-17). The Name field displays the file's title, but is inactive; GoLive doesn't allow you to edit a DTD's name.

Type a brief description of this DTD file in the Description field. If you're configuring an imported DTD file, the MIME Type, Extensions, and Kind fields are blank. (If viewing a default GoLive DTD, these fields are filled in and MIME Type is inactive.) To give your DTD file a proper MIME Type, type "application/x-compiled-dtd" in the field.

XML DTD Element Inspector

Much like the WebDB Tag Inspector (brought up when selecting a tag from the HTML tab's list), the XML DTD Element Inspector displays the name of the XML element and allows you to type a brief note in the Comments field.

However, that's about it for the Basic tab. The Is Document Root checkbox is inactive, and only checked for the element that previously has been selected as the root. In the case of GoLive's Compiled DTD.dtd file, the Compiled element is selected as the root. For DTD files that have been imported, if an element has been selected as the root, this option is checked and inactive. However, you can check this option on another element, and checking it switches the root to that item.

Click the Output tab to configure how the tag displays within the XML code. For instance, selecting X Large from the Outside popup menu places more space before the start tag and after the end tag. Selecting X Large from the Inside popup menu places more space between the start and end tags and the content they contain. Check Indent Content to place space at the beginning of each line of content (see Figure 28-19).

XML DTD Attribute Inspector

Toggle an arrow or plus sign to the left of an XML element to reveal its list of attributes; the inspector then switches to become the XML DTD Attribute Inspector. Again, you find the Name field inactive and a Comment box ready for a brief de-

Figure 28-19
XML DTD
Element
Inspector

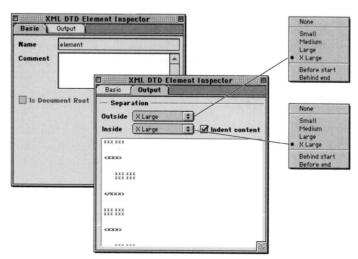

scription (if not already supplied). The Attribute Is and Value Type popup menus are inactive and don't seem to become active for editing. And while the Default field is active for you to type in, its popup button doesn't bring up anything (see Figure 28-20).

Figure 28-20
XML DTD
Attribute
Inspector

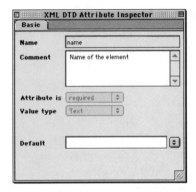

XML Item Inspector

If you want to see what an XML file looks like in GoLive, double-click a DTD file (for instance, Compiled DTD.cdtd from the XML folder in Web Database Modules). In the Layout Editor, you see a gaggle of foreign item tag icons. View and edit the XML elements here in tandem with the XML Item Inspector, or, for an even better view of your XML, switch to the HTML Outline Editor (see Figure 28-21).

Notice that each element and attribute includes a Name. Attributes include a field for Type; if assigned, an element also includes Output information. To add new elements and attributes, use the Outline Toolbar buttons, or the Outline-specific items found in the Special menu.

Unlike code viewed in the HTML Outline Editor, the attributes or values associated with a particular element can't be revealed by clicking a handle or button. Remember, XML is not a preset, defined language, as HTML is—anything you want to modify here must be typed in the text field.

QuickTime Editing

Thanks to Adobe's partnership with Apple, authoring and editing QuickTime files in GoLive is relatively powerful and painless. QuickTime movies and sound files can be opened directly within GoLive from the Site window or by double-clicking the plug-in placeholder in the Document window while in Layout mode. New QuickTime files can be created by choosing the New QuickTime Movie from the New Special section of the File menu.

Figure 28-21
XML DTD
Element
Inspector

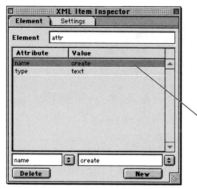

*Viewed in Layout
Editor (top right)
and Outline Editor
(bottom)*

When opened, GoLive opens the new or existing file in the Movie Viewer, which includes the basic QuickTime control bar. To access GoLive's editing capabilities, click the colored film icon in the top left corner of the Movie Viewer and the QuickTime Track Editor appears. This looks somewhat similar to the Timeline Editor (accessed by clicking the movie icon in the Layout Editor), but instead of configuring DHTML animations within a page, the Track Editor allows you to edit the individual tracks (sound, video, text, etc.) within a QuickTime file. (See Figure 28-22; also see the "Track Editor" section of Chapter 3, *Palettes and Parts* for a breakdown of all the editor's buttons and pieces.)

Tip: Playing
Tricks

On Windows, you can start playing a QuickTime file in the Movie Viewer by pressing Enter. To pause, press the 0 (zero) key on your keyboard's keypad. To start back up again, press Enter, or press 0 again to return to the beginning of the file. On both Windows and the Mac, double-click within the movie's image once to begin playing, then double-click a second time to pause.

QuickTime Inspector

Opening a QuickTime file in the GoLive Movie Viewer also brings up the Quick-Time Inspector. The inspector's Basic tab provides information about the file,

Figure 28-22
QuickTime
Movie Viewer
and Track
Editor

Movie Viewer

Determines
window size

Track Editor

including file size, window size, data rate and duration. These values are inactive, and can only be modified using the QuickTime application.

The Annotation tab allows you to enter background information about the movie that gets embedded into the file. To add an annotation for, say, author name, select Author from the popup menu, enter the name in the text area, then click the Add button. If Add is not clicked, the information entered into the text box isn't saved once you select another annotation. When making edits, click Replace when finished, or click Delete to clear all text from an annotation (see Figure 28-23).

Figure 28-23
QuickTime
Inspector's
Basic and
Annotation
tabs

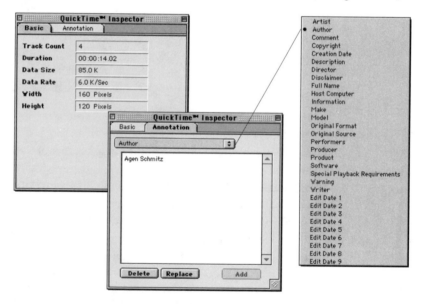

A file's annotations can be viewed when opened in QuickTime by choosing Get Info from the Movie menu (see Figure 28-24).

Tip: Flat QuickTime Files   When saving the QuickTime movie in GoLive, you're given two options: Flatten or Fast Save (the GoLive default). If you're just saving annotations or edits as you're working on a movie, choose Fast Save. However, you should choose Flatten when the movie is publish-ready, as this compresses the data and creates a self-contained QuickTime movie. (It also takes some time to save.)

Figure 28-24
Movie viewed
in QuickTime,
with Info
dialog box

Track Editor and Inspectors

To edit an existing QuickTime file, click the movie cell icon in the upper left corner of GoLive's Movie Viewer dialog box to open the Track Editor. Within the Track Editor, you can add and edit attributes within the QuickTime file by using the various individual tracks (as shown in Figure 28-25), which are controlled using their respective inspectors. To call up an inspector, simply click one of the individual track lines. To toggle back to the GoLive Movie Viewer and its QuickTime Inspector, click the movie icon in the top left corner of the Track Editor. To delete tracks, select an item in the Track Editor (it turns a dark gray) and press Delete.

Track Editor icons. Below the corresponding track icon in the right column of the Track Editor, you see an eye icon, which signifies whether the track is visible or not within the QuickTime file. To make a track invisible, click the eye icon to make it inactive. In addition, some tracks include a toggle arrow, which, if clicked, expands to show additional content (such as the HREF Track's URL in Figure 28-25).

Video Track Inspector

Select a video track in the Track Editor, or drag in the Video Track icon from the QuickTime tab of the Palette, to bring up the Video Track Inspector (see Figure 28-26). An Open dialog appears through which you can navigate to another movie (or QuickTime compatible video file) to place as your video track.

In the inspector, start by entering a name for the track in the top text field. In the Left and Top fields, type pixel coordinates to position the video within your selected screen area. In the Width and Height fields, type pixel values for the horizontal and vertical dimensions of the movie. Check Constrain Proportions to proportionally resize the movie (i.e., the Height value is automatically adjusted when the Width value is edited), thus keeping the original aspect ratio.

Figure 28-25
QuickTime
tracks in Track
Editor

Click to toggle back to Movie Viewer

Time slider

Indicates visible track

Indicates invisible track

Indicates total track length and starting point

Toggle to reveal track items

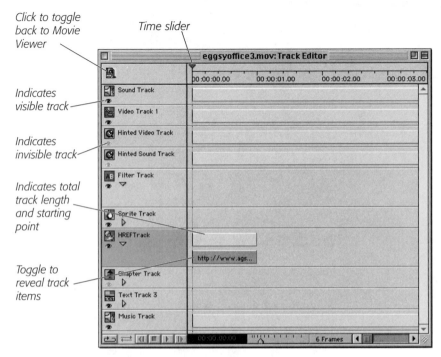

Figure 28-26
Video Track
Inspector

Palette icon

Example of Video Track Inspector attributes

Navigating to a QuickTime file to add as the video track

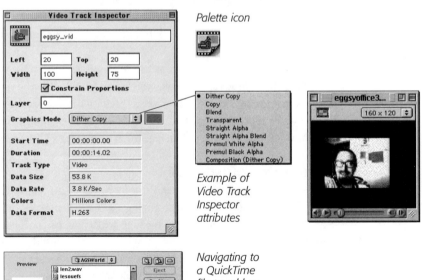

If you have a number of visual layers within a movie, enter a value in the Layer field to place it in the stacking order (the lower the number, the closer it is to the front).

In the Graphics Mode popup menu, select how you want a video track to overlay other tracks in the movie. Your options include:

- **Dither Copy:** (GoLive's default) lays the video track over the track directly beneath it and applies dithering to improve how it looks to the viewer. (Dithering creates additional colors and shades by varying the proportions of colors from an existing palette.)

- **Copy:** essentially performs the same job as Dither Copy. However, because it does not dither, this isn't optimal for display using 256 colors (though it might be a good solution for viewers with low system memory).

- **Blend:** makes the track translucent, allowing you to see the track lying beneath the current track; in the Track Editor, a track at the top of the list is overlaid by tracks added to the list below it. To change the degree and color of the transparency, choose a color from the Color Palette and drag its swatch into the Graphics Mode color field.

- **Transparent:** allows you to define a transparent color as you did for Blend.

- **Alpha channel options:** with 32-bit graphics, you have three 8-bit color channels (red, green, and blue) and one 8-bit alpha channel. The alpha acts as a mask and specifies how the pixel's colors should be merged with another pixel when the two are overlaid. Thus, you are specifying what part of a visible image should be left out. With Straight Alpha, the color components of each pixel are combined with the background pixel. Straight Alpha Blend combines straight alpha with the properties of Blend, causing the masked areas to be transparent and the non-transparent areas to be translucent. Premul White Alpha works with images created on a white background with a premultiplied alpha channel, while Premul Black Alpha does the same with images created on a black background.

- **Composition (Dither Copy):** similar to Dither Copy's properties, but works best when adding animated GIFs as video tracks.

Note that these options can be found in the other visual track inspectors, including Filter, Text, HREF, Sprite, and Chapter Tracks.

The remaining fields are not editable, but are updated as you edit a track within in the Track Editor. For instance, to change the start time of the video track, click and drag the track's bar to a desired point with the grabber hand. The Video Track Inspector isn't automatically updated; however, if you click on another track and click back to the original video track, the new time appears in the Start Time field.

Sound Track and Music Inspectors

Select either a music or sound track to bring up its respective inspector. When you drag either icon in from the Palette's QuickTime tab, GoLive asks you to navigate to the file you want to bring into the movie; sound tracks accept a wide variety of sound files (from .aiff to .wav), while music tracks only accept MIDI files. Both inspectors are largely informational, allowing you to only name the track in the text field at the top (see Figure 28-27).

Figure 28-27
Sound Track
Inspector

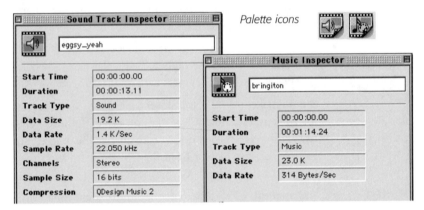

Video Effect Inspector

Select a video effect track from the Track Editor (the name defaults to Filter Track), or drag the Filter icon from the Palette, to bring up the Video Effect Inspector. The Basic tab features the same controls found on the Video Track Inspector, allowing you to add a name and configure dimensions and positioning. Note that the Basic tab on the other track inspectors follow this model as well (see Figure 28-28).

To set up an effect for the movie, click the Effect tab, then select either Generic (which includes such basic effects as clouds and fire), Filter (which adds effects similar to Photoshop filters to a single track), or Transition (which fades from one track to another). Choosing Filter makes the Source A popup menu active, while Transition makes the Source B popup menu active as well; both popup menus list the video tracks found in your movie. Select a track you want to add an effect to. (For Transition, choose your beginning track in A and your ending track in B.)

Clicking the New button brings up the Select Effect dialog box for the type of effect you chose above. Select from the list in the menu pane on the left, then configure its attributes. The preview pane in the lower left corner gives you an idea of what you're doing to your video track. If you want to add this effect to other tracks or movies, you can save its attributes by clicking the Save button. To add previously saved effect files, click Load. When finished, click OK.

Figure 28-28
Video Effect
Track Inspector

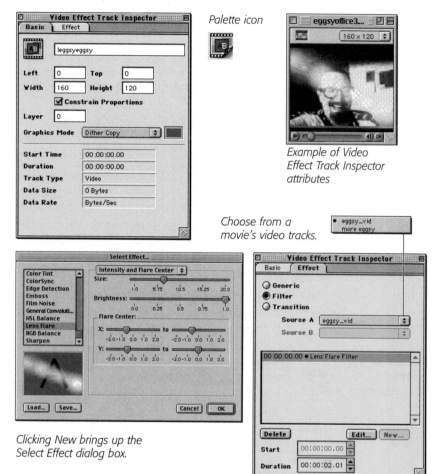

Palette icon

*Example of Video
Effect Track Inspector
attributes*

*Choose from a
movie's video tracks.*

*Clicking New brings up the
Select Effect dialog box.*

**Tip: Track
Inspector
Super Tips**

The tips listed here apply to all Track Inspectors. With the first video effect you create (or any other attribute on any other track inspector), GoLive defaults to making the Start time field inactive at 0:00:00.00 on the timeline. To adjust the beginning point to a later time, click the blue track bar and drag to a desired point with the grabber hand.

The orange track bar below doesn't move until the blue bar is released. To modify the starting point, click and drag. Unless otherwise specified, the video effect you add (or any attribute added to any of the other track inspectors) begins at 0:00:00.00 in your timeline. To specify another starting point, drag the timeline slider to a desired point.

To add another item to any of the track inspectors, you must first move the time slider to any point past the starting point of the initial track attribute you set. After setting the new point, simply repeat the necessary steps for the inspector you're working in.

On the attribute tab of a track inspector (i.e., Text, HREF, etc.), you can modify the Start and Duration time fields of an individual attribute by selecting a time measurement (minutes, seconds, milliseconds) and clicking the up and down arrows. If you have one attribute followed by another and want to change the duration time of the first item, you must change the starting point of the second item.

In the Track Editor, click the toggle arrow to reveal the orange track bar displaying the name of your effect; if you have multiple effects within a track, clicking on each highlights the item in the inspector's Effect tab.

HREF Track Inspector

To add a destination URL to your movie—one that either automatically causes the browser to jump to the new page or allows the viewer to click a link—drag the HREF Track icon from the Palette into the Track Editor. Again, the Basic tab allows you to configure the usual suspects, however, the name text field is inactive (see Figure 28-29).

To add a link, go to the HREF tab and either type in a URL in the Link field or navigate to it using Point & Shoot or Browse, then type a frame name or select an item from the Target popup menu. If you don't add information to either of these

Figure 28-29
HREF Track Inspector

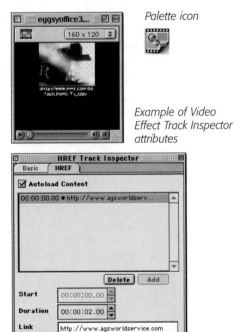

Palette icon

Example of Video Effect Track Inspector attributes

fields before clicking the Add button, GoLive displays an error message. When you're finished specifying information for these fields, click the Add button. To edit an added URL, type your changes in the Link field and press either Return or Tab to accept the edit; the change then appears in that field. Check Autoload to move your viewers automatically to your selected destination (rather than waiting to have them click the link).

Text Track Inspector

To add a text message to your movie, drag the Text Track icon from the Palette into the Track Editor and add any necessary information into the Basic tab's fields. Click the Text tab and enter your message in the Text field. Click the New button when finished, and your message is added to the list field above (see Figure 28-30).

Figure 28-30
Text Track
Inspector

Palette icon

Text track revealed in GoLive Movie Preview

Chapter Track Inspector

You can divide a QuickTime file into sections by dragging the Chapter Track icon from the Palette into the Track Editor, bringing up the Chapter Inspector. These chapters appear in the status line of the QuickTime Player; in version 4.0, the chapters are accessed by clicking the up and down arrows (see Figure 28-31).

After entering information on the Basic tab, click the Chapter tab, type a chapter title in the text field and click the New button.

Sprite Track Inspector

Sprite tracks are handy tools for adding low-impact animation to your movies. Unlike adding an animated sequence as a video track, which streams a continuous set of pixel images, sprite tracks place individual references to images placed into a common gallery, which helps to keep the file size down.

Drag the Sprite Track icon from the Palette to the Track Editor and set up your baseline attributes on the inspector's Basic tab. On the Properties tab, check Visible

Figure 28-31
Chapter Track
Inspector's
Chapter tab

Figure 28-31
Chapter Track
Inspector's
Chapter tab

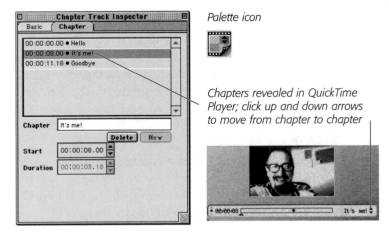

Palette icon

Chapters revealed in QuickTime Player; click up and down arrows to move from chapter to chapter

to display the sprite track in the Movie Viewer; if this is unchecked, the sprite track can be temporarily hidden to display any tracks below it. Check Scale Sprites When Track Is Resized if the images you include are vector graphics; if left unchecked, vector graphics could look jaggy after a movie is resized. To add a background color, drag a color swatch into the Background Color field (see Figure 28-32).

Figure 28-32
Sprite Track
Inspector's
Basic and
Properties tabs

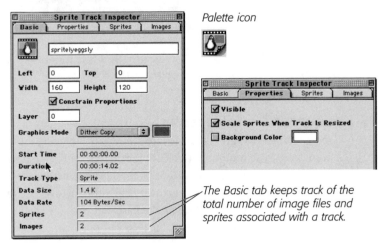

Palette icon

The Basic tab keeps track of the total number of image files and sprites associated with a track.

Next, go to the Images tab to import graphics into the track (see Figure 28-33). Click the Add button, navigate to an image file, and click Open. You're then met with the Compression Settings dialog box, from which you can select an appropriate image format compressor from the top popup menu. Select a color depth from the second popup menu, which offers choices based upon the compression method selected; most format compressors offer just grayscale and color (256 colors), while some offer more choices (such as Cinepak, offering 256 grays, 256 col-

Figure 28-33
Sprite Track
Inspector's
Images tab

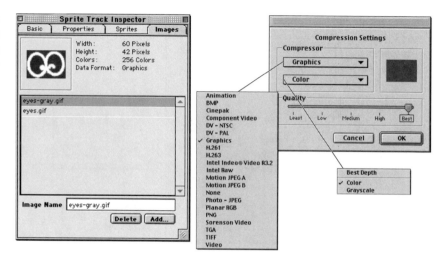

ors, and millions of colors). To modify the quality of compression, drag the slider to one of the preassigned settings. If you click the slider and hold it while dragging, you can view the numerical scale.

Select the image from the list for a preview and summary of its file properties.

Tip:
Importing
Image
Formats

Unlike importing images into a Web page, which must be of a certain file format (like GIF, JPEG, etc.), all the following file formats can go into a QuickTime sprite track: BMP, GIF, JPEG, Photoshop (PSD), PICT, PNG, SGI, Targa, TIFF, and QuickTime Image Format. Mac users can also import MacPaint and QuickDraw GX images.

Go to the Sprites tab and click the Add button to add a sprite to the track (see Figure 28-34). At this point, the track has nothing to show within the movie, just a source file that was brought into the Images tab. Select the generically named sprite from the list and type a title in the Name field. Select your desired image from the Initial Image popup menu at the bottom of the inspector, which lists all images that have been imported into the track. The image now appears in the Movie Viewer with a black background. Modify its placement by typing values in the Top and Left fields. Check Visible if you want the sprite to be seen at the beginning of the track, and select how you want the image to be displayed by selecting an item from the Graphics Mode popup menu.

Click the toggle arrow on the Track Editor's Sprite Track to reveal the list of keyframes (essentially the items you just configured in the Sprite Track Inspector's Sprites tab).

Sprite Sample Inspector. Now that you've set the initial, static sprite images (which reside at 0:00:00.00 on the timeline and are denoted by small boxes with a

Figure 28-34
Sprite Track
Inspector's
Sprites tab

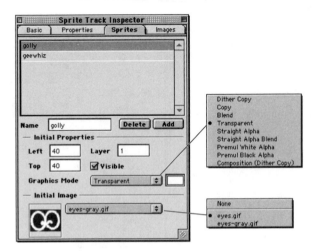

dot in the middle), it's time to create some rudimentary animation. Click a box listed under the Sprite Track (which turns it from blue to orange), to call up the Sprite Sample Inspector.

Here on the Basic tab you can modify many of the same attributes found on the Sprites tab of the Sprite Track Inspector (see Figure 28-35). However, the real fun is on the Actions tab, where you can configure "wired sprites," which can respond to actions performed by the viewer (see Figure 28-36). Note that wired sprites require QuickTime 2.0 or higher to work.

Select the type of viewer input by selecting an item from the Events pane (such as Click, Click Button, Mouse Enter, etc.), then click the "+" (plus sign) button above the Actions pane. Next, select an item from the Action Kind popup menu. Some actions are self-explanatory and don't need any more information (such as Movie GoTo End), while others bring up a set of text fields and/or popup menus

Figure 28-35
Sprite Sample
Inspector's
Basic Tab

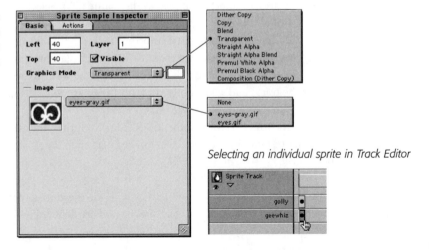

Selecting an individual sprite in Track Editor

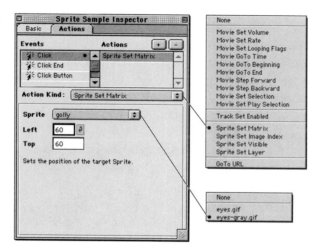

Figure 28-36
Sprite Sample
Inspector's
Actions Tab

that allow you to configure the actions attributes (such as Sprite Set Matrix, which sets the position of a target sprite).

If you click and drag one of the keyframes, it pops back to its initial placement; to add a new keyframe, Option-click (Mac) or Alt-click (Windows) the initial item and drag it to a desired position on the time line. Once a new sprite has been created, you can drag it to any position on the timeline. Configure its attributes as you did for the initial sprite, changing its position, image reference, or associated action, and continue to animate your spritely movie in this manner.

ASP Support

ASP (Active Server Page) is a scripting language and technology developed by Microsoft for use with their Web server, Internet Information Server (IIS); it's also beginning to be supported by other servers, like the free Apache Web server. The term ASP refers to pages that have programming code embedded in an HTML page. When a user requests a page, the server looks through the page on the local hard drive, finds ASP code (if any), and executes it. The server might take any kind of action as a result of ASP code, including just feeding out the HTML part of the page, modifying parts of the HTML (dropping in custom information, for instance), setting a cookie on the user's browser, or redirecting the user to another page on the site or the Web. This makes it easy for a Webmaster or site developer to put their programs and pages in the same file, rather than requiring lots of server configuration or perl scripts.

The problem, of course, is that Microsoft introduced ASP without warning anybody sufficiently. So, suddenly, visual Web page editors had to cope with oodles of code that needed to be left alone to work. However, GoLive takes a hands-off approach. You can read ASP code and write it back to file, as well as work with any number of other codes and proprietary languages (JScript, VBScript, Visual Basic, etc.) that are used in Web pages. You just can't do it visually with fancy icons and helpful inspectors.

If you open a file with ASP code in it, GoLive uses a placeholder icon to indicate where the code exists and the Foreign Item Inspector allows you to edit it; you can also edit ASP code directly in the HTML Source Editor or HTML Outline Editor (see Figure 28-37).

By the way, GoLive doesn't preview or execute ASP code; you have to upload your files to a server that supports ASP to test it out directly.

Figure 28-37
ASP editing in
three modes

Editing ASP code in the Foreign Item Inspector in the Layout Editor (top), using the HTML Outline Editor (center), and HTML Source Editor (bottom)

```
<body bgcolor="white">
    <%%Response.Cookies("MyFavTVShow")="I Dream of Jeannie"%%>
</body>
```

WebObjects

The GoLive manual doesn't mention WebObjects much and we intend to follow suit—no offense to any of you WebObjects users, which is an elite (read: fairly small but truly devoted) group. WebObjects is a system that integrates database information and the World Wide Web fairly efficiently and seamlessly, allowing ordinary users to manipulate and retrieve information between a database and a Web server handling user transactions without a lot of messy coding. This system was developed by NeXT Computer, later acquired by Apple Computer, Inc. (For a great example of a site built and maintained with WebObjects, visit the Apple Store at http://store.apple.com.)

GoLive offers tight integration of WebObjects controllers and its Layout Editor. If you turn on WebObjects in the Modules pane of the Preferences dialog box—and we only recommend you do if you actually use a WebObjects server—GoLive adds an additional tab to the Web Database, the Document window, and the Palette (see Figure 28-38).

Figure 28-38
WebObjects
support with
extra tabs

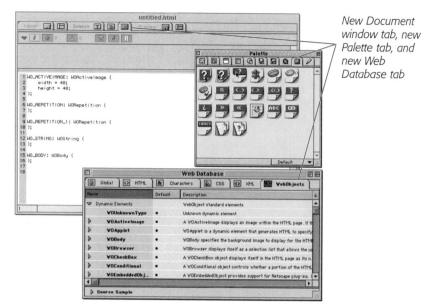

*New Document
window tab, new
Palette tab, and
new Web
Database tab*

If you're a WebObjects user, all these controls and options make great sense, and you're probably ecstatic to see them. For the rest of us, it's important to just leave the WebObjects Module turned off to keep memory usage low.

Plug In, Log Out, and GoLive!

You've reached the end of another thrilling installment in the Real World series of books. But, as you probably know, it's never the end. For more information about where to find more information… see the Preface… and start reading the book all over again….

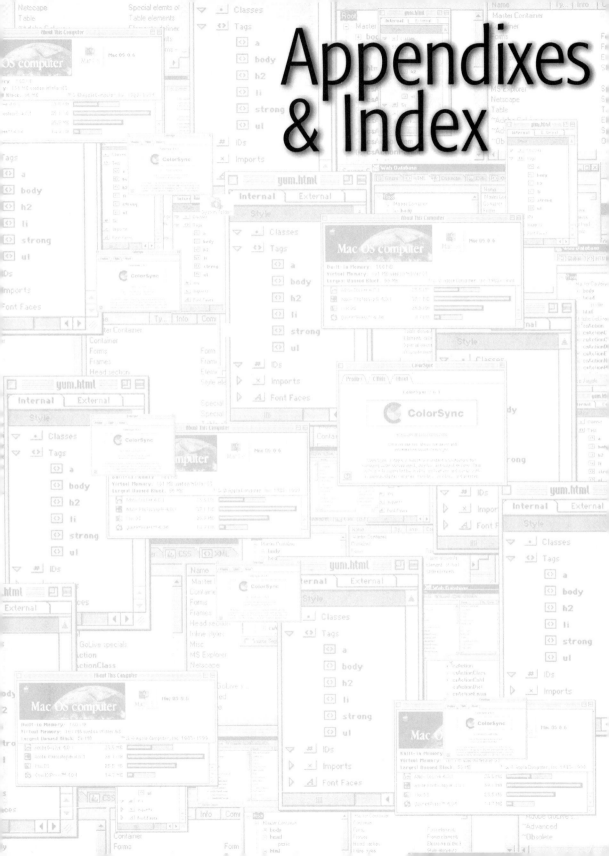

Appendixes
& Index

APPENDIX A

Macintosh Issues & Extras

Even though GoLive appeared first on the Macintosh (as versions of GoLive CyberStudio, the product's previous name), Adobe has done a fairly seamless job of making sure the Macintosh and Windows versions of the product are in parity.

This is a nice touch, as it would be frustrating for users of either platform to see the bright, shiny ball that's waved in front of them but that they can't use.

Most of the Macintosh-only features in GoLive relate to operating system details, not functionality in the program itself. That is, GoLive taps into some items that the Mac OS has built into it or that you extend the Mac OS to support, rather than GoLive for Macintosh having some kind of site-mapping view not found on Windows.

The main areas of difference are:

- **File details.** The Mac stores extra information with each file, such as the program that created it and a label in the Finder (on the Desktop) that Windows files don't include settings for.

- **Mac OS 8.5 specials.** With Mac OS 8.5, Apple introduced a couple of extras that programs could take advantage of: an extended file select dialog box for opening and saving files, and a method of changing the appearance of all interface elements to be consistent throughout all applications. (Don't worry; you can turn both these features off if you don't like them.)

- **Search engine simulation.** GoLive taps into Apple Information Access Technology (AIAT) to provide a simulation of what an Internet search engine might come up with when indexing and searching on your pages.

- **ColorSync.** Apple offers a system-level color-management system called ColorSync that, ideally, lets you scan, edit, view, and output images in a variety of programs, on a variety of machines, with some semblance of consistent color and tonality. Windows offers limited support for this in the current releases, although the potential for cross-platform use is increasing.

- **Internet Config.** The Macintosh version of GoLive can leverage a set of common Internet settings modified and stored by a freeware program called Internet Config. This includes file mappings for files opened via GoLive or downloaded via FTP, and preferences for configuring proxy servers.

- **AppleScript.** The Mac OS has a built-in scripting language that lets you control a lot of the functions of the Finder and various AppleScript-savvy programs. GoLive supports AppleScript in its HTML Source Editor view, and you can use AppleScript to automate page creation, or to provide advance features to end-users through scripts you distribute.

File Features

GoLive inserts Macintosh-specific differences in a few of the Inspector palettes used to examine files.

Finder Label

The Finder label can be set up on the Macintosh Desktop by selecting Label from the Control Panels folder (Mac OS 8.1 or earlier) or by selecting the Labels tab of the Preferences dialog box chosen from the Edit menu (see Figure A-1).

Figure A-1
Setting Label
color and text

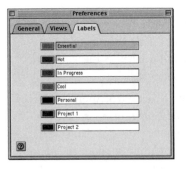

Pre-8.5 Mac OS (above)
Mac OS 8.5 and later (left)

You have seven possible labels preset to some generic names like "Essential" and "Project 1". The color may also be changed by clicking the color swatch next to the name. The order in which the items appear in the Label control panel or Labels tab affects the sorting order in the Finder when you sort the view by Label.

Labels may be assigned in the Finder by selecting one or more items and choosing the label from the Label menu (Mac OS 8.1 and earlier) or by right-clicking and selecting Label from the popup contextual menu (see Figure A-2).

Figure A-2
Label
submenu in
Mac OS 8.5
and later

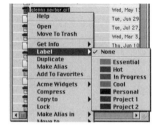

Folder Inspector. In the Files tab of the Site window, selecting a folder brings up the Folder Inspector. The Label popup menu shows the existing choice, and can be set to a new choice that gets applied to the folder on the desktop (see Figure A-3).

Figure A-3
Folder
Inspector's
Label popup
menu

File Inspector. Selecting any file or alias in the Files tab of the Site window brings up the File Inspector which displays the Label menu, identical to the Folder Inspector's menu. As with folders, the inspector shows the current label assigned and lets you choose a new one.

Site View Controller. In the Site tab, clicking the eye icon at the upper right brings up the Site View Controller. In the Color tab, in the Item Color section, GoLive for Macintosh offers Finder Label as a third option for coloring the items that appear in the site map (see Figure A-4).

Figure A-4
Site View
Controller's
Item Color
settings

Type and Creator

When you create or import HTML files from many sources, you can wind up with funky icons in the Macintosh Desktop and in the Site window's Files tab. Worse, double-clicking the file opens it in Microsoft Word, BBEdit, or SimpleText. GoLive provides a simple way to fix this.

The Macintosh stores two pieces of information with every file: its creator and its type. The creator and type are four-character-long codes that correspond to the program which created the file and the type of file it is. Each application on the Macintosh has a unique creator code so that every file knows exactly to which program it belongs. Each application can define any number of its own types so that the application knows what kind of file it's looking at—TIFF image, GIF image, JPEG image for an image-editing program, etc.

Select a file in the Files tab in the Site window and bring up the File Inspector's File tab. The two fields labeled Type and Creator correspond to the Finder's type and creator. To change an HTML file so that it thinks it was created by GoLive, make sure Type is set to "TEXT" and creator is set to "GoMk" (case is important). As soon as you click the Return button on the field or press Return, the icon in the Files tab changes immediately to the GoLive icon (see Figure A-5).

Tip: Change Creator Freeware   CTC (change-creator-type) is a freeware program that lets you batch process a set of files to change their creator or type to something else. You can download it from http://www.eureka.ca/rmf/Docs/ctc.html.

Figure A-5
Changing Creator code to fix program association

The icon was created in some bizarre program with a wacky Creator code; GoLive assigns it a generic document icon, but does recognize it as HTML.

Changing the code to GoMk causes the right icon to appear.

Mac OS 8.5 Specials

Apple added two significant user-interface changes in Mac OS 8.5 and subsequent systems that (supposedly) improve a user's ability to find files and to change the appearance of the system. We're not the biggest fans of either, as the former feature chews more processing power while delivering less performance, and the latter feature doesn't always result in a consistent appearance.

GoLive controls both of these 8.5 additions in the Preferences dialog box under the General pane in the Display settings. The two top boxes on the Mac are Appearance Themes Savvy and Use Navigation Services.

Appearance Themes Aware

In the Appearance control panel, Apple lets you choose a "theme" that affects the color and kind of windows, icons, and other doodads that the Desktop and standard applications use (see Figure A-6). The trick is that the applications have to be "appearance aware": that is, they have to know to read the settings and use them.

Figure A-6
Appearance
control panel

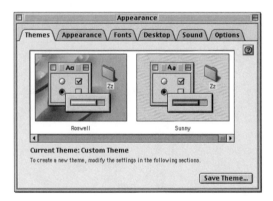

If you uncheck Appearance Themes Savvy, GoLive uses default settings for all of its interface elements. If you check it, it picks up the settings in the Appearance control panel. At present, Apple has provided a few appearances, but new ones can be created along the lines of—but not as detailed as—Microsoft Windows's Desktop Themes (see Figure A-7).

Use Navigation Services

Navigation Services were introduced by Apple to improve how users navigate through their hard drives and other resources when trying to open and save files,

Figure A-7
A Windows
Desktop
Themes setting

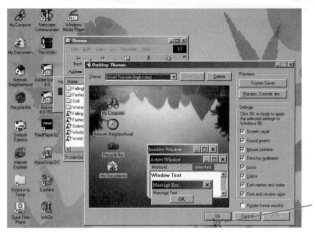

*Yes—the twig is the
cursor in the Fall
Theme.*

and select destination folders. Unfortunately, the current incarnation seems more confusing, and it's certainly more time-consuming. For some reason, the feature takes a substantial amount of time to bring up the dialog box.

With Use Navigation Services checked, the dialog box has been enhanced with extra popup menus: Shortcuts, Favorites, and Recent (see Figure A-8). Shortcuts points to all the currently mounted drives and removables (like CD-ROMs), and lets you connect to network resources. Favorites contains a list of all the files you've designated as Favorites; you can add and remove files from the Favorites menu itself. Recent shows folders and files accessed most recently, segregated into folders at the top, files at the bottom.

Figure A-8
Navigation
Services

*Shortcuts to other volumes
and the network   Favorites*

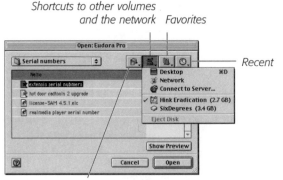

Recent

Default Folder icon inside Navigation Services

We recommend unchecking Use Navigation Services and, instead, installing Default Folder 3, available from St. Clair Software at http://www.stclairsoft.com/DefaultFolder/index.html (see Figure A-9). It's shareware, and we recommend you pony up and register it. It can also work with Navigation Services by enhancing the

Figure A-9
Default Folder

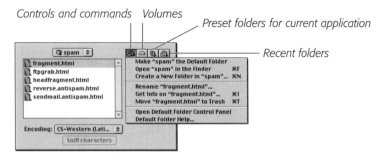

Controls and commands   Volumes

Preset folders for current application

Recent folders

options and flexibility of the built-in features—see its icon in Figure A-8—but we prefer using it on its own. (In fact, we think Apple should just have bought the rights and used Default Folder instead of Navigation Services.)

AIAT

GoLive uses Apple Information Access Technology (AIAT) to create a simulation of Internet search engine indexing and matching, like that done by AltaVista or Google. AIAT is encapsulated in a Module for the Macintosh that is not loaded by default. (See Chapter 22, *Advanced Features*, for details on loading Modules.)

This simulation doesn't claim to match how search engines really perform indexes and searches, but it certainly gives you a little insight into how your pages are structured and what words you're using. It's a good tool for making some decisions about what's important to have on a page.

If you have the AIAT Module loaded and have a Site window as the frontmost window, bringing up the Find dialog box reveals an extra tab: Search in Site Index. Select this tab, and click Build Index to create a word-based index of all of the HTML files on the site. You can click Update Index if you've built it previously and don't have Auto Index checked; if you check Auto Index, the index gets newly updated every time you save.

Searching is straightforward: enter some keywords and click Search (see Figure A-10). Select an Encoding if you have text in another language than that selected in the popup menu. If you have multiple sites open at once, you can select them from the Site menu; closing a Site window removes it from the menu.

Checking the Double Click Opens… button provides some visual feedback by highlighting any matched words in red in an untitled document window if you double-click a match (see Figure A-11). (It's untitled so that the formatting can overwrite the file's content without making that change in the source file itself.)

The results in the Search in Site Index tab are scored by an algorithm that assigns percentages to how close the file is to containing the keywords in the form they appear. There must be other, undocumented factors at work, since two files

Figure A-10
Searching via
AIAT in GoLive

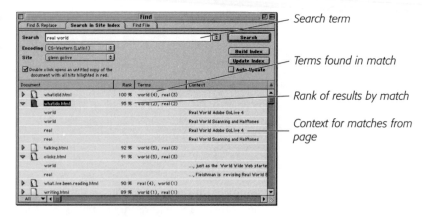

— Search term

— Terms found in match

— Rank of results by match

— Context for matches from
page

Figure A-11
Highlighted
words in
untitled match
document

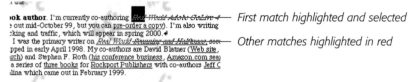

First match highlighted and selected

Other matches highlighted in red

containing the same words get scored differently, perhaps based on the proximity of the words and their frequency. (This mystery is fine, because it parallels the mystery of how Internet search engines rank results.)

Please note that the AIAT module doesn't add site searching to your Web site; it only works locally inside of GoLive as a simulation. To add Web site searches, you have to install special software like Excite for Web Servers (EWS) that scans files' contents and creates a searchable index on the Web server itself.

ColorSync

ColorSync, as noted above, tries to provide consistent color across machines, programs, devices (scanners, monitors, and printers), and platforms. It eliminates the variables and differences between systems and devices so that you're looking at the closest approximation to a standard image as possible.

Because Apple has announced its intention to extend ColorSync onto Windows, and because Microsoft built ColorSync support in the Macintosh release of Internet Explorer 4.5, we've opted to write about ColorSync in Chapter 8, *Images*. We believe in future updates of GoLive and Windows, ColorSync will be either an integral part or a simple add-on. In either case, we aren't gung-ho about its use on the Web *yet*, but see Chapter 8 for more on this subject, including installing ColorSync, updating it, and using it in GoLive for Macintosh.

Internet Config

Internet Config was written by Peter N. Lewis and Quinn "the Eskimo" as a gift to the Internet community to help standardize the use of preferences—for email addresses, mail servers, etc.—and file mappings; it's mostly worked, as virtually every Macintosh program supports the use of Internet Config in some fashion.

Internet Config gets used in three ways in Macintosh GoLive: to supplement and manage file mappings for opening files directly from GoLive; for correctly handling file uploads and downloads; and to set up proxy server settings for environments in which you need those settings.

Tip: Getting Internet Config	Although Internet Config is bundled with virtually every piece of Macintosh Internet software, you can download and quickly install the latest version by heading off to http://www.stairways.com/ic/ where they maintain a page devoted to the topic.

File Mappings

In Chapter 14, *Page Specials*, we talk about File Mapping: GoLive's built-in ability to know which applications should open which files when you double-click them in the Files or Site tab, or select and open them directly from a page.

GoLive for Mac offers an additional feature: you can tie in a list of file extensions, MIME types, and programs associated with them from Internet Config.

Most Internet files have their type determined in part by their file extension—a three- or four-letter code after a period or dot at the end of their name. Windows users have handled extensions for years: filenames, even under Windows 95 and 98, still require a three-letter extension to let Windows know what program created and/or should open a given file.

Under Windows the extension is the only clue to a file's creating application. The extension gets mapped to an application that can open and edit the file through the Windows Registry, a kind of low-level database of program information. The Registry contains a single association for each extension.

If you install Photoshop, CorelDraw, and PhotoImpact one after another, TIFF files you double-click will only open in PhotoImpact, the last one to install its entries in the Registry.

Internet Config tries to bring some of the management features of the Registry without any of the craziness. It comes with a number of mappings built in for standard Internet programs.

In the File Mapping settings of the General pane in the Preferences dialog, checking Use Internet Config instantly imports all of the settings from that utility (see Figure A-12). In fact, it instantly overwrites any customized settings you might have applied, so be aware. (You can apply settings via Internet Config itself and then, when you import, those settings are brought in as well.)

Figure A-12
Internet Config
and GoLive's
File Mapping
settings

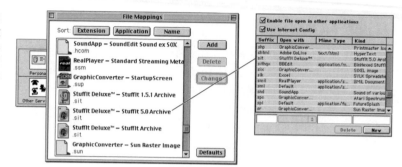

If, for some reason, you think you made a mistake by using the Internet Config settings, uncheck Use Internet Config and GoLive reverts to its built-in settings.

Tip: **Programs** **You've Never** **Heard Of**	Internet Config specifies default programs for lots and lots of extensions that you've probably never heard of. It also lists programs you certainly don't have installed on your machine. But these settings are only invoked if a file with the appropriate extension is encountered. Even then, if you don't have the application, GoLive prompts you or tries to open with the most likely application depending on what other software you have installed.

FTP Up- and Download Mapping

Completely separate from File Mapping is a Macintosh-only setting under the Network panel of the Preferences dialog named Up-/Download (see Figure A-13). The Up-/Download settings provide a mapping separate from the File Mapping settings that get applied only when uploading and downloading files to and from your Macintosh.

Uploading and downloading have separate settings that apply.

Downloading

As explained earlier under "Type and Creator" in the "File Features" section, Macintosh files have both a creator that corresponds with an application that can open or modify it, and a type which identifies the content of the document.

When you download a file from an FTP server, this information is not sent, as Apple stores these details in a special structure nested inside files; this structure doesn't get conveyed through FTP or to other platforms. The files themselves work fine, but their "Macintoshness" has been removed.

The settings in Up-/Download allow you to download a file with any extension listed there, and have GoLive automatically apply the correct Type/Creator pair to it. For each item, GoLive notes an extension (such as .GIF), a Type (like GIFf), creator (like 8BIN for Photoshop), and the application assigned (if any). (In "Uploading," below, we explain the Transfer column's function.)

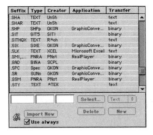

Figure A-13
Up-/Download
settings

Internet Config settings. GoLive comes with some basic types built in, but if you want to have a heaping list of mappings, either click the Import Now button to bring in Internet Config's settings, or click Use Always and GoLive updates the settings at launch when anything changes since the last time you ran the program.

Tip: Use Always Can't Be Added To   If you check Use Always, you have to add new mappings to Internet Config rather than directly in GoLive. The Use Always option disables the Delete and Add buttons.

Adding mappings. You can also add programs to this list easily. You can either click New and add the details yourself, or you can drag and drop an application or file type directly from the Desktop into the list in Up-/Download and GoLive drops the appropriate details in place. If the file you drag has an extension, GoLive adds it; otherwise, you have to enter the extension yourself.

Modifying mappings. Selecting a mapping lets you modify its settings. You can't drag a file or application that's already in the list onto the mapping list; the existing settings are sticky.

Deleting mappings. You can delete specific settings by selecting them and clicking the Delete button.

Committing or cancelling changes. Clicking OK in the Preferences dialog box commits changes you've made, but you can override all of them by clicking Cancel.

Uploading

GoLive uses Up-/Download settings to provide the detail for the manner in which a file should be uploaded to a server, too. In the olden days, text and binary data was differentiated because text only used seven bits of a byte to represent any character, while binary data used all eight bits and might contain program code.

This difference is, unfortunately, preserved into our present day. If the file you're uploading is an HTML file using standard encoding for US English (or Western languages), the contents are entirely text; but if you're uploading a GIF, it's 8-bit binary data.

However, if you upload a file as binary, even if it's text, it always works fine. The eighth bit may be empty, but that doesn't affect text-based file formats at all. If you're adding new applications, GoLive makes them binary uploads unless the file's Type is "TEXT".

The only time you should encounter this as a problem is if a file that's uploaded appears corrupted. If the setting for its type/creator in Up-/Download are set to Text instead of Binary, that's your culprit.

Proxy Servers

GoLive also relies on Internet Config as an option for linking to a proxy server. If you don't know what a proxy server is and you've never set anything to do with one, you can ignore this section entirely. But if you work in an institution or corporation, your Web requests may have to go through an indirect method. A proxy server generally sits on your local or corporate network; it receives requests from browsers or FTP clients inside the network, goes out on the Internet to retrieve the requests pages or items, and then sends them back to the machine that requested them.

GoLive for Macintosh can import your proxy settings from Internet Config in the Network panel of the Preferences dialog box (see Figure A-14). Clicking Import Now brings the current settings in, but checking Use Always keeps the settings current whenever you change them in Internet Config and then launch GoLive.

You can click the Launch Internet Config button to set your proxy addresses and features in Internet Config and then return to GoLive to see them applied.

Figure A-14
Proxy settings

AppleScript

Apple offers a simple scripting language that most Macintosh users barely notice. It's an easy-to-learn programming language, but it is programming, and it's not for every user. However, for automating behavior that requires some flexibility or conditionality, AppleScript can create entire publishing and production systems that wildly extend the abilities of ordinary programs.

Many publishing companies combine AppleScript and QuarkXPress to create a system that allows them to automate workflow from word-processing files through to final laid-out pages.

GoLive offers control only over items in the HTML Source Editor, but it does provide tools to allow you to select, insert, and format text according to HTML specifications, as well as create and name documents.

The reference provided by Adobe in the GoLive manual is extensive and specific enough to avoid repetition here. You can also find much of the same detail built into GoLive's internal AppleScript dictionary definitions. Find the program called Script Editor that should have been installed along with your system. (If it's not on your hard drive, you need to go back and reinstall AppleScript from your Mac OS disk or download it from http://www.applescript.com/.)

Run Script Editor and select Open Dictionary from the File menu. Then select the GoLive application itself, and the Script Editor displays the reference of events that GoLive knows how to work with (see Figure A-15).

Figure A-15
GoLive
AppleScript
dictionary

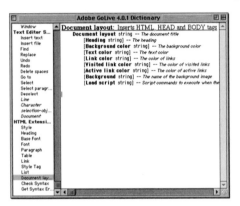

A couple of ideas of how you could use AppleScript include:

- Scripting FileMaker Pro to create output that's used along with a template to create static HTML pages with content extracted from the database. Combined with Anarchie Pro (http://www.stairways.com), another AppleScript-able program, you could set up a system that, on demand, created new pages and uploaded them to your Web site via FTP.

- Creating a standalone AppleScript that prompted for a folder location and then performed a find-and-replace operation on every HTML file in the folder to fix standard HTML problems described in Chapter 20, *Importing a Site*.

For more details on AppleScript, consult Apple's site at http://www.applescript.com/, or buy *Danny Goodman's AppleScript Handbook*, the definitive book on the subject; these links are also found at http://realworldgolive.com.

Text Clippings

Another of the Mac OS's varying methods for storing snippets of text (like the Scrapbook and Stickies utilities) is the Clippings feature. Simply select a block of text and drag it to the Desktop to create a new read-only file containing that text, which the Finder can open directly without the aid of a third-party word processor (see Figure A-16).

Figure A-16
Clippings

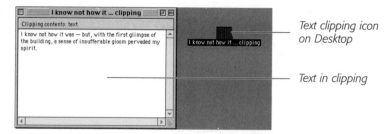

Text clipping icon
on Desktop

Text in clipping

One advantage to creating text clippings is the easy availability of frequently used text. But you could also use them as temporary storage for information that can't all fit on the Clipboard at once. Clippings also retain most of the basic formatting applied to the original text, such as font, bold, italics, and underlines, without having to create a new file with a word processor.

Once you've created a clipping file, you can copy its contents by opening the file and selecting Copy from the Edit menu (or pressing Command-C). But what's nice about clippings is that you don't even have to open them to get to their text: simply drag the clipping file onto an open window for the text to be placed at the location in a document where you release the clipping file.

Master List of CSS Compatibility

Cascading Style Sheets offer a lot of promise for the future of design inside a browser window. However, despite a fully fleshed-out specification (described in Chapter 26, *Cascading Style Sheets*), every version of every browser on every platform does things just a little bit differently. We found ourselves turning again and again to Eric Meyer's excellent Master List on Webreview.com: it's an incredibly detailed chart that describes every major and minor feature of CSS and then assigns a code—see Table Key at right—for how well the feature is implemented in that browser, platform, and version. We liked the chart so much that we licensed it to appear here. The compatibility chart appears first, followed by a glossary.

Table Key on Implementation

Y	Yes
N	No
P	Partial
B	Buggy
Q	Quirky

Win95 Browsers

Nav4	Netscape Navigator 4.5
IE3	Internet Explorer 3.02
IE4	Internet Explorer 4.01
IE5	Internet Explorer 5.0
Opr3	Opera 3.6

Macintosh Browsers

Nav4	Navigator 4.5
IE3	Internet Explorer 3.01
IE4	Internet Explorer 4.5

This material appeared originally at Webreview.com, a publication of Songline Studios, Inc., was written by Eric Mayer, and is copyright ©1999 Songline Studios, Inc. We gratefully acknowledge Songline Studios's cooperation in allowing us to license this material to appear in this book. For the latest version of this chart, which is updated several times a year, we recommend that you visit Webreview.com at http://webreview.com/wr/pub/guides/style/mastergrid.html. This page also links to a complete glossary of the terms used in Cascading Style Sheets (also included in this appendix), as well to other practical articles about using HTML, XML, CSS, JavaScript, and other more advanced features discussed in this book. The version appearing here was last updated July 7 ,1999.

		Windows					Mac	
	Nav4	IE3	IE4	IE5	Opr3	Nav4	IE3	IE4

Basic Concepts

		Nav4	IE3	IE4	IE5	Opr3	Nav4	IE3	IE4
1.1	**Containment in HTML**	P	P	P	P	Y	P	B	Y
	LINK	Y	Y	Y	Y	Y	Y	B	Y
	\<STYLE\>...\</STYLE\>	Y	Y	Y	Y	Y	Y	Y	Y
	@import*	N	N	Q	Q	Y	N	N	Y
	\<x STYLE="dec;"\>**	B	Y	Y	Y	Y	B	Y	Y
1.2	**Grouping**	Y	N	Y	Y	Y	Y	Y	Y
	x, y, z {dec;}	Y	N	Y	Y	Y	Y	Y	Y
1.3	**Inheritance*****	B	P	Y	Y	Y	B	B	Y
	(inherited values)	B	P	Y	Y	Y	B	B	Y
1.4	**Class selector†**	Y	B	Q	Q	Y	Y	B	Y
	.class	Y	B	Q	Q	Y	Y	B	Y
1.5	**ID selector††**	B	B	B	B	B	B	B	B
	#ID	B	B	B	B	B	B	B	B
1.6	**Contextual selectors**	Y	Y	Y	Y	Y	B	P	Y
	x y z {dec;}†††	Y	Y	Y	Y	Y	B	P	Y
1.7	**Comments**	Y	B	Y	Y	Y	Y	Y	Y

*   WinIE4 and WinIE5 both import files even when the @import statement is at the end of the document style sheet. This is technically in violation of the CSS1 specification, although obviously not a major failing; thus the "Quirky" rating.

**   Navigator 4 has particular trouble with list items, which is most of the reason for the B.

***   Navigator 4's inheritance is unstable at best, and fatally flawed at worst. It would take too long to list all occurrences, but particularly troublesome areas include tables and lists.

†   WinIE4/5 allows class names to begin with digits; this is not permitted under CSS1.

††   WinIE4/5 allows ID names to begin with digits; this is not permitted under CSS1. All browsers apply the style for a given ID to more than one instance of that ID in an HTML document, which is not permitted. This is properly an error-checking problem, and not a failing of the CSS implementations, but I feel it is significant enough to warrant the ratings shown.

†††   MacNav4 has the most trouble with contextual selectors involving tables. For example, HTML BODY TABLE P is not properly handled.

	Nav4	IE3	IE4	IE5	Opr3	Nav4	IE3	IE4
				Windows			Mac	

	Windows					Mac		
	Nav4	IE3	IE4	IE5	Opr3	Nav4	IE3	IE4
/* comment */	Y	B	Y	Y	Y	Y	Y	Y

Pseudo-Classes and Pseudo-Elements

		Nav4	IE3	IE4	IE5	Opr3	Nav4	IE3	IE4
2.1	**anchor**	**P**	**N**	**Y**	**Y**	**P**	**P**	**B**	**Y**
	A:link	Y	N	Y	Y	Y	Y	B	Y
	A:active	N	N	Y	Y	N	N	N	Y
	A:visited	N	N	Y	Y	Y	N	B	Y
2.3	**first-line***	**N**	**N**	**N**	**N**	**Y**	**N**	**B**	**N**
	:first-line	N	N	N	N	Y	N	B	N
2.4	**first-letter***	**N**	**N**	**N**	**N**	**Y**	**N**	**B**	**N**
	:first-letter	N	N	N	N	Y	N	B	N

The Cascade

		Nav4	IE3	IE4	IE5	Opr3	Nav4	IE3	IE4
3.1	**important**	**N**	**N**	**Y**	**Y**	**Y**	**N**	**N**	**N**
	!important	N	N	Y	Y	Y	N	N	N
3.2	**Cascading Order****	**B**	**P**	**Y**	**Y**	**Y**	**B**	**P**	**Y**
	Weight sorting	B	Y	Y	Y	Y	B	Y	Y
	Origin sorting	B	Y	Y	Y	Y	B	B	Y
	Specificity sorting	B	P	Y	Y	Y	B	B	Y
	Order sorting	B	N	Y	Y	Y	B	N	Y

Font Properties

		Nav4	IE3	IE4	IE5	Opr3	Nav4	IE3	IE4
5.2.2	**font-family**	**Y**	**P**	**Y**	**Y**	**Y**	**Y**	**P**	**Y**

*   IE3 incorrectly applies styles to the entire element.

**   Again, there are simply far too many instances of problems to list here.

Nav4	IE3	IE4	IE5	Opr3	Nav4	IE3	IE4
		Windows				Mac	

			Windows					Mac	
		Nav4	IE3	IE4	IE5	Opr3	Nav4	IE3	IE4
	<family-name>	Y	Y	Y	Y	Y	Y	P	Y
	<generic-family>	P	P	Y	Y	P	Y	P	Y
	…serif	Y	Y	Y	Y	Y	Y	Y	Y
	…sans-serif	Y	Y	Y	Y	Y	Y	N	Y
	…cursive*	N	B	Y	Y	N	Y	N	Y
	…fantasy	N	B	Y	Y	Y	Y	N	Y
	…monospace	Y	Y	Y	Y	Y	Y	Y	Y
5.2.3	**font-style**	**P**	**P**	**Y**	**Y**	**Y**	**P**	**P**	**Y**
	normal	Y	Y	Y	Y	Y	Y	N	Y
	italic	Y	N	Y	Y	Y	Y	Y	Y
	oblique	N	N	Y	Y	Y	N	N	Y
5.2.4	**font-variant**	**N**	**N**	**P**	**P**	**Y**	**N**	**N**	**Q**
	normal	N	N	Y	Y	Y	N	N	Y
	small-caps**	N	N	Q	Q	Y	N	N	Q
5.2.5	**font-weight**	**P**	**P**	**Y**	**Y**	**Y**	**P**	**P**	**Y**
	normal	Y	N	Y	Y	Y	Y	N	Y
	bold	Y	Y	Y	Y	Y	Y	Y	Y
	bolder	Y	Y	Y	Y	Y	N	N	Y
	lighter	N	Y	Y	Y	Y	N	N	Y
	100 - 900	Y	N	Y	Y	Y	Y	N	Y
5.2.6	**font-size**	**Y**	**P**	**P**	**P**	**Y**	**Y**	**P**	**Q**
	<absolute-size>	Y	Y	Q	Q	Y	Y	B	Q

* Despite a preferences setting for cursive fonts, Opera does not seem to apply the preference, but instead substitutes another font.

** IE4/5 approximates the small-caps style by making all such text uppercase. While this can be justified under the CSS1 specification, visually, it does not render the text in small caps.

		Windows					Mac		
		Nav4	IE3	IE4	IE5	Opr3	Nav4	IE3	IE4
	…xx-small–xx-large*	Y	Y	Q	Q	Y	Y	B	Q
	\<relative-size\>	Y	Y	Y	Y	Y	Y	N	Y
	…larger	Y	Y	Y	Y	Y	Y	N	Y
	…smaller	Y	Y	Y	Y	Y	Y	N	Y
	\<length\>	Y	P	Y	Y	Y	Y	B	Y
	\<percentage\>	Y	Y	Y	Y	Y	Y	P	Y
5.2.7	**font**	**P**	**P**	**P**	**P**	**Y**	**P**	**P**	**Q**
	\<font-family\>	P	Y	Y	Y	Y	Y	P	Y
	\<font-style\>	P	P	Y	Y	Y	Y	P	Y
	\<font-variant\>	N	N	P	P	Y	N	N	Q
	\<font-weight\>	P	Y	Y	Y	Y	Y	N	Y
	\<font-size\>	Y	B	Q	Q	Y	Y	B	Y
	\<line-height\>	B	Y	Y	Y	Y	B	B	Y

Color and Background Properties

5.3.1	**color**	**Y**	**Y**	**Y**	**Y**	**Y**	**Y**	**Y**	**Y**
	\<color\>	Y	Y	Y	Y	Y	Y	Y	Y
5.3.2	**background-color**	**B**	**P**	**Y**	**Y**	**Y**	**B**	**N**	**Y**
	\<color\>**	B	B	Y	Y	Y	B	N	Y
	transparent***	B	N	Y	Y	Y	B	N	Y

* IE4/5's values for absolute sizes assigns small to be the same size as unstyled text, instead of medium, as one might expect. Thus, declaring an absolute font size (such as font-size: medium) will almost certainly lead to different size fonts in Navigator and Explorer. While this is not incorrect under the specification, it is confusing to many authors.

** Nav4 does not apply the background color to the entire content box and padding, but rather just to the text in the element. This can be worked around by declaring a zero-width border.

*** Nav4 insists on applying this value to the parent of an element, not the element itself. This can lead to "holes" in the parent element's background.

		Windows					Mac		
		Nav4	IE3	IE4	IE5	Opr3	Nav4	IE3	IE4
5.3.3	**background-image**	Y	N	Y	Y	Y	Y	N	Y
	\<url\>	Y	N	Y	Y	Y	Y	N	Y
	none	Y	N	Y	Y	Y	Y	N	Y
5.3.4	**background-repeat**	P	N	P	Y	Y	B	N	Y
	repeat*	Y	N	B	Y	Y	Y	N	Y
	repeat-x**	P	N	B	Y	Y	P	N	Y
	repeat-y***	P	N	B	Y	Y	P	N	Y
	no-repeat	Y	N	Y	Y	Y	Y	N	Y
5.3.5	**background-attachment**	N	N	Y	Y	N	N	N	Y
	scroll	N	N	Y	Y	N	N	N	Y
	fixed	N	N	Y	Y	N	N	N	Y
5.3.6	**background-position**	N	N	Y	Y	Y	N	N	Y
	\<percentage\>	N	N	Y	Y	Y	N	N	Y
	\<length\>	N	N	Y	Y	Y	N	N	Y
	top	N	N	Y	Y	Y	N	N	Y
	center	N	N	Y	Y	Y	N	N	Y
	bottom	N	N	Y	Y	Y	N	N	Y
	left	N	N	Y	Y	Y	N	N	Y
	right	N	N	Y	Y	Y	N	N	Y
5.3.7	**background**	P	P	P	Y	P	P	P	Y

* WinIE4 only repeats down and to the right. The correct behavior is for the background image to be tiled in both vertical directions for repeat-y, and both horizontal for repeat-x. Nav4 gets this property correct on a technicality: since it does not support background-position, there is no way to know whether or not it would tile in all four directions if given the chance, or instead emulate WinIE4's behavior. Opera 3.6, MacIE4.5, and WinIE5 all behave correctly.

** WinIE4 only repeats to the right, instead of both left and right.

*** WinIE4 only repeats down, instead of both up and down.

| | | Windows | | | | | Mac | | |
		Nav4	IE3	IE4	IE5	Opr3	Nav4	IE3	IE4
	\<background-color\>	B	P	Y	Y	Y	P	P	Y
	\<background-image\>	P	Y	Y	Y	Y	P	Y	Y
	\<background-repeat\>	P	B	B	Y	Y	P	B	Y
	\<background -attachment\>	N	N	Y	Y	N	N	Y	Y
	\<background-position\>	N	N	Y	Y	Y	N	P	Y

Text Properties

		Nav4	IE3	IE4	IE5	Opr3	Nav4	IE3	IE4
5.4.1	**word-spacing**	**N**	**N**	**N**	**N**	**Y**	**N**	**N**	**Y**
	normal	N	N	N	N	Y	N	N	Y
	\<length\>	N	N	N	N	Y	N	N	Y
5.4.2	**letter-spacing**	**N**	**N**	**Y**	**Y**	**Y**	**N**	**N**	**Y**
	normal	N	N	Y	Y	Y	N	N	Y
	\<length\>	N	N	Y	Y	Y	N	N	Y
5.4.3	**text-decoration**	**Q**	**P**	**P**	**P**	**P**	**Q**	**P**	**P**
	none*	Q	N	Q	Q	Y	Q	Y	Q
	underline	Q	B	Q	Q	Y	Q	B	Q
	overline	N	N	Y	Y	Y	N	N	Y
	line-through	Y	Y	Y	Y	Y	Y	Y	Y
	blink**	Y	N	N	N	N	Y	N	N
5.4.4	**vertical-align**	**N**	**N**	**P**	**P**	**P**	**N**	**N**	**P**

* According to the specification, if an element is decorated, but one of its children is not, the parent's effect will still be visible on the child; in a certain sense, it "shines through." Thus, if a paragraph is underlined, but a STRONG element within it is set to have no underlining, the paragraph underline will still "span" the STRONG element. This also means that the underlining of child elements should be the same color as the parent element, unless the child element has also been set to be underlined.

In practice, however, setting an inline element to none will turn off all decorations, regardless of the parent's decoration. The only exception to this is Opera, which implements the specification correctly.

** Since this value is not required under CSS1, only Navigator supports it (surprise).

Nav4	IE3	IE4	IE5	Opr3	Nav4	IE3	IE4
		Windows				Mac	

		Nav4	IE3	Windows IE4	IE5	Opr3	Nav4	Mac IE3	IE4
	baseline	N	N	Y	Y	Y	N	N	Y
	sub	N	N	Y	Y	Y	N	N	Y
	super	N	N	Y	Y	Y	N	N	Y
	top	N	N	N	N	B	N	N	Y
	text-top	N	N	N	N	N	N	N	Y
	middle	N	N	B	N	B	N	N	Y
	bottom	N	N	N	N	B	N	N	B
	text-bottom	N	N	N	N	N	N	N	B
	\<percentage\>	N	N	N	N	Y	N	N	B
5.4.5	**text-transform**	**Y**	**N**	**Y**	**Y**	**P**	**Y**	**N**	**Y**
	capitalize	Y	N	Y	Y	Y	Y	N	Y
	uppercase*	Y	N	Y	Y	B	Y	N	Y
	lowercase	Y	N	Y	Y	Y	Y	N	Y
	none	Y	N	Y	Y	Y	Y	N	Y
5.4.6	**text-align**	**Y**	**P**	**Y**	**Y**	**Y**	**P**	**P**	**P**
	left	Y	Y	Y	Y	Y	Y	Y	Y
	right	Y	Y	Y	Y	Y	Y	Y	Y
	center	Y	Y	Y	Y	Y	Y	Y	Y
	justify**	B	N	Y	Y	Y	B	N	N
5.4.7	**text-indent**	**Y**	**Y**	**Y**	**Y**	**Y**	**Y**	**Y**	**Y**
	\<length\>	Y	Y	Y	Y	Y	Y	Y	Y
	\<percentage\>	Y	Y	Y	Y	Y	Y	Y	Y

* Opera 3.6 sets to uppercase the first letter in each inline element within a word, which (according to the CSS1 Test Suite) it should not do.

** In Nav4, this value has a tendency to break down in tables, but generally works in other circumstances.

		Nav4	IE3	IE4	IE5	Opr3	Nav4	IE3	IE4
				Windows				Mac	

| | | Windows | | | | | Mac | | |
		Nav4	IE3	IE4	IE5	Opr3	Nav4	IE3	IE4
5.4.8	**line-height***	P	P	Y	Y	Q	P	P	Y
	normal	Y	Y	Y	Y	Y	Y	Y	Y
	\<number\>	P	N	Y	Y	Y	P	B	Y
	\<length\>**	B	Y	Y	Y	Y	B	B	Y
	\<percentage\>	P	Y	Y	Y	Y	P	B	Y

Box Properties

5.5.1	**margin-top***	P	B	P	P	Y	P	B	P
	\<length\>	P	B	P	P	Y	P	B	P
	\<percentage\>	P	Y	P	P	Y	P	B	P
	auto	P	Y	P	P	Y	P	B	P
5.5.2	**margin-right***	B	P	P	P	Y	B	P	P
	\<length\>	B	Y	P	P	Y	B	Y	P
	\<percentage\>	B	N	P	P	Y	B	Y	P
	auto	N	N	N	N	Y	N	N	P
5.5.3	**margin-bottom***	N	Y	P	P	Y	N	N	P
	\<length\>	N	N	P	P	Y	N	N	P
	\<percentage\>	N	N	P	P	Y	N	N	P
	auto	N	N	P	P	Y	N	N	P
5.5.4	**margin-left***	B	P	P	P	Y	B	P	P
	\<length\>	B	Y	P	P	Y	Y	Y	P

*   Nav4 incorrectly permits negative values for this property.

**   Opera 3.6 applies background colors to the space between lines, as opposed to just the text itself, when the background is set for an inline element within the text. (See the CSS1 Test Suite for more details.)

***   All margin properties seem to be problematic, or else completely unsupported, on inline elements. In the case of margin-top, -bottom, -left, and -right, support is pretty good on block-level elements in IE4 and IE5, while with inline elements, IE4 and IE5 ignore this property completely. Navigator does fairly well so long as margins are not applied to floating or inline elements, in which case major bugs can be tripped.

	Nav4	IE3	IE4	IE5	Opr3	Nav4	IE3	IE4
			Windows				Mac	

			Windows					Mac		
		Nav4	IE3	IE4	IE5	Opr3	Nav4	IE3	IE4
	<percentage>	B	Y	P	P	Y	B	Y	P
	auto	N	N	N	N	Y	B	N	P
5.5.5	**margin***	**B**	**B**	**P**	**P**	**Y**	**B**	**B**	**P**
	<length>	B	B	P	P	Y	B	B	P
	<percentage>	B	Y	P	P	Y	B	B	P
	auto	N	Y	P	P	Y	N	B	P
5.5.6	**padding-top***	**B**	**N**	**P**	**P**	**Y**	**B**	**N**	**P**
	<length>	B	N	P	P	Y	B	N	P
	<percentage>	B	N	P	P	Y	B	N	P
5.5.7	**padding-right***	**B**	**N**	**P**	**P**	**Y**	**B**	**N**	**P**
	<length>	B	N	P	P	Y	B	N	P
	<percentage>	B	N	P	P	Y	B	N	P
5.5.8	**padding-bottom***	**B**	**N**	**P**	**P**	**Y**	**B**	**N**	**P**
	<length>	B	N	P	P	Y	B	N	P
	<percentage>	B	N	P	P	Y	B	N	P
5.5.9	**padding-left***	**B**	**N**	**P**	**P**	**Y**	**B**	**N**	**P**
	<length>	B	N	P	P	Y	B	N	P
	<percentage>	B	N	P	P	Y	B	N	P
5.5.10	**padding***	**B**	**N**	**P**	**P**	**B**	**B**	**N**	**P**
	<length>	B	N	P	P	B	B	N	P
	<percentage>	B	N	P	P	B	B	N	P

* All padding properties seem to be problematic, or else completely unsupported, on inline elements. In the case of padding-top and -right, support is pretty good on block-level elements in IE4 and IE5. Opera correctly ignores negative padding values, but will alter the line-height based on values of padding applied to inline elements, which is incorrect. Navigator does fairly well so long as margins are not applied to floating or inline elements, in which case major bugs can be tripped.

	Nav4	IE3	IE4	IE5	Opr3	Nav4	IE3	IE4
			Windows				Mac	

		Windows					Mac		
		Nav4	IE3	IE4	IE5	Opr3	Nav4	IE3	IE4
5.5.11	**border-top-width***	**B**	**N**	**P**	**P**	**Y**	**B**	**N**	**P**
	thin	Y	N	P	P	Y	Y	N	P
	medium	Y	N	P	P	Y	Y	N	P
	thick	Y	N	P	P	Y	Y	N	P
	<length>	Y	N	P	P	Y	Y	N	P
5.5.12	**border-right-width***	**B**	**N**	**P**	**P**	**Y**	**B**	**N**	**P**
	thin	Y	N	P	P	Y	Y	N	P
	medium	Y	N	P	P	Y	Y	N	P
	thick	Y	N	P	P	Y	Y	N	P
	<length>	Y	N	P	P	Y	Y	N	P
5.5.13	**border-bottom-width***	**B**	**N**	**P**	**P**	**Y**	**B**	**N**	**P**
	thin	B	N	P	P	Y	B	N	P
	medium	B	N	P	P	Y	B	N	P
	thick	B	N	P	P	Y	B	N	P
	<length>	B	N	P	P	Y	B	N	P
5.5.14	**border-left-width***	**B**	**N**	**P**	**P**	**Y**	**B**	**N**	**P**
	thin	Y	N	P	P	Y	Y	N	P
	medium	Y	N	P	P	Y	Y	N	P
	thick	Y	N	P	P	Y	Y	N	P
	<length>	Y	N	P	P	Y	Y	N	P
5.5.15	**border-width***	**B**	**N**	**P**	**P**	**Y**	**B**	**N**	**P**
	thin	Y	N	P	P	Y	Y	N	P
	medium	Y	N	P	P	Y	Y	N	P
	thick	Y	N	P	P	Y	Y	N	P

*   Navigator will create visible borders even when no border-style is set, and does not set borders on all side when a style is set. Things get really ugly when borders are applied to inline styles. IE4 and IE5 correctly handle borders on block-level elements, but ignore them for inlines.

	Nav4	IE3	IE4	IE5	Opr3	Nav4	IE3	IE4
			Windows				**Mac**	

		Windows					Mac		
		Nav4	IE3	IE4	IE5	Opr3	Nav4	IE3	IE4
	\<length\>	Y	N	P	P	Y	Y	N	P
5.5.16	**border-color***	**P**	**N**	**Y**	**Y**	**Y**	**P**	**N**	**Y**
	\<color\>	P	N	Y	Y	Y	P	N	Y
5.5.17	**border-style**	**P**	**N**	**P**	**P**	**Y**	**P**	**N**	**Y**
	none	Y	N	Y	Y	Y	Y	N	Y
	dotted	N	N	N	N	Y	N	N	Y
	dashed	N	N	N	N	Y	N	N	Y
	solid	Y	N	Y	Y	Y	Y	N	Y
	double	Y	N	Y	Y	Y	Y	N	Y
	groove	Y	N	Y	Y	Y	Y	N	Y
	ridge	Y	N	Y	Y	Y	Y	N	Y
	inset	Y	N	Y	Y	Y	Y	N	Y
	outset	Y	N	Y	Y	Y	Y	N	Y
5.5.18	**border-top****	**N**	**N**	**P**	**P**	**P**	**N**	**N**	**P**
	\<border-top-width\>	N	N	P	P	P	N	N	P
	\<border-style\>	N	N	P	P	P	N	N	P
	\<color\>	N	N	P	P	P	N	N	P
5.5.19	**border-right****	**N**	**N**	**P**	**P**	**P**	**N**	**N**	**P**
	\<border-right-width\>	N	N	P	P	P	N	N	P
	\<border-style\>	N	N	P	P	P	N	N	P
	\<color\>	N	N	P	P	P	N	N	P
5.5.20	**border-bottom****	**N**	**N**	**P**	**P**	**P**	**N**	**N**	**P**

*   Nav4 and Opera do not set colors on individual sides, as in border-color: red blue green purple. Explorer cannot apply border colors to inline elements, since it does not apply borders to inlines, but this is not penalized here.

**   Opera does not apply border styles to table elements, which is the reason for the "P" rating. IE4 and IE5 do not apply borders to inline elements.

Nav4	IE3	IE4	IE5	Opr3	Nav4	IE3	IE4
		Windows				Mac	

			Windows					Mac	
		Nav4	IE3	IE4	IE5	Opr3	Nav4	IE3	IE4
	<border-bottom-width>	N	N	P	P	P	N	N	P
	<border-style>	N	N	P	P	P	N	N	P
	<color>	N	N	P	P	P	N	N	P
5.5.21	**border-left***	**N**	**N**	**P**	**P**	**P**	**N**	**N**	**P**
	<border-left-width>	N	N	P	P	P	N	N	P
	<border-style>	N	N	P	P	P	N	N	P
	<color>	N	N	P	P	P	N	N	P
5.5.22	**border***	**P**	**N**	**P**	**P**	**P**	**P**	**N**	**P**
	<border-width>	B	N	P	P	P	B	N	P
	<border-style>	P	N	P	P	P	P	N	P
	<color>	Y	N	P	P	P	Y	N	P
5.5.23	**width****	**P**	**N**	**P**	**P**	**Q**	**P**	**N**	**Y**
	<length>	P	N	P	P	Q	P	N	Y
	<percentage>	P	N	P	P	Q	P	N	Y
	auto	P	N	P	P	Q	P	N	Y
5.5.24	**height**	**N**	**N**	**Y**	**Y**	**Y**	**N**	**N**	**Y**
	<length>	N	N	Y	Y	Y	N	N	Y
	auto	N	N	Y	Y	Y	N	N	Y
5.5.25	**float****	**P**	**N**	**P**	**P**	**B**	**P**	**N**	**B**

*   Opera does not apply border styles to table elements, which is the reason for the "P" rating. IE4 and IE5 do not apply borders to inline elements.

**   Navigator applies width in an inconsistent fashion, but appears to honor it on most simple text elements and images. WinIE4/5 applies it to images and tables, but ignores it for most text elements such as P and headings. Opera 3.6, weirdly, seems to set the width of images to 100 percent—but this is largely an illusion, since minimizing the window and then maximizing it again will reveal correctly-sized images.

***   Float is one of the most complicated and hardest-to-implement aspects of the entire specification. Basic floating is generally supported by all browsers, especially on images, but when the specification is closely tested, or the document structure becomes complicated, floating most often happens incorrectly, or not at all. The floating of text elements is especially inconsistent, although IE5 and Opera have cleaned up their act to a large degree, leaving WinIE4 and Nav4 the major transgressors in this respect. Authors should use float with some care, and thoroughly test any pages employing it with great care.

Nav4	IE3	IE4	IE5	Opr3	Nav4	IE3	IE4
		Windows				Mac	

		Windows					Mac		
		Nav4	IE3	IE4	IE5	Opr3	Nav4	IE3	IE4
	left	B	N	B	B	Y	B	N	Y
	right	B	N	B	B	Y	B	N	Y
	none	Y	N	Y	Y	Y	Y	N	Y
5.5.26	**clear***	**P**	**N**	**P**	**P**	**B**	**P**	**N**	**Y**
	none	Y	Y	Y	Y	Y	Y	Y	Y
	left	B	N	B	B	N	B	N	Y
	right	B	N	B	B	Y	B	N	Y
	both	Y	N	Y	Y	Y	Y	N	Y

Classification Properties

		Nav4	IE3	IE4	IE5	Opr3	Nav4	IE3	IE4
5.6.1	**display**	**P**	**N**	**P**	**P**	**P**	**P**	**N**	**P**
	block	B	N	N	Y	Y	B	N	P
	inline**	N	N	N	Y	B	N	N	N
	list-item	B	N	N	N	N	P	N	P
	none	Y	N	Y	Y	Y	Y	N	Y
5.6.2	**white-space**	**P**	**N**	**N**	**N**	**N**	**P**	**N**	**N**
	normal	Y	N	N	N	N	Y	N	N
	pre	Y	N	N	N	N	Y	N	N
	nowrap	N	N	N	N	N	N	N	N
5.6.3	**list-style-type**	**Y**	**N**	**Y**	**Y**	**Y**	**P**	**N**	**Y**
	disc	Y	N	Y	Y	Y	Y	N	Y
	circle	Y	N	Y	Y	Y	Y	N	Y

* Like float, clear is not a simple thing to support. Again, basic support is there, but as things get more complicated, browser behavior breaks down. Thoroughly test pages using this property.

** Opera 3.6 almost gets inline right, but seems to honor the occasional carriage return as though it were a <BR> element, instead of plain white space.

Nav4	IE3	IE4	IE5	Opr3	Nav4	IE3	IE4
		Windows				Mac	

| | | Windows | | | | | Mac | |
		Nav4	IE3	IE4	IE5	Opr3	Nav4	IE3	IE4
	square	Y	N	Y	Y	Y	Y	N	Y
	decimal	Y	N	Y	Y	Y	Y	N	Y
	lower-roman	Y	N	Y	Y	Y	Y	N	Y
	upper-roman	Y	N	Y	Y	Y	Y	N	Y
	lower-alpha	Y	N	Y	Y	Y	Y	N	Y
	upper-alpha	Y	N	Y	Y	Y	Y	N	Y
	none*	Y	N	Y	Y	Y	B	N	Y
5.6.4	**list-style-image**	**N**	**N**	**Y**	**Y**	**Y**	**N**	**N**	**Y**
	\<url\>	N	N	Y	Y	Y	N	N	Y
	none	N	N	Y	Y	Y	N	N	Y
5.6.5	**list-style-position**	**N**	**N**	**Y**	**Y**	**Y**	**N**	**N**	**Y**
	inside**	N	N	Y	Y	Y	N	N	Q
	outside	N	N	Y	Y	Y	N	N	Y
5.6.6	**list-style**	**P**	**N**	**P**	**Y**	**Y**	**P**	**N**	**P**
	\<keyword\>	Y	N	Y	Y	Y	P	N	Y
	\<position\>	N	N	Q	Q	Y	N	N	Q
	\<url\>	N	N	Y	Y	Y	N	N	Y

Units

6.1	**Length Units**	**P**	**P**	**Y**	**Y**	**Y**	**Y**	**B**	**Y**
	em	Y	N	Y	Y	Y	Y	Y	Y
	ex***	Q	N	Q	Q	Q	Q	Q	Q

*   MacNav4 displays question marks for bullets when using this value.

**   The positioning and formatting of list-items when set to this value are a bit odd under MacIE4.

***   All supporting browsers appear to calculate ex as one-half em. This is arguably a reasonable approximation, but it is technically incorrect.

Nav4	IE3	IE4	IE5	Opr3	Nav4	IE3	IE4
		Windows				Mac	

		Windows					Mac		
		Nav4	IE3	IE4	IE5	Opr3	Nav4	IE3	IE4
	px	Y	Y	Y	Y	Y	Y	Y	Y
	in	Y	Y	Y	Y	Y	Y	Y	Y
	cm	Y	Y	Y	Y	Y	Y	Y	Y
	mm	Y	Y	Y	Y	Y	Y	Y	Y
	pt	Y	Y	Y	Y	Y	Y	Y	Y
	pc	Y	Y	Y	Y	Y	Y	Y	Y
6.2	**Percentage Units**	**Y**	**Y**	**Y**	**Y**	**Y**	**Y**	**Y**	**Y**
	\<percentage>	Y	Y	Y	Y	Y	Y	Y	Y
6.3	**Color Units**	**P**	**P**	**Y**	**Y**	**Y**	**P**	**P**	**Y**
	#000	Y	Y	Y	Y	Y	Y	B	Y
	#000000	Y	Y	Y	Y	Y	Y	B	Y
	(RRR,GGG,BBB)	Y	N	Y	Y	Y	Y	N	Y
	(R%,G%,B%)	Y	N	Y	Y	Y	Y	N	Y
	\<keyword>*	B	Y	Y	Y	Y	B	Y	Y
6.4	**URLs**	**B**	**Y**	**Y**	**Y**	**Y**	**B**	**B**	**Y**
	\<url>**	B	Y	Y	Y	Y	B	B	Y

*   Navigator will generate a color for any apparent keyword. For example, color: invalidValue will yield a dark blue, and color: inherit) (a valid declaration under CSS2) comes out as a vaguely nauseous green.

**   Navigator determines relative URLs with respect to the HTML document, not the style sheet.

	Nav4	IE3	IE4	IE5	Opr3	Nav4	IE3	IE4
		Windows					Mac	

Basic Concepts

1.1 *Containment in HTML*

1.2 *Grouping*

Grouping allows the author to assign a single style declaration to multiple elements.

```
H1, H2, H3, H5 {color: purple;}
```

1.3 *Inheritance*

Inherited values are passed from parent to child.

1.4 *Class as selector*

Class selectors may be used to define types of data. A class selector is a string preceded by a period, and is called using the STYLE= attribute. The period does not appear in the value of STYLE.

```
.example {color: brown;}
    <P class="example">This is an example.</P>
```

1.5 *ID as selector*

ID selectors may be used to define types of data. An ID selector is a string preceded by a hash mark (#), and is called using the ID= attribute. The hash mark does not appear in the value of ID.

```
#i5 {color: brown;}
    <P ID="i5">This is text with an ID of 'i5'.</P>
```

1.6 *Contextual selectors*

These are used when styles should be applied to a given element under specific circumstances. Given in the form parent child, where the style is applied to the child element when parent is its parent.

```
H1 EM {color: red;}
    <H1>This is <EM>red</EM>.</H1>
    <P>This is <EM>not</EM>.</P>
```

1.7 *Comments*

Allows the author to add comments to the style sheet. The format is identical to that used in most variants of C/C++.

```
/* This is a comment. */
```

Pseudo-Classes and Pseudo-Elements

2.1 *anchor*

Applies to hyperlinks, but not named anchors.

2.3 *first-line*

Applied to the first displayed line of text in the given element. This persists even if the window is resized and the text reformatted. Should be applied to block-level elements only.

```
P:first-line {color: red;}

    <P>The first line of this paragraph is red. blah blah
blah...</P>
```

2.4 *first-letter*

Applied to the first letter in the given element. Can be used to generate drop-cap effects, among others. Should be applied to block-level elements only.

```
P:first-letter {color: purple;}

    <P>The capital 'T' at the beginning of this paragraph is
purple.</P>
```

The Cascade

3.1 *important*

Style declaration is declared important. Important declarations override all others, regardless of origin or specificity.

```
H1 {color: maroon ! important;}
```

3.2 *Cascading Order*

The way in which rules are combined and chosen; see the CSS1 specification for a detailed explanation.

Font Properties

5.2.2 *font-family*

Used to declare a specific font to be used, or a generic font family, or both.

```
P {font-family: Helvetica,sans-serif;}
```

5.2.3 *font-style*

Selects between italics, oblique, and normal.

```
EM {font-style: oblique;}
```

5.2.4 *font-variant*

Currently has two values: small-caps and normal. Likely to acquire more values in the future.

```
H3 {font-variant: small-caps;}
```

5.2.5 *font-weight*

Sets the weight of a font, making it heavier or lighter.

```
B {font-weight: 700;}
```

5.2.6 *font-size*

Sets the size of the font. This can be defined in absolute size, relative size, or percentage.

```
H2 {font-size: 200%;}
H3 {font-size: 36pt;}
```

5.2.7 *font*

Shorthand property for the other font properties. The order of values is important, and is as follows: font {font-style font-variant font-weight font-size/line-height font-family;}. Any of these values may be omitted.

```
P {font: bold 12pt/14pt Helvetica,sans-serif;}
```

Color and Background Properties

5.3.1 *color*

Sets the color of a given element. For text, this sets the text color; for other elements, such as HR, it sets the foreground color.

```
STRONG {color: teal;}
```

5.3.2 *background-color*

Sets the background color of an element. This background extends out to the edge of the element's border.

```
H4 {background-color: white;}
```

5.3.3 *background-image*

Sets an image to be the background pattern. In conjunction with the other background properties, may tile or repeat in one direction only.

```
BODY {background-image: url(bg41.gif);}
```

5.3.4 *background-repeat*

Sets the repeat style for a background image.

```
BODY {background-repeat: no-repeat;}
```

5.3.5 *background-attachment*

Defines whether or not the background image scrolls with the element. Generally applied to BODY only, as it makes little sense with most other elements.

```
BODY {background-attachment: scroll;}
```

5.3.6 *background-position*

Sets the starting position of the background color or image. If a color, the color fill continues from the set position. If an image, the first image is placed at the set position, and repeating is determined by background-repeat.

```
BODY {background-position: top center;}
```

5.3.7 *background*

Shorthand property for the other background properties. The values can be written in any order.

```
BODY {background: white url(bg41.gif) fixed center;}
```

Text Properties

5.4.1 *word-spacing*

Sets the amount of white space between words, which are defined as strings of characters surrounded by white space.

```
P {word-spacing: 0.5em;}
```

5.4.2 *letter-spacing*

Sets the amount of white space between letters, which are defined as any displayed character.

```
P {letter-spacing: 0.5em;}
```

5.4.3 *text-decoration*

Sets certain effects to the text, such as underline and blink. Combinations of the values are legal.

```
U {text-decoration: underline;}
.old {text-decoration: line-through;}
```

5.4.4 *vertical-align*

Sets the vertical alignment of an element's baseline with respect to its parent element's line-height. May only be applied to inline elements; negative values are permitted.

```
SUP {vertical-align: super;}
.fnote {vertical-align: 50%;}
```

5.4.5 *text-transform*

Changes the case of the letters in the element, regardless of the original text.

```
H1 {text-transform: uppercase;}
.title {text-transform: capitalize;}
```

5.4.6 *text-align*

Sets the horizontal alignment of the text in an element. May only be applied to block-level elements.

```
P {text-align: justify;}
H4 {text-align: center;}
```

5.4.7 *text-indent*

Sets the indentation of the first line in an element. Most often used to create a tab effect for paragraphs. Only applies to block-level elements; negative values are permitted.

```
P {text-indent: 5em;}
H2 {text-indent: -25px;}
```

5.4.8 *line-height*

Sets the vertical distance between baselines in an element. Negative values are not permitted.

```
P {line-height: 18pt;}
H2 {line-height: 200%;}
```

Box Properties

5.5.01 *margin-top*

Sets the size of the top margin of an element. Negative values are permitted, but exercise caution.

```
UL {margin-top: 0.5in;}
```

5.5.02 *margin-right*

Sets the size of the right margin of an element. Negative values are permitted, but exercise caution.

```
IMG {margin-right: 30px;}
```

5.5.03 *margin-bottom*

Sets the size of the bottom margin of an element. Negative values are permitted, but exercise caution.

```
UL {margin-bottom: 0.5in;}
```

5.5.04 *margin-left*

Sets the size of the left margin of an element. Negative values are permitted, but exercise caution.

```
P {margin-left: 3em;}
```

5.5.05 *margin*

Sets the size of the overall margin of an element. Negative values are permitted, but exercise caution.

```
H1 {margin: 2ex;}
```

5.5.06 *padding-top*

Sets the size of the top padding of an element, which will inherit the element's background. Negative values are not permitted.

```
UL {padding-top: 0.5in;}
```

5.5.07 *padding-right*

Sets the size of the right padding of an element, which will inherit the element's background. Negative values are not permitted.

```
IMG {padding-right: 30px;}
```

5.5.08 *padding-bottom*

Sets the size of the bottom padding of an element, which will inherit the element's background. Negative values are not permitted.

```
UL {padding-bottom: 0.5in;}
```

5.5.09 *padding-left*

Sets the size of the left padding of an element, which will inherit the element's background. Negative values are not permitted.

```
P {padding-left: 3em;}
```

5.5.10 *padding*

Sets the size of the overall padding of an element, which will inherit the element's background. Negative values are not permitted.

```
H1 {padding: 2ex;}
```

5.5.11 *border-top-width*

Sets the width of the top border of an element, which will inherit the element's background, and may have a foreground of its own (see border-style). Negative values are not permitted.

```
UL {border-top-width: 0.5in;}
```

5.5.12 *border-right-width*

Sets the width of the right border of an element, which will inherit the element's background, and may have a foreground of its own (see border-style). Negative values are not permitted.

```
IMG {border-right-width: 30px;}
```

5.5.13 *border-bottom-width*

Sets the width of the bottom border of an element, which will inherit the element's background, and may have a foreground of its own (see border-style). Negative values are not permitted.

```
UL {border-bottom-width: 0.5in;}
```

5.5.14 *border-left-width*

Sets the width of the left border of an element, which will inherit the element's background, and may have a foreground of its own (see border-style). Negative values are not permitted.

```
P {border-left-width: 3em;}
```

5.5.15 *border-width*

Sets the width of the overall border of an element, which will inherit the element's background, and may have a foreground of its own (see border-style). Negative values are not permitted.

```
H1 {border-width: 2ex;}
```

5.5.16 *border-color*

Sets the color of the foreground of the overall border of an element (see border-style), which will inherit the element's background.

```
H1 {border-color: purple; border-style: solid;}
```

5.5.17 *border-style*

Sets the style of the overall border of an element, using the color set by border-color.

```
H1 {border-style: solid; border-color: purple;}
```

5.5.18 *border-top*

Shorthand property that defines the width, color, and style of the top border of an element.

```
UL {border-top: 0.5in solid black;}
```

5.5.19 *border-right*

Shorthand property that defines the width, color, and style of the right border of an element.

```
IMG {border-right: 30px dotted blue;}
```

5.5.20 *border-bottom*

Shorthand property that defines the width, color, and style of the bottom border of an element.

```
UL {border-bottom: 0.5in grooved green;}
```

5.5.21 *border-left*

Shorthand property that defines the width, color, and style of the left border of an element.

```
P {border-left: 3em solid gray;}
```

5.5.22 *border*

Shorthand property that defines the width, color, and style of the overall border of an element.

```
H1 {border: 2px dashed tan;}
```

5.5.23 *width*

Used to set the width of an element. Most often applied to images, but can be used on any block-level or replaced element. Negative values are not permitted.

```
TABLE {width: 80%;}
```

5.5.24 *height*

Used to set the height of an element. Most often applied to images, but can be used on any block-level or replaced element, within limits. Negative values are not permitted.

```
IMG.icon {height: 50px;}
```

5.5.25 *float*

Sets the float for an element. Generally applied to images in order to allow text to flow around them, but any element may be floated.

```
IMG {float: left;}
```

5.5.26 *clear*

Defines which floating elements (if any) are allowed to exist to either side of the element.

```
H1 {clear: both;}
```

Classification Properties

5.6.1 *display*

Used to classify elements into broad categories, although there may be limits. The most popular value is probably none.

```
.hide {display: none;}
```

5.6.2 *white-space*

Defines how white space within the element is treated.

```
TD {white-space: nowrap;}
TT {white-space: pre;}
```

5.6.3 *list-style-type*

Used to declare the type of "bullet" or numbering system to be used in an unordered or ordered list. Applies to elements with a display value of list-item.

```
UL {list-style-type: square;}
OL {list-style-type: lower-roman;}
```

5.6.4 *list-style-image*

Used to declare an image to be used as the "bullet" in an unordered or ordered list. Applies to elements with a display value of list-item.

```
UL {list-style-image: url(bullet3.gif));}
```

5.6.5 *list-style-position*

Used to declare the position of the "bullet" or number in an unordered or ordered list with respect to the content of the list item. Applies to elements with a display value of list-item.

```
LI {list-style-position: outer;}
```

5.6.6 *list-style*

Shorthand property condensing all other list-style properties. Applies to all elements with a display value of list-item.

```
UL {list-style: square url(bullet3.gif) outer;}
```

Units

6.1 *Length Units*

Used by various properties to define size in absolute terms; i.e., distances that will be consistent regardless of their context.

```
width: 50px;
margin-left: 2em;
```

6.2 *Percentage Units*

Used by various properties to define size in relative terms; i.e., distances that will be calculated with regard to their context.

```
width: 80%;
```

6.3 *Color Units*

Used by various properties to define colors.

```
color: #FF00FF;
color: rgb(100%,0%,100%);
```

6.4 *URLs*

Used by various properties to define the location of images. Partial URLs are extrapolated relative to the style sheet, not the HTML document.

```
url(picture.gif)
url(http://www.pix.org/lib1/pic278.gif)
```

Index

Page numbers marked in bold, like **357**, *indicate that the reference occurs in a tip.*

(%+=$*!?)

" (quotation marks), 462–463, 514–515, 590

(pound signs), 571

$ (dollar signs), 496

% (percent signs), 327, 611

() (parentheses), 496, 497

* (asterisks), 494

+ (plus signs), 445

. (periods), 494, 570

/ (forward slashes), 415

= (equals signs), 327

? (question marks), 405
  next to fields in Action tab, 546, 547
  next to files and folders in Files tab, 374
  next to files in Missing Files folder, 395
  on plug-in placeholder icons, 609, **610**
  using in Find and Replace feature, 494

\ (backslashes), 493–494, 496

∧ (carets), 495, 496

| (vertical bar), 496

π (pi symbol), 354

A

Absolute links. *See* relative references (Absolute links)

absolute references, 78, 208, **371**, 371, 463–464, 484

accessibility settings. *See* alternative text (Alt attribute)

Action Group Action, 552

Action Headitem Inspector, 100–101

Action Item Inspector, 542

Actions. *See also* CSS (Cascading Style Sheets); DHTML (Dynamic HTML); event handlers; JavaScript
  browser compatibility and, **538**
  combining, 554–558
  configuring, 545–554
  editing and writing by hand, **538**, 545
  grouping together into containers, 552

for JavaScript, 503–505, 510–516, 556

links necessary for, **544**

order of execution, 544

overview, 537

samples of, 554–558

triggering, **527**, 533–535, 541–545, 552

variables, 553–554

Actions Plus, **538**

Actions tab (Button Inspector), 99

Actions tabs, 537, 546

Actions tab (Sprite Sample Inspector), 636–637

Actions tab (Text Inspector), 51–52

Action Track, **519**, 534–535. *See also* Timetracks

Active Server Pages (ASP), 504, 637–638

ActiveX, 616

ActiveX Inspector, 619–620

addresses
adding to global FTP list, 35
creating new, 362
deleting, 363–364
linking to, 393
text format, 218

Adobe ImageReady, adjusting gamma settings, **255**

Adobe Photoshop, **255**, **237**

ads, banner, 547, 554–556

AIAT (Apple Information Access Technology), 161–162, 649–650

alert dialog boxes, 515, 549, 550

aliases, 376, 423, 487–488. *See also* pointers

aligning
images, 24, 42–43, 53, 243–246
layout grids and grid objects, 313, 315, 316
lines, 60, 61
multimedia objects, 611
overview, 42–43
tables, 19, 21, 270–272
text, 218–220, 271, 272, 590
in Web Database, 185

alphabets. *See* languages

alternative text (Alt attribute), 54, 55, 56, 239–240, 618, 619

Anchor Inspector, **34**, 67

anchors, **34**, 298, 383, 582–583. *See also* links

animations. *See also* DHTML (Dynamic HTML); images, animating
Actions stopping, 551
Actions triggering DHTML animation timelines, 551
adding intermediate keyframes to, 527–528
adding to movies, 633–637
attaching Actions to, 545
creating, 523–535
file size affected by, **521**
floating boxes and, 69, 70, 310, 321, 518–523, **530**
layers and, 530
layout grids and, 310
multiple elements in, 528–531
paths, 521, 522, 523, **526**, 527, 528
previewing, 527

scenes, 531–534, 532
settings, 321
speed of, **521**, 527, 536
starting after pages load, **521**, **527**
timetracks, 518–523
triggering, 519

Annotation tab (QuickTime Inspector), 626

Anton, Travis, 284

Appearance control panel (Mac), GoLive using, 647, 648

Appearance Theme Savvy option, 157

Apple Colors tab (Color Palette), 260

Apple Information Access Technology (AIAT), 161, 162, 649–650

Apple Macintosh. *See also specific topics in this index*
conventions explained, xi
desktop, 5
File Mapping behavior specific to, 350
installation, 3, 4
managing windows and palettes, 8, 9
minimizing palettes and changing monitor resolution, 8–9
OS 8.5, GoLive special features using, 647–649
permissions and remote access to files, 424, 425
turning on Tool Tips, 5

AppleScript, 654–655

Area elements, 580

Arrange tab (Site View Controller), 86–87, **443**, 445, 446

arrows
in site maps, 439, 440

in Timeline Editor, 519

ASP (Active Server Page) code, 504, 637–638

associations between files and programs. *See* File Mapping

asterisks (*), 494

Atribs tab (Plug-in Inspector), 611–612

attributes of HTML tags. *See* HTML tag attributes

Audio tab (Plug-in Inspector), 613–614

authorization. *See* permissions

authors
confessions about snap judgments, 451
fulfilling users' every need, GoLive coming pretty darned close to, 500
hair, v, x
idols of, **230**, **609**
it's not *how* you use your mouse…, 274
nonconformity encouraged by, 218
ongoing search for link validation solutions, **394**
urging restraint in using floating boxes, 322
URL Mappings making their heads hurt, 487

B

backgrounds. *See also* colors, background; images, background
CSS and, 576
playing multimedia objects in, 611

backslashes (\), 493–494, 496

bad idea, 284, 285

banner ads, 547, 554–556

Base Inspector, 77–78

Base tag, 207

Basic Palette tab, 7

Basic tab (ActiveX Inspector), 616–617

Basic tab (Java Applet Inspector), 616–617

Basic tab (Marquee Inspector), 65–66

Basic tab (Palette), 7, 124

Basic tab (Plug-in Inspector), 610–611

Basic tab (QuickTime Inspector), 625–626

Basic tab (Site Button Inspector), 98

Basic tab (Video Effect Inspector), 630

Basic tab (Web Database Tag Inspector), 112–113

Basic tab (WebDB Attribute Inspector), 594–595

Basic tab (WebDB Tag Inspector), 594

bits and bytes, 254

Blank item (New Site submenu, File menu), 354

Blink tag, most derided HTML tag ever, **216**

block elements and CSS, 571, 572, **579**

Blockquote tag, 219–220

Body Script Inspector, 70–72, 506–508

Body section of pages, 206–207, 505, 506

Body tag (HTML), 466–467

Border Frame field (Frame Set Inspector), 80

borders

around form elements, 339

around frames, 80, 304–305

around imagemaps, 55

around images, 54, 599–600

around links and images, 56

CSS and, 575

resizing tables using, 20–21

brackets, square ([]) used in Find and Replace feature, 494–495

Break Text (Global tab, Web Database), 589

browsers. *See also names of specific browsers;* previewing; testing
   Actions and compatibility, **538**
   alternate pages for older versions, **538**, **540**, 540
   defaults, GoLive assumptions about, **565**
   forcing windows to reload, 209
   history, 548
   opening new windows, 548
   plug-in creation and use, 608
   preferences, 163, 172–173, 179–180
   remote control subwindows, 556–558, 559
   resizing windows, 552
   scripts and, 506–507
   sending data to servers, 327
   speed of page loading, **53**
   status bar windows, 549–550
   styles overriding CSS style sheets, 577–578
   title bars, 45

browser support
   for Browser Switch, **540**
   for color names, 590
   for CSS, 402, 563–564, 564–565, 583
   for CyberObjects, **538**

for DHTML, 518, **519**

for embedded fonts, 574

for floating boxes, 310, 311, 313, 318

forms testing, 324

for frames and frame borders, 297, 304

for layout grids, 310, 311, **313**

Web Database changes and, 586

for wrapping text in forms, 329

Browser Switch Action, **519**

Browser Switch CyberObjects, 540

Browser Switch icon, 137–138

Browser Switch Inspector, 101–102

Button CyberObject Inspector, 541

Button (Forms palette), 338

Button Image CyberObject, 540–541

Button Image Inspector, 541

Button Inspector, 98–99

buttons. *See also specific buttons*

changing types of, **105**

creating new, 98, 337–338

highlighting, 510–512

image changing when cursors hover over, 510–512, 540–541

images as, **98**, 246

media, 338

radio buttons, 105, 106, 331–332

rollover, 510–512, 547, 583

C

cache, 158, 327

Call Action and Call Function actions, 552

capitalization

Find and Replace feature, 341, **492**

in suffixes (Mac), 178

of tags and attributes, 590

in URL preferences (Mac), 159

of usernames and passwords, 432

in Web Database, 185

Caption checkbox (Table tab, Table Inspector), 57

captions in tables, 21, 58, 272

carets (^), 495, 496

Cascading Style Sheets. *See* CSS (Cascading Style Sheets)

case. *See* capitalization

Castro, Elizabeth, 266, 336

cells, table. *See under* tables

Cell tab (Table Inspector)

adding and deleting rows and columns using, 280

alignment options, 271, 272

cell spanning and, 282

color applied using, 270, 283

configuring attributes, 19, 21

configuring headers, 269–270

overview, 58–59

text wrapping, 270

CGI (Common Gateway Interface), 339, 340

Change References feature, 382, 385–386, 391–393, 395, 444

Chapter Track Inspector, 633, 634

characters. *See also* languages

adding to GoLive, 601–602

counting number of, 345

CSS and, 571, 572

cutting and pasting from outside sources, **212**

GET request limits on, 327

number shown in text fields, 328

reserved in Find and Replace feature, 493–494

supported by HTML, 600–601

symbols in Find and Replace feature, 493–496

WebDB Character Inspector, 115, 601–602

Characters tab (Web Database), **588**, 600–602

Charset Info option, 166

child pages in site map hierarchy, **436**, 453

Circle tool (Map tab, Image Inspector), 248

CJK Encodings module, 498

CJK (Windows), 162

classes, 565, 570, **571**, 577, 578–580

Clear Site feature, 397–398, 479–480

Clickable Image Map Inspector, 54–55

client-side imagemaps, 467–470

client-side scripting, 503

Clippings feature (Mac), 656

CMS (color management system), 203. *See also* ColorSync

CMYK tab (Color Palette), 260

code

for Action samples, 554

appearance in HTML Source Editor, 589–590

behind floating boxes, 309–310, 314

behind layout grids, 309–310, 312

for converting server-side imagemaps to client-side, **468**

copying and pasting into new pages, 31

for CSS, 563

Find and Replace feature and, 474

hand coding

Actions for animations compared to, 556

Actions for JavaScript compared to, 503–505, 510–516, 512, 513

editing Actions, **538**

triggering functions, 552

writing components, 485

HTML editor, 195, 196, 197, 198, 199, 200, 201

indenting (nesting), 589, 595

line breaks in, 589

moving large sections of HTML, 197, 198, 199

paragraph-by-paragraph formatting, 590–591

pointing to components, 486–487

of polygons in imagemaps, 249

preferences, 179–182

removing tabs in, 170

for tables, 265

for testing forms, 340

Color Group Inspector, 93

Color Inspector, 92, 405

color management system (CMS), 2512, 255. *See also* ColorSync

Color Name Translation (Global tab, Web Database), 590

Color Palette

applying colors to text using, 12–13, 226–227

changing color of keyframes using, 521–523

color palettes compared to, **258**

dragging colors from, 257
editing colors using, 405
opening, 257
overview, 42, 132–136
tabs in, 260–262
visibility of, 6, 162

color palettes, Color Palette compared to, **258**

Color Picker (Mac), 162

colors
adding used, 480
applying, 257–258, 406–408
background
Actions changing, 552
adding Body tags using Find and Replace feature, 466–467
applying, **257**
floating boxes and, 321
layout grids and, 63, 64, 313
overview, 13–14
setting for QuickTime files, 613
of site maps, 449
in tables, 22, 268, 270, 271
bits and bytes, 254
of borders around linked images, 339
browsers affecting, **13**
centralizing usage in CSS, 402
copying when creating new sites, 26–27
creating site objects, 362
deleting, 363–364
Desktop, **134**
editing, 405
editing in Site tab, 89
extracting, 404
of frame borders, 305
gamma settings, 255–256

hexadecimal values of, 590
image formats and, 234, 235
of keyframes, 521–523
list of active, 404–405
of lowsource images, **341**
monitors affecting, 254–256
names of, 26–27, 360, 404, 405, 590
overview, 253
platforms affecting, 254–256
preferences, 157–158, 171, 172, 185
refreshing, 363
removing unused, 408
selecting, 258–262
sets, 402–403, 402–408
shading, 440–441
in site maps, 440–441, 449–450
sitewide, 402–408
in Source pane, 181
tables using, 268, 270, 271, 283–285
of text, 45–46, 226–227, **257**
viewing those in use, 404–405
Web-safe, 255–256

Colors and Fontsets tab, 404

Colors dialog box, 162

Colors tab (Site window), 359–360, 363, 402–408

ColorSync, 47–48, 166–167, **253**, 351–352, 650. *See also* CMS (color management system)

Comment Inspector, 62

comments, 273, 478

Common Gateway Interface (CGI), 339, 340

Component CyberObject, 539

Component Inspector, 99

components, 129, 482–487. *See also* CSOBJ tag; stationery; templates; *specific components*

Components feature, 470–472

Components folder, 480, 481

compression levels for images, 156

Condition Action, 552

Confirm Link Action, 549

containers, 324, 325–327, 552, 553

container tags, 197, 198, 201

Content menu (Basic tab, WebDB Tag Inspector), 594

Content tab (File Inspector), 84–85, 378, 436

Content tabs of inspectors, **388**, 442

Controls popup menu (Audio tab, Plug-in Inspector), 614

cookies, 553, 554

COOL tag, 312

Copy Files dialog box, **26**

copyright, **346**, **483**

crashes
in Macs caused by PDFs, **387**
preventing Preferences from being saved, 154
really good ways to crash GoLive, **284**, 292

cryptography (private key), 333–334

CSOBJ tags, 466, 486–487. *See also* Components feature

CSS (Cascading Style Sheets). *See also* Actions
applying, 578–581
browser support, 564–565

character and paragraph styles, 571, 572

coding, 563

configuring, 50–51

CSS2, **561**, 575, **578**

designing, 566–578

DHTML and, 518

floating boxes and, 314

font specifications, 406

list bullets and, **225**

Netscape bug, 552

overview, 116, 402, 561, 563–564

previewing, 564–566

specification, **561**, 568

structural definitions and, 216–217

support for, 402, 561

CSScriptLib, 167

CSS Master List, 565, 657–683

CSS Roots, 202

CSS Selector Inspector
default settings in, 605
designing CSS using, 569, 570
multiple selectors, 582
nested selectors, 582
options in, 572–576
overview, 118–121
pseudo-selectors, 582–583
typography options in, 574, **575**

CSS Style Sheet Inspector, 116–117, **565**, 603–605

CSS tab (Web Database), 116, 186, 192, 586, 587, 603–605

CTC (change-creator-type) freeware, **646**

cursors
CSS controlling, 583

eyedropper, grabbing colors using, **261–262**

grabber hand (glove), 275–276, 319, 320, **525**

I-beam, 274–275

magnifying glass, 30

minus and plus signs next to, 578

Custom tab (Palette), 132, 264

CyberFlash and CyberMovie modules, 162, 399–400

CyberObjects, **499**, 538–545

CyberObjects inspectors, 97–102

CyberObjects Module, 162

CyberObjects tab (Palette), 130–131

CyberStudio, v, xi, **325**, 359, 484

D

database, of files and links, 363, **461**, 476–477. *See also* Web Database

.data folder extension, 357

Date and Time Inspector, 97

dates

changing images or references based on, 548

uploading all files during synchronization despite date, **430**

Date & Time CyberObject, 538–539

Default Folder 3 shareware, 648–649

defaults

displaying Site toolbar, 361

encoding in Form Inspector Encrypt field, 327

File Mapping, 347

folder names, 30, 354

fonts, 14–16

FTP Directory, 415

GoLive assumptions about, **565**

Reference field value, 338

site maps, 447

table settings, 264, 272

text wrapping, 330

Upload Options dialog box settings, **428**

definition files for user-defined plug-ins and Java applets, 614–616

definitions, CSS inline and block, 571

Depth field (Floating Box Inspector), 69, 320, 521

Depth values, 530

Desktop themes (Mac), GoLive using, 647, 648

DHTML (Dynamic HTML), **519**, 167–168, 517–518. *See also* Actions; animation

dialog boxes, opening, 549. *See also specific dialog boxes*

dictionaries for spellchecking, 175, 344

dimensions

of floating boxes, 320

of frames in site maps, 449

of images, **24**, 238–239

measurement units supported, 572–574

of multimedia files in Plug-in Inspector, 611

of tables, 266, **269**

of text areas, 328–330

of thumbnails in site maps, 449

of TV Screen display option in site maps, 449

directories. *See also* folders

creating new, 362

dragging contents of site map, 438

enclosing site pages in, **26**

subsite paths, 464–465

disability settings. *See* alternative text (Alt attribute)

disabled fields, 336–337

Display regions buttons (Map Tab, Image Inspector), 55

Display tab (Site View Controller), 88, 89, 444–448

division elements (Div tag), 314, **518**, 579–580

DNS errors and FTP hostnames, 414, 432

Document Layout Controller, 44–45

Document Layout inspectors, 43. *See also specific inspectors*

Document Object Model (DOM), 509, 510

Document/Site Switch, 137

Document Statistics feature, 345

Document window, 5–6, 187, 188, 189

Document Window roll-up Tab, 188

document windows, switching between, 34

Document Write Action, 549

dollar signs ($), 496

DOM (Document Object Model), 509, 510

downloading
copyright and, **346**
files and folders to FTP servers, 420
files from FTP file list, 419, 433
Mac issues, 178–179

mapping and, 652–653

synchronization affected by deleted or moved files, 431–432

synchronizing sites and, 431–432

time estimates for, 345

Web pages or images from other pages, 164, 346

Drag Floating Box Action, 550

DreamWeaver compared to GoLive, xii

Duncan, Geoff, 222–223

Dynamic HTML, 167–168, 517–518, **519**. *See also* Actions; animation

E

EasyOpen (Mac), 350

ECMA Script, 502. *See also* JavaScript

editors, 144. *See also specific editors*

Effect tab (Video Effect Inspector), 630–632

empty documents and files, **294**, 380

Empty Font Set items, 15

empty references, 14, 193

empty values of text fields in forms, 514–515

encoding. *See also* Form Inspector; MIME (Multipurpose Internet Mail Extensions)
default, 327
Find and Replace feature and, 474
preferences, 162, 163, 164, 165–166
transmitting files to servers using multipart/form-data, 327

encryption, **328**, 333. *See also* Form Inspector

End Tag Inspector, 68

Endtag Inspector, 68

end tags, setting, 594, 595

enumerations for HTML tag attributes, 592, 593, 597. *See also* WebDB Enum Inspector

equals signs (=), 327

Error Inspector, 94, 95, 395–398

error messages. *See* troubleshooting

Errors tab, 394–398

Errors tab (Site window), 374

Event Code (Events tab, JavaScript Inspector), 509

event handlers. *See also* actions; *specific event handlers*
adding to scripts, 511–512, 515
associating objects with JavaScripts, **508**
attaching, 542–545
list of, 508–509
overview, 508
triggering scripts in head, 505

Events tab (JavaScript Inspector), 71, 72, 506–507, 508–509

Execute box (Remote/FTP Inspectors), 422, **423**

exporting
preferences, 169–170, 171, 361
stripping comments out before, 478
uploading compared to, 431

Export Site feature, 476–479

eXtensible Markup Language (XML), 620–624. *See also* Web Database

Extension field (Generic Pages option), 361

extensions. *See also specific extensions*
adding, 348
default, 17
Macs storing information about, 646
overview, 347
Plug-in Inspector gathering information based on, 610
preferences, 163, 178

External Group Inspector, 92–93

Externals tab, 464

External Style Sheet Inspector, 117–118, 569–570

External tab, 389–393, **444**

External tab (Site window), 359, 362, 363

External tab (Style Sheet Editor), 578

Extra tab (Site window), 357

Extra tab (Folder Inspector), **85**

eyedropper cursor, grabbing colors using, **261–262**

F

Fieldset icon, 339

Fieldset tag, 339

File and External tab, 439

file associations. *See* File Mapping

File Browser element, 333

File Exchange dialog box (Mac), 350

file extensions. *See* extensions

File Inspector
Mac settings, 645
naming files using, 30

overview, 27–28

Show Object Information compared to, 373–374

tabs in, 82–85, 376–378

File Mapping. *See also* URL mapping

enabling, 347

Internet Config and, 161, 178, 651–652

opening files while on, 349–350

overriding Finder flags, **375**

overview, 346–347

preferences, 159, 160–161, 178–179

setting HTML editor alternates, **375**

settings, 348–349, 610

updating, 160, 179, 363

file permissions. *See* permissions

files, 421. *See also* pages

adding, 479, 480

adding to sites, 378–380

creating links to, 381–384

creator information about, 646

deleting, **32**, 421, 430, 431–432, 444

in Desktop, 363

editing, 27–28, 381–384, 419–420

finding in multiple sites, 474

icons in Files tab, 374

information about, 368, 370–378

installed, 4

live, 419–420

moving, 381, 430, 431–432

opening, 348, 363, 372–376

orphaned, 397–398

plug-ins, **609**

publish state, 425–426, 428

Remote/FTP Inspector for, 422

removing, 479, 480

renaming, 30, 421, 423, 472

root location, 368–370

in site maps, 444

size of, 423, **521**

synchronizing, 428–429, 430, 431–432, 433

transferring to servers, 36, 327

tuning up, 386–388

updating references to, 368

viewing list of those comprising sites, 358, 433

Files tab

adding files and folders to FTP servers from, 420

adding pending links from, 456

dragging new pages into, 456

renaming files using, 472

Stationery and, 482

Files tab (File Inspector), 364, 376–380

Files tab (Site window)

accessing FTP client using, 413

adding content to, 378–380

creating new directories, 362

downloading files using, 420

icons in, 374

information shown in, 370–378

overview, 357, 358

root location, 368–370

updating, 363

File tab (File Inspector), 27–28, 82, 83

File Transfer Protocol. *See* FTP (File Transfer Protocol)

file translators (Mac), 350

fills, 575

Filter tab (Site View Controller), 87–88, 446, 452

Find and Replace feature

absolute references replaced with relative references using, 464 adding attributes to Body tag using, 466–467

adding quotations to attributes using, 462–463

alphabets and, 474

case ignored, 341, **492**

components created using, 470–472

controls in, 341–343

creating backup files before using, 409

encoding and, 474

Find dialog box, 341–342

imagemaps and, 468–470

impressing onlookers when using, **474**

irreversibility of, 409, **473**

languages and, 474

large sites and, 476

optional characters in searches, 495–496

options in dialog boxes, 462

overview, 341–343

pattern matching, 462–463

preferences, 174, 175

regular expressions, 342, 344–345, 365, 492–497

Replace dialog box, 342–343, 476

reserved characters, 493–494

sitewide, 409–410, 473–476

table cells and, 365

wildcard characters in, 493–496

Finder flags, File Mapping overriding, **375**

Finder label, 644–645

Finder Label (Color tab, Site View Controller), 449

Flash, 399

Flat (Export Site feature), 477, 478

Flatten (QuickTime movies), **626**

Flip Move Action, 550

Floating Box Controller, 6, 10, 320, 321–322, 530–531

floating boxes. *See also* CSS (Cascading Style Sheets)
adding objects to, 319

animating, 310, 518–523, 519, 528–531, 530

background images, 321

browsers supporting, 310, 311, 318

coding behind, 314

colors of, 321

complexity of, 309

coordinates of, 546

creating, 318

CSS and, 314

division container and, 314, **518**

dragging onto pages, 524

images and, 523, 524, **525**

keyframes set using, 520

layers of, 320, 321–322, 521, 522, 530

layout grids and, 310, 313, 318

lists of, 519, 530–531

locking, 531

movement cursor, 319, 320

moving, 314, 319, 550–551

naming, 320, 524

overview, 518–519

reshaping, 314

resizing, 319, 320, 525

restraint in using, 322

selecting, **525**, 530

text turned into, **580**

users dragging and resizing, 525, 550

visibility, 320, 321, 322, 521, 531, 551

Floating Box Inspector, 68–70, 319–321, 520, 521–523, **525**

focus, 334–337

Folder Inspector, 85, 376–378, 645

folders. *See also* directories
creating, 354, 355–357, 420–421
Export Site feature using, 477
in Files tab of Site window, 372–376, 374
imported, 460
importing sites from, 355
naming, 361, 454, **477**
default in Files tab, 30–31
permissions, 422–423, 434
publish state, 425–426, 427, 428
Remote/FTP Inspector for, 422
rescanning, 479
Spring-loaded, **382**

Font Faces (Style Sheets Editor), 574

Font item (Style menu), 406

Font Names List, 15

fonts. *See also* text
centralizing choices in CSS, 402
default, 14–16
designed for onscreen reading, 229
downloading new, **230**
embedding, 574
font sets and fontsets compared to, **402**
naming uses for, 360
preferences, 16, 165–166, 180–181
removing unused, 408
specifying, 227–228

Font Set Editor, 15–16, 405

Font Set Group Inspector, 93

Font Set Inspector, 93–94, 405

font sets, **402**

fontsets
applying, 228, 406, 408
compared to font sets and fonts, **402**
creating, 14–16, 229, 362, 402–408
deleting, 363–364
editing, 228–230, 405
extracting, 404
font name placeholders, 408–409
global changes to, 409
list of active, 363, 404–405
local, global and sitewide compared, **228**
names of, 404, 405
refreshing, 363
removing unused, 408
sitewide, 408

Fontsets tab (Site window)
creating fontsets, 362
creating groups in, 403–404
difficulty of using, 406
dragging items from, 406, 407
editing fontsets using, 405
features on, 402–408
Group icon (Toolbar) and, **402**
updating, 363

Font tab (CSS Selector Inspector), 574, **575**

Font tag, 227–228

footers and headers in site maps for printing, 451

Force Frame Action, 548

format menu shortcuts, 190

Form Button Inspector, 103–105, 338

Form Check Box Inspector, 105

Form End Tag Auto Insert, **103**

Form Fieldset Inspector, 106

Form File Inspector, 106

Form Hidden Inspector, 106–107, 333. *See also* hidden items

Form Image Inspector, 54, 107

Form Inspector, 102–103, 325–327, 333

Form Keygen Inspector, 107–108

Form Label Inspector, 108

Form Listbox Inspector, 108–109

Form Password Inspector, 110

Form Popup Inspector, 108–109

Form Radio Button Inspector, 105, 106

forms. *See also* JavaScript
  actions that are mailto tags, **326**
  building using tables, 288
  buttons, 103–105, 331–333, 338
  CGI and, 339
  checkboxes, 105, 331, 332
  containers, 324, 325–327
  dragging from Palette, **324**
  elements on, 327–334
  fields and field modifiers, 323, 324, 334–337
  fields associated with legends, **339**
  getting value or contents of, 546
  hidden elements, 106–107, 333
  JavaScript handlers added to, **324**
  key generator, 333–334
  lists, 330–331
  menus, 323
  naming, 325, 328, 510
  overview, 324–334
  radio buttons, 105, 106, 331–332
  scripts linked to, 326
  servers processing, 323, 324
  settings for, 328
  tabbing chains and, 335–336
  tables and, **325**
  targets, 326
  testing, 324, 334, 340
  text areas, 109, 110, 328–330
  validating, 512–516

Forms tab (Palette), 125, 324, **324**, 325, **333**, 338

Form tag, **325**

Form Text Area Inspector, 109, 110

Form Text Field Inspector, 110

forward slashes (/), 415

Frame Border popup, 157

Frame Editor, 193, 194, 294, 299–300

Frame icon, 294

Frame Inspector, 300

Frame Inspectors, 79–82, 193, 194

Frame Layout icon, 294

frame layout icon (Palette), **126**

Frame Preview, 164, 203, 292

frames
  borders, 80, 157, 304–305
  creating, 292, 294–300
  dimensions in site maps, 449
  displaying in site maps, 448
  editing, 193–194, 300–307
  framesets compared to, 291–293
  linking in framed pages, 298–299
  linking to, 306–307
  multiple, 549
  naming, 306–307
  overview, 291
  previewing content, 299–300
  resizing, 81, 82, 301–304, 449
  scrollbars, 303, 304

self-referencing, 292
specifying content of, 298–299
targeting, 306–307

Frameset icon, **295**

Frameset Inspector, 79–80, 294, 300, 304–305

framesets
building and populating, 294–300
creating, 296
form targets and, 326
frames and, 291–293
multiple open, **307**
Noframes versions, 297
overriding other sites linking to yours, 548

Frames tab (Palette), 126–127

FTP Directory, 415, 416, 417

FTP File Inspector, 95, 96, 422, 423, 424, 434

FTP (File Transfer Protocol). *See also* synchronizing sites
aborting processes, 419
clients, 412–414, 418, 419–421, 423, 432–434
connections, 414, 432–433
directories, 23–24, 417, 419–423
editing live files, 419–420
error codes, list of, 432
file handling, 419–423
file list, 419, 433
importing sites, 355
overview, 411, 412
passive connections, 416–417, 433
preferences, 176, 177–178, 183, 417–418
properties of items accessed through, 422–423

sending files to chips in our heads using, 411
servers, 35, 36, 413–421, 423, 430, 432, 433
settings for accessing Web server, 35
Site toolbar controls, 364
status of current connection, 419
troubleshooting, 432–434

FTP Folder Inspector, 95–96, 422, 434

FTP Inspectors, 422–423

FTP Link Inspector, 95, 96, 97, 422, 423, 434

FTP pane (Settings dialog box), 413–414

FTP Proxy options (Network pane), 176

FTP tab, accessing, **95**

FTP Up-/Download Mapping, 652–654

FTP Upload & Download feature, 346, 413

full HTML references. *See* references, absolute

G

General setting, 364

Generate button (Basic tab, Image Inspector), **24**

generic language setting for Script tag, 507–508

Generic Page icon (File tab, Site tab), 128

Generic Pages options, 361

GET method, 327

getters, 546

GIF images, 13, **24**, 156

GL Encodings module, 163

Global tab (Web Database), 185, **478**, 586, 587, 588–591

Go Last Page Action, 548

Goto Link Action, 548

graphics. *See* images

Graphics Mode popup menu (Video Track Inspector), 629

gray options on menus, toolbars, 362

Grayscale tab (Color Palette), 260

grid objects. *See* layout grids

Grid Size fields, Layout Grid Inspector's, 63, 64

Gridx tag, 312

Group icon (Toolbar), **402**

grouping
    creating groups for fontsets and colors, 403–404
    Fieldset icon and, 339
    items on different Site menu tabs, 362
    list hierarchies and, 338
    palettes and windows, 9

Group Inspectors, 92–93, 389

H

hand, cursor. *See* cursors

hand coding. *See* code, hand coding

handles
    for image resizing, 23, 242–243

on multimedia placeholder icons, 611

Head container, 205

headers and footers of site maps for printing, 451

header styles for tables, 269–270

Head Inspector icons, 79

Head Inspectors, 72–73. *See also specific Inspectors*

Head Palette tab, 7

Head Script Inspector, 70–72, 79, 506–508

Head section of pages, **189**, 205–206, 505, 506

Head tab (Palette), 7, 126

Height field (Floating Box Inspector), 69–70

Height field (Table Inspector), 21

Height option (Line Inspector), 60, 61

Height tab (Table Inspector), 267

hexadecimal values, 327

hidden items, 333. *See also* Form Hidden Inspector; visibility

Hidden tab (Table Inspector), 59–60, 272–273, **276**

hierarchy of sites, 436, 441, 444, 476–477. *See also* Link Hierarchy; Navigation Hierarchy

highlighted items, 334–337. *See also* focus

highLightOn and highLightOff functions, 512

home pages
    changing, 364

default for new sites, 361

default names of, 28

Export Site feature placement of, 477

overwriting, **431**

parent and sibling pages, **453**

Honor Publish State of checkboxes (Site Settings dialog box), 35

Honor Publish State preferences, 169, 170

Honor Publish State (Upload Options dialog box), 425–427, 428

horizontal lines, adding to pages, 24–25

HREF Track Inspector, **631–632**, 632–633

Hspace option (Spec tab, Image Inspector), 54

HSV tab (Color Palette, Windows), 260

.htm and .html file extensions, 361

HTML. *See also* code; *names of specific attributes and tags*
clicking on pages in site maps, 440–441

for colors, 404

displaying files in site maps, 446

focus and field modifiers, 334–337

labeling and grouping, 338–339

new buttons, 337–338

setting alternate editors, **375**

support for, 334

syntax checking, 179, 195–196, 197

HTML Options dialog box (Export Site feature), 478

HTML Options preferences, 170

HTML Outline Editor, 163, 197–201, 258, 600

HTML Source Editor
AppleScript used in, 655

colors set using, 258

components written using, 485

controlling previews of tags in, 595

Find and Replace feature, 496

Hidden tab of Table Inspector, 273

overview, 195–197

HTML specs (Version tab, WebDB inspectors), 596

HTML tab (Page Inspector), 46–47, 484–485

HTML tab (Web Database)
adding tags, 596–599

changing defaults, 599–600

examining tags, 591–596

previewing effects of changes made in, **588**

HTML tag attributes. *See also specific attributes*
adding quotations to, 462–463

adding to Body tag, 466–467

creating new, 597

inspectors controlling, 41–43

overview, **462**

previewing, **595**

spaces preceding, **462**

Web Attribute Inspector and, 593, 594–595

WebDB Inspector and, 592

HTML tags. *See also specific tags and tag functions*
adding to Web Database, 597–599

controlling previewing in HTML Source Editor, 595

creating new, 597–598

default settings in GoLive, 599–600

GoLive-specific, 312. *See also* CSOBJ tag

most derided tag *ever* (Blink), **216**

WebDB Inspector and, 592–593

WebDB Tag Inspector and, 592, 594

HTTP Proxy options (Network pane), 176

I

icons. *See also specific icons, inspectors, tabs and toolbars*

customizing, **129**

displaying in site maps, 447

funky, on Macintosh Desktop, 646

for plug-ins, 609, 610

previews and, 442, 443

status, 374

using Tool Tips for, 5, 6

visibility in site maps, 450

Idle Action, 554–556

IDs, **149**, 565, 571, 577, 580–581, 582

IE Extension preference, 163

if statements in JavaScript, 511

Image event handlers, 543–544, 545

Image icon (Basic tab, Palette), 236

Image icon (Basic tab, Image Inspector), 22

Image icon for plug-ins, 610

Image Inspector, 7, 23, 52–57, 236, 239–240, 242

imagemaps, 55, 56, 247–250, 467–470

images

Actions controlling, 533–534, 547, 554–556

aligning, 24, 42–43, 53, 243–246

alternative text for, 239–240

animating, **241**, 528–531, 533–534

attributes, 238–240

background, 13–14, 321, 466–467, 528–531, 576

borders around, 239, 599–600

browsers affecting, **13**

changing based on dates, 548

changing into buttons, **333**

ColorSync and, 251–252

compression levels for, 156

downloading during FTP connections, 419

event handlers attached to, 543–544, 545

in floating boxes, **525**, 523, 524

foreground, 528–531

formats, 233–236

importing, **635**, 155–157, 237–238

inserting, 236–252

linking, 56, 57, 336, 339, 346

low-resolution, **24**

lowsource, **24**, 44, 53, 240–241

naming, 26–27

preloading, 511, 547

previewing, 442, 443

resizing, 23–24, 53, 241–243

slide shows, 551

storing in cache, 158

in tables, 22–24, **288**

temporary, 337–338

thumbnails of, **388**

transparent backgrounds, **524**

Images tab (Sprite Track Inspector), 634–635

Img tag, 599–600

importing

images, 155–157, **635**

links from bookmarks and favorites files, 390, 391

pages as home pages, 26

script libraries, 167

sites, 355, 459–461

table content, 57, 58, 285–286

Import item (Web Database submenu, Specials menu), 586

Import method, linking to external style sheets using, 569

Import Old Web Database menu (HTML and Characters tabs, Web Database), 586

Incoming Links, 439, 440, 447

indentation. *See also* spacing
coding, 589, 595
in source code, 179, 180
of text, **139**, 219–220
using transparent images for margin control, **244–245**
in Web Database, 185

Indexed Color tab (Color Palette), 260

index numbers, 509, **510**

In Explorer submenu (Site menu), 372–374, 444

In Finder submenu (Site menu), 372–374, 444

Information window (Mac), 373–374

Inline Action CyberObject, 549

Inline Action Inspector, 100–101, 542, 543

inline elements and CSS, 571, 572, 579

Input Image icon (Forms tab, Palette), **333**

Inspector palette, **525**, 543–544

Inspectors. *See also names of specific Inspectors*
common attributes, 41–43
document layout, 43–45
overview, 5–6
palette and list of, 40

installation, 3, **4**

Internet Config, 161, 178, 184, **348**, 651–654

Internet Explorer. *See* Microsoft Internet Explorer

Invisible items option, Document Layout Controller, 44–45. *See also* visibility

irreversibility, **274**

IsIndex Inspector, 77

Item Color (Color tab, Site View Controller), 449

J

Java Applet Inspector, 616–617, 618, 619

Java applets, 614–616, 618, 619

JavaScript. *See also* Actions; forms
adding, 505–510
blocking when browsers don't support, 507, 511, 515, **538**
client-side, 503
ECMA Script, 502
event handlers, **324**, 507, **508**
events, 508–509, 545
external, 508
form verification, 328
GoLive support for, 503–505
JScript (Microsoft), 502

languages, 70
overview, 501
preferences, 182, 191, 201
references from components, **483**
sample scripts using, 510–516
server-side, 503
storing in external libraries,
    558–559
support for, 501–503, 504, **538**
testing, 502–503, 508, 512

JavaScript Editor, **71**, **72**, 144–145, 337

JavaScript Functions options (HTML
    tab, Page Inspector), 46, 47

JavaScript Inspector
    Change Password checkbox, 336
    handlers added to form elements
        using, **324**
    naming scripts using, 507
    overview, 70–72, 505
    Script Editor and, 509, 510

JavaScript Objects, 509–510

JPEG images, 13, 156, 234–235

JScript (Microsoft), 502

.js file extension (JavaScripts), 508

changing timing between, 520, 521
connectors in Timeline Editor, **526**
creating, 520
creating animation paths, 523
Depth values of, 530
overview, 519–520
paths originating from, 521, 522
pixel locations of, 525
positioning for animation, 525–526
selecting in Timeline Editor, 530
setting, 520–523
tweening and interpolation,
    519–520
Visible settings of, **531**

Key Generator icon, 333–334

Keywords Inspector, 74, 75

Keywords tag and Keywords Inspector,
    209

Kill Frame Action, 548

knobs connecting objects in site maps,
    439, 440, 447

Kvern, Ole, xiii

K

KeyColor field (Floating Box
    Inspector), 521–523

keyframes
    adding intermediate to animations,
        527–528
    animating multiple elements,
        528–531
    changing attributes, **526**
    changing color of, 521–523

L

Label attribute, 338

Label in List Item Editor, **331**

Label popup menu (File tab, Site File
    Inspector), 83

labels, **171**, 338–339, 449–450, 644–645.
    See also Finder label

language attribute of Script tag, 506,
    507–508

languages. *See also* characters
    Asian text encodings preference,
        162, 163

choosing for scripts, 506, 507–508

Find and Replace feature and, 474

non-English character encoding preference, 162, 163, 164, 165, 166

spellchecking and, 343

latency and time estimates for downloading files, 345

Launch File button, 363

Launch File (In Finder and In Explorer submenus, Site menu), 374. *See also* File Mapping

layers

of animations, 530

of floating boxes, 320, 321–322, 521, 522, 530

of imagemap regions, 350

of images, **337**

in movies, 629

Layer tag (Netscape), **518**, 518

Layout Editor

colors set using, 257

components edited in, **483**

default settings in, 600

Find and Replace feature and, 496

overview, 5–6, 189–193

tables and color displayed in, 284

viewing XML files in, 624, 625

Layout Grid Inspector, 63–64, 311, 312, 313

layout grids

aligning, 313, 315, 316

animation and, 310

background color, 313

browsers supporting, 310, 311

distributing grid objects, 315–317

floating boxes and, 310, 313, 318

grid units, 312

grouping grid objects, 317, 318

moving, 311–312, 314, 315

overview, 309, 313

resizing, 312–313, 314, 315

tables converted into, 289

Layout Grid Toolbar, 7, 139–140

Layout Preview, 164, 608

Layout Preview tab, 527, 565

Layout Textbox Inspector, 64, 65

Layout View Controller, 29, 43–45, 192, 603–605

Learn button (in the Spell Checking, Preference feature), 175

Leftmargin and Topmargin tags, 598–599

legends, 338, **339**, 339

libraries, 167, 168, 558–559

Line Break Character (Global tab, Web Database), 589, **590**

Line Break Inspector, 61

linefeeds, 170, 478

Line Inspector, 24–25, 60–61

Link Hierarchy. *See also* site maps

color coding in Site tab, 436

customizing, 444–450

moving around in, 437–439

selecting, 436–437

uploading items to FTP servers based on, 426

Link Inspector

external links and, **391**

fixing missing and problem files, 395, 396–397

Head Link Inspector compared to, **76**

keyboard shortcut, 10

linking to files in site maps using, 439

list of colors and fontsets in use, 405

media link management, 399–400

opening, 384, 439, 440

overview, 76-77, 90–91, 210, 384–386

site maps and, 436

visibility on desktop, 6

link objects, 389–394, 511–512

links. *See also* anchors; references

absolute, 326

Actions controlling, 548–549

adding Point & Shoot, 32–34

borders around, 56, 239

changing references based on dates, 548

color of, 12–13

creating, 363, 381–384

database of, rebuilding, 363, **461**

downloading and uploading using FTP, 431

external, 388–394, 464, **483**

to files, 32–34, 381–384, 384–386, 439

full, 326

to images, 56–57, 236

images as, 56, 239, 246

internal, 464

lines in site maps, 440–441, 447–448, 449, 452

maintenance preferences, 157, 158, 159, 162, 163, 164, 168, 177

in media files, 399–400

modifying and examining, 384–386

pending, 384, 452

publish state, 425, 427, 428

refreshing, 363

remote control, 556–558, 559

scanning new files for, **378**

in site maps, 442, 450, 452–454, 455–456

symbolic, 423

testing, 201, 202, 203

viewing relationships between objects in site maps, 439–442

visibility in site maps, 447

Link tab (Button Inspector), 99

Link tab (Image Inspector), 56–57, 246, 252

Link tag, 209–210

Link View Controller, 90, 91

Link Warnings checkbox (Layout View Controller), 43, 44

Link Warnings icon, 397

Link Warnings option, 45

Link Warnings (Toolbar), 137

List & Others tab (CSS Selector Inspector), 574, 576

lists

creating, 224–225

CSS and, 576

on forms, 330–331

hierarchies, 338

LiveObjects, 167–168, **499**

LiveScript. *See* JavaScript

M

Macintosh. *See* Apple Macintosh

MacOS Encodings, 162, 163, 164

macros, 499–500

magnifying glass, 30, 438

mailto, **326**, 389

Map Name option, (Map tab, Image Inspector), 55

mappings. *See* File Mapping; URL Mapping

Map tab (Image Inspector), 54–56, 248–250

Marginheight and Marginwidth tags, 598–599

marking preferences, 157, 158

Mark Style and Mark Tag menus, 565

Marquee Inspector, 65–67

marquees, 438–439, 528

media files, managing and viewing, 359, 399–400, 608. *See also* plug-ins; *specific file types*

Media folder, 477

memory, **4, 394**

menu bars, components used for, 482

menus, 338, 541. *See also specific menu and submenu names*

messages, Actions triggering, 549–550

Meta Inspector, 73, 74, 207

Meta tags, 73–75, 155, 166, 207–209, **301**. *See also* search engines

Meyer, Eric, 565, 568

Microsoft Internet Explorer
  Actions compatibility, **538**
  adding attributes to Web Database, 598–599
  CSS features unique to, 583
  DHTML support, 518
  embedded font support, 574
  frame border support, 304
  HTML 4.0 support, 334
  importing favorites as external links, 390, 391
  JavaScript testing and support, 502, 504
  plug-ins, 608
  tables and color displayed in, 284
  wrapping form text support, 329

Microsoft VBScript, 504

Microsoft Windows
  conventions explained, xi
  desktop, 6
  permissions and remote access to files, 424, 425

MIME (Multipurpose Internet Mail Extensions), **609–610**, 610

mirror sites, 421, **430–431**

modules, 161–164, 182, 201, 497–499. *See also specific modules*

monitors
  browning marshmallows over, v
  colors, 254–256
  floating boxes and, 525
  resolution and minimizing palettes, 8–9
  size and resolutions recommendation, 10

More button (Export Site feature), 478

More tab (Plug-in Inspector), 611

mouse actions and event handlers, 511–512, 541, 547

Move By and Move To actions, 550, 551

movies, 629, 633–637. *See also* Video Track Inspector

multimedia, 550–551, 611. *See also* animations; floating boxes; plug-ins

Multipurpose Internet Mail Extensions (MIME), **609–610**, 610

Multisection Inspector, 64–65, 315

Music Inspector, 630

N

names
    adding object references to JavaScripts using, 509, **510**
    of animation scenes, 532
    case of, 159
    of colors, 404, 405, 590
    of CSS styles, 568
    of documents, 10–11
    of external links, 390
    of files, 30, 82, 83, 421, 423, 472
    of File tab items, 376, 377
    of floating boxes, 69, 320, 524, 530–531
    of folders, 30–31, 170, 171, 354, 357, 361, 454, **477**
    of fonts and fontsets, 15, 404, 405, 408–409
    of forms and form elements, 325, 328, **510**
    of frames, 306, **307**
    grouping sounds together using, 613
    of IDs, 571
    of multimedia objects, 611
    of objects in Script Editor, 514
    of objects in site maps, 443–444
    of scripts, 507

Name attribute, 338

NATURALSIZEFLAG (attribute added by PageMill), 465–466

Navigate History Action, 548

Navigation Hierarchy. *See also* site maps
    adding links using, 452–454
    adding pages using, 454–455
    color coding in Site tab, 436
    creating flowchart-like map using, 28–29
    customizing, 444–450
    modifying, 451–457
    moving around in, 437–439
    overview, 451–452
    selecting, 437

Navigation Services (Mac), 647–649

Navigator Palette, 365

Negrino, Tom, 502

nesting
    abominations, **313**
    classes, **571**
    code, 589, 595
    CSS selectors and, 582
    folders, 421
    framesets, 296
    layout grids in floating boxes, 313
    site folders, 356
    tables, 277–278, **284**, 286

Netscape browsers
    Actions compatibility, **538**
    embedded font support, 574
    JavaScript support, 501, 502, 504
    support for DHTML, 518

Netscape Communicator, frame border support, 304

Netscape CSS Fix Action, 552

Netscape DevEdge (Web site), 502

Netscape Navigator
adding attributes to Web Database, 598–599
bookmarks imported as external links, 390, 391
cell spanning misbehaving in, 282
HTML 4.0 support, 334
plug-ins, 607–609, 608
tables and color displayed in, 284
wrapping form text supported, 329

Network preferences, 163, 176–179

Noedit tag, 220

Noframes versions of framesets, 297

non-English character encoding preference, 162, 163, 164, 165, 166

O

Object Deletion preference, 168, **169**

object handles, resizing images using, 342–343

object references, 509–510

Objects tab (JavaScript Inspector), 506–507, 509–510

onClick, 533–534

onLoad, 516, **521**

onmouseout and onmouseover, 511–512, 512

onSubmit, 512–516

Open Alert Window Action, 549

OpenRecent (Mac) preference, 163

Open Window Action, 548, 556–558, 559

Optgroup tag, 338, 339

Optimize button (Layout Grid Inspector), 63, 64

Optional menu (Basic tab, WebDB Tag Inspector), 594

option-dragging keyframes, 520

Option tag, 338

Orientation options (Frame Set Inspector), 80

orphaned files and pages, 184, 397–398

Outgoing Links, 439, 440, 447

Outline Editor, 163, 198–201, 624, 625

Outline Editor Toolbar, 140–141

Outline mode shortcuts, 200

Outline view, 445–446, **451**, 453–454

Output menu (CSS tab, Web Database), 605

Output tab (WebDB Tag Inspector), 113, 595

overwriting files and home pages, 420, **431**

P

Page Font Sets menu (Windows), 15

Page icon, 11, 15, 45, 189, 295

Page Inspector
creating components using, 484–485
in Layout Editor, 189, 190
moving code from existing pages to library files, 167, 168
options in, 45–48
overview, 7, 11, 12–14

PageMill NATURALSIZEFLAG attribute, 465–466

pages. *See also* files
adding content to, 31–32
adding to site maps, 454–455
adding to sites, 362
attaching event handlers to, 542, 543
blank, 454
creating, 29, 30, 362, 456–457, **519**
editing, 450, **452**
moving to different positions in hierarchy, **452**
statistics about download time and size, 345
structure of, 205–207, 287–290

Page Setup dialog box, 451

Pages folder, 477

page status preferences, 171, 172

Page tab (File Inspector), 28, 83, 84, 377–378, 450

Page tab (Page Inspector), 13, 45

Page Title field (Page tab, Page Inspector), 10–11, **45**

Palette, 6, 7, 454–455, 609

Palette icons (Inspector), 41

palettes, 5–6, 8–10, 123. *See also specific palettes*

paragraphs, 217–218, 571, 572, 583, 590–591

Par elements and CSS, 579, 580

parentheses (()), 496, 497

parent pages in site map hierarchy, **436**, 441, 453

passive connections, 416–417, 433

passive mode (PASV), 177, 184

Password Action, 549

Password field, encryption compared to, **328**

passwords. *See also* permissions
Change Password checkbox sample script, 336–337
displayed on screen, 327. *See also* security
FTP and, 414, **415**, 417–418, 432
saved in cache, 327
Site FTP client saving, 35, **415**

PASV (passive mode), 177, 184, 416–417, 433

paths. *See* animations, paths; directories

Pavoni, La, xiii

PDF Module, 163, 399

PDFs crashing in Macs, **387**

Pending tab (Page Inspector), 47, 455–457

percentage measurements, 20, 21, 25

percent signs (%), 327, 611

periods (.), 494, 570

permissions. *See also* passwords
categories of, 425
on FTP servers, 419, 421, 422–423, 432–433, 434
remote access and, 424, 425

PhotoHTML, 284, 285

Photoshop, **388**, 443

Photoshop Actions, **51**

.pi (π) file extension, 354

pipe sign (|), 496

pixels, **575**, 20, 21, 23, 25, 573

placeholders, 30, 318, 336, 408–409, 609, **610**, 611

Play on Load button, **527**

Play Scene Action, **521**, 551

Play Sound Action, 551

Plug-in Inspector, 609–614

plug-ins. *See also* media files; multimedia; *specific plug-in types*
   adding objects to pages, 609–616
   configuring attributes, 611–612
   creating user-defined, 614–616
   history of, 608
   icons for, 609, 610
   placeholder icons, 609, **610**

Plug-ins folder, 176, 608

plus signs (+), 445, 494

PNG (Portable Network Graphics). *See* Portable Network Graphics (PNG)

Pointer field and Remote/FTP Inspector, 423

pointers
   connecting linked sites using, 487–488
   downloading and uploading using FTP, 420, 423, 430, 431
   Remote/FTP Inspector for, 422, 423

Point & Shoot
   changing home pages using, 364
   creating anchors, 383
   creating associations between legends and objects, 338
   editing links, 49
   entering Source (URL) references using, 41
   fixing missing files, 395

keyboard shortcuts killing Mac targets, **306**
   linking frames in framed pages using, 298
   linking to files in site maps using, 439, 444
   linking to files in Site window using, 194
   linking to pages and files using, 32–34
   linking to URLs and addresses using, 393
   overview, 381–383
   preferences, 183

Polygon tool (Map tab, Image Inspector), 248–249

pop alerts, 515, 549, 550

popup menu lists on forms, 330–331

Portable Network Graphics (PNG), 156, 163, 336

Port field (Site FTP client), **415**

Position tab (CSS Selector Inspector), 575, 576

posting to sites, 34–37

POST method, 327

pound signs (#), 571

preferences, 153–154, 155. *See also under specific topics*

Preferences dialog box (Photoshop), 443

Pre tag (Preformatted text), **478**

previewing. *See also* Frame Preview; Layout Preview; testing
   animations, 527
   browser preferences, 172, 173
   CSS, 564–566, 603–605
   frames, 80, 81, 82, 203, 299–300

HTML tags, 595
images, 442, 443
layout, 201–202
module preferences, 164, 201
thumbnails, **388**, 442, 443
Web Database changes, 586–588

printing, 181, **441**, 450–451

privacy. *See* passwords

programs. *See* scripts

Progressive compression, 156

Properties window (Windows), 373–374

proxy servers, 176, 418, 433, 654

Publish flag, 426–427, 428

Publish popup menu (File Inspector), 28, 83, **425**

Publish popup menu (Group Inspector), **425**

Publish state, 425–428, 477–478

Q

question marks (?)
next to fields in Action tab, 546, 547
next to files and folders in Files tab, 374
next to files in Missing Files folder, 395
on plug-in placeholder icons, 609, **610**
using in Find and Replace feature, 494

QuickTime
adding text messages to files, 633
CyberMovie and, 162
dividing files into sections, 633, 634

dragging images from Site window, **85**
editing movies using, 624–637
importing images, 156
managing links in, 399–400
plug-in icon for, 610
previewing files, 84
saving movies, **626**

QuickTime icon, **148**

QuickTime Inspector, 625–627

QuickTime Movie Viewer, 625, 626

QuickTime tab (Palette), 131

QuickTime tab (Plug-in Inspector), 612–613

QuickTime Track Editor. *See* Track Editor

quotation marks ("), 462–463, 514–515, 590

Quote Attribute Values (Global tab, Web Database), 590

R

radio buttons, 105, 106, 331–332

read-only elements, Disabled compared to, 336

Real Web Colors tab (Color Palette), 260–261

realworldgolive.com (Web site), x

Rebuild button preference, 167

Rectangle tool (Map tab, Image Inspector), 248

Recursive box (Remote/FTP Inspectors), 422

Recycle Bin (Windows), 169, 361, 398. *See also* trash

referenced files
Export Site feature and, 477
Upload Options dialog box and, 425, 427, 428

Reference field, 338

Reference Inspector, 91–92, 391–393

references. *See also* links
absolute, 208, 371, 463–464, 484
external, 359
extracting, 464
internal, 358, 476–477
JavaScript, **483**, 509–510
relative (Absolute links), 14, 208, 371, 463–464
renaming files affecting, **421**

refreshing colors, fontsets and links, 363

Refresh tag and Refresh Inspector, 75, 209

regular expressions in Find and Replace feature, 342, 344–345, 365, 492–497

relative links, **384**

relative references (Absolute links), 14, 208, **370–371**, 371, 463–464

remote control links, 556–558, 559

Remote File Inspector, 422, 423, 424

Remote Folder Inspector, 422

Remote Link Inspector, 422, 423

reparsing, 168, 387, **461**, 472

repeated elements, turning into Components, 470–472

rescanning, 363, 386–387, 479

reset buttons, 105, 332–333

Resize Window Action, 552

restraint, authors urging, 322

Reveal Object button (Site toolbar), 363

RGB Profile, default preference, 166–167

RGB tab (Color Palette), 260

Rights checkboxes (Site FTP Link Inspector), **96**

rollover effects, 510–512, 547, 583

Root folder, 479, 480, 481

root pages, 183, 202, 368–370

Root popup menu, 565

Rows field (Table tab, Table Inspector), 20

Row tab (Table Inspector), 59, 270, 271, 272, 283

ruler, 192

S

Save As dialog box, 17, 31–32

saving
changes using carriage return, 11
to Components and Root folders, 480, 481
passwords, 327, **415**
plug-in additions, 176
preferences, 154
QuickTime movies, **626**
site file, **356**

screens. *See* monitors

Script Editor, 505, 507, 509, 510

scripts, 167, 326, 507, 510–516. *See also* DHTML (Dynamic HTML); *specific languages*

Script tab (JavaScript Inspector), 71

Script tag, 506, 507–508

scrollbars in frames, 81, 303, 304

Scroll Down, Scroll Left, Scroll Right, and Scroll Up Actions, 552

scrolling lists on forms, 330–331

Scrolling tab (Marquee Inspector), 66–67

search and replace tool, renaming frames using, **307**. *See also* Find and Replace feature

search engines and indexes, 45, 161–162, 209, 649–650

security. *See* passwords

Selection tool (Map tab, Image Inspector), 248

Separate Pages and Media (Export Site feature), 477

servers
    adding to list of favorites, 417, 418
    connecting to, 35, 36
    copying files to, 411
    information sent to, 327, 330
    processing forms, 323, 324
    synchronizing sites with, 411
    transmitting files to, 327

server-side imagemaps, **247**, 467–470

server-side scripting, 503

shading, 440–441. *See also* color

Shockwave Flash, 162

shortcuts, 423, 487–488. *See also* pointers

ShowHide Action, 551

sibling pages in site map hierarchy, **436**, 441, 453

Sideknobs option, 157

Side-Knots, 86, 87, 439, 447

Site Colors tab (Color Palette), 261, 408

site data folders, 357

Site Extras tab (Palette), 129–130

Site file, 427, **435**

.site file extension, 354

site files, 355–356

site folders, 356

Site FTP client, **415**, 416–417

site maps. *See also* Link Hierarchy; Navigation Hierarchy; Site tab (Site window)
    arranging items in, 365, 447, 448
    building, 436–437
    customizing, 444–450
    editing and accessing items in, 440–441, 442–444
    examining links in, 439–442
    modifying, 437
    moving around in, 437–439
    overview, 435–436
    printing, **441**, 450–451
    resetting, 450, **452**
    viewing, 436–437

Site menu, 361–365. *See also specific options and tabs*

Site Module, 164

Site Navigator palette, 362, 365, 436, 438–439

sites
    adding files to, 378–380

collapsing for using Export Site feature, 476–477
defined, 446
exporting, 169–170, 171
files comprising, 358, 433
folders created for new, 355–357
importing, 404, 459–461
linked, 487
local copies of, 356
mapping, 184
page status, 171, 172
preferences, 360–361
settings dialog, 183, 184
setting up, 354–357
updating, 184, 461–467
view, 172

Site settings, 34–35, 425

Site tab (Palette), 128, 361, 362–365

Site tab (Site window). *See also* site
maps
changing view size of, 30
clicking to access file icon, 28
customizing attributes of, 444–450
managing placeholder files in, 30
naming files, overview, 30
overview, 359, 435
Site tab (Palette) compared to, **362**
Stationery and, **482**
thumbnail previews in, **388**

Site toolbar, 7, 141–142, 361, 362, 363,
364

Site Trash folder, **32**

Site View, 453

Site View Controller, 28–29, 85–89,
444–450, 645. *See also specific tabs*

sitewide changes, 402–410, 473–476

Site window, 357–360. *See also specific
tabs*

Size field (Frame Inspector), 81

Size field (Frame Set Inspector), 80

sliders on Color Palette tabs, 260

slide shows, creating, 551

Smith, Dori, 502

Soft wrap button (in HTML Source
Editor), 197

Sound plug-in icon, 610

sounds, 551

Sound Track Inspector, 630, **631–632**

source code. *See* code

Source Mode, 474

Source pane, 179–182

Source reference, 41

Source Sample (Web Database), 586,
587, 588

Source view, **331**

Spacer Inspector, 62–63, 225–226

Spacer tag, 312

spacing. *See also* indentation
adding spaces around plug-ins, 611
checkbox layout and, 332
CSS and, 575
of items in site maps, 449
plain and non-breaking, 332
preceding attributes, **462**
radio button layout and, 332
stripping extra spaces, 478
in tables, 267–269, **276**

Special tab (ActiveX Inspector),
619–620

Special tab (Multisection Inspector), 315–317

Special tab (Plug-in Inspector), 612–614

Spec. tab (Image Inspector), 54, 239–240

speed
of animations, **521**, 527, 536
of keyframes, 520, 521
of page loading, **53**

spellchecking, 164, 173, 175, 343–345

Spring-loaded Folders, 168, **382**

Sprite Sample Inspector, 635–637

Sprite Track Inspector, **631–632**, 633–637

square brackets ([]) used in Find and Replace feature, 494–495

squares in Timeline Editor, **526**

squishing and shrinking. *See* resizing

St. Clair Software, 648–649

Stagger Items checkbox (Arrange tab, Site View Controller), 448

staging sites. *See* mirror sites; synchronizing sites

Start Tabulator Indexing, 335

Stationeries folder, 480, 481

stationery, 31–32, **155**, 481–482. *See also* components; templates

Stationery checkbox (File tab, File Inspector), 28, 82–83

Stationery/Components tab (Palette), 454–455

Stationery folder, **129**

status bar of browser windows, 549–550

Status Label (Color tab, Site View Controller), 449

Status labels, 450

status of FTP sessions, 419

Status tab (Site Button Inspector), 99

Stop Complete Action, 551

Stop Preview button (Frame Set Inspector), 80

Stop Scene Action, 551

Stop Sound Action, 551

Stop Tabulator Indexing, 335

Structure menu (Basic tab, WebDB Tag Inspector), 594

Style menu (Layout Editor), 190, 215–216

Style option (Line Inspector), 60, 61

Styles Can Contain Blocks (Global tab, Web Database), 590

Style Sheet Editor, 117–118, 149–151, 567–570

style sheets, 186, 562–564, 578, **571**, **580**. *See also* CSS (Cascading Style Sheets)

Style Sheet Toolbar, 143

Style tab (Text Inspector), 50–51, 578–580

submit buttons, 104–105, 332–333

subsite paths, 464–465

symbolic links, 423. *See also* pointers

symbols. *See* characters

synchronizing sites. *See also* FTP (File Transfer Protocol) choosing files, 428–429, 430, 433

downloading, 431–432

images and, 238

overview, 411, 424

preparing for, 425–429

timezones and, 426–427

troubleshooting, 432–434

uploading, 238, 425–428, 429–431

syntax checking, 512, 586, 595–596

syntax errors, 179, 195–196, 197, 200, 201

T

tabbing chains, 335–336

Table Inspector, 7, 18–20, 57–60, 266–273, 280, 365

table of contents, creating, 86, 87, 447

tables

adding and deleting rows and columns, 280–281

alignment, 270–272

borders, 266–267, **284**

captions, 272

cell formatting, 286–287

cell spacing and padding, 19, 20–21, 267–269, **276**

cell spanning, 281–283

coding for, 265

color in, 22, **257**, 268, 270, 271, 283–285

columns in, 19, 20, 21, 265, 277, 280

creating, 264–266

default settings, 264, 272

dimensions, 266, 267, **269**

dragging and dropping, 18

editing, 278–287

floating boxes using, 309

form elements in, **325**

forms built using, 288

headers styles, 269–270

images in, 22–24, **288**

importing content, 285–286

inserting, 18

layout grids converted from, 57, 58, 289

layout grids using, 309

nesting, 277–278, **284**, 286

resizing, **274**, 20–21, 278–279

selecting, 19–20, 274–278

as structure of pages, 287–290

text wrapping, 270

tab numbering, 336

Tab option (Map tab, Image Inspector), 55, 56

tab order, 335–336

tabulator indexing, 336

Tag and Endtag Inspectors, 68

Tag Case, Attribute Case (Global tab, Web Database), 590

Tag Inspector, 68

tags. *See also specific tags*

mixing with selectors and IDs, 582

nested, **571**

style sheet selectors, 570, 577

Target Attribute Inspectors, 42

Target destination field (Map tab, Image Inspector), 55

Target Remote Action, 549, 556–558, 559

Target Two Frames Action, 549

TCP/IP, 416

templates, **288**, 31–32, 480–487. *See also* Components feature

testing. *See also* previewing
  animation speed, **521**
  colors, 173
  CSS, 566
  CyberObjects, **538**
  forms, 324, 334, 340
  JavaScript, 502–503, 508, 512
  links, 201, 202, 203
  uploads using mirror sites, **430–431**

text. *See also* fonts; fontsets
  adding, 212
  adding messages to movies, 633
  aligning, 218–220, 271, 272
  alternative, 339–340, 618, 619
  applying fontsets to, 406
  Asian encodings preference, 162, 163
  on buttons, 333
  clicking on labels to select buttons, 332
  colors applied to, 226–227, **257**, 449
  converting to tables, 58
  creating links, **49**
  event handlers attached to, 543–544
  finding, 473–476, 474
  flow of, 575
  formatting, 365
  on forms, 328–330
  indents, 219–220
  lists and indents, 224–226
  navigating, 213–214
  paragraphs, 217–218, 571, 572, 583, 590–591
  resizing text areas, 328–330
  size, 220–224, 572–575
  storing, 553, 656
  structure, 216–217

  styling, 215–216
  in tables, 271, 272
  wrapping, 329–330, 343–346

Text Colors section (Page tab, Page Inspector), 12–13, 45–46

Text event handlers, 543–544

Text Inspector, 48–52, 578–580

Text Modules folder, 499–500

Text tab (CSS Selector Inspector), 574

Text Toolbar, 5–6, 7, 16–17, 138–139

Text Track Inspector, **631–632**, 633

thumbnails, **388**, 438–439, 442–443, 448, 449. *See also* images, previewing

TidBITS article on varying text size, 222–223

time
  changing images or directing users to pages based on, 548
  estimates for downloading files, 345

Time Cursor, 530

Timeline Editor
  confusing features of, 530
  for DHTML animations, 191
  floating boxes listed in, 519
  keyframe connectors in, **526**
  overview, 145–147, 519–520
  recording animation scenes, 532, 533
  time scale in, 520, 521

timelines. *See* Timetracks

Timeout Action, 554–556

Time Redirect Action, 548

timestamp CyberObject, 538, **539**

Timetrack Editor, 162

Timetracks, 518–523, 530. *See also* Action Track; Track Editor

time zones, synchronizing sites and, 426–427

titles
of objects in site maps, 443–444
of pages, 10–11
setting tags for, 45

Title text field (Map tab, Image Inspector), 55, 56

toolbars, 5–6, 136–138. *See also specific toolbars*

Tool Tips, **5**, 6

Top field (Floating Box Inspector), 69

Topmargin and Leftmargin tags, 598–599

Track Editor, 148–149, 548, 625, 626, 627, 628. *See also* Timetrack

Track Inspectors, **631–632**

transferring files. *See* FTP (File Transfer Protocol)

Trash, 169, 361. *See also* Recycling Bin (Windows)

trash, 358, 398. *See also* files, deleting

triangles
in Layout Editor and Layout Preview, 486
in site maps, 441, 445, 446
in Web Database window, 586–588

troubleshooting. *See also* warnings
associating legends and objects, **339**
background colors in tables, **270**
cell spanning misbehaving in Netscape Navigator, 282
checking external links, **394**
crashes in Macs and PDFs, **387**

creating fontset defaults, **230**
creating multiple folders using FTP client, **421**
cursors in tables, **274**
Date & Time CyberObject, **539**
Find and Replace feature, 493–495
font sizes changed after reparsing, 220
FTP, 23, 432–434
items on lists, preselecting, 331
Layout Editor empty, **294**
mailto tags, **326**
plug-in files appearing as text links, **609**
radio button groups, displaying, **332**
saving preferences, 154
synchronizing sites, 432–434
tab numbering and tabulator indexing, 336
text turned into floating boxes, **580**
upgrading GoLive for Mac, **375**
Upload Options dialog box settings, **428**
URL length, **393**, **396**
URL Mappings, **488**

TV Screen display option, 448, 449

tweening and interpolation (keyframes), 519–520

Type menu (Floating Box Inspector), 521, 528

typography, 574, **575**. *See also* fonts; text

U

unethical acts, **346**

Unix permissions and remote access to files, 424, 425

Update, Rescan compared to, **386**

Update anchor warning, 34

Update button (Keywords Inspector), **74**, 75

updates, software, x

Up-/Download settings (Network pane), 178–179

uploading. *See also* FTP (File Transfer Protocol); synchronizing
exporting as alternative to, 431
Mac issues, 178–179
mapping and, 653–654
overview, 36
temporary images and, 238
using FTP, 23–24

Upload Options dialog box, 36, 425–428, 429–431

Upload Referenced Files Only (Upload Options dialog box), 425, 427, 428

URL field (Frame Inspector), 81

URL Handling feature, 158, 159–160, 168, **396**, 397

URL Mapping, 184, 487–488. *See also* File Mapping

URL Popup CyberObject, 541

URL Popup Inspector, Site, 100

URLs
creating new, 362
deleting, 363–364
displaying, 422
errors caused by changing, **444**
hand editing, 49
of objects in site maps, **444**
parts of, 208
% (percent) signs in, 327
in site maps, 446

Userdef Inspector (Mac), 614–616

Userdef tab (Java Applet Inspector), 617, 619

usernames for FTP servers, 414, **415**, 417–418, 432

V

Value attribute (HTML), **331**

Value Type (Basic tab, WebDB Attribute Inspector), 595

variables (Action), 553–554

VBScript, 504

Version tab (Web Database Tag Inspector), 113

Version tab (WebDB inspectors), 595–596

vertical bar (|), 496

Video Effect Inspector, 630–632

Video plug-in icon, 610

Video Track Inspector, 627–629, **631–632**. *See also* movies

view popup menu (Site tab, Site Window), 30

visibility
of floating boxes, 320–321, 322, 521, 531, 551
of grid lines, 312
of JavaScript section in Preferences, **182**
of site map sections, 438–439
of tracks, 627
viewing invisible borders, 267

Visibility option (CSS2), 575

Visible

settings of keyframes, **531**

text wrapping, **330**

Visitor Cookie Action, 554

visually-impaired audiences. *See* alternative text (Alt attribute)

Vspace option (Spec tab, Image Inspector), 54

W

warnings. *See also* troubleshooting
colors of, 157–158
deleting files without, 398
empty references, 193
false Size attribute of HR tag, 196
image resize warnings, 23–24, 242
memory, **394**
preferences, 157, 158, 159, 169
update anchor warning, 34

W3C (World Wide Web Consortium)
specifications, 336, 518, 568, **621**

Web Attribute Inspector, 593

Web browsers. *See* browsers

Web Database. *See also* XML
(eXtensible Markup Language)
adding new HTML tags, 596–599
changing settings in, 586
overview, 585
preferences, 185–186
previewing changes in, 586–588
toolbar, 142

Web Database folder (Modules folder), 586

Web Database inspectors, 111, 593–595. *See also specific Inspectors*

WebDB Attribute Inspector, 113–114, 594–595, 595–596

WebDB Character Inspector, 115, 601–602

WebDB Enum Inspector, 114–115, 593, 595–596. *See also* enumerations for HTML tag attributes

WebDB Inspector, 111, 112, 592–593

WebDB Section Inspector, 112, 597

WebDB Tag Inspector, 112–113, 592, 594, 595–596

Web Download feature, 178–179, 346

web download preference module (Mac), 164

Web Named Colors tab (Color Palette), 12–13, 261

WebObjects, 164, **499**, 638–639

WebObjects Module, 498, 499

Web pages. *See* pages

Webreference.com, 329, 334, 336, 568

WebReview.com, 565, 568

Web servers. *See* servers

web site management module, 164

Web sites. *See* sites

Width and Height fields (Basic tab, Image Inspector), 52–53

Width and Height fields (Floating Box Inspector), 69–70

Width field (Table tab), 20, 21

Width option (Line Inspector), 60, 61

Width tab (Table Inspector), 267

wild abandon, diving into Web Database with, 586

wildcards
    in Find and Replace feature,
        493–496
    search preferences, 174, 175
    in spellchecking, 344

Windows. *See* Microsoft Windows

windows (browser), 8–10, 549, 552

Windows Colors tab (Color Palette),
    260

Windowshade box (Mac), 8

Wipe Transition Action, 551

word and character counts for pages,
    345

World Wide Web Consortium. *See*
    W3C (World Wide Web
    Consortium)

Write Cookie Action, 554

Write Page Tags (HTML tab, Page
    Inspector), 46–47

X

XML DTDAttribute Inspector, 621,
    623–624

XML DTDElement Inspector, 621, 623,
    625

XML DTD Inspector, 621, 622–623

XML (eXtensible Markup Language),
    620–624. *See also* Web Database

XML Item Inspector, 624

XML tab (Web Database), 621–624

Xpos attribute (TD tag), 312

Z

Z–Index, 320, 530. *See also* Depth val-
    ues

Zoom menu (Site tab), 437–438. *See
    also* magnifying glass

Keep in Touch!

We love to hear from our readers—it's through your feedback that we learn about what you're most interested in, where we covered things in too much depth, and where you want even more information. We try to answer all the email we get, although a prompt answer isn't always possible.

Check out http://realworldgolive.com for the latest information about GoLive, updates to the book, and other details, including links to email and online discussions of GoLive.

Here's how to reach us:

Snail mail
7300 E. Green Lake Dr. N., Suite 200
Seattle, WA 98115-5304
Fax (206) 528-2999

Email
authors@realworldgolive.com

—Jeff Carlson, Never Enough Coffee creations, http://necoffee.com
& Glenn Fleishman, Unsolicited Pundit, http://glenns.org